SUPER BOWL

THE GAME OF THEIR LIVES

Also by Danny Peary

Cult Baseball Players
We Played the Game: 65 Players Remember Baseball's Greatest Era, 1947–1964

SUPER BOWL

THE GAME OF THEIR LIVES

DANNY PEARY

Macmillan • USA

MACMILLAN
A Simon & Schuster Macmillan Company
1633 Broadway
New York, NY 10019-6785

Photo credits: Bart Starr, courtesy of the Green Bay Packers; Jerry Kramer, courtesy of the Green Bay Packers; Matt Snell, courtesy of the New York Jets; Len Dawson, courtesy of the Kansas City Chiefs; Jim O'Brien, courtesy of the Indianapolis Colts; Roger Staubach, courtesy of the Dallas Cowboys; Nick Buoniconti, courtesy of the Miami Dolphins; Jim Langer, courtesy of the Miami Dolphins; Franco Harris, © 1997 Pittsburgh Steelers, photograph by Mike Fabus; Rocky Bleier, © 1997 Pittsburgh Steelers, photograph by Mike Fabus; Mark van Eeghen, Official Raiders Photo by Don Honda; Randy White, UPI/Corbis-Bettmann; L. C. Greenwood, © 1997 Pittsburgh Steelers, photograph by Mike Fabus; Jack Youngblood, courtesy of the St. Louis Rams; Jim Plunkett, Official Raiders Photo by Russ Reed; Ken Anderson, courtesy of the Cincinnati Bengals; Joe Jacoby, courtesy of the Washington Redskins; Todd Christensen, Official Raider Photo by Greg Cava; Joe Montana, courtesy of the San Francisco 49ers; Mike Singletary, courtesy of the Chicago Bears, photograph by Bill Smith Photography; Phil Simms, courtesy of the New York Giants; Doug Williams, courtesy of the Washington Redskins; Eric Wright, courtesy of the San Francisco 49ers; Matt Millen, courtesy of the San Francisco 49ers; Ottis Anderson, courtesy of the New York Giants; Mark Rypien, courtesy of the Washington Redskins; Troy Aikman, courtesy of the Dallas Cowboys; James Washington, courtesy of the Dallas Cowboys; Steve Young, courtesy of the San Francisco 49ers; Neil O'Donnell, © 1997 Pittsburgh Steelers, photograph by Mike Sabus; Desmond Howard, courtesy of the Green Bay Packers.

Library of Congress Cataloging-in-Publication Data
Peary, Danny, 1949–
    Super Bowl, the game of their lives / Danny Peary.
        p.   cm.
    ISBN 0-02-860841-0
    1. Super Bowl (football game—History. 2. Football players—United States—
        Interviews. I. Title.
GV956.2.S8P43   1997   97-3904
796.332'648—dc21   CIP
Manufactured in the United States of America

10 9 8 7 6 5 4 3 2 1

Design by Amy Peppler Adams—DesignLab

For Robert L. Rosen, Nova Lanktree, and Steven Herz

It is who you know. When I embarked on this project, I knew none of the 31 players I wanted to interview for this book, but it was my good fortune to know these three helpful people who made my impossible project into a reality.

CONTENTS

CONTENTS

ACKNOWLEDGMENTS

It is safe to say that this book would still be a work in progress if it weren't for the many terrific individuals I will mention below. However, this book wouldn't have even gotten off the ground if it weren't for two good friends, my agent Chris Tomasino and editor Jeanine Bucek. I thank them for the faith they had in my unusual concept for a book about the Super Bowl and for giving me so much support along the way. That they both entered motherhood while the contract was still being drawn up was, I believe, a sign that my book was charmed.

Many other important people were in the picture for the long run. At Macmillan I am especially grateful to publisher Natalie Chapman for her kind feedback, my in-house editor John Michel, and super assistant editor Olga Herrera Moya. Others deserving to be singled out for praise are Ken Samelson, Denise Coursey, Margaret Durante, Kristin Sampson, Mike Freeland, Jennifer Feldman, Glenn Mastro, Nancy Wolff, Mary Dorian, Chris Kensler, and Amy Peppler Adams.

At Robert L. Rosen Agency, Craig Foster, Maria Hettinga, Gail Lockhart, Maureen Casey, John Fuller, and especially Jonathan Diamond did vital behind-the-scenes work that kept the project afloat even when its captain contemplated abandoning ship. You all have my deepest gratitude.

Of course, I am eternally grateful to the football players who served as the narrators for this unique Super Bowl history. It was a real treat being able to speak to these particular players. I thank them for their time and trust. Special thanks to Len Dawson for being the first person to agree to be interviewed by a total stranger.

I have to admit that I didn't really know what I was getting into when I came up with the idea of bringing together 31 high-profile athletes whom I'd never met to participate in one project. Who knew that football stars aren't so easy to get hold of? Or that they aren't so keen about returning phone calls? I was quite fortunate that so many old and new friends were there to bail me out. I again thank the three people to whom I dedicated this book: Robert L. Rosen of R.L.R. Agency; Nova Lanktree of Nova Lanktree Sports; and Steven Herz of If Enterprises, who either called the players directly on my behalf or introduced me to the proper contacts.

I am equally indebted to those other individuals who went out of their way to help me reach players who were essential to this book. My sincere gratitude goes to Ira Silverman; Gil Pagovich; Bob Page; Jamey Crimmins, Nick DeBellis, and Russell Spielman at Integrated Sports International; Dave Rahn of the San Francisco 49ers; Abbe Ruttenberg and Nick Buoniconti of the Miami Project (212-489-3555); Debbie Eben of Steiner Sports; Todd Christensen; Bob Bryan; Marty Blackman; Mary Knox, Roz Cole, and Lisa Ratliff of Personality International; Angela Manolakas of the NFL Players Association; Karen Arnold; Peter Johnson; Brett Daniels of the Dallas Cowboys; Candace Finnerty of TruSports; John Flood; Dan Edwards of the Jacksonville Jaguars; Kurt Robinson; Tony Wyllie of the St. Louis Rams; Reggie Saunders and Phyllis Hayes of the Washington Redskins; Renae McNabb of the Pittsburgh Steelers; and coaches Bill Walsh, Terry Donahue, and Chuck Knox. I suspect that several of these people still fear that it's me on the line every time their phone rings.

I also acknowledge the kindness of Peter Abitante, Jackie Harris, Carol Hitt, Jeff Cordel, Sue Barnett, Bill Pidto, Marian Gianico, Sandy Sedlack, Robert Newhouse, Wanda Anderson, Myron Cope, Carol Hopkins, Dexter Bussey, Barbara Thompson, Samantha Young, Gloria Ashcroft, Jane Walsh, Kim Singletary, Michelle Warren, Mark Arteaga, Verna Riddles, Laurie Wilson, Rich Dalrymple, P. J. Combs, John Bellow, Steve Kay, Tom Mortensen, Jeff Blumb, Paula Martin, Aaron Popkey, Jimmy Walsh, Al LoCasale, Bill Smith, Vernon Biever, Harvey Greene, Margie Rosnick, George Wolff, Bob Nowacki, Rhea Tabakin, Jeanie Dooha, Cory Gann, Emma Bucek, Al Daniels, Julie Weiss, Barbara Haynes, Berj Najarian, Kimberly McIntyre, Jenny Ross, and Fred Glueckstein.

I thank my photo researcher Kent Reichert and those teams that supplied us with pictures for this book: the Green Bay Packers, New York Jets, Kansas City Chiefs, Indianapolis Colts, Dallas Cowboys, Miami Dolphins, Pittsburgh Steelers, Oakland Raiders, St. Louis Rams, Cincinnati Bengals, Washington Redskins, San Francisco 49ers, Chicago Bears, and New York Giants. I am grateful to the people in various public relations and media departments, some of whom I mentioned above. I also acknowledge the photographers who have allowed us to use their work.

Special thanks to my parents, Joe and Laura. They have been great cheerleaders, although they can't even recognize a football game, much less tell you how it is played.

And, finally, my love goes to my wife Suzanne and daughter Zoë, the most highly recommended Super Bowl–watching companions.

INTRODUCTION

The Super Bowl is such a colossal event it seems inconceivable that its origins were modest. Yet, as Bart Starr reminds us in the first chapter of this book, the inaugural "Super Bowl" between his Green Bay Packers and the Kansas City Chiefs—officially titled "The First AFL-NFL World Championship Game"—was not even close to being a sellout. The thirty thousand vacant seats at the Los Angeles Memorial Coliseum that January 15, 1967, pretty much reflected the indifference the American public felt toward the game. Yes, two rival networks broadcast that one historic encounter, but I remember how even the most ardent football fans had no predilection to spend that Sunday in front of the television set. (The NFL wouldn't even assign someone to film the entire game.) This new competition came across as a profit-motivated exhibition game, much like an ersatz annual Chicago College All-Star Game set in January. Even those of us who enjoyed AFL games, with the intriguing NFL cast-offs and wide-open play, believed that a matchup between mighty Green Bay and the AFL champion was as big a mismatch as Goliath versus David sans slingshot. Also, it was hard to take seriously a football game with a nickname inspired by a little round black rubber ball. (At a time when the only "Superstars" played for Andy Warhol, if there had been no faddish superball, we might just as easily have seen the birth of the "Slinky Bowl.") There were no Super Bowl parties, but, as it turned out, the curious among us did tune in, only to watch a Packers runaway that seemed to confirm our worst suspicions.

Of course, what altered our perception were the successive wins by the New York Jets and the revenge-minded Chiefs in Super Bowls III and IV. We realized that the AFL had quickly caught up with the NFL, and we even reexamined the first two Super Bowls and suspected that the crushed Chiefs and Raiders would have held their own against any NFL team but the Packers. The annual game took on legitimacy and began to build its own history and tradition, with records set and broken and tremendous teams and players (many of whom are included in this volume) creating indelible memories. Fan interest increased accordingly, fueled by the jump in popularity of pro football itself because of the NFL-AFL merger, the increase of national television exposure, and the advent and ritualization of *Monday Night Football*.

The Super Bowl has become America's biggest sports spectacular and is, in fact, so big that it transcends sports. Die-hard football fans are merely a small minority of its viewers. For one Sunday in January each year, the entire country shuts down and nearly everyone—except the newly broke spectators at the stadium—gathers around television sets in sports bars or at Super Bowl parties. Eerily and wonderfully, there is convivial bliss, and we are all of one tribe in a three-hour celebration.

The appeal of the Super Bowl to fans is self-evident, but I have always considered it a game for the players rather than the masses. I think of it as essentially an in-house function (much like the Academy Awards to the movie industry) that, because so much money can be generated, is shared with (and marketed to) 800 million viewers around the world. Those 800 million people may thrill to the Super Bowls they watch, but only the players themselves know exactly what it is like to play in a Super Bowl and what it takes to get there in terms of hard work, dedication, and sacrifice. Without question, on Super Sunday, players want more than anything to achieve glory in the eyes of all the other players in the NFL, the only other individuals who could understand what it means to be playing that game. Their satisfaction comes from knowing, as Matt Snell pridefully states, "that all the other teams that started out with us [are] at home watching us play." They want those players whose season has ended to envy the tremendous public exposure only the two Super Bowl opponents enjoy. The fans? The players see us as being witnesses to, even testaments to, their success.

The first players-only oral history of America's premier sports event, *Super Bowl: The Game of Their Lives* is intended to be a tribute to the hard-earned accomplishments of all players who have reached the championship game. I have brought together 31 tremendous players from the past and present who have left their marks on football history to reminisce about all the previous Super Bowls from their unique perspectives. I also asked them to relate their experiences leading up to those games, so we can better understand the significance that one day had in their entire careers. I want readers, particularly young football fans, to learn about these particular individuals who have made the Super Bowl as gigantic as it is, so by design this book is equally about what happened on the field on those historic Sundays and what was going on in the minds of these men as they played the games of their lives. I trust that readers will find these insider accounts make even the blowouts more interesting.

In my search for a wide array of accounts, I interviewed players who manned every position on the field; who came from different backgrounds; and who had diverse NFL experiences on their way to Super Bowls. The narrators include many Hall of Famers, as well as several will-be and should-be Hall of Famers, All-Pros, stars-for-a-day, and/or personal favorites. I limited myself to interviewing 14 of the 28 Super Bowl MVPs, bypassing a few others for players whose stories haven't been told as often, if at all. Three players represent losing teams.

Ironically, after assembling my supposedly disparate group of narrators, I realized that their stories had a common central theme. As you will discover, success for the players in this book did not come easy. Each player was motivated to overcome some form of adversity to reach the pinnacle of football success, be it undeveloped or unrecognized talent, injuries, rejection, or failure. That was their challenge. So it is that even the greatest and most successful players take on underdog status. Whether it's Rocky Bleier being told he can't play football again after suffering debilitating war wounds; Jim Plunkett (and others) finding himself released and on the NFL scrap heap; Joe Montana realizing impatient 49ers fans expect him to carry his team to a Super Bowl victory every year; Doug Williams being burdened with the unfortunate, much-inferred belief (expressed only behind closed doors) that an NFL team can't win with a black quarterback; or Troy Aikman trying to rise from the ashes of a 1–15 rookie season, every player overcame major obstacles. For each player, the Super Bowl "story" began long before kickoff. Now they all share the realization that without the struggle and, in some cases, damage to body and psyche, there would be far less significance to a Super Bowl appearance or victory.

An appearance in the Super Bowl finally allows the players a proper worldwide showcase for their special talents. For a winning player, it is the ring that assures peer respect, and it is the Vince Lombardi Trophy, which recalls those first two Super Bowls, that assures him that he and his entire team have secured a lofty place in sports history. Ironically, a player can have a long, great career, yet only a victory after 60 minutes on Super Sunday can give him the vindication, validation, and/or justification that he has sought for so long while enduring so much. A Super Bowl victory is the one goal in a football player's career that turns out to be even better than expected—"much better," says recent Super Bowl hero Desmond Howard—and that is why it has such a lasting impact.

While the annual Super Bowl resulted from a decision by pro football's power elite three decades ago to stimulate fan interest and generate profits (and, as the first step in the merger, to eliminate competition), that spurious title game immediately took on a life of its own and became legitimate in the eyes of all players (and us fans as well). Indeed, its existence has been necessary for all goal-oriented players because, fortunately, winning the Super Bowl has proved to be the only goal that is worth the long, blood-and-sweat effort NFL players make as a matter of course. It is a proper reward for a player's endeavors because it does show everyone that he is the best in his profession or, as Todd Christensen attests, the "king of the mountain." Jack Youngblood, whose championship dream was never fulfilled, speaks for all players when he says, "In our society, you're measured to a certain degree, right or wrong, by whether you win or lose. And there's only one winner every year in the National Football League. Unfortunately, that's how we measure success, but it's also why we play—we want to be the one winner."

Danny Peary

SUPER BOWL

THE GAME OF THEIR LIVES

SUPERBOWL
1

BART STARR
GREEN BAY PACKERS

SUPER BOWL I

GREEN BAY PACKERS 35
KANSAS CITY CHIEFS 10

BART STARR

*S*uper Bowl was the term that Kansas City Chiefs owner Lamar Hunt coined when a big game between the champions of the National Football League and American Football League was first proposed. However, when the Green Bay Packers played the Chiefs in the first title game between the two leagues on January 15, 1967, at the Los Angeles Memorial Coliseum, few reporters referred to the event as the Super Bowl. Its official name was the *First AFL-NFL World Championship Game.*

Vince Lombardi didn't have to sell us on the fact that we were about to play in an important game. The game sold itself. We knew it was special because we were receiving far more media attention than we did before any of our NFL championship games. Scores of reporters were at our training facility and they were even coming to our hotel in Santa

1

Barbara for interviews. Also, both CBS, which covered NFL games during the season, and NBC, which broadcast AFL games, were there to televise this one game. So we realized it was the most significant game we had ever played. However, Coach Lombardi did inspire us—and this is what I reflect on most today—by impressing upon us that it was appropriate that we, the Green Bay Packers, represented the National Football League in the first of these title games. We had won that opportunity, that right, by winning NFL titles in 1961, 1962, 1965, and now in 1966. He said that the NFL's long-established reputation was now at stake and that the Green and Gold was meant to carry all its history, tradition, and prestige into the game, and to fulfill our obligation. We were convinced. We felt privileged and blessed to be in the NFL and to be part of its growth, and now we took great pride in being its standard bearer.

Coach Lombardi wanted to win this game very, very badly and treated it like a personal mission, yet I didn't detect worry. He approached the game as he always did, from a positive standpoint, so it was never, "What if we lose . . . ," but was instead, "We must win; we can't lose." I don't know that I ever saw worry in him—that wasn't in his makeup. But I'm sure there was inner concern and that may be what Frank Gifford, who was on CBS's broadcasting team, was describing when he said Lombardi was shaking when he interviewed him prior to the game. Because of the magnitude of the Super Bowl, and the high expectations everybody associated with the NFL had for us, we were all anxious and maybe he was feeling more of that because of his position as head coach.

I'd say that before the championship game, Lombardi was primed after having prepared himself during the week for the new task and unique challenge. And he and his coaches had prepared us extremely well, both offensively and defensively, so we were supremely confident. Let me stress that there's a huge difference between being supremely confident and arrogant. Arrogance will bury you whereas supreme confidence will take you to heights you may not have reached before.

Confidence is what Coach Lombardi instilled in us. He was a tremendous salesman in that from the time he took over a very bad Packers team in 1959, he had the style and ability to sell us on the idea that his system was so fundamentally sound that it had to work if we executed properly. He had been the offensive coordinator of the Giants, and before his first season with us, he invited some of our players to an indoctrination of his offensive system, with the single-wing formation, pulling guards on sweeps, crossblocking, double-team blocks, and so on. When we broke after about 90 minutes, I ran downstairs in the Packers office building and called my wife Cherry in Birmingham to tell her, "We're going to begin to win." That's all I said. He could have stopped after 15 minutes and I would have made that same phone call. It was so obvious that he would teach us how to win and I was thrilled.

We had a winning record in Lombardi's first season and reached the NFL title game the second year. We got so ticked off after losing to the Eagles, 17–13, that we developed an insatiable appetite to win and hadn't lost a postseason game since. We had such success because we responded to Coach Lombardi's approach, which was extremely demanding but very rewarding. I've always believed that your best people will respond well to discipline because they recognize it is an asset, not a hindrance. And this proved to be correct, because under Lombardi so many players who hadn't had any success on the pro level became All-Pros. He and the people he hired, like defensive coach Phil Bengston, recognized skills in various players that other coaches overlooked and then harnessed and honed those skills with discipline. I'm sure it was very rewarding to Lombardi when we thrived under his coaching.

Coach Lombardi was a drillmaster who had uniquely high expectations of all his players, often criticized us unmercifully, and made it frustrating to try to win his approval. Yet, while it was difficult for some players to adjust to him, particularly at the beginning—he infuriated some and intimidated others—I had no problem. Over the years, when people in the media would ask me about Lombardi's toughness, I'd say, "He's a piece of cake," and they'd look at me like I was nuts. Then I'd add, "Now playing for Ben Starr would have been hard." Then I'd have to explain that I was raised in a military family and that my dad, Ben Starr, was the toughest SOB I had ever known. He more than prepared me for Lombardi. After him I relished playing for Lombardi!

Even before I heard Lombardi give his frequent motivational speeches—in which he talked about life, not football—I had heard his favorite Douglas MacArthur stories and quotes from my father, who had been with MacArthur in the Philippines and thought he hung the moon. I followed MacArthur's "Will to Win" philosophy, tried to motivate myself to excel, and had great personal pride, so I would say I was a good candidate for Lombardi to mold into his type of quarterback and field general. It would have been marvelous to have been a rookie under him, but I'm happy that the experience unfolded as it did, with him coming in after I had several unspectacular years trying to win the Packers' quarterback job. It made me appreciate his arrival even more. I think it was important that he gave me the starting job during his first year and I had the opportunity to develop with him. He was an outstanding teacher and took great pride in that because he thought coaching was the epitome of teaching. Over the years, he had diagrammed so many plays on blackboards that he could do it without losing eye contact. We all learned great lessons from Vince Lombardi and he earned our respect and love. He maintained his position well without overdoing it. For instance, even before that first Super Bowl—when practices were thorough—he wasn't the type who would call me at night to discuss plays. He planned so well during the day that it wasn't ever necessary.

Lombardi sought to have everyone on our team grow into responsible leaders. I'm not certain what he wanted from me exactly in terms of leadership, but what I tried to do was lead by example. Go out and perform and the rest would take care of itself. I wasn't interested in talking or gesturing and no one else on our team was either. I saw no need to yell at, or jump on, anyone on the offense, except maybe a young backup player who was a bit too flippant and wasn't concentrating on what he was doing. All our veterans were very disciplined and self-starters.

When I was developing as a quarterback under Lombardi, and even before, I tried to compensate for not having the strongest arm. I wanted to learn how to put more zip on the ball and anything else that would make me a better pro quarterback. That's why I watched my idol Johnny Unitas, who was a star at Baltimore before I began to have my success at Green Bay. I had three reels of Unitas that I studied all the time, shot after shot. He was a much deeper passer than I was, but I wanted to see his technique on his dropbacks, his footwork, his play-action, his style. I also tried to detect how he was reading coverages and what he did on fakes. I think much of my improvement had to do with studying him.

I also would listen to players like Paul Hornung and Max McGee when they had suggestions for plays to run. We liked to throw to backs coming out of the backfield, involving them in our passing game, and Hornung knew how to read defenses so he could tell me how he could get open. McGee, a veteran receiver, studied defenders as well as anyone we had. Although I felt I could beat the defensive backs based on what I was observing, it was possible they were making slight adjustments that I wouldn't have been aware of without my receivers informing me. McGee and Hornung were the two guys who were always right on the money.

I also improved because I learned about the tendencies of defenses by talking to defensive players on the Packers, particularly my roommate Henry Jordan. Henry, who played right tackle, and the others would give me the different perspective I needed when attacking defenses. A good thing about our team was that you could talk to other players and get an assessment, get an opinion. Players on offense and defense really bonded.

I think we had a very strong feeling of oneness as a result of living in Green Bay, which was so much smaller than the cities where the other teams played. We were part of the community and weren't only team-mates but neighbors and really got the chance to enjoy each other away from the field. After practices, many of us would flock to a local pub and have a cold beer or two, and large numbers of guys and their wives would go to dinner after games. Jordan and I were very close, as were our wives, and the four of us would socialize or would join others in larger groups. Zeke Bratkowski, who did an exceptional job backing me up at quarter-back, and I also became great friends, as did our wives. There were a lot of friendships formed that continue today.

Lombardi didn't really socialize with players, but he always organized a Thanksgiving dinner for us and our families, and there would be an occasional gathering at his home, maybe once a year after a ball game. I think Paul Hornung and Max McGee played golf with him at times. I was invited, too, but I never went because I enjoyed my relationship with him so much that I didn't want to taint it with socializing.

Lombardi's relationship with Hornung and McGee was unusual. They were funny, fun-loving single guys who were the team's curfew breakers, which wouldn't seem to sit too well with a disciplinarian. But Coach Lombardi saw beyond that to two players who worked at least as hard as anyone else at practice and in games performed as well in the clutch as anyone we had. That's why he simply fined them rather than being harsher with them. It didn't bother him, so they might just go out the next night, and then he'd just give them a heftier fine and go about his business. We joked that they paid for our team party every year by not making curfew. Max and Paul were a perfect fit for our team. We had a lot of serious play-ers who needed to loosen up. Because of my upbringing, I was a bit rigid and their humor helped me a great deal.

Any successful person or organization must be goal oriented or nothing will be accomplished, and the Packers under Lombardi were always goal oriented. In 1966, we knew there was going to be this Super Bowl prize at the end of the year and that was our objective. As I'm sure the Chiefs were aware, our 1966 team was very strong and talented.

As it had been since Lombardi's arrival, we had a strong running game led by Hornung at halfback and Jim Taylor at fullback—although Hornung would miss the Super Bowl because of a pinched nerve in his neck. Paul was an extremely versatile player. He was a very hard runner, could catch passes, throw option passes—he had been a star quarterback at Notre Dame—and until we got Don Chandler, he kicked field goals for us. He was very talented and a consummate clutch player—the greater the pressure, the more he wanted the ball. Taylor was another great player, who was even capable of outrushing Jim Brown when the Packers and Browns played. He absolutely loved to plow into defenders and went out of his way to make contact with them. He became an excellent blocker. It's true he had been an effective blocker for Billy Cannon at LSU, but he learned how to make all the different blocks that were necessary in the pros. He also became a good pass receiver. That's how we could catch defenses by surprise. He beat the Browns in Cleveland by making receptions on flare patterns. He made a couple of guys miss and then took a couple more with him into the end zone to give us the lead late in that game.

Before the season, Taylor had informed the team that instead of returning to Green Bay in 1967, he would become a free agent and sign with the expansion New Orleans Saints. As a result, Lombardi didn't speak to him during the entire season. Taylor had been such a big contributor for many years and was still our top gun, especially with Hornung sidelined for much of the season, so it was a concern. It was something we had to quietly work our way through and not let become disruptive. Taylor had a good year.

Hornung and Taylor made the "Green Bay Sweep" famous, but Elijah Pitts, who replaced Paul in the Super Bowl, and all our other backs learned to run it. Hornung and Taylor were big scoring threats, but there were many other guys you could count on in the clutch. If we had thrown the ball as much then as teams do today, we'd have had some receivers in the Hall of Fame. McGee and the younger Boyd Dowler and Carroll Dale, who both learned from Max, were exceptional wide receivers. However, we didn't throw enough so that they could try "ups" or "goes" or "flys" on the outside.

What made our offense work so well was a tremendous line that made few mistakes. The two best-known players were right guard Jerry Kramer and right tackle Forrest Gregg. They were great blockers and smart players.

Kramer had almost shot off his arm when he was a teenager and had undergone serious surgery about twenty times to remove everything from splinters of wood in his intestines to tumors, yet he kept coming back. Gregg was 6'4" and weighed 250 pounds and could run like hell for a big man. He was an intense, proud competitor who never had a bad game. He would become a Hall of Famer.

Kramer and Gregg were so good that the guys on the left side of the line didn't receive commensurate applause. When we needed a clutch performance, we could go to either side. Fuzzy Thurston was a great pulling left guard. He wasn't that big, but he was agile and tough—I thought of him as a rotund stick of dynamite. Bob Skoronski, in particular, was overlooked, maybe because he wasn't flamboyant. He was an exceptional left tackle who always hustled, and he was one of the team's strongest, most capable leaders during that era. The players knew what he meant to the team because he was one of our captains. If the players had problems, they knew they could go to him, if it was appropriate.

The defensive players could go to Willie Davis, who was their captain. Willie was a class act who was much respected by everybody. He also was a great, great player. When he came out of Grambling, the Browns decided he wasn't big enough to play defensive end in the pros, but Lombardi and Bengston knew better and acquired him. He wasn't big, but he had quickness, tenacity, and intelligence.

Another guy who was considered too small by the Browns was my roommate Henry Jordan. He was very small for a defensive tackle, but Lombardi and Bengston saw that he was so strong for his size, so quick, so smart, so alert, so swift to adapt, that he, too, could become a great player. Like Davis, he was a perennial All-Pro and future Hall of Famer. In Phil Bengston's defensive scheme, Jordan was the freewheeling, slashing, aggressive tackle. He created havoc because the offense didn't know where he was going to be. He went where he felt he could get to the ball best—toward the center, outside the guard, or straight over the guard. Jordan was the penetrating tackle, while Ron Kostelnik, on the left side, was the line-of-scrimmage tackle. Jordan could get caught in a trap and be taken advantage of, but Kostelnik read the draws and screens and covered for him.

Ray Nitschke, our middle linebacker, would also cover for Jordan. His official job was to control the defense and call out the plays, but on his own he joined Jordan in creating chaos. He was a wild man, a real intimidator who loved to knock down opponents with his forearm. Ray was a good, smart person, but he wasn't self-disciplined prior to Lombardi's arrival.

Experience was a great factor in his development. Over the years with Lombardi, he learned that there was a way to do things and another way not to do things. He became a model citizen, an exceptional performer, and a future Hall of Famer.

Dave Robinson was as fine an outside linebacker as I have ever seen. This man was big, strong, very smart, tough, a real hard hitter. Because he could run like a deer, he could stick with backs going out for passes or run down quarterbacks. He's the one who pressured Don Meredith into being intercepted by Tom Brown in the end zone late in the 1966 NFL title game when a completion would have sent the game into overtime.

Willie Wood and Herb Adderley were the same: very hard-driving, aggressive, tenacious, big-play defensive backs. Willie was our strong safety and our best punt returner until Donny Anderson joined us. He was only 5'10" but he was a great athlete. He had been a quarterback at USC, but Lombardi converted him into a safety and he never missed a tackle. Adderley was our left cornerback. He was big, strong, fast, and mentally tough, and as polite as he was off the field, he was that ornery on it. He and Wood were the finest covermen I ever saw. They could cover, react, and hit. They did a lot of things well, which is why they would both make the Hall of Fame.

I'd say the defense was both businesslike and emotional. It was disciplined from the standpoint that Coach Bengston prepared it so well, but it was emotional because of guys like Jordan and the linebackers, Nitschke, Robinson, and Lee Roy Caffey. They were gentlemen off the field but were reckless, nasty, and aggressive on the field. To me, that was the perfect disposition for defensive players.

The Packers were changing in that Taylor was moving on—we didn't yet know that Hornung had played his last game because of his pinched nerve—and we'd signed rookie backs Donny Anderson and Jim Grabowski to huge contracts. But the structure that had been in place for so long was still intact and we still had a great core of unique, talented, and committed individuals, so we wouldn't let anything distract us from our objectives.

We had a very good year, losing only twice, by a point in San Francisco and by three points to Minnesota. We went into the postseason with five consecutive victories. The 1966 season was challenging, but it was fun, more fun than 1967 and the following years. A shoulder injury would really affect the last years of my career, but in 1966 I was as healthy as I ever was. My passing statistics reflected that I was at my peak. Teams were concentrating too much on our run and leaving themselves vulnerable to our passing game. That happened during the year and the postseason, when we passed more than we had since the 1960 title game. We were throwing more effectively.

Obviously there were weaknesses somewhere on the Packers, but there were only hints at most. The age factor wasn't there yet. There was the maturity factor, which was an asset. Our years together had made us stronger, and we didn't make many mistakes. The Cowboys had an excellent football team, but what helped us beat them, 34–27, in the NFL title game was maturity, and against Kansas City, another young team we didn't take for granted, that would be a deciding factor as well.

Our hotel was in Santa Barbara, where we practiced. The wives came to L.A. later in the week and stayed at separate hotels. The media came around a lot. It wasn't structured as it is today with special media times, and after practice the reporters would try to track you down and visit with you. I'm sure the Kansas City players also were taken aback by the attention they were getting.

On the final night, the team moved to a hotel in L.A., so we would be closer to the Coliseum. The morning of the game, I got up, had a quick shower, read the paper, and had breakfast. When I came out of the elevator into the lobby, I ran into Max McGee, who was returning from his big night out with a blond from Chicago he'd met the day before. He'd missed curfew despite the much higher fine Lombardi had imposed and was going upstairs to try to get a little sleep before the game, which would begin a little after 1 P.M. He didn't worry about his late night out affecting his performance, because with his career winding down, he hadn't played much during the season and didn't expect to play in this game at all. Boyd Dowler would be in the game—*unless* something happened to him.

We had played the NFL title game for over 70,000 fans in Dallas. They sold fewer seats in the Los Angeles Coliseum, only about 61,000 in a stadium that had well over 90,000. I had to buy tickets for people and fortunately they weren't hard to get or costly, maybe $12 for the most expensive seats. I didn't think too much about so many empty seats because of the newness of the game. I still was reflecting more on the tremendous amount of media coverage and all the elaborate pregame festivities at the Coliseum. We had no way of knowing how big the game would become in a few years, but we knew that it was already special in terms of football history.

We were heavy favorites and were expected to win the game with ease. But I don't think people realized how much talent the Kansas City Chiefs had. If you looked at their roster, you had to be impressed—they were just three short years away from having their own Super Bowl victory. They were an excellent team that had lost only two games early in the season and had easily beaten Buffalo in the AFL Championship Game. They were well coached by Hank Stram, and his quarterback was Len Dawson, an excellent passer and field leader. Dawson had a great receiver in Otis Taylor, who was a deep threat, as well as Chris Burford, who would have a good game against us. And he had a strong and versatile running game with fullback Curtis McClinton and halfback Mike Garrett, who'd won the Heisman Trophy at USC the year before. Plus they had huge, mobile players on both lines. Their rush was led by tackle Buck Buchanan, who was about 6'8", and on offense Dawson had tackle Jim Tyrer and guard Ed Budde blocking for him on the left side against Henry Jordan and Lionel Aldridge—they were bigger than our guys and they could play. We recognized what maybe other people didn't until the AFL started winning Super Bowls—that the AFL and the Chiefs had some quality people.

Before the game, our locker room was businesslike as usual. There were no pep talks. We sort of sat and reflected and got into the mood to play. But it wasn't quiet or uneasy in any way. There was mild conversation; players would be reviewing certain things. I didn't really talk over plays with anybody except maybe by exchanging a word or two on the way to and from the training room. Despite my respect for the Chiefs, I had good feelings going into the game. Despite my butterflies, I was confident that we could carry out our game plan.

The First AFL–NFL World Championship Game began with the Chiefs kicking off. The first time we got the ball, we couldn't move it. We may have been a little tentative, but there was nothing wrong with trying to get a feel for how the Chiefs were playing and to see if our impressions of them were right after having watched them on film. It wasn't a concern that we didn't have success right away—it just verified that this was a quality team we were playing. However, it was a concern that on our second play, Boyd Dowler reinjured a bad shoulder while attempting to block for Taylor on a sweep. That meant Max McGee, who had been out all night, would have to play the entire game as a wide receiver. He was as surprised as anyone.

On our third possession of the first quarter, with the game still scoreless, we had moved to the Chiefs' 37 when I threw a pass across the middle to McGee. It was thrown behind him because I was hit by Buck Buchanan just as I released it and all the oomph came off the ball. And Max still caught it, with one hand. The defender, Willie Mitchell, might have intercepted

January 15, 1967, at the Los Angeles Memorial Coliseum
Paid Attendance: 61,946
AFL Champion: Kansas City Chiefs (12–2–1)
Head Coach: Hank Stram
NFL Champion: Green Bay Packers (13–2)
Head Coach: Vince Lombardi

STARTING LINEUPS

OFFENSE			DEFENSE		
Kansas City		**Green Bay**	**Kansas City**		**Green Bay**
Chris Burford	LE	Carroll Dale	Jerry Mays	LE	Willie Davis
Jim Tyrer	LT	Bob Skoronski	Andy Rice	LT	Ron Kostelnik
Ed Budde	LG	Fuzzy Thurston	Buck Buchanan	RT	Henry Jordan
Wayne Frazier	C	Bill Curry	Chuck Hurston	RE	Lionel Aldridge
Curt Merz	RG	Jerry Kramer	Bobby Bell	LLB	Dave Robinson
Dave Hill	RT	Forrest Gregg	Sherrill Headrick	MLB	Ray Nitschke
Fred Arbanas	TE	Marv Fleming	E. J. Holub	RLB	Lee Roy Caffey
Len Dawson	QB	Bart Starr	Fred Williamson	LHB	Herb Adderley
Otis Taylor	FL	Boyd Dowler	Willie Mitchell	RHB	Bob Jeter
Curtis McClinton	RB	Jim Taylor	Bobby Hunt	LS	Tom Brown
Mike Garrett	RB	Elijah Pitts	Johnny Robinson	RS	Willie Wood

SUBSTITUTIONS

Kansas City: K—Mike Mercer. P—Jerrel Wilson. Offense: Receivers —Frank Pitts, Reg Carolan. Linemen—Tony DiMidio, Dennis Biodrowski, Jon Gilliam, Al Reynolds. Backs—Bert Coan, Pete Beathard (QB), Gene Thomas. Defense: Linebackers—Walt Corey, Smokey Stover, Bud Abell. Linemen—Aaron Brown. Backs—Emmitt Thomas, Fletcher Smith, Bobby Ply.

Green Bay: K—Don Chandler. P—Chandler, Donny Anderson. Offense: Receivers—Max McGee, Bob Long, Bill Anderson, Red Mack. Linemen—Steve Wright, Gale Gillingham, Ken Bowman. Backs—Zeke Bratkowski (QB), D. Anderson, Jim Grabowski, Phil Vandersea. Defense: Linebacker—Tommy Crutcher. Linemen—Bob Brown, Jim Weatherwax. Backs—Doug Hart, Dave Hathcock. DNP—Paul Hornung.

Kansas City	0	10	0	0—10
Green Bay	7	7	14	7—35

GB	McGee 37 pass from Starr (Chandler kick)
KC	McClinton 7 pass from Dawson (Mercer kick)
GB	Taylor 14 run (Chandler kick)
KC	FG Mercer 31
GB	Pitts 5 run (Chandler kick)
GB	McGee 13 pass from Starr (Chandler kick)
GB	Pitts 1 run (Chandler kick)
MVP:	Bart Starr (Green Bay)

it, but Max somehow stuck his hand way behind his back and snagged it at about the 20-yard line. He then outran Fred Williamson into the end zone for the first score of the game and in Super Bowl history. It should be pointed out that Max had also caught the game-winning touchdown pass against Dallas.

McGee's touchdown came on a blitz. The Chiefs may not have realized that we loved when teams blitzed. We had a very good adjusting process for dogging linebackers and safeties. Guys like McGee could read a blitz and let us know it was coming, which gave us the time to think up a play to exploit it. Although Buchanan nearly got to me on that play and I was sacked early in the game by him, and then by Bobby Bell and Jerry Mays, overall I had great protection on blitzes. Our line allowed me to remain in the pocket rather than bootlegging or scrambling.

After we scored first, I didn't expect Kansas City to be discouraged. Dawson's running game couldn't get going, but he was having success with play-action early on and was able to bring his team back that way. The Chiefs had one long drive that ended with Mike Mercer missing a field goal, but then Dawson drove the Chiefs the length of the field. He completed one long pass to Taylor, and later hit McClinton on a slant across the middle for a short touchdown to tie the game, 7–7.

We came back with a long drive of our own, taking 11 plays. We scored when Taylor swept to the left, to the weak side, behind our guards, and ran in from 14 yards out. With the extra point, that put us ahead to stay, 14–7.

On the third play of that drive, we thought we had a quick touchdown on a pass of over 60 yards to Carroll Dale, but it was nullified because we had been offsides. That was on a third-and-1 and the Chiefs were expecting a run. We were basically a running team and knew defenses thought of us that way. We'd take advantage of that by faking a hand-off to the back going into the line and then throwing long to a receiver in single coverage. The completion to Dale was a different kind of play-action in that instead of faking a slant to Taylor, one of our most successful short-yardage plays, Taylor became a blocker and I faked a pitch to Elijah Pitts, who looked like he was going to take it off tackle. Everyone jammed into the center and I threw long to Dale. There was nothing I loved more than throwing long on third-and-short or fourth-and-short, when it was even more effective because of our conservative image. Another reason we had success with long passes on short-yardage plays is that defenses knew that my passes were typically in the middle to short range. They thought I wasn't strong enough to throw it very deep.

After our slow beginning, we were starting to get untracked. There weren't new wrinkles to our running game because we had confidence in what we had developed over the years. We knew that we had to sustain our blocks very well because they had good, strong guys who were quick to get off a block. The line did a heck of a job tying them up to create holes for Taylor and Pitts. Our passing game was also beginning to come together and we were having success throwing on third down, particularly when they'd blitz. Still, we weren't able to put up any more points in the first half, while the Chiefs added a field goal by Mercer to narrow our lead to 14–10. We weren't satisfied with our performance, but they had played well, so give them credit for the close halftime score.

We were disappointed and maybe even concerned that we hadn't played better in the first half. That made us think back to one of the most memorable games we ever had against Detroit. We were far behind at halftime, but I'd never seen Coach Lombardi calmer and more sure of what we had to do. He said that there was nothing wrong with our game plan and that all we had to do to turn the game around was to start executing according to our abilities. He said, "We aren't going to change one thing in the second half and we're going to win." And we did. Against the Chiefs at halftime, it was basically the same thing. He said we just had to tweak a few things and improve the quality of our play, and we'd be fine.

We played better in the second half and got a couple of breaks. On the Chiefs' first possession, there was a turnover that turned out to be the biggest play of the game. Kansas City was playing well and driving the ball when we surprised them with a rare blitz on third-and-5. Dave Robinson and Lee Roy Caffey put pressure on Dawson and he had to get rid of the ball quickly. He threw to his tight end, Fred Arbanas, but the ball wobbled and Willie Wood intercepted and took it back 50 yards, down to their 5. When I saw Wood make the big interception, I wasn't at all surprised. Our defense had so much experience and had made subtle adjustments at halftime, so there was bound to be a payoff. That's how we were trained; that's what we believed; that was the confidence factor working within us.

On our next play, Pitts sliced through their line for our third touchdown and Don Chandler's extra point made it 21–10. All teams have certain plays that they run at different locations on the field on certain downs and that hand-off to Pitts was one of our lead plays. Everyone knew exactly what we were going to run before I called it. I called all the plays that game but I was aware of what Lombardi wanted in every situation. He did a marvelous job getting us ready for each opponent and that was one of the joys of working with him.

There wasn't an exact moment when I thought, "We're clicking; now we're the Packers again." But at some point in the second half, we began to move the ball like I knew we could. Our running game was working better because we had a better feel for their defense. It takes awhile. A lineman learns about a defender after attempting to block him a few times. So you might come back to plays that you tried earlier and see if you can execute better. You get into that "zone," as they say today. You get that feeling, and you're throwing completions to McGee or Pitts or Fleming or Dale, and you're running the ball well with Taylor and Pitts. And defensively we got the turnover. We were getting into a good balance.

Now we were ahead, 21–10, but we didn't stop passing. On a drive of over 50 yards in the third quarter, I hit McGee three times for good gains, the last being a 13-yard post route into the end zone. He was the primary receiver and I made an accurate pass. He juggled this good pass but caught it, after having made a great stab of the first one that had been 2 feet behind him. We teased him about that. Here's a guy who didn't expect to get into the game and then steps in and plays one of the finest games of his life at a time we needed it badly. He was just superb. He caught seven passes for almost 140 yards and two touchdowns—after having caught only four passes all season!

Attacking the strength of the other team was not only discussed, it was a philosophy of Lombardi's. It would frustrate and cripple opponents if we beat them at their strengths. We would match up our strengths against their strengths, and then take advantage of the weaknesses we exposed. One of the Chiefs' strengths was their linebackers, who made it very hard for us to run inside. However, we had studied the Chiefs' linebacker formation and felt confident that our passing game could benefit from their look. They had two of their three linebackers situated inside their defensive ends—Sherrill Headrick was the middle linebacker so he had to be there, but they had either Bobby Bell or E. J. Holub stuck inside also. That gave us the opportunity on one side or both sides of the field to get our receivers into one-on-one situations with their backs. A defense could play double-zone coverages with that linebacker look as some teams did, but it couldn't play a strong-side zone coverage when its weak-side linebacker was stuck inside. There was no one to help a defensive back cover a receiver. So our plan was to isolate our wide receivers, McGee and Dale, on their cornerbacks, Willie Mitchell and Fred Williamson. They tended to tip their coverages and it was usually man coverage—and that was one of the keys to our success. The way they played their linebackers weakened their pass defense to the outside—so we threw to the outside. I don't think they could have adapted in a way to beat us, but they could have made some subtle changes coming into the game and that could have thrown us for a while and created some problems.

It was a physical game with a lot of big hits. On one play near the end of the game, Anderson ran behind our guard Gale Gillingham, and Fred Williamson was knocked unconscious and had to be carried off the field. During the week leading up to the game, Williamson had boasted that he'd use his "Hammer"—that was his nickname—arm blows to knock off the heads of our receivers. In those days, players didn't do much taunting and the Packers had never been spoken of in that manner, but our guys took it in stride and laughed it off for the most part because it was one thing to talk, another to perform. There wasn't any attempt at retaliation, but when he was knocked unconscious, some of our guys were happy and said, "Well, that's what you get. Tit for tat."

At one point, Taylor and Buchanan had words and almost got into a scuffle after Taylor was slammed to the turf following the whistle. On the next play I gave it to Taylor, who ran directly at Buchanan and picked up a few yards. That was just part of our scheme, part of our game plan. Taylor had a solid game for us, with that second-quarter touchdown and several important third-down runs. On third-and-short, we liked to use him on a slant off tackle because it was tough to stop him from making a few yards when he had blocking up front. He also made a couple of first-down runs on sweeps, with Fuzzy Thurston leading him around the end. I'm sure we also used Taylor as a decoy. We knew the Chiefs were looking for him because he was our lead guy, so we were able to sneak past them a few times with Pitts carrying the ball. Pitts gained almost as many yards as Taylor and had two touchdowns. His second touchdown came in the fourth quarter from 1 yard out on a slant to the left.

If the pressure was on any player, it would have been on Pitts, because he was replacing the injured Paul Hornung. When he joined the Packers in 1961, he was a bashful, insecure young man and Hornung took him under his wing and made him feel that he was part of the team. He would play for the Packers until 1969 and most of the time he didn't know if and when he was going to play, yet he *never* made a mental error, not once. He was almost always in a backup capacity, yet he always prepared himself as if he were going to be the starter. You have to tip your hat to someone like that. The man was always ready and that's the highest compliment that can be paid to a person.

I didn't sense that Kansas City was wearing down. I'm sure they were disturbed that they were falling farther behind, but I didn't detect them relenting in any way. However, as the Super Bowl went on, we were feeling more in control. We were increasingly enthusiastic because we could sense that all we worked for all year was building to a finish. We wanted to keep it going, keep the momentum going, but we made sure not to let everything get out of control. I was thinking about my leadership role and making sure I kept everything at an even keel. That's the discipline factor—Lombardi had drilled us all year to keep everything at a level pace. Nothing foolish, no early celebrating, no arrogance, and none of that flaunting—that's the one thing I dislike in today's pro game.

I personally didn't ever think "This game is over," but the lead increased to 28–10 and 35–10 with decreasing time to play, and we sensed that we were dominating the game. You know the end is there but you just continue to play and try not to make any foolish errors. We were disciplined not to take things for granted, but there's a swelling inside because you have reached a point you sought all year long, game by game. "Here it is; now it's happened." It's a wonderful feeling; it's hard to describe. When the gun goes off, it's exhilarating. You're tired in that you put forth this great physical effort and all the mental strain and emotion and all the practices and all the things that had built up to the game itself are there in the back of your mind. But you're so emotional at this point that you haven't begun to feel any of that yet. It will hit you later.

When the game ended, there was a lot of noise and excitement in the locker room. We didn't necessarily show it on the field—maybe we would today—but we were a very emotional group. Winning was never a mundane thing. I had really enjoyed playing that game. When you're in a competitive situation, it's fun. You don't win them all, but it's still fun while you're in there and working your butt off to win. That's what it's all about. I never thought in terms of personal accomplishment. I was picked the game's MVP and I don't want to dismiss that, but so many other people contributed to what I did. I had great protection, excellent runners, great pass receivers, and a superb defense. Our defense may have been my greatest asset. You have to execute, granted, but you need the opportunities.

After the game, Coach Lombardi was pressed by the media into comparing Kansas City with NFL teams and he admitted that Dallas was better. I think he regretted he said that; it was just said at an emotional moment and wasn't his style. That wasn't him. I'm sure I was asked the same thing and I hope I answered in a way that wouldn't make me want to apologize later. The Packers recognized how talented the Chiefs were. It's just that we had much more team maturity than them, and when you look at that game from all perspectives, you realize how big a role that played in our victory.

At the postgame party in Santa Monica, Lombardi would say complimentary things, put his arm around you, smile, shake your hand. He was an emotional person and you could tell he was very touched. He was so proud of his team and what he had brought to it. I have never seen as large a group of men who were so team oriented and unselfish as those on the Lombardi-coached Packers teams of the sixties. We had an unbelievable commitment from everyone to the team. When you have that with egos put aside in every instance, you win and you build. Near the end of his time with us, Coach Lombardi would make a very soft and profound statement about us as a team: "Long after these rings that you're so proudly wearing are tarnished and those fur coats which we've given to your wives are frayed, what you will remember most about these years are these people around you." He was exactly correct. Those people are what I remember best.

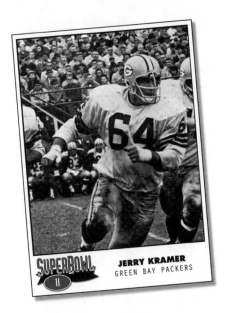

JERRY KRAMER
GREEN BAY PACKERS

SUPER BOWL II

GREEN BAY PACKERS 33
OAKLAND RAIDERS 14

JERRY KRAMER

The 1967 NFL Championship Game between the Packers and the Dallas Cowboys was played in Green Bay on December 31. At game time it was 13 degrees below zero, but the wind chill made it feel 30 degrees colder. This was the first time I ever wore gloves on the field. Because of the weather and the drama, the "Ice Bowl" would be remembered at least as much as our Super Bowl games. We took a 14-point lead, but as often happened with the Packers, we let up and let them back in the game. In fact, Dallas was ahead 17–14 late in the fourth quarter when we began our final drive.

Bart Starr saw that their linebackers were having trouble with traction so he brought us downfield with short passes to Donny Anderson and Chuck Mercein coming out of the backfield. Then with less than a minute left we had the ball at the Dallas 3 or 4. The field was icy and the footing was difficult. We ran a straight hand-off to Anderson between me, the right guard, and Forrest Gregg, the right tackle. Not much. Time out. Bart to the sidelines. Comes back. Straight hand-off again to Anderson. Nothing. Time out. Starr to the sidelines. Comes back. There is time for one more play. Coach Lombardi doesn't want Don Chandler to attempt a game-tying field goal to prolong the game, maybe because of the bad traction Don would have or maybe because he had confidence in our winning the game right then and going indoors.

Bart and I have different versions of what happened next. In my mind, he asked, "Has anybody got anything? Anybody?" Normally when he asked we were like a bunch of crows—I might ask for a sweep or Forrest might want to trap and Max McGee might want a slant pass, and everybody would be yapping. This time 10 guys checked their shoeshines. There wasn't a sound. Finally, Gale Gillingham, the left guard, said, "Run it over there with Jerry and Forrest; they'll get it for us." I had pointed out in Thursday's short-yardage film that Jethro Pugh, the Cowboys' left defensive tackle and my man, stood higher than Bob Lilly, their right tackle, and that if we needed to wedge somebody we could wedge Pugh. Coach Lombardi looked at the film three times and said, "That's right, put in a 31-Wedge." It was designed for Mercein, the fullback, to carry the ball. So now on our final play, Bart called either a 31-Wedge or a 61-Wedge. I talked to Chuck later and he thought he was going to get the ball, as we had discussed at that meeting. He wasn't aware that Starr was going to keep it. I just knew it was a wedge play and that I was the point of attack and the ball carrier would follow me.

It was so cold but everybody was alive, awake, intense, excited, and totally aware of what was going on. I felt a heavy responsibility to the team. I always blocked with my helmet rather than my shoulder and the perfect way for me to block in a critical situation was head up, eyes open, back straight, and the front of my face mask squarely between the numbers of the defensive tackle's chest. Lots of times I could use a fake or mess with the guy a little bit, or just cut him off, going down to his ankles and taking the chance he'd fall. But when I really couldn't afford to fail, then the best way to do it was to keep my eyes open until the point of contact. It's difficult to hit someone with your face and not shut your eyes or blink, even for a 265-pound guy like me. But it's the most effective way to block. I don't know—if Jethro Pugh had just fallen on the ground it might have been impossible for me to move him. But if I was going to move him, the best way to do it was to come off the ball as quickly as possible. I found a little divot, so I got a good start and broke as quickly as I ever had—I still don't know if I beat the snap but there was no flag. The Pugh block was designed as a double-team block and Kenny Bowman, our center, joined me. I still have the mental photographs. My first is of contact with Jethro, which was so critical, getting my face into his numbers and the jolt and the feeling of him starting to slide. Then lying there and just turning over in time to see Bart tumble into the end zone and Chuck jump onto the pile with his arms in the air. The feeling after that was "Whew! Oh, boy! Got it done, got it done!" It wasn't really exhilaration I felt but relief that I had done what I was asked to do and hadn't let my teammates down. We got to our feet routinely. We were a mature team and didn't dance or sing or hit the goalpost or play with our peters or do the antics the young boys go through today. We expected to score and we expected to win. We expected to go to the Super Bowl.

A week before the "Ice Bowl," *Esquire* had published a very derogatory article on Vince Lombardi by Leonard Schecter. He was said to be a tyrant and described as a little pigeon strutting on the sidelines. I had heard that his mother was crying about it and it was difficult for everybody. So I decided to set the record straight. After the Dallas game, I was interviewed on television, before 50 million people, and after talking about that block and my teammates, I said, "Coach Lombardi is misunderstood by a lot of people. We know him and we love him. He's a beautiful man." I had never called anyone in my life "a beautiful man." But it came out and he was very moved and said something nice about my having said something nice. He was an emotional man and really appreciated what I had said, and I felt good about it because I totally meant it.

Lombardi became our coach in 1959, a year after I came to the Packers out of the University of Idaho. He had played guard at Fordham and it was the perception of Fuzzy Thurston, the left guard, and myself that he seemed to focus on us, especially since we were the most visible linemen in Lombardi's power sweep. And since he had played right guard, I felt that I was his main focal point. He never showed me what he used to do or demonstrated his bullfrog stance or technique, but he did chew my ass out with regularity. For a couple of years, we had a very antagonistic relationship and our winning didn't make him ease up. In fact, he was more critical after a victory, which meant that he was rarely in a complimentary mood. So it was growl and mash your teeth and get in each other's face.

I viewed Coach Lombardi as negative and demanding, and thought he motivated through fear and anger. I didn't see his positive side.

Our relationship completely turned around one day in the early sixties. It was muggy and about 96 degrees and we were having a goal-line scrimmage. I was offsides a couple of times, and he gets in my face and gives me his concentration lecture: "College kids have a 15-minute concentration period, high school kids have a 10-minute concentration period, and 6-year-olds can concentrate 1 minute—so where the hell does that leave you?" He chews my ass the whole practice and I'm sitting in the locker room afterward thinking that it was maybe time to give up this game. He finally had beaten me down and I was there for 20 or 30 minutes, elbow on my knee, chin in my hand, looking at the floor. Then he comes by and pats me on the neck and says, "Son, one of these days you're going to be the best guard in football." And that just absolutely filled me up with an energy burst and a vision and a goal, the whole thing. His words got my motor started and from that point on I just worked my ass off to try to be the best guard in football.

My whole life changed in that one moment. And similar positive words had the same impact on Willie Davis, Herb Adderley, and other Packers as well. I've talked only to Willie and Herbie about it, but I'll bet that in other one-on-one conversations Coach Lombardi painted positive pictures for everybody on that team to motivate them. I don't know if it was his timing or that he was such an honest man that made us believe what he said about us was true. In any case, players who never had accomplished anything with the Packers or had been rejected by other teams became All-Pros for Lombardi.

After observing Coach Lombardi for a number of years I had gone from being a rebel to a convert. I had become a Lombardi disciple who bent to his will and believed in his concepts, philosophies, and principles. How the hell can you argue against preparation, commitment, consistency, discipline, perseverance, or giving 100 percent and playing as well as you can possibly play? If Lombardi saw a gap between your performance and what you were capable of, he thought it was his God-given responsibility to get on your ass night and day and get you more emotionally involved and get more out of you than you would get out of yourself. Bart Starr didn't have that much natural ability but Lombardi didn't get on his ass because he was giving him everything he had, without saving anything. Those players who closed that gap and got close to their potential performances—and Bart came closest—were treated differently.

By 1967 his criticism of me wasn't as piercing as it had been. After I really started busting my hump, he became much more supportive and patted me on the back more often. If I had a bad day, he felt bad for me and would say, "God, I hate to see you having a bad day like that. You're better than that." So his whole method of communicating with me changed. Even film days weren't quite as bad for me. In the middle of a game, in the heat of the battle, there would be a screwup and Kenny Bowman would say, "Oh, God, that's going to look bad Tuesday." You're right there fighting to win the damn game, yet you're worrying about Tuesday and how Lombardi would view your performance. So film day was omnipresent. In 1967, I still dreaded film days, but at least he didn't holler at me as much.

However, his training camp, which began in mid-July, was just as strenuous as it had ever been. Those Lombardi drills—especially the one-on-one "nutcrackers" and the up-down "grass drills"—were just as brutal. We older guys wouldn't get into the front row where we were too easy to see. We'd get together further back and cheat. When he faced us, we'd go like hell—up down, up down—but when he turned his back we were on one knee and breathing like mules, trying to get a blow and survive the son of a bitch. He knew what we were doing.

After the first Super Bowl, several Packers showed up for training camp in 1967 with book contracts. I certainly didn't play one of the team's glamour positions but I was offered a book deal, because after nine years in the league and several seasons as an All-Pro, I was pretty well known. My book, *Instant Replay,* which was influenced by pitcher Jim Brosnan's best-selling baseball diary, *The Long Season,* would chronicle my 1967 season with the Packers. Coach Lombardi knew I was doing a book but he didn't interfere. He did say, "There are too many damn blue shirts around here," in reference to all the players' outside business interests, including book writing. He wanted us to think only of football but couldn't come down on us as heavily as he once would have because by then he had outside interests as well. We thought about football so much under Lombardi that it was essential to get away when we could. I cherished my free time playing poker with Ron Kostelnik, Tommy Joe Crutcher, and three or four other guys; or golf—Donny Chandler and I would lose regularly to Max McGee and Zeke Bratkowski; or hunting quail with Carroll Dale, Doug Hart, and Bob Skoronski; or just staying up into the early morning, drinking and talking with my closest friends, Fuzzy and Boyd Dowler, and maybe Max.

For the first time since I had become a Packer, Jim Taylor and Paul Hornung were not in camp. Lombardi had thought Taylor disloyal for signing a free-agent contract with New Orleans and told us that he could be replaced. However, Lombardi was visibly upset that he'd lost Hornung in the expansion draft to the new Saints and said Paul would be missed. Everybody on the team really enjoyed and loved Paul. He was a hell of an athlete and he was fun and beautiful and a hot shot and a star and had a great way of spending time with you and making you feel good.

A couple of years into my career I learned a great lesson about the Packers from Paul. I was the type of player who had to go into a mental mode to get myself ready to play, and started to work up my anger from early in the week so that at 1 P.M. on Sunday I was ready to explode. The night before one game, I'm with Paul in Palo Alto and he's got a couple of fiancées and a couple of martinis and he's having a wonderful time. And I go, "Hey, jerko, we have to win this ball game tomorrow. This is critical to us. Goddamn, don't you think you ought to start thinking about the ball game?" He says, "Watch me. Watch me tomorrow inside the 10. Watch me on short yardage and then tell me what you think I ought to do." So I backed off and I watched his ass closely the next day and I realized, "Paul comes to one o'clock by a different route, but Paul comes to one o'clock"—and that was all that was important. On the Packers we didn't care if you were a saint like Bart or Carroll Dale or a sinner like Paul Hornung or his bookend Max McGee or a lot of us other guys. We didn't care about the color of your skin. We judged people solely by their performances on the field on Sunday afternoon between 1 and 4.

Because of the absence of Taylor and Hornung—who retired because of the pinched nerve in his neck without playing for New Orleans—and a season-ending knee injury to Elijah Pitts, many of our young backs, especially Donny Anderson and Jim Grabowski, got a lot of playing time in 1967. Otherwise, we were pretty similar to the Packers from the previous year. The biggest change was that Gillingham, who was big and fast, replaced Fuzzy as the starting left guard. I felt for Fuzzy, who had held that position since Lombardi came to Green Bay. He was a great guy who loved life and football. It killed him to be sat down, but rather than resent Gillingham, Fuzzy helped him learn the position.

To play guard on the Packers meant you had to pull on the sweep. In the early sixties, the "Green Bay Sweep" was a magnificent play where we'd average about 9 yards per carry. But it had deteriorated a bit by this time. It wasn't the weapon it had been, but it was always part of the repertoire. We could run the sweep strong or weak to Gillingham's side. If I'm the right guard and both guards are pulling right, my blocking assignment is the left cornerback, while our flanker takes on the strong-side safety, and our tight end blocks their left linebacker. Gilly or Fuzzy would pull from the left side and come all the way around our right end, to the left of my path. The ball carrier could either follow us around or cut inside if their left defensive end has been pushed to the outside. We didn't want the defensive end to penetrate or pursue. The tackle on my side, Forrest Gregg, would have a call—and it would be an odd or even call with the center Kenny Bowman—and in most cases he would hit the defensive end with his right shoulder and try not to get tangled up by him but just distract him momentarily. He'd set up the defensive end and then go on to block the middle linebacker. If it worked properly, the defensive end focused on Gregg going inside and that set him up for the onside back to cut him down with a crossbody block before he got off the line.

Under Lombardi I always strove for perfection. In 1967, I was still trying to achieve a perfect game. I had come close but had never done it. After a rough opening game against Alex Karras of the Lions, I had a good season, better than 1966 I thought, and good enough to make All-Pro. The team struggled more than in the previous year and had season-ending injuries to Pitts and Grabowski. We lost four games and tied another and it could have been worse because Bart missed a few games. But as it had been in the past, Zeke Bratkowski stepped in and was up to the task. Bart was back in time for the postseason, but we would have had confidence with Zeke in there.

Personally, when I looked at our playoff schedule, I was looking ahead to the Super Bowl, or the AFL–NFL World Championship Game as it was officially called. In my reading of the situation, the three games ahead were going to be in the inverse order of difficulty. I thought the first game against the Los Angeles Rams would be the most difficult game and that we would have a slightly easier time against the winner of the Dallas–Cleveland playoff game. We felt confident that we could win the Super Bowl if we got there.

The Rams had beaten us a couple of weeks earlier, they'd beaten the hell out of Baltimore, and they were flying. We were a little concerned for the first time. Ray Wietecha, our offensive line coach, said, "What the hell. Sometimes you can't win them all." I wanted to kick his ass. The Rams went ahead 7–0, but we came back to win 28–7. Bart had a great game, completing over 70 percent of his passes, and our speedy rookie back, Travis Williams, scored two touchdowns and picked up a lot of yards. I would be surprised that Williams wouldn't get many carries against Dallas or Oakland.

The Cowboys turned out to be a much tougher opponent than the Rams, but we did beat them in the freezing NFL title game. We could then focus on playing in the Super Bowl against the Oakland Raiders, who had killed the Houston Oilers later that day. We especially looked forward to playing at the Orange Bowl in the warm weather of Miami. However, we didn't pack our bags right away. For the first week, we practiced in Green Bay, in awful weather. It must have been because of budgetary reasons because I can't think of any other explanation for our practicing in 6-below temperatures. Ray Nitschke's toes had been frostbitten in the Dallas game and he still had to go out there to practice. And soon everybody else was suffering with blistered and peeling toes and frosted ears, and we had to try to go out there and "warm up." Lombardi actually told Nitschke to go out and work up a sweat. Right. I'm still angry about that.

Finally, we flew to Florida and the 75-degree temperatures. Only we didn't stay in Miami. Lombardi had booked us into the Galt Ocean Mile Hotel in Fort Lauderdale. This was his way of telling us that we were there to prepare for the game, not to have fun. He intended to keep us too busy to get into trouble, so he'd try to schedule a meal, a meeting, a practice, or some function every hour or 90 minutes so we didn't have much free time. Once in a while we'd have a few hours off and have fun. Did Lombardi cramp McGee's style? Hell no. That was impossible. Max contacted all his acquaintances down there and made the rounds, going to the Bombay Club and all the other clubs in town. The rest of us had fun when we got a few hours off, and altogether I look back on the week with fond memories.

We worked hard to prepare for Oakland. We knew a little about them, but nowhere near like we knew the Chicago Bears or Detroit Lions. We had played Kansas City the year before, so the AFL—that inferior league—was part of our business now and we'd watch the teams on film every now and then. At our offense meetings, we watched the Raiders' defense on film and studied them intently. Depending on the defense, we'd prepare four or five blocking schemes. We'd plan to counter their short-yardage defense, middle-of-the-field defense, sometimes the four-man front, the five-man front. The Raiders didn't have as many variations as a team like the Bears, which would have up to 14 defensive setups that we'd have to prepare for. We wouldn't be surprised by whatever they had in mind. We had run our offense for nine years and it was unusual for us to make mental errors.

I realized I'd be spending most of my time blocking Dan Birdwell, their left tackle. It was my practice to learn my guy's stance to see if he had any tendencies that would give away which direction he was going. Sometimes if a tackle wanted to go to his left, he'd bring his left foot up a little and have his feet a little more parallel, or his weight on his hand, or his weight back. So I watched every aspect of Birdwell's play. I also watched their left end Ike Lassiter and left linebacker Bill Laskey, because I knew I'd also be blocking them a lot. On film, I'd study a guard who had played against Oakland to see how Lassiter would react to a trap or how Laskey would react to a drive block, and things like that. Overall, in our plan to attack a defense, I rarely got into anything else. I was a specialist. It was enough to know we could throw the ball against certain people and run the ball on just about anybody. Otherwise, I really needed to know only about my assignments and the defenders I would take on. Like all the Packers, I was well prepared by game day.

I always had a hard time sleeping before games. I took a sleeping pill almost always the night before. For breakfast, I'd pick. I didn't eat much and ate very little meat. I was big on toast and I'd pour half a glass of honey into a potato and then smother my toast in honey and try to eat as much honey as I could.

To relax, I went on the field to watch the pregame show. I remembered the program from Super Bowl I with the guys flying around the stadium with their jet packs. That was exciting as hell. This time they rolled out these two great big statues, each 25 to 35 feet high, one Packer and one Raider, and they had smoke coming out of their nostrils. They were on a rail so they could get close together and appear to be in combat. That was kind of fun. They did such a wonderful job of promoting the game and creating hoopla that if you weren't pumped, you had to be dead.

We had a pregame tradition where the coaches would leave the team alone in the locker room and the team captains, Bob Skoronski and Willie Davis, would get up and speak their piece. They talked about how the game was going to determine what would be said about the Packers the next day and how we had to win another title because it meant recognition, prestige, and money. They were right about the money. Getting $15,000 per man was a big incentive for us to win the Super Bowl. We had thought of that money all year long because it would double some of our salaries. That was certainly something we all wanted. It was huge, but it wasn't bigger than our pride or responsibility or our teammates.

After the captains spoke, Forrest Gregg, another veteran, said that the Raiders were a little bit afraid of us and that we had to go at them from the very first whistle and put it to them every play. Then McGee said that he wanted to win the last game of his career and Ray Nitschke told us, "Let's play with our hearts." Carroll Dale, who was very active in the Fellowship of Christian Athletes, then led us in the Lord's Prayer and we ran out onto the field for the pregame warm-ups, hooping and hollering.

We then returned to the locker room for some final words from Coach Lombardi. During the previous two weeks, he'd delivered a conflicting message: That it would be a disgrace to lose to a team from a "Mickey Mouse" league; and that the Raiders were a hell of a team and would be hard to beat. Now, in his final speech, he told us, "You are the world champions. You are the champions of the National Football League for the third time in a row, for the first time in the history of the National Football League. That's a great thing to be proud of. But all the glory, everything that you've won, is going to be small in comparison to winning this one." We listened carefully. Some of us sensed that it was the last time he would address us before a game. Although he had told us nothing, he had hinted that he would retire as Packers coach after the game. That certainly pumped us up.

Super Bowl II was played before over 75,000 fans at the Orange Bowl on a hot day. We were two-touchdown favorites and our overall feeling was: We're the champions, we're the best, and we should win this game. Just go out and do your job, take care of business.

Oakland received the opening kickoff but we quickly got the ball. The defense we faced had some good players. We knew their massive right end Ben Davidson because he had tried out with us several years earlier. He was known for his handlebar mustache. He was a very tall, strong kid, but we knew Skoronski, who had been named to the Pro Bowl for the first time, could take care of him. Next to Davidson at right tackle was Tom Keating. He was playing hurt but he still impressed me. On the other side, Dan Birdwell, my chief assignment, didn't have the quickness or strength of Alex Karras or Merlin Olson, the two left tackles who gave me the most trouble in the NFL. But he was a good competitor and made a couple of tackles during our first two possessions. Their linebackers, Bill Laskey, Dan Conners, and Gus Otto, were active and good, but they didn't compare to Dick Butkus, Joe Schmidt, or our guys— Ray Nitschke, with that forearm of his, Dave Robinson, and Lee Roy Caffey. They certainly weren't as tough. There wasn't any one defensive player who stuck out, like Buck Buchanan, Jerry Robinson, E. J. Holub, and Bobby Bell had on Kansas City the year before. They weren't of that caliber.

They often used a 5–2 defense—five linemen and two linebackers. It was a bit confusing but not that effective. Their odd-man line at times would force me to become a utility blocker because there wouldn't always be a defensive lineman directly on me. At times I'd be uncovered and it seems like I was picking up linebackers or backing up the center quite a bit. I played between Forrest Gregg, who was as solid as they come, and Kenny Bowman, who hadn't started at center in Super Bowl I and had only recently won back his job. Like all of us, Bowman had some weaknesses, and he went the wrong way a couple of times because of nervousness, but his attitude was great and he busted his ass.

Our plan was to run on them. To the left, we would run a lot of plays directly at Ben Davidson, successfully attacking their strength. We had some plays designed for our backs Donny Anderson and Ben Wilson, who was in there at fullback ahead of Mercein. We got short on people, and Wilson, who weighed about 230, was one of those guys who comes along and rises to the occasion, like Chuck had done against Dallas. Anderson and Wilson were steady, solid. Donny was flashy, with a little speed. He wasn't a great blocker but he could get the job done. Ben was a workhorse. He'd get 4 or 5 yards, which was our game. We used him as we had Jim Taylor: He'd do the slant off tackle, and there were several variations off that. We were the Packers, so we were going to run the sweeps, the traps, the backs off tackle, the same stuff we'd been running for nine years. We weren't going to change—it was up to Oakland to line up and stop us. I guess we stuck to the ground game because it worked.

On our first two possessions we ran a lot of plays and ate up the clock. In fact, the second time we covered 80 yards in 16 plays and held the ball almost 9 minutes, taking us into the second quarter. Yet both drives were stalled and we had to settle for field goals by Don Chandler. In the mid-fifties, when Chandler was a young punter with the Giants, he would have gotten out of pro football entirely if New York's offensive coach Vince Lombardi hadn't chased him down at the airport. Chandler and Lombardi had rough times in New York, but after Lombardi brought him to Green Bay a few years later, their relationship became warmer. Don felt he owed Lombardi a lot and in 1967, his final season, he was repaying him with the best kicking of his career, making the Pro Bowl for the first itime. Now my close friend and roommate was having the best game of his career.

It wasn't all that frustrating that we had only 6 points so far because we had been able to move the ball and to score both times we had possession.

January 14, 1968, at the Orange Bowl in Miami
Paid Attendance: 75,546
NFL Champion: Green Bay Packers (11–4–1)
Head Coach: Vince Lombardi
AFL Champion: Oakland Raiders (14–1)
Head Coach: John Rauch

STARTING LINEUPS

OFFENSE			DEFENSE		
Green Bay		**Oakland**	**Green Bay**		**Oakland**
Boyd Dowler	LE	Bill Miller	Willie Davis	LE	Ike Lassiter
Bob Skoronski	LT	Bob Svihus	Ron Kostelnik	LT	Dan Birdwell
Gale Gillingham	LG	Gene Upshaw	Henry Jordan	RT	Tom Keating
Ken Bowman	C	Jim Otto	Lionel Aldridge	RE	Ben Davidson
Jerry Kramer	RG	Wayne Hawkins	Dave Robinson	LLB	Bill Laskey
Forrest Gregg	RT	Harry Schuh	Ray Nitschke	MLB	Dan Conners
Marv Fleming	TE	Billy Cannon	Lee Roy Caffey	RLB	Gus Otto
Bart Starr	QB	Daryle Lamonica	Herb Adderley	LHB	Kent McCloughan
Carroll Dale	FL	Fred Biletnikoff	Bobby Jeter	RHB	Willie Brown
Donny Anderson	RB	Pete Banaszak	Tom Brown	LS	Warren Powers
Ben Wilson	RB	Hewritt Dixon	Willie Wood	RS	Howie Williams

SUBSTITUTIONS

Green Bay: K/P—Don Chandler. Offense: Receivers—Bob Long, Max McGee, Dick Capp. Linemen—Fuzzy Thurston, Bob Hyland. Backs—Zeke Bratkowski (QB), Travis Williams, Chuck Mercein. Defense: Linebackers—Tommy Crutcher, Jim Flanigan. Linemen—Bob Brown, Jim Weatherwax. Backs—John Rowser, Doug Hart. DNP—Jim Grabowski, Don Horn, Steve Wright.

Oakland: K—George Blanda. P—Mike Eischeid. Offense: Receivers—Warren Wells, Dave Kocourek, Ken Herock. Linemen—Bob Kruse, Jim Harvey, Dan Archer. Backs—Larry Todd, Roger Hagberg. Defense: Linebackers—John Williamson, Bill Budness, Duane Benson. Linemen—Carleton Oates, Richard Sligh. Backs—Dave Grayson, Rodger Bird. DNP—Rod Sherman.

Green Bay	3	13	10	7—33
Oakland	0	7	0	7—14

GB	FG Chandler 39
GB	FG Chandler 20
GB	Dowler 62 pass from Starr (Chandler kick)
Oak	Miller 23 pass from Lamonica (Blanda kick)
GB	FG Chandler 43
GB	Anderson 2 run (Chandler kick)
GB	FG Chandler 31
GB	Adderley 60 interception (Chandler kick)
Oak	Miller 23 pass from Lamonica (Blanda kick)
MVP:	Bart Starr (Green Bay)

I was thinking we should have scored more points but that we probably would soon. And on our very next play, Boyd Dowler got behind cornerback Kent McCloughan and caught a pass from Starr about 20 yards upfield and ran the rest of the way for our first touchdown. That play covered 62 yards and made the score 13–0. Dowler was always a big-play receiver. He had caught two touchdown passes from Bart in the Dallas game.

To be honest, when we prepared for this game I didn't pay too much attention to the Raiders' offense, which was more impressive than their defense. I knew that Daryle Lamonica had a strong arm and good receivers like Billy Cannon and Fred Biletnikoff, and that Oakland had some tough runners and solid interior linemen like Gene Upshaw and Jim Otto. I figured Herb and Willie Wood and the rest of our defensive guys would study them and shut them down.

The Raiders were known for their power sweep, but our ends Willie Davis and Lionel Aldridge and our backs Willie Wood, Tom Brown, and Bob Jeter contained Pete Banaszak and Hewritt Dixon every time they went wide. Supposedly they couldn't pull their second guard, Upshaw, because he had to stick with Henry Jordan. However, Oakland put together a good drive with Banaszak and Dixon running inside and Lamonica throwing short passes, often to the two backs. Finally, Lamonica hit Bill Miller with a touchdown pass down the right sideline. When they scored I was a bit surprised. I'm sure we marked it down and realized we had our hands full. But there was never panic or deep fear or great concern. I thought we had gotten lazy and careless.

George Blanda, the one-time Bear, missed a long field goal that would have narrowed the score to 13–10. Then with 45 seconds left in the half we got a big break when Anderson's punt was fumbled in Oakland territory and recovered by Dick Capp, who had just been promoted from our taxi squad. Starr hit Dowler with a big third-down pass, and with one second left, Chandler kicked a long field goal, his third of the half, and we led 16–7 going into the locker room.

There wasn't anything to discuss at halftime. We knew we had to stop making silly high school mistakes and execute. Our game plan was fine. I got together with Ski and Gregg and said, "Let's play the last 30 minutes for the old man." I don't recall if I said it loud enough for everyone to hear, although I was trying to be loud enough. You didn't make speeches in front of the guys—I didn't at least.

On our second possession of the second half we put together another long drive. The big play was a 35-yard pass from Starr to McGee on a third-and-1. Just like last year, Max came in when Dowler got hurt and that was his only reception of the game and final reception of his career. We got the ball to the 1, on a first and goal. Anderson lost a yard going to the left, so the next play was to go to the right. I had to get past the defensive linemen and then make an abrupt right to get to Laskey, the linebacker I was supposed to block. Normally I would shield him from the path the ball carrier would try to take, getting between him and the ball carrier. But in this situation, Laskey was in an awkward position, in the hole waiting for Anderson, so I had to drive him past the hole and out of the way. I was able to do that without getting my feet tangled up and I got there before Donny did, so he scored easily. It was a good block.

The score was 23–7. Chandler kicked another field goal to make it 26–7, then early in the fourth quarter, Herb Adderley sealed the victory by stepping in front of Biletnikoff for an interception and running it back 60 yards for a touchdown. The Raiders managed to get another touchdown, again on a pass from Lamonica to Miller, and that closed out the scoring. It was a game where Oakland made several costly mistakes while the Packers had no interceptions or fumbles and were penalized only once.

Although our lead increased, Birdwell and the rest of the Raiders' defense never quit like I felt some of the Chiefs did the year before when they fell far behind. Late in the game, he congratulated me on nailing him with a good block, then on the next play, he got around me and sacked Bratkowski.

Zeke was in there because Bart had jammed his thumb when Davidson fell on him. Rather than going to the air, he kept handing the ball off, using up the clock. Wilson did a lot of the running until sometime in the fourth quarter when he was crawling around the sidelines looking for a missing contact lens. Then Travis Williams got a few carries. I was too concerned with my running plays and my pass blocking, my responsibilities, to not be aware of the other guys, like Bart. I did know that our runners were doing well but I wasn't aware that Bart was having a good game. I didn't think he had a particularly hot hand. I was surprised by his numbers, although he didn't complete 60 percent of his passes as he usually did. I halfway wanted Chandler to be MVP because he kicked four field goals and had 15 points. I thought that might at least get him the game ball. It would have been a great way to end his career.

Our captains were supposed to carry Coach Lombardi off the field at the end of the game, but Davis was on the field. So Forrest Gregg and I, the closest players to him, lifted him up and carried him to the dressing room. He was grinning and slapping us on the shoulders and head.

The first thing we did in the locker room was recite the Lord's Prayer, which was traditional. Then we had a burst of emotion. Then we congratulated everybody, slapped everybody, and hugged everybody. We hugged a lot—we still do. Good feeling, good game, way to go. Winning a game that big results in a wonderful, wonderful euphoric feeling. There was a feeling of a job well done, a responsibility met. We had performed as we were supposed to, did the things we should have. We didn't clutch; we didn't get the lump; we didn't choke. We had played a good solid football game. It was a satisfying way to end the year, being on top. It would have been absolutely devastating to have lost what turned out to be Vince Lombardi's last game as our coach.

I would wear the large Super Bowl II ring, not the one from the first year. For me it was our most difficult year and our most rewarding year. I love the appearance of the ring. There are three diamonds on the ring, symbolic of our being the only team to win three NFL titles in a row, within an emerald football. There's a Green Bay helmet inside an NFL shield, and five flags above the shield, representing our five NFL titles. And there are the scores of the three postseason games we had just won. Best of all: way down at the bottom of one side of the ring is a chevron that says *Challenge*. At the beginning of the season, Coach gave us about an hour lecture on the challenge ahead and how difficult it would be to win our third consecutive title. The players always talked about that challenge and then we met it. On the other side of the ring, there's another chevron that says *Run to Win*. When we went into the Rams game, the first playoff game, we weren't sure we could win. Coach Lombardi gave us a wonderful, emotional talk in the locker room, from Saint Paul's Epistles. Paraphrasing: "Of all the runners who run in the race, only one can win. So run not just to be in the race, run to win." That's on the ring. So those memories of the season, the team, the difficulty. . . . That ring kind of sums it all up.

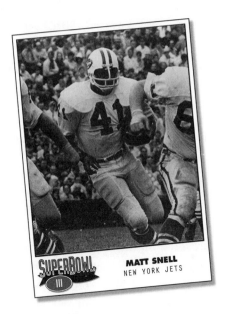

MATT SNELL
NEW YORK JETS

SUPER BOWL III

NEW YORK JETS 16
BALTIMORE COLTS 7

MATT SNELL

In 1964 I was the New York Jets' first pick in the AFL draft and the second player taken by the New York Giants in the NFL draft. Timmy Mara came out to talk to me about the Giants' tradition and how they were an established team and all that, and I'm saying, "What about the money?" They were offering me $10,000 less than the Jets. Also, I figured I'd have to sit a couple of years behind the Giants' backs Alex Webster and Frank Gifford, while I could start right away in the Jets' backfield. So I signed with the Jets. Paul Warfield, who was drafted by the Cleveland Browns, said, "How can you go to the AFL instead of the NFL?" I said, "Paul, you and I played together at Ohio State, and I don't think you're better than I am just because you're going to the NFL. The only reason the NFL is better now is that it has guys with 10 or 12 years' experience, but once those guys get old or retire and the AFL gets a lot of other good guys out of college, we'll be equal." By 1968, the Jets' championship year, the AFL was on the same level as the NFL.

I did get to play immediately for the Jets. In 1964 I led the team in both rushing and pass receiving and was voted the AFL's Rookie of the Year. But the Jets finished only 5–8–1. My goal for the team was to get enough quality players so that we could unseat the Bills and Patriots as the best team in the AFL East. That's what we began to do in 1965, when we drafted Joe Namath and Emerson Boozer. You have to understand that when they first dreamed up the Super Bowl—or World Championship Game, as it was called the first couple of years—the Jets' players never gave it much thought. Our goal, even in 1968, was to win the AFL championship.

The AFL had always been considered a bit of a joke, like the Follies, because you had all these crazy plays. But the one thing it was bringing to football was a lot of passing. Before the merger, the ball we used was a lot more streamlined and made aerodynamically for passing. And they brought in some strong-armed quarterbacks like Len Dawson, Daryle Lamonica, and John Hadl, and when those guys made some noise the AFL started to get noticed. Then, when Joe Namath was drafted by the St. Louis Cardinals yet chose the New York Jets over them, the entire league really started to get press. Particularly the Jets.

To outbid the St. Louis Cardinals for Namath, the Jets made the first big investment in a quarterback. At that time no quarterback got $400,000, which is what Sonny Werblin paid Joe when he came out of Alabama. Before he arrived at our training camp there was all this publicity in the papers, so Weeb Ewbank, who was the general manager as well as coach, called the players together and said, "I have no control over what Sonny wants to give in bonuses, but I promise you that Joe Namath's yearly salary is in line with everybody else's." I think Joe's first-year salary was probably no more than $25,000. I was making $22,000, other guys were making $20,000 or maybe $27,000, so we were all right there together. We couldn't feel any animosity toward Namath because the owner decided to give him an enormous bonus. I think by calling that meeting, Weeb diffused some hard feelings. It might have happened privately, but I have no memory of Joe addressing the whole team to ease friction. I do remember that when he reported to our facility at Peekskill Military Academy, he arrived in a big limo! We'd never heard of such a thing.

The only players who seemed to resent Joe were some over-the-hill guys, and they would be gone soon. I thought Joe and I got along well. A lot of people thought there was friction just because we didn't hang out together, but I didn't hang out with too many people. In truth, the Jets were never a close team with lots of players going out together and everybody hanging out at everybody else's house. Besides, I couldn't afford to hang out with Joe because I didn't have the kind of money he had. (Later, I couldn't hang out with him if I wanted to make my new marriage work. Broadway Joe had that playboy reputation and also loved that Johnnie Walker Red.)

I hate to admit it, but early on there was a lot of black–white divisiveness on the Jets. Some players who I would call "borderline rednecks" pulled stuff against some of the black guys. One night they pulled a real nasty trick on a little wide receiver named Al Dawson in the dormitory at Peekskill. They had white sheets over their heads and they pulled him out of bed. I happened to hear a commotion and went into Al's room after they'd sneaked out and found Al tied up and gagged, with a noose hanging over him. Weeb called a meeting and Sonny told the players, "The only two people in this whole room who are important to this team are Joe Namath and Matt Snell. The rest of you can all pack up your bags and leave. I won't put up with this kind of stuff." He really reamed out the whole squad. So we never had another incident. But there were really strained relationships—it was so intense. (I heard it was like that throughout the AFL.) Weeb would always say, "I'll put up with anything until I find someone to replace you," and the next year those guys who pulled the "prank" were gone. That eased the tension and black and white players got better acquainted and hung out more together. I know some other black players on the team would hang out with Joe at his East Side clubs. The whole team got along better, yet, as I said, we never became as close-knit as people would like to believe, even in our championship season.

Joe came out of college with a bad knee, so the Jets became big proponents of protecting the quarterback. Blocking came natural to me because I'd done it for Woody Hayes at Ohio State. (Hayes taught me head-first "spear" blocking, so I did so many neck exercises that I wore an 18-inch shirt collar.) But Weeb told Boozer that if he couldn't block he wouldn't play. I knew Boozer was too good of a runner not to be out there with me, so I worked with him, teaching him how to block by keeping his head up and eyes open. And he became quite a blocker.

On the line, our guards Dave Herman, Randy Rasmussen, and former Oiler Bob Talamini—the first person Weeb traded for who could still play—were geared to protect Namath. They were short, stocky guys who could really dig in. They didn't have the speed to pull out and lead on the sweep, like Jerry Kramer and Fuzzy Thurston did at Green Bay, so Boozer and I, who didn't have the speed to get outside on our own, were pretty much limited to running between the tackles.

Joe had great wide receivers in Don Maynard and George Sauer. Early in his career Maynard had been cut by the Giants and had gone to play in Canada. Then he came to us and became a Hall of Fame receiver. He was an ole country boy who rarely said anything. He was our speed guy, who we'd turn loose on fly patterns. George was one of the best pattern receivers you'll ever find. He worked at it and worked at it. If Maynard became a harder worker and more skilled receiver it was because he watched Sauer. Everything with George was timing. He would count his steps and make the same sharp break every time, cutting on a dime. I'd ask him, "How do your knees take that?"

Our offense improved, but to become a championship team we needed a better defense. And in 1966, we signed Johnny Sample, which I thought was a good move. He had been on the Colts when they won the 1958 and 1959 NFL championships under Weeb Ewbank and had played with the Steelers and Redskins before he came to us. Johnny had been around a long time, but he still had a lot of desire to play and a lot of athletic ability and speed, and he had that reputation. He brought us that toughness, that NFL mentality. Randy Beverly, our other corner, was a rookie in 1967. We already had Jim Hudson at strong safety—he came in with me—and Billy Baird at free safety, so we had good depth in the defensive backfield.

On the defensive line, Verlon Biggs came in the year after me and our other end Gerry Philbin. Biggs weighed about 275 and was one of the most intimidating defensive linemen in the league. Weeb converted John Elliott, who had been a linebacker at Texas, into a defensive tackle. You probably couldn't get away with that today because Elliott never weighed more than 240–245 pounds. He gave us more speed and versatility than our other tackle Paul Rochester. In the Super Bowl, Elliott would catch the Colts' tight end John Mackey from behind twice on plays that should have gone for touchdowns. So moves like that really helped.

Weeb didn't need Elliott at linebacker because he already had a good group with Larry Grantham, Ralph Baker, and our middle linebacker Al Atkinson. Baker would make big fumble recoveries in both the AFL title game and the Super Bowl. He and Atkinson were drafted in the mid-sixties, while Grantham had a lot more experience. Larry weighed just 210–215, but he was a great linebacker.

Grantham was the defensive captain and a veteran leader. Sample also gave us leadership on defense. He was a talker, but he had the experience to back it up. He always had something to say, whether it was relevant or not. Jim Hudson also gave us a lot of leadership, though he wasn't the talker Sample was. Billy Baird was another silent leader who just did his job and led by example.

On offense there were a lot of leaders other than Namath; just no one talks about them. There was me, Dave Herman, Winston Hill, John Schmitt. . . . It wasn't so much that Joe provided leadership, but that we had confidence that he was going to be there for us, that he was going to do his part. Joe's feeling was, "Look, if you do your job and I do my job, we'll win. I don't have to set an example for you." A lot of times, Joe would be hanging out at parties and you'd wonder if he was capable of doing his job, but when he got on the field he worked hard.

The Jets improved each year, but it wasn't until our 1968 opener against Kansas City that I saw we had the potential to be a championship team. I think Namath grew up so much in that game. Joe was prone to throwing a lot of interceptions, especially in key situations, but in that game he called smart plays. They weren't necessarily low-risk plays, but he knew he had a good shot at completing them because of the strength of his arm. We were ahead 20–19 late in the game but were backed up inside our 5-yard line. Namath was able to hit a couple of slant-in passes to Don Maynard, who wasn't known as a tough, over-the-middle receiver. I can still see those catches. We ran when we had to—draws, traps—and we marched right down the field and held the ball for the rest of the game. Hank Stram said, "I never believed a team would ever do that to my team." That made all of us sit back and reflect: If we could do that to the Chiefs, we could probably beat anybody.

We lost only three games during the season to win the AFL East for the first time. Then we played the Oakland Raiders in the AFL Championship Game. Everything was against us because Oakland had won all the close games we'd played, including the "Heidi Bowl" that year, when NBC switched to a "Heidi" special just before we blew our late lead and lost 43–32. (People told me that when they found out the final score, they couldn't believe we had lost. I told them I couldn't believe it and I was in the game.) I think Oakland felt that if they played us close they'd win as they'd done in the past, but Maynard had a couple of touchdown catches and we pulled it out, 27–23. I've always told people that beating the Raiders in New York was a bigger thrill to me than beating the Colts in the Super Bowl. To me, the AFL Championship was the crowning victory in my season. The Super Bowl was like an extension of the season that I didn't really need. I didn't even care if I played in it. None of us realized how important it was. Who knew that 30 years later people would be talking about that Super Bowl?

Super Bowl III was going to be played in the Orange Bowl in Miami and I can honestly say that I didn't even think about how we were representing the AFL until we arrived in Florida. But a lot of AFL players were down there during the week, and guys like Buck Buchanan from the Chiefs and Daryle Lamonica from the Raiders were coming by and saying, "Win it for the AFL." That put some pressure on us because they were asking us to do something that they couldn't do themselves. Kansas City and Oakland, our best teams in the previous two years, had been badly beaten in the first two Super Bowls. I'd told people that I didn't feel ashamed that they lost because nobody in the NFL could beat the Green Bay Packers either. The Packers were a powerhouse. I wouldn't have wanted to play them, but they were no longer at their peak and we were lucky that the Baltimore Colts had become the NFL's best team in 1968.

We watched all the Colts films, including the 34–0 win over the Browns in the NFL title game. They had won 15 of 16 games, including 10 in a row, 4 with shutouts. But we realized that they weren't as strong as everybody made them out to be, especially on defense. The thing you have to understand: The NFL as a whole refused to play a zone defense. The exception was the Colts, who were forced to play a zone because they didn't have two good cornerbacks. That minus turned into a big plus because all the NFL teams who lost to the Colts that year were inexperienced in facing the zone and didn't know how to attack it. Baltimore was lucky that offenses went against their zone with plays designed to attack man-to-man defenses. However, we wouldn't do that. The AFL didn't have many good cornerbacks, so everybody used a zone defense and we played against zones all year. So unlike the teams the Colts had beaten, we knew the intricacies, the holes, how to flood zones. . . . The Colts played the zone very well, but we knew how to attack it. Weeb emphasized to the receivers, "Find the dead spots in the zone, hook up, and Joe will hit you."

That we were 18-point underdogs was an insult to everyone. There was no way we could be 18-point underdogs to the Colts or anyone else.

Maybe a field goal, a touchdown, . . . but putting us 18 points below them was like saying we were no better than a high school team. It made everybody angry, not just Namath.

I wasn't at the Miami Touchdown Club when Namath "guaranteed" a Jets victory. I think some of us were deep-sea fishing: me, Winston Hill, Emerson Boozer, Mike D'Amato, and a couple of other guys. (We caught enough fish to feed the whole team at our hotel in Fort Lauderdale.) When we got back we saw the headlines with Namath's quote. People don't know that Joe got that "I guarantee it" line the day before from our tight end Pete Lammons. We were sitting and watching film and our offensive coach Clive Rush, who was devising the offensive game plan with Weeb and our line coach Chuck Knox, was running the films back and forth and going on and on. Finally, Pete Lammons stood up and said, "Clive, please don't show us anymore. I *guarantee* we'll beat these guys if they play the same way." So Joe took that and said it when he was getting his AFL MVP Award and the press picked up on it. I don't think that put more pressure on our team because we already felt that we could win the game if we got our running game going and Joe didn't throw interceptions. We were just glad Joe didn't go any further and say, "I guarantee we'll win . . . if they play the zone that they've been playing all year."

That was a pretty laid-back week. There were light workouts and Weeb didn't even make us wear pads that often. We had played our whole schedule so Weeb knew we were in shape. Most days were pretty much taken up by practice and team meetings, but otherwise we were on our own. You'd lie around, play cards, go fishing. . . . I had some friends in the area, so I did a lot of visiting. Weeb relaxed the curfew and did away with bed checks. Practice wasn't until 10 or 11 the next day, so even if you hung out till 1 or 2 in the morning you still got enough sleep. Everybody did their own thing. He didn't treat us like children, and I think the guys responded.

I seem to remember something about missing Photo Day. I think Boozer and I did miss it. Maybe Namath, too. I don't remember getting any bad feedback. If anything, we probably caught hell from Weeb. I don't even think we got fined because I would remember that. You didn't consider those things to be important back then because we weren't under nearly as much media scrutiny as there is today. A lot of the press people didn't even get down to Florida until Wednesday or Thursday, so it wasn't really a high-pressure thing. Anyway, the only guy the press seemed to care about was Namath. They'd write about how he went to a club every night. I doubt that Joe did as much drinking as people claimed and still performed as well as he did. He was serious about the game.

When we had our final team meeting on Saturday, we just tried to reinforce what we were down there for. We had a nice week and everybody had a lot of fun, but now it was time to take care of business. I remember that night because Emerson Boozer and I made an agreement. We were rooming together for the first time that week prior to the game. The papers came out with a comparison between the two teams and I think the only position where we were even rated equal was at quarterback, with Namath and Earl Morrall, who had been the NFL's Most Valuable Player. At every other position they were rated better. Boozer and I took that as an insult, especially when we looked at the Colts' running backs. I said, "I know Tom Matte because he was Ohio State's quarterback my sophomore year. Maybe he's been playing longer, but I'm as good as Tom." Boozer said, "Well, I know I'm as good as Jerry Hill." We decided, "Let's show 'em." The two of us said, "I'm going to do my best to make every block I can for you and you do the same for me." We agreed to show the world that we were as good as Hill and Matte.

The team arrived at the Orange Bowl the next day and everybody was uptight. We knew we would be playing a big game with the whole world watching. I guess we also thought about how Kansas City and Oakland had been slaughtered in the first two games and how we were now 18-point underdogs. Weeb didn't relax us any because he was wrestling with whether it was better to introduce the offense or defense before the game. He was going around in the locker room, mumbling, "What should I do?" I don't know if he was taking a poll. The pregame festivities dragged on and on, but finally it was almost time to go out on the field, and Weeb still couldn't make up his mind. I think it was Namath who spoke up and said, "Hey, Weeb, why don't you just introduce the seniors?" Everybody had a big laugh and that cut the ice a bit.

People tried to portray Joe as a yelling, screaming emotional leader, but as I said, the extent of his leadership was telling us to do our job and that he would do his. Everybody, more or less, led by example. We didn't have many rah-rah leaders or speech makers, so there weren't real pep talks before the game. That wasn't needed. We weren't that close and we weren't that emotional, but we were professional. That's how I'd characterize that team. We counted on each other to do their jobs.

I don't remember who Weeb decided to introduce, so it must have been the defense. It didn't matter because it was just an honor to run out on the field and realize that all the other teams that started out with us were at home watching us play. I never thought about the $15,000 winner's share. Money wasn't everything back then. It was just the AFL against the NFL, let's find out who's best. We did think a lot about the ring and how it should be designed.

We got the ball first and I ran off-tackle on the first play, which was the first of three or four plays that we had scripted for our first series. On the second play I ran a sweep to the left. That wasn't in the script. In fact, all week long, Weeb harped, "We cannot run wide on these guys." So what happens? We're in the formation and Joe saw something and checked off, but he checked off to a sweep, which was exactly what we weren't supposed to do. I looked at Boozer, Boozer looked at me, but we didn't want to call time-out to show people we were nervous. So I moved over and ran the sweep. And it broke for 9 yards and a first down. And I happened to meet the Colts' safety, Rick Volk. I don't think I went into the game with the idea of punishing anybody and it was a fluke what happened to him. His mistake was that he came up to tackle me and ducked, and I kneed him in the head. He'd spend much of the game on the sidelines and later went to the hospital with a concussion. I came back to the huddle and said, "Those guys aren't so tough." If anybody thought they were tougher than us or that we were up against impossible odds, I think that dispelled that. My words eased the tension and made us relax.

The sweep set the tone and showed we could run the ball. But I don't know if our first series was successful otherwise. We were more or less just picking plays to see if they'd work, but we still didn't know which running play would work best. We'd wanted to find that out quickly so we could pass off that play on play-action. So that series didn't answer a lot of questions.

The first time the Colts got the ball they came out with a lot of confidence and anticipation and moved right down the field, getting first downs on almost every play. They were running well and when we tried to stop that they'd go on top. My heart sank. I figured it was going to be a disaster. It's one thing to score in 10 or 12 plays, but if they could do it in just a few plays, you gotta figure there's nothing our defense could do to stop them.

Then when we do stop them, they say that's okay because it's a short field goal and Lou Michaels will kick us ahead. But Lou Michaels misses it! When Lou Michaels missed that easy 27-yard kick you could almost feel the steam go out of them.

On our second series, Namath got the passing game going a little bit. The Colts were known for their strong pass rush, especially by their huge left end Bubba Smith, but Weeb made two smart moves that gave us a solid, solid front. He had our left guard Dave Herman replace Sam Walton at right tackle in order to go against Smith and he inserted Bob Talamini at left guard. Herman wasn't nearly as big as Smith, but he was a fighter and could hold Smith off long enough for Namath to throw passes that were gone in three or four seconds. Namath started to open up a bit in that possession and got a few completions but, oddly enough, the pass that helped us the most was the one he didn't complete to Don Maynard.

We knew they were scared to death of Maynard's speed. They just didn't know that he had pulled his hamstring. Maynard was in there only as a decoy to make them rotate their zone to help their cornerback Bobby Boyd cover him. That rotation resulted in their other corner, Lenny Lyles, being forced to guard George Sauer one-on-one, which he couldn't do. We wanted to throw one deep in Maynard's direction early in the game, even if we didn't come close to completing it, to make them think he was going to be a major part of our attack. The reason Namath overthrew him by so much is that Don couldn't run that fast, even going full tilt. And they said, "Ah ha, we knew they were going to do this." Fine, we knew they knew it. Maynard didn't catch a pass all game, but because of that one play they kept rotating their zone to help Boyd cover him. Meanwhile Namath went to work on the back side, with Sauer going against Lyles. And Sauer gained over 130 yards.

Sauer had a tremendous game. His only mistake came later in the first quarter when he fumbled deep in our territory after catching a short pass. After the Colts recovered, they moved the ball inside our 10 and it looked like they would definitely score this time. But then Morrall threw a pass into the end zone that hit Tom Mitchell on the shoulder pads and flew into the air. And Randy Beverly made the interception. Beverly had the most talent and best speed of our defensive backs, but at some point in every game he'd give up the big play, the big bomb. In this game he intercepted two passes in the end zone. So he made up for it, didn't he?

Not only are we beginning to think that Baltimore is snakebit, but they're starting to think that, too. All year long they had made the plays. Now, all of a sudden, nothing is going right. It's not just that Morrall is having a horrendous day passing—Michaels can't kick and Mitchell can't catch. It's just a disaster up and down the line. So now they're thinking

January 12, 1969, at the Orange Bowl in Miami

Paid Attendance: 75,377

AFL Champion: New York Jets (12–3)
Head Coach: Weeb Ewbank

NFL Champion: Baltimore Colts (15–1)
Head Coach: Don Shula

STARTING LINEUPS

OFFENSE			DEFENSE		
New York		**Baltimore**	**New York**		**Baltimore**
George Sauer	LE	Jimmy Orr	Gerry Philbin	LE	Bubba Smith
Winston Hill	LT	Bob Vogel	Paul Rochester	LT	Billy Ray Smith
Bob Talamini	LG	Glenn Ressler	John Elliott	RT	Fred Miller
John Schmitt	C	Bill Curry	Verlon Biggs	RE	Ordell Braase
Randy Rasmussen	RG	Dan Sullivan	Ralph Baker	LLB	Mike Curtis
Dave Herman	RT	Sam Ball	Al Atkinson	MLB	Dennis Gaubatz
Pete Lammons	TE	John Mackey	Larry Grantham	RLB	Don Shinnick
Joe Namath	QB	Earl Morrall	Johnny Sample	LHB	Bob Boyd
Don Maynard	FL	Willie Richardson	Randy Beverly	RHB	Lenny Lyles
Emerson Boozer	RB	Tom Matte	Jim Hudson	LS	Jerry Logan
Matt Snell	RB	Jerry Hill	Bill Baird	RS	Rick Volk

SUBSTITUTIONS

New York: K—Jim Turner. P—Curly Johnson. Offense: Receivers—Bake Turner, Bill Rademacher, Mark Smolinski. Linemen—Jeff Richardson, Paul Crane, Sam Walton. Backs—Babe Parilli (QB), Bill Mathis. Defense: Linebackers—John Neidert, Carl McAdams. Lineman—Steve Thompson. Backs—Earl Christy, Jim Richards, Mike D'Amato, John Dockery, Cornell Gordon.

Baltimore: K—Lou Michaels. P—David Lee. Offense: Receivers—Ray Perkins, Tom Mitchell, Alex Hawkins. Linemen—John Williams, Cornelius Johnson, Dick Szymanski. Backs—Johnny Unitas (QB), Tim Brown, Preston Pearson, Terry Cole. Defense: Linebackers—Sid Williams, Ron Porter. Linemen—Roy Hilton, Michaels. Backs—Charley Stukes, Ocie Austin. DNP—Jim Ward.

New York	0	7	6	3—16
Baltimore	0	0	0	7— 7

NYJ	Snell 4 run (Turner kick)
NYJ	FG Turner 32
NYJ	FG Turner 30
NYJ	FG Turner 9
Balt	Hill 1 run (Michaels kick)
MVP:	Joe Namath (New York)

about what else can go wrong. One thing we didn't want is for them to get so desperate that Don Shula would replace Morrall with Johnny Unitas. We didn't know that Unitas's arm was so bad. The longer Morrall was in the game, the better we felt we would do.

Meanwhile, the Colts' coaches and defensive players had to be surprised by what a conservative game Joe was calling. They probably figured that after his brash statements he was going to come out winging it. They figured that was the only way we thought we could beat them. They knew Joe threw a lot of interceptions and I'm sure they had all kinds of visions of running some back for touchdowns. I'm sure they were very, very shocked that he called mostly running plays and threw only high-percentage passes.

The game plan wasn't necessarily for me to run left and for Joe to throw to Sauer, although that's what happened for the most part. To win the game we knew that we had to get a running game going, but we didn't know which play was going to go well and prepared many running plays for both me and Boozer, left and right. We did figure that we'd probably run to the right only enough to keep Bubba Smith honest, because it would be hard for Herman to repeatedly block him on running plays. And we hoped to run behind our left tackle Winston Hill, and as it turned out, he had a great day blocking their right defensive end Ordell Braase. Braase must have been over 35 and it was a hot, sunny day, and that made it easier for Winston, who was 6'5", 275 pounds, to overpower him. Braase pretty much faded out. So we stuck with what worked best: our off-tackle play to the left, which we called "19-Straight." Once that worked, we could fake me running off-tackle and throw to Sauer.

The other defender we knew we had to control for our left-side running to work was Mike Curtis, their best linebacker. I would read Curtis even more than I would Braase. It was center John Schmitt's job to get whatever kind of block he could on him. Curtis was very quick, so if John couldn't cut him off, I would reverse myself and cut back over the middle while John tried to push him past the hole. When those counterplays worked, Curtis ran himself out of plays.

I ran the ball more than I expected. In fact, I ran the ball on the first four plays of our touchdown drive. I kept running our basic "19-Straight," which meant there was straight-on blocking by everyone on the line. Boozer led on their outside left linebacker. In those days, the hash marks were closer to the sidelines and we'd set our formation into the closed, or short, side of the field. Most teams would run to the wide side, but we ran toward the short side, which was left. Everyone was blocking one-on-one and I broke it wherever I saw it open.

Namath completed a couple of big passes to Sauer in the drive and one to Bill Mathis out of the backfield. Then I caught a 12-yard pass that brought us inside their 10. I think that was on an option play where both Boozer and I flared out of the backfield, and when Curtis went left with Boozer, Joe threw to me on the right. I remember that because I fumbled the ball when somebody hit me. It was our day because it rolled out and rolled right back into my arms. Nobody even knew it happened.

My 4-yard touchdown run came on the same "19-Straight" play. I just happened to break it outside. Because we had been pounding the ball inside pretty good, John Schmitt told me that he thought he could cut Curtis off. He didn't cut him totally off, but he tied him up a little bit and that let me get outside. I didn't know anything about the Colts always playing a certain defense when Lou Michaels was inserted at tackle, as happened on that scoring play. Namath probably didn't tell me, so I wouldn't do anything other than run the play that was drawn up.

It was great to go ahead 7–0 because they would have to play catch-up and get a little out of their game plan. But it was just early in the second quarter, so I didn't think that touchdown was that big at the time. We were up only by seven points and Tom Matte and Jerry Hill were having a lot of success running. People forget that Matte ran for 116 yards that game. Tom was a good athlete and tough as nails. His one failing was that he didn't have breakaway speed. He should have run all the way on his 58-yard run in the second quarter, but Bill Baird, John Elliott, Johnny Sample, and a couple of other guys all caught him from behind. Tom and Johnny almost got into it after that play.

Matte's run brought them deep into our territory for the third time in the half. But then Morrall threw a pass to Willie Richardson that Sample picked off right in front of the end zone. Then Johnny had to go rub it in someone's face. That's Johnny for you. He still resented that the Colts released him years before. Johnny was our trash talker and was doing his normal talking. I know that upset the Colts because on their side of the ball there wasn't a lot of chatter or any trash talking. They didn't have anyone like Johnny Sample. Or Verlon Biggs, our other guy who would talk a little bit. He had what he called "the Chop," which was a takeoff on Freddy Williamson's "Hammer." When Biggs was chasing a running back, he wouldn't tackle him but would take one of his big arms and chop him in the back of the legs.

We had to punt again and they got the ball back just outside our 40. On the final play of the half, they ran a flea flicker in which Morrall got the ball back from Matte and should have thrown a touchdown down the field to Jimmy Orr, who was all alone and waving at him near the end zone. But Morrall didn't see Orr and was intercepted by Jim Hudson when he tried to throw a shorter pass across the middle to Jerry Hill. I was watching on the sidelines but I didn't see Orr behind our secondary, either. Of course, it wasn't up to me to see him. When our defensive guys came off the field and we all headed for the locker room, they were talking about Morrall making the big mistake. And I'm saying, "What mistake?" And they said, "You didn't see Orr? He was 15 yards behind us!"

I wasn't aware of what the Jets' defensive game plan was, but I saw that they were doing everything so well. Everybody was staying in their lanes; everybody was trying to contain; guys were hustling. Of course, it helped that Earl Morrall wasn't having a very good game. God, didn't he have the worst game of his career? I don't know if it affected him when Namath told the press that week that several AFL quarterbacks, including Joe's backup Babe Parilli, were better than him. But he picked the biggest game of his life to have the worst game. Morrall had come in after Johnny Unitas hurt his arm and had a Cinderella year. But that day he crashed and burned.

At halftime everybody was tired as heck because it was awfully hot. We were a younger team, so if the sun was affecting us to this extent we knew it had to be killing them. We made no changes in the game plan for the second half. We just had to keep our poise and take pride in what we did and not make stupid mistakes. As a matter of fact, Weeb ended up putting that on our Super Bowl ring: *Poise and Pride*. We also wanted to score a few more points to make it harder for them to catch up. We were very confident. It was funny that they did stress to the defense not to let someone get that far behind them again.

So much went wrong for the Colts that game that I'd forgotten that on their first play of the second half, when they hoped to get back on the right track, Tom Matte fumbled when Biggs jumped on his back and Baker recovered for us. That just reconfirmed that it wasn't their day.

In the first half Boozer hadn't carried the ball as much as me, but he had been doing a great job blocking. When we got the ball in the second half, we shared the running. What we also had to the left side was what we called the "Lag Draw" play to Boozer. It had the same look as that off-tackle play I ran, but I went first and blocked for him. Hill blocked

Braase whichever way Boozer wanted to go, and I had to read that and pick up the linebacker.

Boozer and I got us a couple of first downs rushing and that led to Jim Turner's first field goal, from 32 yards out. That put us ahead 10–0 and was very big because now they had to score twice and they hadn't proved they could score once. Every point we put on the board was one more mountain they had to climb.

With a 10-point lead, we didn't think we had to become even more conservative. We already had a conservative game plan and needed to just keep to that. We still wanted a run–pass balance. We definitely didn't want to get pass happy because if we threw even one interception we'd be in trouble. Not that we couldn't fumble and have the same result, but we felt we had better control of things by running the ball. We worried that if Joe started to throw interceptions, he'd call similar pass plays. In previous games, when he felt he threw one bad, he had to prove he could throw one good. He knew his arm was so strong that sometimes he'd try to force passes into double or triple coverage. He'd start doing crazy things. I'd been in games when Namath threw 5 interceptions—up in Buffalo, for instance—so we didn't want to get into that. That day we felt Joe was "on" because he wasn't out there trying to throw 35 or 40 passes—instead he was calling for that many running plays and throwing much less. I couldn't say anything about Joe's emotions in the second half. I couldn't say that he was either loose or close-to-the-vest in the huddle. He just stuck to the game plan and everything was working.

The Colts got the ball back but had to punt after three plays. Then we put together another little drive and Jim Turner kicked his second field goal to increase our lead to 13–0. Near the end of that drive Joe hit his thumb against somebody's helmet and had to come out. So Babe Parilli came in. There was no real concern that Joe wouldn't come right back because we knew it wasn't broken. I didn't even realize he hurt his thumb until later on.

By this time, the Colts were pressing. You saw the frustration and worry on all their faces, and they were asking, "What do we have to do to get a break?" Everything was going against them after a year when they had nothing but success. The most distinct image I have from that whole game is of Ordell Braase and some other guys—not so much Mike Curtis—having a bewildered look. I don't remember anybody on the Colts having a longer face than Braase. The sweat is pouring down; he's all red in the face; he's breathing through his mouth. Winston Hill was doing a great job on him and the heat had got to him, too. You figure, "Jesus, I know I'm tired, but this poor guy's like to die."

The crowd was mostly on Baltimore's side and had come to see how badly we'd get beat. We took the crowd out of the game when we started scoring. As we fought the game out, I think they began to root for the underdog or just be neutral. A lot of fans were just numb because they couldn't believe what they were watching.

Just before the end of the third quarter, Don Shula finally took Morrall out of the game and brought in Johnny Unitas. Of course, I'd seen Unitas play for years on television, but only a couple of the Jets who'd played in the NFL had seen him in person. You've got a legend walking onto the field. A man who was known for clutch plays and for bringing the Colts from behind. We just stopped and watched. We were in awe. When he came in, there was real concern, but when he tried to pass, he couldn't get anything on the ball. It was just a shame that his arm was shot. It wasn't the Johnny Unitas you expected to see.

Our last scoring drive began late in the third quarter. We got down to their 10, I think, on a long pass from Namath to Sauer. George had been killing Lyles all game by running outs and a couple of post patterns on him, so now George told Joe that he could beat Lyles on a fly pattern, which Lyles wouldn't expect. So we ran the play-action pass off the same off-tackle play I'd been running all game and George went down and faked the out and broke it deep down the middle. And Joe read it and laid it up there, and that was 39 yards, our longest play of the game.

That pass play led to Jim Turner's third field goal early in the fourth quarter. That made the score 16–0, which meant they were in a big hole, having to score three times to beat us. We still didn't think the game was over because Johnny Unitas was in at quarterback for them, but on his second series we began to think he didn't have the arm to bring them from so far back with the little amount of time that was left. However, I must say that with Unitas in the game, the rest of the Colts seemed to get a big lift. That's what we were afraid of. We weren't afraid of him throwing long for a quick score once we saw his passes fluttering, but we saw that the rest of their guys were inspired by his presence. Now we had problems. Unitas couldn't throw but he still brought the Colts downfield. Fortunately, when he threw into the end zone, the ball died and Beverly got his second interception.

When the Colts got the ball back after we missed a field goal, Unitas took the Colts 80 yards downfield with some good passing. He did show some flare, some of his old self, some of his greatness. And I was glad that they hadn't brought him in earlier, back in the first half. We might have been in trouble if he'd come in earlier. But it was late in the game that he finally got the Colts on the scoreboard, on a short touchdown run by Jerry Hill. They had to run a lot of plays, including four running plays from inside our 2, and we were glad that our defense didn't just give in because of our lead but forced them to use up a lot of time. We just didn't want to give up a quick touchdown. Make them work for it. We're in the fourth quarter; the clock's on our side. We didn't care if they scored if we won. We didn't care if we won 16–0, 16–7, or 16–14.

Once they had scored, they tried an onside kick and were able to recover it. Naturally, you're shocked when that happens because you're supposed to have your "good-hands" players on the field to make sure you get the ball. That gave the Colts a little more time. Unitas didn't have the arm for a quick strike, but he threw a couple of short completions and got one first down. Then they lost the ball on downs.

When they had the ball fourth-and-5 inside our 20 with about $2^1/2$ minutes left, they tried a pass that went incomplete. At the time, they needed a touchdown and field goal on two possessions to beat us and it didn't matter which they got first. But they went for a difficult touchdown on that play instead of having Michaels attempt a short field goal that would have made it 16–10 and brought them to within a touchdown and extra point of a victory. Maybe Shula didn't send in Michaels because he blew that earlier short kick. Or maybe they felt Johnny Unitas had some magic left. I never really thought about it. But it seems to me the pass was the wrong play to call, especially since they'd get the ball back once more.

At this point, we're just running out the clock. I ran the ball five or six times on our last possession. We ran a number of sweeps and I made sure to stay in bounds to keep the clock running. Now we were running to the right. We weren't that interested in gaining yardage, although we wanted first downs to move the chains. We felt Bubba was frustrated and Dave could block him now because he was probably going to make a charge one way or the other, and I could go to the outside or inside of him. I just told myself, "Don't fumble!"

When the game ended, I thought, "Wow!" If I didn't know who won and just saw the final score, I would have thought the Colts won it. If they're 18-point favorites and you see 16–7, you figure there's no way there's that big a swing. But there was. The best Jets team I ever played on had won Super Bowl III, 16–7. Leaving the field, I saw the Colts were exhausted and in a state of shock. I don't remember any Colt coming over to congratulate me. I don't know if any of us knew what we had accomplished. Maybe Joe did, because I've seen films of him waving his index finger at the crowd and shaking his hand. It hadn't sunk in yet. But I knew we had proved to the NFL players I knew that we could play them head-to-head.

I don't remember the trophy presentation afterward when Pete Rozelle gave it to us. I think I was in the training room getting treatment because I was beat up and exhausted. That game really took it out of me. I had my bad knee drained just a few days before the game, and oh, yeah, it hurt during the game. Luckily it hadn't hurt too badly because of the hot weather. I'm sure Joe felt the same about his knee.

It wasn't really a big deal that Joe got the MVP award over me. That's where supposedly a lot of that animosity between the two of us came from. I didn't feel that way about it. I'd gained 121 yards on 30 carries and scored our touchdown, but it was very hard for them not to give the MVP trophy to someone who guaranteed a victory and had fulfilled his prophesy. It didn't mean that much to me. The Jets leased me a Cadillac because they told me they thought I was probably the game's MVP. That was a better car than Joe got. It meant more to me than the MVP trophy because it showed the team appreciated what I did.

The night of the game, after we showered and went back to the hotel in Fort Lauderdale, there was a party. It was nothing special. We just got together as a team to savor what we had accomplished. We understood that the Colts had a big party planned and had even invited Weeb Ewbank to attend—too bad they had to cancel their party! Some of the Chiefs and Raiders came by. Buck Buchanan had to go around and shake everybody's hand and say, "Thank you for redeeming us." They told us how important our victory was. So we started thinking that many of those guys appreciated what we did more than we did ourselves. You start realizing what you've done. And we've been reminded ever since.

I suppose most of the Colts don't like to remember Super Bowl III. But I got to be friends with Bubba Smith later on when we did all those Lite Beer commercials, and we'd talk about the game. Even today, Bubba teases me. He'll say, "You guys didn't win the game; we gave it to you. If we played you 10 games, we'd win 9 times." I say, "Bubba, didn't they tell you where the game was and when it started? That day is all that counts." Then I tell him, "I will loan you my ring." That just eats him alive.

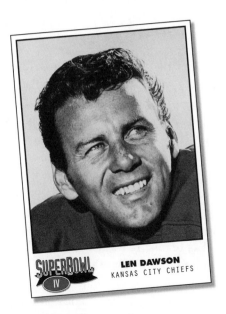

LEN DAWSON
KANSAS CITY CHIEFS

SUPER BOWL IV

KANSAS CITY CHIEFS 23
MINNESOTA VIKINGS 7

LEN DAWSON

In the first four years of the Super Bowl, nobody was neutral about the two teams who were playing. You were either an NFL fan or an AFL fan, and you rooted wholeheartedly for your league's representative and hated the other team. AFL fans were particularly supportive because they wanted to prove wrong those NFL fans who stubbornly contended that no AFL team could compete with the champion of the much older league. When I had sat in the stands at the Orange Bowl during Super Bowl III, everyone around me believed in the vast superiority of the NFL and insisted the Jets were going to be slaughtered by the mighty Colts. Finally, in the fourth quarter, with the Jets comfortably ahead, I asked, "How the hell does that other league look now?" I wasn't surprised that the Jets won. I knew how strong they were. I had thought the Raiders had a good chance to beat the Packers the year before. And I sincerely believed Kansas City had a good chance against the Packers in Super Bowl I, and I would have loved to have had another shot at them.

The Jets' victory made me very happy and gave all the Chiefs a lift as we went into Super Bowl IV against Minnesota. Yet, it didn't put extra pressure on us to win—we felt no burden—because we were considered such big underdogs, by as many as 13 or 14 points. Even though the Jets' win had been decisive, most football "experts" thought it was a fluke and that Baltimore would have won 9 out of 10 games between the two teams. The Jets, Chiefs, and other top AFL teams still weren't regarded as the equals of the best NFL teams. It wasn't until we had handled the Vikings—and really handled them—that the strength of the 1969 Jets was affirmed and the American Football League was given real credibility.

In Super Bowl IV, we proudly wore patches on our jerseys that commemorated the American Football League's tenth year in existence. It was a huge deal to represent the AFL, especially in its final game before the merger of the two leagues. When the AFL began in 1960, it was regarded as an upstart league—the hobby of rich owners. A lot of people thought it wasn't going to last, but it had survived despite much adversity and had become successful enough to force the merger. The Super Bowls, from I to IV, weren't just played for Kansas City, Oakland, or the New York Jets, but for every team and player in the American Football League. To get all of us a little respect, because we didn't have any. In the NFL, they had never stopped saying that the AFL was a league of castoffs, players who either were not good enough to ever play in the NFL or were over the hill. AFL players who were told we were unqualified for the NFL tended to band together. We developed a genuine affection for each other and this league that wanted us and let us showcase our talents.

Unlike Daryle Lamonica and Joe Namath, the AFL quarterbacks in Super Bowls II and III, I had played in the NFL, and my experience there gave me additional motivation to play well against the NFL champions, be it Green Bay or Minnesota. I got absolutely no respect in my three years with the Steelers and two years with the Browns. I never opened and finished a game, even in preseason. I started only twice and then played only the first halves. I can't say I resented the NFL because of that treatment, but I got out of that league because of it, moving to the AFL in 1962 to play quarterback for Hank Stram with the Dallas Texans—a year before they became the Kansas City Chiefs. It was said that I went to the AFL because I wasn't good enough to play in the NFL. In truth, because of the inactivity, my skills had deteriorated to the point where Stram, who had recruited me out of high school and been my backfield coach for two years at Purdue, said, "Jeez, what happened to you?" I was so rusty that it took me a few games to win the starting job. The AFL saved my career. If I had chosen to remain a backup in the NFL, I was destined for obscurity. I went on to be the league's MVP in 1962, when Dallas beat the Houston Oilers in the AFL title game, and an AFL All-Pro for several years. Yet, I hadn't earned real respect because I hadn't proven myself against the NFL. I had hoped that would change in Super Bowl I.

To understand my feelings going into the Minnesota game, you have to go back to that game against Green Bay. When we approached Super Bowl I, Hank and the players kept saying we had a chance if we didn't make any mistakes. I don't know how many guys thought we could win it—remember this is when Vince Lombardi, Bart Starr, and the Packers were dominating the NFL—but we would have liked to have kept it close. The Packers were ahead just 14–10 at halftime. We were holding our own and it truly was a competitive football game. But then I threw an interception on a deflected ball and they returned it to the 5-yard line and scored soon after. And then it was us trying to play catch-up. We were a young team and they were a veteran team, particularly on defense. We weren't able to do it. We got beat 35–10. People looked at the final score and said, "There you have it!" Lombardi was badgered to compare us to NFL teams, and he stated that the Cowboys and several other NFL teams could beat us. The Chiefs had to live with that statement. And everyone in the AFL had to live with it. As for me: The monkey on my back got heavier.

The next year they started having preseason games between the leagues and everyone treated those like they counted because the media was doing the same. Players read the sports pages, so they knew those games were more than exhibitions. We wanted to win those games very badly. Of course, a victory in the Super Bowl is what all of us wanted most. My main goal in football was to have a second opportunity to win a Super Bowl and erase Lombardi's cutting remark about our team and league. Fortunately, I had to wait only three years.

The road to Super Bowl IV was difficult, although we lost only three times. I hurt my knee in the second game of the year against the Patriots. The next day it really got sore, and I didn't know if it was just strained or if it was torn and needed to be sewn back together. Back then, doctors examined your knee simply by moving it and looking at it. They did x-ray my knee, but that didn't tell them anything. Hell, I saw six or seven orthopedic surgeons and they all recommended surgery. One even did it over the phone, having never seen me. In those days, even if you had a successful knee operation, you knew you were out for the year. Since I was already 34, I worried that an operation could end my career. Personally, I didn't think it felt as bad as the knee injury I had earlier in my career that had required surgery, but I went along with the doctors' advice. I was on the operating table. I was out. When I woke up I thought I'd been operated on. But Hank said, "Hold on, I've got another doctor I want you to see."

It just so happened that the doctor in St. Louis had a new idea on how to treat these kinds of knee injuries. His idea was for me to just stay off the leg for two weeks and do a few leg lifts each day. It was a simple treatment and it worked. I missed just six games, while Mike Livingston started at quarterback. I came back and played with tape around it in Buffalo. Just before halftime I took a couple of snaps to get it acclimated. I came out for the second half and never had any problem after that. The offense wasn't told to adjust to protect me—no one took an injury into consideration. If the bone wasn't sticking out, they'd say, "Hell, just get back in there."

The toughest games turned out to be the two playoff games that got us to the Super Bowl. We played the Jets in New York in terrible conditions. They had a very good team and it wasn't easy beating them twice in a row on their home field. But we pulled out a victory, 13–6. Then we played the Raiders in Oakland after having lost to them twice late in the regular season. They had lost only once all season and were the only team that had beaten us in Kansas City during the year. This was another difficult, hard-fought game, but we broke a tie in the second half and won, 17–7. I think the Jets and the Raiders could have both beaten the Vikings.

We were peaking as a team just as we headed to New Orleans to play the Vikings. The team Minnesota would face was much stronger than the one that lost to Green Bay in Super Bowl I. On defense, our real strength, we still had big Buck Buchanan at one tackle, Bobby Bell—the best open-field tackler I ever saw—at left linebacker, and Johnny Robinson at one safety, but there had been wholesale changes. On the defensive line, we added Aaron Brown at right end and Curley Culp at tackle. Culp would become more famous years later with the Houston Oilers, but he was already a tremendous player. Willie Lanier, who, like Buchanan and Culp, was a future Hall of Famer, became our new middle linebacker, and Jim Lynch, another outstanding player, moved in at right linebacker. Emmitt Thomas, who had been on the Super Bowl I squad, had become the starter at one cornerback spot, and newcomer Jimmy Marsalis became an All-Pro on the other side. They both had speed and were tough, and their bump-and-run style would be a major factor in our victory over the Vikings.

Offensively, we had pretty much the same people, but guard Mo Moorman had really bolstered our offensive line, joining tackles Jim Tyrer and Dave Hill and guard Ed Budde to form a huge and formidable front foursome. Our offensive linemen going one-on-one? Any defense that tried to overpower these big guys was playing right into our hands. E. J. Holub had become our center. He had so many knee operations that he was no longer mobile enough to play linebacker in those days when linebackers had to get into the pass coverage.

My two major weapons on offense were wide receiver Otis Taylor, who had developed into a full-fledged star, and halfback Mike Garrett, who had been only a rookie in Super Bowl I. Taylor was a thoroughbred. He had great speed, was strong, and was athletic. At 6'3" and 220 pounds, Otis was one of the first big wide receivers who could run a 4.4 or 4.5 40-yard dash. He loved to run with the ball after making a catch and would often turn short passes into long gains—as he would do against Minnesota. In those days, receivers took a pounding all over the field, even when the ball was in the air, and Otis was the type who liked to hit defenders back every once in a while. He wasn't fun to cover. If he had a defender man-on-man going down the sidelines, I'd let it go because I knew he had a much better chance than the other guy to come down with the ball. It became a jump ball and he was a great leaper.

Garrett, who had won the Heisman Trophy at USC, was pretty much a flat-footed runner but had great balance and good speed. In our offense, our halfbacks—Warren McVea was a solid backup—ran the ball more than our fullbacks, Robert Holmes and Wendell Hayes. So, at 185 pounds, Mike had to be tough to withstand so many poundings. He also was a strong blocker and an excellent receiver, which might have gone back to his base-ball days. He was an all-around football player.

Guys like Garrett displayed finesse—I myself was a soft passer, easy to catch, who relied on timing and touch—but overall, this was a very physical team, on both sides of the ball. We had an awful lot of plays that relied on speed and finesse, but when you got down to the real nitty-gritty, we were a power team. The Vikings, even with their vaunted Purple People Eaters defense, had nothing on us.

Where we were definitely superior to them was in the kicking game. We had added Jan Stenerud to be our placekicker, and with him and Jerrel

Wilson, who would average over 48 yards per punt against Minnesota, we had the best kickers in football. Stenerud, who came from Norway, was very much part of the team and was a loner only in the sense that kickers are usually off by themselves. We probably worked on the kicking game as much as any team did, but in those days teams didn't really work much on the kicking game. So Stenerud and Wilson were just off on their own, kicking or having a lot of coffee and donuts while the rest of us were sitting through one of Hank Stram's meetings.

This team was not only better than the one that played in Super Bowl I but also much closer. We had strong feelings for each other that still exist today. We played together during a time when there were racial problems in our country, but we never had them on our team. There was no friction at all; everyone got along. A lot of the guys lived in Kansas City all year-round, including me. We'd socialize and after home games there would be parties to which players would invite their wives, girl-friends, and families. My best friend was probably Johnny Robinson, but I was friends with all the guys. If you became closest to one player it was usually because your wife was compatible with his wife.

On the field I was the leader of the offense. Even in my first year in the AFL I had strong leadership credentials, although it had been six years since I had been the starting quarterback at Purdue. Playing behind Bobby Layne for two years at Pittsburgh, I had learned nothing about technique—he never threw a spiral—but I had learned about competitiveness, about never giving up, about playing intelligent football (his strength) and about orchestrating the two-minute drill, at which he was as good as anybody. I had the respect of the players from the beginning and that continued as I gained experience and had success.

I wasn't a loud guy in the locker room. I left that up to others. Some guys would be banging their heads and that kind of stuff, so somebody had to maintain composure and know what was going on. I had to think about what we had to do as a team and what plays I was going to call. I was quiet—yet there was no question who was in charge. But there were other leaders, as well. Tight-end Fred Arbanas was outspoken. The offensive players also listened to Jim Tyrer and E. J. Holub. Jerry Mays was a big influence on the defensive line, as was Johnny Robinson in the second-ary. Buck Buchanan was a vocal guy—he got your attention when he had something to say—but he also was a leader by example. He was a guy we could count on because he never had a bad game. Buchanan was one of the captains, and he, Robinson, and Jerry would call plays. Mays was a different personality on the field than off. He had been number one in his class at SMU in engineering. Phi Beta Kappa. But on the field he'd go nuts sometimes. He was an emotional leader, the opposite of me.

I was Stram's coach on the field. I called between 80 and 90 percent of the plays. Hank had only four coaches, so he was his own quarterbacks coach and offensive coordinator and was always designing plays for me to run. That was his shtick. He couldn't even go into a restaurant without writing plays on the tablecloth. They hated to see him walk in! Hank would give the quarterbacks tests every week for the offense he'd devised for the upcoming game, including the Super Bowls. We had to know everybody's assignment on every play. I'd take Hank's tests during a two- or three-hour plane trip and they would last the entire flight. We had a ton of plays—I think about 100 available for the Minnesota game, including a few new ones and, like an end-around designed for Frank Pitts, a few old ones with new wrinkles.

I would say Hank and I had developed together over time, coach and quarterback. I got to know his thinking after being in quarterback meetings with him all those years. And he designed plays to utilize my skills, including my ability to throw quick play-action passes and to throw on the run. He had started moving my pass pocket a few years earlier when we played the San Diego Chargers and they had Ernie Ladd at tackle and Earl Faison at end. Ladd, who became a professional wrestler, was the biggest human being I ever saw—he was about 6'9" and weighed 325 pounds—and Faison was 6'5" and weighed 270 pounds. Ladd was one of the few guys who would talk to the other team before snaps, and he'd tell me something funny like, "Your guy can't block me and I know you gotta throw, so soon I'll be back there with you." Because our guards back then weren't big enough to block him or Faison, we decided I could avoid their rush by not always dropping back 7 to 9 yards directly behind the center. So at times I'd roll out left or right and we'd block down on the defensive end, perhaps with our tight end. That would give our offensive tackles the chance to get set so they could handle the rush. This moving pocket was an important part of our offense in 1969 and the 1970 Super Bowl.

Leading up to Super Bowl IV, Stram talked a lot to the media about the Chiefs having "the offense of the seventies." In those days, pro offenses were very simple, particularly in the NFL. Every team, including the Vikings, copied the Packers, who had been very successful using a basic formation. They didn't have motion; they didn't have double or triple wings; they didn't have slot formations. They just got into a fullback–halfback position or a split backfield and would do their well-known sweep. They'd say, "This is what we're going to do—try to stop us." They would try play-action passes occasionally, but they didn't do anything to disrupt the defense. There was little imagination at work in the NFL. Hank's theory, which would prove correct against the Vikings, was this: If we could force the defense to be moving forward or laterally at the beginning of each play rather than be set or anchored, it wouldn't be so easy for them to stop us. If we got them to move, it would be because they wouldn't yet know exactly who their assignments were and where to line up. They would be at a great disadvantage.

So Hank, the sole architect of our offense, set out to create new formations to disrupt the timing and positioning of the defense. He came up with what was called the "Tight-I Formation," from which we would shift into the final formations for each play. He moved both wide receivers next to the tackles, and instead of having the tight end, usually Fred Arbanas, start out on the line of scrimmage, he positioned him directly behind me in the backfield. Directly behind him would be the fullback and the tailback. Defenses were used to lining up their strong- and weak-side linebackers and safeties according to the side where the tight end lined up, but if Fred started out behind me, they had to guess where he'd go. I'd take a look at how those defenders positioned themselves after guessing where our tight end would go and then I'd send him the other way. So they had to adjust quickly and were in disarray when the ball was hiked. The "Tight-I Formation" worked in all situations, including when we moved the pocket. We had used the moving pocket against Green Bay in Super Bowl I, but now that it developed out of Hank's new "Tight I," it would be much more effective against the Vikings in Super Bowl IV.

There was just a week between the league championships and the Super Bowl, which was to be played on January 11. We arrived in New Orleans and checked into the Fountainebleau Hotel. The coaches tried to keep us to the routine we had in Kansas City before all games, including lifting weights and attending meetings. They gave us a curfew of 10:30 or 11 P.M. and went around checking our rooms to make sure we were there. After Tuesday, the French Quarter was off-limits. It turned out that I couldn't go out anyway.

During this week, there were distractions all our players faced. First of all, we had to take care of our families who were coming to town on Friday and Saturday. That meant getting them tickets to the game and rooms in other hotels. We had to do this ourselves. Then there also were friends and casual acquaintances, who were calling us to ask for tickets and accommodations. Fortunately, in those days we could get tickets easily and not at outrageous prices.

Of course, we all had to deal with the army of reporters who arrived from all over America. There wasn't as much media hoopla surrounding the game as there would be years later when it became an international event, but it was pretty hectic and demanding. Tuesday afternoon was "Picture Day," and we had only a light workout because we had to make ourselves available to the media. After that, I assumed I'd be able to buckle down and fully concentrate on the game ahead of us. But then "the gambling story" broke. . . .

It was reported on television that night—I think first by Huntley–Brinkley on NBC—that I was going to be subpoenaed to go to Detroit and talk about my relationship with an alleged gambler, whose name was Dawson, too. He was being investigated by the Justice Department. Hank told me that the league had informed him that they had thought about breaking the story a week before, but it came out that night and suddenly I had reporters beating on my door and asking for a statement.

It was then that I discovered that anyone in America could be subpoenaed for any reason, whether they know anything or not. I also learned that just because I was being subpoenaed, I was considered guilty by the media. There were about 12 others who were being subpoenaed, but since I was the quarterback on a Super Bowl team, nobody paid attention to them. I was now the central figure in a national story and was being hounded by reporters from all over the country. NFL Security had to sneak me down the back stairs of the hotel so they could interview me without reporters knowing. It was like a cheap movie.

I was interrogated by NFL Security in their hotel room for a couple hours. The man in charge of security for the league interviewed me, and I fell asleep. He said, "I've interviewed rapists and murderers and I've never had anybody fall asleep on me. That in itself tells me that you can't be concerned about it."

They were trying to figure out what to do, and I said, "Why the hell don't we tell the truth? Which is: I do know Donald Dawson, but don't know him that well and haven't seen him in years. He called me twice this year, when I hurt my knee and when my father passed away. That was it."

Hank and Lamar Hunt, the Chiefs' owner, handled it like I wanted. I read my statement, which took about a minute, and they passed it out to the press. Then they told the reporters that they could ask me only about football for the rest of the week.

But reporters still wanted to get to me and I couldn't even leave the hotel at night. It was a tremendous distraction. My wife, 9-year-old son, and 14-year-old daughter, who stayed in Kansas City until the weekend, were affected as well. My son couldn't even go to school because he was being pestered. I had an outlet in that I could go to meetings, and beginning on Wednesday, to some park each day for heavy workouts. My family had to go out in public.

I'm thinking this is the biggest game of my career and all this crap is going on all week long. It was very difficult. My teammates helped. They knew me and knew the suspicions were unfounded. They made fun of it all, saying I'd do anything to get additional publicity. Freddie Arbanas joked that he was jealous because he was from Detroit yet they were talking about me going back to his hometown to testify.

Fortunately, the Super Bowl hadn't yet become a two-week event and we didn't have many days to spend in New Orleans. Finally, the day of the game arrived and it was a relief to everyone, especially me. When I put on my uniform, all my off-field problems disappeared.

Because many of us had already experienced a Super Bowl, we were much looser in the locker room before the game. Against Green Bay, we had been extremely nervous waiting to face Lombardi and his team in the very first Super Bowl. It would have been tough to have driven tenpenny nails up some of the guys' asses because they were that tight. We were serious before going out to play the Vikings, no question about that, but we didn't feel so much pressure this time around. I think this was because we really felt we could beat Minnesota, despite what the oddsmakers said.

The Vikings were considered a great team, having lost only two games during the year. They had beaten the Rams and Browns to reach the Super Bowl for the first time. Their offense was led by Joe Kapp, who had come out of the Canadian Football League. He was a good, gutty quarterback who was tougher than hell. Kapp had a couple of strong running backs in Bill Brown and Dave Osborn, but he did a lot of running himself. He didn't look pretty throwing the ball and his passes fluttered but they went where they had to go. His deep threat was Gene Washington. The offense had scored over 50 points in three games, but the Vikings' strength was undoubtedly its defense. The Purple People Eaters, led by ends Jim Marshall and Carl Eller and tackles Alan Page and Gary Larsen, were considered the most intimidating defensive unit in the NFL.

The Vikings were a good team, but so were we. Johnny Robinson, who was my roommate on the road, said to me: "Okay, I've heard all this stuff from the coaches and read the papers about how we don't have a chance against their defense. But you've been studying them all week—can you score points against them?"

I told him, "Yes. We've got a game plan and if we do the things we want to do, putting our strengths against their weaknesses, we can score points. But what about defensively?"

And he said, "I've been looking at them on film all week. We might shut 'em out!" That was his attitude and the attitude of the entire defense. And they damn near did it.

Super Bowl IV was played in the afternoon at Tulane Stadium, before over 80,000 fans. (As the years went on, more than that number of Kansas City fans alone claimed they were there.) It had been so cold that week that a fountain had frozen at the Fontainebleau, but on game day it wasn't bad. There was a light mist for a while, but it wasn't a factor. The field was slightly wet but in good shape. Overall, the conditions were fine. I also felt fine after a rough night.

We played well from the start. The first time we had the ball we scored on Stenerud's 48-yard field goal. We're looking over at the Vikings and they're saying, "What the hell is this?" First of all he was a sidewinder, and other than Pete and Charlie Gogolak, they had straight-ahead kickers in the NFL. They're watching this little soccer-style kicker line up for the field goal attempt and saying, "Midfield, oh sure." And then bang, he kicks it through. And now they know they really have a problem—if we get to midfield we have a weapon. Stenerud was a major factor. He kicked two more field goals in the second quarter.

Then with the score 9–0, we took advantage of a fumble by Charlie West on the kickoff—that was a key, key play. Suddenly, we have the ball on their 19-yard line. We soon scored from the 5-yard line on a trap play. We had a split backfield with our fullback, Robert Holmes, flaring out. My job was to fake a toss to him and then hand the ball to Mike Garrett, slicing through our left side. Meanwhile, as on real toss plays, Tyrer pulled to his left. Jim Marshall took the bait and didn't even have to be blocked. Moorman slid down the line and took out someone, but the key block was thrown by Fred Arbanas, who just about annihilated their middle linebacker, Lonnie Warwick, the one guy who could have tackled Garrett.

That made the score 16–0 at halftime. This thing was history! We knew it was over! With our defense, all our offense had to do was make sure not to screw up and give the Vikings the ball.

The game was going as we had planned it. Our strategy against their defense was to use the running game to set up everything. If it came, we would throw play-action passes, one of our strengths. We knew that their strength was rushing the passer, particularly with their ends Carl Eller and Jim Marshall. They'd bat down balls. Then they had Alan Page coming up the middle. He was a hell of a player and could give our big lineman trouble because he was quick enough to go one way, stop, and go the other way to get to the quarterback. As was our style, we'd move the pocket right or left, rolling away from their pass rushers and making it easier for our people to handle them. They got to me a couple times, but in general, I had good protection. Because of their strong rush, our receivers couldn't be running plays with patterns that took time to develop. I had to get rid of the ball in a hurry. Fortunately, I could throw in front of their cornerbacks, Earsell Mackbee and Ed Sharockman, because they were off our receivers by 8 to 10 yards. That loose coverage allowed me to complete short passes in quick fashion, which is exactly what I had to do.

We had a big offensive line and they weren't so big on defense. Alan Page weighed just 230–235. And both our guards, Mo Moorman and Ed Budde, were about 270–275, and our tackles, Jim Tyrer and Dave Hill, were about 280. And Fred Arbanas was a terrific blocking tight end. We thought we should run right at 'em with Garrett, McVea, Holmes, and Hayes, and once in a while run reverses with wide receiver Frank Pitts. We ran the end-around because of the way the Vikings pursued the ball, because they would chase like crazy. We had to run something like that even if it wasn't successful, just to keep them honest and give them something to think about. It just so happened that we guessed right on the reverses and caught them unprepared, and Pitts gained big yardage.

Page and Eller were playing extremely well and the Vikings' defense as a whole was doing a pretty good job. But it was obvious that their offense had never seen a defense like ours. In the NFL in those days, teams played a 4–3 defense. The center blocked occasionally but didn't have a big defensive lineman on his nose that he'd have to handle on runs and passes. Now Hank put either of our tackles, Buck Buchanan, who went 6'7" and 280 pounds, or Curley Culp, who weighed 275 pounds and was quick—he had been the NCAA heavyweight wrestling champion at Arizona State—in front of Mick Tingelhoff, who weighed only 230 pounds. He couldn't be expected to handle our guys on every play. By trying to adjust to this mismatch, the Vikings' running game was disrupted and for the most part was highly ineffective.

January 11, 1970, at Tulane Stadium in New Orleans

Attendance: 80,562

NFL Champion: Minnesota Vikings (14–2)
Head Coach: Bud Grant

AFL Champion: Kansas City Chiefs (13–3)
Head Coach: Hank Stram

STARTING LINEUPS

OFFENSE				DEFENSE			
Minnesota		**Kansas City**		**Minnesota**		**Kansas City**	
Gene Washington	WR	Frank Pitts		Carl Eller	LE	Jerry Mays	
Grady Alderman	LT	Jim Tyrer		Gary Larsen	LT	Curley Culp	
Jim Vellone	LG	Ed Budde		Alan Page	RT	Buck Buchanan	
Mick Tingelhoff	C	E. J. Holub		Jim Marshall	RE	Aaron Brown	
Milt Sunde	RG	Mo Moorman		Roy Winston	LLB	Bobby Bell	
Ron Yary	RT	Dave Hill		Lonnie Warwick	MLB	Willie Lanier	
John Beasley	TE	Fred Arbanas		Wally Hilgenberg	RLB	Jim Lynch	
John Henderson	WR	Otis Taylor		Earsell Mackbee	LCB	Jim Marsalis	
Joe Kapp	QB	Len Dawson		Ed Sharockman	RCB	Emmitt Thomas	
Dave Osborn	RB	Mike Garrett		Karl Kassulke	LS	Jim Kearney	
Bill Brown	RB	Robert Holmes		Paul Krause	RS	Johnny Robinson	

SUBSTITUTIONS

Minnesota: K—Fred Cox. P—Bob Lee. Offense: Receivers—Bob Grim, Kent Kramer. Linemen—Steve Smith, Ed White. Backs—Gary Cuozzo (QB), Lee, Clint Jones, Bill Harris, Oscar Reed, Jim Lindsey. Defense: Linebackers—Dale Hackbart, Mike McGill, Jim Hargrove. Lineman—Paul Dickson. Back—Charlie West. DNP—Mike Reilly.

Kansas City: K—Jan Stenerud. P—Jerrel Wilson. Offense: Receivers—Gloster Richardson, Curtis McClinton. Linemen—George Daney, Remi Prudhomme. Backs—Mike Livingston, Warren McVea, Wendell Hayes, Ed Podolak. Defense: Linebacker—Bob Stein. Linemen—Gene Trosch, Ed Lothamer, Chuck Hurston. Backs—Goldie Sellers, Willie Mitchell, Caesar Belser. DNP—Tom Flores.

Minnesota	0	0	7	0— 7
Kansas City	3	13	7	0—23

KC	FG Stenerud 48
KC	FG Stenerud 32
KC	FG Stenerud 25
KC	Garrett 5 run (Stenerud kick)
Minn	Osborn 4 run (Cox kick)
KC	Taylor 46 pass from Dawson (Stenerud kick)
MVP:	Len Dawson (Kansas City)

Our secondary also was doing a superb job. Gene Washington caught only one pass all game and that was a short gainer he fumbled. And he was their big receiver. Kapp had to throw more often to John Henderson, who wasn't as big a scoring threat. While their cornerbacks played way off receivers, our cornerbacks were up in their faces. Both Emmitt Thomas and Jimmy Marsalis had the quickness to be able to do that, so, unlike the Vikings, we didn't have to play a soft man-to-man or zone defense. They changed the patterns for their wide receivers.

At halftime, Stram didn't tell us to become conservative and sit on our lead. A good coach would never say that. He wanted us to continue to control the line of scrimmage and run the ball, and to keep their offense on the sidelines. As I said, our main worry was turnovers. We didn't want them to get an easy score. If they were going to put up points, we wanted them to work for them. And that is what happened. It took time for them to go downfield and score Dave Osborn's touchdown.

We immediately came back with a 46-yard touchdown pass to Otis Taylor. That was the biggest play of the game because it immediately canceled their score and took away their momentum. I threw it out of the "Tight-I," but with two receivers split wide. I later looked at the game film and saw that it was the only play that could have worked. They had an all-out blitz, with the linebackers and safety coming, and we didn't have enough people to block them. Two or three got through, and our backs were behind me so they couldn't intercept them before they reached me. If I'd attempted to drop all the way back into the pocket, I'd have been sacked. But we'd called the right play under those circumstances: I dropped just one step back and got rid of the ball, a little hitch pass to the right side. Taylor went about 6 yards, stopped and looked back, and the ball was on its way. Then he was on his own and made a terrific run into the end zone, 40 yards downfield.

So they were behind 23–7 and had to play catch-up, which was difficult because their style was to run with the football, bang at people, and have Joe Kapp throw only occasionally. Now Kapp had to throw it on nearly every down—and we ended up with three interceptions for the game. With the stacked formation and our cornerbacks' ability to play strong man-to-man, this freed safety Johnny Robinson to play way back and prevent the long play. Meanwhile, our guys were putting pressure on Kapp, so he didn't have time to wait while his receivers worked away from our bump-and-run cornerbacks. Early in the game there was a series when Kapp threw the ball on first, second, and third downs and completed them all and still didn't have enough for a first down. He'd throw a swing pass, but Bell, Lanier, or Lynch would come up and make open-field tackles. Today, defenders like to hit people just to get on highlight films, but our guys made tackles.

Our defense was rock solid. What it did in the postseason was amazing. We held the Jets to six points and Oakland to seven, and now these guys were being held to seven. I don't think Bud Grant could have adjusted his offense during the game to do anything better against our defense. You can't change what had been a successful offense during the last game of the season.

Throughout the game it was businesslike in our huddle. There was no talk by anyone but me. If a player said something, he did it before we reached the huddle or if I asked him a question. On the sidelines I'd go to my players to find out what they thought they could do and learn how the Minnesota defense was playing them. I did that every game, particularly with the receivers. I also might ask the linemen how we could run, say, a back off tackle, or do something else I had in mind.

During time-outs I'd go to the sidelines to talk to Stram. Through our years together, I'd always do that and typically we would discuss what I was working on. He might ask what I was trying to accomplish and then I'd explain that I was working on something in order to set up a particular play. Once in a while, he'd tell me to not forget about a play even though it didn't work because someone missed a block or something. That was about it—end of discussion. But all of a sudden during this game, he's chirping at me, you gotta do this, you gotta do that. And I'm thinking, "Damn, I'm the one who has all the pressure on me—what's he so nervous about?" I knew he was an emotional guy and this was a big game, but he was out of character a bit, really overdoing it with his constant chatter. I didn't realize that he was wired by NFL Films. Nobody knew that he was wearing a microphone, and that was the reason he wouldn't stop talking and making wisecracks. I didn't know about the wire until the next spring when I saw the grand premiere of NFL Films' Super Bowl film in Kansas City. (Bud Grant also saw the film and he didn't like some of the uncomplimentary things Hank said about his team. In the fall we opened the season against the Vikings in Minnesota, and just before they left the hotel, Grant showed his team the film to motivate them.)

I still remember looking up at the clock and seeing that there wasn't much time left and knowing that we'd won. I could sense the pride that all the players felt—it had been there all season with these guys and would never go away. When the gun sounded, I felt that there was a huge—and I mean *huge*—weight lifted off of my shoulders. I don't know if there was as much joy as relief. We had finally done it—for ourselves, our fans, and the entire AFL. The feeling eventually changed to joy—I still feel it.

We would have a team party later on, but there was already a party atmosphere in the clubhouse. We had a lot of guys who were thrilled. There were also many guys who were emotional—guys like Jerry Mays and Otis Taylor. Most everyone was elated because many of us had been in Super Bowl I. Of course, Hank was ecstatic. Even Lamar Hunt was excited. He wasn't the type of owner who made sure his face was on television and in the papers. He was quiet and very low-key. But that game excited him. When he formed the American Football League, one team was supposed to be in Minnesota. Then the NFL promised the state of Minnesota an expansion team if it stayed out of the AFL. The state took that offer and dumped the AFL. What made it worse was that the AFL was actually having its owners meeting in Minneapolis when Minnesota bailed out of the league. So they were suddenly down to seven teams— that's how the Oakland Raiders came in. Lamar didn't forget, so you can imagine his happiness that we had won at Minnesota's expense. He never showed emotion, but he showed emotion that day.

During the celebration, someone told me, "The president wants to speak to you." I asked, "The president of what?" "The United States." In those days, it wasn't traditional for the president to call the victorious locker room. It actually was President Nixon congratulating me on our victory. He even mentioned that I shouldn't worry about the gambling allegations, which I appreciated. Here I was, a guy not considered good enough to play in the NFL, getting a call from the president. That was a thrill.

My son stood with me when I spoke at the postgame news conference. The reporters who had been harassing me all week were there. They asked how the gambling story affected me during the game—I said it didn't affect me at all—but for the most part they asked questions about the game. It's my contention that when you win, you don't have to explain anything. Only when you lose do they expect explanations.

Ironically, Bart Starr, who had been the winning quarterback against us in Super Bowl I, was there reporting for some Midwest station. And he requested to talk to me one-on-one. I said I'd do it only if I could bring my son along with me. You see, Bart was my son's favorite player.

My children were elated. My wife, who has since passed away, was also, but she was ready for me to quit. She'd had enough because there had been so much pressure on the family, particularly at that time with the gambling thing going around.

Kansas City went bonkers. They had a parade for us on Monday, the day after the win. It was something to be seen because this town had never experienced a championship in anything. Those Chiefs would remain the only team from Kansas City that has ever won a Super Bowl. We would always hold a special place in Kansas City's sports history and in the hearts of its people.

I was named the MVP of Super Bowl IV. I think I found out in the locker room. There was no presentation. However, I did receive a car from *Sport* magazine the following week in New York. While I was there, Hank and I were on *The Tonight Show* with Johnny Carson—that was exciting. I also appeared with Dick Cavett and David Frost. After that there were banquets all over the country, by which time I had been cleared of all suspicions of consorting with a gambler.

I had been an MVP of the AFL, but quarterbacking the Chiefs to a Super Bowl victory was much bigger because it was against the National Football League. I think this win and being the MVP of the game had a lot to do with my getting into the Pro Football Hall of Fame in 1987. I'm sure the judges looked at that. Because I had done nothing in my five years in the NFL, this was necessary.

After that Super Bowl Week, after I handled all that pressure, I figured I could handle most anything. To go through that and walk away with the Super Bowl title and MVP award was such a victory for me personally. What's frightening is, what if I'd have had a lousy game? I could have thrown four interceptions. I would never have heard the end of that. That's why I say it was rather an important game for me.

This was the greatest game of my career, which ended in 1975. It's my greatest thrill, along with being enshrined in the Pro Football Hall of Fame. That was the ultimate. That's what it's all about. Everybody wants to win the Super Bowl.

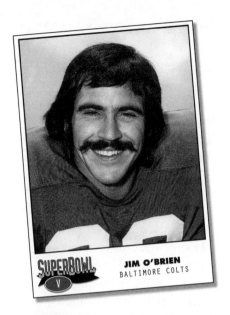

JIM O'BRIEN
BALTIMORE COLTS

SUPER BOWL V

BALTIMORE COLTS 16
DALLAS COWBOYS 13

JIM O'BRIEN

When I was about 9 or 10, I became a kicker by default. Whoever could kick the best kicked, and I was the only kid who could do it. I wasn't much of a pro football fan, but Cleveland was the nearest team to Cincinnati and my favorite player was the Browns' Lou "The Toe" Groza. I definitely didn't want to play tackle like him but I liked that he also was a kicker. I kicked straight-on, like him, and when I got into high school my dad actually bought me one of those Ridell kicking shoes, which was like a big black boot with a square toe. I probably practiced two or three days a week during the summer for an hour each time. I'd kick a bunch of balls and then my dad and I would retrieve them and start all over. I kicked all through high school but it wasn't because I was hoping to get a football scholarship.

I kicked for the University of Cincinnati but I was better known as a receiver. Greg Cook was the quarterback and I set the NCAA record for yards per reception that wasn't broken until a few years ago. I also led the nation in scoring because of all the field goals and extra points. I wasn't really thinking of making the pros as a kicker, but that I could kick in addition to playing wide receiver improved my credentials.

The Baltimore Colts drafted me in the third round. When I came to camp, I didn't know if I was there to kick or play receiver or do both. I was actually a receiver and then I'd kick for about 10 minutes after practice. Kicking was a sideline at first. David Lee, our punter, punted during practice and that was it, but I ran pass routes the whole time. I wore the number 80, a receiver's number, and did everything receivers did, from blocking to pass catching. I went to receivers' meetings and had a playbook and did the drills and caught passes from Johnny Unitas—all that stuff.

I think the fact that I could catch passes had a lot to do with my making the team. However, it became increasingly evident that the Colts were more interested in me as a kicker. They didn't tell me I was there to replace Lou Michaels, but I think they were looking for someone to do that because he was coming to the end of his career. Maybe his missing that short field goal in Super Bowl III had something to do with it.

The fact that I was competing in camp with a popular player made things a bit difficult for me with some of the veterans. Lou Michaels was one of their buddies and was an old-timer like them—and here comes this young kid. It was a bit stressful for me. I don't know if I was kept out by them or I stayed out on my own. They were older and very conservative and most of them were married and here I was young and single and feeling my oats, so to speak. I exuded a lot of confidence and probably that was seen as my being brash or cocky. Also, I let my hair grow an inch longer than anybody else's. Throughout the whole society in 1970, everybody had longer hair, sideburns, mustaches, but the Colts were among the most conservative teams and both quarterbacks, Unitas and Earl Morrall, had crewcuts. I just went ahead and did what I wanted to do, but I always showed up at practice, never late, and I worked just as hard as everybody else—although those veterans were probably suffering more because they were older.

There was no real serious antagonism. Nobody gave me lectures. There were a lot of pranks, but most of what went on was in jest more than anything else. I'm sure the press made a lot more out of it than there really was. What you do on a football team is rib everybody and try to get their goats. For instance, Billy Ray Smith, our defensive tackle, nicknamed me "Lassie" because of my longer hair. I got along with Billy and didn't mind. All that stuff was in fun and nothing really terribly personal. The fact that I played wide receiver helped me gain some acceptance. Still I was different from what the veterans were used to. But some guys were supportive and helpful, and all in all, they were really nice people. Earl Morrall, my holder on kicks, was a very nice guy.

Finally, I beat out Michaels for the kicking job. But I don't think I did it convincingly. In preseason, I had a few good games kicking and one or two really bad games. I hadn't really proven myself, but I think they hoped I could do the job because they cut Michaels before our final preseason game. Then against Washington in that final game I was nervous and kicked badly and I'm sure they were all saying, "Uh, oh."

The next game was the season opener against San Diego. The first official kick of my pro career was from the 10-yard line. In those days the goal posts were on the goal line, so it really was a 10-yard kick and was pretty much an automatic. Morrall was my holder and I kicked it straight through, except, of course, it was called no good. As they admitted later, the referees weren't looking, and when the Chargers signaled that the kick was wide, they believed them. Earl just about went ballistic. He knew I'd had such a rough game the week before against Washington and here I was nervous as hell making my first real kick from only 10 yards out and being told it was no good. He was afraid I would lose my confidence entirely. Fortunately, I got to kick a 19-yarder with not much time left to win the game, 16–14. So it worked out okay, but it was kind of scary.

Now that I was the Colts kicker, I became merely a backup receiver. I probably got into only a game or two during the year. I caught only one pass and don't even remember it. Only if too many people got hurt was I in the game because they didn't want me to be injured and be unable to kick. Because of my kicking I would never devote myself to becoming a good professional receiver. My rookie year and the Super Bowl ended any desire I had to play receiver.

Don Shula drafted me that spring, but then he left to become the coach of the Miami Dolphins. Don McCafferty, who had been on Shula's staff, replaced him as our head coach. Don McCafferty was casual and relaxed and would also like to joke around, so I liked him. He had a managing style, where he'd say, "You have a job to do, so go do it. I'm not going to get into your face, unless you don't do it." He respected the fact that his players knew what to do and how to do it and left them alone for the most part. For this group of guys who had played together for quite a while, he was probably the best kind of coach. He could be critical if you screwed up something, but he would be like a father figure instructing you rather than a tyrant yelling at you. I really enjoyed playing for him.

We had nine rookies who made the team. Norm Bulaich, who became the starting fullback, was probably the best known. I was pretty good friends with Norm and most of the other rookies as well. We also mixed with some of the veterans, particularly the younger guys. Of course, married guys tended to hang out together, as did single players. Bubba Smith, our 300-pound defensive end, and linebacker Ted Hendricks, who was a tall guy himself, befriended me. Ted was unusual, but I was unusual too, so it worked out. Bubba, who was our most feared player, wasn't conservative by any stretch of the imagination either, but he still was respected as being a leader on the team, so it helped me fit in when he accepted me.

The Colts were a fun team to be on, except the day of the game. Not that it wasn't fun, because we did really well, but everybody always had his game face on. It was serious business—probably more serious to most of the guys on the team than it was to me. Of course, being primarily a kicker, I didn't have a lot of say about how my teammates were supposed to get ready for a game. If you're not a team leader, you don't go around telling everybody to lighten up.

Obviously, the leaders of the Colts, especially of the offense, were Johnny Unitas and Earl Morrall. Unitas, who had spent his entire career with the Colts, was pretty quiet, but he was opinionated and guys tended to go along with his opinions. When you were in the huddle with Johnny Unitas, you didn't say anything. He made it very clear that you didn't say anything. He ran the show. Earl was more casual and easygoing. I was never a big football fan, so while I knew of Johnny Unitas, playing on the same team with him didn't have the same effect on me that it probably had on other rookies. Maybe that's another thing that made me different.

Unitas's leadership skills were still there, and though his abilities weren't equal to what they'd been maybe five years before, the players knew he could still lead them to a victory. He had smarts and a lot of times that makes up for one's physical failings. He took us to the Eastern Conference title ahead of Miami, and though he didn't have great playoff games, we won both of them anyway because he made enough big plays.

I had a 40-yard field goal in our 17–0 win over Cincinnati in the divisional playoff and a couple of shorter field goals when we beat Oakland, 27–17, to win the AFC championship. Daryle Lamonica got injured for

Oakland and George Blanda came in, and it was Unitas going against Blanda, two guys who had been around a long time. Unitas hit a long bomb to Ray Perkins that gave us our lead in the fourth quarter, and George tried to make up too much ground too quickly and we intercepted him twice in the end zone to preserve the win.

Because of the merger between the National Football League and the American Football League, there was now the National Football Conference and the American Football Conference. The Colts, Browns, and Steelers had agreed to join many of the old AFL teams in the AFC. In Super Bowl III, the Colts had represented the NFL, but in Super Bowl V they were going to represent the AFC. Some of the Colts veterans who had always been part of the older league resented the move to the AFC and having to play against one of their old NFL rivals in their second Super Bowl. I'm sure they would have preferred representing the NFC.

I know the Colts were a whole lot more serious about going to Super Bowl V than two years before. I think the Colts had taken Super Bowl III too lightly. That was the feeling I got from everybody who had played in that game. They didn't think the Jets were a good team and didn't approach that game seriously enough. They still were angry about losing and wanted to win Super Bowl V to make up for it. We would be playing Dallas, a former NFL rival, and no one doubted they were stronger than the Jets had been. There was no danger of complacency. This time we stayed at the Miami Lakes Country Club, whereas the Super Bowl III team had stayed in a beach hotel. They wanted us to be in a less active, quieter place. We had curfews at 11 P.M. or earlier. The night before the game, we had a 10 P.M. curfew and stayed together as a team. There wasn't any goofing around during Super Bowl Week. Even I was serious.

The coaches were businesslike. They told us that it was going to be a fierce game defensively, but I'm sure everybody already knew that. The two offenses were only satisfactory, but both teams had great defenses. The Cowboys had defensive stars like Bob Lilly, Lee Roy Jordan, Chuck Howley, Herb Adderley, Jethro Pugh, Mel Renfro. . . . They were tough. But we had just as strong a defense with Bubba Smith, Ted Hendricks, Mike Curtis. . . . Both teams had shut out opponents during the season and in the playoffs. On offense, we wanted to do different things and we even devised trick plays—which Don liked—but I don't remember if we planned to emphasize either the pass or run or just mix it up. We knew it was going to be a hard-fought game and that we had to play it to the best of our ability. That was basically it. Obviously we weren't supposed to have as many turnovers as we would.

We had a regular practice routine at Biscayne College. I'd be working with the receivers and Earl was playing quarterback, so we'd have to wait to practice kicking until afterward. I'd kick 10 or 15 minutes a day, that's all. Usually I'd start out at 25 yards and move back to 50 as I warmed up. And I'd go from angle to angle. The press didn't bother me too much because I was still a rookie kicker. However, Unitas and Bubba Smith and some of the other well-known players probably spent hours with reporters. I guess if someone couldn't find anyone to interview they'd talk to me.

It was just a normal week. I wasn't that nervous, even the night before the game. The locker-room scene the next day was no different than it was before a regular season game. I don't think anyone was particularly nervous. It was pretty quiet in there, so I guess everybody was just thinking about what they were supposed to do. I wasn't going to be the guy to change the demeanor of the group. Usually Coach McCafferty would say something to put things in focus. The players who might have said something would be Bubba Smith, Billy Ray Smith, or halfback Tom Matte, who was out with an injury. But there weren't guys who'd give pep talks. Whatever was said would be very short, nothing long-winded or overly inspirational like, "Let's win one for the Gipper," or "Let's avenge ourselves for Super Bowl III." There was none of that kind of stuff. There was no mention of Super Bowl III before the game. Maybe it's because this was a different team. About a fourth of the players were new, we had a new head coach, and we were in a new conference.

As I told the media later, I dreamed that week that the Super Bowl would end with a field goal. But I couldn't tell if the game-winning kicker was me or the Cowboys' Mike Clark. Going into the Super Bowl, I wasn't thinking "I hope it comes down to me." Usually kickers hope that it doesn't come down to them. I know I wasn't looking forward to winning the game as part of my Super Bowl dream. You'd rather your team scores a touchdown so you can kick an extra point rather than attempt a field goal. To be honest, you'd rather win more handily, a 35–0 route, where you don't have to win it with a field goal. Then you know it's a lot more secure. As it turned out, it wasn't like that and you do what you have to do.

One of our two games during the season was against Don Shula's Dolphins at the Orange Bowl, the site of the Super Bowl. But we didn't worry because we weren't playing the Dolphins there again but another visiting team. It didn't matter where the game was played as long as we were in the Super Bowl. We wanted to win the Super Bowl, to finally win the big game. Of course, so did Dallas, who after several frustrating losses in the playoffs over the years, finally made it to the Super Bowl.

As expected, both offenses struggled in the first half. Then the Cowboys broke through with two field goals by Mike Clark. But we tied the game, 6–6, on an unusual play in the second quarter. We were on our own 25 when Unitas threw a hard pass over the middle to Eddie Hinton. The ball went off Eddie's hands and flew farther downfield and our tight end John Mackey grabbed it in full stride. It would have been illegal to have had two receivers touch the ball consecutively, but the officials ruled that the Cowboys' cornerback Mel Renfro had slightly deflected the ball after Hinton touched it. It happened so fast that it was hard to tell that Renfro hit it—and he argued that he hadn't—but the ball seemed to speed up. The films would show that the referees were correct. At the time we weren't worrying if Renfro touched it—we were just watching Mackey run all the way down the field by himself for a touchdown.

I got excited on the sidelines and then had to change gears and think about going in to try the extra point. That was my first placekick of the Super Bowl and I hesitated a second too long and Mark Washington came in and blocked the kick with his chest. It was my fault more than anyone else's. If I'd been a split second sooner I may have gotten it off. I remember being awfully nervous and letting my nerves affect my concentration. When you're kicking you want to put your mind on automatic pilot. You don't think because you can think of bad things as well as good things. On that kick, I was thinking rather than being in a zone.

Dallas's place kicker Mike Clark had given his team its first six points with two field goals, while I had missed my only kick, that extra point. I would have liked to have matched Clark, but I didn't feel like there was competition between us. In fact, I was happy he was attempting field goals instead of them scoring touchdowns. You just cross your fingers and hope he misses.

Super Bowl V was a defensive struggle that resulted in lots of interceptions and fumbles. We weren't thinking "What's going on?" We were just hoping the ball would bounce our way. Sometimes it did and sometimes it didn't. It was like a roller-coaster ride, where we'd have ups and downs with every possession.

After recovering Unitas's fumble deep in our territory in the second quarter, Dallas scored its only touchdown on a short pass from Craig Morton to Duane Thomas. On our next possession, Unitas was hit hard again and

January 17, 1971, at the Orange Bowl in Miami

Paid Attendance: 79,204

AFC Champion: Baltimore Colts (13–2–1)
Head Coach: Don McCafferty

NFC Champion: Dallas Cowboys (12–4)
Head Coach: Tom Landry

STARTING LINEUPS

OFFENSE			DEFENSE		
Baltimore		**Dallas**	**Baltimore**		**Dallas**
Eddie Hinton	WR	Bob Hayes	Bubba Smith	LE	Larry Cole
Bob Vogel	LT	Ralph Neely	Billy Ray Smith	LT	Jethro Pugh
Glenn Ressler	LG	John Niland	Fred Miller	RT	Bob Lilly
Bill Curry	C	Dave Manders	Roy Hilton	RE	George Andrie
John Williams	RG	Blaine Nye	Ray May	LLB	Dave Edwards
Dan Sullivan	RT	Rayfield Wright	Mike Curtis	MLB	Lee Roy Jordan
John Mackey	TE	Pettis Norman	Ted Hendricks	RLB	Chuck Howley
Roy Jefferson	WR	Reggie Rucker	Charley Stukes	LCB	Herb Adderley
John Unitas	QB	Craig Morton	Jim Duncan	RCB	Mel Renfro
Norm Bulaich	RB	Duane Thomas	Jerry Logan	LS	Cornell Green
Tom Nowatzke	RB	Walt Garrison	Rick Volk	RS	Charlie Waters

SUBSTITUTIONS

Baltimore: K—Jim O'Brien. P—David Lee. Offense: Receivers—Tom Mitchell, Ray Perkins. Linemen—Sam Ball, Cornelius Johnson, Tom Goode. Backs—Earl Morrall (QB), Sam Havrilak, Jack Maitland, Jerry Hill. Defense: Linebackers—Bob Grant, Robbie Nichols. Lineman—Billy Newsome. Backs—Ron Gardin, Tom Maxwell. DNP—Jimmy Orr, George Wright.

Dallas: K—Mike Clark. P—Ron Widby. Offense: Receivers—Dennis Homan, Mike Ditka. Lineman—Bob Asher. Backs—Calvin Hill, Dan Reeves, Claxton Welch. Defense: Linebackers—D. D. Lewis, Tom Stincic, Steve Kiner. Linemen—Pat Toomay, Ron East. Backs—Richmond Flowers, Mark Washington, Cliff Harris. DNP—Tony Liscio, Roger Staubach.

Baltimore	0	6	0	10—16
Dallas	3	10	0	0—13

Dall	FG Clark 14
Dall	FG Clark 30
Balt	Mackey 75 pass from Unitas (kick blocked)
Dall	Thomas 7 pass from Morton (Clark kick)
Balt	Nowatzke 2 run (O'Brien kick)
Balt	FG O'Brien 32
MVP:	Chuck Howley (Dallas)

threw an interception. This time Unitas was knocked out of the game. He was hit in the ribs by George Andrie's helmet, but I think if we hadn't been playing on the hard Astroturf he wouldn't have been hurt. Because all day he'd taken a pounding and he'd run out of energy—he couldn't avoid being hit and he couldn't withstand more punishment.

There was no letdown when Unitas was sidelined because Earl Morrall was a damn good quarterback, too—just as good as Unitas in the players' opinion. He moved the team pretty well, and on our last possession of the half, he took us down to the Dallas 2. However, Bulaich failed to gain any yardage in three attempts, which brought up fourth down. I thought we should have gone for a field goal and so did most of the players, but McCafferty wanted to go for the touchdown. I wasn't insulted, but I won't say I wasn't upset that I didn't get the opportunity to kick. I would have liked an easy field goal under my belt to build my confidence. I did wonder if they didn't want to try a field goal because of my blocked extra point, but I could see where the coaches might think we were too close to the goal to not try tying the game with a touchdown. Unfortunately, Morrall threw an incompletion into the end zone and the half ended. Everybody was disappointed we came out of it with no points. We would have been down 13–9 instead of 13–6.

At halftime there didn't seem to be a lot of worry in the locker room. We were down by only a touchdown and an extra point. We just got out the chalkboards and went over what the linemen had to change in their blocking and what the receivers had to change in their patterns, stuff like that. One thing that wasn't changed was quarterback. Unitas could have returned in the second half, but McCafferty decided to stick with Morrall.

We fumbled the opening kick of the second half and Dallas got the ball deep in our territory. They moved the ball to the 2-yard line and had a first-and-goal, and they looked like they were going to go up 20–6. But on the next play Duane Thomas had the ball knocked loose by Jerry Logan and Ray May, and Jim Duncan came up with it to stop their drive. That was a key play. It was just one of many hard hits in the game.

It was really a hard-hitting game. Those mistakes everybody was seeing didn't just happen. Two bodies in motion coming at each other results in mistakes. There's a mistake by one guy but a great play by another guy. It was just one hell of a defensive battle. Even on the sidelines you could hear real crunches from people getting hit. It wasn't just guys dropping the ball. They fumbled because they got the snot knocked out of them.

We moved the ball into Dallas territory and I got my first field-goal attempt. It was from our 48-yard line, which meant it would have been a 52-yarder. The chances of making it weren't great, but in those days if you didn't reach the goal post, you could down the ball on the field. My kick was short, but I kicked it well and it worked out like a great punt, because the ball was downed on the 1 by my snapper, Tom Goode. That gave me some confidence.

Our next scoring opportunity came early in the fourth quarter. Sam Havrilak took the ball on a reverse and was supposed to throw it back to Morrall. But Earl was covered, so Havrilak, who had been a quarterback in college, completed a pass to Eddie Hinton. Eddie was running toward the end zone for our game-tying touchdown when the ball was punched out of his grasp from behind by Cornell Green and bounced toward the Dallas end zone. The ball kept bouncing and bouncing, and though some of the players touched it, nobody could stop it from going out of the end zone. So we lost a chance to tie the game. That was certainly another upsetting moment for us, but everybody just said an expletive or two and went back to work. The good news was that Dallas got the ball on their 20. Field position is so important, especially when you have defensive teams battling it out. We were happy they had to start 80 yards from our goal line. If we felt disappointed or snakebit, we soon got over it.

We got the ball back when Morton had a pass tipped by Jim Duncan and intercepted by Rick Volk, who had a long return to their 3. Then Tom Nowatzke scored over left tackle and I kicked the extra point to tie the game, 13–13. Now we felt a lot more relieved. We felt a surge of momentum and felt we could win the game.

Making that second extra point was very important to me. The field goal I'd missed earlier had given me some confidence because I hit it solid. Then on the point after, I went back to what I was supposed to be doing—concentrating and then going on override—it was a lot easier. As long as you're on automatic, you'll make most of them. If I'd missed that second extra point, obviously it would have made me think a little more on my important field goal attempt later in the game . . . which wouldn't have been a good thing.

We had two top defensive teams playing against two adequate offensive teams, and from my perspective, the defenses were what was determining the outcome of the game. Obviously, the better your defense, the better your chance of winning, because you can stymie a good offense. I think our defense was doing a better job than Dallas's as the game wound down. By this time everybody was tired because it was so hot and humid. Our offense had more than its share of turnovers during the game—four fumbles lost and three interceptions—but Dallas lost that big fumble by Thomas and was intercepted three times late in the game. At times their receivers couldn't hang on to passes because they were hit so hard.

The biggest play of the game was a Dallas turnover with a minute left. Morton threw the ball to Dan Reeves and he jumped to catch it, but it was thrown a bit hard and was a little behind him. The pass went off Reeves's hands just as he was hit from behind and the ball was intercepted by Mike Curtis, who ran it back into field-goal range. When Curtis intercepted that pass, I knew we would soon be going for a field goal because we were too far away to make it into the end zone with so little time left.

The coaches said to get the field-goal team ready. I started warming up. I say "warming up," but it wasn't like it is today. There was no net then so I couldn't actually kick. But someone would hold a ball and I'd go through my steps. And I could stretch and practice my follow-through. I wasn't all that superstitious so I didn't go through any ritual. Before games, I'd always put one sock on first and each shoe on in the same order, but that was about it. When I would go out on the field to kick, I had a clear mind.

I was watching the field as we ran the clock down with a couple of short running plays. I was kind of hoping that someone would break through for a 35-yard touchdown, but on the other hand I was thinking that I will get the chance to attempt the game-winning field goal in a Super Bowl. With nine seconds left, I was sent onto the field.

I came on the field and went to the huddle. Even before we were lined up, guys on the Cowboys were yelling, calling me a rookie and telling me I was going to miss, and making derogatory comments. They kept yelling as we lined up, and then before we could snap the ball, they called time-out. So we went back to the huddle.

Once and for all, I would like to dispel the notion that I then leaned over to pick up grass to test for wind and was so nervous that I had forgotten it was Astroturf. I was pretty nervous but I did not pull up Astroturf. It's very hard to do that—I think you'd need a knife. On an Astroturf field you can always find a lot of lint that has rubbed off from jerseys, and that's what I gathered and threw up in the air. Earl said, "Just kick it straight," because he wanted to make sure I realized there wasn't any wind.

In that second huddle, Earl kept talking to me. And from that point on I didn't hear the Cowboys yelling anything. It was like I was deaf. Time didn't slow down, but I was concentrating so hard that I didn't hear any noise from Dallas, the crowd, or anybody. I had hurt a leg going downfield on a kickoff and had been stretching it for the rest of the game—but I was no longer thinking about that either. Once you get your adrenaline going and are in a pressure situation, you forget about that stuff. It doesn't exist.

I always felt I performed better under pressure. Even in high school, on every practice kick I'd pretend I was kicking for a college team, and then in college I'd pretend I was kicking for a pro team. After kicking 45 minutes or an hour, the most important practice kick was the last kick. I'd concentrate as if I were in a championship game. I wasn't going to make every one, so if I missed what was intended to be my final kick, I'd say, "Hey, there was a penalty," and I'd get to kick it over. So I'd practiced this kick I was about to attempt in the Super Bowl ever since I was a teenager.

We broke our huddle and lined up for my kick, which was from 32 yards out. Tom Goode would hike to Earl Morrall. I always had a regimen of thoughts that I went through before I kicked. The step count is automatic, but I went through four thoughts, in the proper order, repetitiously: concentrate, watch the ball, head down, follow through. I did that three or four times in a row. Then I took my steps back from where Earl was going to place the ball. I felt numb and didn't think of anything. I wasn't brain dead, but I was on automatic. I didn't hear any noise and I really didn't see anything. I didn't even see the ground. I didn't see Earl. All I saw was the ball. It was like the purest form of concentration. It was about 180 degrees different from my first extra-point kick, where I didn't concentrate and there was noise and everything was in motion. This time I saw only the ball and I kicked it hard. And I was lucky enough that the snap was good, everybody blocked good, the holding was good, and it was just one of those perfect plays.

It was the best kick of my life as far as accuracy and distance. It was the culmination, I guess, of all those years of practice. I knew it was good as soon as I kicked it. It would have been good from 52 yards out. The officials quickly signaled that it was good, but there wasn't any doubt. Then I turned to our sidelines and started jumping high in that direction with my arms high in the air. I wasn't looking at anybody in particular. I was happy. Just happy. That's all. Earl grabbed me from behind and many of the other players from on the field and the sidelines ran over and circled me and hugged me and congratulated me.

I'm not sure if I saw Bob Lilly fling his helmet into the air in disgust or if I only saw that on film later. I probably wasn't looking in his direction.

After everybody came down to earth, we knew we had the game won. However, there were still five seconds on the clock, so I had to kick off. They said to make sure I squib kicked it because they didn't want them having a chance to set up a wall for a long run back. It was just as well I didn't kick deep because I was a much better placekicker than I was as a kickoff guy. So I just did a good squib kick and we downed the guy who caught it. There was time for one more play and we intercepted Morton again as time ran out. We had won 16–13 and were Super Bowl champions.

I wasn't thinking about being voted the game's MVP after I made my kick. That didn't cross my mind, even after the game in the locker room. They could have given it to some of the guys who made big plays for our defense—Mike Curtis, Rick Volk, one of our linemen. The award did go to a defensive player, linebacker Chuck Howley of the Cowboys. He made two interceptions and a lot of tackles, so he got the award. I don't know if he deserved it because I wasn't really paying any particular attention to anybody on the Cowboys. Obviously he had a great game. Most of the Cowboys' defensive players played well. Their offense had a harder time, but that's not surprising, because it wasn't nearly as good as our defense. I know Craig Morton didn't have such a great game. Duane Thomas scored their only touchdown and had a few good runs, but he didn't do anything that impressed me. I think Walt Garrison had a better day running and didn't fumble.

I was proud of our team. We had come back to win with five seconds left after not having led the entire game. I really think that everybody on our defensive team stepped up. I don't think you could say any guy played twice as good as he ever played before. That wasn't what happened. Everybody just did what they had to do. The defense stuck in there and gave us good field position. We didn't always capitalize on it, but their defense gave them good field position and they didn't capitalize on it every time either. They lost the ball a lot. Many people in the press would complain about all the mistakes, but I thought it had been a good game to watch—especially since we won. The fact is that most of those errors the media criticized were caused by good, hard defensive plays and weren't accidental. I think it was a damn good game—13–13 with nine seconds left is a pretty darn good game. It all came down to who had the ball last.

Everybody was pretty happy, but we couldn't have champagne in the locker room. They did not have hats made up with "Super Bowl V Winner" or anything like that. But they did give us all our jerseys, which was kind of nice. Then we had a party that night that our owner Carroll

Rosenbloom had arranged. It was basically for friends and family, but Muhammad Ali was there. Everybody had a great time.

The guys on the team were going to cut my hair after the Super Bowl. I don't remember if it was going to happen if we won or lost or either way, but they couldn't wait for the Super Bowl to be over to do it. But after we won on my field goal, Billy Ray Smith said, "Okay, we're not going to cut your hair anymore; we're going to let you go." So I got a reprieve.

Baltimore was a football-crazy town, so I'm sure the fans were thrilled by the Colts' only Super Bowl victory and gave the returning players a tremendous welcome. But I didn't go back. I went to Nassau and Freeport. Some of the single guys went over there for a couple of days to relax. It was a great way to end the season.

Suddenly, people knew who I was. I didn't really do talk shows, but I did go on *The Ed Sullivan Show*, believe it or not. I went on by myself and talked about the kick. It was a fun thing to do. Also I got an endorsement from Life Savers, the candy company. They had a "Life Saver of the Year" award and I went around to different radio stations to promote that. It was a publicity thing, a way to make a few bucks. Had I played for the Giants, Jets, or Rams, I could have gotten a lot more stuff to do. There was attention paid to me, but it was fairly low-key and I wasn't aggressive about it. I probably didn't realize I could have marketed myself more. Looking back: that I had longer hair probably hurt me in getting endorsements.

I think what resulted from my kick was 98 percent positive, and I don't know what the other 2 percent was. I'm sure it changed my personality to some extent and that caused some negative things, but it did make me stronger and told me that I could accomplish whatever I wanted to, not only in football but in anything. I would have a fairly successful life. It's true that I wouldn't have had the notoriety without that kick, although, obviously, that fame was fleeting.

I still enjoy watching my kick if I come across it being shown on TV. But I don't take the tape out and play it. I don't say, "Gee, I'm going to watch that kick because I need to feel good again." How long does it take before you come down from something like making the game-winning kick in the Super Bowl? Well, reality hits when you report to training camp the next summer and there are two or three guys there trying out as kickers. That's when you come down. The lead balloon hits.

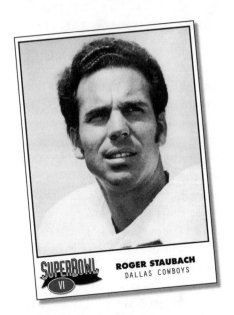

ROGER STAUBACH
DALLAS COWBOYS

SUPER BOWL VI

DALLAS COWBOYS 24
MIAMI DOLPHINS 3

ROGER STAUBACH

When I played football at Navy, I thought that I had the ability to be a pro quarterback. That was particularly true after my junior year when I won the Heisman Trophy and the pro scouts at the College All-Star Game told me they liked my strong arm and that I could run. However, I doubted that I would ever play professionally because after graduation from the academy I was committed to four years of active duty. When you're young, four years seems like a lifetime. I was considered a long shot to ever play in the pros, but both the Kansas City Chiefs in the AFL and the Dallas Cowboys in the NFL made me a late draft pick. Because I was drafted by two teams, I had a little leverage financially, although not as much as I would have had if I were going directly to the pros. I ended up signing with Dallas.

While in the service, I stayed in shape by working out and playing a lot of basketball. At Sherman Field, we had a base football team and played some small colleges, and that helped. In Vietnam, I ran on the base—of course, I couldn't run too far. I also lifted weights. Dallas kept in touch with me during those four years. In fact, in 1968, after my third year in the service, I took a leave and went out to Thousand Oaks, California, and had two weeks of training camp with the Cowboys. Tom Landry and the other coaches realized that I hadn't lost anything and was actually a little bit stronger physically. At that time I made up my mind that I was going to leave the service the following year and join the Cowboys.

After completing my military obligation, I came to Dallas's camp in 1969 as an older rookie. Don Meredith had just retired and Landry promoted Craig Morton to starting quarterback. Now Landry needed a backup for Morton. It was unlike Landry to pick a rookie to fill that role, but he already knew from the previous camp that I was physically capable and now he decided that I also had the maturity to be a backup right away instead of starting out as a third stringer. So I would get a chance to play if Morton got hurt.

I actually had the opportunity to start the first game of the season after Craig hurt his finger in an exhibition game. We beat the St. Louis Cardinals, 24–3, in my debut. Then Craig came back the next week and did just a fantastic job. He was playing at a high level and we were winning. However, he hurt his shoulder against the Atlanta Falcons in our fourth game. It was a partial separation, but they didn't think it required an operation. I would have liked to have started again, but instead of resting him, they played him the next week. We won that game, too, and went to 6–0 before the Browns beat us badly. Craig got away with it for a while, but then his arm started bothering him. I don't think he ever totally recovered.

As a rookie, I was just happy to be there, although I hadn't realized how frustrated I'd be sitting on the bench. I'd never done it. But I understood that Craig was playing very well and it wasn't as if they needed me in there—our record was 11–2–1 and we easily won our division. However, after we were eliminated by Cleveland in the opening game of the playoffs, I really wanted a chance to be the starter the next year. I had anxiety because Tom Landry believed that you needed three or four years to become a starting quarterback. In fact, Craig had waited four years behind Meredith. But I was already 27 and I didn't want to wait until I was in my thirties. Anyway, that a quarterback needs years of experience to develop is somewhat of a myth. It just depends on the individual. I really expressed to Landry that I could play sooner.

I worked real hard just to get a shot. However, Craig Morton was such a fine quarterback that I might never have played if it weren't for his injuries. Craig finally had an operation after the '69 season, but at the camp the next year he struggled with his shoulder and elbow, so I again opened the season as the quarterback. I started the first two games and we beat the Philadelphia Eagles on the road and the New York Giants at Texas Stadium. I also started the third game against the Cardinals. By that game, Craig seemed ready to play again and I sensed that Landry was going to get him back in there no matter what I did, because he felt I wasn't ready to be his starter. In the second quarter we were behind something like 3–0 or 6–0, and I threw a pass into the end zone that hit Lance Rentzel right in the hands. That would have put us ahead, but he dropped it. My next pass was intercepted by Larry Wilson. So Landry took me out. And I didn't get much chance to play the rest of the year.

Craig wasn't quite the same because of the nagging injuries and he had a lot of trouble in the middle of the year. Our whole team was struggling then and we lost one game by over 40 points to Minnesota and another 38–0 to St. Louis. I wouldn't have minded sitting, but it was really frustrating because Craig was hurting and we were playing badly. But then we really turned it around. I don't know if our defense gave up another touchdown all year. Craig was still having arm problems, but he had some good games and we ended up real strong. We won our final five regular season games to beat out the Giants for the Eastern Division title, and then we shut out Detroit to open the playoffs and defeated San Francisco in the NFC Championship Game.

Unfortunately, we then lost to Baltimore in Super Bowl V, 16–13. After so many years of falling short of winning the title, the Cowboys really were disappointed by that loss. The reports of our frustration were not exaggerated. Even going back to the year before, I don't think Tom Landry was ever more down than after we had lost to Cleveland in the playoffs. We had to reexamine our whole operation after that, from our coaching staff to everything else. There were a whole lot of changes. But now we had lost again, to Baltimore, in the final seconds. Bob Lilly hurling his helmet across the field pretty much represented how all the Cowboys felt. I don't know if it was before or after we lost that Super Bowl, but we did see the headline: THE TEAM THAT CAN'T WIN THE BIG GAME. That kind of tag was horrible and unfair really because you're still a winner even if you don't win the title. But the fan and media perception is greater than the reality, and we knew that success was translated as winning the Super

Bowl. Until we had done that, Dallas would never get the recognition it deserved of being a winning team. That was the mentality we had. It was grating on the team, especially on the veteran stars like Bob Lilly, Mel Renfro, Chuck Howley, and Lee Roy Jordan. (Only Herb Adderley, who had won two Super Bowls with Green Bay, didn't have that concern.)

There had been a story in *Sports Illustrated* about Dallas being "a team without a quarterback." I was thinking, "Jeez, here I am. . . . " On a personal level, I continued to be pretty frustrated. Even though I had filled in occasionally during the '69 and '70 seasons, Landry had never thought I was capable of being a starter. However, when we were flying back to Dallas after losing to the Colts, Landry told me that he would give me a chance to become the starter in 1971. When he told me that, I knew he was going to give me a real chance, because he was a man of his word. If Landry made up his mind against you, you were in trouble, but if he made up his mind for you, at least you had a chance.

I think that if we had won Super Bowl V, Craig Morton would have been the starting quarterback the next year. Landry would have stuck with him and I don't think there would have been what developed into a quarterback controversy. If we win the Super Bowl, the job should be his. All I can say is that I was sure hoping we were going to win and was cheering like everybody else.

In 1971 Craig came back the healthiest he had been since his injury. I also was ready. We both played really well in the exhibition season and I think the team went undefeated. Landry couldn't make up his mind between us, so he announced before the season began that we were going to have two starting quarterbacks. That was kind of a weird turn. For me, playing half the time was better than not getting the job at all, but I was still a bit uneasy, as I'm sure Craig was. Leadership is a major quality at the quarterback position and you need to have one person at that spot. He must be so much in control and be so involved—the one person everyone comes up to—and be somebody who comes through at the end of the game. So a coach must pick somebody that he has total confidence in.

I thought Tom Landry was phenomenal as a coach and as a person, but sometimes you start believing so much in your system that you don't realize the difference in players. Tom's feeling was: Hey, we've got a great system, and if we execute the system, it doesn't really matter who's out there. Craig and I used essentially the same system. The coaches put in a few roll-out-type plays for me, a couple of bootlegs, and a couple of other things, but I was pretty much in the same dropback quarterback system that Craig played in. We weren't a run-and-shoot offense and wouldn't really use the shotgun until 1975. When I ran, it was off dropbacks.

I was selected to start the opening game. But I had a weird injury—a vein had broken in my leg in an exhibition game against Kansas City—and in the middle of the week the doctors told me I couldn't play. I couldn't believe it. I was so angry. So Landry announced Craig would start the first week and I'd start the second week. Craig started against the Buffalo Bills and we beat them pretty good. I started the next week against the Eagles and on the third play of the game I got knocked out when a defensive end named Mel Tom hit me on the side of the head. So Craig came in and finished that game and we had another win. In the third game, Landry started Craig in what became a loss to the Redskins. It looked like Craig was back in the driver's seat, but I started the fourth week against the Giants. We were ahead 13–6 at halftime, but Landry took me out. I thought that was it for me. I wasn't really vocal, but Landry knew how upset I was. That was the lowest I'd ever been as a player. I was thinking that I hadn't done anything to not still deserve the chance to be the starting quarterback, but that Landry just wanted Craig back in there.

The next week we played the Saints and Landry started Craig. We were losing 17–0 and Landry sent me in and we scored twice to make it 17–14. We were going to get the ball back with the chance to pull it out, but our punt returner fumbled the ball and the Saints went in to score another touchdown and make the final score 24–14. We had lost, but I had played really well and Landry announced that I was starting against the New England Patriots the next week. We easily beat New England in Dallas. The next week we were going to play the Chicago Bears and it was Craig's turn to start, but at a team meeting Tom Landry announced that we were going to have alternating quarterbacks instead. Craig and I were going to switch after every play. Craig and I were just looking at each other, shaking our heads and wondering, "What is this deal?" It was just a horrible decision. It was saying that the quarterback is just a coach's tool and not a leader. And it just didn't work.

Against the Bears, Craig and I would go back and forth, bringing in the plays. However, in the last two minutes of the game, Landry kept Craig in. So I thought this was it. We lost to the Bears and we were 4–3 and everybody was on our case and we were pretty much written off. It was obvious that Landry had to make a final decision on who his starting quarterback was if we were going to have any hope of salvaging the season.

Either decision would have been the right decision. I could have seen Landry choosing Craig or me. If Landry had picked Craig, I'm sure it would have been my last year in Dallas, but I would have accepted that decision. I wouldn't have walked out, because I was still a team player. I thought Landry would choose Craig, so I was surprised when he decided that I was going to be his starting quarterback for the rest of the season. Landry didn't call us in, but I got the word through some of the coaches. That was probably the most exciting moment in my life. An announcement confirming Landry's decision was given to the press on Tuesday.

Craig was healthy and I know the decision had to hurt him. But he didn't express that to me or the press—he was just a class act, as good a guy as you could be. Craig and I were never close friends, because that would have been difficult, but we handled the situation as well as we could under the circumstances. He supported me the rest of the year. We went to meetings together; we worked out together; we never had disagreements. We had never discussed our situation, but I think Craig and I always had a lot of respect for each other as players and people and there were never ill feelings about trying to win the job over the other guy. I think we both realized that we were each capable of being starting quarterbacks. (Ironically, I got hurt in 1972, and when I came back in 1973, Craig and I were back into the same controversy again. Landry met with us both and said that I was healthy again so I would again be the starter. Craig was really disappointed then and had to gut it out in the '73 season before being traded to the Giants so he could start again.)

We were playing in St. Louis the first week after Landry's decision to go with me and I remember leaving my hotel room and going downstairs. I was a nervous wreck and was going to go out and get something to eat and go back and look at the game plan some more. My roommate, Chuck Howley, was in the restaurant with Bob Lilly and they called me over and settled me down. It was a tough time for a quarterback to come in and assert leadership, but what helped my confidence was that my teammates really showed their support for me. Howley, Lilly, and a lot of guys on defense were behind me, as were the guys on offense. Nobody came out and said, "I'm glad it's Roger, not Craig," but having one quarterback made a difference in the team's attitude and helped us start playing better. If it had been Craig who was chosen as the starter, I've no doubt that the team would have rallied around him as well.

I hadn't given up on the season because I knew we had a good team. Our "Doomsday" defense was outstanding and I had confidence in our offense, especially with the addition of receiver Lance Alworth and the return of our star back Duane Thomas from his early season holdout. As a team, we had always shown resilience, so I believed we had the ability to rebound from our poor start. Even so, I didn't expect that we wouldn't lose another game all year. We beat St. Louis and won all our remaining games to finish the regular season at 11–3 and win the Eastern Division title ahead of the Redskins. I don't know if any of the excitement the players were feeling was due to Landry making me his quarterback, but I think the guys had confidence in me and knew I would do whatever it took to win. The fact that I was kind of a running, hell-bent-for-leather-type quarterback might have had an impact.

I don't think Landry was ever fond of my scrambling. He never believed that a quarterback should run. He didn't feel that it was the smart thing for me to do because it would make me more prone to injuries, but he knew he couldn't change my style of play. So he just accepted that it was part of my game and put up with it. I really feel that Landry and I were different in many ways—I know I was never his prototype quarterback—yet we had a tremendous amount of respect for each other because we were both so competitive and willing to work so hard in order to win. Landry knew that I had the same passion he had to win—and that I did win.

It helped so much to know that he would no longer pull me during a game, as had happened against the Giants. I knew that once Landry stuck with me, I could do well. I was the type of quarterback who could screw up for three quarters and then have a big fourth quarter. Knowing that I'd get my chance in the fourth quarter no matter what happened earlier in the game brought my confidence level way up. Now that I had security, my level of play also went up.

The team's great play, especially on defense, continued in the playoffs. We beat Minnesota 20–12 in a snowstorm and, for the second straight year, defeated the 49ers in the NFC Championship Game, this time by a score of 14–3. We weren't satisfied after we beat San Francisco and there was hardly any celebration. We just knew we had to beat whoever won the AFC title game in the Super Bowl in New Orleans. It would either be the Baltimore Colts again or the Miami Dolphins. Miami had reached the AFC title game when Garo Yepremian kicked a field goal in the second overtime to beat Kansas City. Now, after we had won our game, Miami shut out the Colts to earn its first trip to the Super Bowl.

We had never played the Dolphins and didn't know anything about them other than that they had turned around quickly once Don Shula took over as their coach in 1970. Leading up to the Super Bowl, we studied the heck out of them, though. Our defense came up with the right ways to stop their quarterback, Bob Griese, and his top receiver, Paul Warfield, as well as the Dolphins' strong runners, Larry Csonka and Jim Kiick. Meanwhile, the offense was devising a game plan to neutralize their key defensive player, middle linebacker Nick Buoniconti.

As far as the game plan went, the coaches really put it together and we would execute it. But I had input to some degree. We'd have quarterback meetings and we'd talk about our running game and about the kinds of pass routes that I was the most comfortable with. For instance, I had the ability to throw the ball in tight situations over the middle. Through my whole career that was the case (including years later when we had Drew Pearson). The guy I might go to over the middle, especially on third down, was Lance Alworth. He was a new guy on the team and we got along really well. Lance was not really tall but he was really smart and a great veteran receiver. If we got to third-and-7 or 8 yards, that's when Alworth did a great job. If it was a zone defense, he could stop quickly and turn around to make the catch. If it was man coverage, he could make a move that would get him open, as he would do against Miami.

Most of the big touchdowns we got on passing plays that year were by Alworth and Bob Hayes. Hayes was still a speedster and a big-play receiver. He'd run deep patterns and do some curls. Alworth was more of a possession receiver. Mike Ditka and his backup, Billy Truax, were also big targets, possession-type tight ends on key downs. With those guys, I had some excellent, dependable receivers.

I would have loved to have thrown the ball 40 times a game but that wasn't the way our offense was set up. Unless we got really behind, we'd run, and the number of passes I'd throw would usually be in the low twenties or high teens. I would throw only 19 passes against Miami, and that was more than I threw against either Minnesota or San Francisco. When Landry felt we were the favored team, as was the case against Miami, he would want us to play conservatively, and as long as our defense played well, we'd stay that way. Other than an occasional pass on first down—which usually got us big yardage because teams expected us to run until third down—the big plays we got weren't designed but usually came off broken plays. For instance, against San Francisco, I was trapped in the end zone and scrambled around until I finally got it out to Dan Reeves, which was a big play because it set us off on a key fourth-quarter drive.

We had several big third-down pass conversions against the 49ers. That was important because I believe third-down conversion percentage is the key stat in football. Long yardage on third downs can be as little as 3 or 4 yards, but most teams won't get a first down more than 40 percent of the time. We did better than that. We might not have thrown a lot, but the significant thing about our passing game is that we were able to complete a high percentage of third-down passes. We used a lot of play action, mixed it up really well, and had great success. Those completions to Alworth, Ditka, and Truax were essential for a team that relied on ball control. If we got good running yardage on first down, we were in good shape, but even when our running game was very, very good, there would be times when we were faced with third-and-long.

Our running game was the key to our offense. We had a very strong group of runners in Walt Garrison, Calvin Hill, Duane Thomas, and myself, and we'd run more than twice as much as we passed. Garrison, Hill, and Thomas rotated at the two running-back positions and all got a lot of playing time. The oldest was Garrison, who was a rodeo cowboy. As you'd expect, he was a tough runner and blocker, but he was also a big part of our passing game, especially when we needed short yardage. In fact, he led our team in receptions during the season. Garrison did most of his running inside and was more in the classic fullback mold than Hill or Thomas, but both those guys played fullback when Garrison wasn't in there. Hill was a big guy, but he had excellent speed and could run to the outside. He had a great rookie season in '69 and it looked like he was going to be our workhorse for years to come, but his playing time diminished because of some injuries and because the Cowboys made Duane Thomas their top pick in the next draft. Although they had Hill, they just couldn't pass him up. It was obvious that Thomas was something special in his rookie season, and in '71 he really came into his own. He was getting many more carries than Hill.

However, something was wrong with Duane's mental state. That was made obvious to the public when he refused to talk to the media prior to the Super Bowl. It was hard for anyone to speak with Duane. He just didn't want to talk. You just wondered what was going through his mind. I've talked to him since, and I still don't know what was going on back then. Of course, we all knew that he had held out at the beginning of the year because the Cowboys wouldn't renegotiate his contract after his fine rookie season. He was traded during his holdout to the Patriots, but they had returned him to the Cowboys because of his attitude. He then came back to play for us only at the insistence of Jim Brown, who had become his agent. Duane expressed dissatisfaction over his contract, but I don't know if that was the entire source of his anger or why he moved increasingly into a reclusive-type pattern.

I couldn't communicate with him that well. I tried to and I think he knew that. For instance, I might kid him that I was going to outrush him the next game, or something similar. But his withdrawal became worse and he seemed to stop talking to almost everybody on the team. (The next year, he wouldn't talk to anybody, and the Cowboys traded him.) Even at meetings, when they'd do roll calls, he wouldn't answer, which is pretty much the extent to which he broke the rules. At those meetings he wouldn't be responsive yet he picked up everything. It was amazing to me that on the field he never missed a beat. Duane must have taken time to study our plays—or else he was a genius—because he never made a mistake. He'd move from tailback to fullback and know the blocking schemes and everything else. I guess I never had any problems with him or thought him disruptive because he was such a great player and always did his job. The only thing that I found uncomfortable on the field was when he'd give me this look when I threw the ball behind him. He was a perfectionist and just wanted everything to be done right.

I don't know if Duane was at all putting on reporters on Super Bowl media day when he sat silently with them until his required time was up. To be honest, none of the players were really worrying about Duane and the media because we had to deal with the media ourselves. That was pretty intense all week because we were being constantly reminded by the media how we'd never won the big game before.

For me, my second Super Bowl Week was a whole different ride. I was now the starting quarterback, so I was a focal point of the media attention. I hadn't played at all in Super Bowl V, but it was helpful to have experienced working out with the team and witnessing all the hoopla surrounding the game. So when I came to Super Bowl VI, I had already been through the motions of the outside activities and it was easier to concentrate on preparing for the game. I studied really hard. I didn't go out, except for one night. It's funny how you remember these things: I went out with Joe Williams, one of our running backs, and we saw *Dirty Harry*, the Clint Eastwood movie. That was my only nightlife during the whole week. I remember going over to Landry's room at night instead and watching film. We did a lot of film study before the game.

So on Super Sunday in Tulane Stadium, I was well prepared to play the Miami Dolphins. I was more nervous than the previous year, of course, but that was okay, because it was a healthy nervousness. I was eager for the game to begin.

Neither team did anything on their first possessions. Then Miami became the first team to cross midfield. However, on the next play, Larry Csonka fumbled for the first time all year and Chuck Howley recovered. We took the ball and moved deep into their territory on runs by Thomas and Garrison and a couple of passes, and went ahead 3–0 on Mike Clark's short field goal. I knew that it was good to get up front in a game like this, but I was disappointed I hadn't thrown a touchdown and given us a bigger lead. We had it third-and-goal at their 2 and ran a play-action pass play where I would look to both our back out in the flat and our tight end in the corner. Thomas ran a little flare and I dumped it off to him for no gain when I probably should have waited for Ditka to break free. In fact, Ditka came back and was yelling at me that he got wide open in the end zone. He was all over my case. In the second quarter I would hit Mike with a third-down pass over the middle, but he would drop it, forcing us to punt. I said, "Nice catch, Mike."

I think Csonka's fumble was a big play in that it showed we had some control. Another real positive play for the defense was Bob Lilly's sack of Bob Griese on the Dolphins' next possession. Griese kept retreating but couldn't get away from Lilly or throw the ball away. I don't know if I saw that whole play, but it lasted a while and I definitely saw the end of it. Of course, I've seen it on film a number of times since, because it was definitely a defensive highlight of that game. It was a big 29-yard sack and it further indicated that we were in charge. A play like that gives you that feeling.

I don't know if the other players thought it was a physical game, but I know I got hit hard a few times. The Dolphins' defense definitely shut me down as a runner. Early on, I did a lot of running, but it wasn't forward. It was evident that they had me marked to prevent me from scrambling. There was always someone holding his position until he saw what I was doing. I don't think this worked to their benefit. When they're so concerned about my running that they design plays to stop it and then sit back there and think about me, then things open up for the other backs. That would be the case the whole game.

The Dolphins' defense was set up to protect Nick Buoniconti at the middle linebacker position and have him be the guy who made their tackles. So the key to our running game plan was to make sure that Buoniconti was taken out of each play. We'd always have two guys on him, usually

January 16, 1972, at Tulane Stadium in New Orleans

Attendance: 81,023

NFC Champion: Dallas Cowboys (13–3)
Head Coach: Tom Landry

AFC Champion: Miami Dolphins (12–3–1)
Head Coach: Don Shula

STARTING LINEUPS

OFFENSE

Dallas		Miami
Bob Hayes	WR	Paul Warfield
Tony Liscio	LT	Doug Crusan
John Niland	LG	Bob Kuechenberg
Dave Manders	C	Bob DeMarco
Blaine Nye	RG	Larry Little
Rayfield Wright	RT	Norm Evans
Mike Ditka	TE	Marv Fleming
Lance Alworth	WR	Howard Twilley
Roger Staubach	QB	Bob Griese
Duane Thomas	RB	Jim Kiick
Walt Garrison	RB	Larry Csonka

DEFENSE

Dallas		Miami
Larry Cole	LE	Jim Riley
Jethro Pugh	LT	Manny Fernandez
Bob Lilly	RT	Bob Heinz
George Andrie	RE	Bill Stanfill
Dave Edwards	LLB	Doug Swift
Lee Roy Jordan	MLB	Nick Buoniconti
Chuck Howley	RLB	Mike Kolen
Herb Adderley	LCB	Tim Foley
Mel Renfro	RCB	Curtis Johnson
Cornell Green	LS	Dick Anderson
Cliff Harris	RS	Jake Scott

SUBSTITUTIONS

Dallas: K—Mike Clark. P—Ron Widby. Offense: Receiver—Bill Truax. Lineman—John Fitzgerald. Backs—Dan Reeves, Calvin Hill, Joe Williams, Claxton Welch. Defense: Linebackers—D. D. Lewis, Tom Stincic. Linemen—Tody Smith, Bill Gregory, Pat Toomay. Backs—Ike Thomas, Charlie Waters. DNP—Craig Morton, Gloster Richardson, Forrest Gregg.

Miami: K—Garo Yepremian. P—Larry Seiple. Offense: Receivers—Karl Noonan, Otto Stowe, Jim Mandich. Linemen—Wayne Moore, Jim Langer. Backs—Mercury Morris, Terry Cole, Hubert Ginn. Defense: Linebackers—Bob Matheson, Jesse Powell. Linemen—Frank Cornish, Vern Den Herder. Backs—Lloyd Mumphord, Bob Petrella. DNP—George Mira, John Richardson.

Dallas	3	7	7	7—24
Miami	0	3	0	0— 3

Dall	FG Clark 9
Dall	Alworth 7 pass from Staubach (Clark kick)
Mia	FG Yepremian 31
Dall	D. Thomas 3 run (Clark kick)
Dall	Ditka 7 pass from Staubach (Clark kick)
MVP:	Roger Staubach (Dallas)

guard John Niland and center Jack Manders. Because Buoniconti reacted so quickly, we'd run a lot of counterplays to get him and the other Dolphins to be running one way, and when they'd come back, we'd lay blocks on them. Our whole offensive line was doing a great job blocking—Niland, Manders, Rayfield Wright, Blaine Nye, and Tony Liscio, who had to come out of retirement late in the season when Ralph Neely broke his leg in a dirt-bike accident. Miami's hustling defense pursued a lot, so counterplays worked well, especially since Duane Thomas was great on cutbacks. Duane read plays really well and had pretty good speed, and he had that instinct to cut back to a hole. Lots of guys have speed, but they don't have that instinct. Gale Sayers had it, Jim Brown had it, future Cowboys Tony Dorsett and Emmitt Smith would have it—and Duane Thomas was potentially in that category if he continued to play as he did in 1970 and 1971. (When he came back to the Cowboys a few years after being traded, for some reason that instinct wasn't there.)

Our field goal was the only score of the game until we mounted a drive late in the second quarter. We got a lot of yardage on runs by Thomas and Hill, but probably the biggest play was a 21-yard completion to Alworth over the middle that took us into Miami territory. It was reminiscent of a big 17-yard completion on third down to Alworth against San Francisco. This was one of only two catches Lance would make against Miami all day. His other catch came at the end of the drive and was good for 7 yards and our first touchdown. It was on a quick out. You take a chance when you throw a quick out near the end zone. He was very close to the sidelines and I wanted to make sure there was no way they could intercept it, so I probably threw that pass harder than any pass I threw in my whole life. He made a heck of a catch just over the goal line and kept his feet in bounds. So we were ahead, 10–0.

Miami managed to score just before the half on a field goal by Garo Yepremian. That cut our lead to just a touchdown, but you have to remember that, lately, it hadn't been easy for any team to score a touchdown against our defense.

At halftime we reasoned that Miami would make adjustments to stop our running game. We had been punching the ball inside so successfully that they would have to discuss how to stop that. We figured that in the first half they were going to stay at home a little bit and in the second half they were going to send everyone and be more susceptible to reverses and going-against-the-grain-type plays. So, on our first drive of the second half, we decided to run outside. Mostly it was Thomas running sweeps, but we even did a reverse with Bob Hayes that got us a first down.

Finally we scored when Duane went over the left side from 3 yards out. That play was on an audible. While we continued to make sure Buoniconti was blocked, the other major part of our offensive strategy revolved around their linebacker, Bob Matheson, number 53. Each time Shula inserted Matheson, I had to make sure I knew where he was, because where he was kind of gave away their defensive scheme. So it impacted on what kind of play we'd run and how we were going to block. I'd audibilize on occasion because of the look Matheson gave them. Whatever side Matheson switched to, we'd have a play set up that would work effectively against that defensive look.

Every time we were stymied and got into a third down, we seemed to convert. As I said, that's the style of play that we had. Personally, I thought we could have opened up and scored more throwing the ball. But our defense had the game pretty well under control, so we didn't try a lot offensively except on third-down situations.

I was watching the defense when I had a chance. The key to our defensive game plan was to stop Paul Warfield, who was a tremendous receiver. Cornell Green would follow him wherever he went and Mel Renfro would double him—Green would have him on the inside and Renfro would have him on the outside. They pretty much shut him down. Csonka and Kiick got some yardage running, but the Dolphins needed a big play from a receiver because they just couldn't get the ball deep into our territory. Every time they threatened to drive downfield, we'd get a turnover.

Early in the fourth quarter, when the Dolphins were down 14 points and desperate to get back into the game, Chuck Howley got his second turnover for us. He got off the ground to intercept Griese's short pass at midfield and returned it all the way to the Miami 9. My roommate was mad at himself for not scoring a touchdown because he had a wall of blockers in front of him and clear sailing to the end zone when he just tripped over his own feet and tumbled to the ground.

We scored our final touchdown on a 7-yard pass to Mike Ditka. That play was only slightly different from the play we ran in the first quarter, where I didn't wait for Ditka to break open and threw to Thomas. It was just a play-action where the fullback goes out into the flat and Mike goes into the right corner. Mike got open a few steps behind the defender and I just tossed it to him as he was running toward the corner. It was a play that worked perfectly. When your running game is working so well that they have to respect that, then your play-action passes are much more effective.

We were up, 24–3, and the outcome wasn't much in doubt. However, Miami finally got the ball inside our 20 and was hoping for a late rally, but

Griese fumbled the snap and we got the ball back and drove all the way downfield with some strong running. Before fumbling the ball back to Miami, we got the ball down to the 1 on a reverse to Ditka. He ran about 17 yards, but got turned around and didn't know where the goal was, and fell down just before he would have picked up 6 points. Ditka might have been the MVP if he had gotten into the end zone—and if I'd also hit him with that first pass for a touchdown, Mike would have had three touchdowns, and then he'd definitely have been the MVP.

As it turned out, I received the MVP award. Probably Duane Thomas's attitude toward the media during Super Bowl Week got me the MVP. I think that's the case. I played a good game and didn't make any mistakes and hit some key passes, but my performance wasn't anything MVP-like. It would have given more recognition to our offensive line if they had given the MVP to a running back. Walt Garrison and Calvin Hill ran pretty well between them, but Duane was the guy Miami couldn't stop. He ran for less than 100 yards, but he ran for big yardage on significant plays. He ran through their defense. He had a great game, but because of his lack of communication with reporters, they probably said, "Well, Roger did okay, so let's give it to him." Maybe they gave it to me because of the whole 10-game-victory span.

It was great to celebrate that victory over Miami. After so many years, Dallas had gotten rid of that tag that it couldn't win the big games. The Super Bowl stays with you the rest of your life and we were world champions, and that old saying is true—it was something no one could ever take away from us. When you look at how many teams and players have played, you realize that a Super Bowl victory doesn't happen to everyone. So it was very special to all of us. I can say that I don't think I ever felt any better as an athlete than how I felt after that game, after the Dallas Cowboys had won Super Bowl VI. You can believe that all the old veterans were thrilled as well. Even Tom Landry was smiling.

NICK BUONICONTI
MIAMI DOLPHINS

SUPER BOWL VII

MIAMI DOLPHINS 14
WASHINGTON REDSKINS 7

NICK BUONICONTI

Super Bowl VI had been a blur, even before I was knocked sense-less. The Cowboys seemed to be moving so much faster than we were, like we were in two-four time and they were in four-four time. This is no reflection on Don Shula, who had been to the Super Bowl before, or his coaches, but we never understood what we had to do to win. Meanwhile, Dallas's game plan proved to be correct. Tom Landry and his offensive coaches decided they were going to put two guys on me every play and it was frustrating because I was shielded from getting to the ball. They had me going 10 different ways and I wasn't a factor in the game. None of our defensive guys were. We were overmatched psychologically as well as physically. Cornell Green, the defensive back for Dallas, later commented, "The difference between the Dolphins and Cowboys was that the Dolphins were just happy to be in the game and the Cowboys came to win the game." That was true. We went there—it was party time in New Orleans, young kids on the town. I'm not sure any of us expected to win the game—and we played like it.

When I arrived at training camp a few months after our Super Bowl debacle, I took the article that included Cornell Green's quote, and I underlined his words and stuck it up on the bulletin board. And all year long I'd stop and read it at least once a week—and that really had an impact. I wasn't the only guy who had an entirely new attitude. We were only a year older and still a very young team, but there had been a major maturation process during the off-season. We had learned a hard lesson: When you go into a Super Bowl you have to realize its magnitude. Fran Tarkenton would have three losses in Super Bowls, and he'd downplay them each time by saying, "It's just another game." Well, it's not just another game.

Winning the Super Bowl is the crowning achievement—what you work for all year. We hadn't considered that going into Super Bowl VI and wasted an opportunity to give meaning to our work and accomplishments during the 1971 season. It was not like anybody on the team had to be told that we stunk up the joint and embarrassed ourselves. Our dreadful performance is what catapulted us to an undefeated season in 1972, culminating in a Super Bowl victory over the Washington Redskins.

It was so clear that we had to get back to the Super Bowl and win to make amends for the disgrace we brought on the name of the Miami Dolphins. What we really wanted was to get the season and the playoffs out of the way. Reaching the Super Bowl was by design, but becoming the first NFL team to go unbeaten was an accident. It just happened. After about the ninth game, we'd sit in front of our lockers and look at our schedule and ask, "Which game are we going to lose?" And we'd tick off the remaining opponents and answer, "Nah . . . Nah . . . Nah . . . Nah . . . Nah." There were a couple of tough games. We edged Buffalo by one point and, later in the season, came from behind to beat the Jets 28–24. Those are the close games you have to pull out if you go undefeated. It's simple: You can't go undefeated if you lose.

The playoff games were dicey. But they just proved the greatness of our team. When we needed it, it was there. With time running out and us trailing Cleveland in the divisional playoff, Paul Warfield makes a big catch, Jim Kiick runs it in from 8 yards out to put us ahead, and then Doug Swift intercepts Mike Phipps and we win the game, 20–14.

In the second quarter of the AFC title game against Pittsburgh, Larry Seiple faked a punt and carried the ball almost 40 yards to the Steelers'

12, leading to an Earl Morrall–Larry Csonka pass that tied the game. That fake punt was, by far, the biggest play of the year for us, because without that, I don't think we would have won the game. It turned everything around. With the score tied 7–7 at the half, Shula made the move from Morrall to Bob Griese, who had been out since October with a broken leg. Bob threw a long pass to Warfield and then handed off to Kiick for a go-ahead touchdown; in the fourth quarter Kiick scored again, and Mike Kolen and I intercepted Bradshaw as the game wound down, and we won 21–17. It would have been hell to have gone 15–1.

We were very emotional on the field, very businesslike off the field. There was no celebrating, even after beating the Browns and Steelers. People would come into the locker room and say, "Jeez, you would think you guys lost." And we'd say, "We haven't done anything yet. We've got to win the Super Bowl." There was no way we were going to lose the Super Bowl; there was no way.

The only skeptics we had were NFC people who still thought that AFC teams weren't up to par with NFC teams. According to Jimmy the Greek, the Redskins were favored by one or two points despite the fact that our record was 16–0 and they had lost three times; despite our having a defense that gave up only 171 points during the season; and despite a running game that was second to none, with Larry Csonka and Mercury Morris becoming the first teammates to each gain over 1,000 yards in a season. Plus our third back, Jim Kiick, added another 500 yards rushing. This was a team with talent on both sides of the ball.

Vern Den Herder had replaced Jim Riley as a starter at defensive end and linebacker Bob Matheson played more, but otherwise our defense was the same as it had been against Dallas. We got the "No-Name Defense" nickname because Tom Landry couldn't recall most of our names when speaking to the press before that Super Bowl. That nickname became kind of lovable. It was fun because after a while it became a challenge for us to become known. We played great the whole 1972 season. I was the oldest guy on defense and I did my best to live up to my reputation for being a player who was good, tough, smart, and reliable. I think the guys respected me and would say that I was the leader of the defense. It's hard to talk about myself—it makes me uncomfortable— but I'd say I was sort of the catalyst who jump-started the defense. When things got tough, I was the guy the other guys would look to. I wanted that role of holding the defense together in tough situations, and if I didn't think somebody was doing his job, I'd get right in his face and tell him.

We were an intelligent unit. Our defensive coach Bill Arnsparger said that we made only 13 mental mistakes the entire season. Even with all the different formations and changes, nobody was blowing assignments. We were known for using a "53" defense and that stood for Bob Matheson's uniform number. He would stand up as either a defensive end or fourth linebacker with me, Doug Swift, and Mike Kolen. As a linebacker, he would either rush or drop back into coverage. I'd blitz, he'd blitz, from every which way—we'd have a myriad of looks. Teams would be totally confused.

We were a lot more structured than the Patriots defense I'd been part of for several years before I joined Miami. With Boston, I had blitzed on my own, but no one freelanced under Arnsparger. Everybody on the defense was accounted for on every play. No receiver or back was uncovered. Even line changes were predetermined, and after getting our plays from Arnsparger, I'd make calls and tell the linemen which way I wanted them to go. We studied films and picked up on the tendencies of opposing teams on certain downs with different yardage needed for a first down. Most teams didn't go away from their tendencies, so all the checkoffs, audibles, and line calls I made were based on what I saw in the offensive formations. It was like a chess match, and it was a lot of fun.

At the pregame meal we'd get our short list of plays down. Arnsparger would have taken our entire game plan and boiled it down from maybe 15 types of blitzes to 5 blitzes, and from maybe 25 different coverages to just 4 or 5, of which we'd concentrate on maybe 2. He made it so simple for us. He was the consummate defensive coach, a real genius and a nice guy who got along with his players and respected us enough to accept our feedback. We had so much confidence in him that he could have put anything up on the board and we would have bought it. That's important, because players have to believe in the game plan wholeheartedly. The game is tough enough physically, so mentally it has to be automatic.

Our offense had really developed under Monte Clark since I joined the Dolphins in 1969. (After several All-Pro seasons, I had just come back from a sprained knee and was fine, but the Patriots had a new head coach and wanted a new look and a new guy at middle linebacker, so I was designated to go.) In my first year in Miami I made All-Pro, but the team finished last in its division and I couldn't tell if we had a chance to improve. We didn't seem to be headed anywhere. On offense we had Csonka, Kiick, and Morris in the backfield, but even they weren't making an impact without good blocking. There was some question whether Csonka would ever play fullback again—not just because of injuries but because he didn't play well. Then Joe Robbie hired Don Shula away from the Baltimore Colts to replace George Wilson as head coach.

I remember when Shula called me because he was putting together his staff. I didn't even know him yet, but he wanted me to tell him about the character of Monte Clark, who had just retired as a player with the Browns and was being considered for the offensive line coach position. I told him Monte was a very tough, studious person and that his teammates had respected his leadership skills because they had chosen him as their player rep. Clark got the job and he turned the entire offense around by putting together a stellar line with players no other team had wanted: center Jim Langer, left guard Bob Kuechenberg, left tackle Wayne Moore, right guard Larry Little, and right tackle Norm Evans. Most of those castoffs became All-Pros. I would get inspired watching them. There was nothing greater than watching Larry Little pull around the end and flatten people. He had been traded by San Diego and had quickly become one of the greatest guards who ever played the game. He would become a Hall of Famer, as would Langer, who had been waived by the Browns. And Kuechenberg, who the Eagles let go, should be voted in someday.

Those guys gave Bob Griese terrific protection and opened huge holes for Csonka, Moore, and Kiick, though, as I said, it wasn't so easy for Csonka initially. When Shula came in he literally had to teach Csonka how to run with the football. He used to run straight up and down and Shula impressed upon him that he had to lead with his forearm rather than his head. Shula and his backfield coach Carl Tasseff basically reengineered Csonka to where he became the Hall of Fame player. Csonka emerged as the offensive leader of the Dolphins, even more so than Kuechenberg or Langer. He let Griese do the talking in the huddle and wasn't a rah-rah guy—we didn't have any rah-rah guys on the team—but he led by his actions, by playing with a broken nose and blood all over his shirt. He loved to be thought of in terms of Bronko Nagurski—he really believed he was out of that mold and that it was his job not only to carry a football but to punish the defensive players who wanted to tackle him. His blockers either moved the defense or got moved themselves from behind, because Csonka was coming. He didn't care—he'd run over the backs of his linemen if they weren't moving.

Jim Kiick, who alternated with Mercury Morris as Csonka's running mate, loved the game and loved clutch situations—where he was at his best. In the postseason he scored several key touchdowns for us. When we needed a first down on third-and-4 or 5, he'd get it. We might get the ball to him on a short option because there was no one better coming out of the backfield to catch a pass. I've never seen anyone put moves on like him. He'd get a linebacker to lean one way and then go the opposite way. Even when they'd double team, he'd get open.

Morris was much more demonstrative. He was a shifty breakaway back who was flashy, flamboyant, and effective. He had style. He was the guy who'd say, "Just give me the football and watch me run. Don't ask me to block too much but just give me the ball." Kiick blocked for Csonka and Mercury made an effort. There was so much respect for Csonka when he carried the ball that even Morris would attempt to block.

Griese wasn't a leader type but he was much respected by his offensive players. He wasn't flamboyant but he directed our team masterfully. He rarely made a mistake and was always calm under pressure. He'd missed almost the entire season, yet stepped into the second half of the AFC title game without missing a beat. We needed a lift and he was our tonic. The Steelers had a terrific pass rush and Shula knew that Bob threw the ball a little quicker than Earl. He also mixed plays a little bit better. He got the running game going and hit some short passes, and got us into a good rhythm. He got us into the Super Bowl.

After we won the AFC title, the first thing Shula did was resolve the quarterback issue. Earl Morrall did such an unbelievable job after Griese had broken his leg, leading us to 11 straight victories. But in football there's a credo: You never lose your job because of an injury. So it was Griese's job once he got well. Shula told Griese he was going to start in the Super Bowl and Morrall that he was going to return to being a backup. There was no worry about this change. Earl understood. He was such a great team person that he was the one guy you could take out of the starting lineup and not worry about him complaining or dampening the spirit of the team.

Griese didn't throw as much as most NFL quarterbacks, but when he went to the air he had a great big-play receiver, Paul Warfield. There was no classier receiver: He was like an acrobat or ballet dancer. A few years before, Paul had been acquired in a trade from the Browns, another running team. He was very quiet, yet had so much respect from the other players, including Griese. If he said, "Bob, I can beat my guy on a 15-yard route," there's no question Bob would throw him a pass on a 15-yard route. He and Griese liked to set up defensive backs. Maybe Paul would run only one deep pattern, but all game long they'd have set up that play so that the back wouldn't expect it or be out of position and be burned. Paul played on the right team to get a Super Bowl ring, but we weren't the right team to take advantage of a receiver with his talents. If he'd been on a passing team, he would have set records that even Jerry Rice would never break. He was that good.

There was the combination of great talent on the field and great chemistry among the players. There were never problems between players. Guys got along well, socialized well. On Monday nights, after a day off, we'd get together and go hang out and have a couple of beers at a particular place in Miami. There would be Manny Fernandez, Jake Scott, Bill Stanfill, Dick Anderson, Bob Matheson, and me. It's typical on football teams that the defense and offense are separate off the field as well, and it was essentially the defensive guys who would hang together. But once in a while an offensive guy would join us. Jim Kiick would be there.

Kiick was one of the quiet guys on the offense. Csonka and Griese didn't have a lot to say either. Morris was the only backfield guy who did any talking. Warfield didn't speak much, but our other receivers, Howard Twilley and tight end Marv Fleming, who had won two Super Bowls with Green Bay, were talkative. Little, Langer, Evans, and Moore were the quiet guys on the offensive line. However, Kuechenberg was very vocal and spoke up, and Doug Crusan was the team comedian—he'd keep everybody in stitches. Crusan, Scott, and our kicker, Garo Yepremian, were witty. I wasn't witty, I was a fiery guy.

I was a team captain and would stand up for the guys in front of Shula. If the food wasn't great, the guys would come to me and I'd go to Shula. If service on the plane or at the hotel was bad, the guys would come to me and complain. We had three captains but I was always the guy who would deliver the message. Little and Griese were the other two captains but they weren't vocal or risk takers. If you went to Shula, it was a risk. I enjoyed that role.

We spent one week in Miami and one week in Long Beach preparing for the Redskins, coached by George Allen. The year before, everything had been so fuzzy that it was hard to distinguish between practicing, studying the game plan, looking at movies, and then going out on the town. It sort of all merged together. The second year, it was very clear what we had to do, when we had to do it, and how much time it would take. We knew exactly how to handle the situation. We shut off phones and the team only allowed interviews at certain times, so the players were protected. Long Beach was quiet at night, but guys went out and had a few beers, had dinner, hung out, played pool. I saw a bunch of my buddies on the Rams—Joe Scibelli and other Notre Dame guys—and we'd go out. It was pretty relaxing. I was glad that we had time to thoroughly prepare for the game and still have a good time.

We conducted our practices exactly like we did during the regular season, only we had more time, so in the first week we put the game plan in and the second week we made modifications. During our defensive practices we put one of our guys in a yellow jersey as a stand-in for Larry Brown, who had gained over 1,200 yards rushing that season for Washington. He was the key guy we were going to stop, the only guy our defense paid any particular attention to. Every defensive formation that we employed was geared to Brown carrying the ball. We did the same thing against Buffalo: We worried about O. J. and put our defense in the best possible position to stop him. If they were going to beat us they'd have to do it through the air. And when we played Cincinnati, we would try to take Isaac Curtis out of the game. Our plan was always to take the opponent's biggest weapon and neutralize him. With Brown shut down, if the Redskins were going to beat us, it would have to be with Billy Kilmer throwing.

Practices were good, but we just wanted the game to begin. The players were prepared. Shula was probably more apprehensive than any of us. He was short-fused and highly critical of all the little things. I think some of his criticism was legitimate but most of it was not. Quite candidly: We didn't pay that much attention to him. We did what he wanted us to do but we never let it bother us. We still went ahead and did what we had to do to prepare. We understood that Shula was under the gun, under a microscope—people were calling him a great coach who couldn't win the big game, simply because he had been a two-time loser in the Super Bowl. That was a pretty tough burden for him to carry and he was under a tremendous amount of pressure to win.

I wouldn't say that one of the reasons the players wanted to win was to give him that victory. Don was much respected by all his players and we all had tremendous confidence in the game plans he'd worked out with Bill Arnsparger and his offensive coaches, but he was never a popular coach. We wanted to win for ourselves. I wouldn't wear the AFC championship ring from the previous year because it was a loser's ring. I wanted a Super Bowl ring on my finger. We all wanted Super Bowl rings.

The day of the game I got up at about six in the morning and went down to the coffee shop at our hotel in Long Beach. Manny Fernandez and Griese were there, so we had coffee. We're sitting there and Bob just looked up and said, "This team can't beat us; we can't lose to this team." Coming from him that meant a lot, because he never said anything and, unlike me, always kept his opinions to himself. This made us feel confident that the offense was ready. Defensively, we knew we were ready.

The Dolphins' locker room in the L.A. Coliseum wasn't loud before the game. In fact, the silence was deadly. Everybody was feeling introspective. If you look at footage of the teams coming through the tunnel and onto the field, you'll see us trotting out as if we were coming out to practice, and you'll see George Allen and his Redskins cheering and hollering and whooping it up. There was a terrific contrast. We were so ready. So intense. We knew we were going to win the Super Bowl, but it just had to start before we could win it.

Finally, before more than 90,000 fans, it started. As we had planned, I looked at Washington's offensive formation on each play and shifted our defense so that we were strongest where we felt Larry Brown would run. And it worked. The Redskins' offense wanted to do the same thing Dallas did, which was to put two men on me. They were intent on blocking me but they forgot about Manny Fernandez. They assumed they could handle Manny one-on-one because he was only a 250-pound tackle, but they couldn't block him. Manny was very quick and he'd get into their backfield before they could react and tackle Brown. He beat their center Len Hauss like a drum. I didn't feel that I was sacrificing myself, because as a team we were just kicking the hell out of them. They didn't even get past midfield in the first half.

Considering that we had success stopping teams' best runners, George Allen probably should have come up with a different game plan. But Larry had such a great year and the line had done such a great job blocking that George probably didn't pay as much respect to our defense as he should have. He probably thought, "We can overpower those guys; we can run." But their offensive line just couldn't get the job done. To get away from Manny, they tried everything, including sweeps, but we didn't give them any lanes to cut back into. We closed down both Brown and Charlie Harraway. I have to say it was total domination. On one third-down play in the game, Dick Anderson came up from his safety position and just killed Brown on a sweep play, knocking his helmet off. I think Brown had to leave the field. It was such a big hit that it fired up our whole team.

Anderson and I worked a lot together on combination coverages, usually on the tight end or the back coming out of the backfield. When the tight end came off the football, Dick always made sure I had him under wraps before making his move. He was not as fast as Jake Scott, our other great safety, but he had incredible football instincts, and after reading the quarterback, he would get to places no one thought he could get to. That's how he made two interceptions against Cleveland in the divisional playoffs. He made one of the greatest interception returns of all time against Baltimore when he weaved his way through its entire offense while nine blocks were thrown (none by me). Anderson was a big playmaker, as he showed when he nearly decapitated Brown.

There was no rivalry in our minds between the two defenses. They'd given up only two field goals in their playoff games, but our offense stacked up real well against them. The Washington defense, like the entire team—the "Over-the-Hill-Gang"—was comprised of veterans. They were a little slow—slower than Miami—but were a good, big, sound group that wasn't going to make a lot of mistakes. They weren't going to beat themselves, so our offense would have to beat them physically. Which it did.

We scored on our third possession after reaching their 28-yard line. They had Pat Fischer at cornerback, and he was a hell of a competitor, but Twilley just beat him badly on the final play of the first quarter. He faked a slant to the inside and then went outside, turning Fischer around. Twilley caught it on the 5 and ran it into the end zone. Rather than a burst of emotion, there was a sense of relief. We didn't expect them to score, so in our minds, we had won the game. The game was over. That's why no one really got upset when we then had a long touchdown pass from Griese to Warfield taken away because our backup receiver Marlin Briscoe had been offside. That touchdown seemed sort of superfluous.

We didn't score then, but we soon got the ball back on a big play. We were in a one-coverage, which meant that I had to pick up the tight end, Jerry Smith. I'd go into deep coverage with Smith if that was necessary. On that play, I saw that our outside linebacker had jammed Smith, and he was having a tough time breaking free. I read Kilmer, who was watching Larry Brown flare out of the backfield. Because Smith, my responsibility, was tied up, I was free to react to Kilmer and go with Brown. I should not have been there, but I stepped in front of Brown and made the interception. I returned the ball over 30 yards, taking it inside their 30. The offense then drove the ball toward their end zone, the key play being a 19-yard pass from Griese to Jim Mandich on the sideline that took us to the 2-yard line. Kiick then took it over. His touchdown was basic; he just followed Csonka. He always followed Csonka—Csonka was a horse. That made the score 14–0 and everything was going according to the script. The defense got the turnover and gave it to the offense and they scored. That's how it was supposed to work.

A few times, Griese might have gotten a play from the sidelines, but he was pretty much in charge. He was doing an exceptional job directing the running game and throwing an occasional pass. Warfield was playing with

January 14, 1973, at the Los Angeles Memorial Coliseum

Paid Attendance: 90,182

AFC Champion: Miami Dolphins (16—0)
Head Coach: Don Shula

NFC Champion: Washington Redskins (13—3)
Head Coach: George Allen

STARTING LINEUPS

OFFENSE			DEFENSE		
Miami		**Washington**	**Miami**		**Washington**
Paul Warfield	WR	Charley Taylor	Vern Den Herder	LE	Ron McDole
Wayne Moore	LT	Terry Hermeling	Manny Fernandez	LT	Bill Brundige
Bob Kuechenberg	LG	Paul Laaveg	Bob Heinz	RT	Diron Talbert
Jim Langer	C	Len Hauss	Bill Stanfill	RE	Verlon Biggs
Larry Little	RG	John Wilbur	Doug Swift	LLB	Jack Pardee
Norm Evans	RT	Walter Rock	Nick Buoniconti	MLB	Myron Pottios
Marv Fleming	TE	Jerry Smith	Mike Kolen	RLB	Chris Hanburger
Howard Twilley	WR	Roy Jefferson	Lloyd Mumphord	LCB	Pat Fischer
Bob Griese	QB	Bill Kilmer	Curtis Johnson	RCB	Mike Bass
Jim Kiick	RB	Larry Brown	Dick Anderson	LS	Brig Owens
Larry Csonka	RB	Charlie Harraway	Jake Scott	RS	Roosevelt Taylor

SUBSTITUTIONS

Miami: K—Garo Yepremian. P—Larry Seiple. Offense: Receivers—Jim Mandich, Marlin Briscoe. Linemen—Doug Crusan, Howard Kindig. Backs—Mercury Morris, Ed Jenkins, Hubert Ginn, Earl Morrall, Charles Leigh. Defense: Linebackers—Bob Matheson, Larry Ball, Jesse Powell. Lineman—Maulty Moore. Backs—Henry Stuckey, Charles Babb. DNP—Otto Stowe.

Washington: K—Curt Knight. P—Mike Bragg. Offense: Receivers—Clifton McNeil, Mack Alston. Lineman—George Burman. Backs—Sam Wyche, Herb Mul-Key, Bob Brunet, Mike Hull. Defense: Linebackers—Rusty Tillman, Harold McLinton. Linemen—Mike Fanucci, Manuel Sistrunk. Backs—Ted Vactor, Alvin Haymond, Jeff Severson, Jon Jaqua. DNP—Ray Schoenke.

Miami	7	7	0	0—14
Washington	0	0	0	7— 7

Mia	Twilley 28 pass from Griese (Yepremian kick)
Mia	Kiick 1 run (Yepremian kick)
Wash	Bass 49 fumble return (Knight kick)
MVP:	Jake Scott (Miami)

a bad hamstring, but he and Griese could still beat double coverage when they tried. Interestingly, those big passes to Twilley and Mandich were their only receptions of the game, so Bob was really picking his spots. He was six for six in the first half, while Kilmer was struggling for the Redskins. Billy had taken over as Allen's starter when Sonny Jurgensen was injured. He was a good quarterback, even if his passes always wobbled, but he never got rolling in the Super Bowl. Once we stopped the running game, that really hurt him, because the Redskins were not a pure passing team. They needed Larry Brown to have a big day in order to free up their wide receivers Charley Taylor and Roy Jefferson, but Larry couldn't get started.

The Redskins finally got into our territory on the first drive of the second half, but Curtis Knight missed a field goal attempt from 32 yards out. That was their first scoring threat, so that was a big play. The score would remain 14–0 late into the game.

I think we could have scored many more points if we had opened up, but the defense was playing so well that there was no reason to put the ball in the air. That week we didn't think that Griese would throw only 11 times for the entire game, but Shula's philosophy never changed: "We'll take what they give us. If they give us the run, we'll take it." They gave us the run. Our offensive line was blocking so well, and Csonka, Kiick, and Morris were picking up first downs—on one play, Csonka broke away for almost 50 yards. Griese relied on our running game to wear them down. Maybe we weren't the most explosive team offensively, but grinding the other team into the ground was a trademark of our team. When the defense was off the field, I was always watching the offense. I saw that we had the game totally under control.

On defense, Manny Fernandez continued to do what he was doing. You could tell they were mystified. They couldn't figure out how Manny was making so many plays and they wouldn't adapt to him until after the game was over. Overall he was credited with 17 tackles for the game, most of them unassisted. It was the game of his life—in fact, it was the most dominant game by a defensive lineman in the history of the game, and he would never be given much credit for it. They should have given out two game balls and made Manny Fernandez the co-MVP with Jake Scott.

We prided ourselves on being able to respond whenever we were challenged, and Scott was one of our big-play guys. In the fourth quarter, the Redskins had driven the ball all the way to our 10-yard line, when Jake jumped in front of Charley Taylor and picked off Kilmer's pass in the end zone and then ran it back over 50 yards into Washington territory. It was his second interception of the game and was such a big play and momentum crusher that it got him the votes in the MVP balloting. Scott had a bad wrist in the Super Bowl but was still in there pounding on receivers. Dick Anderson may have been a bigger hitter, but Jake wasn't shy about hitting people. He also was one of the most intelligent guys you'd ever want to meet. His IQ was almost at a genius level and he was very opinionated and vocal, and he had a great football mind. Like Anderson, Scott never made a mental mistake. What he saw in front of him was like what a computer sees. He'd see everything developing and always end up in the right place, like in front of Kilmer's pass.

Scott's big interception led to a field goal attempt of over 40 yards by Garo Yepremian. In the game's most famous play, Garo had his kick blocked by Bill Brundige, and then, instead of falling on it, picked it up and tried to throw it—only he didn't know how to throw a football. It slipped out of his hand and then he batted it into the air, and the 'Skins' Mike Bass took it and ran about 50 yards for a touchdown. That one play took a team that was being totally dominated and put them back into contention. We should have shut them out, and he put them into position to ruin possibly the greatest season in the history of the NFL. It was like someone above was moving around the players on the field and had decided that the Dolphins had basked in glory enough that year. I pictured this whole awful scenario where Washington was going to have the opportunity to tie the game. It was probably the only time in the entire season when I was absolutely disgusted. If I had a rope, I would have hanged Garo right then and there.

It took awhile for the players to get over that play, because everybody projected what could have happened. Now we all laugh about it, but it wasn't funny then. We'd have hung him, but I gotta say that Garo was very well liked by the guys. He endeared himself to us when he was trying to make the team after being cut by Detroit. That was the strike year, and Garo was fighting for a job but would not cross our picket line. The players really respected him because of that.

After their touchdown, I was surprised that George Allen didn't try an onside kick. I was thrilled he didn't because you just never know what will happen on an onside kick. He obviously figured the Redskins would hold us back by our goal line and force us to punt. But we held onto the ball long enough so they had no time to score when they got it back. Miami had beaten the Redskins in the Super Bowl, 14–7, and we were going to get our rings.

After the game I was absolutely exhausted mentally and physically. I'm sure I was exhilarated somewhere along the line, but I don't remember when I finally was able to relax and enjoy it. I remember I was the last one out of the locker room and my wife and mother and father were there. They handed me a beer and I had a swig and finally started to unwind. The team party was almost a downer because it was difficult to get back the emotion that was spent on that field. I couldn't celebrate that night. We were staying in Los Angeles for that one night and I ended up at Trader Vic's with my wife and the Mathesons. Both Bob and I were so emotionally drained from having gone 14–0, then going through the play-offs, and then exonerating ourselves in the Super Bowl and becoming the only team to go 17–0.

The next year it was totally different because we had gotten the monkey off our back. That team was better than the 17–0 team and should have gone undefeated also. We killed Cincinnati and Oakland in the play-offs and then killed Minnesota in the Super Bowl. But I would never wear the ring for Super Bowl VIII, only the one from Super Bowl VII. The win in VIII was anticlimactic.

That 1972 team was special. Maybe we didn't have the best talent ever to play in the NFL, but we have always been terribly underrated. We had a great line, great running backs, a great quarterback, and great wide receivers. And defensively? There are five or six Steelers in the Hall of Fame off their Super Bowl years and we don't have one—I'm not even sure any of us has made it as high as the top 12 in the voting so that we'd seriously be considered. It's ludicrous, stupid. For some reason, we've just never gotten the credit we deserve.

SUPERBOWL
VIII

JIM LANGER
MIAMI DOLPHINS

SUPER BOWL VIII

MIAMI DOLPHINS 24
MINNESOTA VIKINGS 7

JIM LANGER

Today I pass the field where I played my high school football and it looks like a parking lot. That's where I started out, playing ball in a small town in Minnesota.

The University of Minnesota didn't even know I existed, so I went to South Dakota State. In college, I weighed about 250 pounds. I started out as an offensive lineman at guard and then played some tackle, but I never played center. In my senior year I was actually a linebacker and even played some noseguard on short-yardage situations. South Dakota State was a good school and we played in a great conference, but because we were in Division II we didn't get much publicity. The only scout I remember coming was Carl Tasseff, who'd later be the offensive backs coach with the Dolphins. I was married with a small son and working part-time at a gas station. One Saturday Carl drove up and asked my boss if he could have a few minutes with me so he could time me in the 40-yard dash. Obviously my time wasn't too impressive because I didn't get drafted by an NFL team.

I graduated in the spring of 1970, and through the ROTC program I was commissioned as a second lieutenant and scheduled to go into active duty in October—of course, that was still Vietnam vintage. That's when my baseball coach Irv Huether told me he could get me a tryout with the Cleveland Browns because he knew one of their scouts. He said, "I know you're scheduled to go on active duty, but it might be the chance of a lifetime just to experience it." At first I thought it might be kind of neat, but the more I thought about it, the worse it sounded. I was growing more intimidated as it drew closer. Gale Gillingham, who had played for the Packers in the first two Super Bowls and was still in the NFL, lived right behind my wife's mother. I asked Gale if the tryout was worth my time. He said, "Shit, there's going to be a strike and we veterans aren't going to show up for six weeks. Go on in there and you'll get a look. What the hell." So I decided to go.

I left for Cleveland with 54 bucks in my checking account. The cab fare in Cleveland turned out to be $32. So I showed up at Hiram College and I proceeded to stick around there for 10 weeks, during which time I received a per diem. Just as Gillingham had predicted, there was a strike. I played some preseason games at guard and they got to take a good look at me. Then Blanton Collier, the head coach, called me in and said that I was going to be on the taxi squad. But, he explained, first I had to clear waivers. I was elated. I called my wife and told her that I was going to look for an apartment. At 10 o'clock that night I got a call from Miami. Joe Thomas, the general manager, told me that the Dolphins had claimed me off waivers and that I was to catch a plane the next day.

Years later I found out how I ended up in Miami. Monte Clark, who at the time I didn't know, was Miami's offensive line coach. He had played for Cleveland for 11 seasons and knew all those guys in the front office. When talking to them, he asked if the Browns had any extra linemen. My name came up, and the minute I was on waivers, the Dolphins claimed me. I wasn't happy about that because I had grown to like Cleveland. I didn't even know Miami had a football team.

I get down to Miami and I'm thinking I'll last a week and then go into the Army. That was okay: It had been a good run and worth the effort. Miami had 20 rookies who had made their roster, but they were still looking for some young linemen. There was myself and Bob Kuechenberg, who was a guard, and Carl Mauck, a center, and we were all kind of battling for jobs. To my surprise, I made the taxi squad, where I remained for about half the '70 season. Meanwhile, I called my university and talked to the military guys there and they got me a "Delay of Duty." So the Army was very cooperative. I wouldn't have to report until January.

While on the taxi squad, I was playing guard for the scout team, which ran our next opponent's plays against our defense in practice. At the time Miami's starting center was Bob DeMarco, who had been to the Pro Bowl a few times. He was a veteran and didn't want to play on the scout team, so Monte Clark said, "Jim, why don't you learn to play center." I had never played center before, but I saw this as an opportunity. There was an adjustment I had to make because I was left-handed and centers have to snap the ball with their right hands to get the ball up to the quarterback the way they like it—it has to do with the way the ball comes up and is turning. We weren't going to change Bob Griese, so I had to start using my right hand. I found a comfort level using my right hand, so soon our quarterbacks were getting the ball with no problems from me on the exchange.

Most head coaches don't pay much attention to unheralded rookie offensive linemen, and Don Shula seemed to notice me only when I'd screw up, and then he'd throw me out of practice. My major motivation that year was to get through practice without Shula chewing my ass off. I was just a body to him that year but eventually I earned his respect. He told me years later that the decision to keep me came about the next year in a preseason game, when I was still fighting to make the roster. I was playing guard against Minnesota when there was an interception late in the game and I nailed the guy pretty good as he was running down the sideline. That's what caught Don's eye. You never know what play is going to make the difference, but that's the one that made Don want to keep me. It was also important that I was a good special teams player, because those things add up, and pretty soon the coach says, "This kid's a player."

Miami carried seven linemen in 1971, when we played in our first Super Bowl. We had one backup for the tackles and I was the backup for the interior. I played right guard, left guard, and center. Bob DeMarco still was the starter at center, but I established myself as a player who was a reliable sixth lineman and a good special teams player.

My third year was 1972. We started training camp and I began playing center only. I found myself competing with Bob DeMarco for the starting position and I'm sure that the age difference benefited me. I won the job in preseason. Bob was traded back to Cleveland and retired after two or three years.

The first game I started was in Kansas City's brand-new Arrowhead Stadium, in the first game ever played there. I was playing against Buck Buchanan, Curley Culp, and Willie Lanier. This was the team we'd beaten in double overtime in the 1971 playoffs. We beat 'em pretty handily, 20–10. That was the first game of our undefeated season. I would play every offensive down in every game that year. I didn't miss one play.

I was the newcomer on the offensive line. Our guards, Bob Kuechenberg, who was my roommate and close friend, and Larry Little, who was probably our leader at that point, and the tackles, Wayne Moore and Norm Evans, had all been starters. So I was the guy to change the makeup. We just really hit it off. We had a lot of fun together and began to gel as a unit. We were a bunch of young guys who kind of came to Miami at the same time after being let go by other teams and found ourselves in a do-or-die situation. We were as hungry as hell and were lucky to have a coach like Monte Clark. Monte was a fiend at film watching and figuring out what our opponents were trying to do, so we all spent a lot of time together working on our game plans. By accident, we were all guys with a similar work ethic—we were willing to work relentlessly. This allowed Monte to mold us into a unit that fit his thinking, which was: "We're going to make you students of your positions—and you're going to learn how to get good position and how to really block somebody." So each of us became experts at playing our positions. Now the center in the Dolphins' scheme of things did coordinate a lot of the blocking assignments, but I don't think I had any more difficult tasks than did our guards or tackles. I was just one notch in the cog.

When I look back, the key to my success as a center was that I was left-handed. When I started to snap with my right hand, I had my left hand ready to go and was able to lead with my left foot on most things, and that just gave me a natural movement forward as I was pushing the ball backward and up. It takes only $^{32}/_{100}$ of a second to snap the ball—we literally timed this—and in that fraction of a second my forward motion was already started while right-handed centers had their strength and quickness up their butts until they could bring their right arms up. There were a few noseguards who were exceptionally quick off the ball, but in most cases I was hitting them before they moved their hands. I could move on the snap as quick as any guard. That led to a lot of things we did that nobody had ever done before, such as the center leading sweeps. I could pull around the corner as fast as any guard in the league and that was due to the fact that my natural motion wasn't encumbered. I looked at our line and thought we had three guards: Bob Kuechenberg, Larry Little, and myself. And the only difference was that I had to snap the ball first.

Manny Fernandez really helped me a lot. The Dolphins were one of the first NFL teams to use a noseguard, out of necessity, because of injuries. Manny was the guy Bill Arnsparger put in the nose. Manny wasn't a big defensive tackle by any means, but he was extremely quick and very smart. He and I had some real battles, literally. We went from what was initially a very adversarial relationship because of the competition in the trenches in practice to a very respectful relationship—and he still is one of my best friends. Manny taught me how to beat a noseguard. As a center you have to be able to split the defense and cut the noseguard off. Ideally, you do that alone. If it takes two guys, you're lessening the impact of the whole deal. Manny's ability forced me to become very good at hooking and cutting off players with great quickness—otherwise I'd get my ass chewed out all the time. He'd tell me everything a noseguard would do to try to take advantage of me—and by using that information, I was able to remove a lot of problems that would have hindered my development. For example, I developed a habit of moving my thumb just before I snapped the ball. Manny used that as a key to get a quick start off the ball. Finally, after he got some job security and figured out that I was going to stick around, he told me that I was doing something that let him know exactly when I'd snap the ball. Those kinds of things were invaluable.

Another guy who really helped me develop was Nick Buoniconti, our middle linebacker. Nick taught me a tremendous amount. I got to realize that if I could cut Nick off when we had scrimmages, I could cut any linebacker off. There was no linebacker quicker than Buoniconti—no linebacker could read a play faster than him. He didn't make it easy for me because he was working on his own game while I was working on mine. There was no animosity between any of us, although sometimes on the practice field you'd get into a fight with somebody because you didn't want to look bad and the other guy was trying to make you look bad. The end result was that it made you both better players.

We started to win, which was a carryover from 1971. Our focus was on winning the AFC and going back and winning the damn Super Bowl. Nothing else mattered and each win was just another rung in the ladder to get us to where we wanted to go. We just won and won and won. We won a few times because we got lucky and the other team did something stupid, but in any event, we didn't lose all season and beat the Washington Redskins in the Super Bowl.

What was I thinking now that I, an undrafted player, had been a starter for the undefeated Super Bowl champions? My biggest realization that season—and even before—was that Division I players were not any goddamn better than Division II players. I saw a lot of Division I guys who were almost mythical when I was going to school, and I found out in the pros, "Shit, they can't do anything I can't do." Suddenly I discovered that if a guy has a reasonable amount of talent and works at it and gets a few breaks, he can make it in the NFL. I was convinced that what weeds out players is not their physical ability but their mental toughness. Pro football pushes players to their breaking points and some guys say, "I just can't do this anymore."

Obviously we had an outstanding team in 1972 because we didn't lose, but Miami was better in 1973, although we lost two games. By then we started to get into the meaning of "It's tougher to stay on top than it is to get there." In the process of getting there, everybody is excited for you and pulling for you because you're the underdog. But once you win the damn thing and go 17–0, everyone expects success. Now, it's not good enough to just win; you have to win convincingly and dominate the other team. But you can't always do that. The motivation then becomes to retain the respect you achieved from your accomplishments. That's when pride and work ethic drive you forward.

We came into training camp and Shula was still tough. If he'd lightened up at all it was only because he knew the players had won a title and knew what it takes to win. He knew what we had accomplished and let us enjoy that some. The whip started to crack the minute our performance dropped off a little bit. These were very small things that you look for: you didn't finish up a block properly; you didn't use your correct foot when you led on that sweep; you could have buried this guy and you didn't. Just because you won one Super Bowl, who do you think you are? There was that kind of approach to keep us in line. So it came down to getting our feet back on the ground and remembering what the hell we did to win last year.

There were several leaders on the team. Obviously Nick Buoniconti and Larry Little were leaders. Griese was a quiet leader and had tremendous respect from the team. Larry Csonka was the guy I really looked up to both on and off the field. Larry was kind of symbolic of the whole offense, which was a no-nonsense, highly capable, great-execution unit. And our defense was the same way. Csonka had the utmost respect of every player on the team, offense and defense. There were all kinds of leaders you could point to, all kinds of guys who had everyone's respect on both sides of the ball. What it came down to was that nobody wanted to let anybody else down. Nobody wanted to be the reason that this team wasn't successful. We kind of wore that attitude like a chip on our shoulder—"God damn it, this is the Dolphin organization, and if you're going to be part of it, you're going to think and act like the other players do." That wasn't going to be the coaches driving that point home but the players themselves. We had nobody who thought he was better than the team. If he did, we'd go to the coach and say, "Get rid of this son-of-a-bitch. He's a problem." We policed ourselves; the coaches didn't have to worry.

We were a very close-knit team where the offensive and defensive guys mixed together. In my case, I had formed strong friendships with defensive players like Nick, Manny, and Vern Den Herder. There was a lot of chemistry on that team and everybody would hang out together and socialize. There are a lot of world-class restaurants in Miami, but our favorite places for congregating were little out-of-the-way, working-man bars. We were really a blue-collar team and we would pick some of the damnedest places. I'm sure when we walked in the owner wondered how in the hell we ever found the place. During training camp, we frequented a little place called the Lion's Tap. It was a 600-square-foot bar that sold beer and sandwiches. We used to go over every single day after the last workout before dinner. It was the place players got to know each other outside of football, where we learned what our teammates were really like and what made guys tick. Those things are really important. During the season, beginning the year we went undefeated, on every Thursday after practice we'd go to a little bar up in Hollywood called Stratford's. It's a place that I go by today when I'm in Florida and I just have to laugh. It was just a little hole in the wall, but we'd have 30 guys there. That's where we started sticking pins in miniature dolls that were dressed like the opponents we were going to play. It was one of the superstitions that our players got into. It got to be a big deal. By God, players would look forward to it, so we had to continue it in 1973.

As we opened the '73 season, everybody's wondering, "When is our winning streak going to be broken?" It didn't take long. We lost our second game, 12–7, to Oakland. The Raiders were on a mission to beat us and they did in a hard-fought game. Miami and Oakland played many good games and this was one of them, and we ended up losing and the bubble was burst and we were back to being mere mortals. That was a little traumatic. In retrospect, it was probably good that we lost. It had to happen. I want to make it clear that the Dolphins who had gone undefeated weren't head and shoulders above anybody in the NFL. We weren't the type of team that won because we were physically able to beat people. We won because we outsmarted 'em or outexecuted 'em or got lucky on a couple of plays. So a loss early the next season was inevitable. Now we had to pick it up. The team matured and we were executing by the end of the season as well as anybody. I'd been in games when we knew that the team we were playing was better and that our only chance was if they didn't play well. In 1973 we didn't have that feeling. We knew that if we played our game there was nobody we wouldn't beat. We ended up by convincingly beating Oakland, 27–10, in the AFC title game. We expected a real dogfight, but were just so pumped up and just coming out of the blocks so well that we dominated them.

As we went into those playoffs against the Cincinnati Bengals and the Raiders, we were, to use the old cliché, peaking at the right time. We were just like a steamroller. We didn't mind the word "machine" to describe the Dolphins offense because that's what we were trying to be. That goes back to Vince Lombardi's theory: We're going to tell you where we're going, but you still have to stop us. The rules favored the running game in those days. You could knock a receiver down until the ball was in the air, so there was none of this "after 5 yards you can't touch me" that we have today. Because of that our offense was run-oriented. Unlike most quarterbacks, Bob Griese didn't need to throw to be happy. I think we threw a total of 21 passes in the postseason. We used ball control to take over games. We had the line and we had the backs to make it work.

Larry Csonka was at fullback and if we gave him any hole at all we had 4 or 5 yards. I don't care what they did, we got those yards. So we had that weapon. Then we had a very heady runner and receiver in Jim Kiick. Then we had Mercury Morris, the burner who could get outside and run a legitimate 4.3 or 4.4 in the 40. We'd get Csonka going first. When the defense adjusted to stop him, the gate was open for Jim and Merc. We'd fake to Csonka and Mercury would pick up big yards on the outside. The minute they overshifted to stop Mercury, we'd give the ball back to Csonka. We'd get this machine moving down the field, and all of a sudden Griese, who'd spend hours and hours studying how to dissect defenses, would throw a play-action pass to Paul Warfield streaking downfield and instead of picking up between 3 and 7 yards, we're picking up 25 or 30 yards and maybe a touchdown. Those plays all looked alike when the ball was snapped so the defense would be just completely demoralized, realizing there was nothing it could do.

It was a blast to do ball control. There were games when you were, as they'd call it today, "in a zone," though back then we didn't know what the hell to call it. You seem to step into another world. You sense the crowd and you know you're in an NFL game, but you're so focused on what you're doing that it's almost like you're moving in slow motion although in reality the game is incredibly fast. You get into this mode with these guys you've spent all this time with and it's just a surreal environment that's hard to describe. Only champions enter that environment.

We were confident when we arrived in Houston to play the Vikings in Super Bowl VIII. I wouldn't say we were in a jovial mood, but we were loose. We had done this before; we all knew the program; we tried to treat it as just another game, although we knew it was the Super Bowl. We maintained a pretty tight discipline. You understood that you'd be in serious trouble with the other players if you jeopardized the game with something you were doing. That doesn't mean players didn't go out and have a good time—hell, that's part of the deal of going to the Super Bowl. But there's a line you don't cross. You don't do something stupid that you'll read about in the paper.

But there's got to be a story and "the story" was that the Vikings were pissed off about their facilities. We were the home team, so we got to practice at Rice Stadium, where the game would be played, and they practiced at some school. They were complaining about having only cold water and no place to hang their clothes and other things. From our standpoint, we could give a shit. We laughed our asses off about that. I had a hard time believing that their conditions were so bad that it would affect their game. It was all hype.

We also laughed about that other story, which dealt with our wives. Jake Scott was the guy who brought that up: "God damn it, you guys get to bring your wives—but what about our girlfriends?" Other single guys asked about bringing their mothers. We were laughing about that, and the media, of course, made it an issue.

Practices were not easy. There was no such thing as a Dolphin practice under Don Shula that wasn't focused. You never went onto the field without having been completely briefed on exactly what the hell you were going to do. And if you didn't run a play properly in practice or with the appropriate amount of intensity, you were in trouble with Shula. That didn't mean that we were killing each other. The linemen went pretty hard but not at full speed. The defensive players never hit the quarterback or tackled the backs. There was no physical need to be beating on each other. It was mental preparation by this point.

I had no problem sleeping the night before the Super Bowl. The whole team always had a snack at 9 o'clock the night before a game, and everybody would get together and we'd eat a couple of burgers and have a malt and about three beers and go to bed. That was another of our rituals.

Kuechenberg and I were both early risers, so the next morning we got up and went down to the hotel restaurant and had coffee with the trainers and equipment manager and whatever players had gotten up. That was our routine. And, as usual, we started talking about the game.

We had a quiet locker room before the game. There wasn't a lot of jumping around or rah-rah speeches and nobody was shouting, "We're going to kick these guys' asses." It was all business. We were an emotional team—hell yes—but we didn't exhibit a false George Allen–type enthusiasm. Every player knew inside and didn't have to say it that we had to go out and turn it loose.

We received the opening kickoff. The fact is that we were in a pattern where we damn near scored on our first drive in every game. As in the two playoff games, we came out and shoved the ball down our opponent's throat. We just hit the Vikings defense so hard and so fast that they didn't know what hit them. Alan Page later said he knew we would dominate them after only the first couple of plays.

We didn't have any big-yardage plays in that first drive, but we kept moving forward and getting first downs. Mostly, Griese handed off to Csonka and Morris, but he mixed in a couple of short passes to Jim Mandich and Marlin Briscoe to keep the defense honest. We drove down to the 5-yard line and there Griese faked a pitch out to Morris and then gave it to Csonka, who ran over right tackle into the end zone. The key to that play working was we had established that Mercury could run those outside plays successfully. Once they know he can do that, they've got to respect that play and go outside after him—so we came back with an inside run. It's very difficult for the defense to stop a play like that when the team it's facing can execute so well.

Our second touchdown came on our second possession after a drive that was almost exactly like the first one. This time our touchdown came on a 1-yard run by Kiick behind Kuech, me, and Csonka. I didn't know at the time it was Kiick's only touchdown of the year. That wasn't something we would be aware of and didn't plan on. Our third score of the half came on our fourth possession, on a short field goal by Garo Yepremian after another pretty good drive. That put us ahead 17–0.

We had gotten the good lead, although Griese had thrown only six passes. He had completed five of them, including one short pass to Paul Warfield. Warfield had a hamstring injury that limited what he could

January 13, 1974, at Rice Stadium in Houston

Paid Attendance: 71,882 (Actual: 68,142)

NFC Champion: Minnesota Vikings (14–2)
Head Coach: Bud Grant

AFC Champion: Miami Dolphins (14–2)
Head Coach: Don Shula

STARTING LINEUPS

OFFENSE			DEFENSE		
Minnesota		**Miami**	**Minnesota**		**Miami**
Carroll Dale	WR	Paul Warfield	Carl Eller	LE	Vern Den Herder
Grady Alderman	LT	Wayne Moore	Gary Larsen	LT	Manny Fernandez
Ed White	LG	Bob Kuechenberg	Alan Page	RT	Bob Heinz
Mick Tingelhoff	C	Jim Langer	Jim Marshall	RE	Bill Stanfill
Frank Gallagher	RG	Larry Little	Roy Winston	LLB	Doug Swift
Ron Yary	RT	Norm Evans	Jeff Siemon	MLB	Nick Buoniconti
Stu Voigt	TE	Jim Mandich	Wally Hilgenberg	RLB	Mike Kolen
John Gilliam	WR	Marlin Briscoe	Nate Wright	LCB	Lloyd Mumphord
Fran Tarkenton	QB	Bob Griese	Bob Bryant	RCB	Curtis Johnson
Chuck Foreman	RB	Mercury Morris	Jeff Wright	LS	Dick Anderson
Oscar Reed	RB	Larry Csonka	Paul Krause	RS	Jake Scott

SUBSTITUTIONS

Minnesota: K—Fred Cox. P—Mike Eischeid. Offense: Receivers—Jim Lash, Doug Kingsriter. Lineman—Chuck Goodrum. Backs—Ed Marinaro, Bill Brown, Dave Osborn. Defense: Linebackers —Amos Martin, Ron Porter. Linemen—Bob Lurtsema, Doug Sutherland. Backs—Charlie West, Terry Brown. DNP—Bob Berry, Godfrey Zaunbrecher, Steve Lawson, Gary Ballman.

Miami: K—Garo Yepremian. P—Larry Seiple. Offense: Receivers—Marv Fleming, Howard Twilley. Linemen—Doug Crusan, Irv Goode, Ed Newman. Backs—Earl Morrall, Jim Kiick, Don Nottingham. Defense: Linebackers—Larry Ball, Bruce Bannon, Bob Matheson. Lineman—Maulty Moore. Backs—Tim Foley, Henry Stuckey, Charles Babb. DNP —Ron Sellers.

Minnesota	0	0	0	7— 7
Miami	14	3	7	0—24

Mia	Csonka 5 run (Yepremian kick)
Mia	Kiick 1 run (Yepremian kick)
Mia	FG Yepremian 28
Mia	Csonka 2 run (Yepremian kick)
Minn	Tarkenton 4 run (Cox kick)
MVP:	Larry Csonka (Miami)

do. Of the athletes on the team, Paul was the thoroughbred, and if anything was ailing him, including a hamstring injury, it might affect his game somewhat. However, he was still a very tough mental player. He ran his routes—he was a great decoy—and he was a great blocker, as were our other receivers Marlin Briscoe, Jim Mandich, and Howard Twilley. Those guys were always knocking people off. We'd get our backs through the line, and when those receivers blocked a little bit, we'd get substantial gains.

By game time our offense understood the Vikings defense as well as the Vikings did. They used a four-three defense, and basically I blocked the middle linebacker, Jeff Siemon. Between Kuech, Larry, and me, we're blocking Siemon and their tackles, Page and Gary Larsen. We had to neutralize that triangle. We had various ways of doing that without making it easy for them to read our keys. For example, instead of just going after Siemon on every play, on occasion I would block back on Page and fend him off and have Kuech go around and get Siemon. All this was successful right away. We kept ripping huge holes into their defense and Csonka kept picking up good yardage, especially to the right.

Our offensive line knew exactly what the hell it was doing, and no matter what they did, we could adjust to it very quickly. The game plan was to take advantage of the Vikings' strength, which was a very good pursuit. They were very quick off the ball, particularly Page. So we'd use a lot of misdirection plays to get Page and the others to commit to going one way and then we'd run back to the other side. Then we'd throw counterblocks to seal them off when they tried to reverse themselves and make the tackles. I might join Kuechenberg in blocking Page.

We did a lot of counterblocking in the first half, but some of our biggest plays came even though we didn't actually block Page. Kuech would just influence him. By that I mean he'd move as if we were going to run a sweep and pretend that he was going to try to cut Alan off from going outside to stop it. Alan would overplay it and try to get outside Kuech to stop the sweep. Only Kuech would then just do a quick stop, flip around, and do what we called "invert the block," and just let Page go. So Kuech would simply turn Page out and seal him off from the inside, and then we'd run Csonka or Morris or Kiick down the middle between Kuech and me. We'd hear Alan cussing because those negative-influence plays were just driving him nuts. He didn't know what the hell to do.

It was obvious from the beginning that our offense could overpower their defense. The only way that they could stay in the game was if their offense did something to our defense. I'd watch our defense. Our defense was smart and studied a lot, and I knew that our defensive coach Bill Arnsparger and guys like Nick Buoniconti had put together a game plan that would neutralize their star running back Chuck Foreman and make passing difficult for Fran Tarkenton. I knew that John Gilliam and Tarkenton's other receivers would have a rough time because our defensive backs were well schooled in knocking down receivers. I also knew that Manny Fernandez would have another big Super Bowl because the Vikings at that time had a real difficult time blocking noseguards. The year before, he had all those tackles against Washington, and I knew he was going to give the Vikings fits. And he did. We had a lot of confidence in our defense, and as expected, they were playing superbly. When their offense couldn't counter what our offense was doing, the Vikings were dead.

The Vikings did have a chance to cut into our lead before the half ended when after a long drive they had the ball on our 6. On fourth-and-1, they tried to run. Oscar Reed was headed for a first down when Buoniconti knocked the ball loose and we recovered. That's the way the game would go for Minnesota. Every time they tried to get themselves straightened out, they'd shoot themselves in the foot.

I remember coming in at halftime and thinking that it was totally different from the halftime at the Super Bowl the year before. Against Washington, we were in a fight and didn't have that sense of dominance we were now enjoying. We definitely knew that this game was over. The focus was: Things are going our way; we're playing well, but we still have to make sure we don't let them back in the game. We've got to keep the hammer on them, keep the pressure on them, and keep focused.

It became increasingly obvious that this wasn't the Vikings' day. They got the opening kickoff and Gilliam made a hell of a return for 65 yards. But they were penalized for holding and the ball went all the way back. After that, the game really was over.

Like all great teams, we capitalized on mistakes. They had to punt soon after the penalty and we got the ball back in Minnesota territory, and that led to our final score. After a couple of runs, Griese and Warfield came up with the biggest offensive play of the game. Griese knew how to set up a game plan and he knew that eventually he was going to burn the secondary with a long pass to Warfield. He chose a time when the defense was softened up and frustrated from trying to stop the run. On our first possession of the second half, when the Vikings were expecting Bob to be even more conservative because of our lead, he hit Warfield streaking up the left sideline for almost 30 yards. I'm sure Bob and Paul devised that play during the first half of the game while Paul was limping through his decoy routes, and when Bob sensed it was time for a big play, Paul took off. That was Griese's last pass of the day, but for the rest of the game their backs had no choice but to follow our receivers all over the field. That pass broke their backs. The wheels came off their defense.

Our final touchdown came from the 1-yard line. Griese forgot the snap count and I could hear him turn around and ask Zonk the count. Zonk got it wrong. They never did know. I knew what it was, so Bob just wisely started the snap count and waited for the ball. Everybody moved on the ball. That was a veteran team, so we knew stuff like that happens—sometimes you just draw a blank.

Csonka would end up with 145 yards rushing, which was a new Super Bowl record. We weren't consciously trying to help him get his record. It just happened. The only time when we consciously went into a game and tried to get anybody anything in terms of personal accomplishment was in 1972 when we wanted Mercury to get 1,000 yards for the season, which Csonka had already done. (We had the division won, so that was our whole purpose that game against Baltimore. I had to block Mike Curtis, and I'll never forget it because he was a bitch to block.) Csonka deservedly won the MVP with his two touchdowns and record rushing day. He was just a great player, as he proved that day.

I don't think Shula stated at halftime that we'd do a lot more straight blocking in the second half. That was just a by-product of what was going on. They were so confused by the influence plays and counterblocking that they just started to play straight up instead of pursuing. Then our physical strength came more into play and completely took over the game. They weren't a physically strong team and we were. By then all of our linemen were benching 400 pounds plus and the Vikings weren't really on a weight program yet. They were great players and had great hustle, but physically they couldn't match up to us on the line. We were physically dominating them. You could see it in their eyes and hear it in their voices. The Vikings were beaten.

The Vikings finally scored on a Tarkenton keeper. That was anticlimactic. We didn't care by that time. Probably we had some substitutes in at that time because we were substituting quite freely in the fourth quarter just to get people in the game. Winning was important, not a shutout.

After the touchdown, they recovered an onside kick, but again they were penalized, so we got the ball instead. When they got the ball for the final time, they took it downfield, but on their last play Tarkenton was intercepted at the goal line by Curtis Johnson.

The Vikings were snakebit, no doubt about it. Some games just go that way, and, unfortunately for them, theirs happened to be in the Super Bowl. The Vikings were a very good, vicious team, and the year before they were the only team that should have beaten us. But for some reason, on that day they weren't the same team. That seems to happen to some teams in the Super Bowl and that's why some of the games aren't very good. We weren't seeing the best Vikings team, but we didn't feel sorry for them. They had the same opportunity we did, and we won the game. We played very, very well and I think we had a lot to do with their inability to get things going. I don't want to minimize that. It wasn't their day, but by the same token, we just flattened them.

Winning a championship at any level is terrific, but certainly at this level, where it's as high as it gets, there is no greater satisfaction a player can have. You just sit back and savor it. And you say, "We've done this and there's nothing else to do now." This victory was the reason for all that work you've done. It's a great relief and you feel so much satisfaction about your accomplishment. You feel good about what you've done for yourself, but, more importantly, you feel good about what this team has done. You go 32–2 over two years—don't tell me that's not a great football team. (And we would be even better the next year although we'd lose in the playoffs to Oakland.) The Dolphins had to be the best team ever.

People think that something magical must happen to take a person with humble roots to success in professional football. But there is no magic involved. And there is no particular mold from which all the great players are generated. My own experience taught me that people who accomplish great things in sports can come from all kinds of backgrounds. They just have to have the opportunity. I'm just grateful that the Miami Dolphins gave me the opportunity to be part of a team that was looked on with such regard. If I'd been on a losing team, people may never have heard of me, much less chosen me for Pro Bowls. There's no question in my mind: If I hadn't played on those great Miami teams that won back-to-back Super Bowls, I never would have been elected to the Hall of Fame.

FRANCO HARRIS
PITTSBURGH STEELERS

SUPER BOWL IX

PITTSBURGH STEELERS 16
MINNESOTA VIKINGS 6

FRANCO HARRIS

Pittsburgh reached the Super Bowl in my third NFL season. The Steelers had drafted me in the first round out of Penn State, where we had lost only four games in three years. Jack Ham was a linebacker there my first two years before being drafted by Pittsburgh, and I played all three years in the backfield with Lydell Mitchell, who was picked by the Colts. My rookie year went way beyond my wildest dreams, although it didn't begin that way. I started the first game of the season because of somebody being hurt and I didn't do too well in the second game—as a matter of fact, I fumbled and it cost us the game and I was yanked. I played sparingly in the next few games and touched the ball only a few times. Then there was another injury and that's when I got back in to stay. I ended up having a phenomenal season, gaining over

1,000 yards and then making the "Immaculate Reception" that beat Oakland in the first round of the playoffs. That catch was more reflex than anything else, but I was a good receiver and prided myself on not dropping the ball. I would have loved to have caught a lot more passes in the following years, but the Steelers were primarily a running team.

In 1973 I got a bruised knee in preseason and missed about five games. When that was healed, I got turf-toe and wasn't able to function as well as I wanted for the rest of the season. So it was a tough year, and when it was over I told myself, "Franco, you have to make sure you don't go up and down. You must be good year in and year out, so that when you look back over your career you can say you maintained a high level of consistency." My first year was great; my second year wasn't—and I didn't want that pattern to continue. I wanted to be consistently on top. Even though you can't control injuries, I wanted to make sure that was my frame of mind as I entered my third season. And I had an excellent year, rushing for over 1,000 yards for the second time.

We'd made the playoffs in my first two years but had been eliminated by Miami in a close AFC title game in 1972 and then by Oakland in the divisional playoffs in 1973. I didn't know how good the Steelers were at the beginning of the 1974 season. Only in the second half of the season, when things pick up and games are played a little tighter, can you tell how good a team is. And the Steelers played extremely well in winning the Central Division title. We then beat Buffalo by a large margin in the first playoff game, but the win that really made us believers was our 24–13 victory over Oakland in the AFC title game.

Going into the Oakland game, I had confidence and sensed we had become a really great team, yet I was so nervous. Most games you stop being nervous after the first couple of hits, but against Oakland I still had butterflies going into the fourth quarter. When we lined up, I didn't feel it that much, but I did feel it in the huddle. Luckily it didn't affect our performance that much because we rallied for three touchdowns in the final period. But I stayed nervous even after we took the lead. I couldn't help wondering if the game was going to get away from us—are we going to lose in some sort of way? Time was running out, and it was so hard to believe that we were so close to going to the Super Bowl—and I was nervous about being so close to going. I was glad when the game ended.

Scoring two touchdowns in the final period against Oakland was very satisfying, but I didn't look at it as my proving anything to myself. I saw the fourth quarter in terms of how tough both our offense and defense were playing and how the Steelers were gelling into a great team. Early in the year, the Raiders had shut us out in Pittsburgh, but we had come back to beat them in Oakland. If I had to pick one big moment in my career it was the "Immaculate Reception" two years before, and if I picked my best season it would be 1976, but the biggest game was that win over Oakland in the AFC title game. It was so important because we showed the league and the entire country how good we were. And we proved it to ourselves. Without doubt, that was the pivotal game in our whole decade.

Because of the Oakland game, I had confidence in our team and . . . let's put it this way: I wasn't as nervous going into the Super Bowl versus Minnesota. We'd made so many tough runs and catches and defensive plays against Oakland that I felt that we were on a roll. I was feeling pretty secure and it never crossed my mind that we weren't going to win it.

We spent a week in Pittsburgh and then came to New Orleans for Super Bowl Week. There was a lot of media in town and lots of reporters wanting interviews. I do remember being interviewed by Fred Dryer and Lance Rentzel of the Rams, who were there for fun, using silly aliases and posing as reporters. I didn't read papers that week and don't remember if the media was trying to create rivalries between the quarterbacks Terry Bradshaw and Fran Tarkenton, me and Vikings running back Chuck Foreman, or the two defenses, which were both highly regarded.

I can't remember where we practiced, but it wasn't at Tulane Stadium, the site of the Super Bowl. I do remember that the hotel we stayed in was terrible, really terrible—in fact, it was in chapter eleven. Fortunately, we were allowed to go out and into the French Quarter until Thursday night, when we started having curfew. Until then we were totally free besides practice and meetings. I felt good about that. We said right from the start, "Let's make sure we don't let these moments get away. Let's make sure that we savor these moments." That's the way we felt. So we had a great time in New Orleans without losing sight of why we were there. We enjoyed each other's company and our time down there to the fullest, and also went out and played a good game of football.

I felt comfortable with everyone, on defense as well as offense—in fact, my roommate that year was J. T. Thomas, who played cornerback—and that made it enjoyable on and off the field. The Steelers were a close team, with great athletes who were also great people. We hadn't been divided because of the changing quarterback situation, where Joe Gilliam was given the job when there was a strike in training camp and Terry Bradshaw had to win it back during the season. Even Terry Hanratty was given a start. We tried not to pay too much attention to what was going on from week to week and stayed out of the politics of the coaches. We all had gone through times in our own careers where there was a question mark up there on who was going to play and who was going to sit, so I don't think it was difficult for any of us to deal with. But in some instances, the Bradshaw-Gilliam thing got to be a problem. It had nothing to do with taking sides or who liked who or anything like that—it was that there were things some people were doing off the field that affected the team and needed to be addressed. Fortunately, our team leaders came through and handled some of those situations before they became disruptive. I can't answer for Bradshaw as to whether he felt it was his team again by the Oakland game or Super Bowl. But I always felt confident and comfortable with him at quarterback. I know there were times he and Chuck lost control when relating to each other, but there was nothing like that between Brad and the other players.

I felt that we were well prepared by Chuck and his coaches. I always liked that there was practice and meetings, but after that we were on our own. Chuck didn't try to monopolize all of our time and make us think of nothing but football. That was really important for the type of people we had. The coaches had something to do with our being a disciplined team, but our discipline was probably more a reflection of our team leaders.

Joe Greene was one of the leaders on the team and had been since his rookie year. He was a great defensive tackle and terrific person, and he set the tone on and off the field for the entire team. We definitely looked up to him. I liked that he could always put things into perspective, so you could understand what something was really about and know how to react. When I fumbled in the fourth quarter of the Super Bowl, he told me that we'd get the ball back and that eased my mind. We did get it back when he caused Chuck Foreman to fumble at the 5-yard line. Joe also had a big interception in the game. He would get very emotional and vocal and made sure everyone else on defense played with the same drive and sense of purpose that he did.

L. C. Greenwood played alongside Greene on the left side of the line. He was quieter than some of the other guys, but he was a great defensive end and an inspirational player. He also was a fun guy to be around. He always treated people well and treated them fair. Mel Blount was a leader and tremendous defensive back. He was another guy who made sure everyone maintained a certain level of performance. Andy Russell was a team leader, a great linebacker, a tough, smart ballplayer. He was a veteran who was having a great career. Jack Lambert, our middle linebacker, was another great player and team leader. He was just a rookie but you knew he was there. He played with extreme emotion and that fired everyone up. Jack Ham, our third linebacker, was quieter. He was a guy who would never get beat—never. So you always felt secure with him. I had played with him in college and always felt that he was the best ever. Russell, Lambert, and Ham were an amazing linebacking core.

Bradshaw was a leader on the offense. At times, you would suggest things to him on the sidelines, but he was the one who ran things on the field. I didn't mind that at all because I always felt that the huddle is where the quarterback should have control—that's his domain and he runs it the way he wants. Brad always was emotional and some people would worry about that affecting his performance, but during games I saw him as businesslike. He could be a calming influence, as he was in the Super Bowl.

At certain times I didn't mind assuming the leadership role and then trying to motivate my teammates through performance. Emotion does play a part in football and I think I was an emotional player, though maybe I didn't show it too much. I didn't do much talking. I could yell "Pick it up!" but mostly I tried to lead the way by doing it myself. I always had the knack for knowing when it was time to step up and try to get things going. That would be the case in the second half of the Super Bowl.

Before the game, we had players say, "We're going to do this" and "We're going to shut this guy down," or something to that effect. It was great to see guys step up. Guys like Joe and Mel. Seeing guys stand up with that confidence and take a position of strength and determination inspired all the rest of us. We fed off their emotion and confidence. In the locker room, we were ready to play. What guys did to get ready depended on the individual, but there was nothing crazy. We were never a crazy team in the locker room. Finally, it was time to go through the tunnel to the field. I remember that moment. I was excited and a little nervous.

I knew that it would be a difficult matchup because Minnesota had many great players. On defense alone they had Alan Page, Jim Marshall, Carl Eller, Doug Sutherland, Wally Hilgenberg, and Paul Krause. I thought, "Wow, we're playing against a pretty tough crew." But we weren't intimidated by them, even though this was our first time in the Super Bowl and they had been there twice before. Especially after beating the Raiders. The Vikings were a good team, but we felt we were the best team in football. And though we rarely played them, it did cross our minds that we had beaten them in my rookie season and, in fact, had a very good game against them.

January 12, 1975, at Tulane Stadium in New Orleans

Paid Attendance: 80,997

AFC Champion: Pittsburgh Steelers (12–3–1)
Head Coach: Chuck Noll

NFC Champion: Minnesota Vikings (12–4)
Head Coach: Bud Grant

STARTING LINEUPS

OFFENSE			DEFENSE		
Pittsburgh		**Minnesota**	**Pittsburgh**		**Minnesota**
Frank Lewis	WR	Jim Lash	L. C. Greenwood	LE	Carl Eller
Jon Kolb	LT	Charles Goodrum	Joe Greene	LT	Doug Sutherland
Jim Clack	LG	Andy Maurer	Ernie Holmes	RT	Alan Page
Ray Mansfield	C	Mick Tingelhoff	Dwight White	RE	Jim Marshall
Gerry Mullins	RG	Ed White	Jack Ham	LLB	Roy Winston
Gordon Gravelle	RT	Ron Yary	Jack Lambert	MLB	Jeff Siemon
Larry Brown	TE	Stu Voigt	Andy Russell	RLB	Wally Hilgenberg
Ron Shanklin	WR	John Gilliam	J. T. Thomas	LCB	Nate Wright
Terry Bradshaw	QB	Fran Tarkenton	Mel Blount	RCB	Jackie Wallace
Rocky Bleier	RB	Chuck Foreman	Mike Wagner	LS	Jeff Wright
Franco Harris	RB	Dave Osborn	Glen Edwards	RS	Paul Krause

SUBSTITUTIONS

Pittsburgh: K—Roy Gerela. P—Bobby Walden. Offense: Receivers—John Stallworth, Lynn Swann, Reggie Garrett, John McMakin, Randy Grossman. Linemen—Sam Davis, Dave Reavis, Rick Druschel, Mike Webster. Backs—Preston Pearson, Steve Davis, Reggie Harrison. Defense: Linebackers—Loren Toews, Marv Kellum, Ed Bradley. Linemen—Charlie Davis, Steve Furness. Backs—Jim Allen, Richard Conn, Donnie Shell. DNP—Joe Gilliam, Terry Hanratty, Jim Wolf.

Minnesota: K—Fred Cox. P—Mike Eischeid. Offense: Receivers—Sam McCullum, Doug Kingsriter, Steve Craig. Linemen—Grady Alderman, Scott Anderson, Steve Lawson, Milt Sunde. Backs—Bill Brown, Brent McClanahan, Oscar Reed, Ed Marinaro. Defense: Linebackers—Matt Blair, Amos Martin, Fred McNeill. Linemen: Gary Larsen, Bob Lurtsema. Backs—Terry Brown, Randy Poltl. DNP—Bob Berry, Joe Blahak, Dave Boone, John Holland, Steve Riley.

Pittsburgh	0	2	7	7—16	
Minnesota	0	0	0	6— 6	

Pitt — Safety, White downed Tarkenton in end zone
Pitt — Harris 9 run (Gerela kick)
Minn — T. Brown recovered blocked punt in end zone (kick failed)
Pitt — L. Brown 4 pass from Bradshaw (Gerela kick)
MVP: — Franco Harris (Pittsburgh)

We hadn't done much passing in the playoffs, so we knew that Bud Grant would have his defense focus on stopping our running game. I don't remember anything specific about how I was expected to run that day, just that I wasn't supposed to do anything out of the ordinary. There wasn't any one defensive player I was going to try to run away from or at. Our line did a good job. We didn't have an offensive line that blew people out, but it was real good at trapping and hooking. We saw how the defense lined up, and if they were in position to stop the play, we'd audible. I would scan the defense and would make my adjustment. Even if no one else on the team made the adjustment, I would. I felt comfortable doing that even when I had been a rookie. I had to improvise because we could run the same play 50 times and the defense would react differently each time.

We always had two backs behind Bradshaw, me and Rocky Bleier. Rocky had won the Purple Heart and other medals in Vietnam and was a real inspiration, not just to me, having come from a military family, but to all of us. It had taken him a few years to recover from the foot and leg injuries he had suffered in the war. Only in 1974 did he come back all the way and become a starter. We got along great and enjoyed spending time together and talking—Rocky could talk; he wasn't quiet—though we're more likely to have deep conversations today than when we played together. Rocky was a tough and unselfish player and there's no doubt that we complemented each other in the backfield. We blocked for each other and, in the Super Bowl, we tried a few sucker plays because Minnesota was so fast and mobile up front. We'd get Page, Eller, Marshall, or Sutherland to commit to going in one direction—maybe I'd be leading with a block—and then Rocky would go the other way. He was a hard runner who would more often slice through the line than go wide. He had an excellent day and that kept them from keying on me.

It was *very* cold that day in New Orleans. There also was an icy wind. I don't know if the weather caused all the turnovers or the failed field-goal attempts that game, or if it changed our game plan so that Bradshaw did even less passing than usual and then threw only for short yardage. Lynn Swann, who was a backup wide receiver and punt returner as a rookie, didn't get a pass all game. He still complains about that to this day. He was so frustrated that he later told me he'd win the Super Bowl MVP the following year—which he did.

When I was on offense, I didn't feel the Vikings' defense was as physical or hard-hitting as Oakland's had been, and that surprised me. However, our defense was playing as well as it had against the Raiders, and when I was off the field I would watch it closely. It would inspire me, setting the tone of the game in my mind. What our defense—which would be nicknamed "the Steel Curtain"—had done to Oakland and was now doing to Minnesota was just incredible. These were teams that were used to running the ball, and our four-three defense, led by Joe Greene, completely shut them down. Our guys held the Vikings to no yards rushing in the first quarter and less than 25 yards for the entire game, and they intercepted Tarkenton three times. The few times that Minnesota threatened, they made the big play to stop them, often causing a turnover. For instance, near the end of the first half, Tarkenton completed a pass to John Gilliam on about our 5-yard line, but Glen Edwards hit Gilliam so hard that he fumbled and Mel Blount recovered the ball. Those guys were just going at it.

The only score in the first half came earlier in the second quarter when the Vikings were backed up at their goal and Tarkenton pitched out to Dave Osborn and then had to cover it in the end zone when it got away. Dwight White downed him for the safety and we went ahead 2–0. Dwight was pretty sick that entire week. He had a bad viral infection and spent a lot of time in a New Orleans hospital. He had lost nearly 20 pounds and was a definite question mark for the game, but he got out of bed and came to play and had a great game. That's how it was on our team: Players did the job they had to do.

I was surprised we didn't score more than two points in the first half. Rather than it being the wind and cold, I think it was probably that we were trying not to make mistakes rather than going out and playing our usual aggressive game. We weren't as loose as we'd like to have been because so much was riding on one game. I was disappointed in our lack of offensive production, but I still wasn't worried, because we were dominating them despite the close score. It's hard to explain Super Bowl IX— it's just that I felt all year that we would find a way to win and that's how I felt during the game. That's how the team felt. Somehow we were going to win.

There always is a change of attitude going into the second half of a game like this. We knew we had to pick it up some. There was no doubt about that. We had to get some points, no doubt about that either. That's what I was thinking. I wasn't told that I'd be running more.

We scored quickly after the break. Bill Brown lost a fumble on the kickoff and we recovered on the Vikings 30-yard line. After two carries, I ran it in from the 9. My touchdown was on a counterplay—nothing they wouldn't have seen on film. It had been a big play for us all year. I would go one step to my right and then reverse direction and go toward the end of the left side. Then I'd read the defense to see where I should make my cut. On the play in the Super Bowl, Rocky blocked Marshall, Gerry Mullins blocked Wally Hilgenberg, and I got in without being touched. We did that play a few other times during the game and we also had a second play off of it. On the play that went for a touchdown we hooked their end and I went around him, and in the other case we would knock the end to the outside and I would cut inside.

We were wearing shoes that were specially ordered by Tony Parisi, our equipment manager, because he was concerned about the slick footing on the artificial turf at Tulane Stadium. I think he gave the shoes to us before the game, but it might have been at halftime. I don't know if they made an actual difference in how we played, but I guess we *thought* they did, and that was a big plus. The footing didn't seem to be that bad, but we had those shoes on, so we might not have realized just how bad it was. However, I didn't feel that the shoes gave us an advantage over the Vikings. I didn't see them slipping or falling down.

Greene, Greenwood, White, Ernie Holmes, and our linebackers continued to make running nearly impossible for Minnesota. But the Vikings might have gained some hope when both Russell and Lambert had to come out of the game with injuries. However, their replacements, Ed Bradley and Loren Toews, both played very well. What happens is that players feed off other players. The two replacements weren't of the same caliber as Lambert and Russell, but our other players on the field and the importance of what was happening brought their play up to the level of the occasion. Watching our defense often made me lift my own game a notch, so I'm sure that's how Bradley and Toews felt playing with those guys.

Minnesota scored its only touchdown early in the fourth quarter when Bobby Walden had a punt blocked and Terry Brown recovered the ball in the end zone. You hate to see things like that. It didn't make us worry, but I'd say we were concerned. Even though our defense was shutting them down, we realized that there was always a threat with their offense, especially with Fran at quarterback. We knew that just one big play could turn the game around. It did help that Fred Cox's extra point attempt hit the upright, because that meant a Vikings' field goal could only tie the game, not put them ahead.

We didn't want to give them a chance to tie us with a field goal or go ahead with a touchdown. We needed to score ourselves. If there was one thing we learned through the years: If you have to do it, you do it. There was definitely a big sense of purpose when we got the ball late in the game at our own 35 and started to drive downfield. We realized this was our one chance to put the game away. I carried the ball six times in the drive, and after I had run it so many times, I'm pretty sure they were surprised that when we got down to the 4, Bradshaw threw to our tight end Larry Brown in the end zone for a touchdown. I think they expected me to keep running. That was a real big drive for us, and after Brown's touchdown we did feel good. We knew we had done that drive in the hard, old-fashioned way. That builds your confidence.

If anyone had told me going into the game I would run more than 30 times, I'd have told them they were crazy. So I was totally surprised when I learned I had run 34 times during the game and 11 times in the fourth quarter. It didn't feel like it—I wasn't tiring—and it didn't even enter my mind that I had run that much. Also, I didn't even know I was approaching Larry Csonka's Super Bowl rushing record until the game was over. It turned out I got the record on my last run when I was thinking only of us scoring, not about a record.

Our 16–6 victory gave Pittsburgh its first title in 42 years. The fans and Steelers owner Art Rooney had waited all that time. I knew Art Rooney no better than any other player did, but I respected him for what he was building in Pittsburgh in the seventies through the draft and for all that he'd done as one of the pioneers of the National Football League. He'd come to work every day and it was always nice to be around him and see him. He always had something nice to say. Part of the joy of winning the title was winning it for Art. Definitely. Art was about 75 then and I was so happy that he was there to enjoy the Steelers' first Super Bowl victory and all the championship years ahead.

I couldn't say we savored all the moments during the game, but before and afterward? Yes! After our victory, we really celebrated—we players, our families, the whole town of Pittsburgh. We flew back to Pittsburgh the next day and there was a big parade. There were so many fans there and it was great to see them so happy after all those years without a championship. During that decade we had the best fans the whole time. They were so supportive of me and all the other players. They were incredible.

There was just an unbelievable feeling about winning the Super Bowl for the first time. The best in the world. In fact, we enjoyed winning so much that we told ourselves: "We have to do this again."

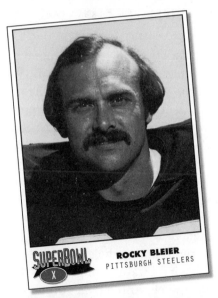

ROCKY BLEIER
PITTSBURGH STEELERS

SUPER BOWL X

PITTSBURGH STEELERS 21
DALLAS COWBOYS 17

ROCKY BLEIER

During every Steelers' training camp in the early seventies, there would be a couple of articles in the Pittsburgh press about "Bleier Coming Back." So I'm sure many Pittsburgh fans were aware of my comeback story to some extent. But it wasn't really until we started winning Super Bowls that my story became bigger and all the fans said they remembered when I first returned to the team. In truth, probably not many fans paid attention when I began my comeback because nothing much was expected of me then. In my brief time with the Steelers before I fought in Vietnam I hadn't done anything to raise the expectations of either the fans or the team.

I doubt that the Steelers expected a whole lot from me in 1968. I had a knee operation coming out of Notre Dame and I was finally taken in the sixteenth round, mainly because I was still available. I made the Steelers primarily as a special teams player. Dick Hoak and Earl Gros were the backs and I carried the ball only six times.

I missed the following season because I was in the service and I came back from the war banged up. I got shot in the left leg, but the biggest damage came from a grenade blowing up under my right foot. I didn't really have to get over any mental trauma from the experience—I guess I felt okay mentally because I hadn't lost anything from my anatomy— but physically it would be a real struggle. I developed a staph infection that went all the way up my leg, and although they never told me, they contemplated taking my leg off. The infection subsided, but then I had to have several operations. I had to have the shrapnel removed, and then I had to regenerate the nerve and get all the strength and flexibility back so that I could move my toes and run off the ball of my foot. There was atrophy of the muscle, bone spurs forming in the joints, and some arthritis. My therapy was just rubbing my feet and doing things like picking up marbles with my toes. I also started lifting weights. I never took the luxury of saying, "I can't do it." The doctors said, "You'll never play again," but what do doctors know? What I learned is that in time injuries will heal and you can go on and play. All athletes learn this. But in 1970, when I came back to training camp, I just wasn't ready. I was just beating myself up.

I made it all the way until the last cut, but then Coach Noll had to make room for his starting roster. Chuck said, "Go home and do what you need to do and come back next year." I was heartbroken. The next morning, Dan Rooney, who was the president of the organization and Art Rooney's son, called and said, "I would like our doctors to take a look at you, and we'll see if something can be done to help you get back to where you can help us." So I was on the Injured Reserve.

I left and started lifting weights again to get strength back in my legs. Then a week before training camp started in 1971, I pulled a hamstring. So I came into camp already hurting, and on the first day of practice I pulled my hamstring and was out for three weeks. I went to see the team's chief surgeon, who had been around for a while. He recommended that I retire because I'd always have problems with my hamstrings. He said he was going to tell the coaches that. I think he just wanted to give the coaches an easy excuse to get rid of a player so they wouldn't have to do it themselves. But I said, "Don't tell them anything yet."

I made the team as a member of the taxi squad. That was a move up from the previous year. I was dressed for three games and played special teams. Maybe they put me into the backfield once. Just being there was encouraging.

In 1972 I came back and my whole thought process was, "Now, I've got to do it. Two years they carried me, they gave me a chance, but now I've got to make it on my own." I was the leading ground gainer in preseason. I wasn't real bright, but it finally dawned on me that they gave me the ball more and more to give me more chances to screw up. They wanted to cut my ass. But I kept having good games and they had to keep me.

Nineteen seventy-two was a turnaround year for the Steelers. Franco Harris came in and ran for 1,000 yards and we made the playoffs for the first time and Franco made the "Immaculate Reception" to beat Oakland in the divisional playoff game. We then lost to Miami in the AFC title game, but it was a very successful year. Once again, my contribution came primarily on special teams. I got only one carry all year. But I was caught up in all the excitement. I was a young guy and it was fun.

Let me digress: After the 1971 season I had gone home to Appleton, Wisconsin, where my father owned a bar. I walked into the family room and there was *my* father in the lotus position. I was stunned: "What are you doing?" He said, "Look at this." And he goes and puts his forehead to his knees. He told me to try it and I couldn't do it. He was compelled to try yoga because he had a lower back and sciatic nerve and muscle problem. I knew I had to do some stretching to work on my own problems, so I borrowed his yoga book and I became very flexible. When I came back to the Steelers in 1972, it so happened that they had hired a stretch coach, Paul Uram. I had been doing yoga exercises with static stretches, rather than the repetitive stretches we had done in our gym classes, so I was already doing what Paul prescribed for the players. He encouraged me to talk to Dr. Robert Kurucz, who was a physiologist doing work with the Olympic track team. Dr. Kurucz talked to me about increasing my speed using the techniques of runners in the Soviet Union. So I worked diligently on those techniques in the off-season.

In 1973 I came back to Pittsburgh in the best shape I'd been in. For one thing, my foot was fine: My strength was there, my flexibility was there, and finally there was no pain. Also, I now bench-pressed 465 pounds and squatted over 600 pounds and had increased my speed in the 40 by two- or three-tenths of a second. I opened some eyes.

However, I still didn't fit into the Steelers' backfield plans. I got only three carries. We had Franco Harris, Preston Pearson, Frenchy Fuqua, and a rookie named Steve Davis. Although Steve was sick and not playing that year, it was obvious that the future for the Steelers was going to be

Franco and Steve starting with Frenchy and Preston as backups. So at the end of the 1973 season, I was thinking that the handwriting was on the wall, and the good Lord was saying it was time to get on with my life. I decided to retire and sell insurance in Chicago. Then Andy Russell, our veteran linebacker, told me, "You can't retire. Those guys aren't worth it. What you're doing is making a decision for them. Back them against a wall. You make them cut you. Don't make it so easy for them." That was the push I needed.

So I came back. And for the third straight year I was the leading ground gainer in preseason, yet began the season on the bench. Sure enough Franco Harris and Steve Davis were the starting running backs. Only Franco missed the first game and Frenchy started in his place, and for the first time I was the backup back, which was encouraging. The second game I didn't play. I got into the third game for a little bit. In the fourth game, against Houston, Preston and I were inserted into the backfield right before the end of the half. I was at fullback and he was at halfback. Thank God, Preston broke one for about 50 yards and we took the lead at halftime. Things were going well, so they decided to start the guys who ended the first half. Preston and I went back in and we won that game.

The following week was against Kansas City on the road, and Preston and I got to start. It was my first start as a Steeler. We won again and I had a nice little game with maybe 40 yards. The following week was a Monday night game against Cleveland. Franco was healthy and was coming back and Preston was playing well, so I assumed I would return to backup. Then at the pregame breakfast the coach said, "Okay, Franco and Rocky are going to start." I found out that Chuck hadn't been pleased with the blocking of the halfbacks. He asked Dick Hoak, who was now our backfield coach, "Who's your best blocker?" "Bleier." "Let's start him at halfback."

It took me by surprise. I couldn't believe it. I'd been playing fullback, so I hadn't even looked at the halfback plays at all. The fullback and halfback were distinguishable in our offense in that there were different blocking techniques and different patterns that were run in the passing sequences. It was just a matter of going back and reminding myself what they were. Then I was ready. I started at halfback, we won the game, and I started the rest of the season.

If a guy averages 4 yards a carry, that ain't bad. That's what I wanted to do. Both Franco and I did a lot of counterplays because our whole system was based on traps. Franco's view was that no situation was ever the same. If he didn't see a hole, he would dance around till he found one. My thing was I had learned very well that the shortest distance between two points is a straight line. I never perceived myself as having speed, so I always tried to use my quickness. If you hit the hole quick, you have the chance to get through. I ran mostly between the tackles and I hit the hole as hard as I possibly could. What I learned was that there were variances as to where the blocks were going to be. It depended on if the defensive tackle played in the two-hole or played the inside shoulder or was hard-charging across the line. The offensive line liked that I made quick adjustments because they didn't have to hold their blocks as long as with Franco. They didn't know where he was going, inside or outside, so they had to keep blocking. But, of course, Franco was a great, great runner. I was primarily a blocking back. We complemented each other so well because I was very happy with my role. I was happy to do anything to keep playing. I enjoyed blocking. I didn't secretly resent Franco running the ball so much more than me. I was just as happy to throw a great block for him and having him make a great run because then I felt I had done my job.

The Steelers won the AFC championship and I like to think I made my contribution as part of the backfield with Franco. I remember before Super Bowl IX began, when we were standing in the tunnel at old Tulane Stadium, I wanted to pinch myself. Here I was, a kid from Appleton, Wisconsin, part of the legacy. We were the underdog against Minnesota but we played a marvelous game and won. It was like, wow—this is the greatest thing! I had a good game and was a contributor, so it was very satisfying. When I went into the locker room, Art Rooney was the first person I saw, and he grabbed my shoulder and put out his hand and said, "Thank you. You did it."

The 1975 training camp contributed a great deal to the Steelers establishing an identity with the fans. Now for the first time in 40 years, the fans had a good team to cheer for. So thousands of people would come daily to watch us practice. At times it would be a pain in the butt, but you were there to say hi, shake hands, sign autographs, and have one-on-one moments with fans. They remembered and our identity started to grow. We were motivated coming off the Super Bowl year to keep up what we started. We had a sense of our own ability and that's the level we played at. The Steelers built entirely through the draft and that rookie crew from the year before—Lynn Swann, John Stallworth, Jack Lambert, Mike Webster, Randy Grossman, about 12 guys—was now a big part of our nucleus. And these were guys who had a winning attitude because they hadn't experienced much losing since they put on Steelers uniforms. We'd even win our preseason games.

I think that the major focus of leadership came from Andy Russell, as it had since I came to Pittsburgh in 1968. He had been in the service, was well educated and well spoken, and everyone respected him. Other guys on defense started to emerge as leaders—Joe Greene, of course. He was the central figure in the awesome front four of the Steel Curtain. In the beginning Jack Lambert was very quiet. But he was one of those guys with a professional aura, who knew what he had to do and went out and did it. That professional attitude didn't take anything away from his desire or intensity. Lambert was intense and it rubbed off.

On offense, our center Ray Mansfield was a leader. He had been around as long as Russell and was called "the Old Ranger." Me? I was just happy to be there. Maybe what I'd done to be there inspired some of the guys.

Of course, Terry Bradshaw's leadership was very important because only one guy spoke in the huddle—the quarterback. In 1975 he was more sure of himself and was able to run the game confidently. In terms of the maturing of our whole team, maybe Bradshaw sitting for a few games in 1974 was the best thing that could have happened. For the only time other than for a few games in his rookie season, he found out what it was like to sit on the bench. He had always been the star in high school and at Louisiana Tech, and then had been a starter and in the limelight in Pittsburgh. Then suddenly, he was forced to play second fiddle to Joe Gilliam, a good quarterback with a lot of moxie and the ability to run the club and take control. When players run into adversity, they can run away and become self-absorbed or, as Brad did, reach out for support and become one of the team members. In 1975 Brad not only had a Super Bowl ring and his ego back intact, but he also had really become one of the guys. Guys related to him much better. When he now played cards with his teammates, it was more of a buddy-buddy type thing. He changed in the huddle, too. He was more secure. Not that he never had to work for his status, but I think he was now more appreciative of having it.

Bradshaw had a great season in 1975. His passing percentage was high and he threw a lot of touchdown passes, especially to Lynn Swann. I still thought of us as a running team, but we definitely did more passing. In 1974 our main receivers had been Frank Lewis and Ron Shanklin, but in 1975 Swann and John Stallworth started and became a major part of our passing game. Also, Randy Grossman got a lot of time at tight end. So we had several quality receivers coming into their own, and when we opened up the passing game, that helped the running game.

I can't say enough about our defense. The Steel Curtain was as great as its reputation. You knew those players were good but you didn't realize how good until you watched them play together as a unit. They were incredible. The offense was so proud of those guys.

We lost only twice during the season and easily won our playoff games from Baltimore and Oakland, both in Pittsburgh, to set up our Super Bowl X match-up with Tom Landry's NFC champion Dallas Cowboys. The game was to be played in the Orange Bowl, so we came down to Miami for Super Bowl Week. We stayed at the Miami Lakes Hotel. It was pretty subdued, so I'm sure a lot of the guys were bored being there, but we weren't a party team anyway. We knew what needed to be done to get through the week from our 1974 experience and from Chuck Noll's approach. He said, "There are going to be a lot of distractions surrounding this game. There will be a lot of media people down here. We'll try to control it the best that we can and try not to let them bother you outside of the designated media times. For the first week, they'll write about the game, so that won't be so bad. By the second week they'll have written everything they possibly could, but since they get paid to fill up columns, they'll write about you personally. But don't worry about it. You'll get the same questions dozens of times, so make up the answers, make up stories, have fun."

I'd say that Chuck Noll's strength as a football coach was to be able to put everything into such simple perspective. Instead of giving pep talks, he would just say, "You prepared so well; you know your assignments; just go out and execute; you know we can win." He maintained that the way you play in the fourth quarter wins or loses football games and that if you aren't in condition you'll get beaten up or become fatigued or not be able to play in the heat. You must be in good shape so you can think rather than just react in a tired manner. Noll also spoke about habits. He said habits are created on the practice field and are carried over to the playing field. That's why we practiced with uniforms and had initial contact.

I can't really say there was bad blood between Pittsburgh and Dallas before the game, although there were things said in the press. For instance, I know they were trying to intimidate Lynn Swann, who had been knocked unconscious in the playoffs. They said they'd go after him. Lynn would have a great game, so obviously their words didn't worry him. I know there was no rivalry between the two teams from past games because we rarely, if ever, played each other, outside of occasional exhibitions. But there may have been a rivalry simply because of the two teams' reputations. We knew Dallas had an excellent team, but in 1975, it was deemed "America's Team," and we, the defending Super Bowl champions, wondered what that meant. They were the *Daaalllaaasss* Cowboys, led by Roger Staubach—very glittery, very shiny. That's how we pictured them. Unlike the Steelers, who were blue-collar, dirty, beer-drinking kind of guys.

We were a group who sat around and talked and had a beer or two. A lot of the guys drank. Lambert was a great drinker. Guys might go out together or in small groups and have a beer after work. Offense and defense, it didn't matter. After a game, after Chuck said his few words while we were taking off our pads and tapes, we'd all go back into the sauna, where there'd be a waste container full of iced beer. We'd sit for 5 or 10 minutes to let our muscles unwind and let the heat take effect on the bumps and the bruises. Each of us would have a cold beer or two and relive the game, this play, that play, when you knocked an opponent on his ass, and so on. That was one of the great things about being on the Steelers.

I was able to sleep the night before the Super Bowl, but the Steelers didn't make it easy. When you were on the road during the regular season, no wives or girlfriends could come stay with you before a game. You had a roommate. Except they switched it, and for the Super Bowl, you could sleep with your wife if you wanted to. The Steelers wanted to save money on rooms so they put the wives with their husbands. Why now would we want to stay with them? I was married then but I didn't want to sleep with my wife the night before the game. So Jack Ham and I stayed together and our wives stayed together. And I was able to sleep.

The next day we had our pregame meal, a typical four hours before the game. Steaks and eggs. The locker room was pretty quiet before the game. We had an emotional group, but I guess we were refined in the sense that there wasn't a lot of yelling and screaming or slamming helmets. Because Chuck wasn't that kind of guy. He was not a rah-rah guy. Enthusiasm was another thing. He had that and his players had that.

I was nervous. Oh, yeah. I got nervous before all games. Of course, this was the biggest game of the year, even though Chuck would say, "Put it in perspective: it is only one of 17 games." I had my little ritual in preparation, from coming in and getting dressed, to the number of sticks of gum that I'd be chewing, to my stretching inside the locker room, to going over all my plays from a mental-visualization aspect, to then going out for warm-ups. I didn't talk to Harris or Bradshaw about what we were going to do in the game. I did go over and say, "Hey, Brad, how are you feeling?" I knew that the key to our success in all games, offensively, was Bradshaw. He'd never say that he wasn't into a game, but sometimes you'd get the feeling that he wasn't really into it, and you'd say, "Oh, Christ, this is going to be a long day; we're going to have to pick up the pieces." Fortunately, on this day I could tell Bradshaw was into the game.

When we were being introduced to the crowd in the Orange Bowl, I glanced toward the sidelines and saw Robert Shaw, the actor. I thought it was kind of strange that he should be standing there, but I never gave it another thought. It was kind of like a flash. I put it away in the back of my mind and didn't think anymore about it until the movie *Black Sunday* came out several months later. Then I did remember seeing Robert Shaw. I don't know if any of the players were aware that a movie was being made about terrorists sabotaging a Super Bowl. I wasn't.

This game was more for ourselves than for Art Rooney and the fans of Pittsburgh, as had been Super Bowl IX. I don't think we had been taken seriously as underdogs in Super Bowl IX, and we now had come back to prove ourselves worthy champions. We felt a certain amount of pride and that feeling had been continually building during the season. Now when we came in to play Super Bowl X, we knew we had the talent to beat Dallas. We were confident. Of course, there was always the possibility that we'd screw up.

Dallas scored first in Super Bowl X on a touchdown pass from Roger Staubach to Drew Pearson. They had gotten the ball deep in our territory when our punter Bobby Walden fumbled the snap and had to eat the ball. We hadn't given up a touchdown in the first quarter all year and didn't give up an offensive touchdown in the previous Super Bowl, but that touchdown didn't upset us at all. We knew that Dallas was capable of scoring because they had done it all season. They had Staubach; they had a great team. It wouldn't have surprised me going into the game that they would score 17 points, although not many teams had scored that many points against us during the season.

We weren't behind for long. On the next drive, we mostly ran the ball except for a long pass to Lynn Swann along the right sideline for 32 yards. Then on a third-and-1 from their 7, instead of calling another running play, Bradshaw surprised the defense by lofting a pass to Randy Grossman for the touchdown. To be honest, the only play I remember of that scoring drive was Swann's great catch. While running down the sidelines, he leapt high in the air over his man and somehow caught the ball and came down in fair territory. It was an exciting play.

Our offensive plan was to recognize the flex defense, with the offset tackle. Most teams tried to run away from the flex, but we decided to attack it rather than be afraid of it. We had studied their techniques on film and tried to pick up tendencies. If they were in the flex and, say, their

January 18, 1976, at the Orange Bowl in Miami
Paid Attendance: 80,187

NFC Champion: Dallas Cowboys (12–4)
Head Coach: Tom Landry

AFC Champion: Pittsburgh Steelers (14–2)
Head Coach: Chuck Noll

STARTING LINEUPS

OFFENSE			DEFENSE		
Dallas		**Pittsburgh**	**Dallas**		**Pittsburgh**
Golden Richards	WR	John Stallworth	Ed Jones	LE	L. C. Greenwood
Ralph Neely	LT	Jon Kolb	Jethro Pugh	LT	Joe Greene
Burton Lawless	LG	Jim Clack	Larry Cole	RT	Ernie Holmes
John Fitzgerald	C	Ray Mansfield	Harvey Martin	RE	Dwight White
Blaine Nye	RG	Gerry Mullins	Dave Edwards	LLB	Jack Ham
Rayfield Wright	RT	Gordon Gravelle	Lee Roy Jordan	MLB	Jack Lambert
Jean Fugett	TE	Larry Brown	D. D. Lewis	RLB	Andy Russell
Drew Pearson	WR	Lynn Swann	Mark Washington	LCB	J. T. Thomas
Roger Staubach	QB	Terry Bradshaw	Mel Renfro	RCC	Mel Blount
Preston Pearson	RB	Rocky Bleier	Charlie Waters	LS	Mike Wagner
Robert Newhouse	RB	Franco Harris	Cliff Harris	RS	Glen Edwards

SUBSTITUTIONS

Dallas: K—Toni Fritsch. P—Mitch Hoopes. Offense: Receivers—Percy Howard, Ron Howard, Billy Joe DuPree. Linemen—Kyle Davis, Pat Donovan, Herbert Scott. Backs—Doug Dennison, Charley Young. Defense: Linebackers—Bob Breunig, Randy White, Tom Henderson, Cal Peterson, Warren Capone. Lineman—Bill Gregory. Backs—Benny Barnes, Randy Hughes, Roland Woolsey. DNP—Clint Longley, Bruce Walton.

Pittsburgh: K—Roy Gerela. P—Bobby Walden. Offense: Receivers—Frank Lewis, Randy Grossman, Reggie Garrett. Linemen—Mike Webster, Sam Davis, Dave Reavis. Backs—Terry Hanratty (QB), John Fuqua, Mike Collier, Reggie Harrison. Linemen—Ed Bradley, Loren Toews, Marv Kellum. Linemen—Steve Furness, John Banaszak. Backs—Donnie Shell, Dave Brown, Jim Allen. DNP—Joe Gilliam.

Dallas	7	3	0	7—17
Pittsburgh	7	0	0	14—21

Dall	D. Pearson 29 pass from Staubach (Fritsch kick)
Pitt	Grossman 7 pass from Bradshaw (Gerela kick)
Dall	FG Fritsch 36
Pitt	Safety, Harrison blocked Hoopes' punt through the end zone
Pitt	FG Gerela 36
Pitt	FG Gerela 18
Pitt	Swann 64 pass from Bradshaw (kick failed)
Dall	P. Howard 34 pass from Staubach (Fritsch kick)
MVP:	Lynn Swann (Pittsburgh)

outside linebacker D. D. Lewis was up on the line or a foot off it, we'd look to see if Lewis gave anything away. Or we'd look at how their safeties, Cliff Harris and Charlie Waters, were lined up. They may have given an indication of doing one or two things. As a back, I'm thinking about who I might have to block if I took a certain path. If I knew the two things a player might do, I could make my adjustments quickly.

The pattern at the beginning was that Franco would run one way and on the next play I'd run the same way. It wasn't something we had planned before the game. Bradshaw just didn't see the need to mix it up. I think our ground game worked fairly well against Dallas's flex, although neither Franco nor I had big running games. I personally had an okay game—although I didn't have any runs that I'd really remember. Franco did have a few good runs to the inside. And even when he was stopped, his carrying the ball served a purpose. Because Dallas set its defense to stop Franco—and to blitz Bradshaw—that opened up things for our receivers. In fact, Swann made an even better catch late in the first half to get us out of bad field position. He was covered man-on-man and collided with Mel Renfro as he went high into the air and he still grabbed the ball as he was falling forward. It was an acrobatic play that gained over 50 yards.

Swann was having a great game that would earn him the MVP selection. He must have been exuberant because the Super Bowl was a great showcase for him. Did he "feel it" and keep asking for the ball in the huddle? You've got to understand that our receivers always wanted the ball. You sometimes hear about how receivers always talk in the huddle and tell the quarterback that they're open every play. Well, that's true. Coming back to the huddle, they're saying, "Brad, I'm open." On the line, Swann would be at one end and Stallworth at the other end, and they'd make that subtle hint, "Hey, Brad, I'm open; throw it over here." There was nothing different this game. Both guys wanted the ball.

The only score of the second quarter was a field goal by Toni Fritsch that gave Dallas a 10–7 lead at the half. We were behind but everything was cool. No worry, no panic. We came into the locker room. We sat down. We had a soda. We smoked a cigarette. We went to the bathroom. We relaxed. And we talked about offensive adjustments. Then we returned to the field to begin the second half.

My adrenaline was pumping, but my emotions weren't as extreme as they had been against Minnesota. After all, that was our first Super Bowl and I'm sure a lot of our players felt the same way. But I realized that the game itself was at least as good. It was a close, hard-fought, interesting game. We hadn't expected a blowout and we weren't getting one.

We had a chance to tie the game in the third quarter, but Roy Gerela missed a short field goal. It was his second miss of the game. Roy had been banged up on the opening kickoff when he had to make the tackle, so you could have blamed that for his kicking problems that day. But Roy hadn't had a great season, and after two misses in the Super Bowl, he was obviously susceptible. So Cliff Harris started celebrating the miss by kind of slapping Roy on the side of the helmet, a mocking that-a-way-to-go gesture. You've probably seen what happened next many times on film: Lambert saw what Harris was doing and spun around and grabbed him and threw him hard to the ground. I was coming off the field and said, "Oh, shit!" It was like: Nobody intimidates my fellow teammates; we're not going to take that crap—boom! After that play, Lambert became an emotional leader. Even with Joe Greene out the second half with an injury, our entire defense was fired up. Lambert made more than a dozen tackles in the middle and our team set a record for sacking Staubach. I know L. C. Greenwood and Dwight White had a few each. So Lambert's reaction to Harris was a big moment in the game.

There was no scoring in the third quarter, so we still were behind by three points going into the fourth quarter. Then we had an unexpected score, which Chuck Noll said was the biggest play of the game. I was on the sideline waiting to see what kind of field position we'd get after Mitch Hoopes punted to us. We put on an all-out blitz and Reggie Harrison went right up the middle and, boom, blocked the punt through their end zone for a safety. That gave us two points to cut their lead to 10–9 and we got the ball back in very good field position after their free kick. No one ever expected such a big play from special teams and it gave us a big lift. Soon after, Gerela kicked a field goal to put us ahead for the first time, 12–10. Right after that, Mike Wagner intercepted a pass and Gerela kicked another field goal to increase our lead to 15–10.

That set the stage for another big play by Swann. It was a 64-yard touchdown pass down the middle that Lynn caught in full stride. He had gotten behind cornerback Mark Washington because Cliff Harris had blitzed from his safety position. I slowed down Harris, but their right tackle Larry Cole came over and hit Bradshaw right in the jaw as he released the ball. Bradshaw kind of looked up to find out if Swann had caught it and then collapsed. He was then escorted to our locker room, finished for the day. Gerela's extra point attempt hit the upright, so we led 21–10.

Then Dallas came right back and drove downfield and scored on a pass from Staubach to Percy Howard. Our defense seemingly had Dallas under control, but I wasn't surprised by anything the Cowboys did to get back in the game. That was only because of my perception of Roger Staubach. I felt he had the talent and ability to make anything happen. He had gotten the Cowboys into the Super Bowl with a "Hail Mary" pass to beat Minnesota, so you could never count him out.

My biggest memory of Super Bowl X was our final offensive series after we had held onto an onside kick at the Dallas 42. Holding just a four-point lead, 21–17, and with less than two minutes left and Bradshaw out of the game, we just wanted to run out the clock. Terry Hanratty, my one-time quarterback at Notre Dame, came in to replace Bradshaw. He handed the ball to Harris twice and it was third-and-10. Then I ran it and it was fourth-and-9. Dallas called its last time-out. Hanratty looked to the sidelines and it was a big surprise that we weren't going to punt. And I'm thinking, what the hell is going on? We've got to kick the ball deep into Dallas's territory. You don't give the ball to Roger Staubach at their 40-yard line. Chuck Noll was scared of our punting because Walden had dropped that earlier snap and nearly had two other punts blocked. He knew Dallas was going to blitz again and didn't want to chance it.

So while Hanratty is talking with Noll, I'm thinking maybe we'll throw it downfield, and even if it is intercepted it would be like a punt. If we're going to run the ball, we've got to give it to Franco. But Hanratty comes back to the huddle and I'm standing next to him and looking at him and saying, "What is it? What is it?" He shook his head but doesn't say anything to me. He says, "All right guys, here it is: 84-Trap, on 2." This was a tackle trap to the right side, in which I carried the football! I couldn't even concentrate on the play because I thought it was ridiculous. Then as we're breaking the huddle, Terry says to me, "Chuck wants you to eat up as much of the clock as possible." That ended any chance of my doing anything. So the ball was snapped, the guard pulls, and I'm underneath him, ball into my guts, boom-bam, 2 yards. If you wanted to eat the clock up, you gave it to Franco, and he'd run all day from sideline to sideline. Not me. Only 5 seconds had elapsed on the clock. We all walked off the field shaking our heads, thinking "What kind of play was that?" It was the stupidest play ever, ever called in history. I didn't look for Chuck on the sideline. It wasn't that I was upset with him. Somehow I felt responsible that we didn't get a first down. I put the onus on myself.

Now I'm on the sideline with the rest of the offense watching Roger, with my heart and stomach in my throat. You knew he could move the ball. And he did. On the first play from the shotgun, he scrambled for a first down to midfield, and on the next play he threw a quick pass to Preston

Pearson for another first down. Because they had no time-outs, Staubach had to throw deep from then on, and fortunately, he didn't connect on his last three passes. The second pass was broken up in the end zone and his final pass was intercepted in the end zone by our safety Glen Edwards, who ran out the clock. It was like, whew, a reprieve! Wow! We got the game! Hey, we're Super Bowl champions; we did it again, back-to-back!

After the game, you certainly wouldn't tease Noll about that call. It was out of mind and everybody was too happy to care. The players wouldn't talk about his decision to run the ball—it was just me. Everybody had a different perspective. I'm sure Lynn Swann wouldn't talk about that play—he'd talk about his big catches and his tremendous Super Bowl performance. It's just that it happened to me, so I never forgot it.

I was beat up after the game and so tired. It had been a hard, physical game in which they blitzed a lot and there had been a lot of tough tackling. We had to fight for everything we got because they were a tough team defensively. Jethro Pugh, Ed Jones, Larry Cole, Harvey Martin, Lee Roy Jordan, Cliff Harris, Charlie Waters—they were all hard tacklers. They weren't dirty players. After the game, Dallas players would come over and congratulate us. No one likes to lose but the players had a mutual respect—I know I felt respect for Dallas.

It was historic that we had won consecutive Super Bowl titles because that had been done only by Green Bay and Miami. It was a distinction that we were proud of as a team. Also, those two wins were very important to me specifically. God, who ever dreamed this would happen to me? I looked at myself: I had been on a state championship team in high school; I had been on a national championship team at Notre Dame. Now in Pittsburgh, I just had another amazing opportunity. I was not a star. I was not in the category of Franco Harris. I was just part of a team and did a job. And I got Super Bowl rings for that. How many guys could say they played and started for the championship Pittsburgh Steelers? How fortunate I was.

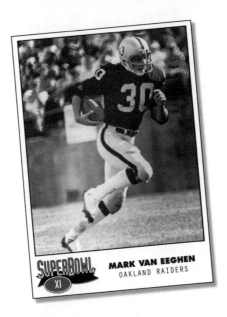

MARK VAN EEGHEN
OAKLAND RAIDERS

SUPER BOWL XI

OAKLAND RAIDERS 32
MINNESOTA VIKINGS 14

MARK VAN EEGHEN

Colgate was hardly the school you went to if your ultimate goal was to play professional football. It was a small, well-regarded liberal arts college in upstate New York with just 2,400 undergraduates. Our football team played a competitive little schedule against a few Ivy League teams and Bucknell, Lehigh, and maybe a couple of bigger schools that we had no chance to beat. There was no winter workout or spring practice; we'd just show up two weeks before the first game and have 10 days of double sessions, play 10 games, and then go back to college life. Football at Colgate was exactly what I wanted it to be. I wasn't on scholarship and regarded it as an extension of my high school football experience in Cranston, Rhode Island.

Although I had played a little bit at fullback as a junior, I was a halfback out of the wishbone. I enjoyed the sport and played hard, but I was kind of lighthearted about it then. But with a few scouts suddenly hanging around your senior year and you hearing enough from enough people, you start to get excited about the possibility of being drafted. Then you decide to go through some testing for the scouts. At one scouting combine, a couple of teams worked me out a little and showed some interest.

I never talked to Oakland, not one word. But later I pieced together that they did a little work behind the scenes. Oddly, Marv Hubbard, the Raiders fullback, had played at Colgate in the sixties, so the Raiders asked Colgate's coach, Neil Wheelwright, to compare how the two of us played for him in our senior years. Neil drew a favorable comparison and that had a lot to do with their interest in me. The big clincher, because of the small arena that I had played in, was being chosen for the East–West Shrine Game. You know what a media circus that is, and all the teams in the NFL and WFL were represented in full force. My exploits on the field that day certainly didn't convince Oakland to take a flyer on me, because I played sparingly, but we were out there for two weeks of practice and, I was told, Al Davis and/or some of his representatives were watching and putting some data together on me.

I remember sitting home on draft day, which was in January in 1974, and the first few rounds went very long. I sat by the phone like you were supposed to do from early morning until late in the afternoon or early evening, when I received a call from John Madden, the Raiders' head coach. It was a very short conversation. "Mark, we've drafted you, third round, congratulations." I fumbled for something to say and that was it.

To play fullback for the Raiders, I had some weight to gain—as a senior I had played at only 192–195—and much to learn very quickly. For instance, blitz blocking wasn't something I had done in a wishbone offense, which rarely passed. That and some other blocking techniques had to be worked on rather hard. Coaches can help you with footwork and put you in the right position to do certain things, but basically I learned the most by observing Marv Hubbard and his backup, Pete Banaszak, as I was told to do. Those were the two guys in front of me who had been through the wars. I saw that what an Oakland Raiders fullback was asked to do at that time had nothing to do with finesse. Raiders fullbacks were collision blockers and your job was to run as hard as you could into defensive players—usually strong backers, middle backers, or defensive ends you were helping out on. It wasn't a fancy style of blocking but more of a "mentality" kind of blocking. You just had to be hard-nosed enough to do it. Hubbard, who weighed about 240, and Banaszak were hard-nosed as hell.

I also learned a great deal from both of those guys' running. Although a running back uses his quickness and his eyes and his instincts, he can be taught certain things as far as reading defenses and understanding what his best opportunities are on given plays. Those guys were great teachers in that regard. They motivated me to play the Raider fullback position the way it had to be played.

In my rookie year, I did a lot of watching and studying. I did a lot of bomb squad coverage and I practiced an awful lot. The first half of the season I was used only on the special teams, but then Marv got hurt. Peter became the starting fullback, but having been coming off the bench, he couldn't carry the whole load at fullback, especially with our halfback Clarence Davis also being hurt. So all of a sudden I'm splitting time with Peter, relieving him just as he had relieved Marv. I had the very good fortune of being able to show what I could do for a handful of games. In my NFL baptism, I played an awful lot and made a good impression. Then Marv came back at the end of the year, and in the playoffs, of course, you put in your proven veteran again. I wasn't disappointed to be going back to my earlier role. I got to experience what it was like to play in the backfield on offense and the coaches got to see what I could do. So my rookie year proved to be a nice training ground.

My real chance came the first game of my second year. We opened the season against the Dolphins and poor Marv blew out both shoulders on one play in the first quarter. So Pete and I finished up that game and we won *Monday Night Football* in Miami, which was a good deal. It was apparent that Marv was down for a long time, and after that game, on our flight to Baltimore, Madden asked Peter's opinion about whether I could replace Marv as the starter. John would make the final decision, but he was asking if Peter would have felt more comfortable starting himself and having me relieve him. Peter basically told John, "Start Mark. Let's keep it going with me coming in."

I got a real quick start in the league due to Marv's sudden injury. I started the next game and I started nearly all the remaining games, with Peter relieving me. I think he came in a little more than he had with Marv because it was just my second year. The Raider fullback position, Peter and I, rushed for about 1,300 yards total. It was an almost even split between us from a yardage standpoint.

It's unlikely I would have played much that second year if Marv hadn't gotten hurt, and my time as the starting fullback ended when he came back with a couple of games to go. After missing the whole season, he didn't play very well. Marv was waived the next training camp and went to Detroit. The decision was made to go with me as the starting fullback in my third year. So 1976, when we went to the Super Bowl, became my first 1,000-yard season. I made it in my last game and became the only Raider other than Marv Hubbard to have reached that milestone. (In 1977 I would have the good fortune to lead the conference in rushing, which really gave me a nice feeling, and I would have my third consecutive and final 1,000-yard season in 1978.)

I became a workhorse in '76, but Peter still got a lot of playing time. He continued to be our short-yardage specialist. That was a very important role that he played on the team. Not that I couldn't do it, but why not bring in somebody fresh? It didn't bother me if I went over the goal line or not; it really didn't. Peter scoring was just as good.

When I was a rookie, John Madden didn't communicate with me very much. That was his way. John was rough on rookies and young guys who hadn't yet earned their spurs, and if he perceived any attitude, he'd be all over you. Until you proved yourself, he had a tendency to ride you pretty hard. It was probably for your own good—I'm sure there was a method to his madness. I'm not saying he was an ogre or unmerciful, because he was polite and kind and all of those things, but until you showed him what you were made of, you couldn't progress to a different level with him and you didn't feel you were part of things. As time went on, I'd say that John was extremely encouraging to me. He liked backs like Marv and Peter, who would put their bodies on the line and get their uniforms all muddy—and I'd do that, too. John was a man of few words in terms of encouragement or motivation, but the words he would say to you would speak volumes. If you got a pat on the back or a "job well done," or if in an offhanded way he complimented you, you knew that you had gotten his attention. I know that he was the best coach that I could have had. He was extremely helpful to this small, back-east school guy who suddenly found himself in the NFL.

John was a tremendous coach, but more than that, he was a tremendous judge who had the ability to read players and determine their different hot buttons. You would think that because we were athletes and getting paid very well that the same effort should be there every practice, but sometimes it wasn't. John expected a certain effort and he expected a certain result, and to get the effort that would produce the result, John had the ability to motivate all kinds of people in different ways. He was a master at that. He earned the complete respect of every player on the team and we would bleed for him. That's what it came down to. We would spill our guts every Sunday for *him* and that's what made winning special. Although we had terrific players and future Hall of Famers up and down our roster, I'm not sure we were the best team in the league top to bottom in those years when we won the most games. He got the most out of us and that's why we won.

We also played for our owner. Al Davis made frequent appearances at training camp, and during the regular season he would be watching most of the practices, especially on Wednesdays and Thursdays—the offensive day and defensive day. He was visible and approachable. In fact, he would approach you—"How are you doing, Mark? How do we look?" I enjoyed him immensely. I know that if you were outside of the Raiders family you looked at him and his organization differently, but if you were on the inside you saw him as a players' owner; you had somebody who would be loyal to you if you busted your butt and tried to "Just Win," as his famous motto went. If you made every effort to be the best Raider you could be and win football games, then you were one of his guys. If you didn't, that was too bad, because you wouldn't be around too long. That's really fair in my mind. Al knew football and that's why we respected him. He didn't run a hamburger franchise or a network. He had come up through the football ranks and knew the game, and because of that you knew there was something different about him.

Even before I came to Oakland, the Raiders had lost several big playoff games that had prevented them from reaching the Super Bowl. Since losing Super Bowl II, Oakland had been knocked out of the playoffs seven times, six times in AFL or AFC championship games by the eventual world champions. It seemed like there was always one thing or another that kept the team from reaching the Super Bowl. There had been Franco Harris's game-ending "Immaculate Reception" that eliminated the Raiders in the 1972 playoffs, and then they lost to Miami in the AFC championship in 1973. Then, in my first two years, the Pittsburgh Steelers beat us in AFC championship games. The first time we lost was on that old iced-down field in Pittsburgh—remember, the sidelines were iced and the tarp was ripped. All the time teams, because of a bad call or unusual circumstances—they're cheated, it's unfair—go into the hopper and never return. But the Raiders didn't feel frustrated or flustered or snakebit. When I came into training camp those first couple of years, I could feel there was a sense of urgency and that anything less than getting back and winning the AFC Championship Game would be an unsuccessful season for the players and coaches. However, we stored that long-range goal in the back of our minds and took each game as one of many on our way back. My hat was off to our coaching staff because that attitude and mentality only came from them.

We had a lot of leaders on our team who motivated guys in different ways. Several motivated me. Marv was gone, but Peter was still there. On the offensive line, at left tackle, was Art Shell, and that guy was a leader. I wrote Art a letter when he entered the Hall of Fame, and the things I told him you usually don't say to people when you're playing with them. He knows now that from afar—the other side of the huddle—that I took great comfort in going into battle with him. Just by the way he prepared himself and handled himself. To me, he was the epitome of focus and professionalism. I just loved Art. To have a player of his stature and ability turn around and say, "Hey, Jeez, great run, Mark, you hit that hole nice, thanks a lot," is all a running back has to hear.

Another player who inspired me to play better was our quarterback, Kenny Stabler. He was my teammate and peer and I loved him and could have a beer or two with him. Yet I was one of many guys on the team who put him a step above the rest of us when we were on the field. He was such a great player and he had a star aura about him. And equally impressive was that he was a professional. If I missed a blitz or someone else missed a pass rush and Kenny got creamed, he would get up, dust himself off, and not say one thing. He'd just get ready for the next play. He knew that we didn't want to let the defense get to him and it was upsetting to us when something like that happened. He didn't see any reason to jump on us. And you know, his silence was worse than if he'd brutally abused us. That made us want to play better for him.

Kenny was a truly marvelous quarterback. All those fourth-quarter comebacks were indicative that in the heat of the battle Kenny was just as cool as you could get. He was just like a gunslinger. Even if we were down, even if we were behind, even if things weren't going too well, there was a confidence that he exhibited in the huddle that we all fed off.

There was no talking in Kenny's huddle, nobody else suggesting plays. There was no bitching and moaning. Art Shell and Gene Upshaw would make sure that we just put our heads down and listened to his next play and moved forward. That's the way it had to be. It was Kenny's huddle and only he talked. He didn't yell, nor was he soft-spoken. He was our leader and our coach on the field.

Another real motivator was Stabler's great veteran receiver Fred Biletnikoff. He was such a great player on the field that it's not surprising that he was also an amazing practice player. He was so disciplined and worked on his skills and routes all the time—before practice a little bit, after practice a little bit. Every time he even played catch, warming up in a circle, he would catch the ball as he would in a game, look it in, and put it away. He was such a good example to us young players because he had been doing it for a while and was as good as you could get, yet was still practicing and working on his skills.

I think that a great strength of our team was that in terms of our camaraderie and guys just hanging together it was very much like it was on a high school football team. We'd all go out together, offensive and defensive guys. Because it wasn't a 9-to-5 job—two days a week it was 9 to 1 and two days a week it was 12 to 5—we had extra time, so guys were getting together for breakfast or playing golf. There were a lot of little traditions: an air-hockey tournament and shuffleboard tournament. I think we all enjoyed each other's company and that we were all different. We were one great group and were not split by either position or color.

It wasn't hard to be a close team, although there were some guys who weren't as disciplined as the rest. There were a couple of guys who almost went out of their way to be wild. Ted Hendricks and John Matuszak come to mind—and I laugh when I think back—and there were some others. You know what I mean? Maybe they did try to match their images.

I guess you could say our defense had a lot of intimidators while our offense exhibited professionalism, but that's pretty much because defense is a different game than offense. An offensive lineman may seem different from a freewheeling, grabbing, clawing defensive lineman, but he can have just as violent a nature. He just has to channel it differently. As a running back, I couldn't get my aggressiveness as charged up as maybe Jack Tatum and Ted Hendricks could on defense.

Just like it was with every other defense in the league, our defense's philosophy was to hit as hard as it possibly could. But beyond that there was an intimidation factor. Whether it was because of our black jerseys or the way we played in a reckless, on-the-edge-of-the-rules way, or the players we had, intimidation most definitely was a factor in the success of our defense. We didn't sit around at meetings planning on intimidating the other team. You just can't say we're going to have a team of intimidators. You're either an intimidator or you aren't an intimidator. The guys on our defense were. Jack Tatum was as tough a player in college as he was in the pros, so there was no change in his game. He brought an intensity and intimidation to our team. John Matuszak came to Oakland in our Super Bowl year already being a physical, intimidating player, and Ted Hendricks had been added to our team the year before because he was like that, too. The defense got its character and personality from players like Tatum, Matuszak, Hendricks, rather than the players changing their style to fit the defense. Jack, who was nicknamed "The Assassin"; Ted, who was "The Mad Stork"; George Atkinson, who was "The Destroyer"; John Matuszak; Otis Sistrunk; and some of the others were responsible for the Raiders becoming known for intimidation.

We had a collection of tremendously talented guys on defense, players you'd remember years down the road. There also was Phil Villapiano, Skip Thomas—"Doctor Death"—Dave Rowe, Monte Johnson, Willie Hall, and the great veteran corner, Willie Brown. When we went to a 3-4 in 1976, Hall was inserted as an inside linebacker and Ted played outside linebacker. They would flop Ted around to both sides of the defense to give him a chance to improvise. Ted was so smart and so tall that he'd always be in the right place to make a hard tackle or, being 6'7", knock down a pass or block a kick. Once we got Matuszak and Hendricks, were we better than we were a few years earlier? I'm not really qualified to answer that. I don't think the defense had ever been the reason we lost a game, certainly not a playoff game. However, I can say that the defense in our Super Bowl year improved as the season went along. I can't say we stepped up just because we brought in some new guys, but the 3-4 defense we switched to, partly to free Hendricks, was very effective.

We opened the season by beating the Super Bowl champion Pittsburgh Steelers and had some other close wins early on before we were clobbered by New England. We didn't lose any more games, and, except for a one-point win at Chicago, the games were basically runaways. Then we went into the playoffs at the top of our game.

Because of the New England embarrassment in Foxboro in September, we knew how good they were when we faced them in the opening game of the playoffs. I would have to say quite honestly that we were confident going into all of our games, but we knew that we were playing our toughest opponent right then. They weren't only talented, they also matched up well against us. The Patriots were riding a crest and had beaten the crap out of us earlier, and we were fortunate to escape with a win, 24–21, on a Stabler keeper with just a few seconds left.

When I spent my last two years in the NFL with New England, they were still talking about their costly penalty in the last minute of the game that gave us a crucial first down. I wasn't on the Pats for a week in 1982 when I sat down with guard John Hannah and had a nice talk about it. What happened was that Sugar Ray Hamilton hit Kenny in the head after he had thrown the ball. It was a late hit, an elbow to the chin. It was a personal foul, but it was more precisely roughing the passer, because a quarterback's head is off-limits. The Patriots' fans, who took a while to get over that—like maybe 10 years—thought the call was so unjust because Kenny's fourth-down pass was errant and the hit hadn't affected the flight of the ball. We get another chance and go in to score and they go home extremely disappointed. Was it a penalty? Yes. Did it affect the outcome of the game? Certainly it did. Should it have been called? I guess so, because it was a penalty, even though it didn't affect the play.

After back-to-back losses to Pittsburgh in AFC title games, we beat them pretty easily, 24–7, in the third meeting, when Franco Harris and Rocky Bleier were both out with injuries. We were at home with our fans, who were so good to us and so supportive, and to be able to celebrate that win with them was just huge. I'd been there only three years, but even so it felt like a big black cloud just blew out of town. We had gotten over the hump and were about to play in the big game, which we always felt we could win if we ever got there. Now was our chance after so many years of disappointment. Finally, Oakland was going to the Super Bowl. It was just such a wonderful feeling: "Now we're there. Now we're there." There was just an other-world kind of excitement.

Super Bowl XI was played in the Rose Bowl in Pasadena. Our opponents were the Minnesota Vikings, another team that had suffered bad fortune in big games over the years. In fact, they had made it to the Super Bowl three times already and had lost all three times. So in this game, either Oakland or Minnesota would end its bad streak and the other team would continue to be thought of as not being able to win the big game. How disappointing would it have been if we had lost? I never thought, "We finally got here, so losing will be awful." I had no foreshadowing of what a loss would mean because we just wouldn't let ourselves think about it. We wanted to play and expected to win.

Super Bowl teams have to be in the city where the game is played a week in advance so the media has access to you. We probably got transplanted in Pasadena Monday morning of Super Bowl Week. There was a media circus. It was just the same as it would be for future Super Bowls. That whole regimentation was in place then and we had to deal with that. The experience was fun only because the coaches and management let it be fun. I think that was the key. Their attitude was, "Hey, you are big guys. You know why we're down here. We're going to practice, but when we're not practicing, you do what you do." We had a normal practice week—there were no extra meetings, no extra practice time, none of that. We could be ourselves. So basically what I remember is practicing, dealing with the media at prescribed times, and then enjoying what the Los Angeles area had to offer until it was time to really focus for the last 36 hours. On Saturday night we had a curfew as all teams do. We may even have had one on Friday.

I didn't think I was nervous even Saturday night. I went to bed and the game still seemed light-years away. But the next morning I was very, very, very nervous and introspective as hell. At the team meal at the hotel, I put this game face on that must have looked so tight. I got on the bus taking us to the Rose Bowl and sat by myself and was staring out the window with that game face on. It must have looked like I had lost my best friend. Jack Tatum came down the aisle and just started laughing at me. He shouted, "What's the matter with you?" He just broke it for me. There was no one more focused and intense than Jack, yet he was able to smile at me and say something that made me laugh at myself and it broke the tension for me. Yes, it was the Super Bowl we were driving to and there would be over 100,000 people watching us, but I now could think that in reality it was just another game and the players had been through it together many times before. So Jack relaxed me some and I knew my nerves would be gone entirely after the first couple of hits.

It was a fairly loose locker room, but I'll qualify that. Saying the importance of what we were about to do didn't affect us would be less than truthful. We knew what we could accomplish that day against the Vikings and had a tremendous amount of focus and confidence, yet the intensity level was up a few notches. We all got ready in our own way. We always had guys who got to the locker room five or six hours before a game, put their uniforms on, and played cards together on their stools. So they did their thing. We had other guys with headphones on listening to music, lying on the floor with their feet up. Fred Biletnikoff would be a nervous wreck smoking and putting Stick'Em all over his hands and uniform. I would be throwing up in the bathroom. I threw up before every game. One time back in Oakland I had that gag reflex and that anxiety that would always play havoc with my guts. It was our routine that before we left the locker room, John would say, "Everybody his own way," and we'd say the Our Father together. That time, he said, "Everybody his own way," and I just blew lunch all over the place. It cracked the place up and from that point forward John would always check: "Hey, is the team ready? Did Mark puke yet? Then we can go."

On our first possession we got a pretty good drive going, but Errol Mann's field-goal attempt struck the left upright. On our next two possessions we played pretty tentatively and ended up punting. Ray Guy, who was the best punter in football, got off one long kick, but the second time he was blocked for the first time in his career. Yours truly takes some responsibility for the blocked punt. My job was to check middle-to-out for guys going after the kick, and I overly checked the middle. I really should have gotten a shoulder or arm on Fred McNeill as he rushed in, but I couldn't get back to him in time, because for some reason I had taken an extra step to the middle. Was that a shock? Oh, my God, you bet it was. When I heard that thud, I can't tell you how sick I felt.

Our punting team came off the field really upset and wondering what the hell just happened. We hadn't scored in the first quarter and now all of a sudden they're at our 2-yard line and we're thinking, "What's wrong with this picture?" But the game turned around in a hurry. On their second play, Phil Villapiano and Dave Rowe slammed into Brent McClanahan before he got back to the line of scrimmage and knocked the ball loose and Willie Hall recovered. I didn't see the fumble, but all of a sudden our offense was heading back out there.

I didn't go back on the field when we were backed up at our goal. Peter did and he had a great block that sprung Davis. It was one of our rare strong-side plays that day: Peter leads at the strong backer; tackle and guard do their thing; Clarence Davis follows Peter right off his block. They popped Davis and he got 35 yards running down the left side. That got us out of bad field position. The slow start wasn't necessarily upsetting, but the blocked punt had been major for all of us, and now so quickly our anxieties were laid to rest with the fumble and the run off the goal line.

Immediately after Davis's run, we started cooking. We went 90 yards on that drive and went up 3–0 early in the second quarter when Mann converted his second field-goal attempt. It was very important to score first. We felt that even if we weren't dominating them, we were playing very well and hadn't had any points to show for it. So to get three on the board was nice.

On our next possession we took the ball downfield with a mix of runs and passes to Dave Casper, Cliff Branch, and Fred Biletnikoff, and then we scored on a short pass to Casper. My roommate had some nice catches and runs in the first half. Not only did Dave catch that pass to put us up 10–0, but in those two scoring drives he caught a couple of short outs and turned them into big gains with guys just bouncing off him. He shredded some people. Dave played a superlative game.

January 9, 1977, at the Rose Bowl in Pasadena, California

Paid Attendance: 103,438

AFC Champion: Oakland Raiders (15–1)
Head Coach: John Madden

NFC Champion: Minnesota Vikings (13–2–1)
Head Coach: Bud Grant

STARTING LINEUPS

OFFENSE			DEFENSE		
Oakland		**Minnesota**	**Oakland**		**Minnesota**
Cliff Branch	WR	Ahmad Rashad	John Matuszak	LE	Carl Eller
Art Shell	LT	Steve Riley		LT	Doug Sutherland
Gene Upshaw	LG	Charles Goodrum	Dave Rowe	MG	
Dave Dalby	C	Mick Tingelhoff		RT	Alan Page
George Buehler	RG	Ed White	Otis Sistrunk	RE	Jim Marshall
John Vella	RT	Ron Yary	Phil Villapiano	LOLB	
Dave Casper	TE	Stu Voigt		LLB	Matt Blair
Fred Biletnikoff	WR	Sammy White	Monte Johnson	LILB	
Ken Stabler	QB	Fran Tarkenton		MLB	Jeff Siemon
Clarence Davis	RB	Brent McClanahan	Willie Hall	RILB	
Mark van Eeghen	RB	Chuck Foreman		RLB	Wally Hilgenberg
			Ted Hendricks	ROLB	
			Skip Thomas	LCB	Nate Wright
			Willie Brown	RCB	Bobby Bryant
			George Atkinson	LS	Jeff Wright
			Jack Tatum	RS	Paul Krause

SUBSTITUTIONS

Oakland: K—Errol Mann. P—Ray Guy. Offense: Receivers—Warren Bankston, Morris Bradshaw, Mike Siani. Lineman: Steve Sylvester. Backs: Pete Banaszak, Carl Garrett, David Humm, Mike Rae (QB), Hubie Ginn, Manfred Moore. Defense: Linebackers—Rodrigo Barnes, Rik Bonness, Floyd Rice. Linemen—Henry Lawrence, Herb McMath, Dan Medlin, Charles Philyaw. Backs—Neal Colzie, Charles Phillips.

Minnesota: K—Fred Cox. P—Neil Clabo. Offense: Receivers—Steve Craig, Bob Grim, Leonard Willis. Lineman—Doug Dumler. Backs—Ron Groce, Sammy Johnson, Robert Miller, Bob Lee (QB). Defense: Linebackers—Amos Martin, Fred McNeill, Roy Winston. Linemen—Mark Mullaney, James White. Backs—Nate Allen, Autry Beamon, Windlan Hall. DNP—Bob Berry, Bart Buetow.

Oakland	0	16	3	13—32
Minnesota	0	0	7	7—14

Oak	FG Mann 24
Oak	Casper 1 pass from Stabler (Mann kick)
Oak	Banaszak 1 run (kick failed)
Oak	FG Mann 40
Minn	S. White 8 pass from Tarkenton (Cox kick)
Oak	Banaszak 2 run (Mann kick)
Oak	Brown 75 interception return (kick failed)
Minn	Voigt 13 pass from Lee (Cox kick)
MVP:	Fred Biletnikoff (Oakland)

Cliff, our biggest deep threat, was a decoy on his long routes because we were trying to establish ball control and Kenny wasn't throwing much downfield. But Cliff caught a few short passes, including a couple on that drive. Of course, Freddy was Freddy. He had been quiet, but then when we needed him on a third down from inside the 10, he made a great catch and did some fancy footwork before going out of bounds to set up a first-and-goal at the 1-yard line. That set up Casper's touchdown.

The passing game started working because Minnesota was having such trouble stopping our running game. Almost all the time we ran to the left. The blocking scheme we came up with for the game was so simple that it had to be boring to play against us. Basically we just used a weak-side running attack. I would lead at the weak backer Wally Hilgenberg, our left tackle Art Shell would block their right end Jim Marshall, our left guard Gene Upshaw would block their right tackle Alan Page—or they'd work in combination—and our center Dave Dalby would take care of their middle linebacker Jeff Siemon. And all game long we ran just two plays for Davis and, in that drive, Carl Garrett. Just two plays. It was just a fullback lead on the weak backer and Davis following him through.

Minnesota's defense had four men on the line and three linebackers and was very predictable. If we put our tight end, Casper, to the right, then they had to honor that because he was so dangerous. So that became their strong side and we'd then go back and run to the left, their weak side. Davis had a great day, going over 135 yards. I got about 70 yards, mostly on runs down the middle and off left tackle. I didn't know that I actually carried the ball more than Clarence, but that's probably because he got all the big gains. I had a feeling going in that my day would consist of a lot of blocking for the halfback. And it worked out real well.

We ran to the left so often, but it's interesting that when we next got down to their goal line, Pete Banaszak scored by running through the right side of our line. Upshaw had his reputation and Art was Art, so it was hard not to think of us as a left-side team, but the guys on the right side of the line were terrific players. George Buehler and John Vella had a tremendous amount of pride and Madden showed his confidence in them by having Peter run to their side for the six points that upped our lead to 16–0.

The biggest play of that drive was a pass to Biletnikoff for 17 yards, again bringing us down to Minnesota's 1. With his man right on top of him, Fred slid feet first right into the end zone to make the catch. We had seen so many highlight-film catches from Fred that it had gotten to the point that such catches didn't faze us too much. Freddy was a one-of-a-kind receiver. He wasn't a big guy and he wasn't a real fast guy, but he certainly was quick and ran such precise routes that it was unbelievable.

All our pieces just kind of fit. The offense was playing well and the defense was shutting out a strong Vikings offense. The defense harassed their star running back Chuck Foreman, with Tatum picking him up across the line, and he didn't have a big game as either a runner or receiver. And Skip Thomas and the safeties took their best receiver, Sammy White, completely out of the game. White didn't make a catch in the entire first half. So Fran Tarkenton didn't have anybody he could go to on the ground or through the air, which obviously makes it tough on a quarterback.

At halftime, we were ahead 16–0, but we wouldn't say the game was over. The Vikings were wobbly but we still had to topple them over. We knew we were dominating them and that all we had to do was push them over the rest of the way. We had to make the kill.

After Mann upped our lead to 19–0, Minnesota finally got on the scoreboard on a touchdown pass from Tarkenton to White at the end of the third quarter. Then they had the makings of another good drive when Willie Hall intercepted Tarkenton. Then we came up with our longest offensive play of the day, a pass from Stabler to Biletnikoff over the middle. I watched Fred catch the short pass and run down the field for nearly 50 yards, and let me tell you, it took him a long time. It was as if rigor mortis was setting in at about their 30-yard line. I tell you, he was humping on that one. He was wide open when he caught the ball but they caught him at the 1. It was the third time in the game he set up a touchdown at the 1, and that is what earned him the MVP award.

John again took me out and sent Peter in for some goal-line plays. John felt that he should say something to me that second time. I didn't think he had to say a thing because all year long Peter was the short-yardage fullback. Would I have liked to have been in there? Sure, but I didn't even question Peter being inserted. But unsolicited, John said, "Mark, I put Peter in because he's been with us a long time and deserves this opportunity. You'll have yours on another day." He went out of his way to tell me that and I thought it was very nice of him. I said, "John, no problem." And it really wasn't a problem, even for a second. I had my share of personal glory with the 1,000-yard year and all of that kind of stuff.

Again, Peter scored by running to the right. It was funny—he didn't know what to do with the ball after he scored those two times, but it was the Super Bowl, so he thought he should do something special. So both times he threw the ball into the stands.

Our final score came on an interception by Willie Brown when he stepped in front of Tarkenton's sideline pass and ran it back 75 yards. It was just great. I've seen the highlight films of that game, and I still hear Bill King's voice in my ears as he described "Old Willie" running for a touchdown—it puts the hair up on my neck every time I hear that. After the career he had, it was very fitting for Willie to make that big play in the biggest win in franchise history.

We had four guys who had played on the Raiders in the Super Bowl II loss to the Packers. Fred Biletnikoff, Pete Banaszak, Gene Upshaw, and Willie Brown had waited a long time to return to the Super Bowl and finally get their victory. It was terrific that they each made major contributions rather than just being spectators. I can't say that I was pulling for them in particular or even thought about their having a second chance. I was just happy for our team and I guess I didn't take time to reflect on all their years of frustration. It was an all-for-one and one-for-all kind of thing.

I don't think Minnesota was terrible. I think our personnel were better and we couldn't have matched up better against them. It was pure and simple: put Shell on Marshall, put me on Hilgenberg, put Upshaw on Page, put Dalby on Siemon, and we're going to win those match-ups. Marshall didn't get a tackle all game. They played intensely, but they weren't able to stop what we did best. They tried and were scratching and clawing, but they just couldn't stop us. It took us a while to get them to the brink of rolling over, but once we did, we felt them collapse. When Willie's interception gave us a 32–7 lead, the bubble burst and everything caved in.

I remember when the game ended. I was standing near Monte Johnson and looking around at the 103,000 people in the Rose Bowl. I thought about the enormity of the game we had just won and understood that this was why we played football. I just had a feeling of well-being that I didn't have too many times. It was just an awesome feeling of accomplishment. I didn't want to leave the field because I was thinking that I was part of a team that is the best in the world. That's an awesome feeling. I had been in other big games and I knew how quickly those feelings leave you, so I lingered on that field for as long as I could, soaking that up.

I finally walked through the tunnel into the locker room. We were all so happy. The team had been knocking on the door for so long and had now won the Super Bowl and had done it in California. There's nothing better than the camaraderie that develops between guys who are dependent on each other for success and their physical well-being—when you achieve a goal together there's nothing better than that. We were many players with different personalities who overcame the long season and years of disappointment, and the feeling at the end of that, as far as sense of accomplishment and pride goes, doesn't have to be spoken. You can just sit there and bathe yourself in it. There was such euphoria all around me and it continued as we celebrated until late at night.

And the next morning it was over. It was over. As I'm sitting in the hotel with my bags, getting ready to go back to Oakland with my wife, I had a solid sense of accomplishment and felt wonderful—but the euphoric feeling can't last that long. It was worth every ounce of blood, sweat, and tears just to have had that feeling for as long as it lasted. The season-long journey to get to the Super Bowl may be more fun than playing in the Super Bowl, but the satisfaction you get from winning the Super Bowl makes any other victory pale by comparison.

Four years later, after we won our second title by defeating Philadelphia in Super Bowl XV, Al Davis said that "was our finest hour." I'm not discounting our victory in Super Bowl XV, but my finest hour took place in Pasadena on January 9, 1977, when we defeated Minnesota. My finest hour as a professional happened that day. My finest memories of professional football happened with John Madden and those Raiders teammates, culminating in that victory in Super Bowl XI.

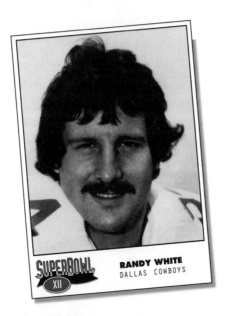

RANDY WHITE
DALLAS COWBOYS

SUPER BOWL XII

DALLAS COWBOYS 27
DENVER BRONCOS 10

RANDY WHITE

The Dallas Cowboys made it to the Super Bowl in 1975, although in many ways it was a year of transition. Bob Lilly, Cornell Green, and several of the offensive stars had retired or gone to other teams and the roster was a mix of veterans and youngsters. I was among the "Dirty Dozen." That's what they called the 12 rookies who made the Cowboys in 1975. Other rookie defensive players included back Randy Hughes and linebackers Thomas Henderson and Bob Breunig, who roomed with me, and Burton Lawless, a rookie offensive guard.

When I broke into the league the Cowboys didn't plan for me to re-place Lilly at right tackle. They had Larry Cole and Bill Gregory on the right side, and Jethro Pugh was still over there at left tackle, so nobody thought about converting me into a tackle at all. I had been a defensive end at Maryland, but the Cowboys already had two great ends, Ed "Too Tall" Jones and Harvey Martin, and they were only a couple of years older than me. Besides, Coach Landry thought I was better suited to play linebacker in the pros. I weighed about 262 when I came to the Cowboys, but he told me to get down to 240 so I could play linebacker. I lost the weight, and in preseason, they put me at middle linebacker.

Lee Roy Jordan was nearing the end of his career and they wanted to groom someone to take his place. Jordan was one of the leaders of the team and was a real help to me. He taught me a lot about football. Also, he was a good friend, and on our days off, I'd hang out with him. Sometimes I'd go with him to his ranch and look at his cows.

That first year, I tried middle linebacker and played backup defensive end. I didn't get in much. I played special teams, short yardage and goal line, and in special situations. I didn't play much in Super Bowl X either, just on special teams and in a few plays at the end of the game, rushing the passer. That was about it. Was the Super Bowl loss to Pittsburgh devastating to the team? Did it inspire us to play harder in Super Bowl XII? To be honest, I don't know what that loss meant. I didn't understand the significance of playing in a Super Bowl and how difficult it was to get to play in one. I was just a rookie and I didn't really know what was going on. All I knew is that I was excited to be able to fulfill the dream I'd had since I was a kid of playing a professional sport. And I knew that all of us rookies were having fun, having a great time, having a blast.

In my second year, I played backup linebacker, but mainly I was on special teams and in special situations. Again, I didn't get much playing time. That year we were upset in the playoffs by the Los Angeles Rams. It would be the only time in my first four seasons that the Cowboys wouldn't play in the Super Bowl.

Lee Roy Jordan retired after the 1976 season, and in my third year I was expected to become the middle linebacker. But they decided that Bob Breunig was more suited for middle linebacker, so they moved me to outside linebacker. The trouble was that in practice I'd be the weak-side linebacker covering our rookie, Tony Dorsett, one-on-one out of the backfield. He had moves and had speed and that experience told me my future wasn't going to be at linebacker. I tried hard and worked hard but I was never comfortable. Then Tom Landry called me into his office and said, "Randy, we're going to move you to defensive tackle." In my first preseason game, I played left tackle. Then they moved me to the right side. At that point I figured, "I'd better make it here because I don't have too many more places I can go."

Once I moved into right tackle, it was pretty much like someone took the handcuffs off and said, "Go!" I picked the position up pretty quickly. Our defensive coach, Ernie Stautner, who had been an All-Pro tackle with Pittsburgh in the 1950s, worked hard with me, teaching me the fundamentals and how to think like a tackle. It was a natural position for me. However, I had lost weight to play linebacker, so my first year at defensive tackle, I had to play at 244–245 pounds. After that I got up to my best playing weight, which ranged from 263 to 267 pounds. That still wouldn't make me as big as tackles were supposed to be, but that's when I felt best. I had natural quickness—which was one of my chief assets—and I lifted weights and kept my strength up.

That was the first year I ever started and I made the Pro Bowl for the first time. I was getting attention and our front foursome—me, Ed, Jethro, and Harvey—was getting attention. I didn't care about publicity and didn't read about us in the papers, but I knew we had a good group that was developing into something special. And it wasn't just us four but the whole unit, which was called the "Doomsday Defense." In fact, the whole team was coming together. The Cowboys had an excellent year, losing only twice. Then we beat Chicago and Minnesota to make it to the Super Bowl against Denver.

By this time the young players had matured and become starters, and though Lee Roy Jordan was gone, we still had quality veteran leaders on defense like Jethro Pugh, Larry Cole, and our safeties, Charlie Waters and Cliff Harris. Jethro Pugh was such a great ballplayer that Larry Cole got overlooked, although the two of them were splitting time at left tackle. Larry was a veteran, too, and had started at defensive end when the Cowboys beat Miami in Super Bowl VI. He was one of the best and most unselfish players I ever had as a teammate. I learned a lot from him. Waters and Harris were great players and solid leaders. Charlie became a coach after he stopped playing, but he thought he was a coach then. He'd be at our defensive meetings and it would be him and Ernie Stautner talking to each other about what we were going to do. Some of the young guys stepped up to become leaders as well, like Bob Breunig, who called our defenses. He was a real intelligent guy and studied hard. He did an outstanding job at middle linebacker, which was a key position in our flex defense.

The most vocal guy on our team was Thomas Henderson, who played outside linebacker. He called himself "Hollywood," and so did some of his buddies and the media. Thomas was a character, but he was also a great football player. He was one of the greatest athletes I'd ever seen. He could run, jump, he could make plays. He was outgoing, which was different than I was. I was kind of quiet and liked to do my job and come sit down and rest and then go out there and do it again; but Thomas liked the attention. He liked to stand in front of the camera and talk to the media and joke around. Most of the time he backed up what he said with his play on the field. He was considered "bad," but if he did what he used to do today, he'd never get noticed. Today, Thomas would be mild.

Roger Staubach was still the guy the offensive players looked up to. And the defensive players regarded him as a good leader as well. Even in my rookie year, he and Lee Roy always were the two guys who stood out when players got together. I didn't get to know Roger too well, but I appreciated when he would come around and pat me on the shoulder and say something like, "Stay ready—we really need a good game out of you today." Hey, he took the time to come over. It meant something to a young player like me to have one of your veterans come over and tell you that. Especially Roger Staubach.

Roger was the best quarterback in the league and he had Drew Pearson and some other great receivers—Preston Pearson, Billy Joe DuPree, Golden Richards—to throw to. He had a strong line and Tony Dorsett and Robert Newhouse in the backfield. Dorsett was our top draft pick out of Pittsburgh and he gained over 1,000 yards as a rookie. He was a breakaway back, and if you gave him an inch, he'd take the whole field. Even on third-and-long, defenses couldn't set up for a pass because Dorsett could pick up that yardage on the ground. He was the player that the coaches thought we needed to become a championship team. He gave the offense a dimension it lacked in the previous few years.

We went to New Orleans for Super Bowl XII. The game was going to be played in the Superdome, which would make it the first Super Bowl ever played indoors. We always had a curfew, but we were allowed to go out to dinner and do some stuff in the French Quarter at night. Some guys were quiet and stayed in the hotel; some guys liked to go out. Everybody prepared for the game in his own way. I suppose some guys would carry film of the Broncos back to their rooms and spend extra time watching at night. I'd done some of that in my time, but during Super Bowl Week, I watched film only at the team meetings during the day. I would study as hard as anybody and then do my mental work. I felt I was ready to go when the game came around.

I didn't prepare for that Super Bowl any differently than I had for any previous game. I was always a big believer in psychocybernetics. Seeing yourself in the situations you're going to be in and seeing yourself being successful and beating the guy across from you. Seeing yourself making the traps, seeing yourself doing everything right. I always felt that if I got the edge on someone I'd be playing against, I'd do it through such mental preparation. You can do that kind of preparation when you're driving home in the car or even when you're sitting and watching television. That's the way I approached every game and the Super Bowl was no different, although there were a lot more distractions and media hype and fanfare. We had veterans on the team, and even most of the young guys had been to a Super Bowl two years before, so we knew it would be like that and couldn't let it distract from the football game. It's hard not to get involved in the Super Bowl Week hoopla to some extent, but you can't get caught up in the celebrating and everything else. When the game's over, you can celebrate as much as anyone else, but during the week you have to stay focused.

I ate the morning of the game. I tried to get something in my stomach. I was pretty uptight but I knew I had to get something down. Actually I liked to eat a bunch the night before a game, because the food you eat the day of the game doesn't really give you any energy—it's what you eat the night before. I used to eat a steak, eat a steak, eat a steak. It wasn't until later in my career that I started eating pasta and felt a whole lot better.

What sticks out in my mind more than the game itself was being in the locker room prior to the game. Everybody was quiet; there was nobody saying nothing. Everybody was just sitting there waiting for Coach Landry. At team meetings, Coach Landry was the main talker. Nobody talked when he was talking. But he never gave any big, big pep talks and didn't prior to this game. Hey, if you need the coach to give you a pep talk to get up and play in the Super Bowl, you're in trouble.

Everybody went out to the field except for us linemen. I remember just sitting there and having a rush. That was a great feeling. You play sports to get yourself into those situations. I don't know—your emotions are going crazy. You're happy, you're mad, you're sad, you're excited, you're scared. You talk about feeling alive. In that locker room before that game— man, I felt alive. Going through the runway and walking out onto the field, I felt like I had wings on and could fly. I don't know if you can get more fired up for one game than another game, but you're playing for the world championship. It's the most important game you're ever going to play in and you have the opportunity to be a world champion.

We had beaten Denver to end the season and then the Bears and Vikings in the playoffs. There wasn't a lot of scoring against us in any of those games. We just played, had some good game plans, and got on a roll.

Our confidence level was way up and we just knew when we walked out there to play in the Super Bowl that we were going to win. Anything can happen, but you're thinking, "Before we come off this field, we're going to win." Of course, I felt that way before every game I ever played, even those we lost. I never walked onto the field thinking, "I don't think we can win today."

It seemed like Denver got most of the tickets to the Super Bowl. Everything in the Superdome seemed to be orange. The Broncos wore orange jerseys and were known as the "Orange Crush," so their fans dressed the part. They had orange clothes, orange hair, orange faces. It was great: Those Bronco fans were really behind their city and their team. But I didn't pay much attention to the crowd. I was there to play a football game and that's what I did.

I had enjoyed Super Bowl Week, but I hadn't liked all the waiting around and all the media attention. Man, I was ready to play the game. I was tired of just preparing to play it. You do a lot of studying, but no matter how much you've prepared yourself mentally, game time comes and you just go out there and play football. You do all your mental work in preparation prior to the game, but once you hit the field you stop thinking. From then on, you are just reacting, changing things as you need to on the field as they come up.

It didn't make any difference to the Cowboys defense if the Broncos ran or passed. Still, before we could start rushing their quarterback, Craig Morton, at will, we knew we had to stop their backs from running. Which we did. When we played our flex defense right, we could stop anybody running the football: Walter Payton and Chuck Foreman in the playoffs, or Otis Armstrong in the Super Bowl.

If all the guys on defense did their jobs the way they were supposed to, it was hard to run on the flex. The flex was a gap-control defense designed for the middle linebacker—Bob Breunig—to make most of the tackles. The philosophy behind it: The defensive players who were at the offense's point of attack—where it was trying to run the play—had to hold their positions. However, if you weren't at the point of attack and you didn't have to contain or cut back, you could go toward the ball. In my spot, I had a lot of freedom. I didn't always play the flex the way it was designed. I played it the best I could within its framework, but a lot of times, especially as I got more experience, I was able to take more calculated risks. If I knew a guy was going to run a play to the other side, I might be quick to pursue; or I might take a chance and take off on a running down when I figured they were going to pass instead. Coach Landry used to get on ya. He'd say, "It's all right to do that once in a while, but you'd better be right a lot more times than you are wrong."

Sometimes I'd be off the line a bit. It depended on which side of the flex I was on. If the flex was to the strong side and I was on the weak side, I'd be up on the ball. If the flex was to my side, I'd be back off the ball. It was just a different position on the line. The interior line played the flex, but the linebackers and cornerbacks, depending on what defense was called, were also involved in stopping the run. They had the responsibility on a cutback or plug. The whole defense worked together. In the flex we were pretty much regimented except if there was a passing situation and we lined up to rush the quarterback. That's when we had a lot of freedom to do what we wanted to do. Then we could play games. I worked with Harvey Martin, or Jethro Pugh at the other tackle, even with Ed. We worked as a unit and would run different stunts that would be effective.

Once you play next to a guy for a while, you can let him know what you'll do with just one word. That's how it was with Harvey and me, although Harvey was a talker. He'd get fired up and into the game. We got along and communicated well. Sometimes we'd get mad at each other and then we'd get glad at each other. It was really enjoyable playing next to him. And we were very successful working together—especially in that Super Bowl. The guy across from me on the line that day was Tom Glassic, their left guard. I think he played at Virginia and he used to re-create battles with miniature soldiers. He was a good player, but he didn't have any more success against me that day than their tackle Andy Maurer had going against Harvey. I don't know what their plan was to stop our defense, but whatever it was, it didn't work real good. We had a pretty good game, both stopping the run and rushing the quarterback.

Craig Morton had become the Broncos' quarterback that year after playing for the New York Giants. He was a veteran who had been the Cowboys' starter until Roger Staubach got the job. Oddly, when the Cowboys traded him to the Giants, they got a first-round draft pick—and that turned out to be me in 1975. (How things could have been different.) Morton was the key to the Broncos' offense. He wasn't mobile, but he had a strong arm, and if we let him sit back and throw the ball, he could be effective and hurt us. So the defense's plan was to put early pressure on him when he dropped back and distract his timing when he was throwing the football.

Harvey and I got into the backfield a lot, and if Morton tried to get away from us by moving to his right to pass, he had Jethro and Ed coming at him. He had to think twice before passing on that side because Too Tall

January 15, 1978, at the Louisiana Superdome in New Orleans

Paid Attendance: 75,804

NFC Champion: Dallas Cowboys (14—2)
Head Coach: Tom Landry

AFC Champion: Denver Broncos (14—2)
Head Coach: Red Miller

STARTING LINEUPS

OFFENSE			DEFENSE		
Dallas		**Denver**	**Dallas**		**Denver**
Butch Johnson	WR	Jack Dolbin	Ed Jones	LE	Barney Chavous
Ralph Neely	LT	Andy Maurer	Jethro Pugh	LT	
Herbert Scott	LG	Tom Glassic		NT	Rubin Carter
John Fitzgerald	C	Mike Montler	Randy White	RT	
Tom Rafferty	RG	Paul Howard	Harvey Martin	RE	Lyle Alzado
Pat Donovan	RT	Claudie Minor		LOLB	Bob Swenson
Billy Joe DuPree	TE	Riley Odoms		LLB	
Drew Pearson	WR	Haven Moses	Tom Henderson	LLB	
Roger Staubach	QB	Craig Morton		LILB	Joe Rizzo
Tony Dorsett	RB	Otis Armstrong	Bob Breunig	MLB	
Robert Newhouse	RB	Jon Keyworth		RILB	Randy Gradishar
			D. D. Lewis	RLB	
				ROLB	Tom Jackson
			Benny Barnes	LCB	Louis Wright
			Aaron Kyle	RCB	Steve Foley
			Charlie Waters	SS	Bill Thompson
			Cliff Harris	FS	Bernard Jackson

SUBSTITUTIONS

Dallas: K—Efren Herrera. P—Danny White. Offense: Receivers—Golden Richards, Tony Hill. Linemen: Burton Lawless, Jim Cooper, Rayfield Wright, Andy Frederick. Backs—White (QB), Preston Pearson, Scott Laidlaw, Larry Brinson, Doug Dennison. Defense: Linebackers—Bruce Huther, Mike Hegman, Guy Brown. Linemen—Dave Stalls, Bill Gregory, Larry Cole. Backs—Randy Hughes, Mel Renfro, Mark Washington. DNP—Glenn Carano, Jay Saldi.

Denver: K—Jim Turner. P—Bucky Dilts. Offense: Receivers—Rick Upchurch, Ron Egloff, John Schultz. Linemen—Bobby Maples, Henry Allison, Glenn Hyde. Backs—Jim Jensen, Lonnie Perrin, Rob Lytle, Norris Weese (QB). Defense: Linebackers—Godwin Turk, Larry Evans, Rob Nairne. Linemen—John Grant, Brison Manor, Paul Smith. Backs—Randy Rich, Randy Poltl. DNP—Craig Penrose.

Dallas	10	3	7	7—27	
Denver	0	0	10	0—10	

Dall	Dorsett 3 run (Herrera kick)
Dall	FG Herrera 35
Dall	FG Herrera 43
Den	FG Turner 47
Dall	Johnson 45 pass from Staubach (Herrera kick)
Den	Lytle 1 run (Turner kick)
Dall	Richards 29 pass from Newhouse (Herrera kick)
Co-MVPs:	Randy White (Dallas) and Harvey Martin (Dallas)

Jones would bat passes down like flies. Ed could make a big difference in that he took away a lot from the offense.

We put so much pressure on Morton that he was intercepted four times in the first half. The first interception came on the Broncos' second possession, when Harvey and I got through to Morton and hit his arm. Randy Hughes got that interception deep in their territory and that led to our first touchdown, on a short run by Tony Dorsett.

The Broncos' first possession had ended when I sacked Morton. I don't remember that play. I don't truly remember many plays that game. It wasn't that I forgot them over time, but I forgot them right after they happened. Which I guess makes me a pretty boring guy to talk about that Super Bowl experience. I tell you something: I was so into that game that it was like a blur to me. I didn't know how much time was left; I didn't know anything. I was focused for that entire game, locked in. I didn't think about anything except the next play. When you're really mentally ready, you don't have time to think about what you're doing or analyze what's happening. The game itself had a lot of fumbles, interceptions, and penalties, but I didn't notice any of that. And I don't know why all that happened. Maybe some of the misplays, especially early in the game, were caused by nerves—everybody was a bit uptight for this game—or, as some people told me, by the fan noise. Because the game was played inside, there was supposedly so much noise that it was hard to hear anything, but since the noise couldn't help me do my job, I really didn't pay attention to it. I didn't find it distracting. I wasn't concerned about the noise; I wasn't concerned about the Orange Crush people; I wasn't concerned about the Dallas Cowboys Cheerleaders. I was barely aware of our offense. When I was on the sideline, I'd glance out there to see what the offense was doing, because I was into the game. But I was probably talking about what we needed to do when we got back on the field, so most of what the offense did was a blur as well. Heck, I was focused only on going out there and doing everything I could to win that football game.

In addition to playing defense, I was still doing blocking and protection when Efren Herrera tried extra points and field goals. I didn't have to take any time off to work on that during Super Bowl Week. I never practiced for that. When the time came for a kick, I just stood out there at the end position and stopped guys from rushing in.

Efren had some missed field-goal attempts in the first half, but he got two over to give us a 13–0 halftime lead. Efren was a good guy. He didn't like that tag kickers get about being apart from the rest of the team. He was one of the guys. The big difference between him and most kickers is that he would make a tackle when he had to. He would run down and cover his kickoffs. He'd hit somebody. In fact, he liked to hit people. Herrera was pretty tough. So he wasn't a typical kicker.

At halftime, we discussed what was working and what we wanted to correct. Of course, it seemed like things were going well, but Coach Landry would always find something that he felt we needed to work on. Maybe we talked about putting a different blitz in or what the Broncos were doing to prevent us from getting to Morton even more. We knew we were doing a good job, but a football game is not 30 minutes long. We had another 30 minutes to play.

Early in the third quarter, Jim Turner kicked a long field goal to give Denver its first points of the game. It didn't upset or worry us. We would have liked to have shut out the Broncos, but they were pros, too. That they scored was no surprise.

We upped our lead to 20–3 soon after that when Staubach made a long pass and Butch Johnson made a super, super circus catch as he crossed the end zone. He was ahead of their backs and dove forward and grabbed the ball with his fingertips and flipped over into the end zone. That was the best catch I ever saw Butch make. Denver complained that he dropped the ball before he crossed the goal line, but he held the ball long enough.

In the third quarter Red Miller took out Morton and brought in Norris Weese. At that time I don't think it would have mattered if they brought in King Kong to play quarterback. After a long punt return by Rick Upchurch, Weese took them the rest of the way for their only touchdown, but we knew it was too late to make any difference. After that, he had just as many problems as Morton. Weese was much more mobile than Morton, but I don't know if he would have given us more trouble if he had started or come in earlier.

Our last score came on a play I do remember. It came after we had recovered a fumble in Denver territory. Robert Newhouse took a hand-off and looked like he was running around the left end, and the defensive backs thought they might have to come up to tackle him. Then Newhouse stopped and threw a bomb up in the air and Golden Richards caught it over his shoulder and went into the end zone. It was a great catch and a great pass—the only pass Robert threw all year. We got six points and I had to go out there with the extra-points team. Herrera kicked the extra point to make the final score 27–10.

Right after the game, Harvey Martin came over to me and said, "Hey, we won the MVP." I didn't remember what I had done. Harvey put his arm around me and people were taking our picture. That Co-MVP thing was nice, but at the time winning the Super Bowl was the great thing. I was excited we won the game. We could have had 10 MVPs that day. Like Randy Hughes, who had that interception and two fumble recoveries. A bunch of guys played great.

Guys talked about getting the money, getting the money. And sure you think about the money, it's nice—back then $18,000 bucks was a pretty good chunk. But heck, I was more excited about getting a Super Bowl ring. It's funny: Today I don't usually wear my ring. If I go somewhere I might, but most of the time I don't.

I still have some contact with Ed, Harvey, and Bob Breunig and I talk to Burton Lawless, who was my roommate for several years. And I'll run into some of the players on that title team at different functions. But I don't have anybody on that team that I really hang around with. Things change, time moves on, guys go their own ways. However, we have a mutual respect and a camaraderie, so that even if we don't see each other for a long time, when we do see each other it's like we were just together.

I look back at getting the chance to play on that team, winning a world championship, getting a Super Bowl ring. There are a lot of great players who never do that in their entire careers. I would play in three Super Bowls in my first four years in the league—Super Bowls X, XII, and XIII— and never get back to another one. I just took it for granted that we'd go back. I played in three more NFC Championship Games after 1978, but we never won one. So to have had the opportunity to play in that Super Bowl in January 1978 and win a world championship was a great, great experience for me. There aren't words to describe the feeling you get from being able to play on a world championship team. It was a great year and a great week and the game itself—what can you say? Hey, that was the highlight of my athletic career right there.

L. C. GREENWOOD
PITTSBURGH STEELERS

SUPER BOWL XIII

PITTSBURGH STEELERS 35
DALLAS COWBOYS 31

L. C. GREENWOOD

When I was drafted by the Pittsburgh Steelers I had never even heard of them. That's the truth. I wasn't a big football fan growing up in Canton, Mississippi, and I wasn't a fan when I played defensive end at Arkansas–Pine Bluff. I wasn't that interested in football other than trying to do the best that I could do at it so that I could maintain my scholarship and get my degree. Because my parents couldn't afford to send me to college, I could go only if I played football. I didn't have any ambitions of playing in the NFL and, besides, I was told I was too thin to play defensive end in the pros because I was 6'6" and weighed only about 215 pounds.

Arkansas–Pine Bluff had only about 3,300 students, but there had been two former players who had made it to the NFL: Bob Brown, a big defensive tackle who was with Green Bay, and Caesar Belser, a defensive back with Kansas City. I don't know if scouts actually came to look at my school play or if they were scouting some of our SWAC Conference opponents like Grambling, Alcorn State, and Jackson State. Maybe when some scouts came to look at some of their great players I happened along and caught their attention.

The Steelers never said they were interested in me, but several NFL scouts were coming around and telling me that I was going to be picked in the first round. Well, you know how much you can count on that. I understand that the Cowboys called my team doctor just before they made their first pick to find out about the knee I had hyperextended at the end of the year. He told them that my knee wasn't strong enough for me to play in the NFL! That's why I slipped down the ladder and wasn't picked until the 10th round. I'm sure that fate had something to do with my going to Pittsburgh and not Dallas. There's no question I went to the right team.

Although some of those scouts said that I would have to be moved to linebacker in the pros, when I arrived at my first Steelers camp in 1969, I was put with the defensive linemen and that's where I stayed. That was also Joe Greene's rookie season. However, while Joe started right away, I didn't. That first year, which was Chuck Noll's first year as head coach, I alternated at left and right defensive end, filling in for the starters Ben McGee and Lloyd Voss. In my second year, when our record improved from 1–13 to 5–9, I split time with them, playing a quarter on one side and a quarter on the other side.

After that year I decided I was better than the other ends and should be starting and making a bigger contribution. My contract had expired and I wouldn't even sign a new one until I found out I was going to start in my third year. I planned on moving elsewhere and would have played out my option. I would have received only a percentage of my salary if I didn't sign a contract, but since I was making only $14,000, I wouldn't have lost much money. But it didn't come to that. After training camp, Dan Radakovich, our new defensive-line coach, told me that the starting job was mine. That was when they finally really noticed me.

At that time, Joe Greene and I were playing on the left side, but what would become the line for the Steel Curtain wasn't in place yet. Dwight White, who became the right defensive end, came to Pittsburgh in 1971, and Ernie Holmes, the right tackle, came along a year later, by which time we had a winning team. That's when we became a defensive line. Our objective wasn't to be known but to be a major part of the program Chuck Noll was building.

Joe was the anchor of the defensive line. Ernie, Dwight, and I realized that Joe was Joe and Joe was going to do what Joe gotta do and we gotta try to do what we had to do. We were just going to go after people from the time the whistle blew until the gun sounded, regardless of the score. We were going to be in everybody's backfield, we didn't care what team we were playing. That was our attitude. And soon we got a reputation for being a defensive force to be reckoned with. When the name Steel Curtain came about for the defense, that was kind of flattering—but it wasn't emphasized that much. It was a long time before we even realized that the working people of Pittsburgh were really into defensive football or would come out and cheer for the Steelers' front four. Not only did our defense get a nickname when we started winning Super Bowls, but the four of us had nicknames of our own. There was "Mean Joe" Greene, "Hollywood Bags" Greenwood, "Mad Dog" White, and "Arrowhead" Holmes—remember Ernie shaved an arrow pattern on his head before we played our first Super Bowl in 1975.

I think initially people thought that the four of us were causing so much trouble simply because we were big bad guys who were good at attacking and beating up people. But we had a defensive scheme. The things we did up front—such as Joe in the hole in a slant position so that his rear end was on the line, and the person on the weak side in a flex position in a three-point stance, and the person on the strong side in what we called a two-gap position—were all designed. All that stuff and more had a purpose. Our job as the front four was specifically to keep the big linemen off our linebackers so they could make the plays. It was all planned; it wasn't a fluke that got good results. I could tell you what every player did in our defensive scheme and why he did it.

When I crossed the white line, my concentration was totally on what I had to do out there on the field. Plus I was hurt most of the time, so I had to keep my head in the game to get the job done. I was listed at 245 pounds but I didn't weigh that much until my twelfth year in the league. My weight fluctuated between 228 and 233. I just couldn't gain any weight. I played on the strong side, so I had to find ways to handle those offensive linemen who weighed 270 to 300 pounds. I couldn't go head-to-head with them on every trip, so I tried to get them tired, frustrated, and confused. I knew what they were going to do because I could read the offensive sets. I knew the flow of the offense and could tell if they were going to pass or run. My strong suit was rushing the quarterback and getting after the running backs. I kept myself in good physical condition so I could run all day. If it was a passing situation and the quarterback was coming to my side, I just kept myself in a position to contain him, so I could force him back to the strength of our defense; if he was running away from me, all I'd need from our other people was to contain him, because most of the time I would catch him from the back. I had more speed than most quarterbacks, so I would often try to lure them into running. I could fake inside and come back outside and catch them from behind.

Joe and I worked together very well, covering each other without having to tell each other. We knew what the other guy was doing and just reacted to that. We also worked real well in combination with linebacker Jack Ham. We played together on the strong side and it was tough because Jack weighed only about 215, I was at 230, and Joe weighed only a little more than that. So we all helped each other make tackles. I'd also help Jack in passing situations by knocking down a lot of balls. As a matter of fact, that became kind of a problem, because Jack would be sitting there waiting for the ball and I'd knock it down before he could intercept. He came back growling, "I was waiting on it. Arrgghh!"

The Steelers had been around for something like 40 years without winning a championship, so winning those first two Super Bowls after the 1974 and 1975 seasons was a tremendous experience. It was a great feeling to be part of that, especially to be a big part of it. The second year we played Dallas at the Orange Bowl. All anybody was saying in Miami was how the Cowboys were going to win Super Bowl X. Nobody on our team listened. We weren't there just so the Cowboys would have a team to beat. We were there to win the Super Bowl again. We were fortunate that it happened that way. Then everybody realized how good we were.

When we lost to Oakland in the 1976 playoffs, both Franco Harris and Rocky Bleier were injured. We had only one healthy running back. That was unfortunate, because before the injuries that was the best football team we ever had. We had some problems at the beginning of that year and lost four of our first five games. But then we won our last nine games. Our defense got five shutouts in those wins and twice gave up only three points. It's unfortunate that we couldn't go through the postseason at full strength because we would have won our third straight Super Bowl.

Despite a 9–5 record in 1977, we didn't feel that our team had already peaked and from then on it was going to be hard to get back to the Super Bowl. It had never been easy, even in the championship yers because we were a young team that didn't have a lot of experience. Only in 1976, when we were experienced and were operating on all cylinders, was it easy, but then we had those injuries at the wrong time. In '77, it was tough again. On every Sunday it was like going out and playing the Super Bowl.

Every team that we played against treated it like that. It's just like when you are the baddest cowboy in the west and everybody is shooting at you. Even in our own division, Cleveland, Houston, and Cincinnati were tough competitors. Maybe we had to take a year off in 1977 so the Cowboys could win. Maybe they sabotaged us somewhere along the way so that we wouldn't win the AFC, and they could win the Super Bowl for a change.

In 1978 we went 14–2, which was our best record. We had a great football team and the only times we lost were when we pretty much beat ourselves. We were real tough. The defense was playing well and our offense was clicking with Franco Harris and Lynn Swann and Terry Bradshaw and John Stallworth and Rocky Bleier. After winning the Central Division, we had easy wins against Denver and Houston in the playoffs. We scored over 30 points in both games and the defense gave up only one touchdown. Still, I wouldn't say we were peaking. I think we played at a steady pace all year. If we played better in the playoffs, it was only because the better the competition, the better we played.

Coach Noll really knew what had to be done on the football field and spent time at practices with not only the offense but also with the defense and special teams as well—trying to do it all—and he'd be screaming and hollering and doing whatever he thought would motivate us. But we'd still just go through the motions and he'd get so upset because it looked like he couldn't light a fire under anybody and make his team look as crisp as he wanted. Then we'd go out and play a great game. I think he was more shocked than anybody on the team that we won a lot of those games, and with such ease. He didn't realize that we played well because we were pretty much motivated by our opponents and by the competitiveness that was present within each and every one of us. We enjoyed playing with each other but we were serious players.

I guess you could say we had some leaders, but guys on our team were pretty intelligent and, as we say, they knew what the deal was when they signed on. They didn't need anybody to come in and give pep talks or motivational speeches. People would say we had a bona fide leader in Joe Greene, and maybe he was because we had guys who would go to him to talk over certain things. But I never really looked at Joe in that way. I mean Joe couldn't motivate me. The only way Joe or anybody else could have motivated me is if they had lined up against that 300-pounder in front of me. But I had to put on the shoulder pads and try not to get my head knocked into the turf and get killed. Joe couldn't do that for me.

Super Bowl XIII between the Steelers and Cowboys was the first rematch in Super Bowl history. We didn't look at the game as the title match for the whole decade. At least I didn't. I've never heard anyone refer to that game like that. Even now I don't feel that way. We just thought that here Dallas comes again, back to the Orange Bowl again, and they think they're going to take it this time because we got away with it the last time. We were up for the challenge. We wanted to get back on the Super Bowl winning track. We had let a couple of years get away—especially in 1976. We thought we had a great chance because we had more weapons and were more experienced than in our earlier Super Bowls. In 1974 and 1975, we didn't have great football teams—we just had great players—but in 1978, we were a great team.

The media really had fun with this game. It was much bigger than Super Bowl X. Both teams got much more exposure and were presented as bitter rivals. There was a lot of coverage of the two teams and our front four had pictures taken, and guys like Terry Bradshaw, Roger Staubach and Hollywood Henderson were on the covers of magazines. Henderson was getting a lot of publicity and there was an emphasis on his nickname. As I said, "Hollywood Bags" was *my* nickname, and I had it before him, so everyone in Pittsburgh was saying he stole my nickname. The two of us still get a kick out of that.

If you'd come into our locker room before the Super Bowl you'd have seen the same activities going on that you'd have seen in the middle of the season. We were loose guys. Chuck would come in sometimes and get so upset because everybody would be doing his own thing. Guys would be playing cards and music would be playing. One activity was a stupid game where everybody'd be in a circle and the guy in the middle would tap whatever he was holding—a little ball or a rolled-up piece of paper—to another player, who'd have to tap it along or be eliminated. There might be 15 guys playing. I'm sure that was going on before the Super Bowl because that was an everyday thing. The first five or six guys who got into the locker room would start it up, before practices or games.

The Cowboys had never beaten us in a Super Bowl, but the media presented them as the defending champions and made them the favorites. It was said that Dallas would come out all fired up and show everyone that they were the champs, but it didn't happen that way. Dallas started out pretty well, but Drew Pearson fumbled on a reverse play that I don't really remember, and we scored first on a pass to Stallworth.

Dallas came back to tie the game, 7–7. There was a third down inside our 40 and we went to one of the third-down blitz packages that we used against all quarterbacks when the offense needed 8 or more yards. We

January 21, 1979, at the Orange Bowl in Miami

Paid Attendance: 79,484

AFC Champion: Pittsburgh Steelers (16–2)
Head Coach: Chuck Noll

NFC Champion: Dallas Cowboys (14–4)
Head Coach: Tom Landry

STARTING LINEUPS

OFFENSE			DEFENSE		
Pittsburgh		**Dallas**	**Pittsburgh**		**Dallas**
John Stallworth	WR	Tony Hill	L. C. Greenwood	LE	Ed Jones
Jon Kolb	LT	Pat Donovan	Joe Greene	LT	Larry Cole
Sam Davis	LG	Herbert Scott	Steve Furness	RT	Randy White
Mike Webster	C	John Fitzgerald	John Banaszak	RE	Harvey Martin
Gerry Mullins	RG	Tom Rafferty	Jack Ham	LLB	Thomas Henderson
Ray Pinney	RT	Rayfield Wright	Jack Lambert	MLB	Bob Breunig
Randy Grossman	TE	Billy Joe DuPree	Loren Toews	RLB	D. D. Lewis
Lynn Swann	WR	Drew Pearson	Ron Johnson	LCB	Benny Barnes
Terry Bradshaw	QB	Roger Staubach	Mel Blount	RCB	Aaron Kyle
Rocky Bleier	RB	Robert Newhouse	Donnie Shell	SS	Charlie Waters
Franco Harris	RB	Tony Dorsett	Mike Wagner	FS	Cliff Harris

SUBSTITUTIONS

Pittsburgh: K—Roy Gerela. P—Craig Colquitt. Offense: Receivers—Theo Bell, Jim Smith, Jim Mandich. Linemen—Larry Brown, Steve Courson, Ted Peterson. Backs—Jack Deloplaine, Rick Moser, Sidney Thornton. Defense: Linebackers—Robin Cole, Dennis Winston. Linemen—Fred Anderson, Tom Beasley, Gary Dunn, Dwight White. Backs—Larry Anderson, Tony Dungy, Ray Oldham. DNP—Bennie Cunningham, Mike Kruczek, Cliff Stoudt.

Dallas: K—Rafael Septien. P—Danny White. Offense: Receivers—Butch Johnson, Robert Steele, Jackie Smith. Linemen—Andy Frederick, Jim Cooper, Burton Lawless, Tom Randall. Backs—Alois Blackwell, Larry Brinson, Scott Laidlaw. Defense: Linebackers—Guy Brown, Mike Hegman, Bruce Huther. Linemen—Larry Bethea, Dave Stalls. Backs—Randy Hughes, Dennis Thurman. DNP—Glenn Carano, Jethro Pugh, Mark Washington.

Pittsburgh	7	14	0	14—35
Dallas	7	7	3	14—31

Pitt	Stallworth 28 pass from Bradshaw (Gerela kick)
Dall	Hill 39 pass from Staubach (Septien kick)
Dall	Hegman 37 fumble recovery return (Septien kick)
Pitt	Stallworth 75 pass from Bradshaw (Gerela kick)
Pitt	Bleier 7 pass from Bradshaw (Gerela kick)
Dall	FG Septien 27
Pitt	Harris 22 run
Pitt	Swann 18 pass from Bradshaw (Gerela kick)
Dall	DuPree 7 pass from Staubach (Septien kick)
Dall	Johnson 4 pass from Staubach (Septien kick)
MVP:	Terry Bradshaw (Pittsburgh)

rushed eight men, which meant their receivers were in man coverage. Roger Staubach just got the throw off and was able to get it to Tony Hill on his left and Hill just outran his man into the end zone. I don't remember the part about Mel Blount covering Drew Pearson so intently that Hill was able to run by him. Or that Blount made an interception late in the half to stop a Cowboy drive.

Mel was just a great athlete. He played man coverage and ran with whatever receiver he had all over the field. He covered Drew Pearson in the Super Bowl. Mel was a big person who could run, and smaller receivers had problems with him because he would just knock them all over the place. Mel was a great competitor and really welcomed the challenge of playing a great team like the Cowboys again. So did other guys, like Jack Lambert, for instance. Jack would always step it up in Super Bowls. He was smart and also could be ferocious. He was an outstanding middle linebacker. Andy Russell was gone from our earlier Super Bowl teams, but Loren Toews had become a starter and we still had Jack Ham, so we were still strong at linebacker.

On the line, Ernie Holmes wasn't with us anymore and Dwight White was alternating with John Banaszak. So Joe and I were now playing mostly with Steve Furness and Banaszak on the right side. They were different kinds of players than Ernie and Dwight. Ernie went 280 to 300 and Steve was about 250 or 260. Ernie was more of an intimidator. I never saw a person stronger than he was. He just beat up on people. Steve tried to be physical but he wasn't big enough to fight with a lot of those guys on the offensive line. Steve had a good game but it was different. Banaszak would fill in for Steve and Dwight. He was a little light to play tackle but did a good job. Teams always tended to run to our right side because they didn't want to run our way. Joe Greene was the best tackler in the league, so naturally they wanted to run away from him. That was the case even when Ernie and Dwight were there and playing as well as they were. Teams didn't want Joe to get into their backfield and mess up everything.

We didn't put any different defenses in against Dallas, although we played Roger differently than we would a quarterback who wasn't so mobile. We knew Roger was a scrambler and that we had to protect the outside. We didn't want him to get out there and have a clear view of his receivers or start running around, so we had to contain. That wasn't so difficult because our defense was pretty much set up for containment. We didn't have to make adjustments. We had what we called "cautious containment." We didn't slow down our pass rush; we just rushed while making sure that he was inside of us instead of outside of us.

Roger and I went back a ways, because on the first play of Super Bowl X, Roger bootlegged and rolled out right to my side and I just went in and sacked him and knocked the ball out of his hand. That play of me and Roger ended up on the cover of *Sports Illustrated*. Roger was a good scrambler, but he wasn't that fast, and I could catch him from behind.

Staubach had a weapon in Tony Dorsett, who had been playing at the University of Pittsburgh when we'd met Dallas in Super Bowl X. I'd hear a lot of reporters say that he wasn't real fast, but I disagree. He hit those holes so fast. He was a little guy going through the hole and he'd get through there. Of course, when you're little you'd better get through there. He had great peripheral vision. If he was going toward or through the hole and saw a hand coming from the side, he could change direction in a heart-beat. Our plan against Dorsett was to just try to hit him as hard as we could. With good, quick backs like Dorsett, Earl Campbell, or O. J. Simpson, we just tried to hit them as hard as we could because we figured they couldn't take that pounding all day. When the ball went to Dorsett, everybody on defense would try to get to him and put a helmet on him. That's the only way you can slow down those kinds of guys. You've got to hit them instead of just dragging them down. They'll know what will hap-pen the next time they carry the ball and won't try to get that extra yard if it means getting knocked out.

Dallas wasn't having much success with their offense, but they did score a second touchdown when Henderson and Mike Hegman stripped the ball from Bradshaw. Their lead didn't last long because we tied the game on a long touchdown pass to John Stallworth. I only knew it was long because I had to go back on the field so quickly. This was the first time that people around the country got to see how good John was and how much he meant to the team. We knew all along what kind of athlete John was. But Lynn was making all those pretty catches—flying for the ball—in Super Bowls, so everybody was putting the emphasis on him. But the guys on the team knew what John could do and how good a football player he was. Everybody knew what we already knew after this Super Bowl.

I didn't see either of Stallworth's touchdown catches or Rocky Bleier's leaping catch in the end zone right before the end of the half. I didn't watch the offense that game. I never watched the offense. After a game, the reporters would ask about the great plays, so that's when I might find out what happened. When I got off the field after each defensive series, I went straight to the bench, where I tried to collect myself and take a deep breath before going back in. I never got into standing on the sidelines and watching our offense or what was going on in the stands. It was the opponent's offense that I thought about, not our offense—it could take care of itself. In 13 years in the NFL I don't think I looked at a whole quarter's worth of what our offense was doing on the football field. In the 1972 playoffs I was standing there on the sidelines looking when Franco Harris made the "Immaculate Reception"—and I still didn't see what was going on. I saw the ball in the air and didn't even know he caught it until I saw him running.

Actually, my biggest memory of the whole Super Bowl was getting a bruised sternum and a painful shoulder injury early on. And I stood up and looked around at the stadium and saw all the people who were cheering and having fun. I said, "Wow!" When I was on the field, few things crossed my mind other than football. It just suddenly hit me that there were over 80,000 people packed into the Orange Bowl and millions and millions of people around the world watching us play. I had never even thought of that until just that moment. This was the middle of the game and I'm hurt like heck, so that kind of brought me into reality. I had been in those two earlier Super Bowls, but that was the first time this kind of thing happened to me. It made it more exciting to be back in the Super Bowl.

We were ahead, 21–14, when we went into the locker room at halftime. The linebackers and defensive backs were off together having a meeting and the linemen were by themselves having a separate meeting. We didn't get involved in what was going to be changed behind us because we were trying to concentrate on what we had to do to plug some holes and stop the plays they were making up front. We worked with our line coach and he went over with us what the Cowboys were doing well and told us how we could adjust. Dallas had scored only seven points on the defense, so I don't think we had to make any major adjustments.

The Cowboys almost tied the game in the third quarter when Staubach threw a third-down pass to Jackie Smith, who was alone in the end zone. I thought Smith caught the ball, but he didn't. He slid and the ball hit him in the chest and fell to the ground. That was a memorable play. It's a shame that a guy with such a great career would have to go through life being remembered most as the guy who dropped that pass. It wasn't as if that pass came at the end of the game. It was only the third quarter, so I couldn't understand how much frustration the Cowboys showed when he dropped it. Everybody on the field and on the sidelines reacted. There were guys on Dallas who later implied that they lost because Smith dropped that pass and they had to settle for a field goal. Who knows what would have happened if he caught the ball. If he had caught the ball, it didn't mean that they were going to win the football game. There was still a lot of time left for us to pull back ahead. Maybe if he'd caught the ball and tied the game it would have only put more pressure on us to play tighter defense—and I think that would have kept them from reaching 31 points.

When we were ahead, 35–17, late in the fourth quarter, after having scored two more touchdowns, our coaches went to our "prevent package," and the Cowboys were able to score twice before the game ended to make the score close. I wasn't used to seeing somebody move the ball downfield so easily against our defense, but I put that all on our defensive coaches because they went with the prevent defense. We'd held Dallas to only a field goal in the whole second half and they hadn't scored an offensive touchdown since the first quarter, and all of a sudden, with a couple of minutes left, our coaches switched our defense. I don't understand that. The coaches' philosophy is that the prevent defense prevents the big plays. But Roger was throwing good and they were getting big plays on almost every play. It made your heart beat a little bit faster.

We weren't surprised at what Staubach could do. We knew what Roger Staubach was capable of before we lined up to begin the game. We'd seen him in Super Bowl X. We knew that he was a great quarterback and could move the ball with consistency and accuracy. And that's what he did. He was on the warpath, but time just ran out on him.

We had a great quarterback of our own in Terry Bradshaw, but I didn't notice that he had a great day. Did he? I knew that he got stripped of the ball, but I didn't know what he did later. I didn't know that he threw four touchdown passes to set a Super Bowl record. Of course, a quarterback probably has done something when the offense scores five touchdowns in a game. But I didn't know how the offense got their touchdowns; I was just glad they got them.

I wasn't watching when the Cowboys' Benny Barnes was called for pass interference deep in Dallas territory when he and Lynn Swann got their feet tangled. And I didn't see Harris then break through the middle for a touchdown to put us up 28–17. Then, after we recovered a fumble on the kickoff, I wasn't watching when Swann scored to put us ahead 35–17. I'm sure it was one of his pretty, leaping catches while running into the end zone, but I didn't even know it was Swann who scored until after the game. I'd find out about those plays later.

Between Staubach's two touchdown passes late in the game, the Cowboys got the ball back when they recovered a fumble on an onside kick. So when they pulled within four points with time almost gone, we knew they were going to try another onside kick. No, I wasn't sitting on the bench then. I was watching the field. This time when they kicked the ball Rocky Bleier was up front and he had good hands and held onto the ball as time ran out. With Roger playing as well as he was, this was the first moment all game when we could feel like champions.

There was a lot of excitement in the locker room after the game, but I wasn't part of the celebration that night. I tried to go to the celebration party, but by the time I found the place, the party was over. I had the bruised sternum and shoulder and didn't know what was going on. Around midnight, my shoulder started hurting more and more. I decided to go back to the hotel because I was going to L.A. the next morning for the Pro Bowl, and by the time I got back there I was in such pain that I couldn't breathe and I couldn't lie in the bed. At that time I was married and my wife thought I was dying—and I felt like I was dying—and she called the doctor. He came and taped up my chest and shoulder and gave me something to help me sleep. I sat in bed with a pillow behind me and pillows on each side and that's how I slept for two hours. Then I got up and flew to L.A. I had treatment for three or four days, practiced one day, and then played in the Pro Bowl.

The Steelers had become the first team to win three Super Bowls and now had the opportunity to win back-to-back titles again. In fact, we assumed we were back on a winning track and would win several more in a row. That didn't happen, but we did win again the next year, beating the Los Angeles Rams. I guess the historic significance of Super Bowl XIII is that it allowed us to move on to win four Super Bowls in that six-year period. But at the time it was just enough to be champions again, and for other teams—and the media and the fans—to realize that we had the talent to keep on winning. Everybody knew that the Pittsburgh Steelers, not the Dallas Cowboys, were the best team in the NFL.

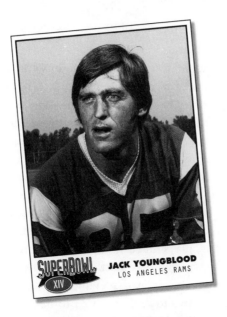

JACK YOUNGBLOOD
LOS ANGELES RAMS

SUPER BOWL XIV

PITTSBURGH STEELERS 31
LOS ANGELES RAMS 19

JACK YOUNGBLOOD

I n all honesty, the Los Angeles Rams were probably a better football team in those years between 1973 and 1978 than we were when we finally made it to the Super Bowl in 1979. We had a more dominating defense and a stronger running game. However, while we won the Western Division those six straight years, for one reason or another—and those reasons were Minnesota or Dallas—we always lost in either the divisional playoff or the NFC Championship Game. It's hard to describe the frustration that players go through after successive years of knowing that you're a pretty good football team and have the majority of pieces in place and then not accomplishing what you projected at each training camp.

After going 12–4 in 1978, we'd been blown out in the NFC title game by Dallas, 28–0. After such a crushing loss, you experience a sense of rejection—you want to go away—but fortunately it's just temporary. At least it was for me. I became even more determined to come back in 1979. After the mourning period, you try to figure out the reasons for your defeat and tell yourself: Let's see if we can eliminate those, get better at what we were good at, and not allow this to happen to us again.

I was a veteran, having joined the Rams as a rookie defensive end in 1971, and from a leadership standpoint, I believed I should stand tall as an individual and say, "If I can do my job a little better, then we'll be better." I wanted the other players to understand that while it's a team game and everybody has to play together and do all the intricate things, it's really how well the individual plays that can make the difference between winning and losing: "Maybe I can play a little bit better on the thirty-first or thirty-eighth play and make a play that changes the course of the game." I'd try to get my teammates to think in those terms.

Of course, our coach Ray Malavasi also motivated the players. Ray had a real bond with the team, especially the defense, because he had been our defensive coordinator for years. Ray was recovering from serious heart problems he'd had the previous year and was briefly hospitalized in the Spring of '79 for hypertension. He was on medication and back on the sidelines. We're thinking, "This tough old bulldog will come back, as he always has. He's come through worse than just quadruple bypass surgery." His health was a concern in the back of our minds, but as players we had our own problems to deal with. For instance, in training camp, I had our right offensive tackle Jackie Slater to look at every day. That's a big enough obstacle in itself. You almost become simplistic: You've got to focus on what you've got to do and try to get better. You understand the bigger picture, but your own perspective is pretty much limited to yourself.

The first part of the '79 season was tremendously discouraging. After losing by wide margins to Dallas, San Diego, and the New York Giants in successive weeks, we were 5–6. We've been pretty good for years and all of a sudden we're losing to teams we should beat and there's a question about whether we'll make it back to the playoffs. Then we started winning some. We felt the team grow and the confidence build. After playing sparingly early in the season, Wendell Tyler was put into the mix and gave us a 1,000-yard breakaway threat; some people who had injuries got back on the field; and when our quarterback Pat Haden went out for the season with a broken finger, Vince Ferragamo stepped in and did a very good job.

There was a lot of pressure on NFL quarterbacks in major market cities and it had always been extremely difficult for Rams quarterbacks. But in his younger days, Vinnie wasn't one to pay much attention to either outside pressure from the media or the expectations of the fans. He was almost insulated from all that stuff by his self-confident, carefree attitude. He was good and had all the tools and loved to play the game and to play pitch-and-catch down the field. And he also had an aura of luck about him. He would do things that were, in football terms, fundamentally unsound, and not only get away with it but make big plays. So we started rallying around this luck: "All right, Vinnie, pull one more rabbit out of the hat. It's time for another one, brother."

This is not to be negative toward any of the many quarterbacks we'd had in the seventies—and maybe this is unfair—but in my opinion the key ingredient we were missing in those years was a dominant quarterback who could take us over the hump and help us win the big games. Vinnie wasn't dominating, but with him at quarterback we finished the season strong to take our record seventh straight division title and finally won our two playoff games to make it to the Super Bowl.

The offense began scoring a lot of points late in the season. Our defense played somewhat better and really stepped up in our first playoff game, when we beat Dallas, 21–19. By then, we had a lot of confidence in our defensive schemes. Ray believed that we had the personnel and the ability to take away the strong points of all the offenses we would face and make big plays. The guys on defense believed we could go out and do enough for us to win as long as the offense produced just a few points. We knew we had to be extremely efficient and couldn't make glaring mistakes that would allow Dallas to get ahead by 14–17 points because we couldn't come back from that. However, our offense could come back from being 5 points down in the fourth quarter. We won when Vinnie hit Billy Waddy with a 50-yard touchdown pass across the middle. Then our defense shut down Dallas for the rest of the game.

The Dallas game confirmed what we already knew, that we were a pretty good football team despite our 9–7 regular season record. When we found out we would play Tampa Bay in the NFC Championship Game, we knew we could shut them out, and we did, 9–0. That was no surprise considering the confidence we had in ourselves by that point.

Finally, we were going to the Super Bowl. That was a wonderful realization, of course, and having been disappointed for so many years, I was thrilled. But in truth, I couldn't personally savor the win over Tampa Bay because I was playing with a broken fibula in my left leg and it was hindering my play. I had broken it in the second quarter of the Dallas game.

Going into the Super Bowl to play the Pittsburgh Steelers, I was probably only capable of playing 60 percent of how Jack Youngblood was supposed to play. When I look back over my 14-year career I see a lot of things I'd have changed, but my only true regret is that when I finally had the opportunity to play in the game I always wanted to play in, I was impaired to the point where I couldn't perform up to my capabilities.

Between the NFC title game and the Super Bowl, I just tried to heal as much as possible. That didn't mean I didn't practice with the defense. There was no question that I would play and try to do my part. We defensive guys were very, very close. Me and Jim, Larry Brooks—who along with my roommate, center Rich Saul, was probably my best friend on the team—Mike Fanning, Cody Jones, Fred Dryer, Jack "Hacksaw" Reynolds . . . Freddie and Hacksaw were definitely characters. They each had their own rules. Guys like our safeties, Dave Elmendorf and Nolan Cromwell, were also characters and super individuals. We had a lot of class guys on our defense and had a lot of good times together off the field—socializing, playing cards—as well as wars on it. We had another war to fight.

In all my years with the Rams, we'd always played in the Los Angeles Coliseum. So I would play in the Rose Bowl in nearby Pasadena for the first time in the Super Bowl. It wasn't an opportunity I was necessarily happy about. I'd gone to different Super Bowls as an observer and I'd been to Miami and New Orleans and all the other places, and then the year I finally get to go as a player, I don't get to go anyplace. As a player, I wouldn't have the chance to go and have fun and experience the extravaganza that the Super Bowl had become. You gotta stay home. How much fun is that? That's what most of us were thinking.

From a logistical standpoint, it was marvelous for us to have the Super Bowl at home because we didn't have to travel and be away for 10 days. But the other thing about being at home is that entire families come in for a visit. I probably had 35 to 40 people there, so I was busy rounding up tickets for about $50 apiece. Everybody in the world showed up at your door. It helped that the players checked into some hotel in Orange County so we could kind of stay away from all the hoopla surrounding the game and all those other distractions.

Going to the Super Bowl was the greatest opportunity we ever had, so we wanted to make the most of it. We were a veteran team and went about trying to make it business as usual. When we were able to get away from those things that weren't normally part of our pregame schedule—like the media crunch—we were able to focus on what we had to do against Pittsburgh. Our coaches worked real hard to make sure that happened.

The Rams were more used to a large media presence than most teams. My own experiences with the local media during the seventies hadn't been bad. The L.A. media was tough and at times had been very hard on the team, the head coaches, and some of the players, but they were always kind toward me. They had always been much warmer toward the defense than the offense. I'll say that they didn't miss much and would point to the bad things we were doing as well as the good things. At least we knew what to expect from the media.

We also knew about the local fans who would be attending the Super Bowl. You've got to understand that L.A. is a demanding market and is not like anywhere else. The fans expect you to come to the ballpark and entertain them, and you'd better win while you're doing that. If you don't both entertain and win, then they let you know you haven't met their expectations. Our attitude going into the Super Bowl was that you couldn't be upset with fans for not having been totally supportive because it was a waste of our energy and thought process. The true fans were going to be with us, the occasional fan would be there if we played well and turn away from us if we played badly, and the idiots who wanted us to play poorly would initiate all the noise from everyone else.

On Saturday they moved us to a new Hyatt Regency right in downtown Los Angeles. I had no trouble sleeping. When we got to the Rose Bowl the next day, we discovered that there were more things going on than usual in the locker room. The TV cameras were already set up and there were more lights and all kinds of little things that were different that you had to acknowledge. Then you decided to stay away from here or there and do this instead of that, and that changed your routine. Everybody had his own way of getting ready. I had to deal with my leg. We had to decide whether we'd try a different type of tape job—all that stuff. My leg was taped and we had built ourselves a special stirrup-like brace that was supposed to keep the fibula from moving more than it normally did. I wasn't taking any shots or painkillers—there wasn't any way that was going to take away a broken leg.

There was a tremendous amount of intensity. I remember talking to different guys about the fact that the Rams and Steelers were the only two football teams still playing. How there had been 28 of us, then 4 of us, and now the 2 of us. That was special in itself. We'd survived the battles and now the final confrontation was Armageddon, so to speak.

It was said that the images of the Rams and the Steelers were as different as any two teams to play in the Super Bowl. We had to constantly fight against the "Hollywood" image with the glitz and glamor and being in the limelight all the time. We had to constantly remind people of how tough we were, whereas the Pittsburgh players inherited that blue-collar, work-ethic image. They were big and burly and wore those black jerseys. They didn't have to worry about being called glitzy because their reputation for toughness preceded them. In the previous five years, they had won all three Super Bowls they had played in.

But we had beaten the Steelers those few times we played in past seasons, so we realized we weren't overmatched by those guys, especially from the defensive standpoint. The things the defense would try to do against the Steelers were the things we did well: Play tough against the run; don't let them control the ball; match up well and go after the quarterback. That meant we wanted to eliminate the Franco Harris and Rocky Bleier factor and then put some pressure on Terry Bradshaw, and not let him scramble around and make big plays like he had been doing for years.

The Steelers came out and did some nice things and were able to drive downfield on their first two possessions. They came up with 10 points on a field goal by Matt Bahr and a short touchdown run by Franco Harris at the beginning of the second quarter. I do remember that we played the Steelers tough in the red zone and made them earn that touchdown. After we held them twice, Harris scored on a third-down sweep, on one of those plays where they just executed better than we did.

Chuck Noll had put some wrinkles into his offense and kept us off balance a little bit. We didn't stop them then, but after we saw something they did for the first time we were able to pretty much neutralize that play. Ray Malavasi was super at making adjustments on the move. Ray and Bud Carson, both. Bud, our defensive coordinator, was calling the plays for Ray, and he and his assistant Dan Radakovich knew that Steelers team because they'd both been part of that organization. Those guys were all great at figuring out what was happening to us on the field and making quick changes that worked.

Meanwhile, we had gotten on the scoreboard ourselves. On our second possession, Wendell Tyler got a long drive started with a 39-yard run to the left sideline. That was the biggest run against the Steelers all season. The coaches felt that if we could get a body on Joe Greene, L. C. Greenwood, and the others, then Wendell had enough talent to get through that initial line of defenders and make things happen in the secondary. Wendell

January 20, 1980, at the Rose Bowl in Pasadena, California

Paid Attendance: 103,985

NFC Champion: Los Angeles Rams (11–7)
Head Coach: Ray Malavasi

AFC Champion: Pittsburgh Steelers (14–4)
Head Coach: Chuck Noll

STARTING LINEUPS

OFFENSE			DEFENSE		
Los Angeles		**Pittsburgh**	**Los Angeles**		**Pittsburgh**
Billy Waddy	WR	John Stallworth	Jack Youngblood	LE	L. C. Greenwood
Doug France	LT	Jon Kolb	Mike Fanning	LT	Joe Greene
Kent Hill	LG	Sam Davis	Larry Brooks	RT	Gary Dunn
Rich Saul	C	Mike Webster	Fred Dryer	RE	John Banaszak
Dennis Harrah	RG	Gerry Mullins	Jim Youngblood	LLB	Dennis Winston
Jackie Slater	RT	Larry Brown	Jack Reynolds	MLB	Jack Lambert
Terry Nelson	TE	Bennie Cunningham	Bob Brudzinski	RLB	Robin Cole
Preston Dennard	WR	Lynn Swann	Pat Thomas	LCB	Ron Johnson
Vince Ferragamo	QB	Terry Bradshaw	Rod Perry	RCB	Mel Blount
Wendell Tyler	RB	Franco Harris	Dave Elmendorf	SS	Donnie Shell
Cullen Bryant	RB	Rocky Bleier	Nolan Cromwell	FS	J. T. Thomas

SUBSTITUTIONS

Los Angeles: K—Frank Corral. P—Ken Clark. Offense: Receivers—Charle Young, Ron Smith, Drew Hill. Linemen—Dan Ryczek, Bill Bain, Gordon Gravelle. Backs—Eddie Hill, Lawrence McCutcheon, Jim Jodat. Defense: Linebackers—Joe Harris, George Andrews, Greg Westbrooks. Linemen—Jerry Wilkinson, Reggie Doss. Backs—Jackie Wallace, Eddie Brown, Dwayne O'Steen, Ivory Sully. DNP—Jeff Rutledge, Bob Lee, Ken Ellis.

Pittsburgh: K—Matt Bahr. P—Craig Colquitt. Offense: Receivers—Theo Bell, Randy Grossman, Jim Smith. Linemen—Thom Dornbrook, Ted Peterson, Steve Courson. Backs—Greg Hawthorne, Anthony Anderson, Sidney Thornton, Rick Moser. Defense: Linebackers—Tom Graves, Loren Toews, Zack Valentine. Linemen—Steve Furness, Tom Beasley, Dwight White. Backs—Larry Anderson, Dwayne Woodruff. DNP—Mike Kruczek, Cliff Stoudt, Jack Ham.

Los Angeles	7	6	6	0—19
Pittsburgh	3	7	7	14—31

Pitt	FG Bahr 41
LA	Bryant 1 run (Corral kick)
Pitt	Harris 1 run (Bahr kick)
LA	FG Corral 31
LA	FG Corral 45
Pitt	Swann 47 pass from Bradshaw (Bahr kick)
LA	Smith 24 pass from McCutcheon (kick failed)
Pitt	Stallworth 73 pass from Bradshaw (Bahr kick)
Pitt	Harris 1 run (Bahr kick)
MVP:	Terry Bradshaw (Pittsburgh)

and Lawrence McCutcheon had several good runs on that drive and brought us down to the Steelers' 1-yard line. Then Cullen Bryant went over for the touchdown that gave us our first lead, 7–3. Bryant was our big, bruising, power fullback and the guy we usually gave the ball to in those short-yardage situations. He also played a big role in protecting Vince. You knew the Steelers were going to come with some blitzes, so you wanted to have a big blocking back in there.

After Harris's touchdown put them back ahead 10–7, the Rams came back again. Our offense drove downfield and we tied the game on a field goal by Frank Corral. After an interception, we got another, longer field goal from Corral to give us a 13–10 lead. It certainly gives a lift to the defensive team when the guys watch the offense drive the ball down the field and execute well. We didn't just have to play within our responsibilities but felt free to go make something *different* happen.

Ferragamo was having a very good half in what was only his eighth game as a starter. He wasn't bothered by the magnitude of the game and wasn't making mistakes. Vinnie had a strong arm, but in the first half he didn't get the chance to throw long to our wide receivers, Preston Dennard (who led our team in receptions) and Billy Waddy. They were being well covered by Pittsburgh's corners, Mel Blount, who was very, very smart, and Ron Johnson. Waddy was as much speed as we had but he wasn't world-class speed. Still, he was a good receiver and had played well at times during the season and playoffs, and we felt he would get away at some point and make a big play. Both Waddy and Dennard would make some big catches in the second half.

Malavasi wasn't at all afraid to let Vinnie pass a lot or go deep, but the plan was to not have him be forced by the defense to abandon the run. Ray wanted us to be able to choose the times we'd pass and where we'd throw rather than having them dictate how we ran our offense. I thought we were mixing it up pretty well with passes and runs in the first half. We were doing almost the same thing Pittsburgh wanted to do. We wanted to run the football with Tyler, Bryant, and McCutcheon and try to control it, and once we had them back on their heels, we were going to throw.

Our defense knew that Chuck Noll also wanted to run the football as much as possible and play keep-away. He also wanted Bradshaw to occasionally throw the ball deep, so we had to constantly change our coverages and keep them from making big plays over our heads to Lynn Swann and John Stallworth. Essentially we wanted to stop the run and force them into situations they didn't want to be in. Then to defend against the pass, we used some special nickel coverages and even went to six backs at times.

I think we were holding our own on the line of scrimmage. All of the linemen were playing exceptionally. Of course, the media had tried to build up a rivalry between the front fours of the two teams' defenses. The Steelers had that "Steel Curtain" mystique. They had accomplished great things and earned their reputations and we had a lot of respect for them, but it was respect and not awe. We felt we were just as good as they were. We certainly felt that as the game went on. Our guys could do pretty good things to their offensive line.

I was trying to be inspirational if nothing else. I was trying to play up to Jack Youngblood's expectations and be the type of player he had been before the injury. I didn't change my style to rush less and contain more. Absolutely not. My job from the left side was to get into Terry Bradshaw's face. He was a big right-handed quarterback and was going to throw it downfield to either Swann or Stallworth, so I had to get to him as fast as possible. I don't think they were trying to take advantage of my condition. They did keep a tight end over there quite a few times, which limits what a defensive end can do. If they'd let me be on the weak side of a set, it would have helped me get into the backfield quicker. Larry Brown, their right tackle, was the guy blocking me. What kind of guy was he? He was a monster. Larry was an athletic offensive lineman, having been converted from tight end. He'd gotten into that whole Pittsburgh regimen of lifting weights and getting as big and strong as possible. So it was no fun playing against him. He was a tremendous competitor.

On both sides of the ball and on special teams it was a very physical game. Anytime you played the Pittsburgh Steelers, it wasn't going to be a finesse game. You weren't going to fool them with razzle-dazzle because they were too intelligent a football team and too good a group of athletes. And you gotta remember who was coaching over there—they were so well coached by Chuck Noll and his assistants. So against Pittsburgh, you had to play on a physical level and beat them one-on-one by doing things better than they did them.

All along you're seeing yourself playing, but it's your team as well that you're watching. The sense was that we could play with these boys, although they had come in with the big rep and we had stubbed our toe many times—we had lost seven games, the most ever by a Super Bowl team. There were questions: Can you survive? Can you do what you think you can do or are you just going to be outclassed? As the game goes along, play for play and drive for drive, and momentum versus momentum, are you going to fold or are you going to rise to the occasion?

As the half drew to a close with us ahead 13–10, I definitely didn't sense that the Steelers were scared they were going to lose, as Jack Lambert might have said later. I sensed that they realized that we were equal to the task at hand and that they had a legitimate game on their hands. It wasn't going to be a waltz and they had to earn what they got.

In the locker room I added a little more tape to my leg. There was nothing else to do. You just bite the bullet harder and hold on.

I had increased confidence in our team, as did the rest of the players and the coaches. We were ahead of the defending champions and that in itself was certainly encouraging. We were happy and excited. Our attitude was: "We can do this. We're the little train that can."

They were notorious for making big plays, and as it turned out, we outplayed them for the whole game, but they made the bigger plays, especially in the second half. That's how I saw it. They went to athletic receivers and made plays in which—and I'm not exaggerating—our defensive backs were literally inches away from making the same plays. For years, their big plays were usually on balls thrown deep downfield to Swann or Stallworth, who could catch the ball no matter how many defenders were going for the ball. The Steelers would have three of those big completions to those guys in the second half.

The first big pass play came on their first possession of the third quarter. It was a 47-yard touchdown that Swann caught at about the 2 while running between two of our backs, Pat Thomas and Nolan Cromwell. Swann leapt into the air and pulled down the ball, which was just slightly out of the reach of Cromwell. Nolan was also in the air but he barely mistimed his jump. Nolan makes that play 9 out of 10 times but, of course, this time he didn't deflect the ball and Swann makes the spectacular catch. I was disappointed because we had a dog on and Reynolds was coming after Bradshaw. But Terry stood in there and didn't flinch at the heat and delivered the ball perfectly 45 yards downfield. That's why I was shaking my head coming off the field. We were so close to Bradshaw but he still made the play.

Again we came back aggressively. Vinnie hit Waddy on a 50-yard pass, and on the next play, McCutcheon threw a halfback pass to Ron Smith for a touchdown. The offense practiced that pass a long time. There again, from an offensive standpoint, we had the assistance of former Steelers coaches who knew what the Steelers were going to do in certain situations.

We knew they'd overreact to a potential sweep and move up their backs and be vulnerable to a pass over their heads, so we put that play into our game plan. Of course, to actually call a play like that in an important situation is a whole different deal than just practicing it. But if you get into a ball game like this one, you can't play close to the vest. You've got to step out and take some risks, as the Steelers did. Ray was willing to call those types of plays.

We were up, 19–17, but then Corral missed the extra point. That meant they would go ahead rather than just tie us with a field goal. That was one of those deals where you don't want to make too much out of one particular play, but certainly that miss tainted the excitement of scoring a touchdown. It was a bucket of water on a fire of coals.

On their next possession, Cromwell almost made a big, big interception. Oh, gosh . . . Oooh, gosh . . . I still hate to think about it. Pittsburgh had the ball in its own territory, coming out, and Bradshaw threw the ball right behind me. We had called a play where Nolan changed his look and wasn't being the free safety he normally was. He had a "sink" situation and he sank right into their pattern, and Bradshaw threw the ball and hit him dead on between the 2 and the 1 on his jersey. Nolan Cromwell was the best athlete I ever played with in 14 years. Nolan Cromwell would make that interception 100 times out of 100 chances. But he didn't catch the ball. He had nobody in front of him and that would have given us a 9-point lead. Believe me, Nolan still sees that one in his dreams.

We went into the fourth quarter still ahead, 19–17. I'm not feeling proud or impressed. I'm thinking, "Here we are on the verge of winning the Super Bowl. Let's do what we're doing just a little bit better for the final 15 minutes." I was trying to encourage the team to keep up our good play and not give them something that could break our back.

Which is what happened . . . right away. On their first possession they had a third down on their own 27 when Bradshaw hit Stallworth with a bomb for a touchdown. There was a mixup in the coverage and our extra back Eddie Brown broke in and let Stallworth go past him down the middle. Still Rod Perry was on John's heels and went up to make the play and once again the ball was literally within an inch of his hand, and John, in Stallworth fashion, went up and made the great catch and scored on a 73-yard play. The players weren't angry at Brown—mistakes on reads and those kinds of things are going to happen. And I didn't see it so much as Eddie making a bad play as John Stallworth making a hell of a play—he was covered by Perry. You just hope that your team can recover.

We were now behind, 24–19, but later in the period Ferragamo again drove us downfield with some accurate passes to Dennard and Waddy. I'm watching as we get into Steelers' territory and I'm thinking we can regain the lead still another time. However, Ferragamo was intercepted by Jack Lambert over the middle at about the 15 for his only turnover. Turning the ball over in that situation, when we seemed to be overcoming what had happened on the Stallworth touchdown was a double back-breaker. Them catching that pass instead of us catching it was going to be tough to overcome. When you have the opportunity to make things happen and you don't, and they do, those are big hills to climb.

Immediately after that, Bradshaw hit Stallworth with another long pass down the middle. John made another amazing catch, in full stride, between two defenders, and got 45 yards on the play. It wasn't as if we didn't know Stallworth was capable of catching the ball down the middle because he'd done it many times in the past. He just beat us on those two plays with great catches. The difference was that John was 6'3" and our cornerback Rod Perry was 5'9". Our defense wasn't surprised by anything Stallworth did, but we were surprised that they threw at all. It was a great call on their part. They had a good running game with Harris and Bleier—although we had been playing them pretty tough all game—but instead of sitting on their lead they were aggressive again, as champions usually are. Champions go for the killer blow, the knockout punch.

They reached the 1-yard line on a disputed pass interference call in the end zone, and again they capitalized. The pass interference was a big play, although if they had ended up just getting a field goal for an eight-point lead, we still would have had to score twice to beat them. The hope was that they would miss the kick and their lead would remain only five points. But the official threw the flag, they got the ball at our goal line, and Harris ran for his second touchdown. That whole drive was painful for us because we felt the game slipping away and just couldn't stop it. That's when I really felt frustrated by my leg injury. It had deprived me of my quickness and ability to run with the explosiveness I usually had.

The Steelers won Super Bowl XIV, 31–19. In the highlight film, you can see me shaking hands and talking with Jack Lambert on the field after the game ended. I was trying to be as respectful as possible in a very disappointing situation. It was part of the game to congratulate the champions. I was friends with Jack and I loved to play against competitors like him in situations where you have to play your best. He had played a terrific game and his interception had helped determine the outcome, which gave the Steelers their fourth Super Bowl victory of the seventies.

It was a thrill to have been part of sports history—Super Bowls, more than any regular-season games or playoff games, are part of sports history. The way that sports history works is that all the great games that the Rams played over the years have been stored away, while that is the one game that is still out there for people to see. So I'm glad we didn't lose 31–0, and there would have been a whole different, much worse storyline. Football fans will always know that the Steelers beat a very good team in the '79 Rams. There have been so many blowouts in Super Bowl history that only a few losing teams have earned similar respect for their effort.

Some of the broadcasters that day were saying how the Rams had achieved a "dignity in defeat that they hadn't known before." I know there had been nothing dignified about our playoff defeats to Dallas and Minnesota in previous years. I'm not sure how dignifying losing is, even to the world champion Pittsburgh Steelers. But I know our effort was dignified and showed that we could play any team, anytime, anywhere.

In our society, you're measured to a certain degree, right or wrong, by whether you win or lose. And there's only one winner every year in the National Football League. Unfortunately, that's how we measure success, but it's also why we play—we want to be the one winner. Before the game, Ray Malavasi was saying to the press that for the team to reach the Super Bowl and not win was worse than not getting there at all. What he was saying was that there is more to being in a championship game than just participating. We weren't there just to play.

The first part of your goal is to get to the Super Bowl and take your opportunity. That in itself is something I'm very happy to have done. I guess if you had to put a number on it from 1 to 10, with 10 being the best, just getting there and participating was a 9. There's no question I'm glad I played in that game despite our losing, and in terms of my career, that really was a momentous day. However, that said, your second goal—which is the absolute goal—is to win the Super Bowl and be able to savor that victory. I know *that* would have been a 10. Ray Malavasi was right: It is somewhat devaluing to get to a championship game and not win it. It's not good enough just to get there.

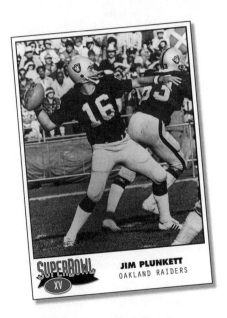

JIM PLUNKETT
OAKLAND RAIDERS

SUPERBOWL
XV

SUPER BOWL XV

OAKLAND RAIDERS 27
PHILADELPHIA EAGLES 10

JIM PLUNKETT

I came to the Oakland Raiders in 1978, after five years in New England and two years in San Francisco. I had just been let go by the Niners and I was at pretty much the depths of my career—my one-time career. It was really hard to take and I wasn't full of optimism or enthusiasm. Some other clubs besides the Raiders contacted my agent and that made me feel a little better. Since I was back in the Bay Area, I thought I would hook on with the Raiders rather than packing my bags and going where it was cold, back east or to the Midwest.

Al Davis signed me, but it was John Madden, the Raiders coach, who sat me down and talked to me. He said, "Every other place you've been, you've had to come in and be the savior. Here we have an established quarterback, so you've just got to learn the system and watch and listen and be prepared when your time comes." Kenny Stabler was the Raiders quarterback, and he was an All-Pro, so they wanted me to sit back and relax and get away from the pressure for a while. I needed some time to resurrect myself, so to speak, and get away from the physical and mental beatings I'd taken over the previous seven years.

After not playing a down in 1978, I came back to training camp in 1979. I felt great, but naturally I had some doubts about my skills. After having been the league's first draft pick and Rookie of the Year with the Patriots, I had been traded by them just four years later and then had been waived by San Francisco, and then had not played for an entire season. So sure, I had to wonder, "Maybe I've lost what I once had." But in 1979 it began to come back. I was throwing the ball as well as ever and felt that I was ready to go. But I wasn't given the opportunity. I could have big games in pre-season and it didn't matter one bit. Tom Flores was now the Raiders' coach but Stabler was still the quarterback.

In 1980, they made a big exchange, with Stabler going to Houston and the younger Dan Pastorini coming to Oakland. Since Dan had been a starter there, he was going to be a starter here, and I wasn't given an opportunity to even compete for the position. As good as I was throwing, I felt slighted. Also, since this was my tenth year in the league, I worried that if I wasn't given a chance to play then, I might never get it. So I asked to be traded before the start of the season. I told my wishes to Tom Flores and he said he'd bring it up to Al Davis. The two of them agreed that they couldn't afford to let me go. I wasn't angry at them because I could see their point. They had drafted Marc Wilson, who had been a star quarter-back at Brigham Young, but I was the only experienced backup they had. So they didn't trade me—fortunately for them, fortunately for me.

During the early part of the season, I was feeling very disgruntled about the situation, though I was not being vocal about it. I still had a job to do, hopefully. One thing that happened really irked me. In our second game against San Diego I came in when Pastorini got hurt. There was time for only one more play, but I threw a TD to Raymond Chester and we tied the game up and sent it into overtime. But all of a sudden Pastorini is back at quarterback in the overtime. I didn't get back in, we lost, and I was really upset.

Pastorini broke his leg in our fifth game, a loss to Kansas City. So I finally got my chance. I don't think my teammates doubted me because I had played well in 1979 and in preseason, but it helped that we did well from the beginning. In my first three starts, we scored 38 points against

San Diego, 45 against Pittsburgh, and over 30 against Seattle, and we won each time. Oakland had opened up its offense before I was the quarterback, but it was a matter of execution. I happened to execute better than Dan did. Plus I realized that if you're given an opportunity, you have to take advantage of it. I had to. Believe me, I was constantly getting ready and preparing myself for each game, and I'd literally be talking to myself: "You've got to concentrate; you've got to be ready for this or that." I'd remind myself of all those kinds of things. Fortunately, I had success right away. After all the beatings I'd taken, my arm was probably not as strong as when I first started, but it was pretty good. I had touch and could take something off the ball or put something on it. I could loft it over somebody and have it drop in between defenders. I could throw short or deep, in the pocket or on the run.

I don't think I had to learn a particularly hard system at Oakland. As it was with any system, you've got to spend a lot of time in repetition and preparation and all that stuff. The only difficult thing was holding the ball as long as they wanted you to. Pastorini had been at Houston early in his career and I'd been at New England, and we'd played behind some shaky lines. Neither of us had the luxury of holding onto the ball while waiting for our receivers to break free, so it was a difficult adjustment for us to make with Oakland. Usually, they didn't want you to throw the ball until you saw the front numbers of the jerseys. Quarterbacks tend to get rid of the ball earlier, but Oakland wanted us to give Cliff Branch and Bobby Chandler the time to get deep downfield and beat their men. The Raiders' passing game wasn't high percentage. It was mostly down the field, which is the reason you needed a strong arm to fit into their system.

By the end of the year, I thought we were the best team in football. But we didn't start out that way and we weren't that way by midseason. If you look at our first five games, our defense was giving up three or four touchdowns a game and our offense had gotten into a scoring rut. So we were just 2–3. After I took over, the offense immediately picked up, and soon after that the defense became the stingiest in the league, holding opponents to only one or two touchdowns a game. It was a dramatic turnaround as far as statistics go. We won my first six games, hit a snag and lost two low-scoring games to Philadelphia and Dallas, and finished the regular season with wins over the Broncos and Giants. We ended up 11–5, which tied us with San Diego for the best record in the Western Division, but we were designated the wild-card team going into the playoffs. By this time, we were the best team, although we hadn't proven that yet.

We ran over Houston in the wild-card game, but the other two playoff games, against Cleveland and San Diego, were nail-biters. We were holding onto a 14–12 lead over the Browns late in the divisional playoff game, and if they would have scored any points, we wouldn't have had time to come back. But they went for the touchdown instead of a short field goal, and Mike Davis intercepted Brian Sipe in the end zone to preserve our lead. In the AFC championship against San Diego we got off to a 28–7 lead, and then all of a sudden we're up by only four points. Ted Hendricks grabs me by the jersey and shakes me, saying, "Goddamn it, keep scoring because we can't stop 'em." He put the fear of God in me. We got a couple of big field goals from Chris Bahr and then we managed to hold onto the ball for more than six-and-a-half minutes, to run out the clock. We kept Dan Fouts and his offense off the field and held on to win, 34–27. We'd been jelling for a long time, but only after we beat San Diego in the championship game did I say, "We are a really good team."

It was hard to believe that we could win with the group of guys we had. They were a bizarre group—I'm not saying I wasn't—but for the most part, when they stepped on the field, they were ready to go to war and get the job done. A lot of things happened during the course of that season— missed practices and stuff—but it didn't seem to bother anybody on game days. If guys had been out drinking at night, they wouldn't try to get out of practice by saying they had bad hamstrings when they really had hangovers, as guys today tend to do. They might go out and party too much on occasion, but they were ready, willing, and able to go to work the next day. These guys paid their dues.

The Raiders had the image of being misfits and individuals and that was pretty accurate, especially back then. We had a crazy bad-boy reputation and sometimes the guys tried to live up to it. Still, I think anybody could have fit in with the Raiders. They did make me feel welcome. They made any new player feel welcome. But they also got on you if you weren't doing your job. They were really loyal to their uniform and sincerely felt that being a Raider was the best thing in the world, something very special. I could sense this attitude as soon as I got there, and I got caught up in it and had a great time. I never ran around with a team that had such strong camaraderie. Every Thursday we'd go out and get to know each other, have some cocktails, play dice. Crazy eights was the game that the Raiders would play on the plane or in the locker room. That year I hung around most with Rich Martini, a young receiver out of U.C. Davis, center Dave Dalby, who's still a good friend, and Bobby Chandler.

John Matuszak, our defensive end, was certainly one of the wilder guys on the team. As they say, he danced to the beat of a different drummer. I wouldn't say we were close, but Tooz and I would talk and make fun of each other, as most teammates tend to do. Everybody got along with him, but I couldn't tell you how close they got to him. We were all glad he was on our team because Tooz was a big part of a very tough, very intimidating, very emotional defense. Especially on defense, the Raiders were a talking group, known for "in-your-face" type of stuff. Other teams were wary of Tooz and some of the other guys.

Ted Hendricks was one of the key figures on the Raiders defense. He was a great, great linebacker who was always coming up with big plays when we needed them. Ted was a unique individual and I really admired him. He was like "Chief Guru" more than anything. He provided comedy relief, intensity, and leadership. He was the type who would get on somebody at practice or during a game for not doing his job. Everybody, including myself, considered Rod Martin, the other outside linebacker, to be one of the team leaders. He really got on people and spoke up in the locker room when he was dissatisfied with what was going on. He did everything well. He was a hard worker, super player, and a good friend. Rod was a real fine fellow who would play great for the Raiders for seven or eight more years.

One of the few new players in the defensive lineup that year was inside linebacker Matt Millen. He was a rookie out of Penn State and let it be known that he came to Oakland to win. He had a big effect on the defense. Matt was fiery and very likable and people rallied around him. He was young, but he was somewhat of a leader, and called the defensive signals.

The best-known player in our secondary was cornerback Lester Hayes. In 1980, he had the most phenomenal season any defensive back has ever had. He had 18 interceptions and two others were called back, one for a TD. He was unique. Lester Hayes was Lester Hayes. He was a talker, on and off the field. Because of his stuttering, when he was being funny it was even funnier. He was always coming up with something, either giving somebody a nickname or relating a silly story—he kept me in stitches. I had a lot of great times with Lester.

The patriarchal leaders of the offense were Art Shell and Gene Upshaw. They were the elder statesmen and longtime All-Pros, and people would look up to them and listen if they had something to say. I think they did a good job of keeping everyone in line, although they had to struggle with a few guys. Art and Gene had to deal with a few difficult personalities. Of course, an offense is not as wild as a defense. Offensive guys have to be more disciplined in order to focus on the many things they are expected to do, while defensive players just need to react.

I think Tom Flores was a good coach. He had a much more aloof personality than his predecessor, John Madden, and some players didn't react well to him because they felt he was a bit standoffish. Fortunately, I related fairly well to him. I thought he was a quiet gentleman. He got angry once, twice, maybe three times a season. Usually that would be at a general meeting when everybody was there, and he would express his frustration at how badly we were practicing or at our lack of preparation or lack of concentration, which was leading to too many mental mistakes. He didn't really focus his anger on one individual.

I think Tom knew how to handle us Super Bowl Week. When the Eagles flew into New Orleans, they were ordered to go directly to practice. The Raiders went directly to the French Quarter. The Eagles were sequestered for the most part by their coach Dick Vermeil, whereas we ran up and down Bourbon Street. Tom knew his players, so he let them out the first night with no curfew, and they went out and probably overdid it. As he figured, they had their fill and there was no longer a need to go out and party after that—although obviously Tooz, with his famous balcony scene with the women and the screaming and stuff like that, still had it. For the most part we got our fun out of the way and concentrated on business. From then on we had an 11 P.M. curfew, which still gave us enough time to do what we wanted, but typically all we did was have dinner with our friends and families. It was no fun for me to go out anyway because I almost couldn't go to the bathroom without hearing a camera shutter. I was too recognizable.

Each day we'd practice at a local high school and there would be group meetings in the morning and afternoon, when we'd watch films and discuss our game plans. At night, some of us would sit in our rooms watching films. Some friends of mine from my Stanford days came out to visit, and when they came up to my room they teased me because I had a bed sheet taped to the wall and an old projector so I could run films. They said, "I thought you guys were a little bit more modern than that."

The Super Bowl was expected to be a defensive struggle. The Eagles defense was strong all year and they had knocked out Dallas, 20–7, in the NFC Championship Game. They had beaten us 10–7 in the regular season with eight sacks, and they came close to getting me about eight other times. Our defense had really come on after the Steelers game. The Eagles had a high-scoring offense with quarterback Ron Jaworski, halfback Wilbert

Montgomery, and their tall receiver, Harold Carmichael, but we had held them to a touchdown and a field goal, their lowest output of the season. In fact, in the first game, both offenses had really been shut down and that's what was anticipated in our second meeting in the Superdome.

I didn't really have expectations. I knew I was going to go out there and execute my end of it. If I ran into trouble, I would find a way to get out of it. That's how I approached the game. I wasn't going to let happen to me what happened in our first game, although I didn't have all the control over that. I was going to get rid of the ball quicker; I was going to make sure that my linemen wouldn't have to block for great lengths of time, play after play. I was going to go to some quick three-step drops and get rid of the ball and go to regular drops as well. I was going to mix it up and keep the Eagles off balance as much as I could.

As always, we went into the game looking for something for our receivers. I don't remember specifically how we intended to approach their cornerbacks, Herman Edwards and rookie Roynell Young, but I'm sure we had a plan for attacking them after having played against them and seen them on film. Edwards was experienced, but Young was the fastest guy they had in the secondary—he was kind of a phenom—so they would put him on Branch. Although he could run, Young still had to be leery of Cliff's speed and experience. We wanted to get Cliff singled up on Young, or have him beat a zone with play-action, by getting the safety to bite on a run-fake. Those one or two steps that the safety would bite on were usually enough to get Cliff behind him. He could beat anybody deep. I liked big plays. One of the most exciting plays in sports is dropping back and hitting the receiver in stride and the receiver running 50 yards down the field for 6. It's a beautiful thing to watch. And Cliff Branch came up with more of those big plays than anybody in the history of the game until the receivers of today. We were always looking for ways in the film study and during the game to get Cliff deep.

Branch was our speedster. But Bob Chandler never liked to hear himself referred to as our "possession receiver." He hated that because he felt he was as fast as anyone—he wasn't Cliff, but he could run down the field, too. Furthermore, during the second half of the season, Raymond Chester, our big tight end, was the guy who was getting deep. He made long receptions almost every game, including a 65-yard touchdown against the Chargers in the AFC championship.

The week dragged on and on. Friday night, my friends and I got together. I'm having a Coke and my friends are drinking, and I'm telling them, "I wish the game were tomorrow. I just want to get this over with. Let's go play, see who the best team is, and get out of here." After two weeks of getting ready—one week in Oakland and one week in New Orleans—and the media driving me nuts after all that time, I was so anxious to play. There's only so much you can prepare.

I was able to sleep the night before the game. It's really bad not to sleep because you really feel the fatigue on the field. So you've got to do it. Before the game, I was in my own world. I was sitting at my locker like I normally did, going over my game plan, though I knew it forwards and backwards. I was pretty oblivious to what was going on around me with the other guys. But as I ran out on the field of the Superdome, I know one thing crossed my mind: After 10 years of thinking I'd never get there, I was there and I wasn't going to be denied.

Super Bowl XV was played during the period when the hostages had returned from Iran and that added a patriotic element to the game, especially during the national anthem. Prior to our introductions, both teams stood in the end zone, and I sensed that the Eagles were tense. That may have been the result of being sequestered all week. They looked dour with glazed eyes. Our guys seemed much looser. I shook Ron Jaworski's hand and he seemed jittery. Of course, that was the only game in my entire life that I forgot to take off my gold chain, so I guess I was somewhat nervous myself and not all there for a while.

The Eagles received the kickoff, and I don't know if it was because of nerves, but Jaworski was intercepted on his first pass. He tried to hit his tight end Jim Spagnola near midfield and Rod Martin picked it off and had a good return. So when our offense took the field for the first time, we were already on the Eagles' 30-yard line, which certainly made things easier for me.

We moved toward their goal, mostly with runs by Mark van Eeghen. Then we had third-and-goal on their 2-yard line. I dropped back to pass. I couldn't find anybody open and I started to take off. That wasn't unusual. I had scrambled quite a bit that year, and against San Diego, when we were on the 5 and everybody was covered, a hole opened up and I took off and scored. I'm sure the Eagles saw that on film, and when I made my move, their linebackers started to converge to stop me before I reached the goal line. They left Cliff open and I was just able to dart it over to him really quickly. Cliff didn't have the best hands in the world and had a history of dropping balls, but he caught that one. Maybe you could say that Chandler, who was a more reliable short-yardage receiver, was my primary target on that play, but that wouldn't be entirely accurate. When I dropped back I would read the entire field—as I had been taught to do—so only once in a while was there a real "primary" receiver. You just try to go to the guy who's open, and Cliff was open on that play. We went ahead 7–0 and that made us feel good because a high percentage of teams that win a Super Bowl score first.

Our second touchdown pass of the quarter went 80 yards—a Super Bowl record. We were on our 20 and it was supposed to be a straight dropback pass where I'd look for Branch, Chandler, or Chester. Kenny King was supposed to come out of the backfield and run a few yards downfield to clear out or maybe catch a dump-off if nobody was open deep. I dropped back and couldn't find anyone open. The clock went off in my head and I couldn't expect my blockers to hold off the Eagles' rush any longer, so I tried to get more time by scrambling to my left. All good receivers are taught to scramble with the quarterback and go to the side he's on and try to help him out, so both Kenny and Bobby went to the left. Kenny broke upfield a bit, to about our 40, and got behind Herman Edwards, and I was able to get it over Edwards' hand by a fingernail and into Kenny's hands. Kenny, another guy not known for his hands, grabbed it and went the distance. Chris Bahr kicked the extra point and we were ahead 14–0 and feeling good since they had scored only 10 points against us in our first meeting.

The Eagles nearly had a touchdown in the first quarter, but it was called back because of an offsides penalty. Jaworski connected with Rodney Parker on a long TD pass, but Carmichael had turned upfield too soon. So they ended up punting. We had come out and were executing our plays and moving the football, while the Eagles couldn't get away from making mistakes, especially early on.

It was just our resolve, having lost to them during the season and getting pretty beat up, that we weren't going to make the same mistakes. We weren't going to let them dominate us this game. When somebody beats you and you have to face them again later in the season, usually they don't make any changes because they figure what worked the first time is going to work the second time. On the other hand, the team that got beat is looking for changes or ways to attack better. I think they were predictable. They did what they did well, so there was no reason to change. We were just more prepared for them the second time around than they were for us. We also were a much better team than the one that had lost to them.

January 25, 1981, at the Louisiana Superdome in New Orleans

Paid Attendance: 75,500

AFC Champion: Oakland Raiders (14–5)
Head Coach: Tom Flores

NFC Champion: Philadelphia Eagles (14–4)
Head Coach: Dick Vermeil

STARTING LINEUPS

OFFENSE			DEFENSE		
Oakland		**Philadelphia**	**Oakland**		**Philadelphia**
Cliff Branch	WR	Harold Carmichael	John Matuszak	LE	Dennis Harrison
Art Shell	LT	Stan Walters	Reggie Kinlaw	MG	Charlie Johnson
Gene Upshaw	LG	Pete Perot	Dave Browning	RE	Carl Hairston
Dave Dalby	C	Guy Morriss	Ted Hendricks	LOLB	John Bunting
Mickey Marvin	RG	Woody Peoples	Matt Millen	LILB	Bill Bergey
Henry Lawrence	RT	Jerry Sisemore	Bob Nelson	RILB	Frank LeMaster
Ray Chester	TE	Keith Krepfle	Rod Martin	ROLB	Jerry Robinson
	TE	John Spagnola	Lester Hayes	LCB	Roynell Young
Bob Chandler	WR		Dwayne O'Steen	RCB	Herman Edwards
Jim Plunkett	QB	Ron Jaworski	Mike Davis	SS	Randy Logan
Mark van Eeghen	RB	Wilbert Montgomery	Burgess Owens	FS	Brenard Wilson
Kenny King	RB	Leroy Harris			

SUBSTITUTIONS

Oakland: K—Chris Bahr. P—Ray Guy. Offense: Receivers—Morris Bradshaw, Derrick Ramsey, Rich Martini, Ira Matthews. Linemen—Bruce Davis, Lindsey Mason, Steve Sylvester. Backs—Arthur Whittington, Derrick Jensen, Todd Christensen. Defense: Linebackers—Mario Celotto, Jeff Barnes, Randy McClanahan. Linemen—Dave Pear, Joe Campbell, Cedrick Hardman, Willie Jones. Backs—Odis McKinney, Keith Moody, Monte Jackson. DNP—Marc Wilson.

Philadelphia: K—Tony Franklin. P—Max Runager. Offense: Receivers—Rodney Parker, Charlie Smith, Wally Henry. Linemen—Mark Slater, Steve Kenney, Ken Clarke, Ron Baker. Backs—Louie Giammona, Perry Harrington, Billy Campfield. Defense: Linebackers—Al Chesley, Reggie Wilkes, Ray Phillips. Linemen—Claude Humphrey, Thomas Brown. Backs—Zac Henderson, John Sciarra, Richard Blackmore. DNP—Joe Pisarcik, Rob Hertel, Bob Torrey.

Oakland	14	0	10	3—27
Philadelphia	0	3	0	7—10

Oak	Branch 2 pass from Plunkett (Bahr kick)
Oak	King 80 pass from Plunkett (Bahr kick)
Phil	FG Franklin 30
Oak	Branch 29 pass from Plunkett (Bahr kick)
Oak	FG Bahr 46
Phil	Krepfle 8 pass from Jaworski (Franklin kick)
Oak	FG Bahr 35
MVP:	Jim Plunkett (Oakland)

I don't think the Eagles had a weak offense. I think our defense was just stopping them, as we did in the first game. I watched our defense from the sidelines. It was playing so well. As it was during the season, anytime we needed a big play, Ted Hendricks or Reggie Kinlaw or Lester Hayes or Mike Davis or Rod Martin or someone else would come up with it. It wasn't always the same person, but somebody inevitably would come up with a play that either stalled a drive, prevented a first down, or prevented a touchdown. I can't speak enough about Charlie Sumner, our linebackers coach. He was a master at calling blitzes at the right times and with the right players.

Once we shut down Wilbert Montgomery, Jaworski had to pass more than he wanted and he wasn't having much luck. I had seen Jaworski play some in L.A. and Philadelphia, but I had never really rated him as a quarterback. I just knew that he had a strong arm and made a lot of big plays in his career, having emerged as a backup with the Rams to become one of the most successful starting quarterbacks in the NFC with Philadelphia. I didn't think in terms of having to outplay him in the Super Bowl. There was no rivalry. In fact, I didn't pay that much attention to how he was doing against our defense. I was more concerned with what the Eagles defense was going to try to do with me.

We didn't really have a different blocking scheme than in the first game, when the Eagles sacked me so often. I still dropped straight back on passing plays—I don't remember rolling out once all game in anticipation of a rush. Maybe I tried to get rid of the ball a little quicker and scrambled better to avoid the rush, but it was more a matter of the guys up front making up their minds that they wouldn't let it happen again. I was sacked once all game and that didn't happen until the second half, and even then I lost only a yard.

Most of our running plays in the first half went up the middle or to the right behind Mickey Marvin and Henry Lawrence, rather than to the left behind Upshaw and Shell. I don't think that was by design. I don't think we planned to run van Eeghen and King primarily one way, right or left. I called the plays, and it's just that when something was working, I tended to stick with it.

King had more speed than van Eeghen and ran outside more. He could break away from the pack once he passed the line of scrimmage, so we hoped to find ways to get him out of there. We liked to free up Kenny by throwing him quick screens, although I think we threw him only one against Philadelphia. Van Eeghan was a power runner. His longest run in his history was 34 yards, so you know you're going to stay between the tackles with him. He wasn't a breakaway back, but he was good down by the goal line or when we needed a first down, and he always managed to gain a lot of yards during the course of a game. Against the Eagles, he picked up 80 yards without gaining over 8 yards on a carry.

I can barely remember the second quarter. The only score came on a field goal by Tony Franklin, which cut our lead to 14–3. Franklin almost had another one right before the half ended, but Hendricks jumped with his arm up at the line of scrimmage and blocked the short attempt. Ted was 6'7" and blocked more kicks than anyone. I knew that was a big play. It would have been an even bigger play if Willie Jones had been able to pick it up for us. He kept trying to pick it up but just kept fumbling it. He was extremely fast, and if he'd been able to run it downfield, they would never have caught him, and we'd have led 21–3 at the half.

At halftime the players went to their individual coaches and discussed what the Eagles were doing in every situation. I got together with Flores. Tom served as our offensive coach and Sam Begosian was the offensive-line coach. Then Tom spoke to the whole team, as he always did. I think he was pleased with our lead and that we seemed to be in control. There wasn't much to say, other than to keep doing what we'd been doing, keep the pressure on, and not make mistakes.

We received the ball to begin the second half. I didn't want to sit on the lead so I went to the air. I hit King with a screen pass for a first down and followed that with a deep pass to Chandler that put us in Eagles territory. Van Eeghen carried the ball to the 29, and on the next play I threw downfield to Cliff. Once in a while even a guy who has been around a lot gets fooled, and I was fooled. I misread the coverage. I thought it was man-to-man, but they ended up backing off into a zone, which I kind of threw into the heart of. But I threw it in a place I felt Cliff could catch the ball. I threw it toward the corner, and Cliff was so quick that he slipped in front of Young and made a great catch, jumping for it and tearing it away from Young. He squirmed into the end zone to make the score 21–3.

On their first possession of the half, the Eagles put together a decent drive and got into our territory. But for the second time, Rod Martin intercepted a pass from Jaworski to Spagnola. We took the ball the other way and Chris Bahr booted a long field goal. Bahr was a good kicker. He missed one every once in a while, but he seldom missed a field goal that mattered, when it was crunch time.

We were ahead by three touchdowns, 24–3, but I was somewhat cynical. I had been in too many games where there had been big comebacks, by us or the other team. I remembered how San Diego had almost come back to beat us in the AFC Championship Game. I certainly felt pleased with the lead but I didn't assume the game was over. I still felt it necessary to keep the pressure on. I still didn't want to sit on the football, unless we were successful just running it. So I continued to mix passes with runs.

In the fourth quarter, Philadelphia finally scored a touchdown on a short pass from Jaworski to Keith Krepfle. It wasn't significant, although I'm sure our defense didn't want them to score. We came back with another field goal by Chris Bahr to give us a 27-point total, so I wouldn't have cared if the Eagles had scored 26 points that game.

They ended up with those 10 points. In their final two possessions, Jaworski fumbled a snap and was intercepted by Rod Martin for the third time. In that Super Bowl, Rod was in the right place at the right time. Part of it was instinct; part of it was Charlie Sumner putting him in the right position to intercept. Both Charlie and Rod had great anticipation. Martin pretty much ruined Jaworksi's day. Ron threw for almost 300 yards and hit some long passes, but he also made those three costly mistakes.

In this Super Bowl, I was disappointed that I missed a couple of passes that I should have hit, but I didn't make mistakes and turn the ball over. Other than that, I just did my job, nothing spectacular. I think our team played a very good game. Our defense played extremely well. You can't take anything away from Philadelphia. You can't say they played poorly. They might have played their best game and not have been able to beat us.

As the game wound down, I was feeling more comfortable. We were certainly in control and I was starting to feel pretty damn good. Everybody on the sidelines was standing up and starting to get into the jubilant mode. We ran the clock out with hand-offs to van Eeghen and Derrick Jensen. When the game ended, everybody ran around hugging each other. Tom and I hugged. I have a vivid memory of Dick Vermeil coming across the field and saying he couldn't leave without congratulating me. We'd known each other since 1965, when he had been my quarterback coach at Stanford.

I looked forward to the locker room celebration and getting back to my friends after the game. A close friend of mine, who took me under his wing when I went to Stanford, rented a place for all the guys who flew out from California. We had our own celebration.

The Raiders had a fabulous celebration at the Fairmont Hotel. Al Davis certainly knew how to throw a party, and the Raiders certainly knew how to celebrate. It capped off our incredible year. It was such a great time. It was just terrific. We would be a dominant team when we won the Super Bowl again in three years, but I was fonder of this Super Bowl victory because of the guys I played with and the way it happened, how with so many new players we evolved from a mediocre team into a great team, the only wild-card team to win the Super Bowl. I was so proud of this team. It was a tremendous effort on everyone's part.

I was happy for everybody. I was particularly happy for Cedrick Hardman, who came over from the 49ers. I had been with him over there and saw how he struggled with teams that weren't very good. Now he had a Super Bowl victory under his belt. I was very, very happy for Bobby Chandler, who came over from Buffalo, and Tom Flores, who had the difficult task of replacing John Madden. I also was happy for Al Davis, who I'm probably closer to today than when we won that Super Bowl. I'm not going to say he was misunderstood, but even then people liked to beat Al Davis when they played the Raiders. It was almost like they had a personal vendetta. I pulled for Al for a lot of reasons. I was thankful to him for wanting me on his ball club, and he was thankful that I was on his ball club, because otherwise it wouldn't have gone all the way.

My MVP award was announced in the locker room. *Sport* magazine was awarding it then and their representative came to me. The actual presentation was made in New York at the Waldorf-Astoria in the off-season. Considering how my first seven years had gone and how I started out on the bench at the beginning of the season, the MVP award was special.

Winning that game instead of losing it made all the difference in the world. I proved that I was back playing as I was capable of playing. It was a great victory for me personally. However, I don't think this one game was a turning point in my career. I'd have kept playing even if we had lost and I would have been the Raiders' starting quarterback based on the good season I had. Still, it was important that I showed I could take the Raiders all the way to the title. I had the chance to prove that I could still play not only to myself but also to the people who had given up on me and thought I should have gotten out of the game. So sure: I would say that my performance in a winning Super Bowl made me feel somewhat vindicated.

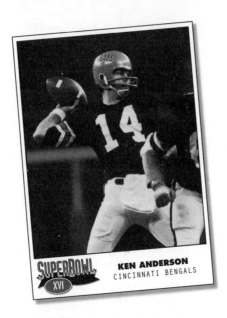

KEN ANDERSON
CINCINNATI BENGALS

SUPERBOWL
XVI

SUPER BOWL XVI

SAN FRANCISCO 49ERS 26
CINCINNATI BENGALS 21

KEN ANDERSON

I don't know if it was *Time* or *Newsweek*, but Joe Montana and I shared the cover in that week leading up to Super Bowl XVI. Certainly the media at that Super Bowl played up the story about the two quarter-backs of the two teams. They made a lot of how both of us hadn't been drafted until the third round and how we both developed under Bill Walsh, who was now Montana's head coach at San Francisco but had been my first quarterback coach at Cincinnati. Montana was the young sensation who, at 25, had the chance to pass Joe Namath as the youngest winning quarterback in Super Bowl history, while my story in the press was that I had come back from several disappointing seasons and an opening day benching to be selected the NFL's Most Valuable Player. After only three years in the league, Joe was written about as the rising star with many Super Bowls in his future and I was the seasoned veteran who had finally made it to the world championship game three weeks before my thirty-third birthday, in my tenth year.

I had played quarterback at Augustana in Illinois. It wasn't a big school, but I wasn't a secret, and scouts came by in the off-season to work me out. When I was drafted in 1971, the Bengals had plans for me to fit into their system. Greg Cook had an excellent rookie season in 1969, but he had hurt his shoulder and Virgil Carter had been the team's quarterback when they reached the playoffs for the first time in 1970. I shared time with him in my rookie season and then became the starter. Paul Brown was the coach and general manager of the Bengals and had made them a playoff team only two years after they joined the league in 1968. When you talk about Paul Brown, you're talking about one of the greatest coaches of all time. It was an experience I'd never forget, just to be associated with him and to see how he directed a football operation, from how he organized practices to how he coached on Sundays to how he decided which players to draft to how he assembled a coaching staff, including Bill Walsh, his quarterbacks and receivers coach.

Bill was there my first five years, until Brown retired as head coach. The training he gave me laid a solid foundation for playing quarterback in the NFL for my entire career. From him I learned about the mechanics and the mental aspects of playing the position, and I acquired an attention to detail. Bill had to convert me into a drop-back quarterback. Much of my success had to do with accuracy, and that's one thing that you can't really be taught. You can either throw the ball from here to there and hit the guy you want to hit, or you can't. Mechanics will only carry you so far. However, what Bill Walsh did to make the best use of my accuracy was to work on the timing I had with my receivers. The precision of the passing game depended on the drop, that third step or fifth step which would allow me to hit an open receiver at the exact moment he reached a designated spot on the field.

Cincinnati had a lot of success through the mid-seventies. We made the playoffs twice, when we won our division in 1973 with a 10–4 record and when we went 11–3 in 1975 to finish one game behind the Steelers and qualify as a wild-card team. Unfortunately, we lost our first playoff games in both years, to Miami in '73 and to Oakland by three points in '75. Nevertheless, we had good teams and good players and I was fortunate enough to lead the league in passing twice and to be selected to a couple of Pro Bowls.

My top receiver in those years was Isaac Curtis. Isaac had world-class speed, but he wasn't a track guy trying to play football. He was a football player who had track speed. There's a big difference. Isaac just had amazing impact when he came into the NFL in 1973—the kind of impact Jerry Rice would have when he came in. Isaac would make 10 touchdown catches a year and was a big-play receiver.

A quarterback is an extension of his team, and during those years when we were good, I was able to play well. When our team got bad in the late seventies and I didn't have a lot of talented players around me, my play at quarterback dropped off. And after having not missed a game in the first seven or eight years of my career, all of a sudden I was getting hit a lot and injuries were starting to pop up. In fact, I hurt my knee in the last preseason game in 1980 and had to play with a brace the whole year. That didn't help my performance. I'm sure there were thoughts in the organization about me being on the downside and possibly needing to be replaced. When Jack Thompson was drafted number one out of Washington State in 1979, I knew it was expected that he'd eventually take my job, perhaps as soon as 1981 if I didn't get off to a good start.

I didn't have a good preseason in '81. Then I played the first quarter of our opening game against Seattle and threw three interceptions and was benched right then. My quarterback rating was 2.9 after that game—I don't know if it's ever been lower for a quarterback. There's no doubt that was the lowest point of my career. In fact, I wondered if my career was over. Will you get a chance to get your job back?

I did get a chance because Thompson had been hurt and wouldn't be ready for the next game. Our third-string quarterback, Turk Schonert, had pulled out that game against Seattle, but Forrest Gregg, who was beginning his second year as our head coach, wanted to go with a more experienced player. So I got the next start. We were playing against the Jets in New York and it was somewhat easier for me on the road. The Cincinnati fans may have been a bit hostile (or a lot hostile) toward me by that point. They had started to turn a few years before. The fans in Cincinnati embraced the football team, but they expected a lot out of us and got frustrated when we didn't do well. When you're not winning, it's no different anywhere else: It's the quarterback's fault. Quarterback is a tough position to play, and negative reactions from fans come with the territory.

Had Jack Thompson been healthy, maybe I wouldn't have started against the Jets; I don't know. But I got the opportunity I needed and had a good game and we won. Fortunately, Forrest Gregg stuck with me. The team came around and I came around. We would win our division and I would win the league passing title and win several postseason awards, including the MVP. One reason for my improvement was that Lindy Infante came in as Forrest's offensive coordinator and helped me get rid of some bad habits I'd acquired the previous year. However, if you talk about my "resurrection" in '81, it mostly had to do with two things: a good head coach in Forrest Gregg and better players.

Forrest Gregg came along at a good time for us. When he became our head coach in 1980, we were a team that wasn't disciplined, wasn't necessarily in great physical shape and wasn't very strong. Forrest grabbed us by the back of the neck as a team and shook us and made us a tough football team physically and mentally. We were physical and did a lot of hitting in practice and certainly that wasn't the Paul Brown style, but Paul let Forrest coach the team his way. And he got results. In 1980 our 6–10 record wasn't impressive, but you could tell at the end of the year we were a much-improved football team. Everybody was excited going into the 1981 season. At training camp, we thought we had the potential to make the playoffs. We had good coaches, we had chemistry—we were an excitable, emotional team with a great blend of young and veteran players—and we had talent. That was a good combination for success.

This was a better Bengals team than the playoff teams of the seventies. We had more overall talent. For instance, all of a sudden we had a very good offensive line. Anthony Muñoz, who would become one of the greatest offensive tackles ever to play in the NFL, was already making a major impact in his second season. What a player he was. And along with him we had guys like Max Montoya, Mike Wilson, and Blair Bush, who, like Muñoz, had been a first-round draft choice. Dave Lapham was a stalwart offensive guard who kind of took charge of an otherwise young line. That was an excellent group on both run and pass blocking.

Our passing game greatly improved. One reason was the addition of Cris Collinsworth. Our number-one draft choice that year was another receiver, David Verser, out of Kansas, and he was going to be the guy who stepped in. But Cris, our second-round pick out of Florida, worked hard and made an impression and won the job. He was tall and lanky, but he was faster than people thought and had tremendous hands and a great love of playing the game. So in he comes as a rookie and has a 1,000-yard season and goes to the Pro Bowl and we go to the Super Bowl—he thought it would always be like that. With Cris on the other side, Isaac Curtis didn't have all the pressure on him for a change. Now we had another guy who could run deep routes and force double coverage. As a result, Isaac would have some big days. For instance, he was the key player with over 100 yards receiving in a pivotal road game against San Diego. Our third receiver was tight end Dan Ross, a Pro Bowler. Danny benefited from having those two guys on the outside and actually led our team with over 70 receptions that year and gained only about 100 yards less than Cris. We had another good tight end in M. L. Harris, who would catch a big touchdown pass against San Diego in the AFC title game. We used a lot of formations with two tight ends, so Harris had an important role on the team.

The only thing we missed from those earlier Cincinnati teams was a break-away back like Essex Johnson, who was a threat to go the distance any time he touched the ball. We were more of a power-running team with Pete Johnson, a 250–260-pound fullback who gained over 1,000 yards, and tailback Charles Alexander, who was a 230-pounder. They were big guys. Forrest Gregg had played on those Packers teams that were famous for sweeps, but that wasn't in our offensive scheme with those backs. Instead we were going to hammer between the tackles.

We had a very reliable kicking game with Jim Breech and punter Pat McInally, and I think our defense was number one in the NFL that year. We had a very strong defensive line with Ross Browner and Eddie Edwards at the ends—they had both been number one draft choices. Glenn Cameron, who was an excellent inside linebacker, also had been a top draft pick. Jim LeClair was a solid middle linebacker and Louis Breeden was at one of our corners . . . so we had some pretty good Pro Bowl–type defensive players. Hank Bullough, our defensive coordinator, would have his players line up in a lot of different places to confuse the offense and blitz a lot to put steady pressure on the quarterback. As the old adage goes, he'd throw everything at you but the kitchen sink—and that would probably come a little bit later.

They say you've got to win in November to make it to the playoffs, and we had five games against playoff-contending teams, and we rolled over every one of them. We had a lot of high-scoring games late in the season, except when we scored only three points in a December loss to San Francisco. I hurt my foot in that game and played only a quarter. If I'd played more, even if we still lost, I have no idea if that experience would have made any difference in the Super Bowl. We had been on such an emotional ride up to that point, so maybe a loss like that helped us. We went into Pittsburgh after that and clinched the division, 17–10, which was maybe the most gratifying win I ever had. They always said that the road to the Super Bowl goes through Pittsburgh—well, we won in Pittsburgh in a big game, after all those years. Then we went to Atlanta for the last game of the season. A victory would up our record to 12–4, the best in the AFC, and guarantee us the home-field advantage throughout the play-offs. So we had to win that game. And we did, 30–28.

We opened the playoffs by hosting the Buffalo Bills. That was a really well-played game without many mistakes. We ended up winning 28–21 when I hit Collinsworth on a touchdown pass in the fourth quarter. That was such a big game for us because it was the first playoff game that the Bengals had ever won.

The AFC title game was played in Cincinnati and the wind chill made it seem like it was 59 degrees below zero. That was the coldest day in NFL history and there was some discussion about postponing the game. I'm sure San Diego didn't like playing in that weather, but I always justify that game by saying that if they'd beaten us during the season out in California, then that playoff game would have been played out there, too. But we crushed them 40–17 and earned the right to play that day in Cincinnati. It wasn't so easy for us either, you know. It hurt to go out there and it was hard to breathe. At that point it becomes a bit mental. I think having a coach like Forrest Gregg who had toughened us mentally gave us a shot to win that game. We got ahead early and eventually pulled away, 27–7. I thought we were peaking going into the Super Bowl.

We were excited. For us to have gotten back to the playoffs for the first time since 1975, and to have beaten Buffalo and San Diego for our first playoff victories in history, was so significant for the franchise that it didn't matter who our opponent would be. We would have been equally happy to have played the Dallas Cowboys or the San Francisco 49ers. The 49ers became our opponent when they won the NFC Championship Game, 28–27, when Dwight Clark made "The Catch" of Joe Montana's pass late in the game.

Super Bowl XVI was the first Super Bowl that wasn't played in a warm-weather climate. Pontiac, Michigan, was almost as cold as Cincinnati had been. It was below zero with the wind chill all week long, but at least we were going to play that game indoors, in the Silverdome. It's not like you have a lot of free time during the week to enjoy things anyway, so the game's location was probably more disappointing for people surrounding the team than the players. Our families arrived on Thursday, and I'm sure they would rather have been in Miami or California. It was too cold for anybody to do anything, so luckily the hotel we stayed at in Dearborn had an indoor pool for the kids.

Fortunately, both teams practiced in the Silverdome, because an outdoor facility would have been out of the question. Bill Walsh and I had remained close and one of the benefits of practicing in the same place was that we had the chance to chat because as we were coming in, his team would be finishing up. The Bengals practiced in the afternoon and the 49ers practiced in the morning. This setup was probably more inconvenient for them, because in a team's normal routine it practices in the early afternoon. And they already had to deal with the three-hour time difference between Michigan and California. Of course, if the game was an indication, it probably didn't affect them too much.

Practices were closed and they would have designated photographers and writers in there with us. There was a lot of media there and they kind of pooled for those spots. They would have access to the players during times that were set aside during the day.

I guess one of the big stories was that for the first time since Super Bowl III both teams were making their first appearances in a Super Bowl. What made us unlikely opponents is that we were both coming off losing records the year before. The 49ers had also gone 6–10 in 1980. But, also like us, they had made a vast improvement in just one year under an excellent head coach. I think the two teams knew each other pretty well from having played earlier and from having two weeks to study each other on film to prepare for this game. There was no need for anybody to ask me if I had advice about the 49ers because I had played for Bill Walsh. Anyway, Bruce Coslet was on our staff and he had played tight end for us under Walsh.

I didn't sleep well the night before the Super Bowl, but I didn't sleep well before any game, even in preseason. I was nervous in the locker room and when we went out onto the field, but I think everybody was nervous, including the 49ers. You tell yourself that it's just another game, but Diana Ross is singing the national anthem and you know she never showed up for games in Cincinnati. So you kind of know that there's something different about this game.

Super Bowl XVI began with our recovering a fumble on the kickoff. Of course, that was a big break we wanted to take advantage of. We quickly got the ball down to the 5 and were moving the ball well, but then I got sacked, and on the next play I threw an interception. We had gotten two first downs on passes over the middle to Curtis and Ross and were tying to throw a little slant pass to Curtis in front of their goal line. But their safety,

January 24, 1982, at the Pontiac Silverdome in Detroit

Paid Attendance: 81,270

NFL Champion: San Francisco 49ers (15–3)
Head Coach: Bill Walsh

AFL Champion: Cincinnati Bengals (14–4)
Head Coach: Forrest Gregg

STARTING LINEUPS

OFFENSE				DEFENSE		
San Francisco		**Cincinnati**	**San Francisco**		**Cincinnati**
Dwight Clark	WR	Cris Collinsworth	Jim Stuckey	LE	Eddie Edwards
Dan Audick	LT	Anthony Muñoz	Archie Reese	NT	Wilson Whitley
John Ayers	LG	Dave Lapham	Dwaine Board	RE	Ross Browner
Fred Quillan	C	Blair Bush	Fred Dean	LOLB	Bo Harris
Randy Cross	RG	Max Montoya	Jack Reynolds	LILB	Jim LeClair
Keith Fahnhorst	RT	Mike Wilson	Bobby Leopold	RILB	Glenn Cameron
Charle Young	TE	Dan Ross	Keena Turner	ROLB	Reggie Williams
Freddie Solomon	WR	Isaac Curtis	Ronnie Lott	LCB	Louis Breeden
Joe Montana	QB	Ken Anderson	Eric Wright	RCB	Ken Riley
Ricky Patton	RB	Charles Alexander	Carlton Williamson	SS	Bobby Kemp
Earl Cooper	RB	Pete Johnson	Dwight Hicks	FS	Bryan Hicks

SUBSTITUTIONS

San Francisco: K—Ray Wersching. P—Jim Miller. Offense: Receivers—Eason Ramson, Mike Shumann, Mike Wilson. Linemen—John Choma, Walt Downing, Allan Kennedy. Backs—Amos Lawrence, Bill Ring, Johnny Davis. Defense: Linebackers—Milt McColl, Craig Puki, Dan Bunz, Willie Harper. Linemen—Lawrence Pillers, John Harty. Backs—Lynn Thomas, Rick Gervais. DNP—Guy Benjamin, Walt Easley, Lenvil Elliott, Saladin Martin.

Cincinnati: K—Jim Breech. Punter—Pat McInally. Offense: Receivers—Steve Kreider, M. L. Harris, Don Bass, David Verser. Linemen—Blake Moore, Mike Obrovac. Backs—Jim Hargrove, Archie Griffin. Defense: Linebackers—Guy Frazier, Rick Razzano, Tom Dinkel. Linemen—Gary Burley, Rod Horn, Mike St. Clair. Backs—John Simmons, Mike Fuller, Ray Griffin, Oliver Davis. DNP—Glenn Bujnoch, Turk Schonert, Jack Thompson.

San Francisco	7	13	0	6—26
Cincinnati	0	0	7	14—21

SF	Montana 1 run (Wersching kick)
SF	Cooper 11 pass from Montana (Wersching kick)
SF	FG Wersching 22
SF	FG Wersching 26
Cin	Anderson 5 run (Breech kick)
Cin	Ross 4 pass from Anderson (Breech kick)
SF	FG Wersching 40
SF	FG Wersching 23
Cin	Ross 3 pass from Anderson (Breech kick)
MVP:	Joe Montana (San Francisco)

Dwight Hicks, just jumped inside and made the play, and he made a nice run, past the 30. We had the chance to get on the scoreboard first and we didn't do it. That was a really disappointing play because I'd had only 10 interceptions all season. But you've just got to go on and not dwell on one bad play. I told myself that I would continue to play well.

As a result of the interception, the 49ers drove downfield and ended up scoring a touchdown by Joe Montana to put them ahead, 7–0. I was watching as Montana did a great job. He came out throwing—a screen to a back, short passes to the wide receivers, Freddie Solomon and Dwight Clark— and then got his running game going, mixing things up really well. That drive exemplified the Bill Walsh style of ball control. You talk about the "West Coast Offense"—a term that is prevalent nowadays—but that offense had its roots in Cincinnati when Bill Walsh coached us there. A big play in that drive came on what we used to call a "triple pass," where they faked a reverse and Freddie Solomon pitched back to Montana, who then threw over the middle to Charle Young for a first down. That was a play I ran back in 1971 with Bill Walsh. I was very familiar with the things they were doing on offense, including the unbalanced lines.

I also knew what to expect from their defense. Chuck Studley was a very innovative defensive coach, which I knew because he had been on our staff until he joined Walsh at San Francisco in the late seventies. I knew Chuck would come up with a few things that we would have to counter. For instance, he let Fred Dean move around on and behind the line so that he could disrupt our blocking scheme. Dean was a great player and certainly that posed problems. However, that tactic was not a surprise to us because we had seen it on film and had a plan for that. Sure, Dean and other 49ers like Jack Reynolds and Keena Turner put some pressure on me and I was sacked a few times, but for the most part our guys did a good job blocking them. I didn't suffer a beating and was able to have a 300-yard passing day. I had enough time to complete 25 passes, and both Ross and Collinsworth gained over 100 yards despite those standout rookie backs Ronnie Lott, Eric Wright, and Carlton Williamson.

On San Francisco's first possession after taking the lead, our defense forced them to punt from inside their end zone, and we got the ball around midfield. We moved the ball inside their 30, and then I threw a pass over the middle to Collinsworth at about the 10. Before he could pull the ball in, he was stripped by Eric Wright and the 49ers recovered. From where I was, I couldn't tell if Cris had possession or not, but it was ruled a completion and a fumble and ended our scoring threat. Cris would probably say he should have held onto the ball. There were so many key plays that contributed to the game's outcome that I had forgotten that one.

Our offense went into the Super Bowl against San Francisco with the same idea we always had: We wanted to have a balanced attack. And we were able to run and pass the ball very effectively, picking up more first downs and total yards than the 49ers and almost doubling what they got through the air. But we kept making mistakes or having miscues, and each time they would capitalize. Cris's fumble was our second turnover, and they turned it into their second touchdown, this time driving 92 yards, a Super Bowl record. Again Montana skillfully mixed short passes with the running of his backs, Earl Cooper and Ricky Patton, and they finally scored on a touchdown pass to Cooper. We were down 14–0 and digging ourselves into a hole.

There would be two more key plays in the first half that helped dig that hole deeper. Right before the half ended, we mishandled two kick-offs and they got two field goals out of it. Those six points turned out to be real big at the end of the game. Ray Wersching's squib kicks were not a total surprise, especially not the second one, obviously. We didn't fear those kicks—you just wish the guys would have caught the ball. It's as simple as that. On the first one, Verser got tackled inside our 5, and when we punted they got the ball back in good field position and drove for a field goal. Then seconds later, Archie Griffin lost the ball inside our 5 and they got another field goal to make it 20–0. And we're thinking, "What the heck is going on here?"

In the locker room at halftime you expected Forrest Gregg to rant and rave, but instead the coaches went off to talk things over, and for most of the break the players were in there by themselves. Nothing was said for a while. Everybody just sat there in disbelief. Jeez, we were embarrassed. We knew we were a better football team than we had shown and we didn't want to continue to embarrass ourselves. When the coaches came back in, we just talked about not making any more mistakes. There was nothing that they were doing that was stopping us; we were stopping ourselves. We just had to start playing tough football.

I don't think our defensive players made adjustments because of the 49ers' successful drives in the first half. Football is a game of players making plays, and in the third quarter the defense made the plays. On their first play of the half, Browner sacked Montana for a big loss and that set the tone for the quarter. They didn't allow San Francisco any first downs in three possessions.

Our offense started making plays as well. To begin the half, we had a drive of over 80 yards. We mixed it up pretty good. I had a first-down end around run to start things off, Pete Johnson carried a few times, and I had a few completions, including one to Curtis after I got a little toss-back from Griffin. There was a penalty for a late hit on Isaac, so we got the ball at about their 10 or 11, and we ran it in from there. Actually, my touchdown from the 5 was supposed to be a pass all the way, but it wasn't open. I eluded one tackler and there was nothing between me and the end zone, so I kept running. Now we were finally on the scoreboard and trailing by only 13 points, 20–7, with a lot of time left to play.

They were playing a zone, but their guy on the backside was almost on an inside technique, and we wanted to try to take him in and then throw outside on him. It looks great in the highlight film where I'm telling Cris Collinsworth not to get caught on the inside and then they cut to a clip of me hitting him with a long pass to the outside, but the play I hit Cris on was something totally different. We had just split 'em on the outside. We had sent somebody down the middle and they kind of looked that guy off a little bit while Cris snuck up the left side. Cris made a great over-the-head catch while running in full stride ahead of the defensive backs. That got us almost 50 yards, down to about their 15. Ross caught a pass up the middle and Johnson ran up the middle on a fourth-down play, and we had the ball first-and-goal at their 3. But then they stopped us. After Johnson failed to score on a couple of runs, their linebacker, Dan Bunz, made a big stop on a short pass to Alexander to bring up fourth down at the 1. That left us with one more chance. All year long we had success pounding our big fullback behind our line. Johnson hadn't been stopped, but now they stopped him with a gang tackle at the line of scrimmage and took over on downs. We had four chances at it but couldn't get it in. When you talk about keys to that game, that was certainly one of them. You have to give the 49ers credit.

They ended up punting after three plays, and this time we did come down and score on a pass to Ross over the middle. But we felt that they had taken away a touchdown we should have scored and we should have been ahead, not still trailing by six points. Fortunately, despite that and how badly we had played in the first half, we had come back. We were behind only 20–14 and there was still 10 minutes to play. We just had to hold them on defense and we'd have a good chance to win.

In fact, we soon had their offense backed up at about their 20-yard line on a second-and-15. If we stopped them, they'd have to punt, and we would get the ball in great field possession. We had been moving the ball, so I expected that we'd then be able to go down and score to take the lead—and I think if we did that we probably would have ended up winning the game. I really believe that. But Montana rolled out and hit one along the sideline to Mike Wilson that got them over 20 yards and a first down. Because of that completion, they were able to keep their drive alive and use a lot of time off the clock, mostly with Patton running. And that drive led to Wersching kicking another field goal to put them up, 23–14, which was a big margin at that time of the game. That pass play was one of the big keys of the game, but nobody really mentions it.

I wasn't surprised by how well Montana was playing. He had the reputation for playing well in big games. He was young but you couldn't rattle him, even with a lot of blitzing. He had been that way coming out of Notre Dame. That poise and confidence certainly helped in that drive when we had the momentum and the game was on the line.

It wasn't desperation time yet, but certainly we had to do things quickly with just over five minutes remaining and being down by two scores. We had to get downfield in chunks and I had tried to force one in there. On the first play after we got the ball back, I tried to hit Collinsworth down the left side. That was pretty much the same play I'd completed to Cris earlier, but this time it was a little shorter and Eric Wright made a nice play, stepping in front of it to make the interception. Wright actually lost the ball on his runback, but the 49ers recovered, and that led to their final field goal, Wersching's fourth of the game.

When we got the ball back, we were down, 26–14, with less than two minutes left and no time-outs. We went right down the field and scored. We completed six straight passes, and Ross, a great receiver who set a Super Bowl record with 11 receptions, made his second touchdown catch from the 3. Some people criticized us for throwing those passes down the middle of the field because that would prevent us from getting out of bounds to stop the clock. But if there's less than two minutes in the game, and you are told you can score a touchdown and still have a few seconds left on the clock to try an onside kick, you'd agree to it. We did exactly what we wanted to do under the circumstances. We made the plays and scored, and then had the chance to recover an onside kick.

I hadn't given up. If we recovered the onside kick, I thought there was still enough time for us to get a touchdown. We'd made a lot of big plays all year long. We just wanted one more chance. Unfortunately, Dwight Clark was able to cover the kick and we lost, 26–21.

I was impressed by San Francisco's performance. We had a lot of respect for that team. They had a great coach and a lot of great players who would get more attention as the years went on: Montana and Clark, the offensive linemen, and the players they had on defense. Ronnie Lott and Eric Wright were rookies, but look at how well they would play for years to come. They were a doggone good football team. Were they a better team than us? On that day they were. Could we beat the 49ers? There was no doubt in my mind that we could. But we didn't do it and they deserve all the credit in the world. They made a lot of big plays when it counted and we made all those mistakes. The first interception I threw, Cris's fumble inside their 10, our mishandling of the two squib kicks before halftime, their goal-line stand, and Montana completing that pass to Wilson. Those were the plays that made the difference.

I guess it's never fun when you lose, so I'd say that Super Bowl loss wasn't fun. It's almost more disappointing as time goes on. At that time we thought we were a pretty good football team and we were going to have other shots to go to the Super Bowl. That shot didn't happen while I was still playing, so my only Super Bowl experience, my only chance to play in a world championship game, was a loss. It was the same for a lot of other guys on that team. Does one game determine whether you had a good career or not? No. Anyway, I played pretty well in that game, although my early interception was one of many things that hurt us. But what you always played for was to win a championship, and I guess that's the one thing I'll always be disappointed about. I won a lot of passing titles and got awards, but we never won the world championship.

The thing I'm probably best remembered for that day is for carrying my son off the field when the game was over. That was the first time anybody had done that. In fact, a picture of us was in the Cincinnati papers the next day, and when you look at a Super Bowl XVI highlight film, the ending shot is of me carrying him. He was six years old and that was something he'd remember for the rest of his life. In fact, that is probably my fondest memory of that day.

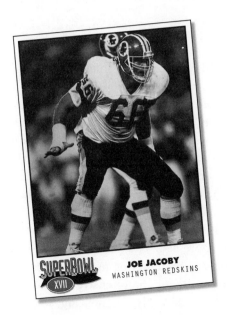

JOE JACOBY
WASHINGTON REDSKINS

SUPER BOWL XVII

WASHINGTON REDSKINS 27
MIAMI DOLPHINS 17

JOE JACOBY

I was already 6'6" or 6'7" in my senior year of high school. I made Kentucky's all-state basketball team, but I realized that my huge mass made me more suited for football. I was an offensive lineman in high school and that's what I played when I went to Louisville. Because Louisville wasn't a major football factory, I was pretty much overlooked by the pros when I played there. That wasn't upsetting because I wasn't really thinking of playing in the NFL until the scouts started looking at people after my senior year. In January, the Redskins, Bucs, and Seahawks worked me out and told me what I needed to do by the time they came back in April, prior to the second round of the draft. So I thought of it seriously for the first time. I had never really worked out, but now I did lifting and running and increased my size, going from 275 to 295. That started it: I would live in the weight room for the next 15 years.

The scouts returned and told me that if I didn't go in the draft and became a free agent, they'd like to bring me in so I could check out their organizations. After I wasn't drafted, Tampa and Seattle called me. In fact, Seattle had a scout sitting in my living room with a three-year contract when the Redskins called to ask me to fly to Washington, D.C. I had never been to the nation's capital and wanted to take the trip, so that night the Seattle scout drove me to the airport. After I landed, I drove down the George Washington Parkway and saw all the national monuments. I was pretty impressed. The next day I went in and met with the Redskins. Joe Gibbs was there, trying to put a team together in his first year as head coach. Joe Bugel, the offensive-line coach, kept me entertained. He still jokes about it: "It was amazing; we got you for just two steak subs."

There were many players coming in, including a lot of free agents. In fact, I was the nineteenth offensive lineman they brought in. Joe Gibbs sat there for 20 minutes talking with me about his ideas and goals for the team and telling me what they were expecting of me. All along he's thinking I'm a defensive lineman. I didn't want to say anything. After he gets up and walks out, I go into another room and sign a two-year contract. After playing 10 or 11 years, I would find out that Coach Gibbs was upset with Joe Bugel for bringing me in and signing me when Gibbs thought I was a defensive player. He was yelling, "How can we get out of this contract?" I bring that up to Joe Gibbs every now and then.

When I showed up at the Redskins' first minicamp, Coach Gibbs wasn't determined to use me now that he was stuck with me. Basically, I just held the practice dummies. However, since the veterans weren't supposed to come to the second minicamp—it was just rookies and free agents—I got a majority of the work. I really didn't put any pressure on myself. I did tell myself that this was probably my only chance at the NFL and would give it my best shot, but I didn't worry if it didn't work out. It did work out because they got to see that they had something. I wasn't surprised that I was doing well—I had just tapped into a natural resource I hadn't used yet. Otherwise, I was just doing what I had always done, which is to play football and enjoy doing it. I got increasingly more work at the next minicamp, before training camp. Then, since the first 7 to 10 days of training camp was basically all rookies, I was in on every snap and getting better and better. They were more and more impressed.

We had injuries early in the year, so I started filling in for people. My first start as a pro came in the third game. I started a couple of games at right guard, one game at left guard, and a couple of games at right tackle. Then at the halfway point of the season, I was switched to left tackle, where I'd play 9 or 10 years until we brought in Jim Lachey and I moved back to right tackle. Russ Grimm, my roommate, was at left guard, and Jeff Bostic was at center, and the three of us would play all those years together. The idea for a very big, mobile offensive line came from Joe Bugel. He had a good offensive line when he was down in Houston and Earl Campbell was the running back. He told Coach Gibbs what was needed to get to the show: "You're going to need big guys up front and you build everything else from that."

In that first year, they were shuffling players around to find out who fit where and what the best combinations of players were. Everybody was getting adjusted to a new system and working with all new people. We opened the season 0–5 but won 8 of the last 11 to finish 8–8. We started to jell as a team. The defense started playing much better and the offense changed its style and started to get good results. Even when we were 0–5, we were number one on offense. We just weren't scoring a lot of points. That drove Joe Gibbs crazy. He was saying, "How can this be going on? We're racking up all these yards and not winning any games. We've just got to get back to the basics." We had been relying on passing, but Coach Gibbs changed us into a team that relied on a good ground game built around his offensive line and the running of John Riggins.

John had held out the year before, so it was good to have him back there. He was a big man at about 6'3" and 245, and even if you didn't get a good block for him or had a stalemate on a play, you knew he would get you at least 3 yards on his own. He was always leaning toward the line of scrimmage and would run somebody over, so you knew he'd get those yards. John wasn't someone who would shake-and-bake—he preferred to go through somebody rather than trying to avoid him. John wanted to win, but I think he wanted to play even more. He loved the physical aspect of running with a football and actually looked forward to the physical beating. In fact, he thrived on it: After 20 carries, he was just getting warmed up.

Because John had so much success running, it opened up our passing game, and after years of struggling to prove himself, Joe Theismann was able to emerge as one of the league's best quarterbacks. He was a very accurate passer and also an excellent runner. We told Joe that we liked it best when he stayed in the pocket, but we knew he liked to scramble. Fortunately, we linemen were young then and could keep up with him. I don't think his running bothered us that much. In fact, Coach Gibbs had some designated sprint outs in there because of Joe's running ability. He wasn't the tallest quarterback, so we also used a lot of deep drops for him, because we needed to get him outside the pocket to throw over it.

Coach Gibbs's ball-control philosophy and how he wanted things done—all of that became ingrained in our minds. I think his biggest strength was to prepare us in the classroom to execute the game plan. It was all laid out for us in our playbooks. Joe allowed everybody on his staff to play an integral part in making sure everybody was ready. Each coach broke down and prepared a different part of the game plan. On the practice field, we combined all those things and everything came together for Sunday.

The young linemen learned a lot that year. Jeff Bostic, Russ Grimm, and I were 22 and right guard Mark May was 21, and not only did we enjoy playing with each other but we also formed friendships that would remain even after our careers were over. I think our abilities were different. Jeff was not very big as far as offensive linemen go. He would probably not like me saying this, but when he says he's 6'2", I don't know where he gets those 2" from. Jeff was an undersized center who probably weighed only 260, but he could maneuver defensive linemen around with his great run-blocking techniques, and he had the great tenacity to get underneath and pass block. Russ played off his athletic abilities. He wasn't highly motivated when it came to working out—he hated it—but would give you 110 percent on the field. He would play until he couldn't do it anymore, and lay his body on the line, as his many scars proved. Mark was not the most gifted athlete, but he was a big guy and had a lot of fight in him. To get the job done, he would go down swinging, kicking, biting, and scratching. For a tall 300-pounder, I was very agile, very good at running, and very good at maneuvering in tight places. I always thought I was a better run blocker—pass blocking was probably the weak part of my game. The veteran on the line was our right tackle, George Starke. He was over 30 and we looked to him as someone with knowledge of other teams' defensive schemes and the players each of us would have to block on the coming Sunday. Off the field, George was a leader who made sure we were entertained but didn't get into trouble.

Our Super Bowl season was interrupted after the second week by an NFL players strike. There wasn't anything to do, so Grimm, Bostic, tight end Don Warren, and I would play cards until four or five in the morning.

All the Redskins players hung together as a group during those weeks we were out and there wasn't much bitching and complaining. The relationships that formed paid off for us when the season resumed.

Theismann and a couple of the other players organized workouts in parks to keep the guys ready. They were useful to the receivers and defensive backs because they could do seven-on-seven skeleton patterns. The receivers could work on their routes and the backs could work on their reads and adjustments. But the offensive linemen couldn't get anything out of it. We went for a couple of weeks, but it wasn't beneficial because we couldn't get our timing down or work on our blocking schemes because there was no physical contact.

I was just about ready to go back home to Kentucky when the settlement was announced. If it hadn't been settled that week, I don't think there would have been a season. So we came back in late November, and after being off for eight or nine weeks, we had to play a game after only three days. Was I in shape? Let's put it this way: During the strike is when I first started to play golf. None of our linemen were in football shape. Fortunately, when we played our first game against the Giants, the linemen we faced were in the same shape we were in.

Nineteen eighty-two, when we went 8–1 to win the Eastern Division, was a unique experience. There were 45 individuals, different characters, who unselfishly played together for one common goal. If there were any personality conflicts between our players off the field, that was left behind when we played together. We had the normal getting on each other, the ribbing, the kidding, but if there was any tension, I didn't see it. It was well known that Theismann and Riggins had different personalities, but they each knew how important the other guy was to the success of the team and—I know because I stood across from John—there was no tension between them in the huddle. Or between anybody else.

During the season, the offensive line got its famous nickname. From then on we were called the Hogs. I don't remember the circumstances of how that name came about and I've heard different stories, but I do know it came from Joe Bugel. He called us different things but basically called us Hogs. He was the one who printed up the Hogs T-shirt. Joe wanted to give his offensive line its own identity and make us feel important. That was his way. He was a motivator and was always trying to keep the guys positive in their outlook. Maybe at the time I was surprised by the tremendous fan response to the Hogs, but looking back I realize that when you're winning, anything catches on. We were winning and it did catch on and keep building and building as we headed into the playoffs. Fans at RFK Stadium had these pig noses on and that's when the Hogettes started, and there were all these men in dresses and in other getups. It was a pretty wild time. I have a lot of fond memories of those loyal Washington fans in the stands. Our fans were a little bit different.

We Hogs wanted to have fun and didn't take ourselves seriously, so we'd do things like go out on the town in tuxedos. We didn't mind the attention. We enjoyed ourselves off the field. We were invited to join the team's "5 O'Clock Club," which was a little after-practice ritual. Sonny Jurgensen told me that it had started—and you may find this hard to believe—back when Vince Lombardi became the Redskins coach and general manager in the late sixties. After practice at camp, Lombardi would buy his players beer so that they would sit around together and build a close-knit camaraderie. That ritual was then passed on to George Allen's "Over-the-Hill Gang" and to future Redskins teams. When Grimm, Bostic, and I arrived on the scene in 1981, we'd like to have a few beers every now and then, so we were adopted by this club. At the time, the other members were John Riggins and offensive guard Ron Saul, who was no longer on the team in '82. The "5 O'Clock Club" didn't just have offensive linemen, but we were in the majority. We'd have a few beers before we went home and have a good time socializing.

The offensive linemen weren't part of the "Fun Bunch" who jumped around in the end zone after touchdowns. That was just the receivers. They were jealous that the Hogs were getting all their limelight, so they had to create their own group. A few were so small that they got another nickname, "The Smurfs." A picture was taken of me holding my arms out, and the Smurfs were standing underneath my arms without touching them. Art Monk, our star receiver, was too tall to be a Smurf, but Charlie Brown was under 6', so he might have fit in there, but the real Smurfs were Alvin Garrett and Virgil Seay, who were 5'8" or less.

The players did have a good time, but we also played good football. Washington made the playoffs for the first time since 1976 by beating the Giants 15–14 on a kick by Mark Moseley, the league's Most Valuable Player. He broke Garo Yepremian's record for consecutive field goals with that kick. Somebody brought that field goal up recently and I said I was out there on the field . . . in the pile somewhere.

Because of the strike, there was an extra playoff round that year. That made for a lot of excitement in Washington because we had the NFC's best record and got to play all our playoff games at home. In our opening game, Riggins had the first of his four consecutive 100-yard postseason games when we beat Detroit 31–7. Then we beat Minnesota 21–7, as Riggins ran for 185 yards. I have a vivid memory of beating the Vikings and hearing our fans yelling, "We want the Cowboys!"

Those two playoff games had been fairly easy, but our only loss during the year had been to the Cowboys, our opponent in the NFC Championship Game. Before that game, we're sitting in the locker room, and Joe Bugel, who had been very even-keeled during the season and was not a smoker, is now chain-smoking and telling us to be calm and not get uptight. Joe Gibbs said we weren't going to do anything fancy; we're going to do what got us that far. The first play was a Gut play, just a simple basic hand-off to Riggins that went off tackle. Fifty-Gut would be off me. John went into the line and it looked as if he was going to be stopped after 2 or 3 yards, but we kept pushing, and when we tumbled down we discovered that it was second-and-1. We'd gotten 9 yards against them without any trouble, so we knew what kind of day it was going to be. Riggins went on to pick up 140 yards and we won fairly easily, 31–17.

One of the biggest plays was when our defensive end Dexter Manley knocked their quarterback Danny White out of the game. Dexter and Lawrence Taylor started that mode of defensive athlete who was big and strong, yet could run and really get after the quarterback. I remember back when we had Dexter on punt coverage. He'd line up wide as the "kill man." He had two or three guys on him, but he was about 6'4" and 250 and could run a 4.5 40, so when those little defensive backs tried to hold him up at the line of scrimmage, he threw them all over the place and ran by them. It was amazing to watch him. I improved as a player because I had to go against Dexter every day in practice. It wasn't easy pass blocking against him—with his speed, I had to backpedal a lot. He definitely helped me prepare to play against a player like Lawrence Taylor.

We flew out to California to play in Super Bowl XVII against the Miami Dolphins, who were coached by Don Shula. Now, you're out there at all these press conferences, sitting at your table and hearing all the questions. . . . It was unbelievable the attention we were getting because there was no game left to be played except the game we were going to be in. I had grown up watching the Super Bowl, and here I was just 23, and now I was going to be one of the players everybody would be watching.

Few reporters brought up that this was a rematch of Super Bowl VII. That was 10 years ago, so the Redskins weren't thinking about avenging that loss. We did talk about the money we'd get if we beat them. Salaries were quite different then, so the winner's share of $70,000 was three times what I made during the season. We talked only about the winner's share because we expected to win, although Miami was considered the favorite. We liked that underdog role. So did Joe Gibbs.

At our first meeting Gibbs said, "We're not going to change our routine. What we did the whole regular season is what we're going to do here." So we did what we normally did. If you went out at night during the season, you went out now. We did have our fun, but we were disciplined enough not to get into trouble. After that we got down to business. We had great practices. Joe Gibbs's philosophy was that you practice full tilt Wednesday, Thursday, and Friday, so you don't have any shocks on Sunday. The only thing we didn't do was tackle, but we went full go until the whistle and we had some hellacious practices. It got so intense that Joe was afraid we were going to hurt each other. He had to slow us down because he was worried about our emotional state. But we were in the right frame of mind; we were ready to play.

I slept fine the night before the Super Bowl. I was nervous but I still slept. The next day we went to the Rose Bowl. Because of the age of the stadium, there wasn't much of a locker room. There were no individual cubicles—it was basically just hooks on the wall. That was astonishing to me considering this was the Super Bowl. Still, I thought it was pretty neat that we were playing in the Rose Bowl. As we waited for the game to start, we were pretty upbeat. Nobody was quiet. Guys were talking about what they had to do: let's not get uptight; let's just play our game. You didn't want to get all the way to the Super Bowl and then lose because people only remember the winner.

I had never played at the Rose Bowl before and it was a rush to go out onto the field. And then to hear the national anthem. There is a special feeling that you get at Super Bowls because of the gala entertainment aspect that the organizers bring to it. It is kind of hard not to be infatuated by the whole event. There is a big-time rush. There were 100,000 people in the stands—at the time, I didn't think about who was in the stands or watching us on television because I was focused on the game. But now looking back on it, it was amazing how many people were watching us play football that day.

We had scored first in all three playoff games, and Miami was the only team to score in the first quarter. Jimmy Cefalo got away from our secondary and caught a 20-yard sideline pass from David Woodley that ended up going for about 75 yards and a touchdown. It was a shocker, but it was still

January 30, 1983, at the Rose Bowl in Pasadena, California
Paid Attendance: 103,667
AFC Champion: Miami Dolphins (10–2)
Head Coach: Don Shula
NFC Champion: Washington Redskins (11–1)
Head Coach: Joe Gibbs

STARTING LINEUPS

OFFENSE				DEFENSE		
Miami		**Washington**	**Miami**		**Washington**
Duriel Harris	WR	Alvin Garrett	Doug Betters	LE	Mat Mendenhall
Jon Giesler	LT	Joe Jacoby		LT	Dave Butz
Bob Kuechenberg	LG	Russ Grimm	Bob Baumhower	NT	
Dwight Stephenson	C	Jeff Bostic		RT	Darryl Grant
Jeff Toews	RG	Fred Dean	Kim Bokamper	RE	Dexter Manley
Eric Laakso	RT	George Starke	Bob Brudzinski	LOLB	
Bruce Hardy	TE	Don Warren		LLB	Mel Kaufman
	TE	Rick Walker	A. J. Duhe	LILB	
Jimmy Cefalo	WR	Charlie Brown		MLB	Neal Olkewicz
David Woodley	QB	Joe Theismann	Earnie Rhone	RILB	
Tony Nathan	RB			RLB	Rich Milot
Andra Franklin	RB	John Riggins	Larry Gordon	ROLB	
			Gerald Small	LCB	Jeris White
			Don McNeal	RCB	Vernon Dean
			Glenn Blackwood	SS	Tony Peters
			Lyle Blackwood	FS	Mark Murphy

SUBSTITUTIONS

Miami: K—Uwe von Schamann. P—Tom Orosz. Offense: Receivers—Vince Heflin, Ronnie Lee, Nat Moore, Joe Rose. Linemen—Mark Dennard, Roy Foster, Cleveland Green. Backs—Woody Bennett, Rich Diana, Eddie Hill, Jim Jensen, Don Strock (QB), Tom Vigorito. Defense: Linebackers—Charles Bowser, Ron Hester, Steve Potter, Steve Shull. Lineman—Vern Den Herder. Backs—William Judson, Mike Kozlowski, Paul Lankford, Fulton Walker. DNP—Richard Bishop, Steve Clark, Mark Duper.

Washington: K—Mark Moseley. P—Jeff Hayes. Offense: Receivers—Clint Didier, Virgil Seay. Linemen—Donald Laster, Mark May. Backs—Nick Giaquinto, Clarence Harmon, Wilbur Jackson, Otis Wonsley. Defense: Linebackers—Monte Coleman, Peter Cronan, Larry Kubin, Quentin Lowry. Linemen—Perry Brooks, Todd Liebenstein, Tony McGee. Backs—Curtis Jordan, Joe Lavender, LeCharls McDaniel, Mike Nelms, Greg Williams. DNP—Rich Caster, Bob Holly, Tom Owen, Garry Puetz, Joe Washington.

Miami	7	10	0	0—17
Washington	0	10	3	14—27

Mia	Cefalo 76 pass from Woodley (von Schamann kick)
Wash	FG Moseley 31
Mia	FG von Schamann 20
Wash	Garrett 4 pass from Theismann (Moseley kick)
Mia	Walker 98 kickoff return (von Schamann kick)
Wash	FG Moseley 20
Wash	Riggins 43 run (Moseley kick)
Wash	Brown 6 pass from Theismann (Moseley kick)
MVP:	John Riggins (Washington)

only the first quarter and it would be a long game. Neither the coaches nor the players worried about it. We knew what we could do on offense.

In our first couple of offensive series, I think we were just caught up in playing in the Super Bowl. It was hard not to be excited. Theismann was probably a little hyper, but I'd say that was true for all of us. We moved the ball pretty well, but we were forced to punt when we let them sack Theismann a couple of times on third down. Then all of us calmed down and we began to play much better. We finally put a scoring drive together on our third possession, which began after Dexter Manley sacked Woodley and Butz recovered his fumble. We got the ball past midfield, and then Riggins just took over, carrying the ball on almost every play.

In our one-back offense, Riggins pretty much ran to the right and middle earlier in the game, but in this drive he mostly ran off left tackle, my position. I don't know if this had anything to do with the game plan, but for the rest of the game he would run to either side, as well as straight ahead. It was quite simple. The Redskins offense wasn't as diversified as it would be as the years went on. Basically we had a dive play to the right and kind of an outside run and we had the same thing to the left—50-Gut was a dive off left tackle—and maybe one or two more running plays, and that was all. In addition, we had a fairly conservative passing game. So there wasn't a lot we did, but defenses had a hard time stopping us.

That drive ended early in the second quarter when Mark Moseley kicked a medium-range field goal to put us on the scoreboard and cut their lead to four points. But Miami came right back to put together what turned out to be its only successful drive of the game. Our defense did shut them down inside our 10 and they came away with only a chip shot by Uwe von Schamann to up their lead to seven points again. I don't know how much I saw of Miami's drive. During the first couple of plays of each series, our offensive linemen were over with the coaches and going over what happened on our previous possession. Only then would I go over to the sidelines and watch our defense. It was still early in the game, so I wasn't worried when Miami upped its lead. Knowing what our defense had done through the year, I figured they'd catch up to Miami's offense and shut down Woodley, Cefalo, and their running backs, Tony Nathan and Andra Franklin. Being in the AFC, Miami was a team we hadn't seen, and with Don Shula as the coach, they had a philosophy that we weren't all that familiar with. So I knew it would take our defense awhile to adjust and stop them. I'm not sure what our defense's game plan was, but I'd say it wanted to shut down Miami's running game and give them only one option: to rely on David Woodley, who wasn't the most fearsome passer. Once the defense had done that, I assumed it would then try to pressure Woodley, who was a very young quarterback, into making mistakes. It did get burned on that pass to Cefalo and had allowed Miami deep penetration on their field-goal drive, but after that, as I anticipated, our defense completely shut them down.

Meanwhile, we were starting to get the best of Miami's "Killer Bee" defense that was named after its six defensive starters whose last names began with the letter "B": their ends Kim Bokamper, who was the guy I played against, and Doug Betters, nose tackle Bob Baumhower, linebacker Bob Brudzinski, and safeties Lyle and Glenn Blackwood. Miami had a good defense, but before the first half was over, we began to wear them down with our size and strength. They didn't match up well against us.

We came back to tie the score after a long drive. We had the ball inside their 5 and were using our "Explode Package," which Coach Gibbs put in that week to be used inside their 20-yard line. I'm still amazed by Joe's offensive input and how he would try innovative things—like what we did that led to our first touchdown. We started in one formation and everybody shifted. All the receivers were in a tight bunch and just moved out, and as a result the Dolphins didn't know what to do with their secondary coverage. I seem to remember that we scored on a little corner pattern to Garrett. Alvin stepped in for Art Monk, who was out the whole playoffs with a foot injury, and he made a lot of big plays for us.

We were still congratulating ourselves for that drive when Fulton Walker, who'd returned our previous kickoff to almost midfield, ran this one back 98 yards without being touched. That was very discouraging from the offensive standpoint. We'd finally put together a good drive, kept our defense off the field, loosened things up with some passing, and had some momentum. We thought we were deadlocked and we were again behind by seven points only 30 seconds later.

We almost came back to score again before the end of the half. In fact, we were in field-goal range, but messed up trying for a touchdown. We'd run out of time-outs, but instead of throwing into the end zone, Theismann hit Garrett on a little pass in the left flat. Garrett was inside their 10, but he didn't get out of bounds and the clock ran out.

Despite what had happened at the end of the first half, we weren't that discouraged at the break. The way our defense was now dominating them, we didn't see how they could score again. We didn't like that we were behind, 17–10, on the scoreboard, but we had 30 minutes to turn that around. As I said before: We knew what we were capable of doing. They hadn't really stopped us yet—we had stopped ourselves with silly mental mistakes and miscues. All we had to do was execute.

On our second possession of the second half we had a big reverse play. We wanted to throw them some misdirection to keep them off-balance so they couldn't just key on our basic running plays and crowd some secondary guys on the line of scrimmage. My job, with the tight end right there with me, was to fake like I was blocking on a play where John was going to run a dive off right tackle or a sweep to the right. Then, when we got the defense to chase John, he handed the ball to Garrett, the receiver coming back around in the opposite direction. I thought Garrett was going all the way, but he got tackled after gaining over 40 yards, and eventually we settled for a short field goal by Moseley.

We were disappointed not to get seven and to be trailing still, but were glad to keep the score tight so we'd be in position to pull it out. I was encouraged because our defense was completely shutting down the Dolphins. They had no ground game by this point and their passing game was worse: a complete zero. Neither Woodley nor his replacement Don Strock completed a pass in the second half, and I think they picked up only two first downs and 34 yards in those 30 minutes.

The teams exchanged interceptions and we had the ball on our 18 when Theismann tried to pass. The play was called Charlie-Ten-Hitch and it was basically a short dropback, two to three steps, and Joe was supposed to throw it to the right. Doug Betters, who was George Starke's man, was 6'7", and when he jumped into the air, Joe didn't have anywhere to throw the ball. So Joe pulled it down and was going to throw it to the left. I had cut down Kim Bokamper on that side, but by this time he'd recovered and gotten back up. This is when Bokamper tipped the pass up into the air directly above him, and Joe made a big play, recovering in time to get his hand in there and knock the ball away before Bokamper got a firm grip on it and ran into the end zone. At the time I wondered what I'd done wrong to let Bokamper deflect that pass. I didn't know until we looked at the film of the game the next year in camp that it wasn't my fault; Betters had made the great play on the other side that forced Theismann to change his play. We were very relieved in the huddle to still have the ball and we were all saying, "Good job, Joe," because they could have gone ahead 24–13 if Joe hadn't reacted so quickly. So we regained our composure.

The other big play of the game came early in the fourth quarter when we were still behind, 17–13. We had fourth down with less than a foot to go on Miami's 43. Rather than punting, Coach Gibbs called a running play for Riggins. Seventy-Chip was one of our short-yardage goal-line plays. It was supposed to go to the left, outside, with myself and a tight end over there blocking. One tight end, Clint Didier, was supposed to come back in motion and then to kick out. Our "I" back, Otis Wonsley, was supposed to lead up and chip into the line and take anybody on. Everybody did their job. Wonsley gave a wicked block and Riggins had a lean little seam to run through. Meanwhile Didier's motion caused one of the Blackwood brothers to slip. Don McNeal, one of their corners, got both hands on Riggins as he came through but couldn't get the clean hit he needed to bring him down. By the time John broke the line of scrimmage, all he had to do was shake the smaller McNeal and he was gone. I didn't watch John run down the field for the go-ahead touchdown because I was covered up by then. But I heard all the horns and I knew what John had done. Needless to say, that was a very big moment, probably the biggest of the game.

We were now ahead for the first time, 20–17, and really pumped up. We knew what we had to do to milk this game out for the final 10 minutes. Our defense would stop the Miami offense, and we would just keep giving Riggins the ball. He ran to the left, to the right, up the middle. By this time our constant beating on their defensive guys had just worn them out. It wasn't easy for 250-pound defensive players taking on 300-pound linemen by that time. After leaning on Bokamper for three and a half quarters, he wasn't having the same success. The rest of their line was just as tired. Now we could get 4, 5, 6, 7 yards at a crack and that kind of running further wears on a defense. Their secondary was now making the tackles and that's something you don't want if you're on defense.

I don't remember if we were aware that John Riggins was approaching the Super Bowl rushing record. It might have been brought up, but I don't think we were trying to get him the record at the time. However, once he set the record with 166 yards, that was a source of enormous pride for the offensive linemen. It was something we could look back on and know we had been a big part of, as was the team rushing record for a Super Bowl. That was 276 yards. We took a great deal of pride in that, as well.

Our final score came on another short pass by Theismann. This one went to our other wide receiver, Charlie Brown. Joe sprinted out to the right, outside the pocket, and we had one of the guards, Fred Dean— who was in for May—pulling out that way. Joe found Brown in the front corner of the end zone. It was a great play and put the game out of reach, 27–17.

Before the final play of the game in which Joe put his knee down, we were all looking at each other and hugging each other. The strike that we had gone through and all the work that we had done and all the games that we had won had culminated in our winning the NFL Championship Game, the Super Bowl. What we had just experienced was something that I never thought would happen when I was a kid growing up. Just to be in this game was amazing, and then all of a sudden you're a Super Bowl champion. You know you're the best in your profession, and your peers will look up to you. It was a great feeling to have, especially in just my second year. To win it in Pasadena, and to win it rushing the ball and with our defense playing great, was just a very big thrill.

We had a lot of pride in how many free agents and nondrafted players were on that team. Most of the guys on the team had been brought in that way. That speaks highly of the Redskins owner Jack Kent Cooke and of the Redskins management. And that speaks highly of Coach Gibbs and his staff for picking the right people who could blend in together and also being able to motivate and inspire them to come so far.

I played in three winning Super Bowls and loved the experience each time, but that first Super Bowl experience means so much. In the later ones I felt, "I've been here and know what it's about." In your first one, you don't know what it's about and you have all those exciting, unexpected feelings, and there are new things around each corner. All those Super Bowls were great, but because I got to experience so many things for the first time that day in the Rose Bowl, I would have to say that I cherish Super Bowl XVII even more than the others.

TODD CHRISTENSEN
LOS ANGELES RAIDERS

SUPER BOWL XVIII

LOS ANGELES RAIDERS 38
WASHINGTON REDSKINS 9

TODD CHRISTENSEN

In January 1981, when the Raiders won the Super Bowl as a wild-card team in New Orleans, I was the special teams captain and called tails when Marie Lombardi, Vince Lombardi's widow, tossed the coin before the game. It was heads. I really thought that was going to be my claim to fame in Super Bowl history.

At the time, playing special teams seemed as far as I would go with the Raiders. That's basically all I had done since I joined the team prior to the fifth game of the 1979 season. At my tryout, Raiders owner Al Davis sat me down and said, "We're looking for some good athletes to play special teams, young people to build us back up." After being cut by the Giants, who had drafted me as a running back out of Brigham Young, and not catching on after tryouts with New England, Green Bay, Philadelphia, and Chicago, I would have shined shoes if he'd asked me. I was listed as a fullback but I didn't play a single down on offense during the remainder of the '79 season. My ability to snap on punts, run under kicks, and play the wedge, and my being young and exuberant, is what kept me in the league until they figured out that I could play.

During the 1980 preseason, Tom Flores said they had to find a position for me. Nobody was interested in me as a running back, so I said, "What about tight end?" In 1979, because of injuries to the wide receivers, both Raiders tight ends, Dave Casper and Ray Chester, caught nearly 60 balls and made the Pro Bowl team. So when I asked to play tight end, that was akin to someone going to the Met when Placido Domingo and Luciano Pavarotti were performing and saying he wanted to sing tenor.

The first preseason game, we're playing San Francisco and they're just kicking the crap out of us, 32–0, after three quarters. So Flores stuck me in along with a has-been quarterback named Jim Plunkett. In one quarter I caught seven passes and two touchdowns. It was an exhibition game and we were going against defensive backs who had numbers like 106 and weren't going to make the team, but they saw I had some ability. I think that's when I made the team. But I wouldn't catch a pass all season.

In 1981 after the Super Bowl win, they stuck me into some funny situations, like as a fullback coming out of the backfield, or they'd line me up in the slot. I wasn't an offensive threat of any consequence, but I did make eight receptions. Suddenly there was frustration, and my special-teams play slipped a bit. I was proud to play special teams, especially on the Raiders, but it was like being a bailiff when you wanted to be an attorney—you're in the courtroom, but it's not like you get big pay or opportunities. I was wondering why I wasn't in there at tight end because Casper had been traded, Chester had just turned 85 or 90, and Derrick Ramsey just couldn't catch the ball. And the Raiders were losing.

In 1982 the team was living in Oakland and traveling to L.A. for games because the franchise had moved, and we were now the Los Angeles Raiders. My frustration had not waned, but this was the last year of my contract, and I was thinking I'd just play and worry about my situation the next year. That's when I got some unexpected and much welcomed playing time because Chester was clearly on his way out and Ramsey got hurt in the preseason. I made only three catches in the first two games against San Francisco and Atlanta, but one beat the 49ers and all were key plays in our victories. So we were 2–0 and the strike came. By the time it ended, Ramsey's knee was better, but Flores decided to start me at tight end in a big game against San Diego.

It was *Monday Night Football* on national television, we were debuting in our new place, and the L.A. crowd wasn't happy with its new team because we're down 24–10 and San Diego's Dan Fouts is unstoppable. We get a drive going and decide to go for it on fourth down—and Plunkett hits me with a touchdown pass. They stuck a hand-held camera in my face at the sidelines, and I looked right at it and said, "We're coming back!" Well, that seemed kind of bold for this nonentity, but in the second half we had a bunch of drives and won 28–24, and I ended up with eight or nine catches for over 100 yards. It was out of a storybook. We got to the airport late at night and as we were getting on the plane, Tom Flores turned to me and said, "You've worked very hard, you've waited your turn, and now it's your time." I remember thinking to myself, *"Yes!"* Finally, it was happening.

So beginning in 1982, I became Plunkett's primary receiver. Defenses had to pay so much attention to Cliff Branch going deep and to rookie Marcus Allen rushing and catching passes out of the backfield that I was able to become a garbage man. I seemed to catch all these 12-yard passes, and at the end of the game the stats said seven catches for 100 yards and a touchdown—it added up. All the way back to Billy Cannon, the Raiders had utilized the tight end, and I knew what to do as a tight end in their system because I had watched Casper and Chester. The genetic gift I was endowed with was that I could catch the football, but the stances, releases, routes, and blocking, I had to learn. I made it a point to the press that "I'm just another slow white guy," but the truth was I was fast.

I had a pretty good 1982 season and was an alternate to the Pro Bowl, which is like being vice president—who cares? Then in 1983, everyone took notice and I made the Pro Bowl as a starter. I'm not the Pete Rose of football players, so I don't memorize all my stats, but that year I had 92 catches for 1,247 yards and 12 touchdowns. At the time, it was the most catches ever for a tight end, the second most yards, and the most touchdowns; and when you combine that with the fact that we would win the Super Bowl, I think I would have to get the nod for having the greatest season for a tight end in the history of the league. I point this out because the Raiders would become the only team to win a Super Bowl with the league's leading receiver.

I knew my reputation of being a pseudointellectual and being deeply religious was not synonymous with the Raider image. But what nobody understood is that the Raiders were concerned with only one thing: Can you play? Beyond that you could do what you wanted and be whoever you were. In that regard, I fit in fine. And because of that freedom, the Raiders had so many other self-motivated people.

Over the years, the press wanted to pick out things about the Raiders that would accrue the most notoriety. So they'd write about Stabler with the women or Matuszak with the machete and ask, "How many girls were in the hot tub?" or "Who's been paroled? Ha, ha." But they didn't take into account what a good team was being assembled and that some of our guys with offbeat reputations, like Ted Hendricks and Dave Casper, were bright, bright people and among the most savvy players in the league. Prior to 1980, the paramilitaristic mode of operation is what the other organizations were abiding by, and only Al Davis was willing to take chances on a so-called problem child. Davis didn't worry about the image of his club. I genuinely believe that was a big edge for us. All of us reveled in our renegade image. We had an "us-against-the-world" attitude, which our coaches played up to motivate us, and we welcomed the opportunity to take on all challengers. There were many games when we were favorites, but even then we played the role of underdogs because we knew everyone wanted to see us get beat. We enjoyed that.

The 1980 wild-card team, which had 22 of 40 players who had been cut or traded by other organizations, won the NFL title because everything went our way, but in truth we were probably about the fifth-best team in the league. However, in 1982, when we went 8–1 during the regular season, and in 1983, we were the best team. Through the draft and trades, the Raiders had become a superior team athletically. There was no contest when we matched up against other teams. That old-style renegade mentality still existed, but fewer players had the desperation of a warrior on his last legs. We had so many good players that there was a different chemistry, as good a chemistry but a different one.

I'd say the leaders included Ted Hendricks, Rod Martin, Mike Davis, and Lyle Alzado, among many others. But none of them would get up and yell, "Come on guys, we've gotta pull together," because they would have been laughed out of the room. We were a group of self-starters, so I don't think we needed someone in charge or an inspirational leader. Instead, we had people like Hendricks who led by example.

Tom Flores was a great fit for our team, where you had so many dominant personalities, so many guys who had TV and radio shows, guys who were high profile. A Mike Ditka–type would have been obnoxious and never worked. Flores had the ability to sublimate his ego. He was a calm guy on the sidelines and behind the scenes. Tom was a very bright man, but because of the way things shook out in the organization, he didn't get much publicity. He was underrated in terms of his knowledge of the game.

Al Davis got most of the publicity. It may have been the impression, due to his manipulation of the press, that we tried to play football the way Al Davis wanted it played, but in truth the guys didn't give him a second thought. He was famous for his 2 A.M. calls to coaches, but he had nothing to do with game plans and on-the-field activities. Through the press, he got credit in a lot of instances when he shouldn't have. In fact, I had conversations with him during the season that led me to believe, "This guy's not in touch." I realized that he was a former coach, but by this time he had other things going off the field. He may have been the smartest owner in football, as many people said, but that's like being the best surfer in Alaska. I don't want this to be misconstrued because I'm not denigrating him. He did bring in great players, and I don't think people appreciate that he was a major, major player at the time of the merger between the NFL and AFL.

Nineteen eighty-two was the year we beat ourselves up because we should have gone to the Super Bowl but we lost to the Jets in the playoffs—in a ridiculous game in which we were just so unlucky. The bad taste in our mouths from that game lingered and, as a result, we were a hungry team in 1983 and did everything we could to get over the top.

Al Davis felt that too, and when he acquired Mike Haynes in November, it was an indication that he wanted to win the title immediately. I think Mike was a free agent, but we had to give the Patriots some picks. At the time nobody did that because a free agent was too costly, but Mike was a great player and Al had already made such a deal years before that had more than a modicum of success—it had brought us Ted Hendricks. This deal solidified our secondary, and there's something about having a great player that rubs off on everybody else—he did for us what Deion Sanders would do for San Francisco in 1994. You had a guy who literally could take away half the field from the offense. He didn't have blazing speed and he didn't hit like a Jack Tatum or Seattle's Kenny Easley, but his coverage skills were beyond superior. There was no one better in man-to-man coverage.

We won six of our final seven regular-season games. Then we crushed Pittsburgh on New Year's Day, 38–10, to get into the AFC Championship Game against Seattle. Guys on our team didn't give pregame speeches, but Lyle Alzado, who had joined us in 1982 after playing for years with Denver and Cleveland and never reaching the Super Bowl, stood up and made this impassioned speech about how Seattle said they were going to beat us and how he had come too far and over too long a period of time to lose now. His speech was laced with expletives, of course, but everybody was in awe as he spoke. It was fabulous, and I say this as someone who never bought into speeches or emotional outbursts before games. Afterward, we went out and just pulverized Seattle, 30–14. Going into the Super Bowl against the Washington Redskins, the Raiders were on a roll.

However, we were installed as five-point underdogs by Jimmy the Greek, although he confessed to one of our players during Super Bowl Week in Tampa, "I know you're going to win by two touchdowns or more, but for the sake of the businesspeople around me I have to make them the favorites." It sounded goofy to me. We had lost to the Redskins 37–35 at their place early in the year, when they scored 17 points in the last seven minutes. People saw the final score and concluded Washington must be better, but they weren't. We had really outplayed them and knew we were tougher physically.

I'm sure that when Joe Gibbs showed the Redskins defense films of the Raiders offense prior to the Super Bowl, they said, "You've got to be kidding!" Because we were so incredibly basic. The Raiders were notorious for not being a team of deception. We didn't have plays with three or four wide receivers; we didn't go with motion; we didn't shotgun; we didn't use a flea flicker; we didn't beat you with a double reverse. We just matched up, ran our plays, and beat the crap out of the defense.

The offensive line was made up of a bunch of hard workers and quality people. Charley Hannah, the left guard, was my roommate, so I can tell you that he had one of the worst bodies in the NFL—but he was still a good player. Not many people had heard about Charley or left tackle Bruce Davis, center Dave Dalby, right guard Mickey Marvin, or right tackle Henry Lawrence, although Lawrence and Dalby would go to Pro Bowls in their careers. They certainly didn't have the notoriety of the "Hogs," the name the media gave the Redskins' offensive line. I don't think you could have picked one guy out, and said, "Boy, this guy's a star," but they did a great job as a cohesive unit, protecting Jim Plunkett, who had won the starting quarterback job back from Marc Wilson, and opening up holes for Marcus Allen, who had his first 1,000-yard season.

In the huddle, Plunkett was businesslike. He was a bright guy, and he threw maybe the best ball of any quarterback I've seen. What I mean is a very catchable ball. He got it to you, and it wasn't a rocket. The first time I went to the Pro Bowl with John Elway, I thought, "Does the word *touch* mean anything to you, John?" Jim was unorthodox in terms of his appearance and how he did things when he scrambled, but he was an accurate passer, called a good game, and as I've said many times, got the job done.

In 1983 Jim Plunkett had 230 completions and exactly 160 of them were to Marcus and me, a running back and a tight end. So it wasn't the case that we had a long-play mentality, as the Raiders once did. Al Davis would snarl, "I want to strike fear in the opponent," so he'd try to convince everyone that we were still a long-ball team when we weren't. We were a conservative offense that didn't make mistakes. Essentially Plunkett was relying on two people at the end of the season. Marcus was running the ball and catching short passes, and I'd catch enough third-down passes to move the sticks. Every now and then Malcolm Barnwell or Cliff Branch would get a big ball.

I give a lot of credit to Cliff Branch for my success. Even though he was aging, he required special attention from the other team's best defensive backs. I would argue that during his tenure he was the fastest guy in football. A lot of guys ran 4.35 until they put on their gear, but Cliff was fast in uniform. He had a gear that was like warp five. He was amazing. When he was in the mood, he was like Richochet Rabbit, all over the field. In 1983 he knew his job was secure, so at 35, he picked his spots.

To use the Hebrew term, Marcus Allen was a *mensch*. He was a man. He might have been the toughest player I've been around, which is saying a lot for a running back. Obviously he had star quality: He was a Heisman Trophy winner at USC, he was L.A., he had all the women, all the attention, the Ferrari, all of that. Why not enjoy that when you're single, and he did. But let me tell you about Marcus. There is a killer hill in El Segundo that comes up Grand Avenue with about a 6-percent to 8-percent grade, and it is about 300 yards up from the bottom to this one spot. So I'm driving down there one Saturday in April and there's Marcus Allen, the L.A. bon vivant, running that hill. I prided myself on being conscientious about staying in shape, so you can imagine how impressed I was. That spoke volumes about how he took care of himself to do his job. Marcus had come from wonderful, wonderful people who instilled in him that work ethic.

When you talk about what Marcus contributed, it's tough to quantify, although the big numbers were all there. He gave us yards and touchdowns, and he gave us confidence. Marcus wasn't all that talkative in the huddle, but I remember a few times he'd actually tell Plunkett, "Throw the ball to Todd," which I liked. I figured he carried some weight. He was young and it wasn't his place to assert his personality, but we pretty much jumped on his back on offense against Pittsburgh and Seattle. After those big games, I'm sure the Redskins defense planned how to shut him down, but there was no way that was going to happen. The scene was set for Marcus to run roughshod over those guys.

The Redskins, like every team in the league, were aware of how good we were on special teams. We had guys like Derrick Jensen, Jeff Barnes, and even myself who could have gone to the Pro Bowl if they'd opened up slots for special-teams players then. We had great special-teams players. I still snapped for punts. I'd use that fact when I'd try to get a raise.

I snapped on punts in the Super Bowl. I made one errant snap, but Ray Guy made a spectacular catch on it and got it off. He was a tremendous athlete, and I'd seen him do such unbelievable things with regularity. He used to kick off, he could throw the ball 80 yards, and he was the best punter in the league. He was just a major contributor for us, yet I'm sure he felt a bit ostracized, as most kickers do. He was a great team player, but he was introverted and usually kept to himself. He would end up with three Super Bowl rings, and many people felt that he deserved to be the first punter inducted into the Hall of Fame.

Chris Bahr, our place kicker and another vital cog on our team, was more loquacious and gregarious. He was a very bright, analytical guy and someone I hung out with on occasion. He participated in some of the funny Raiders games and we were barrel-toss partners—Matt Millen still owes me $300 for that.

When Joe Theismann looked at films of our defense, he probably had the same response that Eagles quarterback Ron Jaworski had prior to Super Bowl XV. "They do all this Cover One, so we'll pick 'em apart." All during Super Bowl Week, we were listening to Theismann talking about what the Redskins could take advantage of and what they would do, and how Riggins was going to have a big game because we didn't stunt or do anything else that could disrupt their running game. Theismann and the Redskins didn't grasp that we had a fabulous defense.

Nobody was going to pass on us. Lester Hayes and Mike Haynes wouldn't even be in the defensive huddle. It was like, "We're covering the receivers; the rest of you do whatever it is you're supposed to do inside." It was just daring and guts, and unbelievable talent. And behind them, just in case, were two outstanding safeties, Mike Davis and Vann McElroy. So there was nowhere a receiver could get open. And nobody was going to run on us, either. We used a three-four, with Howie Long and Lyle Alzado at the ends and Reggie Kinlaw in the middle, and Ted

Hendricks, Matt Millen, Bob Nelson, and Rod Martin behind them. A rivalry was building up before the game between those seven guys and the "Hogs." They took umbrage to the idea the "Hogs" were so dominant, and said, "Bring it, bring it, we'll see." The key to stopping Riggins was having Kinlaw and our inside backers, Millen and Nelson, defeat their people up front—and that's just what would happen. This was a great unit, and its strategy against Washington was simply to kick ass. Man coverage and we are going to come and get you.

We had no fear of the Redskins offense, but we had to respect it. They had scored 541 points—the greatest output in the history of the NFL. Riggins had run for over 1,300 yards and scored a record 24 touchdowns, Theismann had put up some big numbers behind that massive front line, and his top receivers Charlie Brown and Art Monk had good years. Both games they lost were by close scores, so they could have conceivably gone undefeated. As it was, they'd won 27 of their last 30 games, which was amazing. I had very deep respect for Joe Gibbs because he could win with teams that were not overly talented. One guy who was talented was John Riggins, and I greatly admired him for doing what he was doing at an advanced football age. I also thought he was an engaging character and would have loved to have had him as a teammate. I like somebody who marches to his own drummer, and that's what Riggins was all about.

The Redskins won with offense and special teams. They didn't have a strong defense, but with that offense, all the defense had to do was hold the other team to 22 points. They had Mark Murphy, who was a Pro Bowl free safety. Dexter Manley at right end was their best pass rusher but was terrible against the run. Dave Butz, their left tackle, and their linebackers, Neal Olkewicz, Rich Milot, and Mel Kaufman, were okay. Corner Darrell Green would develop into the best of their backs, but he was just a rookie then. A lot of those guys were decent players, but in the Super Bowl they'd be overmatched and outplayed.

I don't know what most of my teammates were doing nights in Tampa as the Super Bowl neared. My own story is ugly: Marc Wilson, who also went to Brigham Young, and I ended up going to a local arcade to play Pac Man. I think back to Vin Scully saying that when Steve Garvey and Orel Hershiser went out it was "to paint the town gray." That was Wilson and I in Tampa—we painted the town gray.

I don't remember any speeches in our locker room before the game. There were some guys who were yelling, but in general, no. There were guys who were—I resist saying "businesslike" because that indicates a degree of sobriety that didn't exist. Yeah, people were excited, but the beating of helmets and jumping on each other was not what the team was about. We understood what we had to do. This particular day there was, for a lack of a less dramatic term, a sense of destiny. Any way you look at it, you're making history. We'd come this far and there was a mission that had to be accomplished. I remember overhearing broadcaster Jim Hall outside our team bus saying, "These guys seem amazingly calm." He was right. Oh, man—the confidence level was so high.

We received the opening kickoff but had trouble moving the ball. I was coming off a slight knee injury—I had a hyperflexion—and hated coming into a game of this magnitude not being 100 percent. But there was no way I wasn't going to play or be in there for that first series. On a second-down play, I ran an in-route and had the man coverage I wanted from safety Ken Coffey. I got caught between steps, tried to cut off my right foot while going right, and slipped and fell. Coffey almost made an interception, but I hit him in the shoulder pad. I wasn't happy and there was concern on the sidelines because my right knee wasn't feeling good. But it would hold up.

Guy punted, and the juggernaut, the Washington offense, took the ball. It got a quick first down, but then our defense did a great job breaking up three straight pass plays. Jeff Hayes came in to punt. The Raiders rarely attempted to block punts early in a game, but Derrick Jensen took it upon himself to try it, much to Washington's surprise. The guy in front of him, Otis Wonsley, just got lazy, and when Derrick took an inside rush, Wonsley just bumped him gently. The fullback who normally would have been in Jensen's path had stepped outside because he was worried about Lester Hayes, who was known to be a tremendous punt blocker. So Derrick had clear sailing and was immediately right on top of Hayes. When we heard that thump of Jensen striking the ball, we went, "Oh, my gosh, this is great!" You could tell this was our lucky day because the ball flew directly backward into the end zone and died there, and Jensen recovered it for a touchdown.

Our defense was doing its job, but our offense continued to do nothing for the rest of the first quarter and in our first possession of the second quarter. Guy kept bailing us out with long punts. Before his third punt is when I almost snapped the ball over his head and he made a leaping one-handed grab. Our offense finally got on track on our next possession. We knew coming into the game that Richie Petitbon, the Redskins' defensive coach, liked to blitz and take his chances with man coverage. Our

January 22, 1984, in Tampa Stadium in Tampa, Florida
Paid Attendance: 72,920
NFC Champion: Washington Redskins (16–2)
Head Coach: Joe Gibbs
AFC Champion: Los Angeles Raiders (14–4)
Head Coach: Tom Flores

STARTING LINEUPS

OFFENSE			DEFENSE		
Washington		**Los Angeles**	**Washington**		**Los Angeles**
Charlie Brown	WR	Cliff Branch	Todd Liebenstein	LE	Howie Long
Joe Jacoby	LT	Bruce Davis	Dave Butz	LT	
Russ Grimm	LG	Charley Hannah		NT	Reggie Kinlaw
Jeff Bostic	C	Dave Dalby	Darryl Grant	RT	
Mark May	RG	Mickey Marvin	Dexter Manley	RE	Lyle Alzado
George Starke	RT	Henry Lawrence		LOLB	Ted Hendricks
Don Warren	TE	Todd Christensen	Mel Kaufman	LLB	
Rick Walker	TE			LILB	Matt Millen
Art Monk	WR	Malcolm Barnwell	Neal Olkewicz	MLB	
Joe Theismann	QB	Jim Plunkett		RILB	Bob Nelson
	RB	Marcus Allen	Rich Milot	RLB	
John Riggins	RB	Kenny King		ROLB	Rod Martin
			Darrell Green	LCB	Lester Hayes
			Anthony Washington	RCB	Mike Haynes
			Ken Coffey	SS	Mike Davis
			Mark Murphy	FS	Vann McElroy

SUBSTITUTIONS

Washington: K—Mark Moseley. P—Jeff Hayes. Offense: Receivers—Clint Didier, Alvin Garrett, Mike Williams. Linemen—Ken Huff, Bruce Kimball, Roy Simmons. Backs—Reggie Evans, Nick Giaquinto, Joe Washington, Otis Wonsley. Defense: Linebackers—Stuart Anderson, Monte Coleman, Peter Cronan, Larry Kubin. Linemen—Perry Brooks, Charles Mann, Tony McGee. Backs—Brian Carpenter, Vernon Dean, Curtis Jordan, Greg Williams. DNP—Bob Holly, Babe Laufenberg, Mark McGrath, Virgil Seay.

Los Angeles: K—Chris Bahr. P—Ray Guy. Offense: Receivers—Don Hasselbeck, Derrick Jensen, Cle Montgomery, Calvin Muhammad, Dokie Williams. Linemen—Shelby Jordan, Don Mosebar, Steve Sylvester. Backs—Frank Hawkins, David Humm, Greg Pruitt, Chester Willis, Marc Wilson (QB). Defense: Linebackers—Jeff Barnes, Darryl Byrd, Tony Caldwell, Jack Squirek. Linemen—Bill Pickel, Johnny Robinson, Dave Stalls, Greg Townsend. Backs—James Davis, Kenny Hills, Odis McKinney, Ted Watts.

Washington	0	3	6	0— 9
Los Angeles	7	14	14	3—38

LA	Jensen recovered blocked punt in end zone (Bahr kick)
LA	Branch 12 pass from Plunkett (Bahr kick)
Wash	FG Moseley 24
LA	Squirek 5 interception return (Bahr kick)
Wash	Riggins 1 run (kick blocked)
LA	Allen 5 run (Bahr kick)
LA	Allen 74 run (Bahr kick)
LA	FG Bahr 21
MVP:	Marcus Allen (Los Angeles)

thinking that we had the chance for big plays seemed to be prescient when Plunkett connected with Cliff on a post pattern for exactly 50 yards, putting us all the way down on Washington's 15-yard line. After Allen gained a few yards off tackle, Plunkett again hit Cliff over the middle, this time for a touchdown. Their cornerback, Anthony Washington, was stuck in man coverage, and Cliff was absolutely abusing him.

We were now ahead, 14–0, and feeling pretty good, but then Washington put together its best drive of the half, aided by a couple of penalties. We finally stopped them, but Moseley kicked a short field goal to close the gap to 14–3. After we had a pretty good drive stalled, Washington got the ball back on its 12-yard line with 12 seconds left in the half. That's when our defensive coach, Charlie Sumner, made a brilliant move.

Charlie remembered that in our regular-season loss to the Redskins they had a similar situation in which Theismann threw a screen pass to Joe Washington and he took it 67 yards. Another play like that would get the Redskins into field-goal position. So Charlie took out Matt Millen, who squawked about being replaced, and brought in a faster linebacker, Jack Squirek. While everyone else played zone, Jack was supposed to play Washington man-on-man—just in case Joe Gibbs was going to call that screen again. With so few seconds left in the half and Washington so deep in its own territory, any pass other than one way downfield might seem like an awful call; but from a surprise standpoint a screen wasn't a bad call, and I would never second-guess Joe Gibbs. So I'll say what happened was less the result of a bad call by Gibbs than a tremendous call by Charlie Sumner. The Redskins lined up with three wide receivers on the right and Theismann dropped back. He looked to his right, trying to get our safeties to go in that direction. He was not paying attention to Joe Washington because that's the idea of surprise. Then he came back to his left and lofted the ball toward Washington on a screen 8 or 10 yards away. Only he didn't anticipate or see Squirek and floated the ball up, and it was an absolute gimme. Squirek made the play of the game, intercepting the ball and running it in for the touchdown. Suddenly, he had increased our lead to 21–3 at the half. Now the Redskins who had been running some at the mouth were suffering from collective laryngitis.

So at halftime the momentum was all ours. The Redskins locker room must have been like a morgue. How do you come back from that? But everybody in our locker room reminded everybody else that we had been way up in the first game against Washington and had lost. Complacency was a concern. We're saying, "We're not going to let that happen again."

Matt Millen, in particular, was very, very vocal about this. He was screaming, "We've come this far . . ." and whacking people. What got us this far was being aggressive and tough, and we wanted to continue to play that way.

When the second half started, they came out and had an impressive 70-yard drive, with Riggins scoring their only touchdown. Moseley's extra point was blocked by Don Hasselbeck, but still our lead had been narrowed to 21–9, and there was a degree of trepidation on our part.

It was important that we had success on our next drive. We were helped on our second play when Plunkett threw a post pattern to Malcolm Barnwell, and his legs got tangled up with Darrell Green's. It was an unfortunate interference by Green, but they had to call it. That resulted in a 38-yard gain and was perhaps the biggest play of the game. If we'd gone three and out after they had scored, who knows? Instead that play set us up in Washington territory. I recall I caught my last pass of the game for a first down, and then Frank Hawkins caught a pass to give us first-and-goal on their 5-yard line. From there, Marcus Allen scored his first touchdown. I think the play was 14-Lead-Man and was designed to go to the right, but Marcus saw an opening and just made an amazing cutback to his left on safety Mark Murphy that, anatomically, he shouldn't have been able to do. That made the score 28–9; and they're looking at themselves and saying, "Jeez, we've got to score three touchdowns," and obviously against our defense that wasn't going to happen.

Our defense made life increasingly miserable for the Redskins, and on the last play of the third quarter, Allen had his biggest play of the game. Seventeen-BOB-TREY-O was the play Marcus was supposed to run to the left behind Bruce Davis and me. Seventeen-BOB stood for backer on backer, Frank Hawkins on Rich Milot; the TREY meant there would be three people involved, two blockers on one defender, and in this case Bruce and I were to throw a double-team block on Charles Mann; and the O represented the offguard, Mickey Marvin, who would pull into the hole. We executed perfectly: Frank had a great block on Milot, Bruce and I just hammered Mann off the line of scrimmage, and Marvin came on the pull. And if Marcus had been right at the hole we opened, it would have been a huge gain. But he went a little too wide and Ken Coffey came up from the strong safety position to challenge him. Even if Coffey merely turned Allen around, the natural pursuit of the other Redskins should have caught up to him in the backfield. But because of our play, there was no penetration and no pursuit, and when Allen cut back against the grain, nobody was there and he was able to run 74 yards in the opposite direction. Obviously it was a great play by Marcus, but when people say he did it on his own, that's bogus, because the people up front, Lawrence, Hannah, and Double D, made some blocks. And down the field, Cliff came out of nowhere to bump off Anthony Washington so Marcus could go the distance.

We were far ahead after Allen's second touchdown, but it wasn't hard playing out the rest of the game. It was great! We got to savor the heck out of it. Football players are trained not to get ahead of themselves, but in the recesses of my subconscious I was saying, "Hey, hey, hey, we're the world champs!" Chris Bahr came over to me on the sidelines and said, "The Redskins are behind us 35–9 with 10 minutes left in the game. . . . I don't think so."

I made four receptions on the day, but there are none I relish to this day. In truth, everybody wants to star in the Super Bowl, and it would have been nice to have caught 10 balls, but getting the ring was the thing. My contribution from a blocking standpoint is what I remember most. Marcus ran behind me quite a bit. I was known as a pass catcher, so I didn't usually get the attention I felt I deserved for my blocking—that was a nice change.

Meanwhile, Cliff Branch picked a very good time to have his best game of the year. He caught six balls, gained 94 yards, and had his last catch called back because the official said I was too quick off the ball. It wasn't a good call. I said, "Jeez, Cliff, I'm sorry, that would have been a 100-yard game for you," and he said, "Ah—we'll get the ring." And we laughed, so that was cool.

I watched the defense all the time I was on the sidelines. I would sit on my helmet in the coaches' zone, where I wasn't supposed to be and could see everything. Their defense wasn't playing a particularly physical game, but our defense was just shutting them down, sacking Theismann, causing him to fumble, intercepting his passes, stopping Riggins on a fourth down. Every time they got into scoring position, we'd take the ball away. Marcus did set a Super Bowl rushing record with 191 yards, but a lot of those yards came after we had the lead, so from a purely football standpoint the MVP should have been Reggie Kinlaw, Rod Martin, or even Bob Nelson. Stuffing Riggins the way that they did was the key to the game. Riggins' longest run was only 8 yards, and for the game he had only 64 yards on 26 carries. Reggie ran wild against Jeff Bostic, which is amazing considering he was just 6'1", 240 pounds. A Lilliputian for his position. They had some outstanding offensive linemen, but on this day our inside people dominated. Nobody could block Kinlaw or Nelson, who did a great job playing the gaps, and Martin had a couple of sacks. They couldn't get inside or outside. We had Hayes and Haynes in Cover One and everything came off of that, including the blitzes by Martin and the safety blitz by Mike Davis to knock the ball loose from Theismann when the 'Skins were deep in our territory late in the game.

After the game, Theismann said, "They handed our asses to us on a tray and the tray was bent." That's true. He was beat up. He was sacked six times and he was knocked down a bunch more. The Raiders defense was intimidating, but intimidation comes from being good. In all candor, you have to say our guys gave the best defensive performance in Super Bowl history. People might argue for the Steelers against the Vikings in Super Bowl IX, but Minnesota was nowhere near the offensive team that the Redskins were.

As the game wound down, we had a final drive that began with another Allen cutback that was good for almost 40 yards. Soon we had first-and-goal on the 1 and Tom Flores felt compelled to put Greg Pruitt in the game because he wanted him to get an honorary touchdown. Defenses aren't stupid, and they saw him come in and they kept stuffing him. I remember Frank Hawkins saying in the huddle, "I've been blocking all game. Why don't I get an honorary touchdown?" And I'm thinking the same thing. So we settled for Greg getting stuffed, and then Chris Bahr came in to kick the field goal, which made the final score 38–9.

They had the ball at the two-minute warning, and I was on the sidelines thinking: We'd won the Super Bowl before in 1981, and it had been exciting, but I could relish this more because I had been a key factor. You start saying, "I'm the son of a University of Oregon professor, I played at the Eugene Boys Athletic Association, I went to Sheldon High School—these are the types of people who don't play pro football, let alone get to this point." I waxed philosophical and the tears came. On the highlight reel for that Super Bowl, you can see me dropping to one knee to thank my maker and my face is covered with my hands as I'm getting emotional. The game was pretty much won for the entire fourth quarter, but for some reason that wave hit me with two minutes left.

After the gun sounded, I joined the celebration in the locker room. I may be getting a little maudlin here, but to re-create that feeling is impossible—if there's anybody who could describe it, it would be me, but words don't do it justice. It's fantastic. I'm not a demonstrative person, but I made a point to hug or shake hands with every person on that team to thank them for being part of this. The players I was most happy for were Lyle Alzado and Greg Pruitt, who were great players but who never before had things go their way. I had a close affinity with Pru because he introduced me to chicken wings and I introduced him to crazy eights, which was the Raiders' card game. Greg and I played before every game.

I remember my big post–Super Bowl celebration: I hugged my in-laws, and we went and had something to eat. I thought not only had we done what was expected, but it was just part of our day-to-day operation. We won a Super Bowl—that's what we were supposed to do. When you're involved in it, you can't afford the luxury of enjoying it because you have to be so completely focused. But now with hindsight, I enjoy it much more and fully appreciate what it took to get there and do what we did against Washington that day in Tampa.

The winner's share was 32 grand. It wasn't a driving force. . . . Wait, of course it was, somewhat. Joe Greene had the best line: "The wife has already spent the money; the ring is the thing." Almost to a man, the players would say that was the case. Players always talk about the ring. Everyone in athletics wants to be considered a champion. In other pro sports, teams become champions after beating the other team four out of seven times, but in football you have that grand moment, that three-hour period where you have to pull it all together and hang it out for everybody to see. So there is a more definitive king-of-the-mountain mentality in football than in other sports. To have the Super Bowl ring is to have instant credibility. You've done it.

That Raiders team might have been the best team to ever play in the Super Bowl. That's an admittedly biased assessment, but just go down our roster man by man, look at the Hall of Fame people, and consider that we scored 38 points and held the Redskins, the highest scoring team in history, to only 9 points. We demolished the other great team in the league, so we were so far above everybody. And as I looked around and saw how young we were and not knowing that the AFC would have a Super Bowl victory drought, I thought, "My gosh! We're going to be on top forever!"

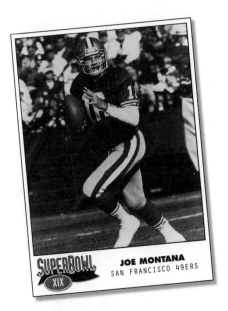

JOE MONTANA
SAN FRANCISCO 49ERS

SUPER BOWL XIX

SAN FRANCISCO 49ERS 38
MIAMI DOLPHINS 16

JOE MONTANA

Sure, it was great to make it back to the Super Bowl after a two-year absence. We nearly got back the year before but had a disappointing loss to Washington in the 1983 NFC Championship Game, 24–21. We tied the Redskins with three fourth-quarter touchdowns only to be beaten on a late field goal after two very questionable calls against our defense. That bitter loss could have motivated us or crushed us. If we had wanted it to bring us down and affect our play in 1984, we could have let it. It would have been easy. But we didn't do that because we had guys like Ronnie Lott who wouldn't allow us to think like that. Ronnie was extra motivated because he had been called for the second penalty before Mark Moseley's winning kick, so he was one of the guys who pushed the team to get back to the playoffs the next season.

In 1984 I was focused on winning the NFC title game and reaching the Super Bowl, but I was able to enjoy the season to a certain degree. You had to, because when you looked back at the year the 49ers had, you'd say, "God, we got a lot accomplished. We did things that other teams weren't able to do." We lost only one game, to Pittsburgh, and finished the season with nine straight victories to end the regular season at 15–1. Then we beat the Giants 21–10 in the first round of the playoffs and the Bears 23–0 in the NFC Championship Game. So going into the Super Bowl against Miami, we had the chance to become the first team in history to win 18 games in a year.

The 1984 49ers were a very close team. And it was the whole team, both offense and defense. That was the great thing about it. We had a game against each other every day at practice and, rather than that dividing us, that made us feel more like one unit. Who better to play against? I guess you could say that Ronnie was a leader and Randy Cross was a leader and there were one or two other guys who would speak up, but everybody on that team knew his job without anybody saying anything to them. You didn't have to tell players to work hard because they saw everybody else do it and they would do it. You could count on each player to be ready for every game, which is why we were able to practice a little lighter and be a little fresher when it was time to play.

Bill Walsh just let the team go and find its own people and its own path and personality. You knew what he wanted from you without being told. For instance, he didn't come out and say that a quarterback should be a leader, but I knew he expected it. He expected you to work the hardest and do the most. That was his standard for the quarterback. I always realized that Bill expected a lot from his starting quarterback, but I didn't fully understand what that meant in our first few years together. There was one time when I'd been playing pretty well, but got hurt, and my backup came in and did a good job. After the game I heard Bill tell him, "Great game," or something like that, and I was a bit upset because Bill never would compliment me in that way, although he would say nice things about me to the press. In time, I came to understand Bill's thinking. When a guy who didn't play a lot played well, Bill thought he deserved to be praised. Bill expected that high level of me all the time, so for him to say something like that to me, I had to do something that was out-of-the-ordinary great. I came to recognize that Bill would compliment me on those occasions when I played over and above what he expected of me.

In Bill's offense, I wasn't going to be throwing the ball down the field all of the time like some other quarterbacks. I wouldn't be making the big plays. I was the "mailman" and it was up to the other guys to make the big plays after I delivered the ball to them. I just had to make the right decisions. That's how I approached it. One guy didn't carry the load—everybody did—and that's what made our offense unique. Our backs Roger Craig and Wendell Tyler—who gave us a much better running game than we had in Super Bowl XVI—and our starting receivers Dwight Clark, Freddie Solomon, and Russ Francis had excellent seasons, but I don't think we had one big gun. On occasion, somebody would have a great game that you wouldn't expect, but we could never say, "We have this one guy who's going to carry us through this tough situation."

Despite everything our offense accomplished in 1984, the media didn't give us any respect during Super Bowl Week. I found that odd. Nobody was talking about our offense and what we had done. Nobody really thought about us because of the great season the Dolphins offense had with Dan Marino and his receivers Mark Clayton and Mark Duper. They'd set records with pass yardage and touchdowns, but it was somewhat of an insult to us to be slighted, because we'd put up some pretty good numbers ourselves and we'd lost one fewer game. We just had a different offense. We didn't throw as many balls as Miami or a lot of other teams—we had pretty much a 50–50 run–pass ratio—or throw a lot of down-the-field touchdowns.

The media assumes that when a team doesn't throw a lot or throw deep it's a sign that they have a weak offensive line. It's not. Our offensive line wasn't given enough credit during the year and it was slighted along with the rest of the offense prior to the Super Bowl. Bubba Paris and John Ayers on the left side, Keith Fahnhorst and Randy Cross on the right, and Fred Quillan at center had been outstanding all year and would play a major part in our Super Bowl victory. They talked about how few sacks Miami's line gave up during the season and how little pressure Dan Marino felt, but that wouldn't be the case in the Super Bowl—our offensive line would outplay Miami's.

I knew how good Danny was, but this was only his second year and I hadn't played against him before the Super Bowl. I had seen Miami a little bit on TV, not very often. Somewhere along the line, Miami would play someone that we were studying and we'd get to see how the Dolphins offense played against that defense. When we studied Miami before the Super Bowl, I didn't really have the time to watch Danny and their offense. I wish I could have because it was always fun to watch another team's offense. Sometimes in the middle of studying you'd catch yourself watching the offense and you'd say, "Dang, what are you doing? You don't have the time to look at the other side of the ball."

I always did a lot of studying. Even in the locker room before the Super Bowl I'd be there with my playbook on the floor. It wasn't a situation where I'd be concentrating so hard that other players couldn't come over or I wouldn't talk to anyone else, but I'd always go over plays. I wouldn't make changes; I'd just try to study more and memorize.

The nice thing is that Bill gave us the plays that we'd run early in the game and that helped us prepare. In fact, we went into a game with a 25-play script, although we always diverged from that. We stayed with the 25 plays only if the game went exactly to plan. If something happened where we went out of our flow or got into third-and-long, then we abandoned it. Later, we'd come back to the plays. In the Miami game we didn't have a lot of third downs on our scoring drives, but we still moved away from the script. There were very few games where we went past 8 or 9—maybe 10—plays of the script.

We did think Miami's pass defense had weaknesses that we could probably take advantage of, but we didn't say that we were going to throw the ball all the time. We were going to play our regular game and mix it up. What was unique about Bill is that he didn't go: "Okay, this is it, this is exactly what we're going to do this game against their defense. Our plan is to only attack this part of the defense." Guaranteed, Bill would find a weakness in the other team's defense and make up some plays that would work against their defensive schemes. But for the most part, he was going to run his regular offense and make the other team stop it. His attitude was: "We're not worried about you; you have to worry about us. We're going to do what we want to do; now you make the changes." He didn't want to make the big changes. He wanted to keep the other team guessing. He liked to keep them on the run as opposed to being put on the run.

In the playoffs I had been intercepted five times, but that wasn't at all on my mind going into the Super Bowl. The Giants and Bears were pretty good teams. Not that I expected to throw interceptions against them, but they played well and put a lot of pressure on me. If they thought it was a problem, believe me, they would have said something, because I had been called up to Bill's office a bunch of times when he thought I was throwing the ball to the other team too much or I was being too cautious in how I was playing. But prior to the Super Bowl, I wasn't called up. Nobody said anything.

Bill didn't really change before a big game, not even the Super Bowl. "Stay on an even keel; don't let any one thing be any bigger than any other." That was his attitude. He tried to keep everything the same as it was during the season, and that was made easier because we were going to play in nearby Stanford Stadium. There was a lot more media attention and hoopla, but it was pretty much like preparing for another home game.

Bill kept the locker room kind of light before the game. Still, I was nervous. I think all the guys had to be nervous. If you're not nervous—what the heck, you don't care about your performance. That's the way I always felt. If I hadn't been nervous about going out there and playing well, then I'd have felt the same if I played bad as if I played good. I was nervous because I didn't want to fail.

I didn't feel any more confident in Super Bowl XIX than I did in Super Bowl XVI just because I was more experienced. The thing about pro football is that you're only as good as your last game. People forget what happened a few years before, and if you lose the big game they're watching now, they get upset. Well, maybe not *upset*, but they do look at it differently: "Well, we won one before . . . but we didn't win this one . . . that shouldn't happen. We should have won this one too; we were good enough; we were better." That's the way it is. If you're good enough to get to the Super Bowl, you're supposed to be good enough to win. Everybody expects you to win, no matter what happens in the game. If you don't believe that, just ask the players on Buffalo.

We punted after our first possession and then watched our defense play, as we always did. Guys like Ronnie Lott, Hacksaw Reynolds, Keena Turner, and Fred Dean inspired us. I'm not sure if they'd played against a no-huddle offense before. I don't remember if I'd seen an opponent use the no-huddle before that game. I think Miami just tried to give us something to think about as opposed to doing it for any specific reason, like keeping Dean and our other second- and third-down players on the sidelines. A lot of times a team will do something early in the game to make you think about a lot of things other than what they are planning to do. So you have to be careful how you react.

We thought our defense would have a tough go of it from the beginning. Just because Danny had such a great year. He'd thrown for over 5,000 yards and 48 touchdowns. Nobody had really stopped him. And our defense didn't stop him at first. He had a bunch of completions in a row and marched the Dolphins down the field on their first two possessions. Miami scored on a field goal by von Schamann and on a short touchdown pass. We didn't dwell on what happened to our defense. We knew those guys would have a letdown here and there, that they were going to make a mistake or two—that's the way it was. We were a team, so we wouldn't say, "You guys are screwing it up." Our defense didn't play well at first, but we just figured the offense had to do its job. It was for us to say, "We've got to keep the ball as much as we can to keep the pressure off our defense and try to keep those guys fresh."

Because Miami was moving the ball so easily, we had the feeling that the game might turn into a shoot-out. We thought that it may reach a point where we had to score every time we got the ball just to stay even. But not because of the lack of defense on our part. Danny was just on a roll. You can feel it when you're on a roll and it doesn't matter what anybody does—they can't stop you. You have it in your own mind that no one is going to stop you. When you go in with that kind of confidence, you're a lot more successful. Fortunately, we would get on a roll ourselves, where we knew Miami's defense couldn't stop us.

Our first touchdown came on a pass to Carl Monroe, who was a backup running back. Like the key completion to Mike Wilson in our big drive against Cincinnati in Super Bowl XVI, this went down the right sideline. It wasn't the same play because Mike was supposed to come straight back to make the catch, while Carl kept running down the line. Also, Mike was a wide receiver and Carl was a back, and either lined up in the slot on the weak side or came out of the backfield. We used that play a bunch during the season, so it wasn't like people hadn't seen it. Carl was the primary receiver, but there was another guy underneath, and if he was open I'd usually just give him the ball. Carl cut through their defenders, caught the ball, and broke free into the end zone. That play went for over 30 yards, which was a big play for us. Actually, it would have been a tight play if one of their defenders hadn't fallen down. We probably would have gotten the completion, but we wouldn't have had a touchdown.

Our second touchdown came early in the second quarter. We were inside their 10 and we ran a play where we had Roger Craig and the other back crossing underneath, and I could take my pick. A tight end also was running a shallow crossing route to help confuse the coverage and that's about what happened. Roger curled across the middle and we got a touchdown. That put us back ahead, 14–10. We liked an early lead because during the year we'd hit lulls in the middle of games that we couldn't explain and let the other team get close. Fortunately, if we had some kind of a lead, we managed to hold onto it.

Miami's defense was set up to give us the short passes. That was fine with us because our game plan was to throw it underneath most of the

January 30, 1985, at Stanford Stadium in Palo Alto, California

Paid Attendance: 84,059

AFC Champion: Miami Dolphins (16–2)
Head Coach: Don Shula

NFC Champion: San Francisco 49ers (17–1)
Head Coach: Bill Walsh

STARTING LINEUPS

OFFENSE			DEFENSE		
Miami		**San Francisco**	**Miami**		**San Francisco**
Mark Duper	WR	Dwight Clark	Doug Betters	LE	Lawrence Pillers
Jon Giesler	LT	Bubba Paris	Bob Baumhower	NT	Manu Tuiasosopo
Roy Foster	LG	John Ayers	Kim Bokamper	RE	Dwaine Board
Dwight Stephenson	C	Fred Quillan	Bob Brudzinski	LOLB	Dan Bunz
Ed Newman	RG	Randy Cross	Jay Brophy	LILB	Riki Ellison
Cleveland Green	RT	Keith Fahnhorst	Mark Brown	RILB	Jack Reynolds
Bruce Hardy	TE	Russ Francis	Charles Bowser	ROLB	Keena Turner
Mark Clayton	WR	Freddie Solomon	Don McNeal	LCB	Ronnie Lott
Dan Marino	QB	Joe Montana	William Judson	RCB	Eric Wright
Tony Nathan	RB	Wendell Tyler	Glenn Blackwood	SS	Carlton Williamson
Woody Bennett	RB	Roger Craig	Lyle Blackwood	FS	Dwight Hicks

SUBSTITUTIONS

Miami: K—Uwe von Schamann. P—Reggie Roby. Offense: Receivers—Jimmy Cefalo, Vince Heflin, Dan Johnson, Nat Moore, Joe Rose. Linemen—Steve Clark, Ronnie Lee, Jeff Toews. Backs—Joe Carter, Eddie Hill, Jim Jensen, Don Strock. Defense: Linebackers—A. J. Duhe, Earnie Rhone, Jackie Shipp, Sanders Shiver. Linemen—Bill Barnett, Charles Benson, Mike Charles. Backs—Bud Brown, Mike Kozlowski, Paul Lankford, Robert Sowell, Fulton Walker. DNP—Pete Johnson.

San Francisco: K—Ray Wersching. P—Max Runager. Offense: Receivers—Earl Cooper, Renaldo Nehemiah, Mike Wilson. Linemen—Allan Kennedy, Guy McIntyre, Billy Shields. Backs—Derrick Harmon, Carl Monroe, Bill Ring. Defense: Linebackers—Milt McColl, Blanchard Montgomery, Todd Shell, Mike Walter. Linemen—Michael Carter, Fred Dean, Gary Johnson, Louie Kelcher, Jeff Stover, Jim Stuckey. Backs—Jeff Fuller, Tom Holmoe, Dana McLemore. DNP—Matt Cavanaugh, Mario Clark, John Frank.

Miami	10	6	0	0—16
San Francisco	7	21	10	0—38

Mia	FG von Schamann 37
SF	Monroe 33 pass from Montana (Wersching kick)
Mia	D. Johnson 2 pass from Marino (Wersching kick)
SF	Craig 8 pass from Montana (Wersching kick)
SF	Montana 6 run (Wersching kick)
SF	Craig 2 run (Wersching kick)
Mia	FG von Schamann 31
Mia	FG von Schamann 30
SF	FG Wersching 27
SF	Craig 16 pass from Montana (Wersching kick)
MVP:	Joe Montana (San Francisco)

time unless they gave it to us down the field. As long as they were going to keep giving us 5 yards, we'd take it. We were able to say, "You want to give short yardage; we'll take short yardage." As long as we were getting first downs, we didn't care how we got them. We were just trying to be patient. That way, we had an edge over other teams. Other teams wouldn't be as patient. We waited until they came up to play close, and then we'd throw the ball over their heads.

I noticed that Miami's inside linebackers, Jay Brophy and Mark Brown, started dropping back in order to stop our short passing game. They would follow our backs into the secondary. They would kind of match up in a zone, so if Craig or Tyler or another back came into that zone, they would play him man-to-man and go with him. (We didn't expect a lot of man-to-man on our receivers, but we ended up getting more than our share.) It's not that Brophy and Brown were turning their backs on me, but when they'd move away from the line of scrimmage, they'd occasionally give me a lane in which to run. I had a few good runs in the first half.

Before a game, the coaches would put in a couple of plays for me to run, but in most cases they didn't make me run unless it was a necessity. Most of the time I ran on my own—the play would break down and I'd get out of the pocket and scramble. My touchdown against Miami from outside their 5 was a breakdown, but the breakdown was more on Miami's part. All of a sudden a big hole opened up in front of me. They blitzed and I stepped up to find a receiver and the hole was right in front of me, so I just took it. I didn't actually think I'd make it to the end zone. My second running touchdown in a Super Bowl—who'd have thought that?

Less surprising is that Roger Craig ran for our next touchdown. I can't really remember that play because it was so routine, with Craig following Tyler over from the 2. He may have even walked over. That was at the end of a drive that began after a short punt by Reggie Roby. In the second quarter, he had three straight line-drive punts, and each time we got real good field position and went on to score touchdowns. I remember that because Roby had punted well all year, so it surprised me that he had such a rough day in the Super Bowl.

We were ahead 28–10 and, yeah, were having fun. When you're playing basically at home and things are going so well, you're definitely having fun. But you're also nervous because Danny was dangerous—and I mean *really* dangerous. That was always in the back of my mind. All of us thought that way. We didn't think that we were putting the game away only because of what Dan was capable of doing. He could do it at any point in time. Because of him there was no way we could just sit back and relax as we had done against other teams that year. We couldn't do that with Danny because, jeez, he was just going crazy all year long. Our defensive backs—Ronnie Lott, Eric Wright, Jeff Fuller—had to just keep playing hard and making big plays.

Our lead was decreased when they got a couple of field goals right before the half. The second came after Guy McIntyre fumbled the kickoff. He should have just downed the ball. So all of a sudden the score was 28–16. Obviously, we didn't assume we had won the game, but we felt pretty good despite their late rally. We had played well in the first half, scoring four touchdowns and containing Marino's passing game in the second quarter. We just made the one dumb mistake on that kickoff, and Guy realized what he should have done and didn't dwell on it. The coaches were satisfied at halftime. They just wanted to make sure we didn't lose an edge. As always, they tried to correct things, making small adjustments here and there.

We tried to keep the same tempo that we had during the first half. We knew if we did that we had a good chance to win the game. And we didn't let up. After scoring on our last three possessions of the first half, we scored on our first two possessions of the second half. The first drive ended with a field goal by Ray Wersching. The second drive began with a 40-yard pass to Wendell Tyler and ended with a pass to Roger Craig, cutting to the left from 16 yards out for his third touchdown of the day.

We were fortunate to have two big, versatile running backs, which we hadn't had in previous years. Wendell Tyler was much more of a running back than a pass receiver. He ran for well over 1,000 yards that year. He could catch the ball but not to the degree where you could rely on him to make a big catch in a game, although he would make a few great catches. I don't know if you could say he made a big catch against Miami, but you could say he made a big play after the catch. It was usually the case that he'd catch the ball short and then pick up big yardage running.

It wasn't a surprise that Roger Craig developed into a pass catcher. He hadn't caught many balls at Kansas, but when the 49ers worked him out, they saw that he had good hands and good mobility. That was probably why they drafted him. I think they were more surprised by his ability to run the ball as well as he could and by how much punishment he could take and still keep carrying the ball.

Craig made some big catches against Miami, but as usual, Dwight Clark was the workhorse. Like Russ Francis, Dwight made a lot of important catches in the game to keep our drives moving. He went out there and found the holes and places to get open. That was how he always contributed. He knew his role and was going to do it to the best of his ability. Unlike a lot of wide receivers, he didn't care about running deep.

Freddie Solomon, our biggest deep threat, caught only one pass in the Super Bowl, but he wasn't used as a decoy for Clark, Francis, and our backs, taking defenders downfield. We didn't just take anyone out of the game. We were always trying to keep everyone involved. If it worked out that someone was covering him well, then we just moved on. We never thought, "God, he hasn't caught any balls; we'd better get him some." Our guys weren't that way. Of course, they all wanted to be part of the game, but in most cases, if it didn't work out that way, they didn't care. We didn't have selfish players.

My philosophy—and the philosophy of the 49ers—always was: if something's downfield, you take it; if not, there are always guys underneath you can throw to. If you have time to get the ball downfield, things will come open, but you don't have to force the ball unless you're desperate at the end of the game. But we weren't in that situation against Miami. When, on second or third down, there wasn't anyone open downfield or it was tight, I would instead make an easy short pass. I would take the sure pass and be satisfied with a second-and-5 or a third-and-2. Those things kill a defense more than a big play where they can say, "Okay, we've had one breakdown and now we can stop them." But when we got 5 yards, then 6 yards, then 4 yards, then 7 yards . . . they hated that—they got frustrated as hell. Many times guys would tell me, "God damn, will you quit dinking the damn ball." My thing was, "Hey, we're having a lot of success and aren't going to stop now." If we had a long pass or run, it was a plus, of course, but on the whole we weren't a long-play offense.

In the second half, we kept eating up yardage and picking up first downs with short passes and the running of Tyler and Craig. Bill Walsh would have us run the same plays until they stopped us. If we ran a bunch of plays the same way, Bill was the reason. It didn't matter what else was going on; our running plays were going well, so he stuck with them. We did have success running to the left behind Bubba Paris, who weighed 40 or 50 pounds more than his man, but Bill also saw we had success running to the right. So we ran both ways.

Miami continued to move the ball well but they couldn't get the ball into the end zone. Our defense managed to keep the pressure on Danny so he couldn't get into his rhythm, and that was really the key to the game. I wasn't surprised that our defense eventually put pressure on him and disrupted his passing game. Our defense had played well over the year, too—that's how we got to the Super Bowl. Those guys played their rear ends off all the time. Watching our guys hit? Shoot, there was nothing like it. It takes a defense to win a championship, and I think, in the end, that's what Miami lacked. They didn't have the depth that we did.

With a 38–16 lead we were in control of the game. Even Dan Marino couldn't bring them back. It was obvious that Miami was getting flustered. It was easy to tell—by how they were getting up after a play and beating their fists into the ground, by the way their guys were talking to us, and by what they said to each other. Anytime you're in that big of a game and things aren't going your way, you get that way. It was frustrating for them, I could tell. I had been in the same position.

After the game, Don Shula would say that his team had a total breakdown. It was probably a combination of that and our team rising to the occasion. We got off to a good start and I think that hurt them. They didn't expect that, and then they probably had a little letdown, and we kept putting up points until it was too late for them to come back. With their offensive personnel, they could have easily had a better game against us. But there's nothing specific their defense could have done because it was really difficult to cover our offense for any length of time. You could stop it for a while but eventually it was going to catch up to you.

As the game was winding down, as I put my knee down—oh, I was ecstatic. I ran off the field and into the clubhouse, congratulating all our players and everyone else. (I wasn't able to hook up with Marino until the Pro Bowl and then we didn't say much about the game.) I was thinking: It's over with now; we played at home; we played a good game both offensively and defensively; we beat a strong team; we won the championship. What more could we ask for! I was thrilled. The sad part is that once the game's over and the celebration in the locker room is over, you have a really big letdown. There were just so many highs in the game, so it was hard to come down. As soon as it's over it's like, "Oh, God, now what do we do?"

The next day, when it was much quieter, I took my parents to the airport. I took the Super Bowl XVI ring off my finger and gave it to my father. It was a nice moment. I wouldn't wear the ring from Super Bowl XIX or the two later Super Bowls. I'm more comfortable just keeping them in a safe. In fact, my father would eventually return that first ring so I could keep it with the other three.

I kind of put all four Super Bowls I played in together, though they each had their own personality. Super Bowl XVI wasn't the greatest game, but it was our first Super Bowl; Super Bowl XIX was nice because we all played well together—and we had fought back from a lot during the year; Super Bowl XXIII wasn't a great game, but what a way to end it on that touchdown to John Taylor—yeah, it was unbelievable; and Super Bowl XXIV stands out because it was my last Super Bowl and because we had such a great game offensively and defensively. I'll probably look back at the last one most of all, but they were all special.

I know that one thing I'll always remember fondly about Super Bowl XIX is that we didn't go away to play it. It's always nice to go to some other place to play a Super Bowl because it is something special, but I don't think I would have preferred going away. It felt good to stay home, despite the many distractions. It gave us an opportunity to play in front of the home crowd and for the people of the Bay area to see us win one Super Bowl in person.

I had downplayed my performance after winning the MVP award at Super Bowl XVI, and though I had better numbers in winning the MVP at Super Bowl XIX, I think my performance was pretty much the same. If you go back and look at this game, there wasn't anything that I did that really stood out any more than what someone else on our team did. After that game wasn't one of those times Bill Walsh came to me with compliments because, like I said, there wasn't anything that I did that was so extraordinary that everybody else didn't do, too. That was the nice thing about it. We had won as a team. We were happy as a team. And after this game, the media stopped talking about Miami and finally recognized how good the San Francisco 49ers were.

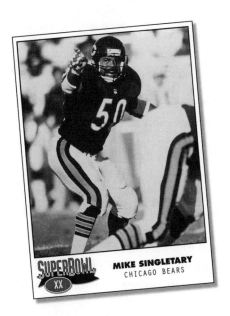

MIKE SINGLETARY
CHICAGO BEARS

SUPER BOWL XX

CHICAGO BEARS 46
NEW ENGLAND PATRIOTS 10

MIKE SINGLETARY

I played middle linebacker all my life. That's what I played at Baylor before the Bears drafted me in 1981. When I came to Chicago, I was very well aware of the Bears' middle linebacker tradition. I knew all about Dick Butkus, Bill George, who pretty much invented the position, and the guy who came before me, Waymond Bryant, who had tried to fulfill that middle linebacker dream but had been hurt. Tom Hicks had the job when I arrived in Chicago, but he was holding out for more money or doing a negotiation ploy, whatever, so he wasn't at training camp. I never met him because at the time of my first scrimmage they cut him. During the season I became a starter and was very excited about having the opportunity to play middle linebacker for a team that appreciated strong defense and had the reputation for building championships through its defense.

I soon met the Bears' longtime owner and former coach George Halas. He was in his mid-eighties then and it was only a couple of years before he passed away, but he was still a pretty powerful individual, and when he came into the room he was larger than life, especially to us rookies. The first time he came in, he talked to us about winning as a team and about the Bears tradition. He asked us, "Do you understand what it means to be here? Do you understand what being a Bear means?" He talked about the importance of defense to the Bears.

Buddy Ryan was the Bears' defensive coordinator, having come in with Neill Armstrong in the late seventies. In my rookie year, he didn't ask the players for any input. We had no quarrel with that because we realized he was a defensive genius and felt fortunate that he was teaching us what it takes to win. We were very concerned when we almost lost him as our coach. We had a losing record and Halas decided he was going to fire all his coaches at the end of the year. The defense got together and wrote a letter to him asking if we could keep Buddy. George came in and said, "You know, in my years of coaching and playing, I've never seen a letter this effective. This letter is so concise in terms of what you want and reveals how much you care for another individual. It really touches me. I'm going to have to think about this." He thought about it and decided to keep Buddy Ryan and the defensive coaching staff.

I think our action humbled Buddy. He could see that he had a group of players who loved him and wanted to play for him. At that point I think he changed his perspective and thought, "This is not just a job." He then became a lot closer to his players, including me. I spent a lot of time with Buddy, talking to him and trying to learn anything I could. Sometimes I'd be picking his brain for so long that he'd run me out of the office, saying, "Let me get my work done, son." While it's true that I became the defensive captain, I really feel that Buddy, rather than me or any of the other players, was the anchor of the great Bears defensive unit of the early eighties. That's because after that first year, Buddy became the one individual who listened to what you said and used that input in his coaching. He let us participate, which is why I believe that Buddy and the players developed that defense together.

After Neill Armstrong was let go, Halas brought in Mike Ditka to be our head coach. Everything began to build off of that move. It definitely mattered to us that Ditka was an ex-Bear and possessed that Bear hardness, that black-and-blue division kind of thing. It also helped that he had played and been an assistant coach with the Dallas Cowboys, because that meant he brought with him some of the tradition of one of the NFL's elite teams. He knew what it took to win from having played the game and from having learned the fundamentals from Tom Landry. Coming back home to Chicago, where he had been an All-Pro tight end, he said, "I'm going to implement all the smarts and wisdom I've acquired over the years into creating a tough, nasty football team."

He said, "I'm going to work you guys harder than you've ever worked in your life. I'm going to drive you and you're going to hate me, but that's okay, because that'll just push you closer to one another." He told us right up front: "One thing I want you to understand is that a lot of you will not make it. But the ones who remain will know what it takes to be a winner and be proud of what they have accomplished and what they have become." It was like a revolving door for a while. He kept bringing in people, changing people, until finally we had what we needed to go to the next level. We worked hard to become a dominant team. Coach Ditka inspired us from the beginning, lighting a fire beneath every one of us. Our goal was to go to the Super Bowl and he felt we could do it in three years. We became a team with a vision, a team with a chip on its shoulder, a team that was ready to knock people out. We were tough, we were smart, and we were very, very controlled. We were ready to go. And in 1985, Coach Ditka's third year, we won 15 of 16 games, easily won both playoff games, and reached the Super Bowl. What he had set out to do had come to pass. It was unfortunate that George Halas wasn't there to see it.

The 1985 Bears were the only team ever to have two head coaches. In Mike Ditka and Buddy Ryan, we had a head coach on offense and a head coach on defense. It's unfortunate that two men with such passion to win had such conflict between them. They were both so strong that there had to be friction but, to be honest, the situation was fine the way it was. They were just like a husband and wife, and no married couple will agree on everything. But they let the disagreements drive them apart. Both men wanted more power and it came to a head in our championship season.

Buddy kept us pretty much insulated from the fury of Mike Ditka, so I'm not sure if Ditka had any specific problems with the defense that could have resulted in conflict between the two. But I think the major rift started over the "Fridge," William Perry, who was a 300-pound defensive tackle out of Clemson. He came in and Buddy Ryan tore into him right away. He called him "one of the worst first-round draft choices I've ever seen." Under Buddy, Fridge just scratched the surface of his potential and never was allowed to come into his own. That was unfortunate, because I really believe that if Buddy had been able to handle Fridge the same way he did most high draft choices, Fridge would have been a truly great player. But Ryan saw him as Ditka's guy. The antagonism started when Coach Ditka said, "If he doesn't want to use you on defense, I'll use you on offense." So he'd insert Fridge as an offensive back because he was so big that he was hard to tackle. The feuding started there. When Fridge started playing for both coaches, the conflict escalated.

If only Coach Ditka and Buddy Ryan had been wise enough to say, "You know what—we need each other, so let's try to put aside our differences and move forward and make history." It didn't bother me much at the time because I thought they were a natural fit and that it would continue that way. I didn't know this would be their final year together.

At the beginning of '85, the defense was a bit rusty. I think we were looking around for Todd Bell and Al Harris, who were holding out. As time went on, we realized we weren't going to get them back. Dave Duerson, who took over for Todd at safety, and Wilber Marshall, who replaced Al at linebacker, had a lot of heat on them to make the defense what it had been with Todd and Al. They really stepped up and the defense began to turn it on. We started out saying, "Let's shut out some people." Then we added, "Let's hold them to less than 100 yards total." In the playoffs we shut out the New York Giants 21–0 and the Los Angeles Rams 24–0. The defense had been awfully good during the year, except in our one loss to Miami, but we were peaking. We were so in tune and so focused as we headed to the Super Bowl in New Orleans to play New England, a team we had already beaten soundly during the season.

Our defense not only wanted to shut out opponents but also wanted to score points. We felt we could create not just turnovers but numbers on the board. What was great about Buddy's "46" defense is that it allowed us to play offense on defense, which was Buddy Ryan's philosophy. The "46," which referred to the jersey number of safety Doug Plank, who played for us until 1982, started out as a nickel defense designed to stop the pass. But we learned we could play run defense out of that thing as well, and we began to implement it with much more frequency. We really liked it because it allowed us so many different looks.

I'd call the defensive signals, and out of the "46" I could choose between as many as 50 plays. Normally, when a quarterback comes to the line and looks at a strong defensive alignment, he says, "Oh, I'm going to check out of this into an offense I can really hurt those guys with." But I could call something else to counter what he was going to do. It was sort of like chess. I could say, "I'm going to put our best defense against that offense, and no matter where you go, I've got you." At any given time, we had one play for every offensive set. So the offense didn't know who was coming or how we were coming. Quarterbacks just couldn't read the "46." They couldn't tell if we were blitzing or who might blitz. They didn't know if guys were coming up the middle, from the outside, from the corners—they had no idea. And receivers didn't know who was going to be covering them—was it going to be a linebacker, a cornerback, a safety, or even a defensive end?

We'd have three guys in the middle: Steve McMichael, Dan Hampton, and maybe Fridge or Tyrone Keys or Mike Hartenstine. Maybe they'd line up over the center and guards, instead of the tackles, and that would throw off the blocking scheme. We'd rush end Richard Dent on one side—he led the league in sacks—and linebackers Wilber Marshall and Otis Wilson would be on the other side. Either Wilber or Otis would take the responsibility of covering the tight end, but they were both going to hit him. Or I was going to take the tight end and one of those guys was going to go get the running back. I'd be on the strong side and we'd have a safety, Dave Duerson, on the weak side. Then you had the two corners, Leslie Frazier and Mike Richardson, and you had Gary Fencik at free safety. From that formation there were just so many different possibilities for us to run. There were times when Leslie wanted to run up to bump the wideout and I would run on top of that and where the receiver went I had to go. I'd say, "Leslie, please get a bump because I don't want to chase this guy all the way up the field." Or I'd get the bump and Frazier would be on top of the receiver. We'd do that on both sides.

Our free safety, Gary Fencik, wasn't the fastest guy in the world, but he didn't have to be because the "46" prevented receivers from running deep routes. We might rush seven or eight guys and there would be only about three-and-a-half seconds before someone was going to get to the quarterback. Every once in a while there would be a quarterback and receiver who could connect on a long bomb against us, but basically we were going to get a jam on those receivers and throw their timing off at the very beginning. Fencik was smart enough to pick out the receiver the quarterback was going to go to first, and where the strong and weak parts of our defense were, so he could put himself into the weak part. All he had to do was read the play and get back. So we had it all down.

I'd use the "46" if I were a coach today, but there's no doubt that the tremendous success we had with it was due to our great personnel. We had smart guys where we needed smart guys, powerful guys where we needed powerful guys, quick guys where we needed quick guys, guys who would hurt and punish people where we needed them, and guys who could run like deer where we needed them. So it was a really well-balanced defense. And we all had a little bit of the dog in us. When you mix that with a lot of pride, ego, intimidation, and everything else, you have something that is really dangerous.

I never thought in my life that I'd ever feel sorry for guys on the other side, but that year I did. I know I felt sorry for Tony Eason in our first game with New England. When I looked into his eyes, I could see his desperation and confusion. He knew he was going to get hit. Quarterbacks would get underneath the center with blood running from their noses or mouths and they had black eyes and they looked like they didn't want to play. They'd be trembling. And our guys would be barking and screaming at them—so it was a sad thing. It was: "Don't hit that guy like that anymore"/"No, I'm going to kill him next time." That's the attitude that our guys had. Steve McMichael, Dan Hampton, Richard Dent, Otis Wilson, Wilber Marshall, and the other guys would be growling: "I'm coming at you; I'm going to get you; you aren't going to know who hit you; you're going to be out of the game." All game long. I was pretty quiet. I was pretty calm unless somebody hit me from the back or something like that, and then I'd talk a little bit. But not much. I was always busy trying to think about what to do next.

The defense didn't have to do it alone in 1985. For the first time the Bears offense rose to championship caliber. It was exciting to see the offense develop so quickly. The biggest reason for this was Jim McMahon. There was no doubt about it. Walter Payton was a great, great runner, a tremendous all-around player, a fierce competitor, and so exciting that I always found myself wanting to get through our defensive series so I could rush off the field and watch him. But while he would get his 1,200 or 1,300 or 1,400 yards every year, it wasn't until Jim came into his own that the offense became great. I'd say that Coach Ditka was the leader of the offense and McMahon was the manager who carried out the policy. Just about every Friday, I would go up to Jim and ask, "What do you think about the next game?" He would tell me exactly what the offense was going to do. He'd say, "We're going to score 20 points," or "We're going to blow these guys out," or "Mike, it's going to be difficult to score, so the defense had better shut them out." He'd always be right. Before the Super Bowl, he told everyone that it would be a blowout. He always knew what the offense could do and he always assumed that the defense would do its job.

Jim was a unique, "neat" individual, one I really enjoyed having the opportunity to know. He had a way of getting along with everybody and the ability to speak everybody's language. He never allowed himself to get higher than the team as some star quarterbacks do even though the media tried to place him higher. The media concentrated on some of the things he did to have fun—like wearing those wild sunglasses and designer headbands—but he was a serious player. He also had a tremendous amount of ability. The only negative thing was that his attitude was tougher than his body. This guy has a bad shoulder and a bad knee, yet he's eager to try to take a cornerback on. I'd tell him, "Jim, please, lay down, slide, run out of bounds." But he'd say, "If he tries to hit me, I'm going to run over him." "Come on, Jim, lay down. Look at the whole picture." "Okay, okay, okay." He did not have a quarterback's mentality. He had a defensive player's mentality and I think that's why he fit in so well. He would get up and head butt the offensive guys and playfully slap them around. Those guys really loved him and happily gave him the leadership he demanded. I think the coaches really admired him, too. I know Buddy did. Buddy appreciated his attitude, that he wasn't intimidated by anyone.

Buddy encouraged the defensive players to get to know Jim, Walter, and the other offensive players. He wanted us to work together and integrate the team as a whole. As a result, we were a very close team. We had accountability and that may have been the strongest focal point of our team. There was no one greater than anyone else. There was no one player who was so outstanding that no one could talk to him. Somebody who got out of shape, I don't care who it was, was going to get pulled aside by a teammate and lectured about what does not happen on the Chicago Bears.

Our defensive and offensive players did a lot together, including making that "Super Bowl Shuffle" video. A lot of the guys were in that. I was in the video—unfortunately, I even sang in it—unfortunately. It was just one of those things where we had the opportunity to raise money for charity, so I thought okay, fine. I felt that the country was excited about football and that video, which became enormously popular, connected people everywhere. I think people took it in good spirits rather than thinking us too cocky for shooting it after we'd gone 12–0, long before we actually qualified for the Super Bowl. But other teams didn't appreciate it. They really hated and resented us after the video. Some vengeful teams could not wait to play us and to try to knock us off. Other teams became even more intimidated. The "Super Bowl Shuffle" definitely had its effect.

During Super Bowl Week in New Orleans, the defense and offense fought a lot during the scrimmages. It was just natural. We were friends, but there'd be one guy who felt his man kept going after the whistle was blown; another guy who felt his man was trying to cut him; another guy who'd think his man was doing something unnecessary for practice. So we'd fight. We were emotional on both sides of the ball. There was so much intensity and rage. There was no way you could put all that combined energy together on that practice field and not have it explode.

The fighting would end when practice ended, and at night, the offense and defense hung out together in New Orleans. I know a lot of guys were having a lot of fun. But I didn't know if there were parties or if guys went to clubs or restaurants in the French Quarter or anywhere else. I must admit I don't know what happened because I didn't go anywhere. I went out to eat only one time. On all other nights, I just stayed in my hotel room and had room service. I just turned around all the pictures on the wall, turned on my projector, and studied film of the Patriots all week.

People would say I was a bit quiet to be on a team with so many wild personalities and to be so close to them. But I was just as wild as they were on the field. I didn't say as much as the other guys when we played, but I was wild. Otherwise, I was a nine-to-five kind of guy. I came to work and did my job. I would always say, "Guys, we've got to stop fooling around; we've got to stop doing this. We've got to get a shutout this week—think about that." They'd say, "Oh, man, here we go again—settle down, Mike." I was always on the edge. Looking back, I think I needed to be that way for the team, since I was the captain, but I sometimes wish that I would have enjoyed it a little more.

The night before the Super Bowl, before we broke off our meetings, Coach Ditka went around the room and called out different guys to say what they were feeling. I remember Walter talking about being on the Bears so many years and finally having the chance to play in a Super Bowl. He said he was going to do everything in his power to bring the championship back to Chicago. Dan Hampton said something similar. McMahon said, "Hey, man, I'm going to go out and lay it on the line," or something like that, to challenge everybody. I don't think I had anything in particular to say that night—though I was always talking—but there were a lot of other guys who gave pep talks. We thought about the whole nine yards.

What is this going to mean to the fans of Chicago? To the Bears organization? To us? To our kids? To our grandchildren?

At the final defensive meeting that night, Buddy told us, "No matter what happens tomorrow, all of you will always be my heroes." That was a great line. At the time I didn't take it as a farewell statement, because I had no idea that Buddy was leaving after the Super Bowl to become the head coach of the Eagles. After Buddy finished speaking, Steve McMichael threw a chair against the blackboard, ending the meeting. I assumed it was out of emotion about the game, not because he was upset that Ryan was leaving. However, I later thought everyone else had a good idea that he wasn't returning. I was so focused on the game that his going anywhere was the last thought on my mind. We had built an unbelievable relationship and I was so naive that I was sure he would tell me if he was doing something like that. I remember Gary Fencik coming in and sitting beside me and saying, "Buddy Ryan is going to leave." And I turned and looked at Gary like he was crazy. I jumped up and went out and found Buddy and said, "Is this true? Are you going to leave? Are you going to leave?" He said, "Aw, son, don't worry about that. Those guys don't know what they're talking about. Just go out and do your job tomorrow."

I did not sleep well before the game. That was pretty normal for me. I didn't sleep well before the playoff games either. I was still nervous when I reached the Superdome and nervous up till game time. I'd say that every player on our team had butterflies. The locker room started out pretty quiet with guys just talking to each other about the game plan. But the closer we got to game time, the louder it got. More guys started hitting their heads and throwing stuff around and kicking things and screaming and there was a let-me-out-of-here kind of atmosphere.

Out on the field, during the national anthem, most of the guys were crying. There was so much emotion. After a week of the media and stuff, you just got tired. And finally here was the real deal, everything we had been talking about at meetings ever since training camp and had worked for since then. We all thought about the importance this game had to us and how we wanted to give it everything we had. We didn't say anything to each other, because if we had we'd have cried some more, so we just looked at each other and from those looks we knew that we were going to go out and win.

We received the opening kickoff. Like us, New England was known for causing turnovers, and on our second play, they really hit Payton and recovered his fumble inside our 20. The Patriots were primarily a running team, but they threw on their first three plays. They hoped to catch us off guard, but Tony Eason didn't complete a pass. On their second play, we were in our "46" defense and I had underneath coverage on their wide receiver, Stanley Morgan, who was going to run a post pattern. The ball was snapped, Frazier got a good jam on Morgan, and I got there just in time to sneak my hand in and deflect the ball off Morgan's fingers at about the 5-yard line. So they had to settle for a field goal by Tony Franklin. They had scored only three points, but we found that jarring. Not that they had scored first but they had scored at all. We fully expected to shut them out, so it was like a wake-up call.

We immediately came back to tie the score on a field goal by Kevin Butler. The big play in our drive was a long pass from McMahon to Willie Gault. That went for over 40 yards, and in the second half they'd connect on a pass of 60 yards. Willie didn't have the great hands but this guy had some speed. He could fly, and teams had to put two or three guys on him to make sure he didn't score a touchdown every play. Dennis McKinnon, our other wide receiver, allowed Willie to be our featured receiver. He knew that Willie could open up the entire offense. I'm sure Willie's presence added two years to Payton's career. I don't think anybody understood how important Willie was until we lost him. Without Willie, defenses could double team McKinnon or give Walter a tough time with an eight-man front. Fortunately, we had Willie in the Super Bowl.

After we tied the score, Richard Dent sacked Eason and caused a fumble. That was the first of their six turnovers, and it set up another field goal, which put us ahead 6–3. Then on New England's next play from scrimmage, Dent knocked the ball loose from Craig James at the 13, and I got the first of my two fumble recoveries of the game. Matt Suhey, who was in the backfield with Payton, ran the ball into the end zone from outside their 10, and we had jumped ahead 13–3. At that point the game was over. Once we got on the board, it was over.

Our game plan had been to shut down the run because we knew they had no chance passing the ball against us. After that first series, they tried to have a balanced offense by mixing a little passing with some running, but nothing had worked and they had fallen 10 points behind. They would have to play catch-up, and they were going to panic because they had to throw more. Eason didn't throw any completions, so Raymond Berry quickly replaced him with the veteran Steve Grogan, but there was nothing Berry could do to turn things around. They couldn't catch us—they couldn't score 13 points. They weren't going to run over us—they didn't

January 26, 1986, in the Louisiana Superdome in New Orleans
Paid Attendance: 73,618
NFC Champion: Chicago Bears (17–1)
Head Coach: Mike Ditka
AFC Champion: New England Patriots (14–5)
Head Coach: Raymond Berry

STARTING LINEUPS

OFFENSE			DEFENSE		
Chicago		**New England**	**Chicago**		**New England**
Willie Gault	WR	Stanley Morgan	Dan Hampton	LE	Garin Veris
Jim Covert	LT	Brian Holloway	Steve McMichael	LT	
Mark Bortz	LG	John Hannah		NT	Lester Williams
Jay Hilgenberg	C	Pete Brock	William Perry	RT	
Tom Thayer	RG	Ron Wooten	Richard Dent	RE	Julius Adams
Keith Van Horne	RT	Steve Moore		LOLB	Andre Tippett
Emery Morehead	TE	Lin Dawson	Otis Wilson	LLB	
Dennis McKinnon	WR	Stephen Starring		LILB	Steve Nelson
Jim McMahon	QB	Tony Collins	Mike Singletary	MLB	
Walter Payton	RB	Craig James		RILB	Larry McGrew
Matt Suhey	RB	Tony Eason	Wilber Marshall	RLB	
				ROLB	Don Blackmon
			Mike Richardson	LCB	Ronnie Lippett
			Leslie Frazier	RCB	Raymond Clayborn
			Dave Duerson	SS	Roland James
			Gary Fencik	FS	Fred Marion

SUBSTITUTIONS

Chicago: K—Kevin Butler. P—Maury Buford. Offense: Receivers—Ken Margerum, Keith Ortego, Tim Wrightman. Linemen—Tom Andrews, Andy Frederick, Stefan Humphries. Backs—Steve Fuller (QB), Dennis Gentry, Thomas Sanders, Calvin Thomas, Mike Tomczak, Perry. Defense: Linebackers—Brian Cabral, Jim Morrissey, Ron Rivera, Cliff Thrift. Linemen—Mike Hartenstine, Tyrone Keys, Henry Waechter. Backs—Shaun Gayle, Reggie Phillips, Ken Taylor.

New England: K—Tony Franklin. P—Rich Camarillo. Offense: Receivers—Irving Fryar, Cedric Jones, Derrick Ramsey. Linemen—Paul Fairchild, Guy Morriss, Art Plunkett. Backs—Steve Grogan, Greg Hawthorne, Mosi Tatupu, Robert Weathers. Defense: Linebackers—Brian Ingram, Johnny Rembert, Ed Reynolds, Ed Williams. Linemen—Smiley Creswell, Dennis Owens, Ben Thomas. Backs—Jim Bowman, Ernest Gibson, Rod McSwain. DNP—Tom Ramsey.

Chicago	13	10	21	2—46
New England	3	0	0	7—10

NE	FG Franklin 36
Chi	FG Butler 28
Chi	FG Butler 24
Chi	Suhey 11 run (Butler kick)
Chi	McMahon 2 run (Butler kick)
Chi	FG Butler 24
Chi	McMahon 1 run (Butler kick)
Chi	Phillips 28 interception return (Butler kick)
Chi	Perry 1 run (Butler kick)
NE	Fryar 8 pass from Grogan (Franklin kick)
Chi	Safety, Waechter tackled Grogan in end zone
MVP:	Richard Dent (Chicago)

have the running backs or the offensive line to do that. They had the *great* John Hannah at left guard, but they didn't have a dominating line. In Eason and Grogan, they didn't have a quarterback who could lead the team down the field to score against our defense. Even getting a first down was difficult, and they didn't get any in the first quarter.

It also was obvious that their defense could not stop our offense. Their line did a good job against Walter the entire game, but we still kept piling up points. McMahon just handed off to Suhey or hit one of our receivers with a long pass or carried the ball himself. Before the first half was over, Jim had a short running touchdown and Butler kicked another field goal to up our lead to 23–3. And we weren't through. I likened us to a bunch of sharks at times, because once we scored, the attack was on. Their bleeding had started and we were going to find the wound and continue to exploit it; we were thirsty for more.

In the locker room, McMahon was saying how we should go out and score 60 points. There was all kind of stuff like that being said. The guys were so hyped that no one wanted to play conservatively. Our attitude was to just go out there and turn it loose. We said, "Let's have some fun and create some enemies along the way." I'm not sure if both our offense and defense wanted to use the Super Bowl as a showcase to the nation, but we did want to create some awe by playing the game as it had never been played before. And we did that.

The defense had held the Patriots to minus 21 yards in the first half. We were playing well but felt that we could play even better. The fact that they had scored three points really frustrated us. So I wasn't satisfied. In fact, after New England got its first first down late in the first half, I really got on everybody. "They got too many yards on that play—what the heck were you doing?" I'd say stuff like that because I didn't want anybody to feel they could let up. I was always angry about something.

As the second half progressed, I looked into the eyes of the Patriots and saw that they were thinking, "We are in the wrong game on the wrong day. We do not belong here. I cannot wait until this is over. This is humiliating." I wanted the game to be over, too. A lot of people enjoy playing when it's not a game anymore, but not me. It was 20–3 at halftime and we quickly scored again on another McMahon sneak, so it was 27–3 and we knew and they knew that they weren't coming back. I preferred a challenge, a close game with our backs against the wall.

In the second half, I almost got my neck broken by the Fridge. Oh, my goodness—I'd forgotten all about that. Fridge was in at defensive tackle and I was going toward Craig James, who was carrying the ball. I was zeroed in on James and it was going to be a sideline hit. Then all of a sudden I saw a shadow out of the corner of my eye. A huge shadow. I knew who it was. I just went, "Oh, no . . ." Wham! I was just lying there on the turf and Fridge is saying, "Mike, please get up, please get up, please get up." I said, "I'm okay, just let me lay here for a minute." I wasn't scared. It was a tough hit, his helmet hit mine, but I didn't think it was a paralyzing blow. I wasn't afraid; I was just kind of knocked silly for a few seconds and had to get my bearings.

Fridge was playing some offense, too, and even got a touchdown by diving over the goal line in the third quarter. At the time, I wasn't upset that Payton hadn't been given the ball instead and been allowed to score a Super Bowl touchdown. To be honest, I wasn't even thinking about who was scoring our offensive touchdowns. All I was doing was looking at the scoreboard and looking at how we were playing defense. I had no idea who was scoring on the offense; I didn't care.

However, when Reggie Phillips scored a touchdown on an interception for the defense, that was good stuff. I think Jim Morrissey hit the receiver and the ball came out to Reggie and he just ran it in. I wasn't on the field by that time, but it was good stuff. I also liked that the defense got two more points late in the game when Henry Waechter tackled Steve Grogan in the end zone. That made the final score 46–10.

After the field goal on New England's first possession of the game, we really didn't want to give up any more points. When the defensive starters began to come out of the game with the score something like 37–3, we told the guys on the second unit to please not let the Patriots score again. As it turned out, Grogan threw a touchdown pass. But it didn't matter.

The game ended. Both Mike Ditka and Buddy Ryan were carried off the field on the backs of the players. I wasn't part of either group. I was so happy that the game was over and that we'd won that I didn't even think about taking the coaches off the field. I just couldn't wait to sit down and let it sink in a bit. I wanted it to just sink in: "We have just won the Super Bowl." That doesn't happen every day. This was something that I had accomplished, and I said, "Lord, thank you for allowing me to win the Super Bowl." A short time after that I thought of Todd Bell and Al Harris not being able to play in the Super Bowl—so it was a little bittersweet.

In the locker room we were on top of the world. We were telling each other, "I love you, I'll do anything for you, just tell me what you want." I thought it was great when Richard Dent was chosen the MVP. He was a great player and he had a great game, causing those two fumbles in the first quarter to help put us ahead and constantly putting pressure on their quarterbacks and running backs. It was the Super Bowl and it was terrific and appropriate that someone from our defense won that award.

I talked briefly to Buddy Ryan. He had tears in his eyes but he didn't say a whole lot. The next time I spoke to him I was in Hawaii for the Pro Bowl, along with a lot of our other players. I had found out while I was over there that Buddy was going to Philadelphia. He called me a couple of times after the announcement, but I didn't return his calls. I was angry because he hadn't told me. Finally, I called him and said, "Buddy, why didn't you tell me you were leaving? Why would you do something like that?" He said, "Son, you've just got to know that I love you and I had to do what was best for me and my family." I said, "Being in Chicago was good for you and your family." I was very childish and selfish about the matter but finally I settled down.

Looking back on what happened with Ditka and Ryan: They were each other's accountability partner and didn't let each other get too big for the team. They were each strong enough to maintain a balance at the top. But when one coach left for Philadelphia, the other coach got too big, and whenever the part becomes bigger than the sum, you're in trouble. Ditka brought in good people after Ryan, but he was so dominating that he swallowed them up. Meanwhile, Buddy had good people in Philadelphia, but not a Ditka. You just can't lose that one person you respect, that one person who can say, "Look, this is the way I see it and the way it's going to be." Both Ditka and Ryan needed someone like that to share the power.

So we won only one Super Bowl. But we did win one and we did it convincingly. I said before that I didn't have as much fun playing football as I should have, but I had a lot of fun that day. I loved that Super Bowl; I just loved it. To me that game exemplified what defense is all about. It also showed what can happen when a team has a lot of talent, leadership, vision, accountability, and love for one another. Despite the conflicts, there was nothing that the 1985 Bears couldn't accomplish. I believe we gave the greatest performance in Super Bowl history.

SUPER BOWL XXI

NEW YORK GIANTS 39
DENVER BRONCOS 20

PHIL SIMMS

I n my sophomore year at Morehead State, I already was pretty sure I'd get a chance to play pro ball. Then I was scouted fairly heavily after my junior year and knew that I was going to be a first- or second-round draft pick. I continued to improve as a senior, and a week or two before the draft I learned that the Giants were probably going to take me as their first pick. So there I was down in Morehead, Kentucky, sitting there and joking, "That'll make the people *happy* in New York." We laughed about it.

I guess I knew about the "Phil Who?" headlines in the New York papers the day after the draft. But I didn't care. The Giants hadn't been to a Super Bowl or won a title of any kind since 1963, so what could one new player, even a quarterback, do about it? And why should that history be a factor in the way he thinks or does anything? It shouldn't.

It's not true that Giants fans were immediately impatient with me. Absolutely not. My first couple of years, it couldn't have been any better. Then when I got hurt a few times, yeah, some of them complained about me and the team. But I never got bad fan mail or felt extra pressure from impatient fans. If the team isn't doing well, the quarterback's not going to have a tremendous fan base. If the team does well, as we did in our Super Bowl season, everybody loves you and you're a hell of a guy. That's just the way it is. I never said, "Oh, Christ, I've got to make the fans like me." That kind of thought never crossed my mind.

When I got to the pros, the Giants' coach was Ray Perkins. He was a former receiver, but it was run first, throw second. We never got to the point of being the passing team we developed into under Bill Parcells from 1984 to 1988, our best passing years. When we reached the Super Bowl in January of 1987, people still regarded us as a running team, but in truth, everything was built around the pass. We had thrown for over 4,000 yards in 1984 and almost that much in 1985 and 1986.

We had been to the playoffs in the previous two years and had high expectations for 1986. So it was a downer to lose our opener, 31–28, to Dallas. We knew we were better than the Cowboys, but there are always surprises in opening games, and this game was on *Monday Night Football* in Dallas, so there was that extra distraction. The big surprise was that they scored so many points against our defense.

For the rest of the season we didn't give up that many points in a game and we lost only one more time, finishing 14–2 and winning the NFC's Eastern Division. Most of those games had close scores except for the blowouts at the end of the season against St. Louis and Green Bay. That's the type of team we were; that's how we were coached. Bill would be aggressive, but once he thought we had enough points to win, he would pull back, rather than taking chances to try to win by wide margins. So some of those close scores were misleading.

The two plays everyone remembers from the 1986 season were a fourth-and-17 completion to Bobby Johnson that helped us beat Minnesota and a long pass to our tight end Mark Bavaro that sparked another comeback victory over San Francisco. They were talked about as being the two plays that helped us become champions. But it's not that simple. I think they were instead two great examples of the team's character. The play against Minnesota was one of the first plays we worked on in training camp every year—it was designed to give me a lot of options. In the huddle, I told Bobby, "Just sit over there by the sideline, and if I have to come to you late, I'm still coming to you." I actually came to him quicker than expected because I got rushed. I saw there was a little hole for me to throw it to him through if I had to, and I had to just before I was hit. First down.

Mark Bavaro's play against the 49ers said a lot about the team. For him to catch the ball and break tackles and carry defenders on his back and never go down just said it all, that we were tough and hardworking. This really was a hardworking team, the most dedicated, highest-effort team I played on in my career.

As the season went on, I tried to get the ball to Bavaro more and more, and he caught many more passes than the wide receivers, Lionel Manuel and Bobby Johnson. I know Lawrence Taylor had a great, great year and was voted the league's MVP, but if there was a signature guy on the Giants who made a difference that season, it was Mark. Whether blocking or catching passes, he was so dynamic it was incredible. We had Joe Morris running the ball well, and we had a solid offensive line, but Mark added a tremendous dimension to our passing game that lifted our whole team over the top. Mark didn't speak, but his personality was so strong because he was silent. As players, we magnified that characteristic—"Hey, the silent, strong man—there he is"—and built that into everything we were trying to be as a team. Bavaro and Phil McConkey, who was definitely the most emotional player on the offense, were the best of friends. They were the perfect match because McConkey did enough talking for two people.

The emotional intensity was totally different on the offense and defense. The entire offensive line—our guards Billy Ard and Chris Godfrey, tackles Brad Benson and Karl Nelson, and center Bart Oates—were all low-key guys. Joe Morris and Mark Bavaro were not speakers, Lionel Manuel was as quiet as Bavaro, and Maurice Carthon, our fullback, did all his speaking by hitting people on the field—he would never say or do anything outrageous. On the field and in the huddle everyone was quiet. But they were the toughest unit I played with in all my years. And very caring. I wasn't shy about telling any of those guys what I wanted from them and it was always accepted. I would chew their butts out in a heartbeat and say things that could really hurt friendships, but they took it the right way and never let it bother our relationship off the field. I wouldn't get into it that way with the defense—I didn't know who was responsible for making bad or good plays, so I was just a fan when the defense was on the field.

There was no question that Lawrence Taylor and I led the team. I led the offensive, and Lawrence led the defense by being emotional and vocal. Harry Carson, the captain, and George Martin, who was another veteran, also were looked up to, but they didn't stir things up like Lawrence. They loved to hold team meetings about once a month to make sure the team was focused and to talk about things that were troubling players. Personally, I just didn't believe in them. In all the years, I don't think I ever stood up and said one word at a team meeting. If I had something to say to an individual, I'd say it to him privately.

A team's chemistry is great when you win, so it shouldn't surprise anyone that we were a close team. Still, you have dividing lines on a football team just as you do elsewhere in the world. On football teams, there's age, race, different positions, whether you're married or single—all those things that divide players into certain groups. On the Giants, there were large cliques, probably consisting of about 8 to 10 players. It wasn't quite offense together and defense together, though it was nearly that. That's the natural thing. You become friends with whom you work.

Our group was me, Carthon, Benson, McConkey, Bavaro, Jim Burt, and Tony Galbreath. Oates was in there, too, hanging around and wanting to know what was going on, getting involved in all the crap we were doing. We hung out together in the weight room, working out, and we'd have dinner every now and then after practice. But mostly there really wasn't a lot of socializing because we spent so much time dealing with football. Burt, our nose tackle, was the one defensive guy in that group. He was a very, very good football player. He also was a character who liked his antics. Jim was Parcells' pet, and he and Bill had a tremendous give-and-take relationship. If Parcells were a player on that team, he would have been Jim Burt, a good football player who could be a tremendous pain in the ass.

My relationship with Parcells took off at the beginning of 1984, his second year as head coach after being an assistant coach. The Giants had a terrible record in 1983 when I was injured, and I think he concluded during the off-season that I was the personality for his team. When we started playing pretty well and he saw how I handled myself, he realized that we were going to mesh together. He knew he could say things to the team through me, which is what he used me for a lot. If the team was doing something wrong, he'd yell at me. That was his way of communicating to the entire team. But let me make this clear: At no time in our years together did our relationship ever go past player-coach. It never became friend-friend, which a lot of people assume. He couldn't do his job properly and it could only have hurt me if we'd have become anything more. Bill Belichick, the defensive coach, Ron Erhardt, the offensive coach, and the position coaches could have friendly relationships with players, but as the head coach, Bill couldn't do that. There has to be fear and all that involved. Bill wouldn't give me free rein at all, hell no, but he absolutely understood my talents. That was his strength as a coach. He had a lot of pieces, so he could get one thing from one guy, another thing from a second guy, and put it all together and make it work.

There was no real back-and-forth between me and Parcells in preparation for the Super Bowl. I was a player; he was a coach. Bill and his coaches designed the game plan. Sure, I would have said we should come out throwing, but quarterbacks are always selfish that way. A coach doesn't quite think like that, especially with a team like ours that could almost win it just with defense and running the ball. So why take the chance of throwing? We'd done very little throwing in beating San Francisco, 49–3, in the playoffs, and Washington, 17–0, in the NFC title game.

Prior to the Super Bowl against the Denver Broncos, I talked to a lot of people who had played in previous Super Bowls. Many of them told me that the bigness of the game really had affected their play. They had been so caught up in the electricity that they couldn't concentrate on what they were trying to do. I found that peculiar and told myself that I wouldn't let that happen to me. I wanted just to concentrate on playing football and not think about things like the game being televised in every country in the world. And I didn't.

Looking back at a lot of games that year and at the Super Bowl, I realize that nothing bothered me. I was so confident and focused. If the bigness of the Super Bowl helped me, it was that in the week leading up to it I was so strong-willed that I allowed nothing to get in the way of football. The other thing is that I was not afraid of making a mistake or being intercepted even though it was a big game. Under Bill, we had been taught to play hard, not worry about mistakes, and talk about winning only in the last couple of minutes.

We practiced one week in Giants Stadium and then we went out to California and practiced at the Rams' training facility for the second week. The team watched films of our victory over Denver during the season and two or three other game films, and I'm sure the coaches broke down more than that. We held quarterback meetings and prepared the plays that we might use during the game. We knew exactly what we wanted to do, what would work and what wouldn't. Our concepts were sound and we became very, very sure of our execution. For two weeks we were about as hot in practice as any team I've been around. Parcells knew that. I'll never forget the Friday before the Super Bowl, which was our last workout, and when we practiced "our game," going over all the situations. And I was throwing strikes. He said, "Goddamn are we hot; we're ready. Save it, Simms, just save it." I had to laugh because that was coming from a man who didn't like to talk in those terms. So we had to be hot.

All my thought processes were positive the entire time. I was very confident in myself and I believe our team was given extra confidence because we were installed as heavy favorites. Denver had a good season under Dan Reeves, but we didn't doubt we could beat them twice in a row. Everything felt great. Practices were just spirited and good and I was thinking I can play out here in this beautiful weather. I even enjoyed the interviews every day. Of course, I was always asked the same question: "Well, Phil, what about John Elway?" Well, shit, here we go again: "Well, John's great, yeah, yeah, yeah." Back then, it was only his fourth year and I was not in awe of him by any means. I honestly believed I was a better quarterback. I'd say in a friendly tone, "You guys keep talking about him, but I'm the one who's hot. I'm the one who's throwing all the touchdown passes." They all laughed and I laughed with them.

When I look back, I find it amazing that the press and the Bronco players didn't talk much about our passing game, because in the previous eight games going into the Super Bowl it had been just dominant. It was as good a stretch as we ever had. Even in the playoff win against the 49ers, we made big plays those few times we did throw. Still the pre–Super Bowl talk about our offense was about Joe Morris and our running game. They did talk about our defense, which was what we were known for and what deserved to be talked about because it was very, very good.

I found it funny when I came home from the Super Bowl and read some of the articles written before the game. Our linemen did interviews where they'd say, "Yeah, our running game's good, but I tell you what, Phil's been hot." They were basically saying, "We're going to come out throwing." They were giving away our game plan! The plan was to come out throwing and in the perfect world we could finish it off with Joe. Just because you come out throwing doesn't mean it will be successful. We would be fortunate that day.

Before the game, the locker room was a little quieter than normal but still fairly loose. We weren't a team where players sat at the lockers thinking about the game. Most of us liked to walk around and talk, BS a lot. I never sat at my locker intensely telling myself, "Oh, man, I've gotta really be good today." Instead, I'd like to talk about college football the day before, anything. Lawrence Taylor was more demonstrative. He liked to talk, but mainly he loved to talk to himself out loud, usually saying something about how wild and crazy he was going to be on the field. We'd all sit around and look at him. It would inspire players or get them going, and we'd get a laugh out of it too because he would be screaming.

It was over 80 degrees in the Rose Bowl in late afternoon and I felt the heat during warm-ups. I started walking because I didn't want to spend any energy. But I felt fine and was really throwing the ball well. Of course, I'd felt great before other games and then struggled. It's never that easy. I just knew that our passing game had been exceptional for several games and that as a team the Giants were solid in every other area. We had a tremendous defense with George Martin, Jim Burt, and Leonard Marshall up front, Taylor, Carson, Carl Banks, our top tackler during the season, and Gary Reasons at linebacker, and backs who could play an effective zone on pass coverage. McConkey was a good punt returner and our kicking game was solid with punter Sean Landeta and placekicker Raul Allegre. And our running game was very strong—Morris ran for over 1,500 yards during the regular season and had big games against the 49ers and Redskins. I'd say that what weaknesses we may have had were minor and were never exposed that season. In fact, at no time during that whole year and going into the Super Bowl did I believe we had a single weakness.

We got the ball after a long field goal by Rich Karlis on Denver's first possession. It was never a trademark of Bill Parcells to plan the first series or first play, but that day we did plan the first play, a pass to Manuel, where he split to the right and cut across the middle for a 15- or 16-yard gain. We knew that he would be open and he was—they played the exact coverage we expected. Then we said we'd hit a pass to Bavaro over the middle. He lined up on the right and gained 8 yards. If you watch a tape of the game, you can see me then say something to the sidelines, because on the third play we were supposed to go for a seam pass all the way up the middle for a touchdown. It was going to go to Lee Rouson coming out of the backfield. Instead they sent in a running play for Morris and Rouson stayed on the bench. And I thought, "Oh, man, they chickened out a little." Which is understandable in a Super Bowl. I did complete that pass to Rouson later in the game for over 20 yards.

Our running game was always just by feel. Call it, and if one thing works, then slowly go with that till we have to counter it and go to something different. We were predominantly a right-handed running team most of the year, and if we did have a signature play, it was the old "Green Bay Sweep." We'd sweep, pull both guards, have the fullback, Carthon, leading with a block and Joe finding a hole. We didn't have any specific plans for where we wanted Morris to run against Denver. We didn't think of it being more advantageous going inside or outside. On the first drive, Morris had good runs to the right, to the left, and down the middle. His second run, where we shifted some people and he ran to the left, was called back because of a penalty. We put that play in for that game. The play was called a "Slant-38 Boss." Boss meant "the back is on the strong safety."

Denver moved Karl Mecklenburg, its top linebacker, around on defense, hoping he'd stop Morris on the run. In preparing for the game, we'd talk about him in regard to our running game, and the coaches decided to run away from him to give us better match-ups. So early in the game, we shifted Bavaro before each hike, because we knew Mecklenburg would follow him, and then we'd run Morris to the side Mecklenburg had been on. It worked well.

I was getting plays from the sidelines more often than from players being sent in. As always, I was the only person to speak in the huddle. There's no time for anyone else to talk. I remember looking at the players during our first drive and thinking these guys were choking to death. They were excited and nervous and affected by the heat and importance of the game, so our whole team was gasping for air. When I came to the line of scrimmage, I saw that Denver's defensive players also were red-faced and breathing as hard as they could, trying to get air but hyperventilating.

I completed six of six passes in the opening drive to five different receivers. Bavaro caught two passes, a seam pass and a little hook, but in this game we didn't have to throw to him as much as usual because we had plays that would work with other receivers, like outside passes to Stacy Robinson. He caught one that drive for a first down on third-and-10. We knew they'd have single coverage on our wide receivers—Manuel, Robinson, Johnson, and McConkey—and they could probably get open. After a Bavaro reception got us down to the 6-yard line, Mark stayed in to block and we brought in his backup Zeke Mowatt, who lined up behind the line. Mowatt went into motion to the left, then cut back to the middle of the end zone and caught my pass to put us ahead.

After the game, Denver was claiming it was surprised when we came out throwing. That sounded good and people bought it, but come on, an offense is either going to run or throw, and a defense just doesn't assume you'll do only one of the two. That we had such success so easily or that I

January 25, 1987, at the Rose Bowl in Pasadena, California
Paid Attendance: 101,063
AFC Champion: Denver Broncos (13–5)
Head Coach: Dan Reeves
NFC Champion: New York Giants (16–2)
Head Coach: Bill Parcells

STARTING LINEUPS

OFFENSE

Denver		New York
Vance Johnson	WR	Lionel Manuel
Dave Studdard	LT	Brad Benson
Keith Bishop	LG	Billy Ard
Bill Bryan	C	Bart Oates
Mark Cooper	RG	Chris Godfrey
Ken Lanier	RT	Karl Nelson
Clarence Kay	TE	Mark Bavaro
Steve Watson	WR	Stacy Robinson
John Elway	QB	Phil Simms
Sammy Winder	RB	Joe Morris
Gerald Willhite	RB	Maurice Carthon

DEFENSE

Denver		New York
Andre Townsend	LE	George Martin
Greg Kragen	NT	Jim Burt
Rulon Jones	RE	Leonard Marshall
Jim Ryan	LOLB	Carl Banks
Karl Mecklenberg	LILB	Gary Reasons
Ricky Hunley	RILB	Harry Carson
Tom Jackson	ROLB	Lawrence Taylor
Louis Wright	LCB	Elvis Patterson
Mike Harden	RCB	Perry Williams
Dennis Smith	SS	Kenny Hill
Steve Foley	FS	Herb Welch

SUBSTITUTIONS

Denver: K—Rich Karlis. P—Mike Horan. Offense: Receivers—Joey Hackett, Mark Jackson, Bobby Micho, Orson Mobley, Clint Sampson. Linemen—Mike Freeman, Dan Remsberg. Backs—Ken Bell, Gary Kubiak (QB), Gene Lang, Steve Sewell. Defense: Linebackers—Darren Comeaux, Rick Dennison, Ken Woodard. Linemen—Tony Colorito, Simon Fletcher, Freddie Gilbert. Backs—Mark Haynes, Tony Lilly, Randy Robbins, Steve Wilson.

New York: K—Raul Allegre. P—Sean Landeta. Offense: Receivers—Bobby Johnson, Phil McConkey, Solomon Miller, Zeke Mowatt. Linemen—Damian Johnson, Brian Johnston, William Roberts. Backs—Ottis Anderson, Tony Galbreath, Lee Rouson, Jeff Rutledge (QB). Defense: Linebackers—Andy Headen, Byron Hunt, Pepper Johnson, Robbie Jones. Linemen—Eric Dorsey, Erik Howard, Jerome Sally. Backs—Mark Collins, Tom Flynn, Greg Lasker.

Denver	10	0	0	10—20
New York	7	2	17	13—39

Den	FG Karlis 48
NYG	Mowatt 6 pass from Simms (Allegre kick)
Den	Elway 4 run (Karlis kick)
NYG	Safety, Martin tackled Elway in end zone
NYG	Bavaro 13 pass from Simms (Allegre kick)
NYG	FG Allegre 21
NYG	Morris 1 run (Allegre kick)
NYG	McConkey 6 pass from Simms (Allegre kick)
Den	FG Karlis 28
NYG	Anderson 2 run (kick failed)
Den	Johnson 47 pass from Elway (Karlis kick)
MVP:	Phil Simms (New York)

threw to so many receivers might have startled them, but we couldn't have startled them simply by throwing.

Denver played defense exactly like we thought it would. Every single coverage was expected. When you scout a team, you know what to expect. That's the reason there aren't upsets in the Super Bowl. After two weeks of preparation, you can't get caught by surprise. So it's just the better team that wins.

On Denver's second possession, we gave up the first touchdown against us in the postseason. On a play that is a trademark for Dan Reeves' quarterbacks, Elway dropped back a step, watched the middle clear, and then ran straight ahead, 4 yards into the end zone without being touched. The Broncos were deep into our territory because of a double penalty, when Carson was called for an out-of-bounds hit and Taylor was penalized for protesting the call. That was uncharacteristic of us, being called for dumb penalties. That was one time when I could say, "Wow, the setting and circumstances are affecting some of our players." All of a sudden we were doing stupid things.

Denver moved the ball easily in the first quarter when building a 10–7 lead. That didn't make me uneasy. Our defense was so great that I just took for granted it would soon catch the rhythm of their offense and then stop them cold. Elway was the most effective runner they had at the beginning, with a couple of first downs and the touchdown, but I knew we'd stop him. We used a zone defense, so running quarterbacks were never a great problem. All our defenders were always facing Elway, so when he took off, the defense reacted. He didn't do much running after the early part of the game.

I loved to BS with referees, especially Jerry Markbreit. I liked Jerry a lot and always loved talking to him on the field, and we did talk after our second drive ended on an incompletion deep to McConkey. Phil was knocked down, but pass interference wasn't called and I took off my helmet and it hit the ground. Jerry goes, "You dropped your helmet, didn't you, Phil?" I said, "What?" He said, "If you threw it, that's a penalty, so you just dropped it, didn't you?" "Yeah, Jerry, I just dropped it." I just walked off the field and there was no penalty. So he was pretty cool.

Denver got the ball back, and after a pass of over 50 yards to Vance Johnson and a few other plays, they had a first down on our 1-yard line. Well, the worst thing you could ever do against the Giants was to get the ball within the 5-yard line. Because it was almost automatic that we would stop them. The Elway touchdown had been a fluke. You couldn't run against us and it was hard to pass because our backs played a zone and could spread around in the small area and make it hard for receivers to get open. In all honesty, I didn't think Denver would score. Taylor threw Elway for a loss going to his right, Gerald Willhite was stopped going down the middle, and Banks, who had 10 solo tackles in the game, stopped Sammy Winder for a loss going left. And I was on the sidelines thinking, "That's no surprise, that's no surprise, that's no surprise; okay we stopped them, what's new?" That's really what I thought. The defense was extraordinary in those types of situations and I loved to watch them. I might be on the phone and miss a play here or there, but I wasn't one of those guys who sat on the bench—at least not until times late in my career when I'd try to relax. I was on the sidelines watching every play, yelling and screaming.

After the goal-line stand, Rich Karlis missed a short field goal, a chip shot. He would miss another field goal from a little farther out at the end of the half. If he'd made those two field goals, would that have had a bearing on the outcome of the game? You never know what would have happened, but I think it might have changed everything: our thought process, maybe the way we attacked them, maybe the way they felt—they might have been more confident with a bigger lead.

Also, there was a controversial call that went our way in the second quarter. Elway had the ball third-and-12 deep in Denver territory and threw a low pass to his tight end Clarence Kay that would have given them enough yardage for a first down. I thought Kay caught it near the ground as he rolled over, but it was ruled an incompletion and the instant replay was inconclusive, so they didn't change it. A later TV replay showed he'd caught it, but it was too late. On the next play, Martin tackled Elway in the end zone for a safety to narrow the score to 10–9. I don't think that miscall was a key play in the game because their free kick rolled about 30 or 40 damn yards and we didn't get good field position. We didn't score as a result of their being forced to punt, so all we came away with was two points, which had no bearing on the outcome.

I audibled a lot during the year—always on third down in passing situations when I could detect the blitz. But I didn't need to audible once this entire game. I was being pressured infrequently by Denver's defense and wouldn't be sacked until late in the game. There was a lot of hard hitting and I saw a lot of tough collisions, but for me it was like one of those games you love to have during the season that allows you the chance to heel. It wasn't rough for me except for one moment after an incompletion that ended our third possession, when Mecklenburg had a hold of my ankle and kept twisting it. That made the cover of *Sports Illustrated*. I remember it hurt at the time and thinking that was close to being underhanded. He wasn't called for a personal foul, which is a little interesting.

Because the game turned into a blowout, people tend to forget that we trailed at halftime, 10–9. But I can't remember a word being said during the break about that. We had a nasty, ugly, old locker room, and I went in and got a drink of water and thought how hot it was. I found a little bench and laid down for about a minute or two and then sat up. I don't remember anything else. I don't remember the coaches telling us anything. Maybe they said, "What we've done is fine; we'll just go out and execute a little better and we'll be all right." We weren't a big halftime team. Our coaches never yelled at us or gave us pep talks. Bill might stand up and say, "Men, you've got 30 minutes. Let's get it done." No more was needed.

On our first possession of the second half, we had fourth down and less than a yard to go on our own 47. When I came off the field, Bill told me, "Stay close." So I wondered what we were going to do now that my backup, Jeff Rutledge, was in the game with our punter, Sean Landeta. We had so many plays that were designed for Jeff: deep passes, short passes, a sweep, a quarterback sneak, an option play. Once the defense was set, Jeff looked to the sideline to know what play to run. They signaled his number, which meant a quarterback sneak. It wasn't a long count and he wasn't trying to draw the defense offside; it just took him a long time to move over the center. I think we all realized it was a pretty big play, but we didn't have far to go and I doubt if we ever failed in such situations during the year. So, after Jeff went over the right side and we made the first down, I don't remember being too excited about it. I thought only that it kept the drive going and that I could go back in and run the next play. But looking back, if Jeff had been stopped in our territory, that could have been a tremendous, tremendous turning point in the game, no doubt.

I didn't at all question the decision to go for the first down. The rap on us was that we were a conservative team, but that was only because we were one of the few teams that could actually run the football. In truth, we were an aggressive team and our coach was not afraid to take chances. Parcells would always say, "This game is not for those who are faint of heart. You can't be worried about failure. If you fail, all right, there'll be another chance." He was really good and philosophical about those things. He knew when to take a risk, and when it didn't work, he wasn't the type to cry, "I shouldn't have tried it!" It was just, "Okay, those things happen, let's move on."

After Rutledge's sneak, we moved downfield on passes to Morris and the seam pass to Rouson, and we scored on a third-down pass from the shotgun that Bavaro caught down the middle at the 1 and took in. That put us ahead to stay, 16–10. The next time we got the ball, we got good field position on a long punt return by McConkey, and ended up with a field goal by Allegre for a 19–10 lead. And we scored on our next possession when Morris ran around right end from the 1, making the score 26–10.

The play before Morris's touchdown was a 44-yard flea flicker to McConkey, which he caught at about the 20 while crossing the field toward the left sideline. We'd done the flea flicker 3 or 4 times during the season and I probably ran that exact play 15 times in the pros, 14 times throwing it to the wide receiver crossing the field in the same direction McConkey ran. Going into the game, I didn't really know if we'd use the flea flicker, but it was almost always in our game plan, a weekly thing. When the coaches called it, I thought, "That's a good call right now, the perfect situation." I handed the ball to Morris, who ran forward and then turned and pitched it back to me, and I threw downfield. After the completion, I remember going, "We've won the Super Bowl." Phil made it all the way to the 1, and I knew we were going to score. That made it 26–10 and we were too far ahead for them to come back against our defense.

By now, our defensive guys were into the rhythm of their offense and were freezing it out. Early in the game, they were playing conservatively, but now they quit worrying about the run. The Broncos weren't going to beat us with Willhite or Winder running the football. So Marshall, Martin, Taylor, Banks, and the others became more aggressive in going after Elway. Boy, did they put pressure on him. That wasn't surprising, because our defense always had stretches where they dominated the other team. That's what happened. It gave the offense a chance to put the game away. As the game progressed, it seemed like Elway was the only player in their offense. When he became their only focus, you knew they were in trouble.

In the third quarter, our offense and defense clicked at the same time, and it led to the rout. At one point, I looked at the scoreboard and we had 200 yards offense for the half and they had 2. Wow! We were going up and down the field and they couldn't make a first down. Twice they punted and then Elvis Patterson intercepted Elway for the only turnover of the game. That led to our most bizarre touchdown, a 6-yard pass down the middle that hit Bavaro's mask and went into McConkey's hands. On the tape of the game, you can see me hugging the closest guy, and it was Dennis Smith, Denver's safety. I think I said something like, "When you're hot, you're hot," and he smiled. Yet I was thinking, "Man, that pass was perfect, Bavaro should have caught it and had an easy touchdown." It is funny how things work out. I'm glad McConkey had the chance to get in the record book after coming 1 yard short on the flea flicker and show that he contributed. That was just a good way to finish it off, especially since the ball bounced off his best friend.

I wasn't aware that I was setting a record with 10 straight completions. I also hit 11 in a row on first downs. It was the strategy to throw on first down early in the game and we stayed with it. Our formations put them into what we called "known coverages," meaning I knew what they were going to do. That made it easier. I was able to throw about half the time to the guy who the play was designed for. When I dumped it off to Joe Morris, that meant the designed play wouldn't work, and I was content with a short gain. I remember when the game was almost over, I was thinking, "Wow, we have been going really good here in the second half." I didn't think any more of it until I looked up at the scoreboard one time and they'd put up that I was 20 of 23. I said, "Man, wow, no shit!" But then I went, "What were my three incompletions?" Not to be funny—if I'd been 3 of 23, I'd have tried to remember the three completions.

Late in the game, I got good yardage on a bootleg to the left. I had run that play quite a few times during the year. It was always late in the game and on third down when the defense was geared for a hand-off to a running back. On previous plays when I handed off, I would always check to see if someone in their backfield was keeping an eye on me. If not, I'd signal to the sidelines what was happening and point to myself. Usually our coaches would watch one more play, and if I wasn't being watched, they'd call the bootleg. Over the years, it was a play the Redskins learned to hate, because I ran it for big first downs six or seven times against them. I ran the bootleg in the NFC Championship Game that got us down to about their half-yard line. In that game, I handed off to Joe for the touchdown, and in the Super Bowl I gave it to Ottis Anderson, who went over from the 2 for our final touchdown.

Then I was out of the game. I finished 22 of 25 for a new Super Bowl completion-percentage record and was chosen the MVP. As I look back on my career, the one thing I should have learned from that game is that positive thinking is the greatest weapon a quarterback has. It is the most valuable tool—forget the strong arm and all that other stuff. If you think positively, it's amazing what your body and mind will let you do. That game was a great example to me. I never once got even close to having a negative thought, so I was never restricted physically or mentally. During that game, I was as free as a player ever could be.

Time was winding down and Parcells and I both had ice buckets dumped on us by our players on the sidelines. It's a good thing I wasn't going back into the game because I could never have played with my uniform soaked. By this time most of the first stringers were being pulled and our defense was playing looser. That allowed the Broncos to narrow the final score to 39–20.

Some of our players celebrated on the field, dancing and mingling with fans. Then everyone went into the locker room, which was fairly loud but not out of control. The league didn't allow the winners to have real champagne. The players were very happy; and I'm sure there was great relief for some of the coaches, who felt we had to take advantage of the opportunity to win the Super Bowl when we were the best team, because we might not ever be that good again.

That Super Bowl was tremendously fun to play. I do remember having fun. Otherwise, I can't remember any extraordinary sensations as that game went on. I wish I did. We all wish that we could pinpoint the moments we will later want to treasure, but we don't realize they are so special while they are happening. That we won the Super Bowl and I played well was, in all honesty, only what I expected. I just took it in stride because I expected great things. Only after I did a few interviews in the locker room and was able to sit back did I start to appreciate what we'd accomplished a little more, but certainly my level of exhilaration still didn't match the magnitude of the game. I was thinking, "We're going to be in a lot of these Super Bowls." As an athlete you think that.

Now I look back on my career with the knowledge of how difficult it is to be Super Bowl champions. You must get all those players and coaches together, put in so much work, avoid injuries—good teams don't get beaten up so easily—and still have a little luck for everything to fall into place. You have to be fortunate. At the end of the television broadcast, John Madden was saying that for football players who win the Super Bowl, "It never gets any better than this." Looking back, I know he was right. I would never be able to match that feeling or re-create that time.

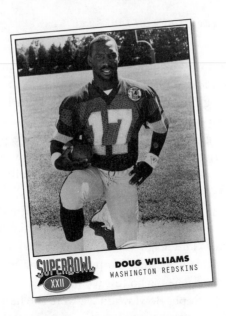

DOUG WILLIAMS
WASHINGTON REDSKINS

SUPERBOWL
XXII

SUPER BOWL XXII

WASHINGTON REDSKINS 42
DENVER BRONCOS 10

DOUG WILLIAMS

Late in Super Bowl XXII, there was an announcement over the loudspeaker that I had been selected the game's Most Valuable Player and many of the Redskins came over to congratulate me. You don't show it, you don't wear it on your sleeve—I didn't—but I felt a lot of emotion. I have wonderful memories of that moment, and when I see it on film, cold chills run through me. When I see it, I don't think of only that championship season, but I look back at my whole career—from 1978, my rookie season with Tampa Bay, until that moment—and remember everything I had to go through in order to be where I was.

I've always thought that the beginning of my professional career at Tampa Bay was similar to Jim Plunkett's at New England. Jim came in several years before me, but we both were first-round draft picks who were starting quarterbacks as rookies and spent years having difficult growing-up periods, playing on young teams and getting beaten up. After a few years, both of us were discarded by our first teams, but we eventually came back to win Super Bowls with better teams. The difference was that New England let Plunkett go because they said he could no longer do it, while Tampa's ownership let me go although they knew I was producing. They just didn't want to pay me.

I spent five years with Tampa Bay and we made it to the playoffs three times, the only times in the organization's history. We then had contract problems in the spring of 1983 and couldn't get it together. I wasn't getting any support for my salary holdout, but I didn't expect it. Players rarely win in the press because most people who buy papers don't understand how players get a lot of money in the first place. So I tried to deal with the press as little as possible. The Buccaneers weren't going to trade me, so either I had to accept their offer or not play at all. I decided to sit out the entire 1983 season.

I had no anger toward the NFL—my problem was with Tampa Bay's ownership—but by leaving the Buccaneers I knew that I might never play in the league again. I didn't really worry about that. There was the new USFL, so I could have played football if I wanted to. But it was a very tough time for me emotionally. You see, my first wife passed away suddenly that April and we had a baby girl. So my state of mind was such that it wasn't important whether I played again. I realized there was more to life than football.

I probably needed that year off to recover from the beatings I'd taken those hard years in Tampa. Then, in 1984, when I was in a better state mentally and physically, I got the opportunity to resume my career in the USFL. I played one year in Oklahoma and another year with the same owner in Phoenix. Then the USFL folded in 1985 and I was out of work.

That's when Joe Gibbs called and asked me if I would come to the Washington Redskins and be back in the NFL for the 1986 season. I was interested because we had a good relationship from years before. He really knew me because he had watched me all the way through college at Grambling, and when I joined Tampa Bay, he was the team's offensive coach. Tampa's offense was creative in my rookie year, but after Gibbs left we became conservative, and what we seemed to do was pitch right, pitch left, run a power play, and it was third-and-long. So I was happy to have the chance to come to Washington, where Coach Gibbs had put together a sophisticated passing game.

Coach Gibbs was candid and told me that being a backup was the only position he had for me. He didn't tell me I'd have a chance to start down the road. Jay Schroeder was a young guy, and at the time, the team felt he was its future. They just needed a veteran backup and that was me. I said that I didn't have a problem with that.

Coach Gibbs was glad to have me, but I'm not sure about Bobby Beathard, the general manager. I don't think he turned flips when I was coming over to the Redskins. Over the years Bobby and I have formed a good relationship, but at the time, I don't think he was a big Doug Williams fan. He didn't think I worked hard, that's what he said. I didn't agree with him but I liked that he was someone who was straightforward and didn't pull any punches.

In 1986 I threw only one pass. But that didn't upset me. The two years I spent in the USFL had been pretty physical. We hadn't had high-priced linemen to protect quarterbacks and that took its toll. I did get kind of banged up and that first year in Washington really gave me an opportunity to slowly get back into the swing of things. In retrospect, it allowed me to find out what the NFL was all about again and got me ready for 1987.

That second year I was a backup again. We played a lot of close games, and it was kind of a bizarre season because I came in about four times in relief of Schroeder and brought us back and won the games. Also I started a couple of games after he had gotten hurt. What finally put me over the top was the last game of the season. We had already made the playoffs, but we were playing Minnesota and were behind. I came in and we came back and won in overtime. After the game Coach Gibbs announced that I was going to be the starter. He said that he felt from a leadership stand-point that going into the playoffs against the Chicago Bears he wanted a veteran at quarterback.

I viewed playing quarterback a little differently than some people. Many people viewed it by numbers, but I viewed it by leadership. The sports-writers were claiming that I was a better quarterback at Washington be-cause my passing statistics were better that year, but it's the amount of respect you get from the players —off the field, on the field, in the huddle, on the sidelines—that will tell you if you got better. The quarterbacks with the best numbers don't necessarily win championships. To be a win-ning quarterback you have to get the confidence of the players and be-come a leader. You have to carry yourself in a way they respect; you have to be a playmaker and make things happen; and you can't mind giving up your body and doing anything else that it takes to win. And when your guys screw up, you don't jump into their faces; you don't point fingers—you take the blame. On the field, I was businesslike and didn't let too much stuff excite me. If something went wrong, I took it in stride, didn't blame anyone, and tried to do better the next time. That was my attitude and I think it rubbed off on the other players.

Now that Washington was winning with me at quarterback, the media was saying that I had improved while in the USFL because I was now completing a lot of touch passes. But my style hadn't changed. It was the same style I had with the Buccaneers, when the media had criticized my passing. I still had the strong arm. When the media criticized me at Tampa Bay, it wasn't about me being young—it was about me throwing the ball hard. While some fans in Tampa disliked me as the quarterback because I was black, the media just complained that I threw too hard—but I believe that also had to do with my skin color. I'm not a crybaby and never have been, but it was evident to me that black quarterbacks with strong arms were judged differently than white quarterbacks with strong arms. Commentators said, "Doug Williams throws the ball too hard," but if you listened to the commentators over the years, they'd rave about how strong Terry Bradshaw's arm was or how strong Dan Marino's arm was or how strong John Elway's arm was, and they didn't say they threw too hard when the ball popped off their receivers' chests. I saw Elway throw a flare pass 100 mph and all they talked about was how great his arm was. If I did something like that, you know they'd have talked about how I threw too hard. So it was hard to please those people and I didn't try. I understood that as a black quarterback, that was what I had to deal with. James Harris, who also had a strong arm, had been the quarterback at Grambling before me and became like an older brother to me. And I saw all he went through with the Rams as the only starting black quarterback in the league. When the Rams lost, they blamed him, so James knew better than anyone how black quarterbacks were judged.

My passing percentage at Tampa Bay went up every year because the team got better every year. And my passing percentage was higher in 1987, when I played on an even better team with a stronger and more innovative offensive concept. But, as I said before, the numbers didn't matter—our winning did. That point was reinforced in the NFC Championship Game. We were playing Minnesota again after having beaten the Bears in the divisional playoff game. They had a very good defense and I didn't have a good game if you were just looking at my numbers. But that wasn't true from the coaches' standpoint. Not once did Joe Gibbs say I was having a bad game. I'll never forget when his assistant coach, Dan Henning, came over to me. He knew I was frustrated because of my numbers, but he sat me down and went over my performance with me. He said, "Doug, I know you're thinking that you had a bad game. Well, let me tell you what you didn't do: You didn't get us beat. What you did do was complete nine passes, and two of them were for TDs and one was a big play that set up a touchdown. You threw some away so you didn't take any sacks."

He knew that I had done a lot of good things that people didn't see. Some of those "bad" passes the broadcasters talked about were throwaways. Some quarterbacks don't want their pass percentages to suffer, so they'll take a sack and hurt the team. I wasn't looking to lead the league in passing, so I felt it was better to throw the ball away and have an incompletion in my stats than to lose 10 yards and be faced with third-and-20. I didn't take sacks. I can still see Minnesota's Joey Browner in that game coming out of the strong safety position and forcing me to throw the ball away. The coaches could see why I got the incompletion, but the television commentators (and newspaper people) couldn't understand.

We went ahead late in the game against Minnesota on a touchdown pass to Gary Clark. It was 17–10, so that when the Vikings brought the ball down to our 6-yard line, the worst thing that could have happened is that they could have tied the game. If that happened, we still would have had the opportunity to win, so I wasn't at the point where I thought we were going to miss out on the Super Bowl. If we had been ahead by less than seven points, I would have worried more. In any case, the Vikings didn't score any points and the clock ran out, and we were the NFC champions and going to the Super Bowl against the Denver Broncos.

Personally it was very gratifying. I think the ultimate goal of some players is to make money—everybody wants to make a decent living—but I think what every player, somewhere in the back of his mind, wants most of all is to be in "the show." That's the Super Bowl. All I was thinking when we beat Minnesota is that I got that right; I got the chance to go. I was very happy, and I was happy for everybody on the team, especially other USFL guys like Ricky Sanders, Gary Clark, and Kelvin Bryant, and some of the other guys who hadn't been to the Super Bowl before.

Everybody in Washington was excited. We'd get visitors at our practices to wish us well during the week before we left for San Diego. Even Ollie North came by for a day or two. It was written up that he gave us a "pep talk." I know Ollie didn't pep me up.

We probably weren't the best team in football or even the second-best team, but we won because we had veterans, strong leadership, a good work ethic, and strong camaraderie. The Redskins were a work-and-more-work blue-collar team that played and practiced well together without any separation between offensive and defensive players. We all got along. At the beginning of the year, when there was the strike and replacement players, not one of the Redskins crossed the picket line. That was a great sign right there. That showed what types of guys we had as far as what they believed in and who they believed in. They believed in each other.

I know the Hogs worked together better than any offensive line in football. I don't know much about Dallas's offensive line of the 1990s, but I can't believe that Joe Bugel didn't assemble a better unit for us in the 1980s. Mark May, R. C. Thielemann, Russ Grimm, Joe Jacoby, Raleigh McKenzie, and Jeff Bostic were very big and very talented. That was a close-knit bunch. They hung together, and when everybody else had gone home after practice, they had their little clubhouse gatherings. They had faith in each other when they lined up beside each other on game days. Their attitude was, "If I do my job, the guy next to me is going to do his, and we're going to be hard to beat." One reason our offensive linemen liked playing in front of me and respected me was because when I was supposed to be in the pocket, I was in the pocket. They knew "Doug is going to make my job easier because we know where he's going to be. He ain't going to be running all over the place. I don't want to get a guy blocked only to have the quarterback run out of the pocket and have my guy escape me and sack him—I'll get the blame for that." They knew I'd be in the pocket, so they had to tell themselves only one thing—"Don't let anybody in the pocket."

In our passing game we had what we called "the posse." That was Art Monk, Ricky Sanders, and Gary Clark, our three great receivers. They all could play. Art was a very, very low-key guy. But he was a smart, big-play receiver. Gary was more vocal. He was very competitive and he didn't care what down it was and how many yards we needed; he felt it was his football. Ricky was the sneaky guy who got things done. Did they get along? Oh, man, they were like three peas in a pod and were always hanging out together. Gary and Ricky looked up to Art, who was the veteran star, and rallied around him, but they had egos, too. Not crazy egos, but egos. What Coach Gibbs had to do to keep all three guys happy was to come up with plays for each of them. So for each, he came up with seven possible plays in which they were the primary receivers. We made sure we spread the ball around to the three of them, short, long, or whatever. They were interchangeable, so they could run similar routes. I never had the problem of receivers in the huddle saying, "I'm open; throw me the football." Coach Gibbs, Joe Bugel, and Dan Henning or whoever was in the press box called the plays. However, after a particular pass play didn't work, a receiver might say, "My guy played me inside and I can beat him on a quick hitch to the outside," and maybe the next time we'd call that play instead.

We scored most of our touchdowns during the year through the air, but we had a pretty effective running game. In fact, with Joe Gibbs, it was run first, pass second. We almost always went with a single-back formation, although on occasion we'd use one of our H backs, Clint Didier or Don Warren, as a fullback. During the regular season, George Rogers, the veteran, and Kelvin Bryant, who had come over with me from the USFL, carried most of the load. Bryant was also part of our passing game and had a touchdown reception in the NFC title game. During the playoffs, a rookie got back a lot of playing time: Timmy Smith.

Tim hardly carried the ball during the season, but he got more time against Chicago and Minnesota and did well. He was a young, energetic good-timer who didn't really understand what the game was all about or what he had to do, but he had some talent that you could see if you watched him closely. He was strong, quick, and had decent speed—which you wouldn't have thought because he looked like a little old fat-legged back. Like all rookies, Timmy was bushy-tailed and wide-eyed when he got to the pros and he didn't really open his mouth until he found a couple of guys he could be buddies with and talk to a little bit. Then we found out that he was not quiet by any stretch of the imagination. He would have loved to have talked to the reporters during Super Bowl Week, but they ignored him because nobody knew that he would be starting.

Before we left Washington, Joe Gibbs had told me that he was going to start Timmy at running back to give us more of an outside threat. It would be Timmy's first start as a pro and Joe told me not to tell him because he feared Timmy would be too anxious all week and be hounded by the media. It was a decision he felt was the best for the team, and he just wanted me to know because I was the quarterback. In practice, George Rogers still got a lot of the plays, but Tim got his share. I don't think Denver knew Timmy was starting even if they saw our practices. Coach Gibbs was worried about Denver scouts spying on us anyway, so we'd have guys wearing different numbers and would run plays where we'd have 12 or 13 guys on the field. We knew who the guys were in correct positions but it would have confused anybody watching us.

Coach Gibbs didn't try to come up with a different offensive game plan against Denver than the one we had used against Minnesota. He wanted to run *his* offense and it didn't matter if we were facing a physical team like the Vikings or a finesse team like the Broncos. No matter who we were playing, he felt we had to do certain things and not get away from that. I never counted the number of plays we had for the game. Anyway, you don't just run 75 or 100 plays; you use more formations than you do plays and run the same plays out of different formations. That's what we did basically. What's important was not how many plays we had but the match-ups and mismatches we created with different formations.

Our defense was well prepared for the Super Bowl by Rich Petitbon. I didn't know much about the other side of the ball, but I could see that Rich did a hell of a job patching it up over there. At one end we had a great pass rusher in Dexter Manley. He was a vocal guy, our shit-talker per se. Then at the other end we had Charles Mann, who was the businessman. And we had old, steady Dave Butz at an inside tackle just causing havoc up the middle. Darryl Grant, on the other side, didn't get a lot of credit but was a big force on the defensive front. Then you had guys like Barry Wilburn, who had a heck of a year at cornerback yet probably couldn't even run a 4.7 in the 40. Barry was smart enough to be in the right place at the right time and would have a couple of big interceptions in the Super Bowl. The other cornerback was Darrell Green, who could outrun a deer and was a tremendous defender. And at strong safety we had Alvin Walton, who would do a good job at disrupting John Elway's passing and running. Also we had some solid linebackers like Monte Coleman and Neal Olkewicz. Petitbon took advantage of each player's strengths and didn't call the defense based on what he wanted as much as on what he thought everybody could do. It worked because our defense was pretty good.

Everybody on the team believed in our coaches, so we never doubted that we were going to win the Super Bowl, even though we were underdogs and nobody gave us a chance. I'd have been a little worried if I didn't think I had a good week of practice, but the whole team, including myself, had the best week of practice that we had all year.

I had come to San Diego with the idea of being relaxed and doing my job. I didn't do all the video-camera scenery stuff; I didn't do the town; I didn't do the limo. After practice I went back to the hotel and watched television and ordered room service. I did that until one of my old Tampa

Bay teammates, Jimmie Giles, came to town and we went to dinner. We walked out of the hotel room, didn't sign autographs or talk to anybody in the lobby, and just got in the car and went to dinner.

What distractions there were came from the media. Super Bowl Week was a long week for me because everybody was talking about the "black quarterback" thing. I think there were a lot of people in San Diego that didn't seem to know I was black until I got there, because all they wanted to ask me about was how it felt to be the first black quarterback to start in a Super Bowl. One reporter asked, "How long have you been a black quarterback?" I think I understood where he was coming from and it just came out that way. I think he was trying to ask me how long people had been *referring* to me as a "black quarterback." I hope that was what he wanted to say. I'm giving him the benefit of the doubt.

My thing was this: For 30-something odd years, I had gotten up and looked in the mirror. So nobody had to tell me what color I was. That part was settled. I already knew that and so did my teammates. The players didn't get caught up in the hype. The hype was with the media. They wanted to make headlines by coming up with a story. It only takes one person to create a story and everyone else follows the lead. For some in the media, the Super Bowl was presented as being a white quarterback going against a black quarterback, John Elway against me. For others, it was simply one quarterback against another quarterback, which wasn't correct either. While I never got into judging me or anybody else at quarterback, it was obvious that Elway had done a great job leading the Broncos to the Super Bowl two years in a row—but I didn't worry about him because he was just one player. It was Denver against Washington, not Elway against me. It was our defense against Elway and the Denver offense, and it was their defense trying to stop me and the Redskins offense. I wouldn't put a blitz on him and he wouldn't blitz me.

The people in the media had the problem with me being the Redskins quarterback and couldn't deal with it. But I could. I didn't even see it as a "controversy." I think if I had gotten caught up in all the hoopla about "the black quarterback," I wouldn't have been able to focus on the game. But it didn't become too much for me. First of all, I didn't read the paper. Second of all, I didn't do any more than I had to do from a media standpoint. I didn't do any extra stuff. When the media's hour was over with, my mind refocused on what we had to do with Denver.

So everything went just fine until I had to have an emergency root canal the day before the game. As I sat in the chair I wasn't worried that I wouldn't feel up to playing the next day. I was having the root canal so I could play. That Saturday evening I had trouble talking, but I went back to the hotel and laid down and watched TV and let the painkiller work. After that I didn't have a problem. But I still didn't sleep well before the game. I didn't sleep well before any game. I would stay up late and usually would eat a lot of chocolate—usually candy kisses—but that night I had to go without eating chocolate.

My mouth felt all right on the morning of the Super Bowl and I was able to eat breakfast. I didn't eat a lot but I put something in my stomach. Then we went to Jack Murphy Stadium, which was hosting the Super Bowl for the first time. I had never played there but it didn't matter. The only stadium that anyone had trouble adjusting to was Candlestick Park because most of the time you don't play on such a soft field.

It was no different in the locker room before the Super Bowl than before any other game. You'd see Dexter Manley marching around with his earphones on, beating on lockers, and breathing hard. You'd see big linemen quietly sitting by their locker looking up into space. You'd see some of the hyper guys like Kelvin Bryant pacing about. You'd see Art Monk making sure that he was neatly put together and Gary Clark looking scraggly. There wasn't a lot of hoopla, but there weren't a lot of heads down either. There were no pep talks. We had a lot of veterans so we didn't need them. Joe Gibbs didn't give any big talk before we went onto the field. He wasn't a preacher or a rah-rah type of coach. He'd just tell you, "We've worked all week; we know what we're doing; we know what they're going to do; let's go out there and do what we have to do to win." He had a great concept: We're going to work when we have to work; we're going to relax when we have to relax. These guys knew it was time to work.

I made sure I used the bathroom before I went onto the field. I was always the type of guy who used the urinal about five or six times before coming out of the locker room, whether I needed to or not. I wouldn't go back in after the national anthem. Once that was over with, peace was out the window, it was time to play football.

Denver scored first on their first play from scrimmage, when Elway threw a long touchdown pass to Ricky Nattiel behind Barry Wilburn. It was for over 50 yards. I was on the telephone with one of the coaches and didn't see what happened until the replay. People have always asked if that play stunned the team. All you had to do was to look back two games before that—people don't remember we were 14 points down in the second quarter against the Chicago Bears in frigid weather but came back to win, 21–17. We knew Chicago was a better team than Denver, so seven points so early in the game was definitely not going to make us think that we couldn't come back.

With the Broncos ahead 7–0, they got inside our 10-yard line on their next possession, but on third down Dave Butz stopped Elway on a delayed run down the middle, and they had to settle for a field goal. In my mind that wasn't such a big play either because we'd have been behind only 14–0, the same score as in the Bears game. Ten to zero was about the same. I don't think that would have changed the game—14 points wouldn't have overcome our 42 points, I don't think.

Denver kicked off and Ricky Sanders was hit hard and fumbled the ball at our 16-yard line. Fortunately, we got it back in the big pileup. Now *that* was a big play. In fact, that was the biggest play of the game. We all felt relieved we had recovered the ball. It could have been 17–0 and we could have been in a treacherous hole to dig out of, and we probably would have had to deviate from our game plan to make sure we scored points quicker than we had in mind. When we got the ball back on the fumble, that set the tone for the rest of the game. That was the play.

There was another big play that came a couple of plays later that a lot of people don't remember. We were backed up on our 10 and it was third-and-16, and we needed a first down or they'd get the ball in good field position. Then I completed a 40-yard pass to Art Monk. He ran a 15- or 20-yard route and made a heck of a play. It was his only catch of the game and people have forgotten about it because they remember the later touchdowns by Ricky and Gary. But that was probably our biggest offensive play of the whole Super Bowl because it got us out of terrible field position and got our passing game going. Before that, our receivers had been nervous and were dropping the ball.

We didn't score on that possession, but I was still confident that we would come back. However, my game almost came to a quick end late in the first quarter. I dropped back to pass and slipped, and when I went down, I twisted my left knee. It had been hurt before and now I hyperextended it. I was in too much pain to know if I'd be able to get back into the game. I wanted to just be able to walk off the field on my own. If I could walk off, I knew I would be able to come back. And that's what I did. I missed just two plays and was ready to go at the beginning of the second quarter. Pain—at that time it was no longer important.

What I remember most in that whole game was what Joe Gibbs said just before we went back out for the second quarter. "Just get in there; we're going to get this sucker running." That's all.

January 31, 1988, at Jack Murphy Stadium in San Diego
Paid Attendance: 73,302
NFC Champion: Washington Redskins (13–4)
Head Coach: Joe Gibbs
AFC Champion: Denver Broncos (12–4–1)
Head Coach: Dan Reeves

STARTING LINEUPS

OFFENSE / DEFENSE

Washington		Denver	Washington		Denver
Gary Clark	WR	Mark Jackson	Charles Mann	LE	Andre Townsend
Joe Jacoby	LT	Dave Studdard	Dave Butz	LT	
Raleigh McKenzie	LG	Keith Bishop		NT	Greg Kragen
Jeff Bostic	C	Mike Freeman	Darryl Grant	RT	
R. C. Thielemann	RG	Stefan Humphries	Dexter Manley	RE	Rulon Jones
Mark May	RT	Ken Lanier		LOLB	Simon Fletcher
Clint Didier	TE	Clarence Kay	Mel Kaufman	LLB	
Don Warren	TE			LILB	Karl Mecklenburg
Ricky Sanders	WR	Ricky Nattiel	Neal Olkewicz	MLB	
Doug Williams	QB	John Elway		RILB	Ricky Hunley
	RB	Gene Lang	Monte Coleman	RLB	
Timmy Smith	RB	Sammy Winder		ROLB	Jim Ryan
			Darrell Green	LCB	Mark Haynes
			Todd Bowles	RCB	Steve Wilson
			Barry Wilburn	SS	Dennis Smith
			Alvin Walton	FS	Tony Lilly

SUBSTITUTIONS

Washington: K—Ali Haji-Sheikh. P—Steve Cox. Offense: Receivers—Anthony Jones, Art Monk, Terry Orr, Eric Yarber. Linemen—Russ Grimm, Rick Kehr. Backs—Reggie Branch, Kelvin Bryant, Keith Griffin, George Rogers, Jay Schroeder (QB). Defense: Linebackers—Ravin Caldwell, Kurt Gouveia, Rich Milot. Linemen—Dean Hamel, Steve Hamilton, Markus Koch. Backs—Brian Davis, Vernon Dean, Clarence Vaughn, Dennis Woodberry.

Denver: K—Rich Karlis. P—Mike Horan. Offense: Receivers—Vance Johnson, Orson Mobley, Steve Watson. Lineman—Keith Kartz. Backs—Ken Bell, Tony Boddie, Gary Kubiak, Bobby Micho, Steve Sewell. Defense: Linebackers—Michael Brooks, Rick Dennison, Bruce Klostermann, Tim Lucas. Linemen—Walt Bowyer, Freddie Gilbert. Backs—Tyrone Braxton, Jeremiah Castille, K. C. Clark, Bruce Plummer, Randy Robbins. DNP—Larry Lee.

Washington	0	35	0	7—42
Denver	10	0	0	0—10

Den	Nattiel 56 pass from Elway (Karlis kick)
Den	FG Karlis 24
Wash	Sanders 80 pass from Williams (Haji-Sheikh kick)
Wash	Clark 27 pass from Williams (Haji-Sheikh kick)
Wash	Smith 58 run (Haji-Sheikh kick)
Wash	Sanders 50 pass from Williams (Haji-Sheikh kick)
Wash	Didier 8 pass from Williams (Haji-Sheikh kick)
Wash	Smith 4 run (Haji-Sheikh kick)
MVP:	Doug Williams (Washington)

Denver was a finesse team, while we had to be a very physical team in order to win the NFC East. We knew that once the Broncos had run all their trick plays, they would be forced to try to play physical football. That's what happened. They used quick counts, shovel passes, Elway even came out of the backfield to catch a pass, all the trickery they could come up with. But once we saw it and were able to cope with it, it was time for them to try to play our type of physical game. And they couldn't do it. When our defense stopped Denver, our offense went to work, and we came back like we knew we would.

If you were playing the Giants, you knew you wanted to have a tight end over Lawrence Taylor most of the time, but this game we didn't go into with the idea of concentrating on stopping one particular defender. We knew that Karl Mecklenburg was one of their key players from a blitz standpoint, but that didn't bother us. Our game plan was to dictate to them, not let them dictate to us. We did that with match-ups, by getting one-on-ones with Ricky Sanders and their corner Mark Haynes, and forcing their safety Tony Lilly to defend the pass instead of blitz. When we ran the ball, we often did double teams on their noseguard, Greg Kragen, and then ran the ball up the middle. We were the ones who created plays. Sometimes we'd run formations just to see how they would play them, and then we'd come back and throw a pass because we saw the match-up we would get with that formation.

Coach Gibbs worked awfully hard to put together a game plan that he knew was going to work, but he still gave his quarterback a few audibles to use in a game for special situations. For instance, if I got to the line and thought our receiver would be one-on-one with a defensive back, I felt that the receiver would win the match, so I'd audible a particular pass play to him. It so happened that none of the four touchdown passes in the second quarter would come on audibles, but I would make automatic adjustments and throw different pass plays than I called at the line. For quarterbacks, audibles and automatic adjustments work hand-in-hand, especially when the defense is able to dictate what the offense will do.

Against Denver, some of our long passes were dictated by the defense and not by the offense. The 80-yard TD pass I threw to Ricky Sanders on our first play of the second quarter was supposed to have been a 7-yard hitch pass where we'd fake the back into the line and I would take a three-step drop and throw a quick short pass to Ricky. But the defense dictated that I change the play. Mark Haynes was playing man coverage on Ricky and came up to the line to bump him. If the DB presses, you can't throw the hitch because he's right there to intercept. Haynes tried to put a hand on Ricky, but Ricky dodged him and ran up the right sideline. He got four or five steps on Haynes and you know Ricky could run. All I had to do was put the ball in the air and he ran under it. Tony Lilly couldn't get over in time, so it was off to the races.

Joe Gibbs said that the sidelines came alive after that touchdown. Well, I wasn't on the sidelines, but I knew it was a play our team needed from an offensive standpoint to get our confidence way up and to show everyone that there were two teams playing this game. We had finally scored and trailed only 10–7.

On our next series we had the ball on Denver's 27 and tried a pass. They brought the linebacker, and I should have thrown to the tailback in the flat. But because they were blitzing it was man-on-man with their backs on our receivers. I made another automatic adjustment and Gary Clark beat his guy crossing to the left. I threw the ball into the corner and he dove for it just over the goal line and it was six points. Good throw, great catch. Ali Haji-Sheikh's extra point put us ahead, 14–10.

I wasn't looking into the eyes of the Denver rushers. They didn't matter to me. I didn't have to worry about them because I knew they were going to be stymied by our offensive line. I had confidence in those guys and they had confidence in me. There's a moment in the highlight film of the game where our huge tackle Joe Jacoby can be seen urging me on in a very emotional and vocal manner. That was unusual because Joe was a very, very quiet guy. But he was aware of all that I had gone through with the media during the week and walked up to me and said, "Black, white, green, yellow, we're going to win this thing with you!" I respected all of those guys on the line, but when a guy comes out and says something like that, it makes you feel a heck of a lot better. It made me feel great.

Our third touchdown was a 58-yard run by Timmy Smith. It wasn't anything but our old bread-and-butter counterplay. Raleigh McKenzie and Joe Jacoby pulled and went to the right side and opened up a big hole for Smith and allowed him to break free down the sideline. Then Tim did a good job of staying in bounds and outrunning those guys. In the trenches our more physical offensive line was just winning the battle.

The score was suddenly 21–10 in our favor, but we weren't looking at each other and saying, "What's going on?" When you work your butt off the whole year and execute, and then spend two weeks executing in practice, you expect to execute in the Super Bowl. That's what we were doing. Perhaps Denver was seeing a team execute better than anybody in history in that quarter, but that's the way the cookie crumbles sometimes. People always say that we were in "a zone" and all that. Not only was I in a zone, it was a team thing. By this time, Denver didn't know how to defend us because we could pass or run. We were able to run–run, pass–run, pass–pass, it didn't matter.

We had just run a touchdown off the counterplay, so on our next series we faked the counter using a different formation. The secondary shifted and Tony Lilly fell for the play-action fake and came up, and that left Ricky Sanders behind him as he crossed the field. Lilly couldn't recover. Ricky was several yards ahead of Lilly when I hit him at the 10-yard line and he ran the rest of the way into the end zone. That was a 50-yard pass and Ricky's second touchdown.

You could tell that Denver was deflated. You could look at the players on the field or could look across the field at Dan Reeves and his coaches and players, and you knew something was going across their minds about how we were scoring every time we got the ball and they couldn't stop us. But even after four quick touchdowns, I still didn't think that anything special was happening. I just hoped we could get a big enough lead to keep Elway from coming back.

We got the ball back when Barry Wilburn intercepted Elway to stop a drive. Then we quickly went all the way downfield. The fifth touchdown of the period was a short loft pass to Clint Didier running to his left in the end zone. We dug in and outformationed them. Didier was in tight and Ricky came across in motion, and that spread the defense and took the cornerback away, and Clint just ran a corner route, in and then out, and was by himself when he caught the pass.

So we had scored 35 points in one quarter for a Super Bowl record—we scored on five consecutive possessions and I think we had the ball less than six minutes. I look back at our success in the second quarter and I see it as the result of hard work and opportunities. You've got to work hard, you've got to execute, and you've got to have luck, and we had all three that quarter. I passed well, but with my receivers as wide open as they were, I shouldn't have been playing if I couldn't complete those passes.

The half ended with us up 35–10. In the locker room we all got together to talk about what we had to do in the second half. Control the ball and all that. Joe Bugel came up to me. He used to call me "Stud," and he just said, "Hey, Stud, you don't have to go back out there if you don't want to. I think we can handle this." At that time my knee was swelling and I could hardly walk. But I said, "No, I started it and I'm going to finish it." That was it.

I didn't worry that we would be complacent in the second half. We knew that if we were capable of having a quarter like we had, some other team could do it too, and we didn't want it to happen against us. All I'm saying to myself is, "Lord, I hope Elway won't have a third quarter like our second quarter."

Joe Gibbs had a lot of respect for Dan Reeves and wasn't trying to run up the score, so I think we got a little conservative in the second half. I attempted only 8 passes compared to 21 in the first half. We just kept the ball on the ground and let the clock run. We mostly gave the ball to Timmy, who scored the only touchdown of the second half with a short run up the middle. We all knew he could run, but no one expected him to gain over 200 yards in the Super Bowl. With the way our linemen were blocking I could have picked up 120 yards on my bad leg. I tell you, I turned around one time and they had completely wiped out the whole middle of Denver's defensive line. I'm saying to myself, "My God."

I don't want to take anything away from Tim because he made a lot of great runs. One of his biggest runs of the day was right up the middle on a bang play where we double teamed the noseguard. And I just turned and handed it to him going straight up the middle and he cut left and had a long run down the sidelines for 30 or 40 yards. Timmy had several long runs. We didn't get caught up in stats, so we weren't trying to help Timmy break Marcus Allen's Super Bowl rushing record with his 204 yards or help Ricky Sanders set a Super Bowl record with 193 yards receiving. That just happened. I threw for 340 yards without passing much in the second half, and I'm sure we could have set a few records passing and everything else if we had wanted to.

Manley, Butz, Grant, and Mann were putting a lot of pressure on Elway and it was obvious that Denver wasn't going to make a comeback. We knew we were going to be Super Bowl champs. I don't think we were making any special effort to keep our emotions intact until after the game was over. I was pretty cool regardless, even when it was announced that I was the MVP. As I said, it was an emotional moment. How couldn't it be? That's the pinnacle of any man's career. Not only to go to the Super Bowl but to then win it and be named MVP. There have only been a few MVPs.

On the last play I just leaned over and put my knee to the ground. Oh, man, as the quarterback you always want to get to that point. It means you've won. That was the exclamation point on the game. Then I stood on the field and I held my helmet up in the air. That was a lot of anxiety being released. There's a lot to be said about that image of me with the raised helmet. But I won't say it. . . .

My whole family was in the stands. There were about 18 people from Zachary. My dad couldn't make it because he was a disabled veteran, but my mom was there with my brothers and sisters and aunties and it was a wonderful thing. Eddie Robinson, my coach at Grambling, was at the game, and we hugged. He said that the proudest moment he ever had in football was to be at that game and watch me perform and be the Super Bowl MVP. Here's a guy who coached over 50 years, so what he said was really big time as far as I was concerned.

After the game, when they held the press conference, I didn't want to deal with the same black quarterback questions. I wanted to be looked at as the quarterback of the Washington Redskins, not as a black quarterback. But I was so happy it was over with that my attitude was: If you want me black, okay, I'll be black. I wanted to tell the media that I was black if only because they didn't seem to know it until that week.

Today, when I'm asked if winning the MVP changed my life, I answer, "I'm still working." No, it did not. That's for sure. I'd have a better golf game if it did. I'd have had more time to play. Even though I was held up in the light and was a role model whether I wanted to be or not—and I accepted that—it was unfortunate that corporate America didn't look at it that way. They picked who they wanted and I wasn't who they picked. I hadn't been to detox, I hadn't had a DWI, I hadn't beat up anybody, so they didn't think I had any appeal. I couldn't get angry at things I couldn't control, but I was disappointed because being the first African-American to play quarterback in the Super Bowl and then to be the MVP . . . I just thought that should have had great appeal to America. But then you realize you are in America and everything isn't the way it should be. Corporate America ignored something that could never happen again—there could never ever be another first black quarterback in the Super Bowl.

I have pride in having played in the Super Bowl. And I have pride to have been the first African-American quarterback in the history of the Super Bowl, which is something that can never be erased. I've got kids and they've got something to grow up with: "My dad was the first black quarterback to play in the Super Bowl, and win, and be the MVP." Even then I knew it was something to be proud of. Without a doubt I was aware of my place in history.

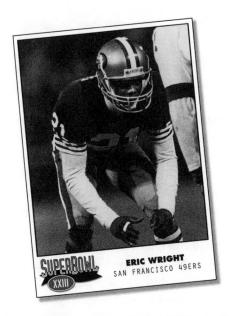

ERIC WRIGHT
SAN FRANCISCO 49ERS

SUPER BOWL XXIII

SAN FRANCISCO 49ERS 20
CINCINNATI BENGALS 16

ERIC WRIGHT

I was chosen in the second round of the 1981 NFL draft, when the 49ers used four of their first five picks on defensive backs. They drafted Ronnie Lott from USC, me from Missouri, and Carlton Williamson and Lynn Thomas from Pittsburgh. Four rookies and three of us started right away. George Seifert was the secondary coach, and he didn't have to get permission from Bill Walsh to go with rookies because that was their plan when they took all of us so high in the draft. There had been something like 30 DBs who had come in and out of there in about two years. The only guy they had been satisfied with was free safety Dwight Hicks. They wanted to improve at the other positions and it so happened that it worked out. Ronnie and I became the corners and Williamson became the strong safety. The funny thing is that I wasn't a

317

cornerback. At Missouri I played free safety. In fact, the only time I ever played corner was in a college All-Star game in Mobile.

The friendships between Ronnie, Carlton, Dwight, and me evolved from day one. We each had high standards and there was competition between us in that vein, but rather than pushing us apart, it made us draw close and play better as a unit. We all wanted us to be the best secondary in the league and that drove us. I don't think it was a great secondary right away. We were just good in my rookie year, when the 49ers went on to beat Cincinnati in Super Bowl XVI. But by 1983 or '84, when the 49ers went 15–1 and beat Miami in Super Bowl XIX and all four of us went to the Pro Bowl, we were at the top of our game, and there was no question that we were the best secondary in the league.

If Ronnie Lott had a philosophy for playing defense—such as an us-against-the-world philosophy—that would be the entire secondary's philosophy. Normally, Ronnie was our spokesman and the focal point when it came to us getting PR. We weren't jealous that he was getting most of the publicity. When people asked me if I minded Ronnie getting the attention, I'd say no because I could leave the locker room and he had to stay around to be interviewed. I didn't want to do interviews—I just wanted to play football and win and be successful.

Ronnie and Keena Turner were probably the most vocal leaders on the team. Joe Montana and myself and a lot of other guys led in a silent way. We showed leadership in the way we came to work every day and by the way we played. But when something needed to be said, Ronnie said whatever he wanted to say to you, to the coaches, to anybody affiliated with the 49ers. He was a driving force, one of the coaches on the field. If Ronnie didn't think you were performing, he was going to jump your ass. In the heat of the battle—yeah, I resented it if Ronnie got in my face. A lot of the players resented it. But we knew that Ronnie was the guy who could raise the level of play of everybody on the team, especially the defense and especially the secondary. If Ronnie didn't do it himself, it might have been different, but we knew that when it counted, Ronnie was going to raise his own level. When the game was on the line, he was the only player I was ever out on the field with who I absolutely knew was going to find a way to make a big play. I've never thought about whether he had the same respect for me as I did for him. I think everybody on our team had respect for everybody else because that is what enabled us to be a close group and to go to four Super Bowls.

We practiced the way we played. We would go after guys. Maybe it wasn't like in a game when you would run into guys, but it was all-out, man-to-man coverage, all-out competitiveness. If a wide receiver caught a ball on me in practice, I was upset. It was not acceptable if a guy caught a pass. Even if that guy was Jerry Rice, who joined the 49ers in 1985. Or John Taylor, who came in a couple of years later. Or Freddie Solomon, who was a very good wide receiver before Rice and Taylor came along. Because if it got to the point where you'd accept a receiver catching even a 1- or 2-yard pass, you were going to accept him catching a touchdown. It was not acceptable in our secondary for any receiver to catch a pass of any kind. That was why we got our paycheck.

So no, it wasn't exciting for me to watch the development of Jerry Rice as an NFL receiver. He was the enemy. When it's break time and you're on the sidelines between drills, you can be friends with Jerry and J. T., but when you're playing against them and preparing for the next game, you can't be their friends. That was the train of thought I had. I didn't want to be a good defensive back, I wanted to be a great defensive back, and that required a certain mentality. I was respected by the guys I played man-to-man against every Sunday because it was evident that, hey, if you were a receiver, you couldn't be my friend.

Were Rice and Taylor friends? I'd say so. I'm not saying they were buddy-buddy and hung out, but they got along. (On the 49ers, you maybe didn't like a guy, but you respected him and made a point of getting along.) I do know there was a difference in their football mentalities. What separated the two of them is that you had to get Jerry the ball—you *had* to do that or Jerry would be a bit upset. With J. T., it didn't matter. J. T. complemented Jerry, like I complemented Ronnie. You needed a player who gave them balance at receiver and J. T. gave them balance. To me, J. T. was the more gifted of the two receivers. He was such a raw talent and athlete that he could have been as good as Jerry or even better, but Jerry worked much harder in the off-season. J. T. was the type who would go out and play basketball and that was his workout. That was how J. T. got in shape for football. Jerry literally worked to get stronger and did anything to improve.

There's no question that Jerry developed his workout habits and became the greatest receiver in the game because of how we trained and because of our established day-to-day workout habits. We set the standard for him. And for everybody else. I believe that our 1981 team, which had the new secondary, set the standard that the 49ers would have from then on, that they still have today. Our standard was: It's not acceptable not to win an NFC championship and not go to the Super Bowl. If you don't do those things in San Francisco, you're a failure. And somebody has to take the blame. What the defense did was make our Super Bowl appearances as frequent as possible so that no blame could be placed on us.

After we won the Super Bowl in my rookie year, we expected to win every year. It was frustrating when we didn't go back, especially when we came close. That's why I remember all those losses so vividly. Nineteen eighty-two was a strike season, but we should have made it back to the Super Bowl in 1983. We lost the NFC Championship Game to the Redskins in Washington because of the officiating at the end of the game, when one call went against myself and another went against Ronnie. We won our second Super Bowl the next year, but then were knocked out of the play-offs the next two seasons by the Giants (who would also beat us in the 1990 NFC Championship Game). In '87, it was Minnesota who upset us in the playoffs.

Immediately following those disappointments, our guys would always rally together. We would always have a meeting spot, like a bar, and all of us would get together and have drinks. It took us a while to recover from some of those devastating losses, but that is what bonded us into a close-knit team and motivated us during the off-season to try to get back there again. We went into the 1988 season not having reached the Super Bowl for three years, and we all felt that had been too long.

By then, our secondary had changed, so that only Ronnie Lott was still starting, and he had moved to free safety. Hicks and Williamson were no longer around, and I was only coming in as the nickel back on third-down passing situations. As the nickel back on the 49ers, I was supposed to take a receiver on the inside, either playing him man-to-man or doubling up on the guy. I was in a diminished role because I had strained my groin against Dallas in the last game of the 1985 season and then missed the Pro Bowl because I reinjured it in the postseason. It got progressively worse. I was able to come back but I felt its effects. It was very frustrating having a nagging injury that wouldn't go away. It just never got back to 100 percent. (That's what eventually got me out of the game.)

When you have an injury, you see the writing on the wall. You don't need somebody to tell you that your job description has changed. One day you're playing every snap; the next day you're delegated to playing sparingly, and you're not one of the major guys anymore. George and Bill wanted me to come back and would have given me my job back as the starting corner if I'd have been healthy. But I could never reach that point where I once was. Mentally, I knew what to do, but physically I just couldn't do it anymore. It was like getting old, like Ronnie did. But when he got older and lost his range, he adjusted by changing positions and moving closer to the line. (Kids today don't believe that Ronnie started off as a corner because he became such a good safety.) You normally go outside and move in, like he did, but I couldn't make that adjustment. I couldn't go from corner to safety, even though I played it in college. I tried that, but I just couldn't do it anymore. So I accepted just being used in the nickel package.

Just because Eric Wright wasn't healthy and wasn't playing much didn't mean he was one of those selfish guys who didn't want the corner who was replacing him to do a good job. I always wanted Tim McKyer to be successful. I wanted the team to be successful. The thing is, they didn't miss a beat without me. And that was good. It made me want to come back even quicker to be part of the team because you want to contribute and be one of the guys.

I was one of several 49ers players who had physical ailments at the beginning of the 1988 season. John Taylor missed the first few games because of a drug suspension. That was hard on the team, but at least in those days most teams had depth at all positions. In fact, another problem we had early on was that Bill Walsh had two quarterbacks, Joe Montana and Steve Young. Joe had hurt his back, so the 49ers acquired Steve from Tampa Bay in the off-season as insurance. Joe was able to come back and we had two healthy quarterbacks, but Bill couldn't make up his mind who should start. Again, instead of dividing us, that quarterback controversy made us closer. I'd say that the guys who had been there, including most of the guys on defense, were very loyal to Joe. We had played with him over the years and in two winning Super Bowls, so we supported him 100 percent.

All that adversity probably had some effect because we almost didn't even win our division. We struggled early in the season, even when we won. We were just 6–5 with five games left to play. I don't know if Bill Walsh's job was in jeopardy, but there was pressure on coaches and everybody else in the 49ers organization when the team wasn't winning. We were expected to win by our owner, Mr. D.—Eddie DeBartolo—and there was a lot of tension for everyone involved when we weren't doing it. Even if we just dropped two in a row, there was extreme pressure.

When Bill decided to stick with Joe Montana as his quarterback, we started playing well again and ran off a string of victories. It's not that it became easy for us, but we had such confidence in Joe getting us wins if we just kept games close. We knew that when he was in there we could be down by a touchdown with two minutes left and he would bring us back.

We knew when Joe was healthy and Joe was on, everybody raised their level of play. Everybody realized that they had to deliver.

We finished 10–6 to beat out the Los Angeles Rams for the Western Division title. And in the playoffs, both the offense and defense continued to play great football. We absolutely crushed Minnesota in the opening round. We beat them 34–9. Then we destroyed the Bears in Chicago for the NFC title. I think they got only a field goal. Bill preached to us that if we were focused when going into an enemy environment like Soldier Field, we would find some way to leave it with a victory. He motivated us and we bonded together to become a great road team. If we hadn't been, we wouldn't have been a championship team.

We were excited to be going back to the Super Bowl. Every Super Bowl I played in was fun, even Super Bowl XVI, when there was such tension because it was so close. My first Super Bowl had been a dream come true. You watch the Super Bowl growing up as a kid, and hey, it's here, you're playing in it.

Super Bowl XIX against Miami came after a season when we lost only one game. I recently asked Bill how the current San Francisco teams would have done against that championship team, and he said, "There will never ever be a team that compared to that team." Many of the defensive players, including me, were pissed off because the offense got all the PR. Joe, Roger Craig, and the rest of the offense played great, but the defense stopped Dan Marino and prevented a shootout. Offense gets you there, but defense wins championships. That was our motto. If they don't score, they don't win. My interception against Marino? That was the best play that Eric Wright ever made. It was prime time in one of the biggest games ever, and I made a great play. Athletically, I don't know how I did it. I was up in the air, facing the other direction. I bit on Mark Clayton's out move; and then I spun around somehow and he was there and the ball was there, and if I hadn't been there, it would have been six points for Miami.

Super Bowl XVI had been played at the Silverdome in Detroit. We were fortunate to play indoors because Detroit was so cold. We were driving on ice. Still, Super Bowl XIX was tougher because the game was in Palo Alto, so we were close to home. There were so many distractions that it was hard to prepare for the game. For our third Super Bowl, we got to go away and it was to a nice, warm place, Miami. But in truth, we were just happy to be anywhere. At that time of the year, if you're still playing, hell yeah, you're happy no matter where you have to play. All the other teams are back home.

It so happened that when we were in Miami there was rioting in parts of the city because a black man had been shot by a Hispanic cop. It got pretty wild, especially at night, when there'd be fires. That scared a lot of guys, and we had to be very careful about where we went and what we did. Cincinnati's hotel was downtown and closer than ours was to Overtown, where the worst rioting was taking place, so I'm sure the Bengals were affected more than us.

Despite the problems in the city, we were able to have a good time. We found places to go and just avoided those areas where there was a ruckus. But we were there to win a football game, so if someone would stay out late and miss a curfew, we'd always have a team meeting. Hey guys, it's getting toward the end of the week, so we've got to come in early, and everybody's ass has to get to work. We buckled down and had a great week of practice.

Super Bowl XXIII was pushed as a rematch of Super Bowl XVI because it was again the San Francisco 49ers going against the Cincinnati Bengals. Of course, the media liked to push Super Bowls as being battles not just of teams but of particular individuals. While Super Bowl XXIII was supposed to be a battle between the two quarterbacks, Joe Montana and Boomer Esiason; and the running backs, Roger Craig and their rookie Ickey Woods; and the two strong defenses; it was mostly billed as a game between the head coaches, Bill Walsh and Sam Wyche. Bill had coached Wyche when he had been a Bengals backup quarterback in the late sixties. Then, Wyche had been Bill's quarterback coach on the 49ers and had coached Joe Montana when we beat the Bengals that first Super Bowl.

We had a lot of players who hadn't been on the 49ers when we'd last won a Super Bowl. But in the locker room before the game, I didn't detect any of those guys being any more nervous than the rest of us. Rice and Taylor certainly weren't that nervous because they went out and played great games. We weren't a team that needed pregame pep talks. In fact, the only pep talk I remember before the game was by Ronnie, I think, or someone else who said we should put everything into Super Bowl XXIII because it could be some of the guys' last game, and we had to make sure they went out the right way. But I don't think that Ronnie or anyone else knew that both Bill Walsh and our veteran center Randy Cross would retire after the game.

We weren't thinking about how a third Super Bowl win would make us the top team of the decade. That wasn't a concern. We just wanted to go out and beat the Bengals, that was all. When we got out on the field, we were so energized. You're so hyped before any Super Bowl, waiting for it to begin, and you don't calm down until it does. There's always some music that really gets you going—in my first Super Bowl, it had been Kenny Loggins singing "This Is It," and there had been another familiar song at Stanford Stadium. So I'm sure there was some song that pumped us up before Super Bowl XXIII. But I don't remember much that happened prior to that Super Bowl other than being sent back inside to cut back my black high-tops. That season it was my thing to wear those high-tops all the way up the socks, but they wouldn't let me wear them like that in the Super Bowl. I remember that.

We received the opening kickoff. Only a couple of plays into the game, our offensive tackle Steve Wallace broke his leg. Not much later in the quarter, their nose tackle Tim Krumrie broke his leg. So there were two casualties right at the beginning. The thing about it was that the night before or that morning they'd left a vacuum system on, and it sucked all the water out of the field. There was bad footing because the field was pretty much tearing up. The bad field condition was a major concern early in the game, but when those guys went down, you had to put it into your mind that was just a normal thing that happened in the course of the football game. We didn't want to be wary about the field because it would slow us down.

The 49ers offense often scored on its first drive. That was a trademark. But when we didn't do it in this game, it wasn't disconcerting. Our offense was stopped by a good Bengals defense, so it wasn't something unusual. It was just up to our defense to stop the Bengals offense. Our defense prided itself on keeping the other team in check until the offense got going—that was a formula for winning.

On defense, we wanted to keep Boomer off balance and force him into doing things that were out of the Bengals' offensive scheme. That way we hoped to keep Ickey Woods from having a productive game on the ground. That was the year of the "Ickey Shuffle"—he was getting a lot of hype, and I know he did a Ford commercial with his mom—and our thing was to not let the Bengals get untracked where Ickey could do that dance on us. If he did his dance, that meant he was scoring touchdowns and having a good day. We were not going to let that happen. He picked up some yardage, but he never got into the end zone.

A lot of teams criticized the 49ers for not being a physical group. The offense always had the "finesse" label. But the defense wasn't like that. We were physical when we needed to be. We were physical against the Bengals. We had high-caliber guys like Michael Carter, Charles Haley,

January 22, 1989, at Joe Robbie Stadium in Miami

Paid Attendance: 75,129

AFC Champion: Cincinnati Bengals (14–4)
Head Coach: Sam Wyche

NFC Champion: San Francisco 49ers (12–6)
Head Coach: Bill Walsh

STARTING LINEUPS

OFFENSE			DEFENSE		
Cincinnati		**San Francisco**	**Cincinnati**		**San Francisco**
Tim McGee	WR	John Taylor	Jim Skow	LE	Larry Roberts
Anthony Muñoz	LT	Steve Wallace	Tim Krumrie	NT	Michael Carter
Bruce Reimers	LG	Jesse Sapolu	Jason Buck	RE	Kevin Fagan
Bruce Kozerski	C	Randy Cross	Leon White	LOLB	Charles Haley
Max Montoya	RG	Guy McIntyre	Carl Zander	LILB	Jim Fahnhorst
Brian Blados	RT	Harris Barton	Joe Kelly	RILB	Michael Walter
Rodney Holman	TE	John Frank	Reggie Williams	ROLB	Keena Turner
Eddie Brown	WR	Jerry Rice	Lewis Billups	LCB	Tim McKyer
Boomer Esiason	QB	Joe Montana	Eric Thomas	RCB	Don Griffin
James Brooks	RB	Roger Craig	David Fulcher	SS	Jeff Fuller
Ickey Woods	RB	Tom Rathman	Solomon Wilcots	FS	Ronnie Lott

SUBSTITUTIONS

Cincinnati: K—Jim Breech. P—Lee Johnson. Offense: Receivers—Cris Collinsworth, Ira Hillary, Carl Parker, Jim Riggs. Linemen—David Douglas, Jim Rourke, Dave Smith. Backs—Stanford Jennings, Marc Logan, Turk Schonert. Defense: Linebackers—Leo Barker, Ed Brady, Emanuel King. Linemen—Eddie Edwards, David Grant, Skip McClendon. Backs—Barney Bussey, Rickey Dixon, Ray Horton, Daryl Smith. DNP—Mike Norseth.

San Francisco: K—Mike Cofer. P—Barry Helton. Offense: Receivers—Terry Greer, Ron Heller, Brent Jones, Mike Wilson. Linemen—Bruce Collie, Bubba Paris, Chuck Thomas. Backs—Del Rodgers, Harry Sydney. Defense: Linebackers—Riki Ellison, Sam Kennedy, Bill Romanowski. Linemen—Pierce Holt, Pete Kugler, Jeff Stover, Daniel Stubbs. Backs—Greg Cox, Tom Holmoe, Darryl Pollard, Eric Wright. DNP—Steve Young.

Cincinnati	0	3	10	3—16
San Francisco	3	0	3	14—20

SF	FG Cofer 41
Cin	FG Breech 34
Cin	FG Breech 43
SF	FG Cofer 32
Cin	Jennings 93 kickoff return (Breech kick)
SF	Rice 14 pass from Montana (Cofer kick)
Cin	FG Breech 40
SF	Taylor 10 pass from Montana (Cofer kick)
MVP:	Jerry Rice (San Francisco)

and Keena Turner. We called Michael Carter "Stump." He was the best nose tackle in the game then, another Randy White. He controlled the line of scrimmage. Haley was a young linebacker in those days, and he reminded me of Fred Dean. No matter how practices went, Chuck came to play on game days. We knew he'd be there rushing Boomer and getting a sack or two. Keena Turner was an undersized linebacker, who played the rush and covered tight ends. He wasn't one of those specialty kind of guys, who you'd take out on passing downs—he'd play on nickel, he'd help double wide receivers, he'd cover running backs one-on-one. Of course, we also had a very physical secondary, with McKyer and Don Griffin at the corners, and Ronnie Lott and Jeff Fuller at the safeties. Ronnie was a vicious tackler and everybody else tried to follow his lead. Fuller could really hit. He was a great athlete and a great player. He was the future of the 49ers defense, and it's too bad that his career would be shortened by injuries. But he was healthy in Super Bowl XXIII and had a big game covering receivers and stopping the run.

I'd come in on passing downs, usually replacing a linebacker, maybe Mike Walter. Haley, Turner, and Jim Fahnhorst would usually stay in. As I expected, I didn't play much, maybe about 20 snaps in the nickel package, helping Lott, Fuller, McKyer, and Griffin with the receivers.

The Bengals had a pretty good passing game to go with what was considered the best running game in the AFC. Esiason, who had been his league's MVP, had a talented group of receivers. We knew Tim McGee, Cris Collinsworth, and especially Eddie Brown could all run, so we couldn't let those guys go unmolested down the field—at all times we had to get a piece of them, as big a piece as possible. We would be very aggressive against them the whole game. I was the most familiar with Collinsworth because when I'd been the starting corner in Super Bowl XVI, I guarded him. He was a rookie then, and I saw that he ran great patterns and "could run for a white guy." He was fast, and if you mistakenly played too relaxed, he'd blow by you. That's what happened on the long pass-play that game. I respected him after that.

In those years when I had been an every-snap player, I got my rest when the defense was off the field. But in Super Bowl XXIII, when I didn't play that much, I watched the offense. I wasn't down because of my limited playing time and stood on the sidelines trying to get the offense going. On our second possession, it started to move some. In fact, we were backed up inside our 5-yard line, and Joe drove us all the way into field-goal range. Then Mike Cofer put us ahead, 3–0. Anytime you can get ahead it's important. That field goal was major because it would turn out to be a close game where every point mattered.

When the offense got the ball again, Joe continued to do ball control with passes to Rice and Craig and hand-offs to Craig and Tom Rathman. Roger Craig was such a big part of the offense. He was a back who could run with power and speed and was a very good receiver. In one year he had gained 1,000 yards both rushing and passing. In '88, I think he caught more passes than Rice. Rog was a powerful runner who believed in punishing guys. He had that high-knee action and would always hit into a defender. You'd better come and hit Rog before he got going, or you would take a blow. I'm glad I just had to practice against him.

The offense moved deep into Cincinnati territory again, but came up with nothing when Cofer missed a field-goal attempt. He'd made a kick from about 40 yards out before, but this time he missed one from half that distance. A chip shot. I don't know what happened on the second kick. But we still led, so we couldn't let it bother us.

Both defenses were playing well, so it was still 3–0 early in the second quarter when their punter booted the ball over 60 yards and John Taylor returned it 45 yards. I think they both set records. J. T. ran for a long time because he stretched the field, going from the left sideline all the way to the right sideline. It was a great run. Early in his career, J. T. did more punt returning than receiving and he was really good at it..

Soon after Taylor's long return, Roger Craig made a nice run but fumbled when David Fulcher gave him a great hit. Fulcher was their strong safety, and in the first half he seemed to be in the middle of every play. He sacked Joe; he made a few tackles; he knocked the ball loose from Roger. You respect those guys who have a nose for the football, and I think the offense would make some adjustments later in the game to stop him from being such a factor.

That turnover brought the defense back on the field. Only bad teams get deflated when an opportunity like that is lost. Great teams rebound. We were a great team at dealing with adversity.

We held Cincinnati scoreless until right before the end of the half, when Jim Breech kicked a field goal to make the score 3–3. As a defensive player you get paid to stop people, so we hated to see that happen. You feel you didn't hold up your end of the bargain with the offense. But then again, the offense hadn't scored much themselves and had given them the ball in our territory to begin that drive. So there are trade-offs. You'd love not to have given them three points, but at least you hadn't given up seven points.

At the break, we were confident we were going to win. We felt the game was starting from scratch and that we'd come out at the beginning of the second half and it would be a different football game. We figured we'd go out and take the game over.

The surprise was that it was Cincinnati who came out strong in the third quarter. After receiving the kickoff, they held the ball for over nine minutes. I remember that because I was in on the nickel plays. They were doing ball control just like the 49ers were known for doing it. Ickey Woods and James Brooks were picking up 3 or 4 or 5 yards at a pop and Esiason was completing some short passes. Our defense finally stopped them, but Breech kicked another fairly long field goal to put Cincinnati in front for the first time, 6–3. It wasn't a relief that we held them to only a field goal because we weren't happy that they scored at all. However, the field goal wasn't the death blow a touchdown might have been. Our trailing in the second half didn't worry us, but we all had to get on the same page quickly and start doing our jobs if we were going to win.

The offense didn't come back and score on its next possession but had to punt. Fortunately it got the ball back in one play when our backup outside linebacker Bill Romanowski intercepted Esiason inside the Bengals' 25-yard line. Romo made a big, big play. I wasn't on the field, but I saw it clearly because it was close to our sidelines. Boomer tried to drill a short pass over Romo—maybe he didn't even see him—and Romo put his hand up and tipped the ball, and then he pulled it in for the interception. I think he and Keena Turner were switching off a lot that game, so he happened to be in on first down. I felt it was finally our turn for something good to happen, for the offense to have a chance to do something. We didn't score a touchdown, but at least Cofer kicked another field goal to tie the game, 6–6.

Again we felt the game was going to be ours. On the sidelines, we're thinking that all we have to do is take it. Then suddenly we're watching Stanford Jennings receive the kickoff inside their 10 and break free up the middle, going all the way for a touchdown. That was a real shocker, especially coming so soon after we had tied the game. We always prided ourselves on good special teams, but he'd run all the way without being touched. We were now behind by a touchdown, 13–6, although the defense hadn't give up a touchdown all game.

We may have been concerned, but we weren't worried yet because our offense had been moving the ball against the Bengals, and we still had Joe Montana going out there on the field. We knew that if our defense could keep the score close, which it had done, there was no question—*no question*—that Joe would pull it out.

Now that we had fallen behind, Joe came out and immediately hit Jerry and Roger with long passes—30 yards, 40 yards—and we were inside their 20. Joe got hot. Then he threw a pass across the middle toward their goal line—to either Jerry or J. T.—that went right into the arms of their cornerback Lewis Billups! But he dropped it! He dropped it! We were watching from the sidelines, and everyone was relieved. I know we all felt that we dodged a bullet, that the game could have been turned around by an interception. That gave our offense another chance, and it came back on the next play to score. Joe hit Jerry over on the left sidelines, and he stretched the ball over the end-zone marker as he was falling out of bounds. That tied the game for the third time, 13–13, early in the final quarter.

The next time we got the ball, Cofer missed a go-ahead field goal from about the 50. That would have been a big kick, but it was from a long way out and wasn't a sure thing by any means. It would have been great to have put the Bengals in the hole because with the score tied, they were able to move slowly downfield once more. Again we stopped them, but Breech booted a 40-yard field goal to put them up again, 16–13. That was Breech's third field goal—he was the major guy in their offense that game because he scored all their points.

I'm looking at the clock and seeing about three and a half minutes left and thinking, "Oh, damn, here we go." You do have doubts, you do think you might lose this one. But then you remember that Joe Montana is in there and he's the best there is at bringing teams from behind in the fourth quarter.

As it turned out, Joe was faced with having to take us 92 yards because we were penalized for an illegal block on the kickoff and had to start out on our 8. And Joe did it. He hit about five passes in a row, several to Rice. We were standing on the sidelines cheering, and there was a lot of praying going on. Some guys were thinking tying field goal to send the game into overtime; other guys were thinking winning touchdown. I was thinking win, and I didn't care how we did it.

The biggest play of our drive was a long pass to Jerry Rice on a second-and-20. He almost broke it for a touchdown but was dragged down. That put us inside their 20, and you know they were getting worried. They knew what Joe could do because he'd done it to them in a comeback win in 1987. Sam Wyche knew what he could do. We were already in field-goal range, but now Montana hit Craig at their 10-yard line. We called time-out with less than 40 seconds left. Now everybody is thinking touchdown.

Everybody knew the next play was going to be a pass into the end zone. I expected Jerry to get the ball because he had been catching passes all game, including that drive. John Taylor hadn't caught one pass yet, but he was someone who could get open and catch the ball. The Bengals expected the pass to go to Jerry and rolled their coverage over to Jerry's side. That meant there had to be something going on with the offside receiver, Taylor. J. T. just shot right into the middle and was open for just a moment. I don't know if J. T. was the primary receiver, but nobody was better than Joe at finding the open guy, and Joe quickly hit him as he ran toward the back of the end zone. The best guys will make the big plays. Joe made the big plays. I'd say J. T. made the big plays, too. Hey, J. T. had a good game with the punt return and that winning touchdown.

Taylor wouldn't get the MVP award. As usual, J. T. was overshadowed. Jerry Rice would win for catching so many passes and gaining over 200 yards. Jerry had a great game, but you have to remember that he was on the receiving end of some great passes from Joe Montana. People forget that Joe threw for over 350 yards to several receivers, completed two touchdown passes, and engineered that amazing winning drive. I think Rice and Montana should have been dual MVPs.

When Taylor caught that ball and we went ahead with only 34 seconds left, there was pandemonium on our sidelines. Everybody was jumping all over each other. We couldn't believe it! We didn't care that they had kept it close and had almost beaten us. When you get in that game and it's the last game for everything, you don't care how close it is. You don't care—20–16 was okay with us. You just want to win.

In the final seconds that the Bengals had the ball, I was one of our guys in a deep zone, playing some prevent defense. It wasn't hard to concentrate after our touchdown. The thing you really didn't want was to be the culprit, to be the guy who gives up the big play and puts them in scoring position with so little time left on the clock. When Boomer's last pass went way downfield to my side of the field, toward Cris Collinsworth, I didn't want to be that guy. I'd had interceptions in my first two Super Bowls and wanted to keep my streak alive. I got there and broke up the final pass. It was exciting because I had the opportunity to make a play on the final play of the Super Bowl.

We had won the game! Now there was pandemonium in the locker room also. That was natural. We were feeling what we wanted to feel. We felt fortunate; we felt blessed. The players gathered around and Ronnie Lott said the victory meant so much because we had struggled so much during the year. This team wasn't as good as the one that won Super Bowl XIX, but because of all we'd been through, he said it was our sweetest victory. Super Bowl XVI will always be special to me because it was the first time we went there and the first time we won. But this Super Bowl was sweet because when you go through a lot of adversity through the course of a 16-game season and three postseason games, and you win a Super Bowl, it makes it even more meaningful. It also became more meaningful when Bill Walsh and Cross-Man retired. It was a real surprise to me when Bill stepped down. I'm glad he could do it with a victory.

The rest of us would come back to win Super Bowl XXIV. Ronnie Lott, Joe Montana, Keena Turner, and myself would get our fourth rings. It's a great memory just to have played in four Super Bowls. But the best part is that we won them all.

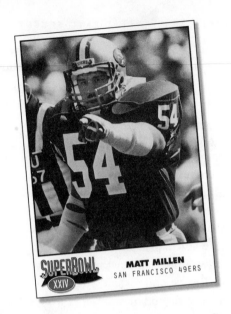

MATT MILLEN
SAN FRANCISCO 49ERS

SUPER BOWL XXIV

SAN FRANCISCO 49ERS 55
DENVER BRONCOS 10

MATT MILLEN

I had one of my best years in 1988 and made the Pro Bowl. Then after off-season knee surgery I reported to the L.A. Raiders training camp in '89, expecting to begin my tenth year with the team. But the Raiders had made some coaching changes and there was a new defensive coordinator, and after three days I called my wife and said, "I'm not going to be here this year." I knew I didn't figure in their plans. I knew the signs. Eventually, they told me they were going to try to trade me and there was talk with Miami, Washington, and a couple of other teams. Maybe those teams were concerned about my knee, but I couldn't show it was okay, because I played only about a quarter in the entire preseason. Then a couple of our people, including the guy they wanted to take my place at inside linebacker, got hurt and they had to play me in the last preseason game. I did well, so I assumed they had to keep me, right? But the next day they call me to say they were going to release me. So they just flat released me. It turned out to be the best thing that could have happened.

I went home to Pennsylvania because it was my son's birthday, and I had all these phone calls from teams that were interested in me. As fate would have it, that last preseason game showed people that my knee was fine and I was the same player. I returned to L.A. because the Rams wanted to sign me, and then I flew up to San Francisco to talk to the 49ers. I went up there because Bob Zeman, who was the linebackers coach and had been the Raiders' defensive coordinator just two years before, had called me on the phone and said, "Matt, I know how you play. You'll fit in great up here." The 49ers' biggest concern was my "madman" image down in L.A., but Bob sold them on the fact that I was nothing like that off the field and would be very easy to work with. So I worked out with them, and all they asked was, "Why were they saying your knee is bad?" I said, "I don't know. Check it for yourself." Well, they did, and saw nothing wrong with it, and they offered me a contract. They really didn't have a position for me to play because they had two healthy starters, but something just told me to sign there. Friday I signed and Sunday I played.

Bill Walsh had retired after the 49ers won their third Super Bowl, and George Seifert, who had been the defensive coordinator, was now in his first year as the head coach. As soon as I got there I realized the team was on a mission. Guys were loyal to Walsh, but wanted to prove, maybe just to themselves, that they had a bigger role in the success of the 49ers than they had been credited with. Joe Montana never talked about it, Jerry Rice never talked about it, but other guys were open about it, particularly on defense. Guys like Ronnie Lott, Charles Haley, Pierce Holt, Kevin Fagan, Michael Carter, Eric Wright, Keena Turner, and Michael Walter had been around and were very aware of what had been going on. It was a very prevalent opinion that, "Hey, we'll win it this year because of *us*."

George Seifert stayed with the defense for the majority of the time and Mike Holmgren coached the offense. George had a quiet manner, and the first thing I noticed about him is that he let his players play. Rather than interfering, he just let us go. Of course, Seifert had Joe Montana as his quarterback, so he didn't want to mess with that, as Walsh had when he played Steve Young a lot in the previous season. George just left it alone. I'd say that maintaining the status quo was a big part of his approach. He didn't rock the boat.

That team had been together for so long that roles were already defined. The guy who stood tallest in the locker room was Ronnie Lott, the 49ers' perennial All-Pro free safety. He was inherently a leader, plus he was reared in the 49ers system with those coaches and defensive players. That was his group. Ronnie would be disappointed—in fact, it drove him crazy—when other defensive guys wouldn't play like he wanted them to play. He stuck to the defense, but I would say that Ronnie was the heart and soul of the entire 49ers team.

Joe Montana was a leader on the field, not so much in the locker room. "Joe Cool" was the perfect nickname for him because he was very cool, very calm. He wouldn't be verbally demonstrative or march up and down the sideline giving guys pep talks. Never. You didn't look to him for that, either. You only looked at him to see how "on" he was. Joe was the leader in the competition. When it came time to compete, you just had to watch Joe and follow his lead. Joe Montana just exuded winning. It wasn't limited to football. Rarely have I been around guys like Joe who compete over anything, whether it's the game itself or a practice scrimmage, quarterback versus quarterback. Even prior to practice you might find him taking part in this stupid game where he and maybe Steve Bono would spend hours trying to throw tape that was still on its spool into a hole on the pipe at the top of the goal posts. After practice, Joe might be part of the competition where guys threw their dirty clothes into the laundry basket—how far away can you toss it from? He wanted to win in everything.

Jerry Rice was the other guy who motivated you without saying anything. Jerry seemed almost inhuman to me. When I first started watching him as a teammate, I thought this guy was a freak of nature. No one could work like that and not be tired. No one could push himself like that. I thought it would come to an end, but it never did. It went the whole year and into the playoffs and his body just kept getting more defined and he was in better and better shape. (In subsequent years he would maintain that pattern.) He was fanatical about taking care of himself. He'd do his stretching, his running, his work on machines; he'd watch what he ate. Jerry did his film work with the team and then by himself. At practice, he'd run before anyone got out there, and then he worked at his trade. When the defense was on the field, he'd be over there catching balls constantly, working on sideline patterns, working on his other routes, working on how he's going to work a guy that week. Before practice even started and while it was going on, he worked on his concentration, using two hands and catching hundreds of balls. While the offense was on the field, he would take every ball that was thrown to him into the end zone, and then he'd run back. When he caught the next ball, he'd run to the end zone again. He always gave a great effort and it shamed—or inspired— other players into working. He had great impact on young players because he was the greatest receiver ever, yet was outworking everybody on the field—they had no excuse not to work.

I never talked to Jerry about his philosophy while we were playing together. But when he was breaking the records in 1995, I sat down with him. He had a great deal of pride and I think that came from his dad, who was a mason. I know he respected his dad's work ethic. He watched his dad work day after day, year after year—and he tells the story about how his dad would throw bricks to him and he'd have to catch them. He learned to concentrate, because if he didn't, he was going to get hit in the face.

Jerry was a model for all the receivers in the league, but John Taylor, the 49ers' other great wideout, was his own guy. I loved John because he was going to do what he was going to do regardless of anybody. He didn't run 5-yard routes, but if he wanted to, he would have. He wasn't going to be swayed.

Roger Craig, our star running back, was like Jerry Rice in that he worked constantly. I had played against Roger and saw how well he ran and how many balls he caught. Now I was practicing with him and was surprised to discover that Roger did not have great hands, but he worked to the point that he made himself into a good receiver with reliable hands. He and our other back, Tom Rathman, complemented each other so well. They were both good blockers, though Rathman had the better reputation, and both were major parts in the passing game. You just had to appreciate how hard they worked and how good they wanted to be. It never was about being a star and all the stuff that goes with that. It was about working. Rathman and Craig epitomized that focus and priority that was such a part of the 49ers' success as a team.

Coming in from the outside, I thought my role was to just stay quiet and gain the respect of the other players. I felt that you have no place to stand on a team unless you first prove yourself. Respect isn't given just because of age or years of service. You have to prove that you still have it and can play. I was getting into only a few plays each game, so all I could prove was that I would practice every day and practice hard every day. But I couldn't be really physical because, traditionally, the 49ers didn't have physical practices. They take a different approach. It was difficult for me to show anything until the fourth game, when I became a starter. The

49ers didn't have any physical backers until I came along, and now all of a sudden some of the defensive leaders like Ronnie Lott, Charles Haley, and Michael Carter would be talking about you when we watched films and saying, "Whoa, watch what Matt did on this play." Then it was there. Then all that other stuff meant something. Until you show you can do it, it really doesn't mean anything.

The 49ers defense supposedly worked out of a 3-4, but it was really a 4-3 with me in the middle. I was calling the defensive signals from the beginning. It wasn't difficult because adjustments were something that came natural to me, and for some reason guys would listen to me. The guys were so accepting of me and also relying on me to do my job—all of a sudden, they're saying, "Matt will take care of it." Now I was in a familiar role again and that made it a lot easier for me. But I also knew going in that there was a defined leader of the defense in Ronnie Lott, so it would have been wrong for me to try to take that leadership role. My role was to fit in with Ronnie, and that was easy because he was so competitive. I'd known Ronnie for years.

The Niners defense didn't situation substitute too much, so I played a lot. We didn't do much blitzing, but I'd play a lot in coverage. We played a lot of match-up zones, which really fit me perfectly. It wasn't a traditional zone where you dropped back to a position and had to rely on your peripheral vision to pick up things. This zone—it really was a "man" concept within the zone—was very rule oriented: if this, then this; if that, then this, then this. It was very logical, which was perfect for me. Just give me what you want me to do and I'll do it.

I could sense the improvement of the defense as the year went along. A few things happened. Chet Brooks, a tough player from Texas A&M, manned the strong safety position because Jeff Fuller had lost the use of his right arm against New England. Fuller was a bigger guy, but Chet played the position very physically and with an attitude. Also, I think Don Griffin, our right corner, really started to play well. That was important because Eric Wright, a real smart corner, was nursing a groin injury for much of the season. And this was the year Pierce Holt emerged as a really fine defensive end. These guys began to play at a higher level, up there with the veterans. There was still nobody better or tougher than Ronnie Lott at free safety, and Charles Haley was having his usual great year at outside linebacker. And when I showed up, they finally had somebody who could be physical inside. What that did was take pressure off our ends, Holt and Kevin Fagan, and our nose, Michael Carter. It was the downside of Carter's career and he had gotten heavy. He also had a foot problem that made it hard for him to redirect and he had started to guess which gap to play. So when I was in there, it freed Michael from always having to be a two-gap player, where he was responsible for taking the gap to his immediate left and the gap to his immediate right. Because I could come in and be physical at 265 pounds, I could do part of his job and he could take only one gap. So that really brought a lot of things together up front. And we just started to come on. We finished the regular season with a shutout of the Bears and we continued to play great in the playoffs.

With the defense getting better with every game and Montana directing the best offense ever to grace the field in the National Football League, we were pretty hard to beat. In fact, we knew that we couldn't be beaten and would win the Super Bowl as early as the first quarter of our first playoff game against Minnesota. The only thing that was talked about prior to facing Minnesota was the game in '87 when the 49ers thought they had the best team in football only to be humiliated by the Vikings. So all everyone talked about was how we couldn't let that happen again. And we didn't. We won in a runaway 41–13. Then in the NFC Championship Game we reversed one of our two losses of the regular season by crushing the Los Angeles Rams, 30–3. It was evident in both games that we were playing with far more intensity. The 49ers players understood that it was time to step up their game in the playoffs. That mindset we had was coupled with our tremendous competitiveness. Nobody had to say, "Hey, this is our season," or any of those trite things wanting-to-win teams say. Teams that have what it takes to win don't say a word about it; they just go out and do it.

I was going to the Super Bowl for the third time, but my first time out of a Raiders uniform. Ironically, Super Bowl XXIV against the Denver Broncos was going to be played in New Orleans, where the Raiders had won Super Bowl XV in my rookie year. It was somewhat strange returning to a Super Bowl in this city, but it didn't feel odd coming in with a different team because I really felt a part of the 49ers by this time. The Super Bowl had changed a ton since the Raiders had won there. It had turned into a real spectacle and had gotten so big that it was like night and day. In 1981, when I sat there in New Orleans, our press day was almost presented as optional. There were things that went on, but it wasn't that big a deal. The media had made a huge deal about John Matuszak going out one night and having a wild time and about guys getting fined, but nothing was really different from what we had done during the regular season. But by the time of Super Bowl XXIV, what the Raiders supposedly had done was legendary in New Orleans. It was said that, "When the Raiders were here, they ruled this town. They did this and they did that." And I'm sitting there thinking, "Wait a second. I was on that team. It wasn't anything like that." Not only had the stories grown, now the game itself had grown. The media had grown. Everything was just bigger and was more intense. I could feel that right away. I hadn't been to the Super Bowl since January of 1984, but it was something the 49ers were comfortable with because they had just been to the Super Bowl the year before. They were very used to this setting.

We had started preparing for the Broncos back in San Francisco. We watched the championship games and they started putting in the game plan almost two weeks prior to Super Sunday. Then we'd go over the specifics with Ray Rhodes, who was the defensive backs coach. We'd go over it man by man, formation by formation, coverage by coverage. Then there'd be a lot of player input, mostly from Ronnie and occasionally from the guys up front. Charles Haley was a great student of the game. After that our input was minimal.

I'd always hear about how a team was really good and how they could do this, this, and this. Then we got the tapes of the Broncos, who supposedly could do all that, and after we watched them, we said, "Well, they can't run the football well and they don't run good pass routes . . . but, well, they've got John Elway." That's all you said. And you say, "Hold on. They've got only one guy? He's got to do it all by himself? Offense and defense?" That was a pretty fair assessment. As I've said on air as a broadcaster, they should have been called the Denver Elways because he was everything to them. They had Karl Mecklenburg at one linebacker and they had all these other guys, but Elway stood head and shoulders above everybody. It's not like we were trying to say anything negative or positive about the Broncos we watched on film; we were just trying to be realistic. We looked at their team and broke it down and came up with this conclusion: "If we play our best game, we're going to kill them. If we play a bad game, we've still got a chance."

We decided that the main thing we had to do was to keep John Elway from making big plays. We didn't feel they could methodically work the ball down the field and score by running the football. They were only going to score by throwing the football. My role was to get them into sure passing situations, where we could set up the coverage to stop Elway.

I developed a habit during the season of asking Joe Montana how many points we would get in the next game. And he usually would say 21 points, or 24, or something similar. Prior to the Super Bowl, I asked, "Joe, how many points are were going to get against Denver?" His passing in practice had just been unconscious, and I'll never forget that he answered, "100, if they'll let me." I said, "How can you say that?" He said, "If they play their safeties the way they've been playing them, we'll eat 'em alive." Well, he was right. Who knows how many points he could have scored if he kept passing after the third quarter and didn't leave the game early.

The night before the game we moved to a different hotel. That wasn't something that happened when I had been to my last Super Bowl in New Orleans. On that night, we had our meetings and did whatever we had done the whole season long. You don't break your routine and that was something the 49ers understood. Everybody did what they always did to get ready and went to bed—I never lost a second's sleep before a game— and then got up in the morning, took part in the pregame meal, and came to the Superdome.

Guys don't really watch the festivities before a Super Bowl or pay attention to the big halftime show. You're so focused that you don't care what's going on. Prior to the game, we had a relatively quiet locker room. There were no pep talks. Nothing needed to be said. What little conversation there was about the game was mental gymnastics, players straightening things out to make sure they didn't make mistakes. There was never anything specific like, "What do you think about what Elway does on third down?" Or, "What routes will Vance Johnson and Mark Jackson run?" Or, "Do you think Bobby Humphrey will be able to run inside against us?" Or, "How will they handle Charles Haley?" It was always, "We know what we're going to do; let's go do it." Before my earlier Super Bowls, the Raiders had been underdogs and we had chips on our shoulders. But the 49ers were big favorites and we were loose. We were confident we were going to win.

We started that game in our basic defense and Elway came out throwing and he was off. In fact, on the first play that they ran from scrimmage he had Jackson wide open and he threw it right in the dirt. Then he overthrew Jackson on the next play. It wasn't a good sign. As the Bronco fans, the Bronco opponents, and maybe the Bronco players themselves knew, Denver had a chance if Elway was on. But we would never let him get started.

The 49ers offense always had its first series mapped out. The defense never knew what that series was. We'd just go and watch to see how "on" they were. If they moved the ball early and went down the field, even if they didn't score, we knew we were fine. If the offense came out and got stoned, then we knew it was going to be tough. So we go into this Super Bowl expecting our offense to not only move the football but to play a particular way. I'm on the sidelines and the first thing that I do is look at the Denver defense. And I'm going, "They're lining up just the way we thought they would." They were playing with that college look, with the wide safeties in a two-deep look, and leaving the middle of the field wide open. Now I remember what Joe told me—if they play it that way, we'll kill 'em.

And all of a sudden, Montana moves the offense right down the field and hits Rice over the middle and it's 7–0. It was like stealing. That was one of the plays where you saw how great Rice was. Steve Atwater came right at him from the blindside to try to jolt the ball loose with a heavy hit, but Rice was a strong guy and Atwater just bounced off. Rice just brushed him away and went into the end zone. Jerry was just amazing.

In their defense, there were guys who were good individually and made a great effort, but they matched up poorly against our offense. They were really going to have to play way above their heads from an individual stand-point to be able to compete against the athletes on the 49ers. Also, philo-sophically, it was going to have to be a different defensive game plan. They couldn't play that type of zone against the 49ers. Although, quite frankly, they didn't have the capabilities to match up man-to-man against Jerry Rice, John Taylor, and our other receivers.

With Denver behind 7–0, Elway had his biggest passing play, a shovel pass to Bobby Humphrey that got them 27 yards down the left sideline. That play wasn't such a surprise because we knew they had it; it was more of a disappointment that it happened to us because it was something we had practiced against. They scored on a field goal by David Treadwell to cut our lead to 7–3. We're thinking we're okay. You know in the game something will happen to you; it always does. That's one of the things the 49ers always talked about. The Raiders' philosophy was to not let any-thing happen to you—if you get into a fight, don't get hit. The 49ers took it for granted that the other team was going to make some plays against us, and that all we had to do was regroup and we'd be okay.

On the first play of the Broncos' next possession, Humphrey was stripped of the ball by Kevin Fagan and Brooks recovered on their 49. They didn't have great running backs and we felt we could take that part of their game away from them. Montana then drove the offense down the field, with the big play being a pass to Rice over the middle again.

We scored on a short pass to Brent Jones, a tight end who had really come into his own that year. In the highlight film, you can see Montana on the sidelines listening to Jones explain how he could make a particular play. (I'm not sure if that turned out to be the touchdown pass.) Joe was

January 28, 1990, at the Louisiana Superdome in New Orleans

Paid Attendance: 72,919

NFC Champion: San Francisco 49ers (16–2)
Head Coach: George Seifert

AFC Champion: Denver Broncos (13–5)
Head Coach: Dan Reeves

STARTING LINEUPS

OFFENSE			DEFENSE		
San Francisco		**Denver**	**San Francisco**		**Denver**
John Taylor	WR	Vance Johnson	Pierce Holt	LE	Alphonso Carreker
Bubba Paris	LT	Gerald Perry	Michael Carter	NT	Greg Kragen
Guy McIntyre	LG	Jim Juriga	Kevin Fagan	RE	Ron Holmes
Jesse Sapolu	C	Keith Kartz	Charles Haley	LOLB	Michael Brooks
Bruce Collie	RG	Doug Widell	Matt Millen	LILB	Rick Dennison
Harris Barton	RT	Ken Lanier	Michael Walter	RILB	Karl Mecklenburg
Brent Jones	TE	Orson Mobley	Keena Turner	ROLB	Simon Fletcher
Jerry Rice	WR	Mark Jackson	Darryl Pollard	LCB	Tyrone Braxton
Joe Montana	QB	John Elway	Don Griffin	RCB	Wymon Henderson
Roger Craig	RB	Steve Sewell	Chet Brooks	SS	Dennis Smith
Tom Rathman	RB	Bobby Humphrey	Ronnie Lott	FS	Steve Atwater

SUBSTITUTIONS

San Francisco: K—Mike Cofer. P—Barry Helton. Offense: Receivers—Mike Sherrard, Wesley Walls, Jamie Williams, Mike Wilson. Linemen—Terry Tausch, Chuck Thomas, Steve Wallace. Backs—Terrance Flagler, Harry Sydney, Spencer Tillman, Steve Young (QB). Defense: Linebackers—Keith DeLong, Steve Hendrickson, Bill Romanowski. Linemen—Jim Burt, Pete Kugler, Larry Roberts, Daniel Stubbs. Backs—Johnny Jackson, Tim McKyer, Eric Wright.

Denver: K—David Treadwell. P—Mike Horan. Offense: Receivers—Paul Green, Clarence Kay, Rickey Nattiel, Michael Young. Linemen—Keith Bishop, Monte Smith. Backs—Ken Bell, Melvin Bratton, Gary Kubiak (QB), Sammy Winder. Defense: Linebackers—Scott Curtis, Bruce Klostermann, Tim Lucas, Marc Munford. Linemen—Brad Henke, Warren Powers, Andre Townsend. Backs—Darren Carrington, Kip Corrington, Mark Haynes, Randy Robbins.

San Francisco	13	14	14	14—55
Denver	3	0	7	0—10

SF	Rice 20 pass from Montana (Cofer kick)
Den	FG Treadwell 42
SF	Jones 7 pass from Montana (kick failed)
SF	Rathman 1 run (Cofer kick)
SF	Rice 38 pass from Montana (Cofer kick)
SF	Rice 28 pass from Montana (Cofer kick)
SF	Taylor 35 pass from Montana (Cofer kick)
Den	Elway 3 run (Treadwell kick)
SF	Rathman 3 run (Cofer kick)
SF	Craig 1 run (Cofer kick)
MVP:	Joe Montana (San Francisco)

one of those guys who listened to his players and also saw what they were talking about when he was on the field. It wasn't like you'd say, "Joe, I can beat this guy," and he'd brush it off with a "Yeah, right, okay," and forget about it. Joe listened to what was suggested and then saw things. Then he could tell if it would work. One of his great strengths was that he could see everything. Nothing got by him.

Tom Rathman had a really good first half. He kept that drive going with a big fourth-down run in Denver territory. On the next drive, Joe rolled out and threw the ball to his right and Tom made a one-handed grab. He really was an excellent receiver. In that drive, you really could see how well Tom and Roger worked together, because Joe went exclusively to them on the ground and through the air, and they took us all the way down to the goal. It was a beautifully executed drive, which Tom finished with a short touchdown run.

Right before the end of the first half, Montana connected with Rice again for a touchdown on a post route. I remember he got so free because one of their backs followed Taylor on a slant. I had watched how brilliantly Rice and Taylor ran patterns together because I'd played defense against them the year before when I'd been on the Raiders. But Taylor's role in the passing game hadn't been as big then, and you were aware of him mostly because of the great things he was doing on special teams. He was just starting to come on. By this year, that kid was really great. He was so strong and powerful. He went out there and never said two words, but he complemented Jerry so well because of his style and because he was so capable. Jerry and John could run the same routes, which really made it tough for any defense. They were still doubling Jerry on every play, so Mike Holmgren started to move Jerry around. He'd put him in motion and put him in different positions on and behind the line. Mike also freed Taylor from double teams like that.

At halftime the score was 27–3 and it seemed like it was worse than that. We had to guard against getting excited, although we knew we were the world champs. We knew we had won the football game. You couldn't spend the break going over adjustments because there was nothing that needed to be done. We just wanted to go out and kick them while they were down. Denver wasn't going to be able to stop our offense or defense. We had some holes, but Denver couldn't have found them.

Denver was just beat. They had been heavy underdogs and some people predicted we were going to kill them. They had the bad experience of losing all three Super Bowls they had played in. I could relate it to when I was with the Raiders and, for some reason we could never figure out, we'd lose in Seattle Monday night every year. We'd go to Seattle and practice extra hard, we knew we had a better team, and knew there was no way to be beaten, and then we're being beaten and we'd fight it and fight it until it hits you that, "We're going to get beat again." At halftime of the Super Bowl, Denver knew it was going to happen again. You play for pride and all those things, but frustration and defeat was just written on their faces. I didn't feel sorry for them, only for Elway.

In the third quarter, we intercepted Elway on Denver's first two possessions. In both cases, Montana quickly threw touchdowns, the first to Rice and the second to Taylor. Of course, both were on passes down the middle. The funny thing: Years later I finally got the chance to sit down and talk to John Elway. We talked about that Super Bowl and he said, "You know, Matt, I've got to tell you what scared me going into that game. All week long I was running the 49ers offense with the scout team against our defense. I must have thrown seven or eight touchdown passes against them. Gary Kubiak and I would look at each other and say, 'I hope we're not playing the 49ers with that defense!'" He said, "All week long our coaches were saying, 'They don't throw the ball down the middle! They don't do it!'" John just started laughing and told me, "How could we be so dumb?"

Probably the most demonstrative we ever saw Joe Montana was after he threw those scoring passes. He would throw both arms up to signal each touchdown. He had good reason to be excited. That touchdown to Taylor was his fifth touchdown pass of the game and gave him a new Super Bowl record. And the third quarter wasn't even over. The whole team took pride in that record, absolutely. For me it was extra special. Although it was just my first year on the 49ers, I had known Joe for a long, long time. I could flash back to just a year earlier after the Raiders had beaten the 49ers 9–3 in Candlestick Park, before they had a hot streak that took them to the Super Bowl. Joe and I had a conversation after that game about whether or not he was going to be traded to the Raiders. Remember that in 1988 they had benched him and put Steve Young in and they were saying Montana's back was no good, that he was too old, that it was time for him to move on, that maybe they'll trade him. There were rumors about him coming to the Raiders, and I said, "Heck, if you come down to play in Los Angeles, it will be great." We had this talk and that was the end of it. Of course, the 49ers get hot with Montana at quarterback and win their division and go on to win the Super Bowl against the

Bengals, and then the next year he wins the MVP and they're talking about him being the greatest player of all time. Montana was the Player of the Year, the Sportsman of the Year, the Super Bowl MVP for the third time, you name it. So people forgot about 1988. But I didn't, and when he set that record it just kind of meant a little bit more to me.

You couldn't be more down than the Broncos were. Still Elway did manage to put together a scoring drive. He was helped by an interference call in the end zone that wiped out an interception by Bill Romanowski. They got the ball on the 1 and we stopped Bobby Humphrey on a couple of attempts to get into the end zone. We dug in and I was in on those tackles. Finally, on third down, Elway ran it in himself on a quarterback draw. That was a typical Dan Reeves call, and I remember saying in the huddle, "They're going to spread us out and try a quarterback draw. Hold the outside, I'll hold inside." And they ran it—John started to his left and broke back out to his right—and I slipped on that Superdome turf. We didn't want them to score—it was just a sense of pride. We weren't worried about them coming back with the score 41–10.

Following Elway's touchdown we had another long drive, with Montana mixing passes with running plays. When we got down close, he didn't try to get his sixth touchdown pass but gave the ball to Rathman for his second rushing touchdown. That ended the third quarter. It was weird because the party on the sidelines had already begun. Even though there was no way they could win, you would look up at the scoreboard and see there's time remaining and you're still in a football game. So while some of our guys were high-fiving and congratulating each other, we still had to go out on the field and play.

I was still in there early in the fourth quarter, but we were using more of the nickel. At that point, they had no other choice but to pass. That's when guys like Haley, Holt, and Fagan were most effective. The Broncos couldn't handle those guys up front and they were getting a strong rush on Elway on every play. And early in the final quarter, we knocked down Elway and recovered his fumble at the 1-yard line.

I looked down at him and he had this look of pain on his face. I picked him up and I said something simple to him like, "Hang in there, John." Basically what I was trying to tell him was to keep his head up. I didn't know what to say to the guy. All those years I played against Elway when I was with the Raiders, he always had a smile on his face. Always. And it used to bug me. But you know, I always misread that smile. I took it as a little bit of arrogance—and there has to be a certain degree of that—but what he does with that smile is hide a lot of things behind it. I watched him in this game and came to understand that what he really was was ultracompetitive, as much as Montana. That game we were just killing them and they had no chance, but he was still trying to do anything he could to make something happen.

It happened only a few times in all the years that I played where my eyes met an opponent's eyes and you "know." For instance, I'd look at offensive guards coming to the line of scrimmage and they'd look back and I knew they knew they could do nothing to stop me. In this particular instance, I looked at John as I helped him up and he looked at me and we just kind of connected. It was the strangest thing, but I knew I understood him then. At that great moment it struck me that what he was really about was winning and I gained a huge measure of respect for him. I've been a John Elway fan ever since.

The 49ers had a killer instinct to score immediately after turnovers and, true to form, we scored again on the play after that fumble recovery on a short run by Roger Craig. So all our major weapons on offense that year—Rice, Taylor, Jones, Rathman, and Craig—got touchdowns in this Super Bowl. They were spreading the glory around. Despite the lopsided score, I was still watching from the sidelines. Now I go from being a competitor to being a fan. And it's fun and I get to enjoy it. Those moments are so rare, especially in big games like that.

I remember hugging George Seifert and thanking him on the sidelines. I was thinking back to before I signed with the 49ers when Bob Zeman told me the organization was concerned that I wouldn't fit in because of the bad image of the Raiders and because I was perceived as a bad guy who was fighting all the time. So I just thanked George for taking a chance on me. What I said was simple, but it was heartfelt.

That was my final Super Bowl as a participant, but rather than dwelling on what I did that game, I look back at that game in terms of team. The 49ers were one really great team, and it still strikes me how many truly great players were on it: Montana, Rice, Lott, Haley, Craig, on and on. I'm so fortunate to have played with those guys. You don't forget something like that. That's what makes this football stuff fun.

OTTIS ANDERSON
NEW YORK GIANTS

SUPERBOWL
XXV

SUPER BOWL XXV

NEW YORK GIANTS 20
BUFFALO BILLS 19

OTTIS ANDERSON

The two highlights of my career were my rookie year with the St. Louis Cardinals in 1979 and winning Super Bowl XXV with the New York Giants in 1991. I have to put them side by side. They were my two most memorable and rejoiceful times in professional football, and what makes them more special is that one came at the beginning and the other came near the end of my career.

The Cardinals selected me as the top pick in the whole NFL draft in 1979, which was quite an honor. But when I came in, nobody really expected anything from me. Especially not as a rookie. I looked at the stats of the backs who had been there before me and all those guys had credentials. I was from little Miami, which had its first winning season in about 10 years. Then it was really something to be an All-Pro, the

Offensive Player of the Year, the Most Valuable Player of the NFC. You can't compare that to the Super Bowl because it's completely different.

I thought I'd always play for the Cardinals, but in 1986, they hired Gene Stallings to be the head coach. When a new coach and staff comes in, 9 times out of 10, they like to rearrange things. Stallings thought I was a good player, but I saw that I wasn't going to be a part of his plan. I had an excellent camp, yet all of a sudden I was going to be splitting time with Stump Mitchell. Stump was a heck of a running back, and if anybody was going to take over the job it should have been him, but I was still healthy and productive, so I didn't see any need for a change. I did use the word *trade*, but I didn't think that would really happen.

It was a shock that the Giants were in the hunt for me. During preseason, I had heard Pittsburgh was interested in me but I had heard nothing about New York. We played the Giants in our fifth game, and afterward Jim Burt asked, "How would you like to be a Giant?" I told him that was impossible, though if I were traded I'd love to be a Giant. That was on a Sunday, and on Wednesday, I was a Giant.

I had just signed a contract extension with the Cardinals and the Giants picked up my contract. It was for the rest of the 1986 season and 1987, so the Giants thought they were going to be obligated for two years and that's what they zeroed in on. They figured that if they didn't win the Super Bowl in '86–'87, they weren't going to win it.

The Giants told me they needed more production from the fullback position, though they knew I was a halfback. It was a way to quickly get me on the field and change their one-dimension offense, which was basically Joe Morris left, Joe Morris right. They already had Maurice Carthon at fullback, but they considered Maurice a blocking back and got me to balance the running attack. So when we got into a split-back formation or I–formation, it would no longer meant that Morris was definitely going to get the ball. That's what I was told about my role, but my main thing was to come in and not be a disruptive force. The Giants were 4–1, and I had left a team that was 1–4, so things were looking up and I wanted to keep it that way. I did everything the coaches asked. I got only a few plays offensively, but I didn't complain, and utilized that year to recuperate and get healthy. I always showed signs of my ability in practice.

When I scored the Giants' final touchdown in Super Bowl XXI, I was excited but somewhat saddened, because I felt I was on a team that I didn't make a major contribution to. It wasn't like it would have been if I had stayed on the Cardinals and they developed into a championship team. On the Giants we had guys like Lawrence Taylor, Joe Morris, Harry Carson, and Phil Simms who had been there from the beginning and watched it materialize. I was just coming in on the tail end of a great thing. Then I realized: Hey, when the Giants gave me the ball so I could score that Super Bowl touchdown, it was a sign of appreciation for the seven years I spent in St. Louis, where I was an enemy and rushed for close to 10,000 yards. I accepted the touchdown as an honor.

In 1987 I still had a year left on my contract. In the preseason, I was pretty much used only for short yardage and goal line. Then the strike came about. When it was over the Giants had a losing record and didn't have much use for me. In fact, I was put on the inactive list, and for the last five or six games I went to the stadium but never dressed. I wasn't injured—they just didn't need me. That was somewhat frustrating. When you're put on that list, you realize they don't expect a whole lot out of you in the future. At that point I felt my career was down the drain.

The next year my contract was cut in half and I was getting what a guy just starting out in the league was making. I was somewhat disappointed, but it was still more money than I would have made on the street, so I swallowed my pride. Every year the Giants have an off-season workout program to make sure a lot of players stay in shape and grow together as a team. In 1988 I was told that I didn't have to come up to the workout program. However, I knew that if I didn't participate, that would really put a damper on my chances for returning. So I stayed up there on my own. I also went to minicamp. I kept busting my butt, so that if it came down to me playing, I'd be ready. I showed good intensity, and Ron Erhardt, the offensive coordinator, decided that I'd be good at short yardage and goal line, so in 1988 I started playing in those situations.

In 1989 there was me, Joe Morris, Lee Rouson, Tony Galbreath, George Adams, and rookies Lewis Tillman and Dave Meggett at the running-back position. I had an excellent camp, better than the other backs. I had maybe lost a step, but the determination and fire to be competitive and win was still there. My chances were very strong for making the team. Then Joe Morris broke his foot in the last preseason game. Parcells had to decide who to go with as his starter, me or Lewis Tillman. Lewis had come in from Jackson State with all the credentials of a great prospect, but Bill didn't like to start rookies. Our first game was to be on Monday night in the nation's capital, and he decided that he'd go with the back with experience, who had done it before and who had a good camp. He chose me. I went on to have a 1,000-yard season.

In 1990 the Giants decided not to re-sign Joe Morris after he came back from the foot injury. So I was kept on to be the featured runner. Erhardt liked to run me best out of the single-back position because he figured out that gave me better vision and I could do more. He'd line me up in the I-formation even though he didn't try to get me outside too much. He kept me in between the tackles. He kept me inside and ran Meggett and Tillman outside. We had a balance.

My relationship with Parcells had changed. In 1986 he was glad to have me. In 1987 I don't think he cared. In 1988 he really didn't care. In 1989 he realized I still could play, and in 1989 and 1990, I went from a guy on the bench to a starter, from a guy who had no clout to a guy who had privileges, from the outhouse to the penthouse. He now talked to me all the time.

Parcells' 1986 team had all the pieces in place. It was a team that expected to win sooner or later. That team had a name, had a purpose. This 1990 team had no true identity. However, the defense continued to be the pride of the Giants and was the reason we were so successful. It kept us in every game and often totally shut down opponents. When George Martin left, he left his mark on Carl Banks, Pepper Johnson, Everson Walls, Mark Collins. These guys had all the tools. They also hit hard, as Bill Belichick ordered them to do. From the Super Bowl XXI team, we still had some well-known players on defense—Taylor, Banks, Leonard Marshall, Pepper Johnson—but we didn't have any big-name players on offense. We didn't have any leaders. Joe was gone; Phil was out with a season-ending injury; Bavaro was hurting and very quiet.

When Simms went down, our season could have been over, but we had confidence in Jeff Hostetler. We knew Jeff deserved to be a starter in the league. Anytime he had come into a game, he moved the ball. He didn't surprise us with his success in the playoffs. When he took over, the backs knew we had new responsibilities. We knew with Phil we had a quarterback who would stay in the pocket until the cows came home. We knew Jeff Hostetler, who could run with the ball, would stay back there, but he ain't gonna wait on the cows. We knew this, so it was no big deal for us to make adjustments in our blocking and receiving schemes.

We had a boring offense. Everybody in the league knew we were boring. It was 2–3 yards and a cloud of dust. Even the receivers hated it. Mark Ingram, Stephen Baker—they complained all the time. They were blocking more than they were running pass routes. We had no deep threat. Defenses would line up eight, nine men on the line, and we'd say, "We know you know we're running, so stop us."

What helped our offense was that we didn't make any mistakes. As a team we made only 14 turnovers in 16 games, which was the fewest in the history of the NFL. It wasn't pride that kept us from fumbling; it was fear. Parcells said, "If you fumble, you're on the sidelines." Everybody knew he meant that because he made examples out of certain people. I wanted to be on the field, so I didn't fumble. I knew Lewis Tillman was on the sidelines licking his bits to get in there. Years before, my friend Willard Harrell, who had been a back with me at St. Louis, told me, "When you've got a young kid on that sideline who's hungry and trying to play, you keep him off the field, whatever it takes, because if you come out you'll be on the bench."

We couldn't tell how good we were until we beat the 49ers in the NFC Championship Game in San Francisco. They were the defending champions and were expected to go to the Super Bowl. I didn't like that game because we had no control over anything. The 49ers controlled the clock; they controlled the ball; they did everything they wanted. Late in the fourth quarter, they led, 13–12. I was standing on the sidelines with Mark Ingram and he was worrying because they were running the ball and eating the clock. He looked at me, almost in tears, and I told him, "Ingram, don't worry about it. It's definite, the Super Bowl is in Florida—so I will be there, and if I'll be there, you're going to be there." It just so happened that Roger Craig fumbled twice. The first time he was able to get it back. Later all they had to do was run out the clock, but they gave it to Craig, and he tried to run and fumbled, and L. T. picked it up. Then we went downfield and Matt Bahr kicked his fifth field goal of the game, from 42 yards out, and that was that. We were the NFC champions.

The next day we showed up at the Hilton in Tampa and the administrators didn't have rooms ready for us because they were expecting the 49ers. We told them San Francisco wouldn't be coming. The 49ers had hotel reservations, sent their equipment, made ticket arrangements, everything. That was great. The city had billboards with the 49ers versus the Bills, with Jerry Rice and Joe Montana's pictures plastered all over. They had everybody but the Giants. It would have been a great Super Bowl in terms of marketing to have the 49ers against the Bills. But the 49ers were not invited to the party.

We knew that in order to beat the Bills we had to keep their offense off the field. We knew that they could put points on the board. Nobody in the NFL could slow down their no-huddle offense. They get Jim Kelly, Thurman Thomas, and Andre Reed on the field and they're going to beat you—that was just as plain as the nose on your face. They proved that when they beat a good Raiders team, 51–3, in the AFC title game. When you looked at the two teams on paper, when you did the mathematics, we weren't supposed to win the game. We knew that to even be in this game toward the end, our only hope was to keep possession of the ball so they didn't have the chance to score.

Our philosophy on offense was to grind it out a couple of yards at a time, take every minute, go down to the last second before we snapped the ball, utilize the clock. However, during practice we didn't work with the clock in mind. We worked on a lot of plays we felt could catch them off guard. A lot of bootleg plays were designed to confuse their right end Bruce Smith and their left outside linebacker Cornelius Bennett, who were both All-Pros. Releasing the tight end, bouncing off the offense with two tight ends, utilizing Dave Meggett's speed, anything to confuse them. We just had all kinds of things. I've got to admit Parcells and Erhardt came up with a heck of a strategy.

Parcells gave us a 1 A.M. curfew on Monday and Tuesday and a midnight curfew on Wednesday. After that we stayed in. There weren't a whole lot of places to go, because when you came down the stairs the lobby was packed with fans who wanted autographs and pictures and you couldn't really walk through. Most of the players just stayed in their rooms and invited up friends and family members. There were things to do in Tampa, but we didn't want to ruin what we were trying to do as a football team.

Super Bowl XXV took place at the outbreak of the Persian Gulf War, so there were security concerns. For the first few days, however, we didn't notice anything. However, on Media Day, L. T. and some of the other guys went early to Tampa Stadium and the security people wouldn't let them in. They didn't care who they were. They made them wait until the rest of us got there on the team bus. Before members of the media could go inside, they took everybody's cameras and opened them up. They made sure nobody was coming in with anything other than what they said they had. That's when you realized how much security there was. Of course, security was extremely tight on the day of the game. They checked everybody who came in.

In the locker room before the game, there was a lot of laughing and talking. Everybody was hyped because we knew the whole world was watching the game, including our troops. Then we ran out onto the field. When they said they were introducing the offense, hey that was my cup of tea there, baby. I was the last person introduced on the Giants before the game. We just lined up that way—at other times it would be Maurice or Jeff. Everybody wanted to see me do my thing—that's the way I looked at it. It was me doing my thing against the Bills. I was excited.

On our first possession, we moved the ball slowly downfield, gaining a few yards at a time and eating up the clock. Just as we had planned. As Parcells said, "We don't need no individual heroes. We got here as a team; let's play as a team. Everybody do only what you are capable of doing and don't try to do more. At the end of this game, win or lose, you should be so exhausted, because you will have given your all. If you're not feeling that way then you didn't do your job." So everybody went that extra yard, extra step. Each player carried his own load, and we were successful.

Parcells knew that for us to be effective running the ball he had to make sure I was fresh as much as possible. It was hot and he respected my age and did different things to save me. He utilized Dave Meggett and ran play-action plays so I could get my breath, and he put me on the sidelines and let Meggett and Maurice go in and run.

Meggett was our punt returner but Ron Erhardt wanted to get him into the offense to give us another dimension. He was a fast, elusive runner who could make big plays, but the problem was to get him in there and not have defenses keying on him. With Meggett in the game, the defense expected him to run with the ball or catch a pass, because he wasn't in to block. So we decided to stay in a split-back formation and run identical plays. I was the lead blocker on one side, and if I went to the opposite side with the ball, Meggett was the lead blocker. The first time we played Buffalo we didn't do that. We had Rodney Hampton at running back and he played out of the "I" with Maurice Carthon blocking, so we didn't have a chance to experiment with the split-back formation. In the Super Bowl, we kind of caught Buffalo sleeping.

I would line up both on the strong and weak sides, and that would confuse them, too. When Maurice came in the game, I was the weak-side running back, and when Meggett came in, I was the strong-side running back. When I was weak side, Maurice would run a few plays and I would lead block for him. Just that formation alone and the personnel really got 'em confused. Most defenses try to substitute according to the offense's personnel, but if your personnel isn't doing what the defense expects, then you're putting yourself in a good position.

We knew from the first time we played the Bills that we had to get to the corners—to get around Bruce Smith and Cornelius Bennett and make those guys run—and to then get them back underneath, inside, with the

January 27, 1991, at Tampa Stadium in Tampa, Florida

Paid Attendance: 73,813

AFC Champion: Buffalo Bills (15–3)
Head Coach: Marv Levy

NFC Champion: New York Giants (15–3)
Head Coach: Bill Parcells

STARTING LINEUPS

OFFENSE			DEFENSE		
Buffalo		**New York**	**Buffalo**		**New York**
James Lofton	WR	Mark Ingram	Leon Seals	LE	Eric Dorsey
Will Wolford	LT	Jumbo Elliott	Jeff Wright	NT	Erik Howard
Jim Ritcher	LG	William Roberts	Bruce Smith	RE	Leonard Marshall
Kent Hull	C	Bart Oates	Cornelius Bennett	LOLB	Carl Banks
John Davis	RG	Eric Moore	Shane Conlan	LILB	Steve DeOssie
Howard Ballard	RT	Doug Riesenberg	Ray Bentley	RILB	Pepper Johnson
Keith McKeller	TE	Mark Bavaro	Darryl Talley	ROLB	Lawrence Taylor
Andre Reed	WR	Stephen Baker	Kirby Jackson	LCB	Mark Collins
Jim Kelly	QB	Jeff Hostetler	Nate Odomes	RCB	Everson Walls
Jamie Mueller	RB	Maurice Carthon	Leonard Smith	SS	Greg Jackson
Thurman Thomas	RB	Ottis Anderson	Mark Kelso	FS	Myron Guyton

SUBSTITUTIONS

Buffalo: K—Scott Norwood. P—Rick Tuten. Offense: Receivers—Al Edwards, Pete Metzelaars, Butch Rolle, Steve Tasker. Linemen—Mitch Frerotte, Adam Lingner. Backs—Kenneth Davis, Carwell Gardner, Frank Reich, Don Smith. Defense: Linebackers—Carlton Bailey, Hal Garner. Linemen—Gary Baldinger, Mike Lodish, Glenn Parker, Mark Pike. Backs—Dwight Drane, John Hagy, Clifford Hicks, James Williams. DNP—Gale Gilbert.

New York: K—Matt Bahr. P—Sean Landeta. Offense: Receivers—Howard Cross, Troy Kyles, Bob Mrosko, Stacy Robinson. Linemen—Bob Kratch, Brian Williams. Backs—Dave Meggett, Lee Rouson, Lewis Tillman. Defense: Linebackers—Bobby Abrams, Johnie Cooks, Lawrence McGrew, Gary Reasons. Linemen—Mike Fox, John Washington. Backs—Roger Brown, Dave Duerson, Reyna Thompson, David Whitmore, Perry Williams. DNP—Matt Cavanaugh.

Buffalo	3	9	0	7—19
New York	3	7	7	3—20

NYG	FG Bahr 28
Buff	FG Norwood 23
Buff	D. Smith 1 run (Norwood kick)
Buff	Safety, B. Smith tackled Hostetler in end zone
NYG	Baker 14 pass from Hostetler (Bahr kick)
NYG	Anderson 1 run (Bahr kick)
Buff	Thomas 31 run (Norwood kick)
NYG	FG Bahr 21
MVP:	Ottis Anderson (New York Giants)

power running. So our plan was to utilize Dave Meggett's speed, to make them play the perimeter, and use me inside. But I also ran outside. It was totally confusing to them because they didn't expect me to go outside at all after watching our playoff games against the Bears and 49ers, where everything I ran was in between the tackles. They kind of bunched everything inside, forcing me to go outside. A few plays I was able to get outside, but most of the time we just had excellent inside blocking.

I ran a lot to the left behind Jumbo Elliott and William Roberts, who were the two best blockers on the team at that time. I'm not taking anything away from Bob Kratch, Doug Riesenberg, and Eric Moore on the right side, but Jumbo and William were playing so well. Jumbo was in his first year and everybody thought Bruce Smith would dominate him. But we had almost a perfect scenario: You put a young guy, Elliott, with an experienced guy, Roberts, and you have them play together and see what happens. They did well on the left side. Bruce didn't dominate anybody.

On that first drive, Meggett and I ran the ball, and Jeff completed a few short passes. Then Matt Bahr's field goal put us ahead, 3–0. But Kelly, Thomas, and Reed came back, and the Bills went ahead, 10–3. They were going up and down the field and we couldn't stop them. They threatened to blow the game open. And they almost did on a key play when we were backed up on our own 7-yard line. Hostetler ran a bootleg action away from myself as I went to the left. Bruce Smith made a hard move on Jumbo Elliott. Rather than taking my fake all the way out, I shortened my path to help Jumbo with Smith. And Hostetler's right foot hit my right foot, and he started to plunge forward into our end zone. I was spun around when I tripped Hostetler, and Bruce was able to get past me. As Jeff was going down, Bruce grabbed his right wrist, and it looked like he was going to yank the ball free, but Jeff had the smarts to use his other hand to pull the ball to his chest. So they got only two points for the safety instead of seven points for a touchdown on a fumble recovery. I'm quite sure that if they had gotten seven, that would have changed the complexion of the game, and I'm quite sure Thurman Thomas would be telling you about this Super Bowl.

We were behind, 12–3, late in the half when we started another drive. Meggett and I were moving the ball successfully, but I wouldn't say it was exciting or fun. For me, it was hard, because I thought the game was pretty boring. I didn't think what we were doing with our ground game was that big of a deal. I really didn't. I was caught up in the fact that they were playing well, and that when they had the ball they were running up and down the field, and when we had it we were barely moving. I always thought they had the advantage.

My first big run of the game came when I started left and used a little footwork to go to the right and break through a hole. Up in the booth, there was some surprise that I could move my feet like that, but Dan Dierdorf knew—he saw me in St. Louis when I first came in as a rookie and saw what I could do. I never lost it. I just got bigger. The footwork was always there, but I never had a chance to utilize my agility with the Giants. Because I never had the opportunity to display that on short runs, whenever I got a chance to shake-and-bake in the secondary I tried to do it.

The drive ended just seconds before the end of the half when Stephen Baker caught a touchdown pass while running to the left side of the end zone. That was the play that was called in the huddle. That was the play Hostetler and Baker were practicing all week long. And they did it in our playoff game against Chicago. The same play and the same result. Success on that play was a given. After being held to five field goals against the 49ers, we finally got a touchdown. It gave us momentum, and opportunity to pull close. We had made it competitive, making it 12–10. We knew we were only a field goal from winning the whole thing.

At halftime, Parcells said that he wanted us to establish ourselves in the third quarter. It was going to set the tone for the fourth quarter and determine whether we were going to win or lose the game. We had to reestablish the momentum we had at the end of the first half. He knew that if we went three downs and out, we would have lost. Instead we had the longest drive in Super Bowl history.

I picked up where I left off in the second quarter. On a third-and-1, I ran down the left sideline for a big gain. I ended the run by giving a forearm to their safety Mark Kelso. They knew from playing against me that I had the forearm. It wasn't unusual, but what caught them off guard was my preparation before releasing it. I usually didn't take much time before releasing the forearm—I called it a "quick 2-inch punch." But I was rope-a-doping and doing the old Muhammad Ali windup. I started telling him from a long ways back that, "If you come close to me, you're going to get hit." And he came closer and I wound up, and he got closer and it happened. The players on the sideline responded to that play. They knew I wanted to win at all costs—so did the Bills. I wasn't one to go around bragging—I showed by example, on the field.

On that drive we just took what they gave us. We weren't going to do anything fancy, any trickery. Other than that run, we just slowly moved the ball. We didn't try to be greedy. We didn't try for any big plays. We knew we couldn't keep dropping back 10 steps and have Jeff throw the deep pass, because we just wouldn't have the time. Bruce Smith was over there and would take that away. Instead, Jeff took the three to five steps and got rid of the football on short passes—that was it.

We worried about Jeff all the time. He would sit by me on the bench, and I saw that he didn't know where he was half the time. Parcells would make the linemen look at Jeff sitting there to see what the Bills were doing to him. He'd say, "Everybody wake up—we better do something different or we aren't going to be in this game with a quarterback of sound mind." In the second half we had to figure out a way to keep Jeff from getting beaten up. We chose to run more often. And we stopped running away from Cornelius Bennett. In the first half we kept running away and he kept hitting Hostetler. So we decided to come toward him to neutralize him. We put a back in front of him to just slow him down. We started bootlegging toward him and then we started bootlegging away from him. He had been playing the way he wanted to, but we started making him play honest.

We relied mostly on the run in the opening drive of the second half, but the play that kept the drive going was a short pass to the right side from Hostetler to Mark Ingram. It was third-and-13 and Mark made one of the greatest catches and runs in the history of the Super Bowl. I didn't realize how much he did until I saw the film. I've only seen bits and pieces of that Super Bowl film, but they showed that play so much in the highlights that it's still fresh in my mind. He broke about five or six tackles—it was unbelievable—and he kept spinning away from guys and moving forward. He was like Mark Bavaro against the 49ers in 1986. He wouldn't go down until he made the first down. That play was inspirational.

We kept moving toward their goal. We used up over nine minutes of the clock and then I ran it in to the left side without being tackled. It was from only 1 yard out and wasn't hard. It wasn't much different than the short-yardage and goal-line plays I'd been running since 1989, when I had 14 touchdowns. It was not unusual, but it was most definitely gratifying. It gave me the chance to make big-time history. I became the only Giant to score in both their Super Bowls.

Buffalo went back ahead, 19–17, in the fourth quarter on a long run to right side by Thurman Thomas. Had the Bills won the Super Bowl, Thurman probably would have gotten the MVP because he gained over 130 yards on the ground and caught a few passes. But I've never known them to give the MVP to the losing team's running back.

We weren't that upset that we'd fallen behind again. By this time I figured we had just as much chance as them of winning. There was time left and all we had to do was to stay within our offense to put up more points. We knew that if we got it close, we'd get seven or Matt Bahr would give us three points. We knew Matt could kick within a certain distance. He was one of the most accurate short-distance kickers that we'd seen in a long time. Early in the season we had Raul Allegre, and he was pretty good, but Raul got hurt and Matt came along and moved out Raul for good. We knew Matt could do it and we just tried to get it within his range. We did that and he put us ahead with a short field goal, 20–19.

The Bills had a lot of time to go back ahead, but other than Thurman, they had a hard time gaining yardage. Our defense pretty much shut down their passing game. And the Bills receivers were dropping passes in anticipation of being hit. Bill Belichick told our defensive players, "Any player goes for the ball, whether he catches it or not, you lay him out." They did what they were told to do. So we had young guys like Myron Guyton and Greg Jackson, who were hitters, as were Mark Collins and Everson Walls. They hit hard. Sometimes they even hit our own guys.

We knew they were getting frustrated and tired. I knew they were getting tired of tackling me. Every time they tackled me it took something out of them. I was 6'2" and about 240 and I was running hard and running low and running with power and running with the intention to hurt anybody who tried to tackle me. I wasn't getting tired. Like I said, it was such a boring game to me that I didn't feel like I was burning any energy. Each time I got the ball I felt stronger and better.

On the Bills' final drive, they got into field-goal range with eight seconds left. It would be from about 47 yards out. Not all the Giants players watched Scott Norwood's final kick. I wanted to see. I didn't want to miss the highlight of the whole game. The same thing with that kick as Matt Bahr's kick at the end of the San Francisco game. Everybody was holding each other's hands. I had my helmet off. From where I was, I couldn't tell if Norwood made it or missed it. In fact, at my angle, it looked more like he made it. What gave it away was the Giants on the field jumping up and down. The ball had sailed just to the right of the goal post and we had won. I looked up and said, "Thank you, God. Thank you, Jesus."

It was in the stars; it was the writing on the wall. There was no way that game could have gone any other way than the way it did. I knew that the Man Up Above wasn't going to deny me that win after he let us beat Frisco. I had predicted the outcome of the Super Bowl. When I was a rookie going to the Cardinals, I told my Miami roommate Kenny Johnson that if I ever played in a Super Bowl and it was played in Florida and I was the featured running back, I'd win the Most Valuable Player. That's what my dream was all about, and it was being fulfilled.

I was fortunate they gave me the MVP. I appreciated the honor and it was one of the greatest awards bestowed on me during my career. I gained over 100 yards, but the MVP could have easily gone to Hostetler. He took the punishment. He was unbelievable to have accomplished what he did. That guy—you saw why he deserved to get paid so much when he later signed with the Raiders.

I think everybody celebrated individually. Back at the hotel, with family members. We as a team never got into the celebration part. Everybody went off on their own. However, I do remember that night when Maurice Carthon, William Roberts, and Pepper Johnson stood outside their hotel doors just laughing and crying and laughing and crying and playing music all night long. It was a happy time.

I look back on that game and I see what a terrific game plan that Parcells, Erhardt, Belichick, and the other coaches came up with to beat a team we supposedly had no chance against. I don't think any of us could imagine that we could hold the ball for over forty minutes and execute those long drives. But we had to do it and we did. It was important that we didn't have any turnovers.

I don't know if you could call it a physical game, although there was a lot of good hitting, especially by our guys. It's hard for me to judge because I didn't think it was that good a game. I think it was the dullest game that anyone could sit down and watch. But everybody else has said that it was the most exciting game in Super Bowl history.

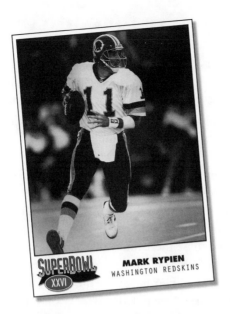

MARK RYPIEN
WASHINGTON REDSKINS

SUPER BOWL XXVI

SUPER BOWL XXVI

WASHINGTON REDSKINS 37
BUFFALO BILLS 24

MARK RYPIEN

I played college ball at Washington State, a school that has a tradition of producing successful quarterbacks. Jack Thompson was there before me and Timm Rosenbach and Drew Bledsoe followed me. We took pride in our passing game and the NFL paid attention. In my senior year, the Washington Redskins became interested in me, and in anticipation of the 1986 NFL draft, Jerry Rhome, their quarterback coach, came to work me out. When you're a young kid with ambitions to go into the NFL, and a guy with the stature of Jerry Rhome comes to work you out, you're pumped up. One of the things that Jerry saw was that I could throw the ball a long way. That was important because the Redskins did a lot of play-action and had fast receivers to get downfield and put a vertical stretch on the defense—so the quarterback had to have a more than adequate arm. At the time, I felt I had one of the strongest arms in football.

The Redskins selected me in the sixth round. Jay Schroeder was their starting quarterback based on the way he performed the preceding season after Joe Theismann had his career-ending leg injury. They knew Jay had a lot of talent but he was kind of green, so they needed a veteran to be his backup. Doug Williams was available. Doug didn't have much mobility, but the guy could throw it out of his back pocket as far as most other guys could throw stepping into it. So they signed Doug, and that was no big deal for me even though it meant I wouldn't play unless both guys were out. I was just excited to be there and learn both the physical and mental aspects of pro football from some pretty good players.

The first year I hurt my knee and spent the entire season on the injured list. The second year, 1987, began with a strike, something no athlete ever wants to go through. After it was over, it seemed that Jay and Doug took turns getting hurt and replacing each other as the starter. Though I never played, I was the emergency guy. I was active but I think I suited only three games. There was the chance they were going to suit me in Super Bowl XXII, but they never did. So I was in street clothes watching Doug Williams lead us to a big victory. That was a great game to be part of anyway. It was always valuable to watch.

Nobody talked about future plans for me. I was always kind of on the outside, but I was very fortunate because for the two years he was there, Jerry Rhome tutored me, and what I learned was very instrumental in my progress. I worked on footwork, reads, and understanding the system. I learned the importance of knowing not only where your main receiver is but where your two and three receivers are. Those first two years I said to myself, "Gosh, this game is a heck of a lot faster than it is in college. Boy, I don't know if I'm cut out for this." Really, you don't know until you actually get the opportunity.

The following season I did get an opportunity. Jay and Doug were at the center of a big old squabble in the off-season. The coaches were going to name Doug the guy, and Jay didn't like it and wanted out. So early in the season, Jay got traded to Oakland for offensive tackle Jim Lachey, and I became Doug's backup. (At the time I didn't realize that Lachey was going to be very important to my success.)

When Doug later went down with appendicitis and had to have surgery, I had to answer the bell. Joe Gibbs said, "This guy's been sitting around for two years; let's see if he learned anything." It was time to show if I was the possible future of this team or another of those guys who they described as "a good college quarterback, couldn't cut it in the NFL." That's how it works in the NFL. There have been lots of guys who failed when they had their opportunity, and some like me who've been fortunate to get it done.

I did a good job and when Doug came back we both got starts. It wasn't uncomfortable, although fans took sides on who the starter should be and did some booing. Having already been through a quarterback controversy with Jay and Doug, I knew how ugly it could get and didn't want to have anything to do with something like that. Doug was a very good guy, and we had a great relationship the whole time we played together and I wanted to keep it that way. Anything else and the media in Washington was going to jump on it and take it to who knows where. My basic train of thought was: If they give me the ball on Sunday, I'm going to play my heart out; and if I'm going to back up Doug, I'll cheer like a son of a gun.

Sharing time with Doug, I threw only slightly more than 200 passes, but 18 of my completions were for touchdowns. That was a high percentage, and the fantasy-football lords thought I was the greatest thing since sliced bread. In the next couple of years I would continue to throw a high percentage of touchdowns.

I became the starter in '89, and Doug eventually gave way to Stan Humphries as my backup. It's always the case that they have somebody behind you in case you can't make it. Because of the winning tradition in Washington, quarterbacks were under pressure to produce quickly. Not getting to the playoffs at all in '88 or '89 was unthinkable in Washington, and even a first-round playoff win over Philadelphia in 1990 wasn't cutting it because the team had already won two Super Bowls and appeared in three in the 1980s. Anything less than an NFC East title and an NFC championship was mediocrity in our town. I understood that, and when the boos came, I knew that was part of the deal. When you don't play well, that's the reaction you're going to get. In the long run, it made me buckle down a little bit. I didn't go out there trying to lose or throw interceptions, but it happens, and probably the first reaction the fan has to something like that is to boo. I wouldn't say anything negative about the fans in Washington because when you're playing in front of a packed house, every time you walk on the field, whether you're 14–2 or 4–12, you appreciate that. (Toward the end of my stay in Washington, the booing did get bad at times. I thought I stunk in certain games and wished I wasn't on the football field, so I couldn't argue with the fans who booed me then. Even my wife, I think, agreed with them a few times. I played my heart out those years in Washington, but because of injuries down the stretch, I might not have looked as good as I would have liked. I think the Washington fans realize that now. They felt that they had a guy who played hard and didn't moan and groan and enjoyed every minute of it, and when it was time to move on, I moved on gracefully.)

Prior to the year we went to Super Bowl XXVI, we had a high winning percentage with me at quarterback and I had good numbers, but there was always something holding me back. There had been injuries and there had been times in '88 and '89 when I had trouble holding onto the football. But I'd come back from the injuries and played full seasons, and my fumbling problems were a thing of the past. So, in Joe Gibbs' mind, all the questions about me had been answered. It was kind of like: "Mark has always done good things here, and though he's had trouble doing some other things, he's corrected that."

I had such gratitude toward Joe for giving me, a sixth-round draft pick, a chance to become a starting quarterback in the NFL. I might not have gotten the chance somewhere else. In the tough times, the bad times, there were times he wanted to ring my neck, but I would put some smiles on his face, too. I had tremendous respect for Joe, but I can't say I was close to him when he was my coach. Knowing him as a good friend today, it was probably the way he wanted it at the time. Apparently he had gotten close to Joe Theismann, and they kind of had a falling out at the end and that left a sour taste in his mouth. He didn't really want to get close to another of his quarterbacks. If that's the way Joe wanted things, I appreciated that, and that's how we kept it. Player-coach relationships can either be good or absolute atrocities, so I just tried to keep it good and be very cooperative with the game plans. I think one of the things that impressed Joe most about me was how I could be given a totally new game plan on a Wednesday morning and be able to go out there at the noon walk-through and spit it out with no problems at all. He kept us guys around who were smart, played with intensity, and had good football instincts.

By 1991 Gibbs had full confidence in me as his quarterback, and finally it all came together. We began the season with 11 consecutive victories. An undefeated season would have been great history-wise, and we were thinking, "Boy, wouldn't it be nice to do what the Dolphins did?" Our streak was ended by Dallas, 24–21, and we lost once more, to the Eagles in our last game of the regular season. We finished the year with a 14–2 record and won the Eastern Division by three games over the

Cowboys. I realized that I was on a great team. I felt we had the horses and personnel to win it all.

A pivotal game for us was in New York against the Giants on a Sunday night. It had been futile trying to beat the Giants in recent years. In fact, we'd lost six in a row to them. In that game, we fell behind 13–0 at the half, but then we came back to win 17–13. We went ahead in the fourth quarter when I hit Gary Clark on a deep post pattern. Earlier in the game, I rolled to the right and threw back to the left and Gary dropped a cinch touchdown. This time I rolled left and threw right and got over the top of the safety and their great cornerback Everson Walls. We beat the Giants again later in the season. The coaches might have looked at the Giants wins and said, "Hey, this might be it. This might be Mark Rypien's 'coming.'" I wouldn't look at it from such an individualistic standpoint, but maybe some people were thinking, "Mark brought us down and was the guy, so this could be a special year for us." And lo and behold, it was.

At our Saturday night meetings before a game, players who had been true Redskins over the years and were respected by their peers would get up and speak and give little pep talks. Guys like Monte Coleman, Joe Jacoby, Russ Grimm, Jeff Bostic, Charles Mann, and Darrell Green would say, "This is a great run we're on guys; this is fun for all of us, and even Joe's having a good time." I think each player could sense that Joe Gibbs was enjoying himself a lot because he was giving us Monday and Tuesday off after a win and had a loosy-goosy attitude. Of course, a good time can end at any time, so we said, "Let's enjoy this while we can," and we did. We fed off each other, players and coaches. A lot of times on a team, it is one side of the football and the other side. But on the Redskins, offensive guys, defensive guys, and special-teams players were all friends. It was a group of guys who believed in each other and enjoyed each other. That was important when playing on Sundays.

It was Joe's way to keep it on the ground because not a lot of bad things can happen when you're running the football. We had a strong running game. Earnest Byner got over 1,000 yards for us that year, but he was still one of our unsung heroes. He played R-back, he played H-back, he played fullback, he blocked, he caught quite a few balls out of the backfield. You could not ask more from a football player. Earnest was our workhorse, the guy we went to between the tackles. Ricky Ervins was our outside guy. Ricky had a tremendous year, too. He was another versatile player who could do his own thing or spell Earnest or Gerald Riggs. Gerald was our banger. We had a lot of specialists and Gerald was our short-yardage guy who we used a lot inside the five. Ron Wolfley, who would be my team-mate on the St. Louis Rams, had one of the funniest comments ever: "If you need 2 yards, Gerald will get you 2 yards; if you need 4 yards, Gerald will get you 2 yards." He may have gotten only 2 yards sometimes, but he got us a lot of touchdowns that year. Byner, Ervins, and Riggs each had their own assets, so we didn't worry, no matter who Joe put in as our back. Very rarely did we go to two backs, although we used tight end Terry Orr sometimes as an H-back.

Joe Gibbs' main philosophy was to control the line of scrimmage with the Hogs, his big offensive linemen. They were a great group who defi-nitely deserved all the accolades they got over the years. It was neat to see your offensive linemen get recognition and even be given a nickname, which was rare. They took pride in it. The one thing about those guys—Mark May, Jeff Bostic, Jim Lachey, Joe Jacoby, Raleigh McKenzie, Mark Schlereth—is that they were smart. Joe Gibbs didn't want a guy who made mistakes in the fourth quarter because he wasn't well prepared. Joe always prepared us so well, but he made sure to have guys who also pre-pared themselves to go out and play.

The Hogs were known for being a bit notorious off the field; they had their 5 O'Clock Club for socializing, they had guys like Jeff Bostic and Russ Grimm playing practical jokes, and they had other ways of enjoying themselves, there's no doubt. But when they crossed the stripes, they meant business. Those guys had been there for a while, and just as they knew how to go against defensive players, they knew what it took to get everything out of our own players. So they were leaders, which didn't mean they wouldn't listen to me when things weren't going good and they needed to strap it on. I'd get in a guy's face in a positive way, and I think they enjoyed that. Even the Hogs had to have their butts jumped at certain points in time, and they respected when I did that.

The Hogs and I worked well together because they knew where I was going to be, and it wasn't going to change from snap to snap. It was my good fortune to have those Hogs up front because they led the league almost every year I was there in fewest sacks allowed. But by the same token, if things did break down and they were having trouble protecting me, which didn't happen a lot, they took comfort in knowing that I would bail them out by throwing the ball away or making a play downfield.

In our passing game, we did have a few trick plays that took a long time to develop, but most of our things were timing routes. If we did have a post route or something similar, I had to wait that extra second for my receiver to get a step on the defender, often knowing in the back of my mind that I was going to get hit. It was ideal for Joe Gibbs' system to have a quarterback who would sit in the pocket and make plays. But it wasn't a deal where we designed plays where the quarterback just stood back there seven steps and waited and waited for a receiver to break free downfield. That was never part of our scheme. Instead, we had offensive progression through our reads, and our reads took us to our deep throws, based on how the free safeties responded to play-action and stuff like that. Play-action and our ability to run the football was the reason we had success with deep passes, not a decision to just be a straight drop-back team that was going to throw deep.

Because of the great way the Hogs blocked the front fours of defenses and the way our backs ran, we were likely to see eight or nine defenders creeping up to the line of scrimmage to get some penetration. That didn't leave a lot of their guys in coverage, so that's what enabled our receivers, Art Monk, Gary Clark, and Ricky Sanders, to become a much bigger part of the offense. It becomes an interesting chess game that you play: When there are a lot of defenders on the line of scrimmage, what do you do? There weren't a lot of places to go, so we were fortunate to have receivers who were playmakers. You can have a lot of great players, but you must have playmakers to win.

Gary Clark was our weak-side receiver, Art Monk was the strong-side guy, and Ricky Sanders was our motion guy. Those guys played the game differently, but they all could make great catches, spin for another 8 or 10 yards, and break tackles. And they were equally creative. Ricky was a real crafty guy, who was great at finding holes and getting open. He did a lot of the middle reads we had. Art was the smart veteran you'd go to on third down or when you needed a big catch. Gary was just a big-play guy up and down the field. He scored a lot of key touchdowns, including two each in our victories over the Giants. He wanted the football, and he'd tell you, too. You've gotta love a guy like that.

Balls were coming their way. In 1989 they each had over 1,000 yards receiving. We didn't say before a game that we were going to go to one guy specifically, but a defense could dictate that. Even a good pass defense could take away only two of our receivers, so we'd still have the third guy open that game. It put a lot of strain and vertical stretch on defenses having those three guys on the field at the same time. I was fortunate to play with a total package like that. Those guys were great friends—Art had children, so he couldn't hang out with Gary and Ricky—but each had his own identity on and off the field, and because of that they blended well together and made it a whole lot of fun for everybody.

Our offense led the NFL in scoring in 1991 and our defense was second in the league in fewest points allowed. Richie Petitbon had done a wonderful job with our defense, and they had played tremendously all year. In the playoffs they would play a major role.

The first playoff game against Atlanta wasn't that easy. We had beaten them earlier that year, 56–17, when I threw six touchdown passes. We were already up by five or six touchdowns when I was asked if I wanted to stay in the game and have the chance to break Sammy Baugh's Redskins' single-game record from the 1940s. I chose not to go back into the game and set a record. Still, the Falcons would later make an issue about us rubbing it in. Because of that game, Atlanta was out for revenge in the playoff and they played us harder. There was a downpour and the conditions were absolutely atrocious, and they had number 21—Deion Sanders—lurking on their side, so you had to be careful. As it turned out, our defense played well and we won, 24–7.

In the NFC Championship Game, we played Detroit, another team we'd beaten badly during the regular season, 45–0, when they were without Barry Sanders. You hate to play somebody you trounced because they're going to come with a little red in their eyes and be ready to play. But we were ready also, and being at R. F. K. Stadium made winning a whole lot easier. Again our defense played great. They picked off Erik Kramer four times and had five sacks, three by Wilber Marshall. Wilber was another flat-out playmaker. As the years went on, he had injuries and wasn't quite the same player, but that year he created absolute havoc. You could look in his eyes and see he wanted to prove something in Washington that he had already proven in Chicago with the Bears.

We beat Detroit, 41–10, and there was no doubt we were peaking as we headed to Minneapolis to play in Super Bowl XXVI against Buffalo, who probably should have won the year before and had another good team. They were in Super Bowls back-to-back, so I think we were made the underdogs by about three points.

Going to the Super Bowl—that's as exciting as anything gets. There are guys who play their whole careers and don't have the opportunity to play in a championship game, never mind a Super Bowl, so I was going to enjoy every minute of it. Yet I wasn't going to get so hyped that I wouldn't be able to mount the proper intensity on Super Sunday. It helped that Joe Gibbs and some of the players like Joe Jacoby, Russ Grimm, Jeff Bostic, and Monte Coleman had been to three Super Bowls. And, of course, I had been on the sidelines for Super Bowl XXII. This time I would be playing.

It was different being in Minneapolis for a Super Bowl. At least it was different for most people because they didn't know what the heck we were going there for in the winter. But me being a northerner, with my relatives being from Canada, I thought it was the greatest thing in the world. We thought that Super Bowls in winter should be about ice instead of palm trees. So I loved it. And Minneapolis and St. Paul did a wonderful job hosting the event.

They expected us to practice, get some rest, and enjoy ourselves—and that's what we did. There were some stories about my teammates being out late, and I'm sure a lot of the opposition was out there with them. But they'd been there before and had a feel for what they could do and what they couldn't get away with. As for me: On Monday night, with Tuesday off, I went to a local pub and had a few beers with one of my brothers and my friend who had been the best man at my wedding. I didn't go out much otherwise. I was going to do every darn thing I could to get prepared for this game, and I figured that for the rest of my life I could worry about enjoying Friday and Saturday nights. Besides, Super Bowls, when you think about it, are for everybody but the two teams playing in them. It's for corporate America and for everyone to have all their parties and festivities. The players must prepare for the game.

Joe and the coaching staff put the offensive game plan together and then gave it to me. If I could explain it to the whole team, then it was a game plan that we could run smoothly. It was a different plan than the ones against Detroit and Atlanta because we decided we were going to try the no-huddle, which we had kind of tinkered with on and off during the year. The no-huddle was Buffalo's trademark, what Jim Kelly ran so well. They were the team that had brought it into the limelight in the latter part of the eighties and into the nineties. I doubted that it would surprise them. I imagine that they had played against it some; anyway, it's likely that word got out that we were practicing with it. Obviously they weren't going to set up their whole defensive game plan based on that because they didn't know to what extent we were going to use it.

It was hard to sleep the night before Super Sunday. The game was in late afternoon, but I was up at six or seven in the morning and got to the Metrodome six hours before the game—it was Chip Lohmiller, myself, and Erik Williams. I took a little nap and slept better there than I had in the hotel bed. There was a lot on my mind.

I had 50 relatives and friends in the Metrodome, so I probably was a combination of being excited and being hyper when I ran onto the field during introductions. Mike Utley, who had played offensive tackle with me at Washington State, was there, and I gave the thumbs-up to him as I was coming out of the balloons. That was the season he got paralyzed at Detroit. I gave that sign to tell him, "Hey, Mike, this one's for all of us Cougars." I was pumped.

In our first drive I hit Art Monk for four completions. It was never designed that way; it evolved to that because of what the defense gave us with their basic roll coverage to the weak and strong sides. In the back of my mind was the fact that Art had been to a couple of Super Bowls, but had been hampered by injuries or something and made only a couple of catches. I wanted to get him a Super Bowl touchdown, and it would have been nice. Of course, Art made a nice catch at the back of the end zone, but it was called back because instant replay showed Art's foot coming down on the back line. Then we fumbled the field-goal snap and came away with no points. Was that a heartbreaker? Yes. And no. We didn't get any points but we had some success moving the ball.

The Bills got the ball, but Jim Kelly was intercepted by Brad Edwards, so we were back in great field position. I was looking at film, and then all of a sudden I had to grab my helmet and go back on the field. As it turned out, we had the ball third-and-goal from the 7, or something like that, and I see Ricky Ervins break free, and he has a gut-cinch touchdown; only my pass hits a defensive lineman's hand and pops in the air, and Kirby Jackson makes the interception. That's one play that makes you wonder what's going on. You had a reversal on a touchdown, you missed a field-goal opportunity, and now you get this interception on a sure touchdown, so you're kind of thinking maybe this isn't the Redskins day. But through it all, we didn't hang our heads. I was just pissed off because there was nothing that I did wrong mentally—just some guy put his hand up at the wrong time for me. You say to yourself, "Put that one behind you."

We had looked at films of the previous Super Bowl where the Giants had done what we were going to try to do against Buffalo, which was to control the ball and try to make big plays. Buffalo wasn't a team that gave up a lot of big plays, but you could get some if you were physical with them and withstood their adrenaline push at the start of the game. I'd thought that Super Bowl XXII was the fastest game possible, but this burst of adrenaline by the Buffalo defense was the most incredible thing I'd ever seen, being in my first Super Bowl playing experience. I tell you

January 26, 1992, at the Metrodome in Minneapolis
Attendance: 63,130
NFC Champion: Washington Redskins (16—2)
Head Coach: Joe Gibbs
AFC Champion: Buffalo Bills (15—3)
Head Coach: Marv Levy

STARTING LINEUPS

OFFENSE			DEFENSE		
Washington		**Buffalo**	**Washington**		**Buffalo**
Gary Clark	WR	James Lofton	Charles Mann	LE	Leon Seals
Ron Middleton	TE	Pete Metzelaars	Erik Williams	LT	
Jim Lachey	LT	Will Wolford		NT	Jeff Wright
Raleigh McKenzie	LG	Jim Ritcher	Tim Johnson	RT	
Jeff Bostic	C	Kent Hull	Fred Stokes	RE	Bruce Smith
Mark Schlereth	RG	Glenn Parker		LOLB	Cornelius Bennett
Joe Jacoby	RT	Howard Ballard	Wilber Marshall	LLB	
Don Warren	TE	Keith McKeller		LILB	Shane Conlan
Art Monk	WR	Andre Reed	Kurt Gouveia	MLB	
Mark Rypien	QB	Jim Kelly		RILB	Carlton Bailey
Earnest Byner	RB	Kenneth Davis	Andre Collins	RLB	
				ROLB	Darryl Talley
			Martin Mayhew	LCB	Kirby Jackson
			Darrell Green	RCB	Nate Odomes
			Danny Copeland	SS	Dwight Drane
			Brad Edwards	FS	Mark Kelso

SUBSTITUTIONS

Washington: K—Chip Lohmiller. P—Kelly Goodburn. Offense: Receivers—John Brandes, Stephen Hobbs, James Jenkins, Terry Orr, Ricky Sanders. Linemen—Mark Adickes, Russ Grimm, Ed Simmons. Backs—Ricky Ervins, Brian Mitchell, Gerald Riggs, Jeff Rutledge. Defense: Linebackers—Ravin Caldwell, Monte Coleman. Linemen—Jason Buck, James Geathers, Bobby Wilson. Backs—Terry Hoage, A. J. Johnson, Sidney Johnson, Alvoid Mays.

Buffalo: K—Scott Norwood, Brad Daluiso. P—Chris Mohr. Offense: Receivers—Don Beebe, Al Edwards, Butch Rolle, Steve Tasker. Linemen—Mitch Frerotte, Adam Lingner, Joe Staysniak. Backs—Carwell Gardner, Frank Reich (QB), Thurman Thomas. Defense: Linebackers—Ray Bentley, Hal Garner, Marvcus Patton. Linemen—Phil Hansen, Mike Lodish, Mark Pike. Backs—Chris Hale, Clifford Hicks, Henry Jones, James Williams.

Washington	0	17	14	6—37
Buffalo	0	0	10	14—24

Wash	FG Lohmiller 34
Wash	Byner 10 pass from Rypien (Lohmiller kick)
Wash	Riggs 1 run (Lohmiller kick)
Wash	Riggs 2 run (Lohmiller kick)
Buff	FG Norwood 21
Buff	Thomas 1 run (Norwood kick)
Wash	Clark 30 pass from Rypien (Lohmiller kick)
Wash	FG Lohmiller 25
Wash	FG Lohmiller 39
Buff	Metzelaars 2 pass from Kelly (Norwood kick)
Buff	Beebe 4 pass from Kelly (Norwood kick)
MVP:	Mark Rypien (Washington)

I got banged around in our first few series. It was intense, the most intense thing I've ever been in in my life. I was a little concerned coming to the sidelines and talking to my guys. We had made a few pass plays and had moved the ball, but I was getting hit and it wasn't characteristic of our guys to let that happen. Jeff Bostic kind of comes over and says, "Calm down, weather the storm. These guys are throwing everything they have at us now, but they're going to tire themselves out." He was correct, but when you're out there taking a few shots from Bruce Smith and guys like Carlton Bailey and Cornelius Bennett are pouncing on your chest, you wonder what's going on? Sure enough, the adrenaline wore off. . . .

It was important just to get on the board and get a lead—it would let us dig in—and we went ahead 3–0 on Chip Lohmiller's field goal. On our next drive we got a long pass play to Ricky Sanders, who was covered by their safety Mark Kelso. I had a double pump called with Art running down the right sideline. The corner on Art stayed pretty deep and didn't bite on the fake, but Kelso, with the pocket moving to the right, kind of slid a little bit with me, and that's when Ricky, in the middle of the field, gave a little hesitation fake and cut back across the field. I put it out there and he made a nice play on it. I then hit Byner with a pass in the flat, and he made a nice catch and run into the end zone to give us a 10–0 lead. After the bad break on the interception, I felt pretty much in sync for the rest of the game. Our guys were finding ways to get open, and I was laying the ball in for them.

Jim Kelly played well the year before in the Super Bowl but had lost a heartbreaker, and I think he felt Buffalo had a game plan that could beat us. But our defense rose to the occasion and played as good as they had all season at this crucial time. Kelly had a lot of trouble. His rushing game with Thurman Thomas started out slow, the Bills fell behind, and he started passing. So our defense did a lot of blitzing. That was Richie's game plan after seeing something on film. I didn't sit in on the defensive meetings, but that was the thing we heard: "Hey this could go one way or the other—we could blitz the heck out of them and surprise them and knock them way into the nickel seats, or they could make the big plays, so we've got to be ready." Fortunately, the blitzing worked to perfection.

On the Bills' next possession, Darrell Green intercepted Kelly. We felt that the momentum was swinging our way. One thing I appreciated about Joe Gibbs is that he never backed down from being aggressive. He didn't want to just grind it out for the rest of the game because we were only in the second quarter. While the momentum was in our favor, he wanted us to jump on top. So we came back with a quick strike to Gary Clark, who made a great catch and cut all the way back underneath everything and ran down the sidelines for over 30 yards. Then we got about 15 more yards on a sweep by Ervins, and Gerald Riggs finished it with a touchdown. We were up 17–0. That's when I just started pumping my fists and running down the sidelines. I had never been so high in my life.

The Bills' frustrations started to show. Just before the first half ended, Bills receiver Andre Reed got angry that interference wasn't called against our defensive back on a play near our goal. When he slammed his helmet into the ground, he was given an unsportsmanlike penalty that took the Bills out of field-goal range. Reed was one of the premier players in the game and I'm sure he felt there was some contact on that play, but there's a better way of voicing your opinion. Maybe he was frustrated about not getting the ball—probably Thurman Thomas felt that way, too because Kelly was passing on almost every down. We've all been there before. I'd been to where I was not throwing the ball well and then when I do throw one well and some defender runs through my receiver and there's no call—yeah, you get pissed. That's one of those things that happen.

At halftime we were feeling good. The offensive and defensive guys were telling each other that they were doing a great job and to keep it up. Then the second half begins, and look what happens: One linebacker, Andre Collins, blitzes Kelly, and another linebacker, Kurt Gouveia, gets a tremendous interception and takes it down to their 2. Riggs ran it in for the second time, and we were on top 24–0. At that point, we were thinking that this might be our day after all.

The Bills did mount a brief comeback behind the passing of Kelly. They scored on a field goal by Scott Norwood and then Thurman Thomas had a short touchdown to pull them within 14 points, 24–10. I don't think any of us were that concerned. We just knew our offense had to go out and sustain a drive. We didn't want to go three-and-out and have our defense have to go out to win this thing for us. We knew that if this game was going to be won, it was going to be on our next drive. So we went 79 yards, of which 60 yards came on passes to Gary Clark. We used a no-huddle until a third-down play. That play was signaled in, and it was a touchdown to Gary. It was a corner route where he got man-to-man coverage. They came with a safety blitz, which they hadn't done a lot of. I dropped back, the protection was great, and just laid the ball out for him.

Whereas in our first possession of the Super Bowl I had kept going to Art Monk, in this drive I went almost exclusively to Gary Clark. That's the way the game went a lot of times. They'd roll up to Gary's side and that would leave a one-on-one type situation with Art; or they'd roll up to Art's side with a two-deep configuration and give you the opportunity to work Gary down the middle. I hit Gary a couple of times with some in routes, and he made some big plays in some big holes. So now all of a sudden you notice that they're rolling weak to Gary and rolling strong to Art and backing it up with two safeties. So its kind of a double team, but now they're giving you a shot with Ricky Sanders down the middle.

We were running the no-huddle and Ricky Ervins was running well and we were passing well. Whatever I called out at that time was based on the defensive alignment. We put three wide receivers out there in a "check with me" situation. If the Buffalo defense lined up "seven in the box," as we called it, we threw the football; but if they lined up with only "six in the box," we ran draws, we ran counters, we ran a little of everything. That was the unique part about it. The plan we had was a total package for our three wide receivers. As it turned out, we used the no-huddle for only two or three series in the game, but I think it wore Buffalo down a little bit and worked to our advantage. We did a pretty good job with it.

Clark's touchdown made the score 31–10, and that was pretty much the end of the game, though we did get two more field goals from Lohmiller to up our lead to 37–10. The Skins were pretty much celebrating. We just wanted to get some rushing first downs and run out the clock, and Ricky and Earnest did a great job. It was just grind this thing out and get it over with. We did not want to do anything stupid that would get us into trouble and give them some quick scores. They were a talented football team and had come striking back in a lot of games. But our defense was so strong and solid that we really didn't think that would happen against us. We just wanted to give them the ball when they had a long field and short time. The Bills did score on a couple of late touchdowns on Kelly passes, but it didn't matter to us whether we won 37–10 or 37–24.

I found out I got the MVP award with about five minutes left in the game. There was no surge of excitement on my part. I thought Brad Edwards could have gotten the award because he had made two key interceptions and played real well. You don't really care. You have been to the Super Bowl, you have played your best, and your team has come out on top. That was the most important thing. The Disney people came over and said you're the guy picked for the MVP, and we need you to say this. From that point on, even in the huddle, I'd be practicing my lines. They're tough lines, you know: "I'm going to Disney World. I'm going to

Disneyland." I enjoyed filming that. I had my daughter out on the field with me during that, and I can say that was an exciting moment.

My father had passed away about four years prior to the game and that was the only thing really missing that day. But he wasn't really missing. He was watching in his own way. Every time we'd score I looked up to the—I think he was in the sky, but who knows because we were in a dome. But, in any case, I looked up and said a little thanks.

After the game there was a happy celebration. I talked to Joe Gibbs. I was up for contract the next year, and I remember him saying, "Well, you sure hit the jackpot there, big fellah." Joe was such a big part of what I had accomplished and would accomplish and I had so much to thank him for. It was said that this Super Bowl was his masterpiece, and I couldn't disagree. I think he did a remarkable job all year long.

I look back at the two previous Super Bowls the Redskins had won, and the one thing I can say is that we were the only Redskins team to win a Super Bowl in a nonstrike year. That's something to be proud of. I don't ever say, "Hey, *I* was able to win the Super Bowl," because it was never about me as an individual. There was not one player who took the spotlight for anything that we did as a team. It was a group of guys who had a team mission that was achieved that Super Bowl Sunday. It's something we'll never forget. I can say in all honesty that I just want to be known for being a part of that group that dedicated itself to the Washington Redskins, to having a great, great season, and to beating the Buffalo Bills in Super Bowl XXVI.

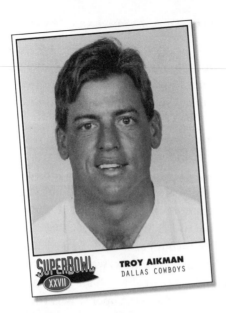

TROY AIKMAN
DALLAS COWBOYS

SUPER BOWL
XXVII

SUPER BOWL XXVII

DALLAS COWBOYS 52
BUFFALO BILLS 27

TROY AIKMAN

I was twenty-six in 1992, my fourth year in the NFL. In 1989, my rookie season as Dallas's quarterback and Jimmy Johnson's first year as the head coach, the Cowboys had gone only 1–15, but we improved to 7–9 in 1990 then to 11–5 with a playoff win in 1991. Our goal had been pretty much as Jimmy had established it, which was to do better every year, and in 1992 that meant winning the NFC Championship Game. But, while that was our goal at training camp, we were still a football team that didn't know how good it was. We didn't know if that goal was attainable. So it was exciting for everybody when we started playing well and winning and putting together a 13–3 record to win the Eastern Division by two games over Philadelphia. The Eagles were a team we had really struggled against ever since I came into the league, and they had beaten us in Philadelphia during the season. Although we had won the second game in Dallas, we knew it would be a real test for us when we met for a third time in the playoffs, which they'd made as a wild-card team. It really helped our confidence to beat them pretty easily, 34–10, in Dallas, to reach the NFC Championship Game against the 49ers. We had gotten to where we had wanted to go back at training camp.

We flew out to San Francisco to play the 49ers. They had lost only twice that year and had just eliminated Washington, the defending world champions, and nobody really gave us much of a chance. I don't even know if we thought we were going to win that ball game, although Jimmy Johnson expressed his confidence. I'm not sure what the general mood of the team was, but it seemed like everybody was loose and just said, "Hey, we'll just go out and play." We didn't really know what was going to take place that game, but the next thing we know, we'd won 30–20 and we're off to the Super Bowl. I remember flying back to Dallas that night and still trying to comprehend that we were actually going to the Super Bowl. When we had gone out to play against the 49ers, we were so focused on that game, I don't think it had crossed anybody's mind that we were only one game away from the Super Bowl. Now it had sunk in, and what an exciting realization that was.

Dallas was the youngest team in the NFL, yet we were such a talented team that we were able to overcome our youth and inexperience. Our youth was a big reason we were considered underdogs against San Francisco, but I think it really was to our advantage because our attitude was to just play. That team, more than any other team I've been on, just went out onto the field and played, played as well as it could, and won games. It really didn't get caught up in the significance of each game or what the impact would be if we won or lost. We didn't worry about who the opponent was or what each game meant. We just went out and played football, and before we knew it we were in the Super Bowl and nobody could believe it.

After a week in Dallas we flew out to Los Angeles for the week leading up to the Super Bowl. It was a very special week for me because we were going to play in the Rose Bowl in Pasadena, and before that we practiced at UCLA, where I had gone to college. At our practice field I got to see a lot of the people I'd known when I was playing ball there. So it was a unique experience for me.

Our opponent was the Buffalo Bills, who had beaten the Miami Dolphins for their third consecutive AFC championship. Of course, I had seen Buffalo's previous Super Bowls against the Giants and the Redskins. Buffalo had lost both games, but I didn't think that would make it any easier for us. From my perspective, I looked at Buffalo as a talented team that had been there before and knew what it was like; and I knew, because they hadn't won when they thought they should have, just how hungry they were going to be on game day. I know that during the week, there was a lot of talk in the media about how they had learned from their Super Bowl experiences and were totally focused on Super Bowl XXVII and beating us.

However, we were confident. We had just had, in Dallas after beating San Francisco and then in California, as good a two weeks of practice as I can recall the Cowboys ever having. We really went into Super Bowl XXVII thinking that we could continue to play at that level. Jimmy Johnson had a lot to do with that. He really set the tempo for our football team, and throughout that postseason and going into the Super Bowl, he was always confident that we'd win. He was pretty cheery before the game began on Super Sunday and that came across to the players. I think that Jimmy was the ideal coach for a Super Bowl; that game against Buffalo was the perfect situation for him. Some coaches get uptight when they realize what is at stake in such an important game, but with Jimmy, it was just the opposite. He would really rise to the occasion and be almost more relaxed than he'd be in games with less meaning. He didn't mind the pressure of the Super Bowl. In fact, even during the game he was having a good time and was very upbeat. That helped the players feel at ease.

Playing in the Super Bowl had been a goal of mine and a *dream* of mine that had come true. And when I went into that game against Buffalo, I said I was going to completely enjoy the experience because I didn't know if I'd get another chance in my life to play in a Super Bowl. And I was able to do that. From the time I got to the stadium until I left after we'd won the game, I was fully aware of everything that was happening.

Everyone's adrenaline was really going at the beginning of the first quarter. I know that I was having a hard time catching my breath after I came on the field and that was the case with everyone in the huddle. We didn't do well on our first possession. Then we had a punt blocked by Steve Tasker, their All-Pro special teams guy. A few plays later Thurman Thomas ran the ball into the end zone and suddenly Buffalo led 7–0. I wouldn't say we were in shock from what had just happened or worried that we couldn't recover from something like that because of our youth, but I think we were all concerned. There was concern when we fell behind because when we had gone out offensively we hadn't done anything

January 31, 1993, at the Rose Bowl in Pasadena, California
Paid Attendance: 98,374
AFC Champion: Buffalo Bills (14–5)
Head Coach: Marv Levy
NFC Champion: Dallas Cowboys (15–3)
Head Coach: Jimmy Johnson

STARTING LINEUPS

OFFENSE			DEFENSE		
Buffalo		**Dallas**	**Buffalo**		**Dallas**
James Lofton	WR	Alvin Harper	Phil Hansen	LE	Tony Tolbert
Will Wolford	LT	Mark Tuinei		LT	Tony Casillas
Jim Ritcher	LG	Nate Newton	Jeff Wright	NT	
Kent Hull	C	Mark Stepnoski		RT	Russell Maryland
Glenn Parker	RG	John Gesek	Bruce Smith	RE	Charles Haley
Howard Ballard	RT	Erik Williams	Marvcus Patton	LOLB	
Pete Metzelaars	TE	Jay Novacek		LLB	Vinson Smith
Andre Reed	WR	Michael Irvin	Shane Conlan	LILB	
Jim Kelly	QB	Troy Aikman		MLB	Robert Jones
Don Beebe	RB	Daryl Johnston	Cornelius Bennett	RILB	
Thurman Thomas	RB	Emmitt Smith		RLB	Ken Norton
			Darryl Talley	ROLB	
			James Williams	LCB	Kevin Smith
			Nate Odomes	RCB	Larry Brown
			Henry Jones	SS	Thomas Everett
			Mark Kelso	FS	James Washington

SUBSTITUTIONS

Buffalo: K—Steve Christie. P—Chris Mohr. Offense: Receivers—Rob Awalt, Brad Lamb, Keith McKeller, Steve Tasker. Linemen—John Davis, John Fina, Mitch Frerotte, Adam Lingner. Backs—Kenneth Davis, Carwell Gardner, Frank Reich (QB). Defense: Linebackers—Carlton Bailey, Keith Goganious, Mark Maddox. Linemen—Mike Lodish, Mark Pike. Backs—Matt Darby, Chris Hale, Clifford Hicks, Kirby Jackson. DNP—Keith Willis.

Dallas: K—Lin Elliott. P—Mike Saxon. Offense: Receivers—Kelvin Martin, Jimmy Smith, Derek Tennell. Linemen—Frank Cornish, Kevin Gogan, Dale Hellestrae. Backs—Tommie Agee, Steve Beurlein, Derrick Gainer. Defense: Linebackers—Dixon Edwards, Godfrey Myles, Mickey Pruitt. Linemen—Chad Hennings, Jim Jeffcoat, Jimmie Jones, Leon Lett. Backs—Kenneth Gant, Clayton Holmes, Issiac Holt, Ray Horton, Darren Woodson.

Buffalo	7	3	7	0—17
Dallas	14	14	3	21—52

Buff	Thomas 2 run (Christie kick)
Dall	Novacek 23 pass from Aikman (Elliott kick)
Dall	J. Jones 2 fumble return (Elliott kick)
Buff	FG Christie 21
Dall	Irvin 19 pass from Aikman (Elliott kick)
Dall	Irvin 18 pass from Aikman (Elliott kick)
Dall	FG Elliott 20
Buff	Beebe 40 pass from Reich (Christie kick)
Dall	Harper 45 pass from Aikman (Elliott kick)
Dall	E. Smith 10 run (Elliott kick)
Dall	Norton 9 fumble return (Elliott kick)
MVP:	Troy Aikman (Dallas)

with the ball. When you have something happen like that quick score off a blocked punt, especially so early in the game, there's a major momentum shift. You don't want things to quickly get out of control and to fall further behind. That can happen. Fortunately for us, our defense played very well and kept Buffalo's scoring down, limiting them to only a field goal for the rest of the half. When the game was still close in the first half, our defense had a great goal-line stand and several big turnovers that shifted the momentum back in our favor.

In fact, our first score came after an interception. We blitzed Jim Kelly and James Washington intercepted to give us the ball in Buffalo territory just past midfield. (Washington, who had been a year ahead of me at UCLA, would also get a couple of turnovers against Buffalo in the next Super Bowl.) Two passes later, the first to Michael Irvin and the second to Jay Novacek, and we tied the game, 7–7.

I had been consulted by Jimmy and his coaches about the offensive game plan we were going to use against Buffalo. Norv Turner, our offensive coordinator, and I had worked closely together, going over the plan thoroughly. I remember that we talked a lot about what we would try to do early in the game. We had discussed their pass defense and expected that they would play us with a lot of two-deep coverage and roll their corners. And when we got out there in the first couple of series, they were doing just what we thought they would do. They were playing two-deep coverage to take our wideouts, Michael Irvin and Alvin Harper, out of the game, and I was forced on a number of occasions to come underneath to the backs or our tight end Jay Novacek. The Bills were also blitzing to try to get pressure on me. And they did that effectively as well. Their guys were moving pretty good.

From what I recall, we ran mostly to the left, with Emmitt Smith behind tackle Mark Tuinei and guard Nate Newton. And we threw mostly to the middle and right, but that wasn't because of anything in our game plan. Early on, we threw those passes down the middle because we wanted to come underneath their deep coverage. If we were going to have success throwing the ball, that's where we were going to have to go. That's what happened on our first touchdown drive, when I hit Irvin coming over the middle for 20 yards and then hit Novacek on a seam pass for a touchdown. On the play to Jay, I didn't think I could get it in to him. But the safety, Mark Kelso, was slow to react to the ball, and Jay made a nice catch while running into the end zone.

People would talk about our big, strong offensive line and about me, Emmitt Smith, and Michael Irvin, but they didn't talk about Jay Novacek in the way I thought that they should. Jay was as big a part of our offense as any of the others, because he did so much at the tight-end position. He blocked, ran great patterns and got free in traffic, had tremendous hands, and was a tough runner once he caught the ball. Defenses talked about trying to stop the other guys, especially Michael, but, as would continue to be the case in future years, Jay was really the one who made everything possible. Defenses had to be very careful what they did against us, especially if they put all their efforts into stopping Michael. They forgot about Jay and he was a great, great player. It has always bothered me that Jay hasn't been recognized as much as the rest of us have been.

Irvin, Harper, and Novacek worked well together, so that at least one of them would get open when we wanted to throw. They knew what each other was doing and what I was doing and where the coverage was, and they could be very creative. We also had Kelvin Martin coming in as our third wide receiver in passing situations and he was an exceptional role player.

In the second quarter, Jim Kelly hurt his leg on a hard tackle by Ken Norton and had to leave the game. The opposing quarterback being knocked from a game wasn't really something I'd be concerned with because I had other things to focus on. I will say that when you were playing some teams, you could make an argument that, "So and so is down; now they're in real trouble." But remember that Kelly's backup, Frank Reich, was the one who had just brought Buffalo back from a record 32-point deficit in the AFC wild-card game against Houston. He had played well in the playoffs up to the Super Bowl. So even when Jim went down, and as good a player as Jim was, our football team didn't relax and think that we now had control of everything. Frank had proven himself to be a good quarterback.

Reich started out well and brought the Bills offense downfield to where Christie could kick a field goal to cut our lead to 14–10. But then our offense started moving the ball better. No question—it all started with our offensive line, with Tuinei, Newton, right guard John Gesek, right tackle Erik Williams, and center Mark Stepnoski. Tuinei, Newton, and Williams would also be part of our line in Super Bowls XXVIII and XXX. They each weighed over 300 pounds but were mobile. For me to have the time to throw that day, and for us to be able to run the football as well as we needed to, that line had to play well. And it did.

Of course, it helped to have a running back like Emmitt Smith, who was the NFL's rushing leader. He had gained over 100 yards against the 49ers and did it again against Buffalo in the first of several tremendous

Super Bowl performances he'd have with us. Emmitt is just a gifted athlete and an exceptional running back. Also, he has a great attitude and is a great competitor. Emmitt wants the ball.

We were running Emmitt a great deal by the second quarter not only because he could pick up yardage but also because we wanted to force Buffalo's secondary out of that two-deep coverage. Our philosophy on offense was that a defense could not stop us from running the football with just seven guys. If the Bills were going to play the two-deep coverage to try to take away Irvin, Harper, and our other wide receivers, we were going to hammer them with running; and when they would then try to take away our running game by bringing up a safety, we were going to be able to go to the wide receivers in man-on-man situations. That's what happened.

We felt that they were at their best when their cornerbacks were up on our wideouts and that we could throw the ball efficiently only if we could get those corners to back off of our guys. The Bills kept their corners up early in the game and limited our passing game to those underneath passes to Novacek and Smith. But after we had gone ahead 14–7, when Haley put on a big pass rush and Jimmie Jones ran in Kelly's fumble, they changed their defense. I guess they were that concerned about us just running the football at 'em once we had a lead. They figured that with the two-deep coverage, they wouldn't get the run support on Emmitt that they'd get if they played a coverage-three or a man-to-man coverage. So to try to stop Emmitt, they stopped doing what had been working, and I think that was a mistake. Had they stayed in the coverages that they were using earlier in the game, the game might have stayed close. But they went to man-to-man and coverage-three and brought a safety up for run support, and then we had them where we wanted them.

We got down to their 19 and then I threw a touchdown pass to Michael Irvin, who now had man coverage on him and could get open easier. The intended play was for Michael to fake to the corner to get cornerback Nate Odomes to bite and then cut back to the center of the field. But Michael felt Odomes was sitting on him a little bit, so he cut the route short. As a result the ball was late getting out. In fact, when I let it go, I thought it was going to come back the other way. I thought Odomes was going to intercept. But Michael was able to catch it and get into the end zone. It was those types of things that just went our way that day. And they didn't have anything going their way. On that particular play, they might have had an interception, but instead we got a touchdown, and on some of their fumbles that we recovered, the ball just bounced our way.

One of those fumbles came on their first play from scrimmage after Irvin's catch. Leon Lett knocked the ball away from Thurman Thomas and we recovered inside their 20. We came back on the very next play with another touchdown pass to Irvin, who made a leaping catch. That was when our killer instinct was evident. We wanted to put them away early.

In fact, with a 28–10 halftime lead, we talked in the locker room about how we were going to receive the kickoff to begin the second half and how we would go down the field and score a touchdown to really put the game away. We almost did it but had to settle for a short field goal by Lin Elliott. So we didn't put the game away and on the last play of the third quarter Reich connected on a long touchdown pass to Don Beebe that pulled them within 14 points.

Going into the fourth quarter, it's safe to say that nobody on our team thought the game was over or that we could afford to stop playing as well as we had been. But I don't know if we felt concerned that Buffalo was now only two touchdowns behind, even though they had big-play guys like Thurman Thomas, James Lofton, and Andre Reed, who made several catches and picked up a lot of yardage that game. We had been having a lot of success offensively against the Bills defense and felt confident that we would go back on the field and do it some more. However, it wasn't until after I completed the 45-yard touchdown pass to Alvin Harper that I felt completely relaxed and knew with total certainty that we were going to win the game. That pass was down the right sideline. They were in a coverage-two on that play, and I pumped to Novacek down the middle and got the safety to freeze in his tracks to watch Jay while letting Harper run by. Their corner just didn't follow Alvin closely enough up the field, so Alvin was pretty free. I was able to just lay it out there for Alvin to run under. That put us up, 38–17, and really put the game away. However, it wasn't hard to keep playing, although the outcome of the game was determined. It was easy to play; it was fun to play. As I said before, I was determined to enjoy every minute of this game in case I never made it back.

Right after Harper's touchdown, an interception by Thomas Everett led to another touchdown, this one a 10-yard run by Emmitt Smith. It was the first of Smith's many career Super Bowl touchdowns. And we scored again when Ken Norton ran a fumble back for a touchdown, making the final score 52–17.

The Bills had a number of turnovers we were able to capitalize on. In those types of games—and we'd been in games where we were the team making the turnovers—it just kind of snowballs on you once things start going bad. You're out there struggling and trying to do everything to get back in the game—and that just lends itself to those types of misplays happening. It just seemed that everything went against the Bills.

You might figure that after two Super Bowl losses the Bills seemed brittle when things began to turn against them, but I didn't sense that in this game. However, I would notice it in Super Bowl XXVIII, the following year. In that game, we played poorly in the first half and headed into the locker room trailing the Bills. Buffalo had played exceptionally well and I was thinking that it didn't look good for us. But I looked over and saw their players go in and you would have thought that they were the team who was behind. At that moment I kind of thought they were a team that just felt that something bad was going to happen, that they were snakebit in Super Bowls. But in Super Bowl XXVII, I never felt that.

Much of what happened to the Bills in Super Bowl XXVII was due to our phenomenal defense. I was watching the defense all game long and Haley, Norton, and so many other guys made big, big plays. Our offense would get a lot of recognition after this Super Bowl, but I think it was really the defense that allowed us to reach the Super Bowl. Our defense had been that good the whole season and maybe didn't get enough credit. In the Super Bowl, because of the number of points we put up, it was maybe assumed that the offense got them all. But the record nine turnovers the defense got led to many of the points the offense put up; and they got two touchdowns of their own on fumble recoveries. They almost got a third fumble recovery touchdown when Leon Lett ran over 60 yards after picking up the ball, only to have it slapped out of his hand when he waved it around before crossing the goal line. I was watching the play and saw Don Beebe catch him from behind at the last moment. I know Leon felt bad about holding the ball up, sure, and would have done it differently if he had a second chance. I don't think he or anybody else expected the scrutiny he would get following that play. Why would he? The game was over already and it didn't matter if he scored or not. It was just one of those things. But, yeah, he felt bad about it.

People always ask me what plays I remember most in that Super Bowl. But you know, it's really not the big plays that stand out in my mind, though I certainly remember them. The thing I recall most about winning that Super Bowl is seeing the faces of all those players who had been on the Cowboys when we were 1–15 three years earlier, when everyone was taking shots at us because we were so bad. There were a number of people who said we'd never do it with the players we had. And we did it.

So that's the thing I remember most. In fact, I have a picture hanging up in my house that was taken on the sidelines after we knew we were going to win, and it really typifies the whole experience. It shows it all, because it shows the happiness and just the satisfaction of knowing what we were accomplishing—the greatest thing in football is winning the world championship. As I said at training camp, we were so young that we really had no idea we were as good as we were or what we were going to be able to accomplish during the season. That win really was special.

Dallas was a team that had certainly improved since I was a rookie. The team had grown considerably and now had a lot of talent. But that talent wasn't the reason we won the Super Bowl. We won because of a group of guys who were very, very close and who genuinely cared about each other and who had great character and who were extremely unselfish. They were good people, and when you have good people with the kind of work ethic and talent that we had, then you are going to win a lot of Super Bowls. We would do that. But I'd say now that winning Super Bowl XXVII was the best for me. That was the most fun I've had playing pro football. That was the happiest time.

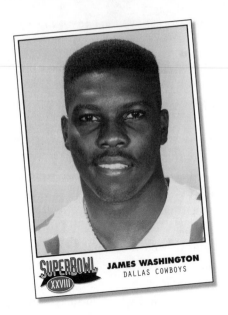

JAMES WASHINGTON
DALLAS COWBOYS

SUPER BOWL XXVIII

DALLAS COWBOYS 30
BUFFALO BILLS 13

JAMES WASHINGTON

I'm the last person back there, the last guy receivers have to get by before getting into the end zone. Everybody else can make a mistake, but I'm the one fans boo, because every time I make a mistake the scoreboard lights up. Even when a corner gets beat they've got to blame it on me. I've been a safety for a long time and it never changes.

I was a free safety for Terry Donahue at UCLA on the 1985 team that beat Iowa in the Rose Bowl and the 1987 team that had Troy Aikman, Ken Norton, Jr., and Carnell Lake. I was projected to be a top draft pick, but I blew my right knee out my senior year and didn't have a chance to rehab it before I performed at the scouting combine. I ended up being drafted in the fifth round. It took my rookie year to recover and then I was ready to go. I was a good 4.4 in the 40 before I hurt my knee, and after I got better I ran a legit 4.5.

After two years on the Los Angeles Rams, I came to Dallas as a Plan B free agent. I joined the Cowboys in Jimmy Johnson's second year, 1990, right after they lost 15 games. We went 7–9 and missed the playoffs by a game because Troy Aikman got hurt and Babe Laufenberg was the backup quarterback. Babe was the kind of guy you don't remember unless you played with him—and in those last couple of games you wish you didn't.

The defense developed as quickly as the offense because we used a system that Jimmy Johnson and his coordinator, Dave Wannstedt, used when they were together on the Miami Hurricanes. Jimmy ran the offense, but he was really a defensive coach, too. He focused on getting defensive backs and linebackers who had quickness and speed, who could really come off the corner. In our system, the safeties were like 10-deep linebackers and thought run first, pass second. We lined up 10 or 11 yards deep in kind of an umbrella-type coverage with four across and the corners about 8 yards deep. People thought we were playing a lot of zone, but after 10 yards we were in man-to-man coverage on the receivers in our areas. The defense used five-man pressure every once in a while, and then we always had a safety in the hole, but we didn't do much blitzing. When I was up on the line getting fumbles I was just playing aggressive. It wasn't a blitz call—it was just run-pass reading. One thing our coaches really tried to teach us was reading keys. The safeties played a big part in the run defense because we didn't have guys two-gapping, but had every guy going to his own slot. It was that simple a defense, but we had a lot of speed and aggressive guys who really wanted to get after the ball. We were able to become a dominant defense, and that as much as our offense helped us reach the Super Bowl so quickly.

In Super Bowl XXVII we played Buffalo. To be honest, that game, like Super Bowl XXVIII, was turned around by myself. Buffalo was already ahead 7–0 early in the game and driving the ball down our throats when Ken Gant came off the corner and put a lot of pressure on Jim Kelly, the Bills' tight end fell down, and I just happened to be where I needed to be when Kelly threw the ball. That particular interception was one of the biggest of my career. I've always been known for making plays come playoff time and in big-game situations, but to have that happen where I grew up, where I played college ball, in the stadium where I'd won a Rose Bowl, in the Super Bowl, in my first Super Bowl—it was like "Wow!" It was incredible. It felt exactly like it should have felt. When we quickly scored the tying touchdown off the turnover, I was on top of the world. But after eight more turnovers by our defense, this key interception just kind of got ignored. I had the turnover that turned the game around, but it was overlooked once we set the Super Bowl record by causing nine turnovers. I said to myself, "If I ever get to the Super Bowl again, I'm going to really turn it out, where nobody will not remember what I've done," and fortunately I had the opportunity to do that the following year.

The next year Jimmy Johnson and I got into it. At the safeties, besides me, we had Thomas Everett and Darren Woodson. He wanted to play Woodson at strong safety, where Everett had been playing, so they were going to move Everett to free safety. I didn't even have the chance to fight to keep my job—it was just taken away from me. I had led the team in interceptions every year that I'd started and had gone through the whole rebuilding process, but now Jimmy was splitting time between me and Thomas Everett at free safety, figuring it would make us more competitive. That's the kind of thing that Jimmy did. I had split time when I first got to Dallas in 1990 and I hadn't really liked it, so I decided just to play nickel defense and let Everett have the job.

I started the first game of the season against Washington because Woodson was out, but I hurt my knee; then Woodson came back and he and Thomas Everett were starting. And I wouldn't start again until the last game of the season. It was a rough experience not starting, but I was smashing people the whole year. Actually, I had more playing time on the field than the starters. I'd probably come in after the first series. We had a lot of formations where I'd go in. The 45 package has five defensive backs in the game, a dime package has six defensive backs in the game, so I'd play in both packages. In the dime package, you'd have all the defensive backs in, and you'd take two linebackers out. In the 45 you'd leave two linebackers in and move a defensive back into a linebacker position to cover the receiver. When we would use the 45 package in Super Bowl XXVIII, Woodson would move to the linebacker position, while Everett returned to strong safety, and I played free safety.

I could feel that it would eventually come apart for the Cowboys. We had a lot of controversy that whole year, especially in the beginning, and it wasn't limited to the defensive backfield. Emmitt Smith, who had led the league in rushing the year before, held out for a new contract. Most people felt that he deserved . . . everything. When they negotiated Troy Aikman's contract right after they finally did Emmitt's, there was no problem giving him $50 million, and all Emmitt had asked for was $15 million. I think it was kind of like a slap in Emmitt's face. I was aware that Emmitt was disappointed that he had to hold out. The two of us were very good friends. In his rookie year we had lived right next to each other and I took him under my wing—before long he became an eagle.

When Jerry Jones wouldn't give Emmitt a new contract right away, I think that's when Jimmy Johnson's conflict with Jerry really started to build. And when Emmitt had to hold out and we lost our first two games, I think that was when the trigger was pulled. I think that was the big part of why Jimmy ended up leaving. When you tell a coach to go win and then you don't bring in one of the best players on the team so that he can win, then you're not giving your coach a fair shot. There was always friction between Jimmy and Jerry Jones, even before. It wasn't just something that happened out of the blue. Jimmy liked to have control over the players he got, but Jerry was the owner. You have two headstrong guys who wanted only their way. We were in the biggest city in a big state, but they both couldn't fit inside.

This upset some guys who were real close to Jimmy Johnson, but it didn't affect me, because it seemed like he had been trying to get me out of there since he got me. Even though he brought me there. Jimmy was a damn good football coach, but personality-wise, off the field, he was a little different. Remember, it was his decision that I didn't start. I wasn't the type of guy who would concern myself with trying to talk to him about it. I just played football. I really enjoyed the game and just tried to play it to the best of my abilities.

Before we beat San Francisco for the second straight year in the NFC Championship Game, Jimmy Johnson called up a radio station to say we were going to win. He wanted everybody to know how sure he was. That was the type of arrogance that his players showed. We were a very young team and took our lead from Jimmy Johnson. It was kind of like being in the military, where you take on the attitude of your general. You see that your general has a lot of confidence, then you begin to have a lot of confidence. That's what we had that year. For instance, after we lost a meaningless game in Atlanta during the season, while all their fans were getting on us, we were saying, "We'll be back here soon." We knew that the Super Bowl was going to be played at the Georgia Dome, so we knew we were going to be back. Wherever the Super Bowl was going to be played, that's where we were going to be. We were destined to get back there; we were determined to get back there.

A lot of players arrive in town a week before the Super Bowl and take off their pads when they go on the practice field. That worked for some guys, but not for us. Jimmy liked a high-tempo atmosphere, so we practiced to the limit, with the same intensity we had when we were play-ing a game. The defense didn't knock Emmitt around in practice or tackle Troy, but receivers knew better than to run posts and in routes on us, because we'd lay them out, even though we were teammates. Michael Irvin, Alvin Harper, and Jay Novacek knew what the deal was and came off the ball as if they were in a game and practiced harder than anybody I've ever seen. We practiced like that until the last day.

Buffalo had lost three consecutive Super Bowls, but they were a tough team. Although we had beaten them badly in the previous Super Bowl and we were a big favorite, a lot of people forgot that we had lost to Buf-falo during the season, 13–10. Before the game, the media tried to com-pare the two teams. It was obvious that we had the better defense, so the comparisons they made were all on offense: Troy Aikman with Jim Kelly, Michael Irvin with Andre Reed, Emmitt Smith with Thurman Thomas. Emmitt and Thurman were real good friends off the field, so those two always wanted to best the other when they played each other. Part of Emmitt's drive was that he wanted to be the best running back on the field in every game. The other players, at least on defense, wanted him to do well, but we didn't concern ourselves with whether he was getting more yards than Thurman in the Super Bowl. Our approach to the game was pretty businesslike.

We hated each other on the practice field, but we were pretty tight off the field. As in any large group, you had cliques where certain guys hung out only with each other, but I'm sure offensive guys and defensive guys were going out together that week in Atlanta. I'm not much of a social person—I'm a loner—so I pretty much always hung out by myself.

I didn't do anything out of the ordinary, but that Super Bowl Week was great because Jimmy told me that I was going to be starting. I knew that after the season the Cowboys were going to decide whether to keep me and start me or to trade me to a team looking for a starting free safety. So I realized I was going to have the chance to market myself in the Super Bowl. So the whole week, the whole process, the whole buildup was real special for me. I couldn't wait to play in the Super Bowl again and was I ever happy to be playing Buffalo again.

Everyone was asking if Troy would be able to play in the Super Bowl after having suffered a concussion in the 49ers game only a week before. To be honest, we thought the defense could win the Super Bowl on its own, but you always get concerned if you don't have your true leader going to the big dance. With Troy I wasn't worried. I had seen Troy take some big, big hits and come back and I'd shake my head in amazement.

He was a country boy with a lot of heart and character, and I knew he wouldn't miss that game for nothing.

What I did mostly that week was watch film, which is what I usually did. I went through a process of breaking down the Bills offense. They had one running back, Thurman Thomas, who was part of their passing attack, and four receivers: tight end Pete Metzelaars and wide receivers Andre Reed, Don Beebe, and Bill Brooks. I studied each receiver, seeing the types of routes they ran, and I focused in on Metzelaars because I would primarily be playing him. As a student of the game, I tried to determine what they could do out of their four-receiver formation and learned there were only a few patterns they could run. I figured out that it was kind of like the run-and-shoot, where they had only four or five routes. I concluded that it was a system where you could tell what was going to happen by reading what the slot receiver was doing.

In the early morning before the game I was still watching film. But that wasn't my intention. For some reason I could hardly sleep, and when I woke up at 5:30 A.M., I got out of bed and went down to the film room and watched film by myself. Man, that was one of the longest nights of my life. Then the bus ride from the hotel to the stadium was the longest bus ride. It was going to be such an important game for me and I just couldn't wait to play.

At the Georgia Dome, I went out early and did my usual ritual of walking through the stadium and doing warm-ups. The day just felt so special to me. In the locker room, we were all looking into each other's eyes and we knew what we had to do. We weren't absolutely sure we were going to win because they had beaten us earlier in the season, 13–10, but we knew that we could beat 'em. That first loss was one of those "we-let-that-one-get-away" games. Before the game, Michael Irvin was upbeat as usual, and he, Ken Norton, and I were sitting together and talking in the training room in the back, away from what was going on with the other guys in the locker room. I remember telling Michael and Ken, "This is the only chance that I'll get. I have to show everybody what I can do." I did have to show the world that I could play. Even though I'd been knocking people's helmets off in the '93 season, you kind of get °lost in the shuffle on a team full of superstars. But I had no doubt it was my day.

It was extremely exciting going onto the field and hearing the national anthem. It was my second Super Bowl but it didn't matter: It was the Super Bowl and you can never take anything away from the Super Bowl. You are standing there, a player on one of the two best teams in the league, and everybody in the world is watching. And we called it "Show Time." Put it on.

The game began with a big play. Kevin Williams received their opening kickoff and took off running down the sideline. He got 50 yards on the return and we were like, "We're going to kill 'em!" But what I think that play did was relax us because our offense went out and got stopped. Now, I was like, "Oh, man . . . the Bills came to play." We got just a field goal from Eddie Murray, so it was 3–0. And then the Bills offense came out and had a pretty good drive. Buffalo used the no-huddle early in the game and they were in a groove. Even when we stopped them, Steve Christie kicked a field goal from over 50 yards away to tie the game. So we're saying, "Wait a minute. . . ."

Minutes later they had the ball back in good field position and were driving. The Bills tried a shuffle pass from Kelly to Thurman Thomas. We'd heard that they had a special play they were going to use, but we didn't know exactly what it was. It was a slow developing play and it really wasn't a great play to run against a defense with our quickness and swarming linebackers and defensive backs. That play would be their downfall the whole game. Thomas did catch that shuffle pass, but I was already there and hit him from the side and got my arm in there and knocked the ball out of his hands.

That fumble was the culmination of how I had been playing—and thinking—all along. Earlier Andre Reed ran a pass route across the middle. I was at free safety and came up and whacked him. He caught the ball, but there was then a "conversation" in which he was told, "Those hits are going to happen all day. And if you choose to stay in this game, you're going to hurt." Thomas Everett was right in line with me because Beebe came out on another route and got splattered. So we were trying to make a statement with our hard hits. And there was a verbal statement, too. That was part of the game. You're not trash talking; you're just trying to tell them: "Don't think you can just come around here and catch passes all day." Eventually our physical play took a toll on those receivers. It was a game for our entire defense. We showed people it wasn't a fluke that we got all those turnovers the year before. We came out roaring again.

We got only a field goal after Thomas's turnover. I wasn't disappointed. In fact, I hadn't even been watching what the offense had been doing because the defense was trying to figure out why no one up front had made the tackle on the shuffle pass. All you can do is handle your own. You have to do your job and make your plays and not concern yourself with the offense.

January 30, 1994, at the Georgia Dome in Atlanta

Paid Attendance: 72,817

NFC Champion: Dallas Cowboys (14–4)
Head Coach: Jimmy Johnson
AFC Champion: Buffalo Bills (14–4)
Head Coach: Marv Levy

STARTING LINEUPS

OFFENSE

Dallas		Buffalo
Alvin Harper	WR	Don Beebe
Mark Tuinei	LT	John Fina
Nate Newton	LG	Glenn Parker
John Gesek	C	Kent Hull
Kevin Gogan	RG	John Davis
Erik Williams	RT	Howard Ballard
Jay Novacek	TE	Pete Metzelaars
Michael Irvin	WR	Andre Reed
	WR	Bill Brooks
Troy Aikman	QB	Jim Kelly
Daryl Johnston	RB	
Emmitt Smith	RB	Thurman Thomas

DEFENSE

Dallas		Buffalo
Tony Tolbert	LE	Phil Hansen
Tony Casillas	LT	
	NT	Jeff Wright
Leon Lett	RT	
Charles Haley	RE	Bruce Smith
	LOLB	Marvcus Patton
	LILB	Carnelius Bennett
Ken Norton	MLB	
	RILB	Mark Maddox
Darrin Smith	RLB	
	ROLB	Darryl Talley
Darren Woodson	B	
Kevin Smith	LCB	Mickey Washington
Larry Brown	RCB	Nate Odomes
Thomas Everett	SS	Henry Jones
James Washington	FS	Mark Kelso

SUBSTITUTIONS

Dallas: K—Eddie Murray. P—John Jett. Offense: Receivers—Scott Galbraith, Kevin Williams. Linemen—Frank Cornish, Dale Hellestrae. Backs—Lincoln Coleman, Derrick Gainer, Bernie Kosar. Defense: Linebackers—Dixon Edwards, Robert Jones, Godfrey Myles, Matt Vanderbeek. Linemen—Chad Hennings, Jim Jeffcoat, Jimmie Jones, Russell Maryland. Backs—Bill Bates, Joe Fishback, Kenneth Gant, Elvis Patterson, Dave Thomas. DNP—Derrick Lassic.

Buffalo: K—Steve Christie. P—Chris Mohr. Offense: Receivers—Russell Copeland, Keith McKeller, Steve Tasker. Linemen—Jerry Crafts, Mike Devlin, Adam Lingner, Jim Ritcher. Backs—Kenneth Davis, Carwell Gardner, Frank Reich. Defense: Linebackers—Monty Brown, Keith Goganious, Richard Harvey. Linemen—Oliver Barnett, Mike Lodish, Mark Pike. Backs—Matt Darby, Jerome Henderson, Kirk Schulz, Thomas Smith. DNP—Nate Turner.

Dallas	6	0	14	10—30
Buffalo	3	10	0	0—13

Dall	FG Murray 41
Buff	FG Christie 54
Dall	FG Murray 24
Buff	T. Thomas 4 run (Christie kick)
Buff	FG Christie 28
Dall	Washington 46 fumble return (Murray kick)
Dall	E. Smith 15 run (Murray kick)
Dall	E. Smith 1 run (Murray kick)
Dall	FG Murray 20
MVP:	Emmitt Smith (Dallas)

I was the hold-up guy on punt returns. I held up the one receiver still out there by myself. So I was on the field when Dave Thomas, one of our rookies, got called for roughing the punter. It wasn't a good call because Dave didn't really run into their punter—Chris Mohr just did a good acting job. That was a big play because our defense had to come back on the field after having just stopped them. We were a bit winded and they were able to drive down the field and score the only touchdown of the half by either team on a short run by Thurman Thomas, who made a great move to get free. They were able to get another field goal by Christie before the half ended, so we were behind 13–6 at the break.

Although I wasn't watching the offense, I kind of figured that Troy wasn't having a great first half because I knew the offense wasn't having a great half—as Troy and Emmitt go, the offense goes. There were a lot of games in which Troy had slow starts and we didn't lose very often.

Kelly had a pretty good first half for Buffalo. The strategy we had going into the game against him was to make him throw deep by first shutting down their running game and then shutting down his short passing game. If you take his short stuff away—take his slots away, take his underneath passing away, take his tackle-box passing away—then you have a pretty good pass defense against Jim Kelly. But first, as in any game, you try to take the run away, because a team that can run dictates what goes on the field. If Thomas could run against us, then we wouldn't know when Kelly was going to pass. So we wanted to take Thomas out of the game and make Kelly throw long. Early on, they were able to pretty much run the ball against us and to stop our run. They could have beaten us if they had continued to do that. But winning teams take away something from the other team, and we were able to stop Thomas with our big boys up front.

We went in at halftime and Jimmy Johnson didn't say one word to anybody. The defense didn't say one word to the offense. The offense didn't say one word to the defense. Michael Irvin didn't say one word to James Washington and James Washington didn't say one word to Emmitt Smith or anyone else. There was silence in the locker room. We just looked at each other. Then the coaches made the adjustments that needed to be made. There was no hurrah, hurrah, no pep talks or tirades, we just went back out.

I walked with Leon Lett back onto the field, and I said, "Leon, you've got to give me something." I meant that he had to give me some plays to get this thing started. I was trying to pump him up. And lo and behold, as soon as Buffalo got the ball to start the third quarter, Leon caused Thomas to fumble, again on the shuffle pass, at the Bills 46. And the rest is history. I saw the ball on the ground and got so excited. The ball was *sooooo* big. That's why you could see me scoop it up so easy. I started to pitch the ball to Kevin Smith because we always did that in practice, but I was afraid to do that because anything could have happened. So I held onto it and the next thing you know I was on *Arsenio Hall.*

As I started to run, the first thing that crossed my mind was, "Where's Beebe?" I flashed back on Super Bowl XXVII when Leon ran toward the end zone with a fumble and Beebe ran him down and knocked the ball away. So I'm thinking, "Where's Beebe?" I was thinking of Beebe when I hesitated for a moment in front of a big, old lineman, and the best thing about it is that Leon Lett, who had caused the fumble, made the first block on my touchdown. I saw Leon coming, stopped, and Leon wiped out the lineman. It would have been funny if he'd wiped out Beebe. I knew Beebe was coming and saw him in front of me and that's when I stopped. He was the only guy I was worried about catching me. But then Everett knocked him out of the way. And Woodson got a block. It was hilarious to me because I was seeing all these Bills around me being wiped out by our guys. I could see all this because everything was so big and so clear in my eyes and it seemed like it was taking forever. I had a clear alley in front of me and I kind of followed Everett into the end zone. That might not have been a pretty run but it had to be one of my greatest runs ever. After that play, I was in a daze for the rest of the game.

We had only tied the game, 13–13, but the momentum had shifted. We were still smashing them, playing real aggressive defense. I remember Jim Jeffcoat making a big hit on a running back, Tony Tolbert coming off tackle and end and making plays on running backs, and Ken Norton and Charles Haley putting pressure on Kelly. You could see our defense just getting better and more aggressive as the game went on. I think our defense gave the offense the momentum they needed. Because we were no longer behind, we could just run the ball with Smith.

Emmitt started running the ball up their tail on almost every play and he put us ahead 20–13 with a 15-yard touchdown run. He was running sweeps behind our big linemen. I wasn't watching the offense but I saw the touchdown on the big monitor.

Early in the fourth quarter, Buffalo got the ball and had the opportunity to drive back downfield and be right back in the game. By this time they couldn't even make 5 yards running on first-and-10, especially with Thurman Thomas out with leg cramps, so when it got to be third-and-5 and the money was on the line, you knew they were going to pass. I think I had knocked Reed out of the game by then when I hit him on his side, so who could they throw it to other than Beebe? And they weren't going to go for a deep ball when they needed only 5 yards. I knew what play was coming and I actually went to our sideline and told our coaches exactly what coverage to be in. On that pass to Beebe, if we'd been in any other coverage than the one I asked for, it would have been wide open for them and the drive would have stayed alive. But what happened was their tight end tried to clear and go across and I was sitting right where I needed to be. I got a great break on the ball and I had an interception and ran it back about 12 yards to inside their 35. I wasn't thinking touchdown on that play. I was exhausted and had leg cramps and I wanted to just fall on the ground and get out of there. That's why Emmitt gets so much money to run the ball. He just kept running and ran away with the MVP.

I don't know if I would have been able to do an "I'm going to Disneyland" commercial if I'd been selected the MVP. I don't think Larry Brown would do one after Super Bowl XXX because they had never expected him to win the MVP award and didn't bother making a deal with his agent. The majority of the time it's either a quarterback or running back who gets to be the MVP. Not many defensive players win the award, so they don't get the chance to negotiate for that Disneyland thing. But I don't think my not getting the MVP award had anything to do with whether I was going to Disneyland.

But I will say that when I intercepted the ball it gave Emmitt the chance to blow it out of the water. He ran on 8 of 10 plays after I gave the offense the ball, and scored his second touchdown to put the game out of reach, 27–13. Murray would add a short field goal to make the final score 30–13.

Toward the end of the game, some of us were talking about the MVP award on the sidelines. Before the award was announced I went over just to congratulate Emmitt on his great game. So we were both on the sidelines while the game wound down. Then I heard that Emmitt had won the award, so I went to congratulate him on that, too. There was no need to be angry that I didn't get the award—although, if it had gone to anybody else but Emmitt Smith, then I would probably have been pissed. In his book, Emmitt said I should have been the co-MVP. I did everything I could possibly do that day—I played the best game that a defensive player could play, not just being instrumental in three turnovers, but as a full player with tackles and aggressiveness all game long. An 11-man defense tries to get three or four turnovers a game and put the offense in scoring position or score itself—we had a full-team defensive effort that day, but I accomplished those goals all by myself. I was personally involved in almost everything that happened that day.

Buffalo had lost for the fourth consecutive time in the Super Bowl and for the second straight time to Dallas. They had blown a halftime lead and been held scoreless by our defense in the second half. You know these guys off the field, and I felt real bad for Thurman Thomas for losing again. You want to go say something, but there's a different time and place for all that. I did talk to him after that year when we did a football camp together. We joked about it . . . but you don't joke about it too much.

I was so relieved that the season was over. We had been strong enough to overcome controversy, injuries, and those first two losses to become Super Bowl champions. But it had been a strain. I still was bound to the Cowboys for another year, so I asked them to trade me or Thomas Everett. It didn't make any sense sitting on the bench when I knew I could make an impact in the league. That Monday morning, Everett was traded. Jimmy Johnson did that before he left as coach—we knew a break with Jones had to come. We would have a pretty good year in 1994 under Barry Switzer, and be number-one in defense with the number-one secondary, and I would lead the team in interceptions again. I would have a Pro Bowl season. Then I would sign with Washington as a free agent. The next year, after Dallas won Super Bowl XXX, many other players would depart. I don't agree with those who say our second Super Bowl team was better than the first, but I think if we had kept that team together, we could have won 7 Super Bowls in 10 seasons.

When I retire and look back on my career, there's no doubt that Super Bowl XXVIII will rank very, very high. I've played better games, but to play that well and have it be in the Super Bowl was very exciting. Everywhere I go people tell me they saw what I did. People now say, "Hey, if Larry Brown deserved the MVP for his two interceptions in Super Bowl XXX, then James Washington definitely should have been the MVP in Super Bowl XXVIII for causing a fumble that led to a field goal, running back a fumble for a touchdown, making an interception that led to a touchdown, and making 11 solo tackles." It was a very special game. It was a day when you're at your best on the day you want to be at your best.

STEVE YOUNG
SAN FRANCISCO 49ERS

SUPER BOWL XXIX

SAN FRANCISCO 49ERS 49
SAN DIEGO CHARGERS 26

STEVE YOUNG

When I came to San Francisco from Tampa Bay in 1987, Joe Montana had the bad back. Bill Walsh told me that '87 was going to be Joe's last year. But he forgot to tell Joe. If I had known I'd come in to back up Joe for four years, I probably would have gone somewhere else. That's what the rub was. I understood the role of backup quarterback, and I filled it the best I could, but I just didn't like it. It wasn't in my personality. I did get a few starts over the years, and I finally started on a regular basis when Joe missed the '91 and '92 seasons with an elbow injury, but Joe was still there, waiting to return. It was very hard, because with my status changing every year, I could never get the control I wanted and be a full-time leader of the offense.

The 49ers were going to trade me. I demanded, they demanded, it was just always off and on. But in the end I kept pushing to stay. I knew I could walk away saying, "Well, I tried," but I didn't want to miss out on the chance of a lifetime, to try to quarterback San Francisco to a championship. Anyone can run away and try something else, but to stand firm and go into the lion's den, that's the ultimate challenge. I think I stayed because I knew I was going to experience something like that. The demands were so great that I knew that I'd find out how good I really was. I knew that was going to be the result, one way or the other, and that was what I wanted. I couldn't do it anywhere else. Being the quarterback of the 49ers, with all the pressure, was the best way to learn about myself.

You probably couldn't understand the pressure on me or feel what I was going through unless you were in San Francisco. The transition from Montana to me as the team's starting quarterback was so wrenching. It wasn't smooth in the sense that our times didn't fit together, with my career starting exactly when his career ended. Joe could still play when the 49ers decided to move him to Kansas City in 1993 and stick with me as their quarterback. He'd led the team to its four titles, so there was a lot of emotion about letting him go when he wasn't finished. I lived in the middle of that. It truly wasn't the case of putting pressure on myself—the pressure came from the outside, primarily from the media. You could put a name on it, you could put a face on it, you could do anything you wanted to it, but it didn't change the fact that it was all about championships. To be a great quarterback in San Francisco, you had to win the Super Bowl.

They didn't believe I was a great quarterback. Absolutely. It was repeated so often—"Steve Young isn't a great quarterback"—that it was like a self-mantra that you keep repeating until you believe it's true. I heard it so often that I couldn't fight it anymore. I kept trying to say, "I'm the MVP in the league; I can do all these things on the field; it's a team game, so you can't just look at me when we don't reach the Super Bowl." But finally I just said, "Nah, I'm not going to fight it anymore. Okay, I can't do anything to change their minds except win a championship." That made it a little easier.

We lost to Dallas 30–20 in the NFC Championship Game at the end of the 1992 season. Then Dallas beat us 38–21 in the NFC Championship Game at the end of the '93 season. That loss catapulted us to the next year, our championship year. We could not deal with that loss. It was too devastating. No one talked about it at all. To this day we still haven't dealt with it and it's probably a good thing. In some strange way, we accepted it.

We've used that game for years. After the first Dallas loss, we'd thought, "Let's just push harder; let's hold on tighter." We did that but we lost again. What that second loss told us was that we had gotten farther away from what we should be doing. We realized that our technique—close-to-the-vest, corporate, no emotion—wasn't working. So everyone from the top of the organization on down, including George Seifert, said "Screw it. Let's not worry about it so much. Let's relax, have a good time, and just let loose." George set the tone. He changed his hairdo and laughed a little bit. So we took it in the opposite direction and had a lighter grip.

Despite having been eliminated by Dallas for the second straight time, I was determined to enjoy the '94 season. I always made a point of enjoying the ride. In fact, the whole team said, "Look, we're going to enjoy this." And we enjoyed training camp and right on through. It's kind of funny how it all worked out. I think our new philosophy took us to the championship. It's true that we brought in some new players, but that wasn't the beginning of the change. The beginning was when the players took to that philosophy. I remember when our young backs Ricky Watters and William Floyd started celebrating after scoring touchdowns. Jerry Rice and I and some of the other veterans weren't used to seeing that kind of emotional display on the 49ers. But we decided to go with it, and I think that had a lot to do with the team having more fun as the season went along. You could sense the change in attitude right away. I'd say that the 49ers who went on to win the championship were very strong-willed yet pretty loose. That was the combination. There was a stark contrast: We had a strong work ethic yet, at the same time, could relax.

After a slow start, we got rolling and went on to have a great season. We finished with a 13–3 record, the best in the NFL, and had a lot of high-scoring games. I wouldn't say we had a really different approach offensively in '94 because we'd had the leading offense in the league every year. However, we improved offensively because William Floyd had a good rookie year and Ricky Watters matured into an All-Pro–caliber back. We didn't do major changes; we just got better.

We brought in several defensive players, including three starting linebackers, Ken Norton from Dallas, Rickey Jackson, and Gary Plummer. There were some other free agents—Richard Dent, Toi Cook—and then early in the season we signed Deion Sanders to play corner. Bringing in Deion was important talent-wise. I think a lot of football is just perception and we were perceived with him as having a much stronger defense. So people were now afraid of us. They had always been afraid of our offense, but now there was something about our defense that seemed to make guys wilt even before the game started. In warm-ups, when those guys came out of our locker room—Norton, Sanders, player after player after player—you could tell that other teams didn't even want to play.

It was said that we brought those guys in specifically to get us above Dallas. It was okay to say that because in the end it probably turned out to be true, but it's not like we went into the season saying that it will be great if we go 1–15 if our win is against the Cowboys. There's a bigger picture. It's an easy statement. It works either way. Because in the end we'd have to beat the best team in the league and everyone knew that team was going to be Dallas.

We played the Cowboys at midseason and our 21–14 victory set the tone for future games we'd have with them. It was kind of like we'd been beaten twice in big games and we needed that win just to gain the confidence. Maybe it wasn't that big a deal, but we needed to get rid of the stigma in our heads that we couldn't get past these guys. After we got past them in that game, we would keep doing it. That was a key game and a tough game and a great game.

We beat Dallas during our 10-game winning streak, which took us to the final game of the regular season. That game was in Minnesota, and it didn't matter to us because we'd already clinched home field in the play-offs. And we ended up losing. There was kind of a sick feeling in the locker room afterward and the guys were thinking, "Why did we let this game go?" even though it didn't mean anything. I didn't want that feeling from the loss to stick around. I told the players not to worry about it. I told them there were 39 days between then and the Super Bowl, and that if we would really commit ourselves to doing what we needed to do in that time, it would be the greatest experience of our lives. The idea was that in a very short time we could make history. People kept saying that I was showing more leadership that year than before. Well, the truth is that the leadership I was asserting had been continually growing since I'd become the starting quarterback. There had been a consistent building of confidence and leadership over time. And it wouldn't stop there but continue to grow after the Super Bowl season.

The loss to the Vikings became a nonissue. We easily beat Chicago in the first playoff game. We crushed them, 44–15. But that game wasn't what it was all about. It was all about the hurdle we hadn't been able to get over. We knew where we were headed: to play Dallas for the third straight year for the NFC championship. When I think back to our NFL championship, it wasn't only about the Super Bowl but also the Dallas game that led up to it. It has to be both games together.

The Dallas game was played in San Francisco and I thought it was a lot of fun. I was thinking that I'd been there—against Dallas in the NFC Championship Game—twice already. So I thought we could loosen up this time. Let's just wing it. And we did. Winging it really made a difference. We made some big plays because of that. There were throws that I made and things that we did that we wouldn't have tried. If we'd held on tight, we'd have tried to win it 17–14, and who knows what would have happened. By just letting it rip, we were able to jump ahead 21–0 early in the game and hold onto our lead and win, 38–28. Who was thinking we could score 38 points against the Cowboys? But we did it, and in front of our home fans, and finally we were going back to the Super Bowl.

Super Bowl XXIX against San Diego was played at Joe Robbie Stadium in late January. We had been to Miami for Super Bowl XXIII and there were riots going on back then, but this experience wasn't completely different. We go to the same city and stay in the same hotel and play in the same stadium, so the only real difference for me was that my role had changed from backup quarterback who did not play to starter. Other than that I thought the whole thing was repetitive. It wasn't overwhelming at all. I did my share of interviews, but I didn't feel there was a lot of media pressure on me. Seriously, by the time I'd gone through the whole thing— taking over the quarterback job from Joe Montana—there was no way anything could ever be like that. Even the Super Bowl. I'd faced real media pressure before. Talking about football and a big game—that was nothing!

I was in a good mood the whole time, whether I was dealing with the media, studying film, or out on the practice field. I have to say that it was the most phenomenal week of practice ever. Ever. The ball never touched the ground in practice. What was great is that I had tremendous coaching from Mike Shanahan, the offensive coordinator, and Gary Kubiak, the quarterbacks coach. I wouldn't say I had input in the game plan. Nah— Mike Shanahan was the guy. He made it happen. He was designer and I was the orchestrator. I knew he had a great game plan for San Diego. I said at the time that Mike was like Albert Einstein with smoke blowing out his ears.

I studied a lot of film, but on the eve of the Super Bowl, it was done. Mike and Gary said, "We're ready; go to bed. Tomorrow, let's go do it." So I just went to bed. That night I shared a room with Brent Jones, our tight end, as I did on the eve of all road games during the season. We were the only guys on the team who ever roomed together on the road. Everybody else got their own rooms. We all had our own rooms throughout Super Bowl Week, including me, but that night we brought another bed into my room for Brent so we could reenact what we'd done all season long the night before a road game. We just went through our normal routine.

I got to Joe Robbie Stadium really early the next day because I didn't like all the Super Sunday hoopla. Once I was inside the cement locker room, sealed away from it, it was just another game to me. I simply reviewed the game plan with Mike about an hour before kickoff and then I was done. I think all of us were loose. We were having a good time, right from the beginning. If I would use one word to characterize our locker room before the game, it would be *experienced*. We had 25 to 30 guys who had been to the Super Bowl before. That makes a huge difference. Our guys had been around and had done it all, so there was not the nervousness that I'm sure was evident in the San Diego locker room. We had a lot of experience and a lot of leadership—it was almost like a whole team of leaders. So there were no pep talks. Everything had been said, and we knew exactly what needed to be done. There didn't need to be much talk.

We were pretty much quiet assassins.

We were big favorites—it was something like 18 points—but I thought that because we had beaten up the Chargers in December, 38–15, that this game would be a little tighter played. Mike didn't. San Diego had some great defensive players like Junior Seau and Leslie O'Neal, so I didn't know if we could score that many points again. I didn't expect a blowout. Mike did. He called just what happened. As decisively as we'd beaten San Diego a few weeks before, that win wasn't as smooth as it would be in the Super Bowl. Nothing was like that Super Bowl. It was like *synergistic nirvana!*

Yes, part of our plan was the quick strike at the beginning of the game. Absolutely. We had scored quickly all season. That was one of our strong points. We got the ball first and Mike wanted us to score in five plays. But we screwed up and it took only three plays. Floyd ran the ball up the middle. Then I completed a pass to John Taylor. Then I faked another hand-off to Floyd to bring up their linebackers and then threw a long pass down the middle to Jerry Rice. He was running a post pattern and he streaked right past their safeties for our first score. I think the Chargers were in shock. They were using a new two-deep defensive scheme, and I later said that for us to score so easily against it, it must have felt like a dagger in their hearts.

On San Diego's first possession, they went three-and-out, so we got the ball right back and went for another quick strike. This time it took four plays. Watters ran up the middle, there was a short pass to Floyd, and I picked up about 20 yards on a scramble. That got us near midfield and then we ran a play-action with Floyd faking into the line and Watters going deep. Ricky was originally supposed to run a corner pattern, but I sent him up the middle instead, and he caught the pass at about their 30 and broke a couple of tackles by their safeties and went the distance. That put us ahead 14–0 with only about five minutes gone in the game.

I guess a lot of people thought the game was over after the second touchdown, maybe even after the first touchdown, because it was obvious that the San Diego defense was going to have a lot of trouble with our offense. I could see that their defense wasn't real happy with what was going on, but I'm sure their offensive players hadn't given up. They had a pretty potent offense with Stan Humphries and Natrone Means, one of the league's biggest backs, and some good receivers, and they probably believed they could come back like they'd done against Miami and Pittsburgh in the playoffs. They were behind, but it was early in the game, so they figured they could still follow their game plan and go with ball control. And they put together a long drive. They scored after eating up over seven minutes and were then only a touchdown behind. That was the time their defense had to make a stand, but they couldn't do it. We moved right down the field and scored on a short pass to Floyd, again over the middle. He hadn't caught a touchdown pass all year, so they were covering our wide receivers, and he slipped through. So early in the second quarter, we went back out in front by 14 points, 21–7.

Three possessions, three touchdowns. Then we took one series off. On our fifth possession, we took over just inside Chargers territory after we deflected a punt. We then put together a short drive and scored again on a pass to Watters from inside the 10. It was nothing fancy, just a swing pass in the flat to Ricky. They had a linebacker on him and he had no trouble getting away from him. Ricky was having a great game. He had really come on during the season. He gave us a breakaway back and also had become a big part of our passing game. After Jerry, he caught the most passes on our team that year, and he'd also made a big touchdown reception two weeks before against Dallas.

At halftime we were up, 28–10. We didn't want to change anything because everybody was playing at a real high level—the offensive line, the defense . . . But I wouldn't say that anybody in our locker room thought the game was over. We couldn't think that way. We reminded ourselves that San Diego was a good comeback team. Still, we were confident that we could keep playing the way we had in the first half, no matter how they tried to adjust to us. We just wanted to continue to be aggressive to

January 29, 1995, at Joe Robbie Stadium in Miami
Paid Attendance: 74,107
AFC Champion: San Diego Chargers (13–5)
Head Coach: Bobby Ross
NFC Champion: San Francisco 49ers (15–3)
Head Coach: George Seifert

STARTING LINEUPS

OFFENSE				DEFENSE			
San Diego		**San Francisco**		**San Diego**		**San Francisco**	
Shawn Jefferson	WR	John Taylor		Chris Mims	LE	Dennis Brown	
Duane Young	TE	Brent Jones		Shawn Lee	LT	Bryant Young	
Harry Swayne	LT	Steve Wallace		Reuben Davis	RT	Dana Stubblefield	
Isaac Davis	LG	Jesse Sapolu		Leslie O'Neal	RE	Rickey Jackson	
Courtney Hall	C	Bart Oates		David Griggs	LB	Lee Woodall	
Joe Cocozzo	RG	Derrick Deese		Dennis Gibson	LB	Gary Plummer	
Stan Brock	RT	Harris Barton		Junior Seau	LB	Ken Norton	
Alfred Pupunu	TE			Darrien Gordon	LCB	Eric Davis	
Mark Seay	WR	Jerry Rice		Dwayne Harper	RCB	Deion Sanders	
Stan Humphries	QB	Steve Young		Darren Carrington	SS	Tim McDonald	
	RB	Ricky Watters		Stanley Richard	FS	Merton Hanks	
Natrone Means	RB	William Floyd					

SUBSTITUTIONS

San Diego: K—John Carney. P—Bryan Wagner. Offense: Receivers—David Binn, Andre Coleman, Steve Hendrickson, Tony Martin, Shannon Mitchell. Linemen—Eric Jonassen, Vaughn Parker. Backs—Eric Bieniemy, Rodney Culver, Gale Gilbert (QB), Ronnie Harmon. Defense: Linebackers—Lewis Bush, Doug Miller. Linemen—Raylee Johnson, Les Miller, John Parrella. Backs—Eric Castle, Willie Clark, Rodney Harrison, Sean Vanhorse. DNP—Curtis Whitley.

San Francisco: K—Doug Brien. P—Klaus Wilmsmeyer. Offense: Receivers—Ed McCaffrey, Ted Popson, Nate Singleton. Linemen—Chris Dalman, Frank Pollack, Ralph Tamm. Backs—Dexter Carter, Elvis Grbac (QB), Mark Logan, Derek Loville, Bill Musgrave (QB), Adam Walker. Defense: Linebackers—Antonio Goss, Kevin Mitchell. Linemen—Rhett Hall, Tim Harris, Charles Mann, Troy Wilson. Backs—Toi Cook, Tyronne Drakeford, Dana Hall.

San Diego	7	3	8	8—26
San Francisco	14	14	14	7—49

SF	Rice 44 pass from Young (Brien kick)
SF	Watters 51 pass from Young (Brien kick)
SD	Means 1 run (Carney kick)
SF	Floyd 5 pass from Young (Brien kick)
SF	Watters 8 pass from Young (Brien kick)
SD	FG Carney 31
SF	Watters 9 run (Brien kick)
SF	Rice 15 pass from Young (Brien kick)
SD	Coleman 98 kickoff return (Seay pass from Humphries)
SF	Rice 7 pass from Young (Brien kick)
SD	Martin 30 pass from Humphries (Pupuno pass from Humphries)
MVP:	Steve Young (San Francisco)

keep the pressure on them and not make any mistakes. We were able to do that. We didn't turn over the ball all game and we were penalized only 10 yards, which made things easier.

Trailing by 18 points, San Diego needed to get off to a good start in the second half. But instead we picked up where we left off. Our defense stopped them cold on their first series, and when our offense got the ball, we moved downfield on catches by Rice and John Taylor. Then Watters scored on a cutback from the 9 for our only rushing touchdown of the game. We'd had two touchdown passes from inside the 10 earlier, so maybe the Chargers weren't expecting a running play. That was Ricky's third touchdown of the game.

Jerry Rice would also score three times. He had suffered a slight shoulder separation on an end-around in the first quarter, and I was glad he came back, because when he'd left we hadn't really put the damage to them yet. I wasn't worrying about his shoulder—once you're in the game, you just play—and was still going to him often. His second touchdown reception came on a 15-yard crossing pattern. The Chargers put on a strong rush and I was on my back when Jerry ran into the end zone to increase our lead to 42–10. That was my fifth touchdown pass of the game and I was excited. I was on the ground but I was still signaling the touchdown with my arms raised.

My record-breaking sixth touchdown pass of the Super Bowl went to Jerry early in the fourth quarter. It was a quick slant pass from about the 7 and Jerry made a diving catch. That was Jerry's third touchdown of the game and it was really something because I had watched him when he also caught three TD passes from Joe Montana in Super Bowl XXIV, when Joe set the record I'd just broken. What more can you say about Jerry Rice other than he is the best receiver ever. After the game I was telling reporters that Jerry was a better receiver with the one arm than all the other receivers in the league were with two.

By this time, the Chargers were out of the game. They scored a couple of touchdowns in the half—one on a long kickoff return—and two two-point conversions to make the final score 49–26. I'm sure that coming into the game Bobby Ross wanted the Chargers' offense to use up a lot of time on the clock to keep our offense off the field, but they couldn't do that in the second half because they'd fallen too far behind. They had to try to score quickly, so they had to pretty much abandon their game plan and go to the air. Consequently, our guys put on a big rush and they were intercepted three times. Our defense would make many big plays. All during the season, that's what I'd watch for on the sidelines.

I spent most of the fourth quarter on the sidelines and watched Elvis Grbac finish up at quarterback. I was having so much fun. This time I was the starter and left the game with the big lead. In Super Bowl XXIV, I had replaced Joe when we were far ahead. Both times it was a great thing. It had been meaningful for me to put my knee down at the end of Super Bowl XXIV. Absolutely. It's the Super Bowl. Either way is great. If there was a difference to the whole experience it was only that those earlier Super Bowl teams I was on weren't my teams. They were Joe's teams.

After the game, in the locker room, everybody was ecstatic. I can't describe the feeling. There was the award presentation ceremony and I was up there holding up and clutching the Vince Lombardi Trophy, which we'd won for being Super Bowl champs. That's why football is the ultimate team game. When you get there, you share it with 50 other guys. The elation you feel is geometric—50 times 50. I was up there shouting to all the players that no one could take that trophy away from us—not ever! I reminded them of the 39-day commitment we made after that loss to Minnesota. Everyone on that team had made a commitment to working hard and a commitment to each other.

I was up there laughing and celebrating and hugging people—Gary Kubiak, Eddie DeBartolo, Jesse Sapolu, Jerry Rice—and everyone seemed genuinely happy for me after what I'd been through. I wish everyone who ever played football could have felt like I did. There was no greater feeling in the world. I couldn't ask for more than to throw six touchdown passes, throw for over 300 yards, win the Super Bowl, and be its MVP. When you get to the biggest game and play your best game ever, you couldn't ask for more. I feel it was my best effort. I'd never thrown six touchdown passes in a game in my whole life!

The two things that were talked about after the game were "the monkey off my back"—which I myself was laughing about on the sidelines as the game wound down—and "exorcising the ghost of Joe Montana." It ended up being the same thing. As I said, it related to there being previous championships in San Francisco and the fact that I hadn't been the one at quarterback. San Francisco was a championship town and it demanded a championship quarterback. Before that Super Bowl I had done everything else but take the 49ers to the championship. The final piece. And now I had done it.

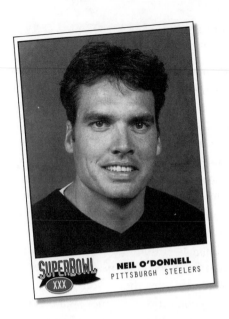

NEIL O'DONNELL
PITTSBURGH STEELERS

SUPER BOWL XXX

DALLAS COWBOYS 27
PITTSBURGH STEELERS 17

NEIL O'DONNELL

I was in my sixth year with the Steelers and fifth year as their starting quarterback when we made it to the Super Bowl. I was one of the few players still there from when Chuck Noll was the head coach. Chuck wanted to draft me out of Maryland, so he was a big reason I went to Pittsburgh in the third round in 1990. I have great memories of my years with him. He was from the old school and didn't play me at all as a rookie, but he watched me develop and started me in eight games in 1991. After that season, Chuck was ready to get out of coaching, so I was fortunate to have played for him. It had really been a great honor because Chuck was a Hall of Fame coach who had taken the Steelers to four world championships in the seventies.

Pittsburgh wasn't an easy place to play because many fans were still caught up in the seventies and Chuck's championship teams. They remembered Franco Harris and Rocky Bleier and Terry Bradshaw and that's who you were always compared to. I guess it took me a while to win them over. Fans will always be fans and they cheered when you did well and were all over you when you were struggling. At first it was tough—all I did was win there and they still found reasons to bad-mouth me a little bit. But I did adapt and became very comfortable in Pittsburgh. There were a lot of people in that city who were behind me and respected what I did in my years there.

Bill Cowher, who had been the defensive coordinator at Kansas City, became our coach in 1992. He was the youngest coach in the NFL. Bill came to a team that people said had players who were too old to play, and players who were too young and not ready to play, and he took us to the playoffs every year. I was his quarterback and the person he would talk to on offense if there was something he wasn't comfortable with or if he wanted to know what was going on back in the locker room. He would never hesitate to call on me. We had a great working relationship; we really did. And we had a lot of success together.

At the time, I thought Bill and Ron Erhardt, his offensive coordinator, also had a very good working relationship. It would be a real shocker to see Ron leave Pittsburgh for the New York Jets after the Super Bowl, preceding me there. It was Ron's offense and Bill just kind of stayed out of it. Bill really tuned in on the defense and would actually run the special teams a lot of the time. I know he would run the projector. Bobby April, the special teams coach, would call out the returns and Bill would be right in there, sitting through every one of them. Most head coaches don't do that, but Bill had been a special teams player himself.

In Pittsburgh, all you heard and read about was our defense. It was still a defensive-minded city and the fans hadn't forgotten Joe Greene, L. C. Greenwood, Jack Lambert, Donnie Shell—the whole Steel Curtain. Now you'd hear about Kevin Greene, Greg Lloyd, Rod Woodson. . . . That was okay, but the offense was doing its job, too—don't forget that. In my final three years in Pittsburgh, playing for Cowher and Erhardt and assistant coaches Dick Hoak, Kent Stephenson, Chan Gailey, and Pat Hodgson, the Steelers were in the top 10 offensively. I'd say, "Let's just keep doing what we're doing and keep winning games, and don't worry, they'll recognize us, too." We were a close-knit group offensively. Which isn't to say that the Steelers were segregated into offense and defense. We'd get involved in the team's socials on Friday afternoons after practice and there would be everyone. When we'd go out, it would be everybody. We had a working-class team and we all stayed together. Everybody got along, and that's why it was so much fun to play on that team and one of the reasons we did so well. We were all in it together.

Bill saw us mature and play into an AFC championship-caliber team. In his first two years we lost to Buffalo and Kansas City in the first round of the playoffs, but we made it to the AFC Championship Game in his third season. We could have gone to the Super Bowl, but we lost to the Chargers in the last 21 seconds, 17–13. That was such a tough loss. We drove all the way down to San Diego's 3-yard line, but my pass got tipped on the final play. I had a great year in 1994, but all they wrote about was the last play of that game. It was frustrating because I wouldn't get to throw again until September.

Then I broke my hand on opening day in 1995. That put me out for four more weeks. It was so hard for me to watch the Steelers struggle. We started slowly and everyone was writing us off. Then I came back and we began to play better. I started telling everyone, "We gotta believe." It was tough, because after we lost Rod Woodson with a knee injury, people were saying the defense would never be the same. He was a great cornerback and, like Greg Lloyd, a veteran leader of the defense, so the reaction was, "Oh, no, we lost Rod." But it was, "Hey, fellahs, if all of us do our jobs, we'll be okay. We may have to shuffle people around, like moving Carnell Lake from safety to corner, but there is enough talent on this team to go to the Super Bowl." All of a sudden we started to get the momentum going, won some games, and people started believing.

You heard so much about our defense, our defense, our defense—and we did have a great defense—but in 1995, I think the offense pretty much carried the defense. In the preseason, the coaches had told me that they didn't get rid of Barry Foster, our most productive rusher, because they intended to change our offense. We were going to keep it pretty much the same because Ron Erhardt believed in establishing the running game and going from there. However, I was told we would spread it out a little more, throw a little more, and I'd be asked to do a little more. I said, "Hey, I'm all for it." I don't know a quarterback who doesn't like throwing it more. But I kind of sat back and waited and didn't get excited because I'd heard that before. At first, we were a running team, but without Foster or tight end Eric Green, we just couldn't pound it like we used to. So as the season unwound, we went more to the passing game. I missed four games yet I still threw for nearly 3,000 yards.

Probably in the fifth or sixth game we started to really spread it out. In previous years, we always had a receiver or two who wanted the ball to go to them every play, but in 1995, there wasn't any one guy calling for the ball. Everybody was happy to play a part. We'd go with three, four, or even five receivers. We wanted to see how the five-receiver set worked and it worked well. Our backs had always been part of the passing game— John L. Williams had caught a ton of passes in 1994—but once we started spreading it out, we just tried to get it to the wideouts. When we'd go with the five wideouts, or just three or four, we did a great job of moving the football, and we had a lot of fun doing it because we had so many people involved. Nobody had ever heard of Yancey Thigpen or Ernie Mills before and all of a sudden these people are making all these catches every game. Yancey gained over 1,300 yards.

What we did wasn't really complex. Because I couldn't get the best protection with so many guys going out for passes, we did a lot of no-huddles and I'd make quick reads at the line of scrimmage and just let it go. We spread out so quickly that—boom—there were suddenly four or five wideouts and the defense would be thrown off balance and not have time to adjust. Some of our receivers, like Yancey and Ernie, would do set routes, while an experienced receiver like Andre Hastings, who was used to running the no-huddle, would make reads and run routes according to whether the defense was playing zone or man coverage. I had several choices of where to go with the ball. Foot-speed-wise, you had to push it deep to Mills or Thigpen. Hastings was definitely an option-route receiver. He didn't have the best speed, but he was a tough little kid who could run the reads and find ways to get open. He really caught the ball well.

Erhardt even began to use Kordell Stewart, who had been a quarterback at Colorado, as a receiver when we'd go to a lot of wideouts. He was a physical guy, a great athlete who could run and could use his hands— you really couldn't coach that. People were afraid to really coach him because he was getting open without having ever played receiver before. He had the advantage of being a rookie because nobody knew what to expect of him. He'd go out there and bang off defenders—they'd try to assault him, but he'd find a way to break free.

Ron didn't need to explain to me why he'd substitute Kordell for me at quarterback on some fourth-and-short plays. He knew I had been in Pittsburgh for a long time and would go along with anything that would help us win. I wasn't going to get upset those times Kordell replaced me on fourth-and-1. Kordell could run, and if he could run the option and get the first down, great. I would get my snaps, I knew that much. Hey, it was a great little attribute we had to throw Kordell in there. He gave our offense some diversity.

That had to be one of the best Steelers teams I played on. We had talent in earlier years, but we didn't play as well as a team. I could definitely see the whole team mature as the season progressed. The offense and defense, without Rod, were playing great football and we got on a roll and went on to have a banner year. We won eight in a row before we lost our last game on the last play out in Green Bay. The fans' slogan for the season was "3 More Yards." We didn't mind hearing that one bit. Those words reminded us of just how close we had come to beating the Chargers and told us just to go that much more. The key to reaching the Super Bowl was to just go that extra step.

We played Buffalo in the first round of the playoffs and that was a big game for us. The Bills were always tough in the postseason and had beaten us in our first playoff appearance three years before. This time we won, 40–21, and we were able to play in our second consecutive AFC Championship Game, this time against the Indianapolis Colts. It was another close title game that went down to the wire. I know it was an exciting game, but I couldn't really appreciate it while we were playing it, and I couldn't even think about it fully until after the Super Bowl. I just knew that we had another opportunity to go to the Super Bowl and I kept reminding myself during that whole game: "It can't happen to us twice." This time the other team was behind at the end and it came down to the Hail Mary pass that Jim Harbaugh threw into the end zone on the final play. I was on the sidelines, way up where the line of scrimmage was. I saw a lot of people go for the ball and then a Colt was on his back holding the ball. But I couldn't tell if he had caught it or if it had hit the ground first. I looked at one ref and he wasn't doing anything, and looked at the other one and he was just watching. Finally, it was ruled an incompletion and we won the game. I saw the tape later and it was the right call. That was a great win for myself and the Steelers. But afterward I asked about Jim Harbaugh to see how he was. I had been in the same situation the year before and knew how devastating a loss like that could be.

Finally we had made it to the Super Bowl, which was going to be played for the first time in Tempe, Arizona. Dallas had made it back to the Super Bowl for the third time in four years by beating Green Bay in the NFC Championship Game. The press wrote about the Steelers and Cowboys resuming their Super Bowl rivalry, but the players really didn't get into that, because Super Bowl X and Super Bowl XIII had been played back in the seventies and the game had changed so much since then. The media was playing up how both teams had won four Super Bowls and were going for a fifth, but that didn't put any extra pressure on me. Everyone was saying, "Win one for the thumb," but I just wanted one ring for my finger. I didn't care which finger I put it on; I just wanted one for myself.

Was the week leading up to the Super Bowl fun? No. That week was both pressure-filled and uncomfortable. There's so much build up to the game. It's unbelievable how big an event the Super Bowl is, how much revenue there is, how much money changes hands—it's really something. I was kind of prepared for how big the Super Bowl was from talking to other quarterbacks about how the media was going to be all over me. And it was. I was ready for it but I hadn't learned to just say no. There are too many people who think you're their best friend and who want your time. Everybody wants your time. I really didn't get a chance to enjoy my family with all that was going on around there. It was really hard just to be yourself and take time to reflect. You have in the back of your head that you have a game to play on Sunday and it's hard to focus. I'm not blaming anything on the week prior to the game, but it was overwhelming at first. I told myself that I wanted to return to the Super Bowl as soon as possible because I would do things differently.

The players stayed at a chain hotel. It was away from our families, and to tell you the truth, it wasn't the nicest accommodation. I thought it would be a lot more secluded. So the most relaxing thing turned out to be going to practice. It would take us away from everything. We'd go to this junior college field and there'd be mountains around us and we'd sit there and stretch, and there'd be times when I'd be saying, "I'd rather just stay right here." It really is beautiful there. It's no wonder that we had very good practices.

I'm sure the Cowboys knew better how to handle the hoopla. Even when the media tried to come up with some negative stories, it didn't bother them. It didn't matter to them because they'd been there before. They knew what it was all about. They knew what they were doing. If they didn't have curfews, that was fine. They could do whatever they wanted because they'd been going there almost every year. The Steelers hadn't been there since Super Bowl XIV, so it was all new to us.

I don't think the media had much regard for the Steelers. I know they were giving the Cowboys the win the whole week. All you kept hearing was "blowout, blowout, blowout." I think the spread was around 13 points. Sure it angered us that we weren't given a chance. We put it on the same as everyone else and we deserved to be there as much as the Cowboys did. When you worked as hard as we did and had been playing this game for so long, you want to get respect. I don't think we got it.

Bill Cowher had a lot of respect for his team. He didn't tell us that we had to overachieve or play mistake-free to beat the Cowboys. He told us, "Go out there and play the way you've been playing the past year and we should be fine. Don't be uptight, play loose, go out there and have fun." He had that open attitude, that open spirit, the whole week.

In preparing for the Cowboys, I think we had every game of theirs cut up. You could drive yourself crazy because there was so much film, so I just really focused on what they did in the playoffs and in beating the Packers. Ron Erhardt gave me a chance to look at his game plan to see if I liked it. He would always say, "I'm not married to anything." Ron gave me a lot of freedom to call plays and also to throw some things out that maybe they thought would work better than I did. I'd have to have the confidence in a play. I'd have to know that this guy is going to run the correct route and things like that. I'm a strong believer in: You put a game plan in and then the players have to execute it. I was satisfied with the game plan. I'd never hold a loss against our game plan. Because you never know; some days our running game may not be going well and we'd throw the ball a lot, or vice versa. The Steelers believed in seeing how games unwound. We didn't go into the game with the attitude: Okay, we're going to run the ball today. You can't do that. Especially against a team as strong as Dallas. You looked at their guys up front. Leon Lett, Tony Tolbert, Russell Maryland, Charles Haley—those guys could bring a lot of heat. I saw that their defense was very talented and confident in their ability and played well together. There really wasn't a weakness. What we had to do was not get caught up in all the hoopla early on and stay in the game. We knew that if the score was close in the third quarter, we could make it an interesting game.

I was asked a lot if we were nervous before the game. It really wasn't *nervous*, it was *anxious*. You want to get out there and play. You want the first snap. In the locker room at Sun Devil Stadium, the players were focused, not loud, there was nobody jumping up and down. Mostly it was people minding their own business and just waiting. That's the tough part, just waiting, all the way through the introductions. They really leave you there for a while. We did our normal routine and Bill Cowher spoke about what we had to do, then we just said our prayers and went out there. There really weren't pep talks or anybody taking control of the locker room and voicing his opinions. That late in the year, everybody knew what it took to win.

The pregame ceremonies were very exciting. There was "the Circle of MVPs" from the previous 29 Super Bowls, the tribute to the *Challenger* with the planes, Vanessa Williams singing the national anthem, the long player introductions. . . . Sure, it was emotional. I'm standing there thinking, "Wow, this is what it's all about, it really is." The Super Bowl is what you really work for. You get to a point in your career where you say, "Okay, I've done everything else. I've broken seven Steelers records; I've played in the playoffs four times; I've played in two AFC Championship Games; I played in the Pro Bowl in '93; I won a Quarterback Challenge. Now I'm just trying to win the Big One." As you stand there you reflect on how hard it was to get there. If the ball bounced one way instead of the other, then you aren't there. I thought about all the great quarterbacks who had never played in the Super Bowl, so I wanted to make the most of my opportunity. You are focused on the game ahead but you think of many things. I lost my father two years before and he would have been a big part of that day. I wished he could have been there in person to really experience it all, because you still play for your father in a lot of ways. So that was hard. But I had 37 other people there from my family and I had plenty of support. What also made it special is that the Super Bowl turned 30 only a few months before my own thirtieth birthday.

The Cowboys got the ball first and I stood on the sidelines watching our defense. Dallas had two big plays on its first possession. Troy Aikman completed a pass to Michael Irvin on the right side for about 20 yards and then Emmitt Smith ran to the left for another 20–25 yards. It would be his only long run of the game. Those two big plays back-to-back didn't shock me. It was early and we had to settle our feet, too. I was thinking, "Okay, stop them for three and let's get some points." I think our defense had a bend-but-not-break mentality. I had the confidence in our defense that they would adjust and stop them. They did hold them after Smith's run and Dallas ended up with only a field goal by Chris Boniol.

So we were down only 3–0 when we got the ball. The field looked beautiful, but it did give a lot. It was a fast track, but it was cut too short and there was some slipping. I don't know how much it affected receivers on pass routes. When you're under the gun, you think about so many other things. After the first play, you stop thinking, "I'm in the Super Bowl." It's out of your system. There's so much more going on than what's happening in the stands or what happened the prior week. You're focused only on what's happening on the field.

On our first possession, we ran Erric Pegram a couple of plays up the middle and then threw a short pass to Hastings. We didn't get a first down and had to punt, but we did get to feel out Dallas's defense a bit. The plan was to go out and see how Dallas would react. They had a lot of talent on that defensive line with guys like Leon Lett and Russell Maryland, and we wanted to see how well we could protect the passer and how we could run the ball early in the game, and just go from there. We wanted to mix it up and see how our one-on-one match-ups would be. When we passed, we were not going to make an effort to stay away from Deion Sanders, as people said we would, and go only to Larry Brown's side. Brown was a good corner, too. We would take our chances with Deion. He was a great athlete—everyone knew that—but you have to use the whole field.

When Dallas got the ball back, they put together their one touchdown drive of the game. Their big play was a long completion to Deion, who also played some wide receiver. It was a concern that he would be playing on offense because when Deion's in there you've got to watch him. I think Willie Williams almost made a pretty good defensive play, but Deion somehow came up with it. Deion made a great play and they got almost 50 yards. Then they scored their first touchdown on a short pass to Jay Novacek. I know people were complaining about the block that picked off our linebacker in the end zone. They were saying it was an illegal pick, but what can you do about it when it's all said and done?

We had led the AFC in time of possession, but we were already down 10–0 and couldn't do ball control. We had to get some points. We started to move the ball, but then we were faced with fourth-and-1 close to midfield. We didn't want to give up the ball, so I wasn't surprised when they didn't send in the punter. Instead Kordell Stewart took the snap. Prior to the game, Bill told us, "We will have to take our chances. We didn't come here just to play close; we've come here to win this thing." So we all thought, "Let's go for it and try to make something happen." Kordell ran for the first down and we continued to put together a good drive by mixing it up. But then there was a bad snap way over my head. I was fortunate to recover it because if I'd fumbled it, they would have gotten the ball on our 40. We kept the ball but lost about 13 yards on the play. That killed our drive, and after Rohn Stark punted into the end zone, the Cowboys put together another drive of their own.

Troy Aikman completed several passes in a row and took the Cowboys all the way down the field. But then they had a touchdown pass to Michael Irvin called back because Irvin was called for interference. Everyone who followed football knew that Irvin used his hands on defenders. He was a physical player and did a good job of getting away with it, but that time he got caught pushing off Carnell Lake. That was a big play because instead

January 28, 1996, at Sun Devil Stadium in Tempe, Arizona
Paid Attendance: 76,347
NFC Champion: Dallas Cowboys (14–4)
Head Coach: Barry Switzer
AFC Champion: Pittsburgh Steelers (13–5)
Head Coach: Bill Cowher

STARTING LINEUPS

OFFENSE			DEFENSE		
Dallas		**Pittsburgh**	**Dallas**		**Pittsburgh**
Kevin Williams	WR	Yancey Thigpen	Tony Tolbert	LE	Brentson Buckner
Mark Tuinei	LT	John Jackson	Russell Maryland	LT	
Nate Newton	LG	Tom Newberry		NT	Joel Steed
Derek Kennard	C	Dermontti Dawson	Leon Lett	RT	
Larry Allen	RG	Brenden Stai	Charles Haley	RE	Ray Seals
Erik Williams	RT	Leon Searcy		LOLB	Kevin Greene
Jay Novacek	TE	Mark Bruener	Dixon Edwards	LB	
Michael Irvin	WR	Ernie Mills		LILB	Levon Kirkland
Troy Aikman	QB	Neil O'Donnell	Robert Jones	MLB	
Daryl Johnston	RB	John L. Williams		RILB	Chad Brown
Emmitt Smith	RB	Erric Pegram	Darrin Smith	LB	
				ROLB	Greg Lloyd
			Deion Sanders	LCB	Carnell Lake
			Larry Brown	RCB	Willie Williams
			Darren Woodson	SS	Myron Bell
			Brock Marion	FS	Darren Perry

SUBSTITUTIONS

Dallas: K—Chris Boniol. P—John Jett. Offense: Receivers: Cory Fleming, Kendell Watkins, Eric Bjornson, Billy Davis. Linemen—Ron Stone, Dale Hellestrae. Back—David Lang. Defense: Linebackers—Jim Schwantz, Godfrey Myles. Linemen—Chad Hennings, Shante Carver, Hurvin McCormick. Backs—Bill Bates, Charlie Williams, Scott Case, Greg Briggs. DNP—Wade Wilson, Sherman Williams, George Hegamin.

Pittsburgh: K—Norm Johnson. P—Rohn Stark. Receivers—Kordell Stewart, Corey Holliday, Jonathan Hayes, Andre Hastings. Linemen—Kendall Gammon, Justin Strzelczyk, James Parrish. Backs—Fred McAfee, Bam Morris, Tim Lester, Stewart (QB). Defense: Linebackers—Jerry Olsavsky, Jason Gildon. Linemen—Kevin Henry, Bill Johnson. Backs—Deon Figures, Chris Oldham, Rod Woodson, Randy Fuller, Lethon Flowers. DNP—Mike Tomczak.

Dallas	10	3	7	7—27	
Pittsburgh	0	7	0	10—17	

Dall	FG Boniol 42
Dall	Novacek 3 pass from Aikman (Boniol kick)
Dall	FG Boniol 35
Pitt	Thigpen 6 pass from O'Donnell (Johnson kick)
Dall	E. Smith 1 run (Boniol kick)
Pitt	FG Johnson 46
Pitt	Morris 1 run (Johnson kick)
Dall	E. Smith 4 run (Bonioil kick)
MVP:	Larry Brown (Dallas)

of going up 17–0, they had to settle for another field goal by Boniol and went up only 13–0. So we didn't have to go to a totally different hurry-up offense. I felt that if we fell 17 points behind, we'd be in real trouble. I knew that when the Cowboys were ahead by a lot of points, they played their best. They were very cocky and would go out and show all their attributes and really hurt you. But if we stay close, it could be interesting. Keep them to three and hopefully we'll go out and get something.

With the score 13–0 everything was pretty quiet. The Steelers fans had watched us move the ball, but we weren't executing the way we wanted to on third downs. We said we had to get points on the board before half-time and we snuck one in there right before the gun. I was even sacked a couple of times and we still made it downfield. It was a great drive and the key was that everybody was involved. Bam Morris started to run the ball well, Kordell had another fourth-down run, and Hastings, Mills, and Thigpen made some great catches. It was one of those times when we had timing and rhythm in our passing game, and once we got things going, completing a few passes felt pretty good. I wasn't trying to compete against Troy, because the only numbers I care about are wins and losses. All I was trying to do was run our offense and do what I had to do. Mills made a terrific catch inside the 10, and then with only about 13 seconds left in the half, we scored when Thigpen cut inside of Sanders on the right side and I quickly completed it to him just over the goal line. Yancey wasn't the prime receiver on that play—it was just a read that I got and I took a chance and fired a slant in down to him. That was a big, big touchdown for us because we were right back in the game at 13–7. That made our fans cheer. We went in at halftime feeling pretty good and knowing we were going to get the ball back to begin the second half.

Bill felt good at halftime. He was glad that Dallas had scored only one touchdown and had to kick field goals the other two times they'd gotten close to our end zone. He thought we'd been jittery at first but had settled down. Our defense was playing well and we'd finally put some points on the board. He wanted us to keep the momentum going because if we were close in the fourth quarter anything could happen. We talked about what we had to do to keep drives going. We didn't go into details, like how many passes we were completing on first or second or third down, or what our stats were using the shotgun. We were aware we were doing well with our hurry-up offense, because that's when we were moving the football.

We got the ball into Dallas territory on our first possession of the second half. Then we stalled. Instead of trying a long field goal, we had Rohn Stark punt, and for the second time he kicked the ball into the end zone.

That he again failed to knock it out of bounds had to frustrate us. If you put the Cowboys at their 10-yard line at a time our defense was getting settled, that could have made a big difference in the game. There were a ton of Steelers fans there—in fact, the majority of the crowd was rooting for us—so if we backed the Cowboys up near their end zone, the fans could have been very loud and made it very difficult for them. It could have changed things around. But we couldn't get mad at Rohn. We didn't get caught in blaming anyone for anything because we were out there as a team. I'm sure Rohn didn't want the ball to sail into the end zone. He had been punting for 14 or 15 years and knew we wanted him to angle it in the corner. It just didn't work out that way.

The Cowboys got the ball on their 20, but got only one first down before our defense held them. This was a different defense than the one that had started the game. That Dallas had played in two recent Super Bowls had definitely been a factor in their favor early in the game. Oh, yeah, their experience had helped them jump to that early lead. But once we calmed down, I think we did fine. I wouldn't say our defense had solved all its problems, but after Dallas had those big plays in their first two drives of the game, they didn't have much luck. The goal of our defense coming into the game was to stop Emmitt Smith. Stop the running game first, because that's what Dallas did best—when they were successful at it, they were at their best. I think our defense did a great job doing just that. Emmitt had the one big run in the first drive and that was it. We had strong linebackers with Greg Lloyd, Kevin Greene, and Levon Kirkland, a big kid, and they were making big plays, but I think it has to start up front. Our defensive line was doing a great job, too. Dallas had Nate Newton, Larry Allen, and all those other 330-pound offensive linemen against our much smaller linemen, and I think our guys held in there pretty good. The entire defense was playing great. Even Rod Woodson played some on third downs after having come back from surgery. The media played up how inspired our team would be if Rod played. I don't think the players got caught up in that. It was great to see Rod come back because it really was a miracle that he was able to step on the field. But was his presence inspiring? I would have to say yes and no. Rod was a great talent and had been there for many years, but we had gotten to the Super Bowl with him on the sidelines.

Dallas's defense was also playing a very good game. A very physical game. The Cowboys were bringing some pressure from their down linemen, and on third downs they were throwing a lot of zone blitzes at me. They were mixing it up pretty good. They didn't show much of that prior to this game, but they did a pretty good job doing those things. I felt pressure and got sacked a few times—Charles Haley had a sack, Tony Tolbert. . . . But I'd give our linemen a lot of credit for hanging in there, especially when they were outnumbered on passing plays. For the most part I was well protected. We had good players on the line, including the best center in the business, Dermontti Dawson, who was someone I had a very close relationship with. He was such a great athlete and did wonderful things. As always I could rely on him.

On our second possession of the half, I was intercepted for the first time. The Cowboys might have blitzed, but I had time. On that play I believe I had three receivers over on the right side. They cut to the middle, but the throw went to the sideline, and Larry Brown picked it off at the Cowboys' 40 and had a long runback. Then Troy hit Irvin on a pass at about their 2 and Emmitt ran it in for a touchdown to make the score 20–7 in Dallas's favor. On that interception, it just wasn't a good throw on my part. I just lost the ball out of my hand. Of course, you're frustrated by a play like that, but you tell yourself to get it out of your mind in a hurry. Because there was still a long way to go in the game and we were only down by 13 points.

Even though the score didn't change by the end of the third quarter, we didn't feel we were out of the game. There were times during the season when we'd struggle in the first half and then in the second half we would get it rolling, and come fourth quarter, we knew we would win the game. I don't care if we were down or not, we believed, "Hey, fellahs, this is ours. Let's play the last quarter the way we are capable of doing it and we'll come out with a win."

We narrowed the score to 20–10 early in the fourth quarter on a long field goal by Norm Johnson, one of the best kickers in the league. Then we got it right back. I didn't know that Johnson would then try an onside kick. I was probably off getting something to drink and talking to Erhardt. So it was a big surprise, a nice present to learn we had tried an onside kick and had recovered the ball. That gave us some momentum.

When we took the field we were businesslike rather than emotional. And once again we had a great drive. It seemed that the whole game we had great drives and great catches by Mills and Hastings and Thigpen, and some good running, but we had trouble scoring. This time we knew we had to get it done. I had great confidence in my receivers and they had great confidence in me. We knew what we had to do. We had some big receptions over the middle, but it wasn't like, hey let's go across the middle every time we pass. We were going to mix it up and do whatever we could against their defense. Mills hurt his knee that drive, but Hastings and Thigpen made some big catches that took us inside the Cowboys' 5. Then I handed the ball to Bam Morris. Sometimes you didn't know if he'd turn it on during a game. But he ran extremely hard that day, as he had throughout the playoffs. He wouldn't go down. Morris scored on one of our basic short-yardage plays to the right. He went in untouched. So with the extra point we had cut the Cowboys' lead to only three, 20–17, and there was still a lot of time on the clock.

When I came off the field I sent a kiss into the stands to my mom. That was as good as we felt all day. At that point we thought we could win. But from Day One, we thought we could win. We had stepped on the field to win, not just make it close.

Unfortunately, when we got the ball back with still over four minutes remaining and started a drive that could have put us ahead, I was intercepted again. There was a blitz on third down and I threw it to the sideline and Larry Brown ran it back again. That second interception was a total . . . there was a miscommunication between Andre Hastings and myself. I can't blame anyone. I will never ever sell anyone down the river because that's not my style. It was just too bad because we were still right in it. It was very frustrating. I made the tackle on Brown on that play. But then Emmitt Smith had his second short touchdown run. That made the score 27–17 and put the game away. Later, all I could do was throw Hail Mary passes. You just let it go and take a shot.

I don't remember what Troy Aikman said to me after the game. It wasn't a blur, but you're frustrated by the loss and just want to get off the field and reflect on everything. In our locker room there was a lot of disappointment. Dallas had played a good game, but everyone knew we had a chance to beat them. We had them right where we wanted them, but in the end, things didn't happen the way we wanted.

I have a lot of pride about our performance in the game. I have a lot of great memories of that game. It was exciting; it really was. When it was over, people said the Steelers really did play a good game and then they started giving us a few accolades. Of course, you'd still hear crap about a couple of plays here and there. That's what they like to write about. But would the Pittsburgh Steelers have been better off getting blown out as everyone predicted, or making it an interesting game, one of the best Super Bowls? I didn't get caught up in all the negative headlines and newspaper stories. After you watch the tape of the game and see how we lost, you just go on. You have to look at the big picture. We had a great year. I had a great year. It was a great year and it's too bad it ended the way it did, but you get over it and you have a whole new beginning. When I moved on to the Jets after the year, I immediately started thinking of playing in another Super Bowl.

During the 1995 season and during Super Bowl XXX, I wasn't thinking about the fact that I'd be a free agent after the game. That was so far out of the picture that it didn't cross my mind. But I knew how it was with free agency. I looked around our locker room and knew that the team wouldn't be the same the following year. It was kind of tough looking at a lot of the guys and thinking that this may be the last time the team would be together. Sure enough, there were a lot of people there, including myself, who wouldn't be wearing the black and gold in 1996. I never thought that so early in my career I would go to New York, but it happened through free agency. It would be hard leaving Pittsburgh after six years. I would miss my teammates. We'd been through a lot and we all played extremely well together and we all really cared for each other. We were really a close group. It's too bad we couldn't all stick together.

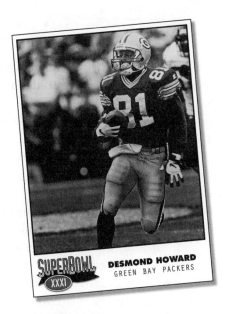

DESMOND HOWARD
GREEN BAY PACKERS

SUPER BOWL XXXI

GREEN BAY PACKERS 35
NEW ENGLAND PATRIOTS 21

DESMOND HOWARD

When I signed a one-year free-agent contract with Green Bay, it was never my purpose to prove to the Washington Redskins or Jacksonville Jaguars that they were wrong for having released me. And it's not necessarily true that I picked the Packers to play for in 1996 because I knew they had intended to choose me fifth if the Redskins hadn't picked me fourth in the 1992 draft. My only desire was to go to a winning team, and it was obvious that Green Bay would again make the playoffs and probably win a world championship. Fortunately Ron Wolf, the Packers general manager, saw through the BS and was willing to take a chance on me.

I don't know the reason Ron Wolf wanted to sign me because we never spoke. He talked to my agent Leigh Steinberg, who told me only that the

Packers wanted to see if I still had what they saw when I'd won the Heisman Trophy at Michigan. So when I signed I didn't know what they expected of me. Wide receiver had been my primary position in college and in my three years with Washington and one year with Jacksonville, but I had also played special teams pretty well so that was an option. I didn't insist that I play receiver before I signed. I knew that Brett Favre already had some great receivers. My concern was to just make the team and take it from there.

Despite my trials and tribulations with the Redskins and the Jaguars, I always had confidence in myself and never quit thinking I'd succeed if given the opportunity. Unfortunately, early in the preseason I had a bad hip pointer and couldn't show the Packers anything. I was worried that I'd be cut. I spoke to Sherm Lewis, the offensive coordinator, and expressed my frustrations about not being able to do what I can do. But I didn't have any sit-down sessions with our head coach, Mike Holmgren (although we did talk a few times). The one player I was able to express my frustrations to was Reggie White. I didn't know anybody on the Packers when I got to training camp and I'd never met Reggie—I knew him like every football fan knew him, as Reggie White the great defensive end—but I saw that he was one of the team leaders and definitely someone I could talk to. I went to him because he seemed to be one of the most serious people in the league. He also had a pretty good relationship with Mike Holmgren, and I was trying to get a feel for the situation. I liked him a lot. He was a good person; he had a great soul; he was a kindred spirit. Reggie was an ordained minister, and we even prayed together about my hip injury.

My hip got better, and I scored a touchdown on a punt return against Pittsburgh in the next to last game of the preseason. I don't know how important that play was, but by the end of training camp I had solidified my position on the team. Our final preseason game against the Colts was on national television and supposedly one of the guys in the booth asked Ron Wolf about me and he said, "Desmond's on the team." I was out there playing so I don't know if that story is true or not, but I did make the team.

From the beginning of the '96 season, I had success as a kickoff and punt returner. There wasn't one factor that made me more successful with the Packers than I'd been with return teams elsewhere. The other teams had good systems too, but they didn't have the personnel that we did on special teams. And under Nolan Cromwell we executed so well that we were the top team in the league at returning the ball. We had guys on special teams who played their butts off, and I gave them a lot of credit for the NFL record 875 return yards and record three touchdowns I got running back punts. We averaged over 15 yards on punt returns.

My relationship with Mike Holmgren became more than it had been during training camp, and he told the whole team, "We have a guy who has a chance to run a kick back every time he touches the ball. All we have to do is carry out our assignments and give him a chance to run." So that was our philosophy, and we'd go out there and score points. It was very nice that he said that about me.

Although I made most of my contributions on special teams, I was also a backup wide receiver. I didn't play a lot, but when Robert Brooks went out for the season in a Monday night game, I came in and made a couple of key third-down catches. Then Antonio Freeman broke his forearm in the Tampa Bay game, and I came in and did well. With both Brooks and Freeman out, Don Beebe and I both got a lot of time. Then Freeman came back, and we acquired Andre Rison after he was cut by Jacksonville in November. I wasn't disappointed when they brought in Rison instead of going with me as the starter. By that time I knew my role on the team, and I was fulfilling it really well. Andre was a Pro Bowl receiver, a guy who had proven himself time and again, so it made sense to get that type of guy, especially at that time of the year. It was a smart move. A lot of sportswriters criticized Ron Wolf for bringing him in because they thought he'd be disruptive, but we became world champs with Rison, so you can't second guess him.

I was glad that Rison and Freeman were doing so well. The wide receivers on the Packers all rooted for each other. We were all very close. In fact there was a great sense of unity on the entire team. The team had a nice mix, a good chemistry. Guys of all ages got along and everybody on offense, defense, and special teams was friends. You pulled for your teammates, even if they played the same position you did—as was also the case with our running backs Edgar Bennett and Dorsey Levens. It didn't matter which player had a big game as long as we were winning. Everybody was just happy to be having a good season and to be accomplishing a common goal, which was to win the first championship in Green Bay since Super Bowl II. Green Bay had been knocked out of the playoffs in three consecutive years by Dallas, and Brett Favre; Reggie White, who had come to Green Bay with the belief he could win a title; Edgar Bennett; tight end Mark Chmura; safety LeRoy Butler, who was another of the team leaders; and the other players who had suffered any of those losses were determined to get over the hump and win the Super Bowl in 1996. That became my goal, too, and the goal of all the other players the Packers picked up that year. The fans were definitely behind us. I'm sure it happened but I don't really remember Packers players from the Vince Lombardi years coming by to give us encouragement; I do know that when I walked onto Lambeau Field I could feel the tradition—I actually could. I was grateful for the opportunity to play there.

I wouldn't say Brett Favre's personal problems affected us because we went on to be the highest scoring team in the league. However, I didn't like the way the media handled the painkiller situation. The Green Bay press was supportive, but every time you'd look at national television there would always be a negative angle. It was like a knock: Every time they'd mention how well Brett was playing, they'd also mention his recent addiction to painkillers, as if he had been hooked on heroin or something. They didn't talk about the great amount of courage he had to come out and say, "I have a problem with painkillers and I'm going to take care of it." The man had acknowledged a problem and fixed it in the off-season, so he should have been commended not ridiculed. But Brett handled it real well. We didn't have to be protective of him because he could take care of himself. He said, "I kicked my problem and you can say what you want about me." Brett got back at everybody by throwing 39 touchdown passes and becoming the league's MVP again. I can't think of a better way to do it.

Because of the injuries and other adversities it wasn't an easy year for us, but we had more peaks than valleys and finished the regular season with a 13–3 record, the best in the NFC. Our offense led the league in points scored, the defense gave up the fewest points, and we were the NFL's most productive special teams unit, so the team was pretty sure we'd make it through the playoffs, especially since we'd be playing in Green Bay.

In the playoffs against San Francisco and Carolina I had the usual butterflies. I'm always slightly nervous before a game, though I'm not sick or anything. I had confidence in how we'd do on special teams. We'd been doing well all year, why would we change now? As long as the guys in front of me executed their assignments, I didn't worry about what the 11 guys on coverage did. We didn't have any letdowns.

In our victory over the 49ers I was able to step up and score on a 71-yard punt return and make some other very big plays. I'm a big, big movie fan and after my touchdown I copied Jim Carrey in *The Mask*, when he ran with his legs way out there with his hands, and then I jumped into the stands with the fans, which is what a lot of the Packers did at home after scoring touchdowns. That was fun. In the NFC title game against Carolina, which had eliminated Dallas, I almost broke a kickoff return, but the guys who really stepped up big were our backs. Dorsey Levens, who really came on late in the year, got about 200 yards running and pass receiving and made an important touchdown catch, a super catch in the end zone; and Edgar Bennett ran the ball extremely well. Brett had another great game and our defense played like it had all year, and we pulled away to win, 30–13. The Packers always won on cold days at home. Everybody was so happy. Green Bay was going to play in its first Super Bowl since 1968.

While we were in New Orleans getting ready to play the New England Patriots in the Superdome, I'd say we were pretty disciplined. That's how Mike Holmgren wanted it, and we didn't have the types of guys who'd get into trouble anyway. We kept to our practice schedules and had curfews, but we still could go out and enjoy the town. Our hotel was pretty close to the French Quarter, and it was fun to hang with some of the guys. I don't drink so we didn't go to bars, but we'd walk around and hear music and go into different shops and restaurants.

We had normal practices, like we would for a usual Sunday game. There was nothing different because we were getting ready to play in the Super Bowl. I practiced a little bit as a receiver, but I didn't expect to do anything but return punts and kicks. With one game left, you've got to go with what got you there. We did special teams work at the beginning of practice for about 40 minutes. We practiced returns, eleven-on-eleven, and everybody executed their assignments. We did a return like we'd do it in the game. We weren't a team that practiced in pads, so obviously it wasn't full-out, but guys were running and hustling. No one was out there hitting and tackling, but it was real quick, real fast. We didn't have play numbers for returns, just right, left, or up the middle, and then you do different things as you go downfield. We'd do specific special teams things on different days, just like it was with the offense and defense.

We had our conferences with the press and I got asked about becoming a free agent at the end of the year. I had been getting a lot of questions about that since I'd started to have success during the season. Obviously when you start scoring touchdowns and having some positive impact on your team, the media starts asking about your plans for the next season. You try not to think about your free-agent status, which is why I tried to deflect the questions and focus on the game. I said, "Look, just let me play in the Super Bowl. Let the Packers become world champs. Once we do that I feel like all the marbles will just fall in place."

Super Bowl Week finally ended. The night before the game there was a team meeting, we watched films and stuff, and then we went to bed, knowing that the next day we'd be playing in the championship game. We were ready. The next day in our locker room at the Superdome we were emotional, subdued, businesslike . . . How we were feeling encompassed all of those adjectives and more. We just wanted to take care of business and have a lot of fun doing it. We were serious, but not overly so. It's not like it was dead quiet. As always guys were playing different types of music, from rap to gospel to oldies. Most guys were talking and joking a little bit. I didn't see anybody banging their heads on the wall, nobody I was aware of. There weren't pep talks, although Holmgren might have said a few words like, "We know what we're here for; you guys know what to do; go out there and let it loose." Something like that. That was all that really needed to be said at that point. There was prayer. A lot of guys went in and prayed with Reggie White, who also would pray with guys from both teams after games. I think the media blew the religious thing out of proportion. A lot of teams pray, and I don't think we prayed any more than they did.

We ran out on the field for introductions, and Luther Vandross sang the national anthem, and I'm thinking, "This is it. This is *the* Super Bowl." I'm thinking we just have to go out and do what we've been doing all year. We respected New England and knew a Bill Parcells–coached team could be dangerous, but we knew that if we played our game there wasn't a team in the NFL that could withstand our best shots and beat us.

New England got the ball first, but after one first down, Tom Tupa came in to punt. So I went onto the field with the special teams unit. Other than normal pregame jitters I wouldn't get nervous before making my first punt return, even in the Super Bowl. I guess the more success you have, the more comfortable you feel. As the ball was snapped to Tupa, I wasn't thinking about me but wondering what the Patriots were going to do. Where are they going to place the ball? That's the big question in my mind. Are they going to kick it out of bounds because I had been having such success returning punts? Or are they going to kick it to the sidelines? Or to the middle of the field? As it turned out Tupa punted it toward our left sideline. As the ball was in the air, I looked back and forth about three times from the ball to the coverage. I wasn't frightened. I could feel them coming but I wasn't worried about getting hit. I wasn't visualizing what I was going to do, but I was thinking about what I could do. I was concentrating on catching the ball, knowing that I would then run with instinct. I was thinking about the ball and the fastest guy coming down, the guy closest to me. I wanted to make him miss rather than take the hit and try to break free. It was a long punt and I caught it near the left sideline. Was it on the 13? I'm not sure. I made the first guy miss and a few others miss. Then I picked up speed and a few blocks and I wasn't brought down until we had gained over 30 yards.

Afterward I was going back and forth with some guys on the New England sidelines. I was telling them, "Keep kicking the ball to me and I'll scorch you sooner or later." I threw a couple of expletives in there also. They had been talking a lot of stuff; they had guys telling me how they were going to hit me, smack me, and then strike the Heisman pose I used to do after scoring touchdowns at Michigan. I was like a bottle of soda that had been shaken up for about two weeks—hearing their comments at press conferences—and come game time, they took the cap off and I exploded.

After the punt return, Edgar Bennett picked up short yardage and on the next play, when it was second-and-long, the Patriots blitzed and got burned. Their defense wasn't expected to blitz so early in the game, but Favre saw it coming and audibled, which was really a credit to him, and sent Rison down the middle on a post pattern in single coverage. Andre got a great break and streaked far ahead of his man, caught the ball at about the 20, and scored easily. Fifty-four yards, I think. So we were ahead, 7–0. To say that our scoring a touchdown right after my long punt return was "exciting" would be an understatement. The roof must have jumped off the Superdome at least two inches.

Then Drew Bledsoe was intercepted for the first time. Norm Evans stepped inside of Terry Glenn and made a nice play, and we had the ball back inside the Patriots' 30-yard line. So we were already in field-goal range. From what had happened so far, I didn't necessarily think it was going to be a runaway for us, but I hoped it would be. I knew we had the capability of blowing out teams. However, I knew New England was a good team and that we couldn't get overconfident and relax on them at any time, and certainly not so early in the game.

New England showed they were a good team. Their defense held us to a field goal after the interception, and then their offense came back from the 10–0 deficit to take a 14–10 lead before the quarter was over. We weren't surprised. On their first scoring drive, they picked up some big yardage on short passes to Keith Byars and Curtis Martin, but their biggest play came on a penalty, when we got called for pass interference in the end zone. That put the ball on our 1-yard line, and then Bledsoe connected on a pass to Byars. Their big play in the second drive was a long pass on third-and-short that Glenn made a heck of a leaping catch on inside our 5-yard line. Then Ben Coates caught a pass in the end zone. They didn't have much success running the ball against us, but they did some play-action and went to the air and had a couple of big plays to put them ahead and shift the momentum in their favor.

On the first two kickoffs following their touchdowns, they did a really good job of containing me. But we were picking up pointers. You can watch films, but you don't know exactly what their coverage team is going to do against you until you actually play against it. Then you have a better feel for what their personnel is like. You can't judge a player's speed from watching him on film, or his determination. But after a couple of returns you understand an individual's talents and determine how to stop him. I was thinking that eventually what we were doing was going to work and we'd break one. I had the confidence where I thought I had the opportunity to break it on every return, on kickoffs or punts.

Although I had that early punt return, they kept punting the ball to me. The next couple of times, I didn't pick up a lot of yardage on the returns. The second time, I got the ball back to our 19. If I'd gotten back to the 20, Favre and Freeman would have only tied the record on the next play for the longest play in Super Bowl history. I didn't tease them about that but I told Freeman, "Every time I return the ball, we score." I don't even know what the play was called. But basically, what happened was that the Patriots' rookie safety, Lawyer Milloy, played up on the line, and Freeman shot right by him on a fly and Favre led him with the ball. Freeman's not superfast, but he got by both Milloy and the free safety coming over. They had safeties who would come up and smack you, but those guys were more hitters than they were speed guys. Bill Parcells wanted to kill our receivers, but he had to catch them first.

I was happy for Freeman. He was my roommate when we traveled, and we were good buddies. He was playing with a soft pad over his injured forearm, so it wasn't painful for him to catch the ball. But I think he concentrated more because he had to wear that thing, because he wasn't dropping any balls after he came back.

We were now back ahead, 17–14. The Patriots had to punt soon after they got the ball, and again Tupa kicked it to the left sideline. They continued to roll the dice by kicking it to me. After the success we had on the first punt return, I could tell that I could run well all day. Definitely. I felt good. Again a few guys missed, and I got my second big return, this time for 34 yards, a couple of yards longer than the first one. I was told going into the game that the Super Bowl record for punt return yardage was only about 55 yards, held by John Taylor. So I knew that if they were going to put the ball in my hands, I was going to pass Taylor. On those two long punt returns alone, I broke the record.

Yeah, my running on that punt return may have been better than on the first return because I had to make a few more moves. I couldn't tell you. I can't appreciate what I do like people watching the game can. When I'm running, everything is instinctive. I don't find a course and stick with it. Most of the times I try to put myself into the position where I'm the initiator, so the defense has to react to my moves. I have to look at how the field is set up and see where I am in relation to my blockers and try to put the defenders in the best position possible to get blocked. It happens so fast that I don't really know what I do until I watch the play on film.

That return took us across the 50-yard line and Chris Jacke soon kicked his second field goal to put us up, 20–14. So I was glad that my return had led to some more points. After those two punt returns, it was hard to keep myself at a calm level. I was so excited and so hyped up and so emotionally into it that I had to tell myself to calm down. That stuff is draining. It will get you tired physically and mentally. I actually had a headache.

The Patriots also had a dangerous punt returner in Dave Meggett, but there was no rivalry between us to see who would do better in the Super Bowl. It's not boxing. I'm not covering him and he's not covering me. People forget that our final two games were against the two Pro Bowl returners, Michael Bates of Carolina and Meggett, and we shut them both down. Meggett didn't even come close to breaking one all game. It wasn't just Nolan's return unit that was *bad*—his coverage unit was *bad*, too. Those guys would get out there and get after people.

Our final score of the half came after another interception. Bledsoe was hurrying his passes because he was getting a heavy rush from our defensive line and from our backs LeRoy Butler and Doug Evans, who were blitzing from the blind side. Our offense capitalized on breaks all game long and after this turnover, put together its best drive of the game, during which Favre connected with Freeman for a big gain, and Levens and

Bennett finally got our running game going. Levens had a nice run down to the 1- or 2-yard line, and Favre took it over himself by diving toward the corner of the end zone and just putting the ball over the goal line. They signaled that it was a touchdown, but I couldn't tell if he reached far enough from where I was standing. He ran toward our sideline, but all the photographers were in the way and I couldn't see what happened. Brett's a good runner but he doesn't run as much as he used to because of the punishment. But he had to run then and didn't worry about his body.

We were up, 27–14, at halftime? I watched the entire game and can tell you about all the plays, but I don't know the scores quarter by quarter. I don't think we were satisfied with our performance so far because teams didn't score points on us like New England had. We had given up the fewest points in the league and they had scored 14 points already. Fritz Shurmur and his defense weren't happy about those points. Although all their scoring came from only one big play and a penalty, we still had to eliminate those kinds of mistakes.

I calmed down to a certain extent during the break. I was thinking that if we took the kickoff that opened the second half and scored a touchdown then there was no way they would come back from such a big deficit. However, we didn't return that kick for a touchdown and we didn't get any points on that first drive. We got inside their 40 but then got into a fourth-and-1 situation. That's when Coach Holmgren decided to have Levens run outside, and he was thrown for a big loss. I don't think that if he had the chance to call that play again he'd make the same decision. We weren't having great success running outside, but maybe he was thinking they were expecting us to run inside so he tried to surprise them. It's like a chess game out there.

Neither team scored on their next possession, but late in the third quarter, New England closed the gap to 27-21. Curtis Martin scored on a run up the middle from inside the 20. It was a strong run. Every time they scored, they did it from within the strike zone. Usually teams didn't score on our defense with long plays.

All of a sudden it was only a six-point lead. The wave of emotion in the stadium—you could feel it—was on their side. They had just scored, they were only a touchdown and extra point from taking the lead, and this was a game. This is what everybody wanted to see. So now we said, "Okay, let's do something. . . ."

On the kickoff I had to go back to the 1-yard line to catch the ball and when you go back on the ball, the blockers in the wedge are supposed to

January 26, 1997 at the Superdome in New Orleans
Paid Attendance: 72,301
AFC Champion: New England Patriots (13–6)
Head Coach: Bill Parcells
NFC Champion: Green Bay Packers (16–3)
Head Coach: Mike Holmgren

STARTING LINEUPS

OFFENSE			DEFENSE		
New England		**Green Bay**	**New England**		**Green Bay**
Shawn Jefferson	WR	Antonio Freeman	Ferric Collins	LE	Reggie White
Bruce Armstrong	LT	Bruce Wilkerson	Mark Wheeler	LT	
William Roberts	LG	Aaron Taylor		DT	Santana Dotson
Dave Wohlabaugh	C	Frank Winters		NT	Gilbert Brown
Todd Rucci	RG	Adam Timmerman	Pio Sagapolutele	RT	
Max Lane	RT	Earl Dotson	Willie McGinest	RE	Sean Jones
Ben Coates	TE	Mark Chmura	Chris Slade	LLB	Wayne Simmons
Terry Glenn	WR	Andre Rison	Ted Johnson	MLB	Ron Cox
Drew Bledsoe	QB	Brett Favre	Todd Collons	RLB	Brian Williams
Curtis Martin	RB	Edgar Bennett	Ty Law	LCB	Craig Newsome
Keith Byars	RB	William Henderson	Otis Smith	RCB	Doug Evans
			Lawyer Milloy	SS	LeRoy Butler
			Willie Clay	FS	Eugene Robinson

SUBSTITUTIONS

New England: K—Adam Vinatieri. P—Tom Tupa. Offense: Receivers—Ray Lucas, Hason Graham, Vincent Brisby, John Burke, Mike Bartrum. Linemen—Bob Kratch, Mike Gisler. Backs—Dave Meggett, Marrio Grier. Defense: Linebackers—Tedy Bruschi, Marty Moore, Dwayne Sabb. Linemen—Chris Sullivan, Chad Eaton, Mike Jones. Backs—Terry Ray, Jerome Henderson, Mike McGruder, Corwin Brown. DNP—Ricky Reynolds.

Green Bay: K—Chris Jacke. P—Craig Hentrich. Offense: Receivers—Desmond Howard, Don Beebe, Jeff Thomason, Keith Jackson, Terry Mickens. Linemen—Lindsay Knapp, Jeff Dellenbach, John Michels. Backs—Dorsey Levens, Calvin Jones, Travis Jervey. Defense: Linebackers—Bernardo Harris, Lamont Holinquest. Linemen—Darius Holland, Keith McKenzie, Gabe Wilkins. Backs—Roderick Mullen, Tyrone Williams, Mike Prior, Chris Hayes. DNP—Jim McMahon.

New England	14	0	7	0—21	
Green Bay	10	17	8	0—35	

GB	Rison 54 pass from Favre (Jacke kick)
GB	FG Jacke 37
NE	Byars 1 pass from Bledsoe (Vinatieri kick)
NE	Coates 4 pass from Bledsoe (Vinatieri kick)
GB	Freeman 81 pass from Favre (Jacke kick)
GB	FG Jacke 31
GB	Favre 2 run (Jacke kick)
NE	Martin 18 run (Vinatieri kick)
GB	Howard 99 kickoff return (Chmura pass from Favre)
MVP:	Desmond Howard (Green Bay)

look back so they can time it right. That's what they did. You're supposed to hit the hole fast and then when you see that open field you go into a different gear. And, oh man, the guys made excellent blocks. You couldn't have drawn it up better. Up front in the wedge, Don Beebe made a good block on the left side, and Keith McKenzie knocked back the kicker in the middle of the field, and I went to cut between them. As I was heading for the hole, Hason Graham grabbed my face mask briefly, and his hand slid down and grabbed my right shoulder and pulled it back. But he fell to the ground and I kept running. I looked and all I had to deal with was their kicker. And then I was in the clear!

I ran down field all alone. I wasn't thinking that I was running for a touchdown in the Super Bowl. I was thinking, I don't want anyone to catch me from behind. Not in front of 800 million viewers. The only guy who could have caught me was Don Beebe and he was on my team. (You know from Super Bowl XXVII that Beebe could do it.)

As soon as I got into the end zone I started my dance. I'm a big Michael Jackson fan so I dusted off an old dance. I got those robot moves from the Jackson 5 on TV's *Dance Machine*. That was my first kickoff return for a touchdown in the pros. I didn't know at the time that I had set the record for the longest kickoff return in Super Bowl history, 99 yards. I didn't know what the record had been. What was so great and exciting was the timing. The other team had been celebrating on the sideline after Martin's touchdown and thinking, "one more touchdown and we've got it won." I was in my own world. I had just an unbelievable feeling. I was running across the field and hitting my chest with my right fist and hugging my teammates and looking up at where my parents and family members were sitting. And I looked at the Patriots bench so they'd know that when you light a fire you get burned—"I told you so." It was great because I had helped our team go up by 14 points, which it did when Favre and Chmura connected on a two-point conversion.

That touchdown was a backbreaker, but I didn't assume the game was over until the fourth quarter and the score hadn't changed. Then it became obvious that they wouldn't be able to catch up because our defense was playing so well. It was great seeing Reggie White set a record with three sacks, all in the second half. What made it special is that he said it was my kickoff return that inspired him. He had two in succession on the Patriot's next possession. After that kickoff return, they didn't have a prayer against our defense. Bledsoe was getting sacked and intercepted. Reggie got another sack and Santana Dotson rushed up the middle and threw Bledsoe for a big loss. We had as many as eight backs in there, so it was hard for him to complete anything. Craig Newsome made one interception and later caused another by knocking the ball loose from a receiver and having it ricochet to Brian Williams. Bledsoe was a good quarterback, but he was young and against so much pressure from our defense he made mistakes. On at least two of his four interceptions, he threw off his back foot. And our defensive backs kept making great plays.

I had one of my best punt returns late in the fourth quarter. I caught the ball in the middle of the field and ran to the right sideline and picked up about 20 yards. Only they called it back because of a holding penalty on Tyrone Williams. I didn't get to see the replay, but Williams said it was a bogus call. The funny thing is that we had defensive guys on the field, like Reggie White, Sean Jones, and Brian Williams, and I was just supposed to fair-catch the ball, not run it back. But it was a short, low punt.

I was still taunting the Patriots and they were still saying a lot of smack to me. One of their guys tapped me on the shoulder after that punt return and pointed to the ground and said, "There's a flag, there's a flag." And I said, "Look at the score, though." It was all in fun. People wrongly criticize players for doing certain things like that. But people who have never done it don't understand what it's all about. Because after it was all over the same guys were walking up to me and saying, "That was a great game." All that other stuff is just in the heat of battle. It's just something that happens. That taunting was very, very uncharacteristic of me; I never did that, especially in the NFL. The last time I was so hyper was in college and that was only in one game. My friends later said, "Man, what was going on with you out there today?"

As the game was winding down and it was obvious we would win, I wasn't thinking about what I'd been through. I knew Jacksonville and Washington were at home watching me play, but I wasn't really thinking about them. I was just so happy that I didn't want to think of anything negative. I was thinking, "This is really happening! The Super Bowl! The whole world is watching! 800 million viewers! Amazing!" Getting the MVP just made it more special.

In the fourth quarter people came up to me and said that I had a chance to be the MVP. They put up my stats and the records I'd broken or tied on the scoreboard, and I thought I might have a chance of getting it. But it wasn't something I wanted to bank on. I should have been picked for the Pro Bowl but I wasn't, so I knew strange things happened. I didn't consider myself a shoo-in, especially since no special teams player had ever gotten the award. Also, we had so much talent on our team, and guys like Brett and Reggie had great games. Nolan Cromwell came up to me before the announcement and said that he had a dream that I won the MVP of the Super Bowl. I said, "Really? Cool, great." Then, just before the game ended, it was flashed on the scoreboard that I was the MVP. That's how I learned I'd been selected.

Basically I was just going around feeling grateful that I was a world champ. Oh, man, we were going to be WORLD CHAMPIONS. That was our goal. That's what we had talked about in training camp. Once the game ended, I realized it was even better than I thought it would be to be part of a world championship team. *Much* better. Maybe it was because I was also the MVP. That was the full scenario I had visualized.

There were other guys I was happy for. Brett—I was very happy for him. He had shown everybody. And Reggie White, my man—if it weren't for him I might not have been a Packer. He had finally gotten his ring. So had Sean Jones, our other defensive end, who had played as long as Reggie. Another guy who had been in the league a long time was Eugene Robinson, who the Packers had acquired from Seattle. Keith Jackson was a good, good friend so I was very happy he got his ring after playing many years with Philadelphia and Miami. And I was happy for Don Beebe, who had lost four Super Bowls with Buffalo.

Also I was happy for Andre Rison. He had been unfairly criticized and misunderstood by the media. It was good to see him just go out there and show everybody what he could do. Early in the first half, Rison and I— yes, we both had been released by Jacksonville and had been written off by many people—were together on the sidelines saying how we were going to shock the world in the Super Bowl. We kept saying it and saying it. Then we did it!

Green Bay was again world champion after 29 years. And what made it so satisfying was that we had beaten a good, well-coached team. You had to respect a Bill Parcells team because he got a lot from his players. There was a lot of hard hitting that game, and it took a real effort by the Packers to win. Somebody's got to lose, but New England did its part because together we gave the fans the best Super Bowl in years.

Because I won the MVP award I did a lot of media events. I flew to Disney World in Orlando to do a promotion and then to New York to be a guest on *The David Letterman Show* and to make a few more appearances. For a few weeks, I did a lot of interviews and signed a lot of autographs. I wasn't surprised by all the attention. Having been the MVP, it just came with the territory. After all, there is no bigger event in sports than the Super Bowl.

INDEX